SHAKE IT UP

SHAKE IT UP

GREAT AMERICAN WRITING ON ROCK AND POP FROM ELVIS TO JAY Z

EDITED BY

JONATHAN LETHEM
and KEVIN DETTMAR

A Library of America Special Publication

Visit our website at www.loa.org.

Some of the material in this volume is reprinted with permission
of the holders of copyright and publication rights.
Sources and acknowledgments begin on page 559.

This paper meets the requirements of
ANSI/NISO Z39.48–1992 (Permanence of Paper).

Distributed to the trade in the United States
by Penguin Random House Inc.
and in Canada by Penguin Random House Canada Ltd.

Library of Congress Control Number: 2106959719
ISBN 978–1–59853–531–0

First Printing

Manufactured in the United States of America

Contents

Introduction

FIFTY SELECTIONS from fifty writers covering approximately fifty years of American rock and pop writing: it's an elegant conceit, you've got to admit. One writer from each of the fifty states, though, proved a bridge too far. Nevertheless, the origin of the practice of writing about the American popular music known as "rock 'n' roll"—a music which, as this book's contents suggest, would come to encompass elements of variants like rhythm and blues, soul, bubblegum, doo-wop, and, later, art rock, funk, punk, glam, disco, heavy metal, and hip-hop—is as distributed, as mongrel, and as intimate as the origin of the music itself.

The music this writing took as its subject emerged over a period of decades, a prodigal stepchild of jazz and the blues, then abruptly coalesced into a teenage sensation in the mid-'50s apotheosis of Fats Domino, Elvis Presley, Chuck Berry, and their cohort. At that moment it became, as much as comic books, the epitome of a vernacular popular culture that was decried, mocked, and ignored, often simultaneously. That the new forms, even when played by whites for whites, unmistakably had roots in black cultural styles hardly went unnoticed, even when it went unspoken; a terror of cultural miscegenation lay behind the scorn. That it should find itself the object of critical response within a decade of its birth might seem miraculous, under the circumstances, but it wasn't the subject of criticism at its inception. Early assessments of this music's value were in the hands of the users; a DJ flipping a 45 to discover a preferred B-Side was engaged in a critical intervention on behalf of an audience he inferred and a tradition he was helping create. Even the phrase "The British Invasion"—a marketing concept that was also a clarion cry—implies some critical-historical awareness, the birth of a language for declaring that these disposable artifacts could be ordered into legacies of influence and impact.

In getting itself on its feet, the field of rock and pop writing resembled the music that inspired it. In both cases, a tiny handful of practitioners working in eccentric isolation became a story of the invention of an embracing collective idea. Think of Sun Records producer Sam Phillips in Memphis, or *Crawdaddy* magazine founder Paul Williams mimeographing in his Swarthmore dorm room, each generating a lonely signal that would inspire thousands of others. The writers who in the mid-'60s began to cobble together the tradition reflected in this anthology started as fans, and the "magazines" in which they published were, to begin with, fanzines or underground newspapers: *Crawdaddy*, *Mojo-Navigator*, and *Rolling Stone*.

Like the musicians, these writers gained their sense of possibility from available parts. These included their immediate predecessors in the lively zine traditions of the folk music, jazz, and science fiction demimondes, as well as the hybrid New Journalism of writers like Gay Talese and Tom Wolfe, and pop-acute film criticism like that of Pauline Kael. In this regard, the early rock magazines were founded on the presumption of a counterculture, even if it was one partly being wished into existence by writers and publishers. *Rolling Stone*, exceptional for its (successful) commercial aspirations, declared in its first issue that it was "not just about the music, but about the things and attitudes that music embraces."

Among the utopian notions in the air was an aesthetic proposition: that the pop music of the time might not only be the next great American art form, but that it might be so precisely because of the elements that had made it eligible for sneering dismissal by an older generation. And further, that some version of "community" was implicit in the artworks themselves—a community founded less on political axioms than on instantaneous recognition of sensory revelations. You had not only to hear the music, but to actually trust what you heard.

An attitude therefore not of defensiveness, but of revolutionary and often joyous defiance, is forged in the prose of the early rock writers.

Sometimes these were close readers—like Robert Christgau, and others like him, with degrees in English—making explicit claims that the songs could sustain and reward persistent study. Other times they were dropouts staking all they had on the belief that rock 'n' roll was part of a new and necessary language for living in the world. In any case, the stakes were high. Even the Dada-interventionist writer Richard Meltzer, whose mock-heroic exegeses of songs by the likes of The Trashmen mocked the academicization of pop before it had begun, stands as confirmation of the aspirations he satirizes.

The earliest writing collected here displays how this scattering of excitable utterances became an actual living discourse. With a startling quickness, these writers (nearly all white and all men at the outset) formed a loose guild of working journalists. *Rolling Stone* and *The Village Voice*—and soon *Creem*, and a revived *Crawdaddy*, and others—made possible, for a while, a rich professional era, one corresponding to what in retrospect was a long heyday for the music industry itself in the '70s and '80s into the '90s. Major newspapers all had working pop critics, and there were many major newspapers; slick magazines, both monthlies and weeklies, joined the party too. As utopian assumptions and capitalist imperatives together dissolved the quarantine between counterculture advocacy and mercantile media, writers like Paul Nelson and Jon Landau began working directly with musical artists on behalf of record labels or management companies.

Such alliances were mostly short-lived, as were the advertising dollars keeping certain magazines not only on the newsstands, but free to commit writers to eccentric long-form pieces. Before long, with a steady erosion of the world of professional journalism generally came a grim narrowing of the career path of the popular music journalist. Even as "pop culture" has in senses both good and bad installed itself as synonymous with "culture," and rock 'n' roll appointed itself with a Hall of Fame, the field of writing this collection celebrates has often had to scatter and relocate itself: in book writing (including special publishing projects like Bloomsbury's 33⅓ series), in academia, and on the Internet, where music sites and individual music bloggers have in some sense reinstated the zine atmosphere of pop music writing's origins.

Nevertheless, the field of operation represented by these fifty examples is a fresh one. The horizon here is still too near for panoramic views. Most of these writers are still alive; many of them might dispute our compass. Anyhow, it's too early for canon formation in a field so marvelously volatile—a volatility that mirrors, still, that of pop music itself, which remains smokestack lightning. The writing here attempts to catch some in a bottle.

When we first conceived of this volume, we were inspired by the opening sentence from Phillip Lopate's introduction to his Library of America volume on American movie critics, in which he calls that writing "a distinctive branch of American letters." Half a century in, rock and pop writing constitutes another. We've assembled a collection of American rock and pop writing—not writing about American rock and pop. Though these American writers may have privileged to some degree American artists, we've chosen our pieces for the writing, rather than attempting some national survey of the music. (An important part of the origin of rock and pop writing is British; it's worth noting that the writers we've gathered were in conversation, implicitly and sometimes explicitly, with British peers like Nik Cohn, Charlie Gillett, and others.)

The book proposes, then, neither a history of rock and pop nor of rock and pop writing. Instead, we tried to make a feast. We sought to reflect the diversity of voices making up the American rock and pop writing scene; the heartbreaking imbalances are rooted in historical actualities, a playing field tilted badly from the start. Women writers, for instance, were subjected to a staggering array of hazings; Ellen Sander's Led Zeppelin piece included here serves as a cautionary account of why more female voices departed (or never joined) the conversation. Ellen Willis is of course the great early exception, though her gifts were nourished and opportunities opened up, at least in part, from within her sympathetic partnership with Robert Christgau. The relative paucity—especially in earlier decades—of voices of color offers an especially bitter irony, given the primacy of black music in this tradition. If the situation is somewhat improved today, it's hardly repaired.

Rock and pop writers embarked on this new kind of cultural journalism and criticism well aware that their subjects might prove to be ephemeral; but the best of the writing, no matter its ostensible occasion, never was. Greil Marcus titled a posthumous collection of Lester Bangs's writing after one of Bangs's essays: *Psychotic Reactions and Carburetor Dung*. That title preserves the name of the only album by The Count Five—an album (and a band) that, without Bangs's loving screed, might have been lost to the dustbin of history. It also provided the name for the Malaysian punk band Carburetor Dung. Sometimes, it's true, reading a piece makes listening to a record feel obligatory: "when Johnny Rotten rolled his r's," Marcus writes in *Lipstick Traces*, "it sounded as if his teeth had been ground down to points." Is it possible to read that without putting on "Holidays in the Sun"?

By the same token, the best rock and pop writing transcends or outlives its nominal occasion. Ezra Pound once described literature as "news that stays news": in this sense, the best rock writing aspires to the condition of literature. The moment of its writing fades into the background as history is transformed into myth. Reading Marcus's own *Mystery Train*, one might feel the need to hear Harmonica Frank, the subject of the book's first chapter. In the opinion of these humble writers, the music of Harmonica Frank is utterly forgettable; it is Marcus's description of it that is unforgettable. Our goal, then, was always writing that conveys such force, that is so rich with implication, that you not only feel compelled to go and find its music to listen to, but you'll never be certain that what you hear there hasn't somehow been planted in your mind by the writer.

Jonathan Lethem
Kevin Dettmar
2016

NAT HENTOFF

Nathan Irving "Nat" Hentoff (1925–2017) bridged the worlds of jazz and of rock and pop writing. His career began at the jazz magazine *Down Beat* in 1952, before he cofounded *The Jazz Review* in 1958. He was a prolific writer on music and political topics since publishing *Hear Me Talkin' to Ya: The Story of Jazz by the Men Who Made It* with Nat Shapiro in 1955, with an output including twenty nonfiction books, nine novels, and two memoirs. Hentoff's greatest influence on popular music criticism may actually have come through his prodigious output of album liner notes; his notes for *The Freewheelin' Bob Dylan* (1963) went a long way toward preparing listeners to listen intelligently to this challenging new music.

▼ ▼

The Freewheelin' Bob Dylan

OF ALL the precipitously emergent singers of folk songs in the continuing renascence of that self-assertive tradition, none has equaled Bob Dylan's singularity of impact. As Harry Jackson, a cowboy singer and a painter, has exclaimed: "He's so goddamned real it's unbelievable!" The irrepressible reality of Bob Dylan is a compound of spontaneity, candor, slicing wit and an uncommonly perceptive eye and ear for the way many of us constrict our capacity for living while a few of us don't.

Not yet twenty-two at the time of this album's release, Dylan is growing at a swift, experience-hungry rate. In these performances, there is already a marked change from his first album (*Bob Dylan* Columbia CL 1779/CS 8579), and there will surely be many further dimensions of Dylan to come. What makes this collection particularly arresting is that it consists in large part of Dylan's own compositions. The resurgence of topical folk songs has become a pervasive part of the folk movement among city singers, but few of the young bards so far have demonstrated a knowledge of the difference between well-intentioned pamphleteering and the creation of a valid musical experience. Dylan has. As the highly critical editors of *Little Sandy Review* have noted, ". . . right now, he is certainly our finest contemporary folk song writer. Nobody else really even comes close."

The details of Dylan's biography were summarized in the notes to his first Columbia album; but to recapitulate briefly, he was born on May 24, 1941, in Duluth, Minnesota. His experience with adjusting himself to new sights and sounds started early. During his first nineteen years, he lived in Gallup, New Mexico; Cheyenne, South Dakota; Sioux Falls, South Dakota; Phillipsburg, Kansas; Hibbing, Minnesota (where he was graduated from high school), and Minneapolis (where he spent a restless six months at the University of Minnesota).

"Everywhere he went," Gil Turner wrote in his article on Dylan in *Sing Out*, "his ears were wide open for the music around him. He listened to the blues singers, cowboy singers, pop singers and others —soaking up music and styles with an uncanny memory and facility for assimilation. Gradually, his own preferences developed and became more, the strongest areas being Negro blues and country music. Among the musicians and singers who influenced him were Hank Williams, Muddy Waters, Jelly Roll Morton, Leadbelly, Mance Lipscomb and Big Joe Williams." And, above all others, Woody Guthrie. At ten he was playing guitar, and by the age of fifteen, Dylan had taught himself piano, harmonica and autoharp.

In February 1961, Dylan came east, primarily to visit Woody Guthrie at Greystone Hospital in New Jersey. The visits have continued, and Guthrie has expressed approval of Dylan's first album, being particularly fond of the "Song to Woody" in it. By September of 1961, Dylan's singing in Greenwich Village, especially at Gerde's Folk City, had ignited a nucleus of singers and a few critics (notably Bob Shelton of the *New York Times*) into exuberant appreciation of his work. Since then, Dylan has inexorably increased the scope of his American audiences while also performing briefly in London and Rome.

The first of Dylan's songs in this set is "Blowin' In The Wind." In 1962, Dylan said of the song's background: "I still say that some of the biggest criminals are those that turn their heads away when they see wrong and they know it's wrong. I'm only 21 years old and I know that there's been too many wars. . . . You people over 21 should know better." All that he prefers to add by way of commentary now is: "The first way to answer these questions in the song is by asking them. But lots of people have to first find the wind." On this track, and except when otherwise noted, Dylan is heard alone—accompanying himself on guitar and harmonica.

"Girl From The North Country" was first conceived by Bob Dylan about three years before he finally wrote it down in December 1962. "That often happens," he explains. "I carry a song in my head for a long time and then it comes bursting out." The song—and Dylan's performance—reflect his particular kind of lyricism. The mood is a fusion of yearning, poignancy and simple appreciation of a beautiful girl. Dylan illuminates all these corners of his vision, but simultaneously retains his bristling sense of self. He's not about to go begging anything from this girl up north.

"Masters Of War" startles Dylan himself. "I've never really written anything like that before," he recalls. "I don't sing songs which hope people will die, but I couldn't help it in this one. The song is a sort of striking out, a reaction to the last straw, a feeling of what can you do?" The rage (which is as much anguish as it is anger) is a way of catharsis, a way of getting temporary relief from the heavy feeling of impotence that affects many who cannot understand a civilization which juggles its own means for oblivion and calls that performance an act toward peace.

"Down The Highway" is a distillation of Dylan's feeling about the blues. "The way I think about the blues," he says, "comes from what I learned from Big Joe Williams. The blues is more than something to sit home and arrange. What made the real blues singers so great is that they were able to state all the problems they had; but at the same time, they were standing outside them and could look at them. And in that way, they had them beat. What's depressing today is that many young singers are trying to get inside the blues, forgetting that those older singers used them to get outside their troubles."

"Bob Dylan's Blues" was composed spontaneously. It's one of what he calls his "really off-the-cuff songs. I start with an idea, and then I feel what follows. Best way I can describe this one is that it's sort of like walking by a side street. You gaze in and walk on."

"A Hard Rain's A-Gonna Fall" represents to Dylan a maturation of his feelings on this subject since the earlier and almost as powerful "Let Me Die In My Footsteps," which is not included here but which was released as a single record by Columbia. Unlike most of his song-writing contemporaries among city singers, Dylan doesn't simply make a polemical point in his compositions. As in this song about the psychopathology of peace-through-balance-of-terror, Dylan's images are multiply (and sometimes horrifyingly) evocative. As a result, by transmuting his fierce convictions into what can only be called art, Dylan reaches basic emotions which few political statements or extrapolations of statistics have so far been able to touch. Whether a song or a singer can then convert others is something else again.

"Hard Rain," adds Dylan, "is a desperate kind of song." It was written during the Cuban missile crisis of October 1962 when those who allowed themselves to think of the impossible results of the Kennedy-Khrushchev confrontation were chilled by the imminence of oblivion. "Every line in it," says Dylan, "is actually the start of a whole song. But when I wrote it, I thought I wouldn't have enough time alive to write all those songs so I put all I could into this one." Dylan treats "Don't Think Twice, It's All Right" differently from most city singers. "A lot of people," he says, "make it sort of a love song—slow and easy-going. But it isn't a love song. It's a statement that maybe you can say to make yourself feel better. It's as if you were talking to yourself. It's a hard song to sing. I can sing it sometimes, but I ain't that good yet. I don't carry myself yet the way that Big Joe Williams, Woody Guthrie, Leadbelly and Lightnin' Hopkins have carried themselves. I hope to be able to someday, but they're older people. I sometimes am able to do it, but it happens, when it happens, unconsciously. You see, in time, with those old singers, music was a tool—a way to live more, a way to make themselves feel better at certain points. As for me, I can make myself feel better sometimes, but at other times, it's still hard to go to sleep at night." Dylan's accompaniment on this track includes Bruce Langhorne (guitar), George Barnes (bass guitar), Dick Wellstood (piano), Gene Ramey (bass) and Herb Lovelle (drums).

"Bob Dylan's Dream" is another of his songs which was transported for a time in his mind before being written down. It was initially set off after all-night conversation between Dylan and Oscar Brown, Jr., in Greenwich Village. "Oscar," says Dylan, "is a groovy guy and the idea of this came from what we were talking about." The song slumbered, however, until Dylan went to England in the winter of 1962. There he heard a singer (whose name he recalls as Martin Carthy) perform "Lord Franklin," and that old melody found a new adapted home in "Bob Dylan's Dream." The song is a fond looking back at the easy camaraderie and idealism of the young when they are young. There is also in "Dream" a wry but sad requiem for the friendships that have evaporated as different routes, geographical and otherwise, are taken.

Of "Oxford Town," Dylan notes with laughter that "it's a banjo tune I play on the guitar." Otherwise, this account of the ordeal of James Meredith speaks grimly for itself.

"Talkin' World War III Blues" was about half-formulated beforehand and half-improvised at the recording session itself. The "talking blues" form is tempting to many young singers because it seems so pliable and yet so simple. However, the simpler a form, the more revealing it is of the essence of the performer. There's no place to hide in the talking blues. Because Bob Dylan is so hugely and quixotically himself, he is able to fill all the space the talking blues affords with unmistakable originality. In this piece, for example, he has singularly distilled the way we all wish away our end, thermo-nuclear or "natural." Or at least, the way we try to.

"Corrina, Corrina" has been considerably changed by Dylan. "I'm not one of those guys who goes around changing songs just for the sake of changing them. But I'd never heard 'Corrina, Corrina' exactly the way it first was, so that this version is the way it came out of me." As he indicates here, Dylan can be tender without being sentimental and his lyricism is laced with unabashed passion. The accompaniment is Dick Wellstood (piano), Howie Collins (guitar), Bruce Langhorne (guitar), Leonard Gaskin (bass) and Herb Lovelle (drums).

"Honey, Just Allow Me One More Chance" was first heard by Dylan from a recording by a now-dead Texas blues singer. Dylan can only remember that his first name was Henry. "What especially stayed with me," says Dylan, "was the plea in the title." Here Dylan distills the buoyant expectancy of the love search.

Unlike some of his contemporaries, Dylan isn't limited to one or two ways of feeling his music. He can be poignant and mocking, angry and exultant, reflective and whoopingly joyful. The final "I Shall Be Free" is another of Dylan's off-the-cuff songs in which he demonstrates the vividness, unpredictability and cutting edge of his wit.

This album, in sum, is the protean Bob Dylan at the time of the recording. By the next recording, there will be more new songs and insights and experiences. Dylan can't stop searching and looking and reflecting upon what he sees and hears. "Anything I can sing," he observes, "I call a song. Anything I can't sing, I call a poem. Anything I can't sing or anything that's too long to be a poem, I call a novel. But my novels don't have the usual story lines. They're about my feelings at a certain place at a certain time." In addition to his singing and song writing, Dylan is working on three "novels." One is about the week before he came to New York and his initial week in that city. Another is about South Dakota people he knew. And the third is about New York and a trip from New York to New Orleans.

Throughout everything he writes and sings, there is the surge of a young man looking into as many diverse scenes and people as he can find ("Every once in a while I got to ramble around") and of a man looking into himself. "The most important thing I know I learned from Woody Guthrie," says Dylan. "I'm my own person. I've got basic common rights—whether I'm here in this country or any other place. I'll never finish saying everything I feel, but I'll be doing my part to make some sense out of the way we're living, and not living, now. All I'm doing is saying what's on my mind the best way I know how. And whatever else you say about me, everything I do and sing and write comes out of me."

It is this continuing explosion of a total individual, a young man growing free rather than absurd, that makes Bob Dylan so powerful and so personal and so important a singer. As you can hear in these performances.

1963

Amiri Baraka

The founder of the Black Arts movement, Amiri Baraka was born LeRoi Jones in Newark, New Jersey, in 1934; his assumption of a new name was characteristic of a life dedicated to public provocation and dynamic change. Baraka's career in letters was centrifugal in its embrace of a multiplicity of forms, activities, and modes—as a poet, fiction writer, and polemicist, an Obie-winning dramatist, a critic, and groundbreaking small-press publisher. His writing was adamant in its commitment to radical social action, including in some cases calls to violent resistance. In the 1970s he broke with Black nationalism in favor of Marxism, and in 2002 his divisive tenure as poet laureate of New Jersey led to the governor's abolition of the post. *Blues People: Negro Music in White America*, published in 1963 under the name Jones, may be the most celebrated study of American popular music by a writer not principally known as a music historian or critic. He followed this with *Black Music* (1968), a groundbreaking survey of the free jazz of John Coltrane, Cecil Taylor, and others. His essay "The Changing Same" (1966), included in that collection and excerpted here, is part cultural history, part polemic, arguing for the continuing importance of artistic and political self-consciousness as African American music goes pop. Baraka's involvement in music included management of a record label, Jihad, and spoken-word recordings of his poems with the accompaniment of leading jazz musicians. He died in 2014.

▼ ▼

from
The Changing Same
(R&B and New Black Music)

THE BLUES IMPULSE transferred . . . containing a race, and its expression. *Primal* (mixtures . . . transfers and imitations). Through its many changes, it remained the exact replication of The Black Man In The West.

An expression of the culture at its most un-self- (therefore showing the larger consciousness of a *one self*, immune to bullshit) conscious. The direct expression of a place . . . jazz seeks another place as it weakens, a middle-class place. Except the consciously separate from those aspirations. Hence the so-called avant-garde or new music, the new Black Music, is separate because it seeks to be equally separate, equally un-self-conscious . . . meaning more conscious of the real weights of existence as the straightest R&B. There are simply more temptations for the middle-class Negro because he can make believe in America more, cop out easier, become whiter and slighter with less trouble, than most R&B people. Simply because he is closer to begin with.

Jazz, too often, becomes a music of special, not necessarily emotional, occasion. But R&B now, with the same help from white America in its exploitation of energy for profit, the same as if it was a gold mine, strings that music out along a similar weakening line. Beginning with their own vacuous "understanding" of what Black music is, or how it acts upon you, they believe, from the Beatles on down, that it is about white life.

The Blues, its "kinds" and diversity, its identifying parent styles. The phenomenon of jazz is another way of specifying cultural influences. The jazz that is most European, popular or avant, or the jazz that is Blackest, still makes reference to a central body of cultural experience. The impulse, the force that pushes you to sing . . . all up in there . . . is one thing . . . what it produces is another. It can be expressive of the entire force, or make it the occasion of some special pleading. Or it is all equal . . . we simply identify the part of the world in which we are most responsive. It is all there. We are exact (even in our lies). The elements that turn our singing into direction reflections of our selves are heavy and palpable as weather.

We are moved and directed by our total response to the possibility of all effects.

We are bodies responding differently, a (total) force, like against you. You react to push it, re-create it, resist it. It is the opposite pressure producing (in this case) the sound, the music.

The City Blues tradition is called that by me only to recognize different elements active in its creation. The slick city people we become after the exodus, the unleashing of an energy into the Northern urban situation. Wholesale.

The line we could trace, as musical "tradition," is what we as a people dig and pass on, as best we can. The call and response form of Africa (lead and chorus) has never left us, as a mode of (musical) expression. It has come down both as vocal and instrumental form.

The rhythm quartet of the last thirty years is a very obvious continuation of Black vocal tradition, and a condensation in the form from the larger tribal singing units . . . through the form of the large religious choirs (chorus) which were initially *dancers and singers*, of religious and/or ritual purpose.

Indeed, to go back in any historical (or emotional) line of ascent in Black music leads us inevitably to religion, i.e., spirit worship. This phenomenon is always at the root in Black art, the worship of spirit—or at least the summoning of or by such force. As even the music itself was that, a reflection of, or the no thing itself.

The slave ship destroyed a great many formal art traditions of the Black man. The white man enforced such cultural rape. A "cultureless" people is a people without a memory. No history. This is the best state for slaves; to be objects, just like the rest of massa's possessions.

The breakdown of Black cultural tradition meant finally the destruction of most formal art and social tradition. Including the breakdown of the Black pre-American religious forms. Forcibly so. Christianity replaced African religions as the outlet for spirit worship. And Christian forms were traded, consciously and unconsciously, for their own. Chris tian forms were emphasized under threat of death. What resulted were Afro-Christian forms. These are forms which persist today.

The stripping away, gradual erosion, of the pure African form as means of expression by Black people, and the gradual embracing of mixed Afro-Christian, Afro-American forms is an initial reference to the cultural philosophy of Black People, Black Art.

Another such reference, or such stripping, is an American phenom- enon, i.e., it is something that affected all of America, in fact the entire West. This, of course, is the loss of religiosity in the West, in general.

Black Music is African in origin, African-American in its totality, and its various forms (especially the vocal) show just how the African impulses were redistributed in its expression, and the expression itself became Christianized and post-Christianized.

Even today a great many of the best known R&B groups, quartets, etc., have church backgrounds, and the music itself is as churchified as it has ever been . . . in varying degrees of its complete emotional iden- tification with the Black African-American culture (Sam and Dave, etc. at one end . . . Dionne Warwick in the middle . . . Leslie Uggams, the other end . . . and fading).

The church continues, but not the devotion (at no level of its exis- tence is it as large, though in the poorest, most abstractly altruistic levels of churchgoing, the emotion is the devotion, and the God, the God of that feeling and movement, remains as powerful though "redis- tributed" somewhat).

But the kind of church Black people belonged to usually connected them with the society as a whole . . . identified them, their aspirations, their culture: because the church was one of the few places complete fullness of expression by the Black was not constantly censored by the white man. Even the asking of freedom, though in terms veiled with the biblical references of "The Jews," went down in church.

It was only those arts and cultural practices that were less obvi- ously capable of "alien" social statement that could survive during slavery. (And even today in contemporary America, it is much the same . . . though instead of out and out murder there are hardly more merciful ways of limiting Black protest or simple statement . . . in the arts just as in any other aspect of American life.)

Blues (Lyric) its song quality is, it seems, the deepest expression of memory. Experience re/feeling. It is the racial memory. It is the "abstract" design of racial character that is evident, would be evident, in creation carrying the force of that racial memory.

Just as the God spoken about in the Black songs is not the same one in the white songs. Though the words might look the same. (They are not even pronounced alike.) But it is a different quality of energy they summon. It is the simple tone of varying evolution by which we distinguish the races. The peoples. The body is directly figured in it. "The life of the organs."

But evolution is not merely physical: yet if you can understand what the physical alludes to, is reflect of, then it will be understood that each process in "life" is duplicated at all levels.

The Blues (impulse) lyric (song) is even descriptive of a plane of evolution, a direction . . . coming and going . . . through whatever worlds. Environment, as the social workers say . . . but Total Environment (including at all levels, the spiritual).

Identification is Sound Identification is Sight Identification is Touch, Feeling, Smell, Movement. (For instance, I can tell, even in the shadows, halfway across the field, whether it is a white man or Black man running. Though Whitney Young would like to see us all run the same.)

For instance, a white man could box like Muhammad Ali, only *after* seeing Muhammad Ali box. He could not initiate that style. It is no description, it *is* the culture. (AD 1966)

The Spirituals . . . The Camp Meeting Songs at backwoods churches . . . or Slave Songs talking about deliverance.

The God the slaves worshipped (for the most part, except maybe the "pure white" God of the toms) had to be willing to free them, somehow, someway . . . one sweet day.

The God, the perfection of what the spiritual delivery and world are said to be, is what the worshippers sang. That perfect Black land. The land changed with the God in charge. The churches the slaves and freedmen went to identified these Gods, and their will in heaven, as well as earth.

The closer the church was to Africa, the Blacker the God. (The Blacker the spirit.) The closer to the will (and meaning) of the West, the whiter the God, the whiter the spirit worshipped. The whiter the worshippers. This is still so. And the hard Black core of America is African.

From the different churches, the different Gods, the different versions of Earth. The different weights and "classic" versions of reality. And the different singing. Different expressions (of a whole). A whole people . . . a nation, in captivity.

Rhythm and Blues is part of "the national genius," of the Black man, of the Black nation. It is the direct, no monkey business expression of urban and rural (in its various stylistic variations) Black America.

The hard, driving shouting of James Brown identifies a place and image in America. A people and an energy, harnessed and not harnessed by America. JB is straight out, open, and speaking from the most deeply religious people on this continent.

The energy is harnessed because what JB does has to go down in a system governed by "aliens," and he will probably never become, say, as wealthy, etc., that is he will never reap the *material* benefits that several bunches of white folks will, from his own efforts. But the will of the expression transcends the physical-mental "material," finally alien system-world it has to go through to allow any "benefits" in it. Because the will of the expression is spiritual, and as such it must transcend its mineral, vegetable, animal, environment.

Form and content are both mutually expressive of the whole. And they are both equally expressive . . . each have an identifying motif and function. In Black music, both identify place and direction. We want different contents and different forms because we have different feelings. We are different peoples.

James Brown's form and content identify an entire group of people in America. However these may be transmuted and reused, reappear in other areas, in other musics for different purposes in the society, the initial energy and image are about a specific grouping of people, Black People.

Music makes an image. What image? What environment (in that word's most extended meaning, i.e., total, external and internal, environment)? I mean there is a world powered by that image. The world James Brown's images power is the lowest placement (the most alien) in the white American social order. Therefore, it is the Blackest and potentially the strongest.

It is not simply "the strongest" because of the transmutation and harnessing I spoke of earlier. This is social, but it is total. The world is a total. (And in this sense, the total function of "free music" can be understood. See, especially, H. Dumas' story in *Negro Digest* "Will the Circle Be Unbroken?" and understand the implications of music as an autonomous *judge* of civilizations, etc. Wow!)

By image, I mean that music (art for that matter . . . or any thing else if analyzed) summons and describes where its energies were gotten. The blinking lights and shiny heads, or the gray concrete and endless dreams. But the description is of a total environment. The content speaks of this environment, as does the form.

The "whitened" Negro and white man want a different content from the people James Brown "describes." They are different peoples. The softness and so-called "well being" of the white man's environment is described in his music (art) . . . in all expressions of his self. All people's are.

If you play James Brown (say, "Money Won't Change You . . . but time will take you out") in a bank, the total environment is changed. Not only the sardonic comment of the lyrics, but the total emotional placement of the rhythm, instrumentation and sound. An energy is released in the bank, a summoning of images that take the bank, and everybody in it, on a trip. That is, they visit another place. A place where Black People live.

But dig, not only is it a place where Black People live, it is a place, in the spiritual precincts of its emotional telling, where Black People move in almost absolute openness and strength. (For instance, what is a white person who walks into a James Brown or Sam and Dave song? How would he function? What would be the social metaphor for his existence in that world? What would he be doing?)

This is as true, finally, with the John Coltrane world or the Sun-Ra world. In the Albert Ayler world, or Ornette Coleman world, you would say, "well, they might just be playing away furiously at some stringed instrument." You understand?

In the Leslie Uggams world? They would be marrying a half-white singer and directing the show . . . maybe even whispering lyrics and stuff from the wings. You understand? *The song and the people is the same.*

The reaction to any expression moves the deepest part of the psyche and makes its identifications throughout. The middle-class Negro wants a different content (image) from James Brown, because he has come from a different place, and wants a different thing (he thinks). The something you want to hear is the thing you already are or move toward.

We feel, Where is the expression going? What will it lead to? What does it characterize? What does it make us feel like? What is its image? Jazz content, of course, is as pregnant.

The implications of content.

The form content of much of what is called New Thing or Avant-Garde or New Music differs (or seems to differ) from Rhythm and Blues, R&B oriented jazz, or what the cat on the block digs. (And here I'm talking about what is essentially *Black Music*. Although, to be sure, too often the "unswingingness" of much of the "new" is because of its association, derivation and even straight-out imitation of certain aspects of contemporary European and white Euro-American music . . . whether they are making believe they are Bach or Webern.) Avant-garde, finally, is a bad term because it also means a lot of quacks and quackers, too.

But the significant difference is, again, direction, intent, sense of identification . . . "kind" of consciousness. And that's what it's about; consciousness. What are you *with* (the word Con-With/Scio-Know).

The "new" musicians are self-conscious. Just as the boppers were. Extremely conscious of self. They are more conscious of a total self (or *want* to be) than the R&B people who, for the most part, are all-expression. Emotional expression. Many times self-consciousness turns out to be just what it is as a common figure of speech. It produces world-weariness, cynicism, corniness. Even in the name of Art. Or what have you . . . social uplift, "Now we can play good as white folks," or "I went to Juilliard, and this piece exhibits a Bach-like contrapuntal line," and so forth right on out to lunch.

But at its best and most expressive, the New Black Music is expression, and expression of reflection as well. What is presented is a consciously proposed learning experience. (See "The New Wave.") It is no wonder that many of the new Black musicians are or say they want to be "Spiritual Men" (some of the boppers embraced Islam), or else they are interested in the Wisdom Religion itself, i.e., the rise to spirit. It is expanding the consciousness of the given that they are interested in, not merely expressing what is already there, or alluded to. They are interested in the *unknown*. The mystical.

But it is interpretation. The Miracles are spiritual. They sing (and sing about) feeling. Their content is about feeling . . . the form is to make feeling, etc. The self-conscious (reflective, long-form, New Thing, bop, etc.) Art Musicians cultivate consciousness that wants more feeling, to rise . . . up a scale one measures with one's life. It is about thought, but thought can kill it. Life is complex in the same simplicity.

R&B is about emotion, issues purely out of emotion. New Black Music is also about emotion, but from a different place, and, finally, towards a different end. What these musicians feel is a more complete existence. That is, the digging of everything. What the wisdom religion preaches.

(But the actual New Black Music will be a larger expression. It will include the pretension of The New Music, as actuality, as summoner of Black Spirit, the evolved music of the then evolved people.)

The differences between rhythm and blues and the so-called new music or art jazz, the different places, are artificial, or they are merely indicative of the different placements of spirit. (Even "purely" social, like what the musicians want, etc.)

For instance, use of Indian music, old spirituals, even heavily rhythmic blues licks (and soon electronic devices) by new music musicians point toward the final close in the spectrum of the sound that will come. A really new, really all inclusive music. The whole people.

Any analysis of the content of R&B, the lyrics, or the total musical will and direction, will give a placement in contrast to analysis of new jazz content. (Even to the analysis of the implied vocalism of the new music: what are its intent and direction, what place it makes, etc., are concerned.) Again even the purely social, as analyzing reference, will give the sense of difference, what directions, what needs are present in the performers, and then, why the music naturally flows out of this.

The songs of R&B, for instance, what are they about? What are the people, for the most part, singing about? Their lives. That's what the New Musicians are playing about, and the projection of forms for those lives. (And I think any analysis will immediately show, as I pointed out in *Blues People*, that the songs, the music, changed, as the people did.) Mainly, I think the songs are about what is known as "love," requited and un. But the most popular songs are always a little sad, in tune with the temper of the people's lives. The extremes. Wild Joy—Deep Hurt.

The songs about unrequited, incompleted, obstructed, etc., love probably outnumber the others very easily. Thinking very quickly of just the songs that come readily to my mind, generally current, and favorites of mine (and on that other *top ten*, which is, you bet, the indication of where the minds, the people, are). "Walk On By" "Where Did Our Love Go?" "What Becomes of the Broken Hearted?" "The Tracks of My Tears," high poetry in the final character of their delivery . . . but to a very large extent, the songs are about love affairs which do not, did not, come off. For God knows how many reasons. Infidelity, not enough dough, incredibly "secret" reasons where the loved and the lover or the lovers are already separated and longing one for the other, according to who's singing, male or female. And all more precise and specific than the Moynihan Report, e.g., listen to Jr. Walker's "Road Runner." And this missed love that runs through these songs is exactly reflect of what is the term of love and loving in the Black world of America Twentieth Century.

The miss-understanding, nay, gap . . . abyss, that separates Black man and Black woman is always, over and over, again and again, told about and cried about. And it's old, in this country, to us. "Come back baby, Baby, please don't go . . . Cause the way I love you, Baby, you will never know . . . So come back, Baby, let's talk it over . . . one more time." A blues which bees older than Ray Charles or Lightnin' Hopkins, for that matter. "I got to laugh to keep from cryin'," which The Miracles make, "I got to dance to keep from cryin'," is not only a song but the culture itself. It is finally the same cry, the same people. You really got a hold on me. As old as our breath here.

But there are many songs about love triumphant. "I feel good . . . I got you . . . Hey!" the score, the together self, at one and in love and swinging, flying God-like. But a differently realized life-triumph than in the older more formally religious songs. The Jordans, the Promised Lands, now be cars and women-flesh, and especially dough. (Like, *power*.) There are many many songs about Money, e.g., Barrett Strong "Money," J.B.'s "I Got Money . . . now all I need is love," among so many others. But the songs are dealing with the everyday, and how to get through it and to the other side (or maybe not) which for the most part still bees that world, but on top of it, power full, and beauty full.

The older religiosity falls away from the music, but the deepest feel of spirit worship always remains, as the music's emotional patterns continue to make reference to. The new jazz people are usually much more self-consciously concerned about "God" than the R&B folks. But most of the R&B people were *really* in the church at one time, and sang there first, only to drift or rush away later.

1966

RICHARD POIRIER

Richard Poirier (1925–2009), cofounder of Library of America, was not a rock writer. A professor of American and English literature at Rutgers University, and editor for the influential literary journals *Partisan Review* and *Raritan* (which he founded in 1981), Poirier was a scholar and a committed public intellectual. His "Learning from the Beatles" (1967), published in *Partisan Review*, marks one of the first serious attempts by the academy to engage critically (and in Poirier's case, enthusiastically) with rock & roll. Throughout his career, Poirier worked to break down the facile exclusion of popular culture from intellectual culture. In a very real sense, this anthology is the offspring of precisely that kind of thinking and writing.

▼ ▼

Learning from the Beatles

HAS ANYONE been able completely to ignore *Sgt. Pepper's Lonely Hearts Club Band*? Probably not. But the very fact of its immense popularity with people of every age and persuasion is almost a guarantee of its not receiving the demanding critical attention that it calls for. It isn't enough to say that it is the latest and most remarkable of the thirteen albums composed and performed by the Beatles since 1964; some such claim could have been made for each album when it appeared. *Sgt. Pepper* isn't in the line of continuous development; rather, it is an eruption. It is an astounding accomplishment for which no one could have been wholly prepared, and it therefore substantially enlarges and modifies all the work that preceded it. It sends us back to the earlier Beatles not for confirmation of the fact that they have always been the best group of their kind. Rather, we listen for those gestations of genius that have now come to fruition. And the evidence is there: in each album which, while being unmistakably theirs, is nonetheless full of exploratory peculiarities not heard on the others; in the way the release even of a single can set off a new surge of energy in their many imitators; in a self-delighting inventiveness that has gradually exceeded the sheer physical capacities even of four such brilliant musicians. The consequent necessity for expanded orchestral and electronic support reached the point where the Sgt. Pepper album had to be wholly conceived in studio with as many as forty-eight instruments. Meanwhile, still in their mid-twenties they have made two movies, *A Hard Day's Night* and *Help!*, which are in spots as good as the Marx brothers, and their most talented member, John Lennon, has written two books of Joycean verbal play that suggest why no one is ever in danger of reading too much into the lyrics of their songs. The Beatles are now beyond patronization, and this is especially satisfying to those like myself who have wondered how much longer the literary academic adjudicators could claim to be taking the arts seriously by promoting a couple of distinguished novels every year, a few films, some poems, maybe a museum show and, if they're really lucky, a play.

Of course to delay a revolution there are ways and ways of finally paying considered attention to the lower orders. One way is to sociologize in the manner, McLuhan or pre-McLuhan, that forces the good and the bad in the popular arts to lie down in the same categories. There'll surely be a piece announcing, say, that the Beatles "represent"—a favorite word in the shelving process—not just the young but an aristocracy of the young. And of course they are aristocratic: in their carelessness, their assumption that they can enact anyone else's life just for the fun of it, their tolerance for the things they do make fun of, their delight in wildness along with a disdain for middle-class rectitudes, their easy expertness, their indifference to the wealth they are happy to have, their pleasures in costume and in a casual eccentricity of ordinary dress, their in-group language not meant, any more than is Bob Dylan's—another such aristocrat—to make ordinary sense. That kind of accommodation is familiar by now, and so is another, which is to admit them into the company of their "betters." You know, the way jazz is like Bach? Well, sometimes they are like Monteverdi and sometimes their songs are even better than Schumann's. But that won't work either. Liverpool boys of their sort have been let into Eton before, and not on the assumption that it would be the style of Eton that would change.

It won't be easy to accommodate the Beatles, and that's nowadays almost the precondition for exciting the pastoral concern of Responsible Critics. Literary and academic grown-ups will discover that their favorite captive audience, the young in school, really have listened to the Beatles' kind of music and won't buy the yarn of significance that ensnares most adult talk about the other arts. Any effort to account for what the Beatles are doing will be difficult, as I've learned from this not very extensive and inexpert try, but only to the extent that talking about the experience of any work of art is more difficult than talking about the theory of it, or the issues in it or the history around it. The results of any such effort by a number of people would be of importance not just for popular music but for all the arts. People who listen to the Beatles love them—what about that? Why isn't there more talk about pleasure, about the excitement of witnessing a performance, about the excitement that goes into a performance of any kind? Such talk could set in motion a radical and acutely necessary amendment to the literary and academic club rules. Since the exalted arts (to which the novel, about a century ago, was the last genre to be admitted) have all but surrendered the provision of fun and entertainment to the popular arts, criticism must turn to film and song if it is to remind itself that the arts really do not need to be boring, no matter how much copy can be made from the elaboration of current theories of boredom.

Critical confrontations initiated in this spirit could give a new status to an increasingly unfashionable kind of criticism: to close-up, detailed concern for performance, for enactment and execution in a work of art. Film and song, the two activities in which young people are now especially interested, and about which they are learning to talk fairly well, may yield something to other kinds of scrutiny, but they yield much more to this kind. So does literature, on the very infrequent occasions when it is so treated. The need is for intense localization of interest and a consequent modesty of description, in the manner of Stark Young's dramatic criticism, or Bernard Haggin's writing about classical music and jazz or Edwin Denby and, more recently, Robert Garis on ballet. Imagining an audience for such criticism, the critic thinks not of a public with Issues and Topics at the ready, but rather of a small group of like-minded, quite private people who find pleasure in certain intensive acts of looking and listening. Looking and listening to something with such a group, imaginary or real, means checking out responses, pointing to particular features, asking detailed questions, sharing momentary excitements. People tend to listen to the Beatles the way families in the last century listened to readings of Dickens, and it might be remembered by literary snobs that the novel then, like the Beatles and even film now, was considered a popular form of entertainment generally beneath serious criticism, and most certainly beneath academic attention.

The Beatles' music is said to belong to the young, but if it does that's only because the young have the right motive for caring about it—they enjoy themselves. They also know what produces the fun they have, by phrase and instrument, and they're very quick, as I've discovered, to shoot down inflated interpretations. They should indeed exercise proprietary rights. This is the first time that people of school age have been tuned in to sounds invented not by composers approved by adults but in to sounds invented by their own near contemporaries, sounds associated with lyrics, manners and dress that they also identify as their own. David Amram, the New York Philharmonic's first resident composer, is understandably optimistic that this kind of identification will develop an avidity of attention to music that could be the salvation of American musical composition and performance. Perhaps in some such way the popular arts can help restore all the arts to their status as entertainment.

To help this process along it isn't necessary that literary and academic grown-ups go to school to their children. Rather, they must begin to ask some childlike and therefore some extremely difficult questions about particular works: Is this any fun? How and where is it any fun? And if it isn't why bother? While listening together to recordings of popular music, people of any age tend naturally to ask these questions, and I've heard them asked by young people with an eager precision which they almost never exhibit, for want of academic encouragement, when they talk about a poem or a story. Their writing about this music isn't as good as their talk, at least in the magazines I've been able to get hold of, like *Vibrations, The Broadside* and, perhaps the best, *Crawdaddy.* In written criticism they display some of the adult vices, including at times a nearly Germanic fondness for categorization: the Mersey beat, the raving style, trip songs, the San Francisco school, the love sound, folk-rock and the rock-folk-pop tradition are typical of the terms that get bandied about with desperate and charming hope. Reviews of popular music in the major newspapers and magazines are much worse, however, and before the Sgt. Pepper album practically no space even for an intelligent note was given the Beatles in any of them. Now that they've begun to appear, any adult easily victimized by a reputed generational gap need only read reviews of *Sgt. Pepper* in the *New York Times* and the *Village Voice* by Richard Goldstein to discover that youth is no guarantee of understanding. In his early twenties, he is already an ancient. Some of his questions—does the album have any real unity?—were not necessary even when originally asked some two thousand years ago, while others are a bad dream of Brooks and Warren: the "lyrical technique" of "She's Leaving Home" is "uninspired narrative, with a dearth of poetic irony." The song is in fact one of *Sgt. Pepper*'s satirically funniest cuts, though someone Goldstein's age mightn't as easily see this as someone older. Recognition of its special blend of period sentimentality and elegance of wit is conferred upon the listener not by his being chronologically young but by his having once lived with that especially English blend of tones from Beatrice Lillie or Noel Coward, and their wistful play about the genteel.

Nearly all the songs on the Sgt. Pepper album and the two singles released here since then—"All You Need Is Love" and "Baby You're a Rich Man"—are in fact quite broadly allusive: to the blues, to jazz hits of the thirties and forties, to classical music, early rock and roll, previous cuts by the Beatles themselves. Much of the comedy in these songs and much of their historical resonance, as in the stately Wagnerian episode in "A Day In the Life," is managed in this way. Mixing of styles and tones reminds the listener that one kind of feeling about a subject isn't enough and that any single induced feeling must often exist within the context of seemingly contradictory alternatives. Most good groups offer something of this kind, like the Who, with the brilliant drummer Keith Moon. In songs like "Don't Look Away" and "So Sad About Us," Moon, working with the composer-guitarist Pete Townsend, calls forth a complicated response in a manner nicely described in *Crawdaddy* by Jon Landau, one of the best of the reviewers I've read: "Townsend scratches his chorus, muffles his strings, or lets the chord stand out full depending on what Moon is doing—the result being a perfectly unified guitar-drum sound that can't help but make you feel happy even while the lyrics tell you to feel sad." The Beatles have often in the past worked for similar mixtures, but they now offer an additional nuance: especially in later songs, one of the interwoven strands is likely to be an echo of some familiar, probably clichéd musical, verbal or dramatic formula. These echoes, like the soap-opera background music of "She's Leaving Home" or the jaunty music-hall tones of "When I'm Sixty-four," have the enriching effect that allusiveness can have in poetry: of expanding a situation toward the simultaneous condition of pathos, because the situation is seen as recurrent and therefore possibly insoluble, and comic, because the recurrence has finally passed into cliché.

Any close listening to musical groups soon establishes the fact that as composers and performers the Beatles repay attention altogether more than does any other group, American or English. They offer something for nearly everyone and respond to almost any kind of interest. The Rolling Stones, the Left Banke and the Bee Gees are especially good, but in none of these is there an inventive productivity equal to that of Lennon, McCartney or their producer George Martin, whose contributions of electronic and orchestral notation really make him one of the group, particularly now that their performances are to be exclusively in studio. Only Dylan shows something equivalent to the Beatles in his combination of talents as composer, lyricist and performer. In performance the Beatles exhibit a nearly total theatrical power. It is a power so unencumbered and so freely diverse both for the group and for each of its members that it creates an element of suspense in whatever they do, an expectation that this time there really will be a failure of good taste—that attribute shared by only the greatest theatrical performers. They never wholly lose themselves in anyone else's styling, however, or in their own exuberance; they never succumb to the excitements they generate, much less those of their audience. It's unthinkable that they would lend themselves for the rock and wreck sequence of the Yardbirds in Antonioni's *Blow-up*. That particular performance, quite aside from what it contributed to a brilliant film, is a symptom of the infiltration even into popular music of the decadence by which entertainment is being displaced by a self-abasing enactment of what is implicit in the *form* of entertainment—in this instance, of group playing that gives way to animosities and a destructive retaliation against recalcitrant instrumental support. When the Beatles sound as if they are heading orchestrally into self-obliterating noise, it is very often only that they may assert their presence vocally in quite the opposite direction: by contrasting choirboy cooing, by filigrees of voice-play coming from each of them, as in the reprise of "Sgt. Pepper," for instance, or, as in "Lovely Rita," the little choral oo's and gaspings—all of these suggesting, in their relation to solo, crosscurrents of feeling within an agreed area of play. Manners so instinctively free and yet so harmonious could not be guided from outside, either by an audience or even by directorial guidance, however much the latter did help in rescuing them from the tawdry enslavement to Elvis Presley, an otherwise profitable influence, in their first, fortunately hard-to-find recording of 1961 made in Hamburg with Ringo's predecessor at the drums, Peter Best.

As is the taste of all great performers—in athletics, in politics, in any of the arts—the taste of the Beatles or of Dylan is an emanation of personality, of a self that is the generous master but never the creature of its audience. Taste in such instances is inseparable from a stubbornness of selfhood, and it doesn't matter that the self has been invented for the theater. Any self is invented as soon as any purpose is conceived.

But the Beatles are a special case in not being *a* self at all. They are a group, and the unmistakeable group identity exists almost in spite of sharp individuation, each of them, except the invisible Martin, known to be unique in some shaggy way. There are few other groups in which even one or two of the members are as publicly recognizable as any of the Beatles, and this can't be explained as a difference simply in public relations. It is precisely this unusual individuation which explains, I think, why the Beatles are so much stronger than any other group and why they don't need, like the Who, to play at animosities on stage. The pretense doesn't communicate the presence of individual Who but rather an anxiety at their not instinctively feeling like individuals when they are together. The Beatles, on the other hand, enhance the individuality of one another by the sheer elaborateness by which they arrive at a cohesive sound and by a musical awareness of one another that isn't distinguishable from the multiple directions allowed in the attainment of harmony. Like members of a great athletic team, like such partners in dance as Nureyev and Fonteyn or like some jazz combos, the Beatles in performance seem to draw their aspirations and their energy not from the audience but from one another. Their close, loyal and affectionate personal ties are of course not irrelevant.

The incentive for what they accomplish seems to be sequestered among them, a tensed responsiveness that encourages from Harrison, as in "And Your Bird Can Sing," what sounds like the best guitar playing in the world and which provokes the immense productivity of Lennon and McCartney. The amount they have composed might be explained by commercial venture but not the daring and originality of each new single or album. Of course the promise of "new sounds" is itself a commercial necessity in their business, as the anxieties of the second album of the Jefferson Airplane indicate, but the Beatles will soon release their fourteenth, and it's not merely "new sounds" that they produce, an easy enough matter with orchestral support, electronics and Asiatic importations. They produce different styles, different musical conceptions and revisions of sentiment that give an unprecedented variety to an artistic career that had its proper beginning a mere four or five years ago. The freshness of each effort is often so radically different from the one before, as any comparison among *Rubber Soul, Revolver* and *Sgt. Pepper* will indicate, as to constitute risk rather than financial ambition—especially three such albums, along with a collection of earlier songs, *Yesterday and Today*, in a period just over eighteen months. They are the ones who get tired of the sounds they have made, and the testings and teasings that produce each new album are self-inflicted. If they are careerist it is in the manner not of Judy Garland, reminding us in each concert of "Somewhere Over the Rainbow" and the pains of show biz, but of John Coltrane who, when he died in July at forty, was also about to give up performance in public altogether, even though his reputation as one of the most influential musicians in jazz and its greatest saxophonist guaranteed him an increasingly profitable concert career. His interest in music was a continually exploratory one, an effort to broaden the possibilities, as the Beatles do now in studio, of his music and his instruments. Like Harrison with his guitar, he managed with the soprano sax to produce a nearly oriental sound, and this discovery led him to an interest in Indian music much as Harrison was led to the study of the sitar. And again like the Beatles, Coltrane's experimentation was the more intense because he and his sidemen, Elvin Jones and McCoy Tyner, achieved a remarkable degree of liberating, energizing empathy. Almost all such champions are extraordinary and private men who work with an audience, as the phrase goes, only when that audience is composed of the few who can perform with them. Otherwise, the audience is what it ought to be: not participants but witnesses or only listeners to a performance. The audience that in the theme song of *Sgt. Pepper* is so "lovely" that "we'd like to take you home with us" is a wholly imaginary one, especially on a record contrived as an escape from public performance.

Aloof from politics, their topicality is of music, the sentiments and the social predicaments traditional to folk songs, and ballads. Maybe the most important service of the Beatles and similar groups is the restoration to good standing of the simplicities that have frightened us into irony and the search for irony; they locate the beauty and pathos of commonplace feelings even while they work havoc with fashionable or tiresome expressions of those feelings. A particularly brilliant example is the record, released some weeks after the Sgt. Pepper album, with "Baby You're a Rich Man" on one side and "All You Need Is Love" on the other. "Baby You're a Rich Man" opens with an inquiry addressed by McCartney and Harrison to Lennon, who can be said to represent here a starry-eyed fan's version of the Beatles themselves: "How does it feel to be / One of the beautiful people?" This and subsequent questions are asked of the "rich man" in a reverentially high but devastatingly lilting voice, to the accompaniment of bursts of sitar music and the clip-clopping of Indian song. The sitar, an instrument Harrison studied in India for six weeks with the renowned Ravi Shankar ("George," he reported, "was truly humble") here suggests not the India of "Within You, Without You" evoked on the Sgt. Pepper album, the India of the Bhagavad Gita. It is rather another India, of fabulous riches, the India of the British and their Maharajahs, a place for exotic travel, but also for josh sticks and the otherworldliness of a "trip." All these possibilities are at work in the interplay of music and lyrics. Contributing to the merely social and satiric implications of the song, the Indian sounds operate in the manner of classical allusion in Pope: they expand to the ridiculous the cant of jet-set, international gossip columns—"one of the beautiful people" or "baby, you're a rich man now," or "how often have you been there?" But, as in Pope, the instrument of ridicule here, the sitar, is allowed in the very process to remain unsullied and eloquent. The social implications of the song carry more than a hint of self-parody since the comic mixtures of verbal and musical phrasing refer us to similar mixtures that are a result of the Beatles' fantastic fortune: Liverpool boys, still in their twenties, once relatively poor and now enormously rich, once socially nowhere and now internationally "there," once close to home both in fact and in their music but now implicated not only in the Mersey beat but in the Ganges sound, in travel to India and "trips" of a kind for which India set the precedent for centuries.

Most remarkably, the song doesn't sort out its social satire from its implicitly positive treatment of drugs. Bob Dylan often puns with roughly the same intention, as in "Rainy Day Women #12 & 35," a simple but effective example:

Well, they'll stone you when you're trying to be so good,
They'll stone you just like they said they would.
They'll stone you when you try to go home,
Then they'll stone you when you're there all alone.
But I would not feel so all alone:
Everybody must get stoned.

In the Beatles' song, the very same phrases that belong to the platitudes of the "beautiful people" belong also, with favorable connotations, to the drug scene. The question, "And have you travelled very far?" is answered by Lennon, the "beautiful" person, with what socially would be a comfortable cliché: "Far as the eye can see." But the phrase is really too outmoded for the jet age and thus sends us back to the original question and to the possibility that the "travel" can refer to a "trip" on LSD, the destination of which would indeed be "as far as the eye can see." Most of the lyrics operate in this double way, both as social satire and drug talk: "How often have you been there? / Often enough to know," or "What did you see when you were there? / Nothing that doesn't show" or "Some do it naturally" (presumably an acidhead by nature) to which the answer is "Happy to be that way." The song could pass simply as social satire, though to see that and that only is also to be the object of satire, of not knowing what implications are carried even by the language you make fun of for its imprecisions. The point, and it's one that I'll come back to, is that the argot of LSD isn't much different from the banalities of question and answer between a "beautiful" person and his bedazzled interviewer. The punning genius of Lennon is evident here perhaps more effectively than in his two books, *In My Own Write* and *A Spaniard in the Works*, with their affinities to Edward Lear as well as to the Joyce of *Finnegans Wake*.

The Beatles won't be stuck even within their most intricate contrivances, however, and they escape often by reminding us and themselves that they are singers and not pushers, performers and not propagandists. The moment occurs in "Baby You're a Rich Man," as it does in other songs, near the end, in the question "Now that you've found another key / What are you going to play?" Necessarily the question refers us to their music while at the same time alluding to the promised results of drugs—a new "key" to personality, to a role as well as to the notes that one might "play." Similar uses of words that can allude both to the subject of the moment and to their constant subject, musical creation, occur in "All You Need Is Love" ("Nothing you can sing that can't be sung"), with implications we'll get to in a moment, and in the second song on the Sgt. Pepper album, "A Little Help From My Friends." Sung by Ringo the "help" refers most simply to affection when there is no one around to love and it also means pot supplied by a friend. However, at the beginning of the song it explicitly means the assistance the others will give Ringo with his singing, while the phrases "out of tune" and "out of key" suggest, in the broadest sense, that the number, like the whole occasion, is in the mode not of the Beatles but of Sgt. Pepper's Lonely Hearts Club Band: "What would you think if I sang out of tune, / Would you stand up and walk out on me. / Lend me your ears and I'll sing you a song, / And I'll try not to sing out of key. / Oh, I get by with a little help from my friends, / Mmmm, I get high with a little help from my friends, / Mmmm, going to try with a little help from my friends, . . ."

One of the Beatles' most appealing qualities is their tendency more to self-parody than to parody of others. The two are of course very close for performers who empathize with all the characters in their songs and whose most conspicuous moments of self-parody occur when they're emulating someone whose style they'd like to master. At such moments their boyishness really does shine forth as a musical virtue: giving themselves almost wholly to an imitation of some performer they admire, their necessary exaggeration of his style makes fun of no one so much as themselves. It's a matter of trying on a style and then—as if embarrassed by their own riches, by a self-confident knowledge that no style, not even one of their own invention, is more than a temporary exercise of strength—of laughing themselves out of imitation. Listen to the extravagant rendering on *Beatles '65* of Chuck Berry in "Rock and Roll Music" or their many early emulations of Presley, whose importance to their development is everywhere apparent, or the mimicry of Western music in "Act Naturally" on one of their very best albums, *Yesterday and Today*, or the McCartney imitation of Little Richard singing "Long Tall Sally" on the *Beatles Second Album*. It's all cowboys and Indians by people who have a lot of other games they want to play and who know very well where home is and when to go there. Parody and self-parody is frequent among the other groups in the form of persistent stylization, but its object is almost always some clichéd sentiment or situation. Parody from the Beatles tends usually, and increasingly, to be directed toward musical tradition and their own musical efforts. This is at least one reason why "All You Need Is Love," recorded on the reverse side of "Baby You're a Rich Man," is one of the most important they have ever done, an indication, along with the Sgt. Pepper album, of so sophisticated an awareness of their historical achievements in music as to make it seem unlikely that they can continue much longer without still further changes of direction even more radical than their decision not to perform henceforth for live audiences. "All You Need Is Love" is decisive evidence that when the Beatles think about anything they think musically and that musical thinking dictates their response to other things: to "love," in this instance, to drugs and social manners in "Baby You're a Rich Man Now" and throughout the Sgt. Pepper album.

I doubt that any of these subjects would in itself prove a sufficient sustenance for their musical invention until first called forth and then kindled by some musical idea. At this point in their career it is impossible, given their and George Martin's musical knowledge and sophistication, that the title "All You Need Is Love" should mean what it would mean coming from any other group, namely hippie or flower love. Expectations of complications are satisfied from the outset: the repetition, three times and in a languorous tone, of the phrase "love, love, love" might remind us of the song of the aging Chaplin in *Limelight*, a song in which he keeps repeating the word throughout with a pitiable and insistent rapidity. Musical subterfuge of lyric simplicity occurs again when the title line, "all you need is love," picks up a musical trailer out of the thirties ballroom. The historical frequency of the "need" for love is thus proposed by the music, and it is as if this proposition emboldens the lyrics: "Nothing you can do that can't be done," "nothing you can sing that can't be sung," "nothing you can know that can't be known," "nothing you can see that can't be shown—it's easy"—this is a sample of equally ambiguous assertions that constitute the verbal substance of the song, even while the word "love" is being stretched out in choral background. And like the ambiguous language of "Baby You're a Rich Man," the phrasing here sounds comfortably familiar—if you had love you could do anything. Except that isn't really what the lyrics imply. Rather, the suggestion is that doing, singing, knowing, seeing have in some sense already been done or at least that we needn't be in any particular sweat about them; they're accepted as already within the accustomed range of human possibility. What has not been demonstrated to anyone's satisfaction, what hasn't been tried, is "love." "Love" remains the great unfulfilled need, and the historical evidence for this is in endless musical compositions about it. Far from suggesting that "love" will solve everything, which would be the hippie reading of "all you need is love," the song allows most things to be solved without it. Such a nice bit of discrimination issues from the music and thence into the lyrics. Interestingly enough, the lyrics were meant to be simple in deference to the largely non–English-speaking audience for whom the song was especially written and performed on the BBC worldwide TV production of "Our World." "Normally," the Beatles' song publisher Richard James later observed, "the Beatles like to write sophisticated material, but they were glad to have the opportunity to write something with a very basic appeal." But so was Shakespeare at the Globe, and we know how unsophisticated *he* could be. The simplicity is entirely in the initial repetitions of title line and the word "love," a verbal simplicity first modified by the music and then turned into complications that have escaped even most English-speaking listeners.

Lennon and McCartney's recognition through music that the "need" for love is historical and recurrent is communicated to the listener by instrumental and vocal allusions to earlier material. The historical allusiveness is at the outset smart-alecky—the song opens with the French National Anthem—passes through the Chaplin echo, if that's what it is, to various echoes of the blues, and boogie-woogie, all of them in the mere shadings of background, until at the end the song itself seems to be swept up and dispersed within the musical history of which it is a part and of the electronics by which that history has been made available. The process begins by a recurrence of the "love, love, love" phrase, here repeated and doubled as on a stalled record. It then proceeds into a medley of sounds, fractured, mingled musical phrases drifting into a blur which my friend Paul Bertram pointed out to me is like the sounds of a radio at night fading and drifting among the signals of different stations. We can make out fragments of old love songs condemned to wander through the airways for all time: "Green Sleeves," a burst of trumpet sound I can't identify, a hit of the thirties called "In the Mood," a ghostly "love you, yeah, yeah, yeah" of "She Loves You" from the *Beatles Second Album* of 1964 and, in the context of "All You Need Is Love," a pathetic "all together now . . . everybody!" of the old community sing. Far from being in any way satiric, the song gathers into itself the musical expression of the "need" for love as it has accumulated through decades of popular music.

This historical feeling for music, including their own musical creations, explains, I think, the Beatles' fascination with the invented aspects of everything around them, the participatory tenderness and joy with which they respond to styles and artifact, the maturity with which they have come to see the coloring of the human and social landscape of contemporary England. It's as if they naturally see the world in the form of *son et lumière*: as they say in a beautiful neighborhood song about Liverpool, "Penny Lane is in my ears and in my eyes." Not everyone their age is capable of seeing the odd wonder of a meter maid—after all, a meter maid's a meter maid; fewer still would be moved to a song of praise like "Lovely Rita" ("When it gets dark I tow your heart away"); and only a Beatle could be expected, when seeing her with a bag across her shoulder, to have the historically enlivened vision that "made her look a little like a military man." Now of course English boys out of Liverpool can be expected, it says here, to be more intimate than American boys from San Francisco with the residual social and cultural evidences from World War II and even from the First World War. In response to these and other traces of the past, however, the Beatles display an absolutely unique kind of involvement. It isn't simply that they have an instinctive nostalgia for period styles, as in "She's Leaving Home" or "When I'm Sixty-four," or that they absorb the past through the media of the popular arts, through music, cinema, theatrical conventions, bands like Sgt. Pepper's or music-hall performers. Everyone to some extent apprehends the world in the shapes given it by the popular arts and its media; we all see even the things that are new to us through that gridiron of style that Harold Rosenberg imagines as a debilitating shield in front of the British Redcoats even as they first entered the American terrain. No, the Beatles have the distinction in their work both of *knowing* that this is how they see and feel things and of enjoying the knowledge. It could be said that they know what Beckett and Borges know but without any loss of simple enthusiasm or innocent expectation, and without any patronization of those who do not know. In the loving phrases of "Penny Lane," "A pretty nurse is selling poppies from a tray / And tho' she feels as if she's in a play, / She is anyway."

It isn't surprising that drugs have become important to their music, that they are leading an effort in England for the legalization of marijuana, partly as a result of the conviction and sentencing on drug charges of two of the Rolling Stones, and that in response to questions, Lennon, McCartney and Harrison have let it be known that they've taken LSD. At least four of the songs on the Sgt. Pepper album are concerned with taking a "trip" or "turning on": "A Little Help From My Friends," "Lucy in the Sky with Diamonds," "Fixing a Hole" and "A Day in the Life," with a good chance of a fifth in "Getting Better." Throughout the album, the consciousness of the *dramatis personae* in the songs is directed more or less by inventions of media or of the popular arts, and drugs are proposed as one kind of personal escape into the freedom of some further invention all on one's own. Inventing the world out of the mind with drugs is more physically risky than doing it by writing songs, films or wearing costumes, but danger isn't what the songs offer for consideration, and it's in any case up to the Beatles alone to decide what they want for their minds and bodies. Instead, the songs propose, quite delightfully and reasonably, that the vision of the world while on a "trip" or under the influence of a drug isn't necessarily wilder than a vision of the world through which we travel under the influence of the arts or the news media. Thus, the third song on the album, "Lucy in the Sky with Diamonds," proposes that the listener can "picture" a "trip" scene without taking such a "trip" himself. Here, as in "Baby You're a Rich Man," the experience of a "trip" is wittily superimposed on the experience of ordinary travel: "Picture yourself on a train in a station, / With plasticine porters with looking glass ties, / Suddenly someone is there at the turnstile, / The girl with kaleido-scope eyes." Of course the images could come as easily from Edward Lear as from the experience of drugs, and Lennon has claimed that the title of the song is not an anagram for LSD but was taken from a draw-ing his son did at school. Lennon, the author of two books of Joycean punning, knows to the point of hilarity that one meaning denies the presence of another, which it has hidden inside, only to all strangers and the police. Still his reticence is obviously a form of the truth. The Beatles won't be reduced to drugs when they mean, intend and enact so much more. "Acid," Harrison told the Los Angeles *Free Press* in August, "is not the answer, definitely not the answer. It's enabled people to see a little bit more, but when you really get hip, you don't need it." Later, to Hunter Davies of the London *Sunday Times*, McCartney announced that they'd given up drugs. "It was an experience we went through and now it's over we don't need it any more. We think we're finding other ways of getting there." In this effort they're apparently being helped by Maharishi Mahesh Yogi, the Indian founder of the International Med-itation Society, though even on the way to their initiation in Bangor, North Wales, Lennon wondered if the experience wasn't simply going to be another version of what they already knew: "You know, like some are EMI and some Decca, but it's really still records."

The notion that we "picture" ourselves much of the time anyway without even willing it, that we see ourselves and the world in exotic images usually invented by someone else, is suggested throughout the Sgt. Pepper album, even on the cover, with its clustered photographs of world-shaping "stars" of all kinds. In "A Day in the Life," the last song and a work of great power and historical grasp, the hapless man whose role is sung by McCartney wants to "turn on" himself and his lover—maybe us too—as a relief from the multiple controls exerted over life and the imagination by various and competing media. The sad little "oh boy" interjected by McCartney's sweet, vulnerable voice into orchestral movements of intimidating, sometimes portentous momentum, expresses wonderfully how the victim is further confounded by the fact that these controls often impose themselves under the guise of entertainment:

> *I read the news today oh boy*
> *About a lucky man who made the grade*
> *And though the news was rather sad*
> *Well I just had to laugh*
> *I saw the photograph.*
> *He blew his mind out in a car*
> *He didn't notice that the lights had changed*
> *A crowd of people stood and stared*
> *They'd seen his face before*
> *Nobody was really sure*
> *If he was from the House of Lords.*
> *I saw a film today oh boy*
> *The English Army had just won the war*
> *A crowd of people turned away*
> *But I just had to look*
> *Having read the book.*
> *I'd love to turn you on. . . .*

The news in the paper is "rather sad" but the photograph is funny, so how does one respond to the suicide; suicide is a violent repudiation of the self but it mightn't have happened if the man had followed the orders of the traffic lights; the victim isn't so much a man anyway as a face people have seen someplace in the news, in photographs or possibly even on film; and while a film of the English army winning the war is too dated for most people to look at, and maybe they don't believe in the victory anyway, the man in the song has to look at it (oh boy—a film) because he has read a book about it and therefore it does have

some reality for him. "Turning on" is at least a way of escaping submission to the media designed to turn on the mind from the outside—
quite appropriately the song was banned on the BBC—and loving to
turn "you" on, either a lover or you, the listener, is an effort to escape
the horror of loneliness projected by the final images of the song:

> *I read the news today oh boy*
> *Four thousand holes in Blackburn*
> *Lancashire*
> *And though the holes were rather small*
> *They had to count them all*
> *Now they know how many holes it takes*
> *To fill the Albert Hall.*
> *I'd love to turn you on.*

The audience in Albert Hall—the same as the "lovely audience" in the
first song that the Beatles would like to "take home" with them?—are
only so many holes: unfilled and therefore unfertile holes, of the earth
and therefore holes of decomposition, gathered together but separate
and therefore countable, utterly and inarticulately alone. Is this merely
a bit of visionary ghoulishness, something seen on a "trip"? No, good
citizens can find it, like everything else in the song, in the daily news—
of how Scotland Yard searched for buried bodies on a moor by making
holes in the earth with poles and then waiting for the stench of decom-
posing flesh.

Lennon and McCartney in their songs seem as vulnerable as the man
in "A Day in the Life" to the sights and sounds by which different
media shape and then reshape reality, but their response isn't in any
way as intimidated, and "turning on" isn't their only recourse. They can
also tune in and play the game, sometimes to show, as in "A Day in the
Life," how one shaped view of reality can be mocked out of existence by
crossing it with another. They mix their media the way they mix musical
sounds or cross lyrics of one tone with music of quite another—with a
vengeance. It's unwise ever to assume that they're doing only one thing
or expressing themselves in only one style. "She's Leaving Home" does

have a persistent cello background to evoke genteel melodrama of an earlier decade, and "When I'm Sixty-four" is intentionally clichéd throughout both in its ragtime rhythm and in its lyrics. The result is a satiric heightening of the love-nest sentimentality of old popular songs in the mode of "He'll build a little home / Just meant for two / From which I'll never roam / Who would, would you?" The home in "When I'm Sixty-four" is slightly larger to accommodate children, but that's the only important difference: "Every summer we can rent a cottage / In the Isle of Wight, if it's not too dear / We shall scrimp and save / Grandchildren on your knee / Vera Chuck & Dave." But the Beatles aren't satisfied merely with having written a brilliant spoof, with scoring, on their own authority, off death-dealing clichés. Instead, they quite suddenly at the end transform one cliché (of sentimental domesticity) into another (of a lonely-hearts newspaper advertisement) thereby proposing a vulgar contemporary medium suitable to the cheap and public sentiments that once passed for nice, private and decent: "Send me a postcard, drop me a line, / Stating point of view / Indicate precisely what you mean to say / Yours sincerely, wasting away / Give me your answer, fill in a form / Mine for evermore / Will you still need me, will you still feed me / When I'm sixty-four."

The Sgt. Pepper album and the singles released here just before and after it—"Penny Lane," "Strawberry Fields Forever," "All You Need Is Love" and "Baby You're a Rich Man"—constitute the Beatles' most audacious musical effort so far, works of such achieved ambitiousness as to give an entirely new retrospective shape to their whole career. Nothing less is being claimed by these songs than that the Beatles now exist not merely as a phenomenon of entertainment but as a force of historical consequence. They have placed themselves within a musical, social and historical environment more monumental in its surroundings and more significantly populated than was the environment of any of their early songs. Listening to the Sgt. Pepper album one thinks not simply of the history of popular music but of the history of this century. It doesn't matter that some of the songs were composed before it occurred to the Beatles to use the motif of Sgt. Pepper, with its historical overtones; the songs emanated from some inwardly felt coherence that awaited a merely explicit design, and they would ask to be heard together even without the design.

Under the aegis of an old-time concert given by the type of music-hall band with which Lennon's father, Alfred, claims to have been associated, the songs, directly or by chance images, offer something like a review of contemporary English life, saved from folksong generality by having each song resemble a dramatic monologue. The review begins with the Sgt. Pepper theme song, followed immediately by "A Little Help From My Friends": Ringo, helped by the other Beatles, will, as I've already mentioned, try not to sing out of "key," try, that is, to fit into a style still heard in England but very much out of date. Between this and the reprise of Sgt. Pepper, which would be the natural end of the album, are ten songs, and while some are period pieces, about hangovers from the past, as is the band itself, no effort is made at any sort of historical chronology. Their arrangement is apparently haphazard, suggesting how the hippie and the historically pretentious, the genteel and the mod, the impoverished and the exotic, the Indian influence and the influence of technology are inextricably entangled into what is England. As I probably shouldn't say again, the Beatles never for long wholly submerge themselves in any form or style, so that at the end of the Indian, meditative sonorities of "Within You, Without You" the burst of laughter can be taken to mean—look, we have come through, an assurance from the Beatles (if it *is* their laughter and not the response of technicians left in as an example of how "straights" might react) that they are still Beatles, Liverpool boys still there on the far side of a demanding foreign experience. This characteristic release of themselves from history and back to their own proper time and place occurs with respect to the design of the whole album in a most poignant way. Right after the reprise of the Sgt. Pepper song, with no interval and picking up the beat of the Sgt. Pepper theme, an "extra" song, perhaps the most brilliant ever written by Lennon and McCartney, breaks out of the theatrical frame and enters "a day in the life," into the way we live now. It projects a degree of loneliness not to be managed within the conventions of Sgt. Pepper's Lonely Hearts Club Band. Released from the controls of Sgt. Pepper, the song exposes the horrors of more contemporary and less benign controls, and it is from these that the song proposes the necessity of still further release. It does so in musical sounds meant to convey a "trip" out, sounds of ascending-airplane velocity and crescendo that occur right after the first "I'd love to turn you on," at midpoint in the song, and after the final, plaintive repetition of the line at the end, when the airplane sounds give way to a sustained orchestral chord that drifts softly and slowly toward infinity and silence. It is, as I've suggested, a song of wasteland, and the concluding "I'd love to turn you on" has as much propriety to the fragmented life that precedes it in the song and in the whole work as does the "Shantih, Shantih, Shantih" to the fragments of Eliot's poem. Eliot can be remembered here for still other reasons: not only because he pays conspicuous respect to the music hall but because his poems, like the Beatles' songs, work for a kaleidoscopic effect, for fragmented patterns of sound that can bring historic masses into juxtaposition only to let them be fractured by other emerging and equally evocative fragments.

Eliot is not among the sixty-two faces and figures, all unnamed and in some cases probably quite obscure, gathered round the Beatles on the cover, a pictorial extension of the collage effect which is so significant to the music. In making the selection, the Beatles were understandably drawn to figures who promote the idea of other possible worlds or who offer literary and cinematic trips to exotic places: Poe, Oscar Wilde, H. G. Wells, along with Marx, Jung, Lawrence of Arabia and Johnny Weismuller. They are also partial to the kind of theatrical person whose full being is the theatrical self, like W. C. Fields, Tom Mix, Brando and Mae West, who has delightfully adapted such Beatle songs as "Day Tripper" to her own style. Above all, the cover is a celebration of the Beatles themselves who can now be placed (and Bob Dylan, too) within a group who have, aside from everything else, infused the imagination of the living with the possibilities of other ways of living, of extraordinary existences, of something beyond "a day in the life." So it is indeed like a funeral for the Beatles, except that they'd be no more "dead" than anyone else in attendance. There they are in the center, mustachioed and in the brassed and tassled silk of the old-time bands, and, with bril-

liant, quite funny implications, they are also represented in the collage
as wax figures by Madame Tussaud, clothed in business suits. Live Beatles in costumes from the past and effigies of the Beatles in the garb of
the present, with the name of the Beatles in flowers planted before the
whole group—this bit of slyness is of a piece with not sorting out past
and present and promised future in the order of the songs, or the mixed
allusiveness to period styles, including earlier Beatles' styles or the mixing and confoundings of media in songs like "When I'm Sixty-four" or
"A Day in the Life." The cover suggests that the Beatles to some extent
live the past in the present, live in the shadows of their own as well as of
other people's past accomplishments, and that among the imaginative
creations that fascinate them most, the figures closest at hand on the
cover, are their own past selves. "And the time will come," it is promised in one of their songs, "when you will see we're all one, and life
flows on within you and without you." As an apprehension of artistic,
and perhaps of any other kind of placement within living endeavor, this
idea is allowable only to the very great.

1967

JULES SIEGEL

Though by the early 1980s he had given up writing about rock and pop—indeed, had pretty well given up writing for publication altogether—Jules Siegel (1935–2012) was early to the field. His piece "The Big Beat" (1965) was an early model of how to write rock history. The essay reprinted here, on the brilliant and doomed Brian Wilson/Beach Boys masterpiece *Smile*, was written for *The Saturday Evening Post* but rejected as "not objective enough": an apt description, in retrospect, for some of the most glorious rock writing in the decades that followed. Soon after, Siegel was made editor-in-chief of the influential but short-lived magazine *Cheetah*, where the *Smile* piece was published in the inaugural issue in October 1967. Rock writing was but a small part of Siegel's journalistic output, but in their sophistication and penetrating intelligence, his articles and essays on the subject continue to exert a substantial influence.

▼ ▼

Goodbye Surfing, Hello God!

IT WAS just another day of greatness at Gold Star Recording Studios on Santa Monica Boulevard in Hollywood. In the morning four long-haired kids had knocked out two hours of sound for a record plugger who was trying to curry favor with a disk jockey friend of theirs in San Jose. Nobody knew it at the moment, but out of that two hours there were about three minutes that would hit the top of the charts in a few weeks, and the record plugger, the disk jockey and the kids would all be hailed as geniuses, but geniuses with a very small g.

Now, however, in the very same studio a Genius with a very large capital G was going to produce a hit. There was no doubt it would be a hit because this Genius was Brian Wilson. In four years of recording for Capitol Records, he and his group, the Beach Boys, had made surfing music a national craze, sold 16 million singles and earned gold records for 10 of their 12 albums.

Not only was Brian going to produce a hit, but also, one gathered, he was going to show everybody in the music business exactly where it was at; and where it was at, it seemed, was that Brian Wilson was not merely a Genius—which is to say a steady commercial success—but rather, like Bob Dylan and John Lennon, a GENIUS—which is to say a steady commercial success and hip besides.

Until now, though, there were not too many hip people who would have considered Brian Wilson and the Beach Boys hip, even though he had produced one very hip record, "Good Vibrations," which had sold more than a million copies, and a super-hip album, *Pet Sounds*, which didn't do very well at all—by previous Beach Boys sales standards. Among the hip people he was still on trial, and the question discussed earnestly among the recognized authorities on what is and what is not hip was whether or not Brian Wilson was hip, semi-hip or square.

But walking into the control room with the answers to all questions such as this was Brian Wilson himself, wearing a competition-stripe surfer's T-shirt, tight white duck pants, pale green bowling shoes and a red plastic toy fireman's helmet.

Everybody was wearing identical red plastic toy fireman's helmets. Brian's cousin and production assistant, Steve Korthoff, was wearing one; his wife, Marilyn, and her sister, Diane Rovelle—Brian's secretary—were also wearing them, and so was a once-dignified writer from *The Saturday Evening Post* who had been following Brian around for two months.

Out in the studio, the musicians for the session were unpacking their instruments. In sport shirts and slacks, they looked like insurance salesmen and used-car dealers, except for one blonde female percussionist who might have been stamped out by a special machine that supplied plastic mannequin housewives for detergent commercials.

Controlled, a little bored after 20 years or so of nicely paid anonymity, these were the professionals of the popular music business, hired guns who did their job expertly and efficiently and then went home to the suburbs. If you wanted swing, they gave you swing. A little movie-track lushness? Fine, here comes movie-track lushness. Now it's rock and roll? Perfect rock and roll, down the chute.

"Steve," Brian called out, "where are the rest of those fire hats? I want everybody to wear fire hats. We've really got to get into this thing." Out to the Rolls-Royce went Steve and within a few minutes all of the musicians were wearing fire hats, silly grins beginning to crack their professional dignity.

"All right, let's go," said Brian. Then, using a variety of techniques ranging from vocal demonstration to actually playing the instruments, he taught each musician his part. A gigantic fire howled out of the massive studio speakers in a pounding crash of pictorial music that summoned up visions of roaring, windstorm flames, falling timbers, mournful sirens and sweating firemen, building into a peak and crackling off into fading embers as a single drum turned into a collapsing wall and the fire-engine cellos dissolved and disappeared.

"When did he write this?" asked an astonished pop music producer who had wandered into the studio. "This is really fantastic! Man, this is unbelievable! How long has he been working on it?"

"About an hour," answered one of Brian's friends.

"I don't believe it. I just can't believe what I'm hearing," said the producer and fell into a stone glazed silence as the fire music began again.

For the next three hours, Brian Wilson recorded and rerecorded, take after take, changing the sound balance, adding echo, experimenting with a sound effects track of a real fire.

"Let me hear that again." "Drums, I think you're a little slow in that last part. Let's get right on it." "That was really good. Now, one more time, the whole thing." "All right, let me hear the cellos alone." "Great. Really great. Now let's *do it*!"

With 23 takes on tape and the entire operation responding to his touch like the black knobs on the control board, sweat glistening down his long, reddish hair onto his freckled face, the control room a litter of dead cigarette butts, Chicken Delight boxes, crumpled napkins, Coke bottles and all the accumulated trash of the physical end of the creative process, Brian stood at the board as the four speakers blasted the music into the room.

For the 24th time, the drum crashed and the sound effects crackle faded and stopped.

"Thank you," said Brian, into the control room mike. "Let me hear that back." Feet shifting, his body still, eyes closed, head moving seal-like to his music, he stood under the speakers and listened. "Let me hear that one more time." Again the fire roared. "Everybody come out and listen to this," Brian said to the musicians. They came into the control room and listened to what they had made.

"What do you think?" Brian asked.

"It's incredible, incredible," whispered one of the musicians, a man in his 50s, wearing a Hawaiian shirt and iridescent trousers and pointed black Italian shoes. "Absolutely incredible."

"Yeah," said Brian on the way home, an acetate trial copy or "dub" of the tape in his hands, the red plastic fire helmet still on his head. "Yeah, I'm going to call this 'Mrs. O'Leary's Fire' and I think it might just scare a whole lot of people."

As it turns out, however, Brian Wilson's magic fire music is not going to scare anybody—because nobody other than the few people who heard it in the studio will ever get to listen to it. A few days after the record was finished, a building across the street from the studio burned down and, according to Brian, there was also an unusually large number of fires in Los Angeles. Afraid that his music might in fact turn out to be magic fire music, Wilson destroyed the master.

"I don't have to do a big scary fire like that," he later said. "I can do a candle and it's still fire. That would have been a really bad vibration to let out on the world, that Chicago fire. The next one is going to be a candle."

A person who thinks of himself as understanding would probably interpret this episode as an example of perhaps too-excessive artistic perfectionism. One with psychiatric inclinations would hear all this stuff about someone who actually believed music could cause fires and start using words such as neurosis and maybe even psychosis. A true student of spoken hip, however, would say *hang-up*, which covers all of the above.

As far as Brian's pretensions toward hipness are concerned, no label could do him worse harm. In the hip world, there is a widespread idea that really hip people don't have hang-ups, which gives rise to the unspoken rule (unspoken because there is also the widespread idea that really hip people don't make *any* rules) that no one who wants to be thought of as hip ever reveals his hang-ups, except maybe to his guru, and in the strictest of privacy.

In any case, whatever his talent, Brian Wilson's attempt to win a hip following and reputation foundered for many months in an obsessive cycle of creation and destruction that threatened not only his career and his future but also his marriage, his friendships, his relationship with the Beach Boys and, some of his closest friends worried, his mind.

For a boy who used to be known in adolescence as a lover of sweets, the whole thing must have begun to taste very sour; yet, this particular phase of Brian's drive toward whatever his goal of supreme success might be began on a rising tide that at first looked as if it would carry him and the Beach Boys beyond the Beatles, who had started just about the same time they did, into the number-one position in the international pop music fame-and-power competition.

"About a year ago I had what I consider a very religious experience," Wilson told Los Angeles writer Tom Nolan in 1966. "I took LSD, a full dose of LSD, and later, another time, I took a smaller dose. And I learned a lot of things, like patience, understanding. I can't teach you or tell you what I learned from taking it, but I consider it a very religious experience."

A short time after his LSD experience, Wilson began work on the record that was to establish him right along with the Beatles as one of the most important innovators in modern popular music. It was called "Good Vibrations," and it took more than six months, 90 hours of tape and 11 complete versions before a three-minute-35-second final master tape satisfied him. Among the instruments on "Good Vibra-tions" was an electronic device called a theramin, which had its debut in the soundtrack of the movie *Spellbound*, back in the Forties. To some people, "Good Vibrations" was considerably crazier than Gregory Peck had been in the movie, but to others, Brian Wilson's new record, along with his somewhat earlier LP release, "Pet Sounds," marked the begin-ning of a new era in pop music.

"They've Found the New Sound at Last!" shrieked the headline over a London Sunday *Express* review as "Good Vibrations" hit the English charts at number six and leaped to number one the following week. Within a few weeks, the Beach Boys had pushed the Beatles out of first place in England's *New Musical Express*' annual poll. In America, "Good Vibrations" sold nearly 400,000 copies in four days before reaching number one several weeks later and earning a gold record within another month when it hit the one-million sale mark.

In America, where there is none of the Beach Boys' California-mystique that adds a special touch of romance to their records and appearances in Europe and England, the news had not really reached all of the people whose opinion can turn popularity into fashionability. With the exception of a professor of show business (right, professor of show business; in California such a thing is not considered unusual) who turned up one night to interview Brian, and a few young writ-ers (such as The *Village Voice*'s Richard Goldstein, Paul Williams of *Crawdaddy*, and Lawrence Dietz of *New York Magazine*) not too many opinion makers were prepared to accept the Beach Boys into the main-stream of the culture industry.

"Listen man," said San Francisco music critic Ralph Gleason who had only recently graduated from jazz into Bob Dylan and was apparently not yet ready for any more violent twists, "I recognize the L.A. hype when I hear it. I know all about the Beach Boys and I think I liked them better before, if only for sociological reasons, if you understand what I mean."

"As for the Beach Boys," an editor of *The Saturday Evening Post* chided his writer, who had filed the world's longest Western Union telegram of a story, "I want you to understand that as an individual you can feel that Brian Wilson is the greatest musician of our time, and maybe the greatest human being, but as a reporter you have got to maintain your objectivity."

"They want me to put him down," the writer complained. "That's their idea of objectivity—the put-down.

"It has to do with this idea that it's not hip to be sincere," he continued, "and they really want to be hip. What they don't understand is that last year hip was sardonic—camp, they called it. This year hip is sincere.

"When somebody as corny as Brian Wilson starts singing right out front about God and I start writing it—very *sincerely*, you understand—it puts them very uptight.

"I think it's because it reminds them of all those terribly sincere hymns and sermons they used to have to listen to in church when they were kids in Iowa or Ohio.

"Who knows? Maybe they're right. I mean, who needs all this goddamn intense sincerity all the time?"

What all this meant, of course, was that everybody agreed that Brian Wilson and the Beach Boys were still too square. It would take more than "Good Vibrations" and *Pet Sounds* to erase three-and-a-half years of "Little Deuce Coupe"—a *lot* more if you counted in those J. C. Penney-style custom-tailored, kandy-striped sport shirts they insisted on wearing on stage.

Brian, however, had not yet heard the news, it appeared, and was steadily going about the business of trying to become hip. The Beach Boys, who have toured without him ever since he broke down during one particularly wearing trip, were now in England and Europe, phoning back daily reports of enthusiastic fan hysteria—screaming little girls tearing at their flesh, wild press conferences, private chats with the Rolling Stones. Washed in the heat of a kind of attention they had never received in the United States even at the height of their commercial success, three Beach Boys—Brian's brothers, Dennis and Carl, and his cousin, Mike Love—walked into a London Rolls-Royce showroom and bought four Phantom VII limousines, one for each of them and a fourth for Brian. Al Jardine and Bruce Johnston, the Beach Boys who are not corporate members of the Beach Boys' enterprises, sent their best regards and bought themselves some new clothing.

"I think this London thing has really helped," said Brian with satisfaction after he had made the color selection on his $32,000 toy—a ducal-burgundy lacquered status symbol ordinarily reserved for heads of state. "That's just what the boys needed, a little attention to jack up their confidence." Then, learning that he wouldn't be able to have his new car for three months, he went out and bought an interim Rolls-Royce for $20,000 from Mamas and Papas producer Lou Adler, taking possession of the automobile just in time to meet his group at the airport as they returned home.

"It's a great environment for conducting business," he explained as his friend and former road manager, Terry Sachen, hastily pressed into service as interim chauffeur for the interim Rolls-Royce, informally uniformed in his usual fringed deerskins and moccasins, drove the car through Hollywood and to one of Brian's favorite eating places, the Pioneer Chicken drive-in on Sunset Boulevard.

"This car is really out of sight," said Brian, filling up on fried shrimp in the basket. "Next time we go up to Capitol, I'm going to drive up in my Rolls-Royce limo. You've got to do those things with a little style. It's not just an ordinary visit that way—it's an arrival, right? Wow! That's really great—an *arrival*, in my limo. It'll blow their minds!"

Whether or not the interim Rolls-Royce actually ever blew the minds of the hard-nosed executives who run Capitol Records is something to speculate on, but no one in the record industry with a sense of history could have failed to note that this very same limousine had once belonged to John Lennon; and in the closing months of 1966, with the Beach Boys home in Los Angeles, Brian rode the "Good Vibrations" high, driving forward in bursts of enormous energy that seemed destined before long to earn him the throne of the international empire of pop music still ruled by John Lennon and the Beatles.

At the time, it looked as if the Beatles were ready to step down. Their summer concerts in America had been only moderately successful at best, compared to earlier years. There were ten thousand empty seats at

Shea Stadium in New York and 11 lonely fans at the airport in Seattle. Mass media, underground press, music-industry trade papers and the fan magazines were filled with fears that the Beatles were finished, that the group was breaking up. Lennon was off acting in a movie; McCartney was walking around London alone, said to be carrying a giant torch for his sometime girl friend, Jane Asher; George Harrison was getting deeper and deeper into a mystical Indian thing under the instruction of sitar-master Ravi Shankar; and Ringo was collecting material for a Beatles museum.

In Los Angeles, Brian Wilson was riding around in the Rolls-Royce that had once belonged to John Lennon, pouring a deluge of new sounds onto miles of stereo tape in three different recording studios booked day and night for him in month-solid blocks, holding court nightly at his $240,000 Beverly Hills Babylonian-modern home, and, after guests left, sitting at his grand piano until dawn, writing new material.

The work in progress was an album called *Smile.* "I'm writing a teen-age symphony to God," Brian told dinner guests on an October evening. He then played for them the collection of black acetate trial records which lay piled on the floor of his red imitation-velvet wallpapered bedroom with its leopard-print bedspread. In the bathroom, above the wash basin, there was a plastic color picture of Jesus Christ with trick effect eyes that appeared to open and close when you moved your head. Sophisticate newcomers pointed it out to each other and laughed slyly, almost hoping to find a Keane painting among decorations ranging from Lava Lamps to a department-store rack of dozens of dolls, each still in its plastic bubble container, the whole display trembling like a space-age Christmas tree to the music flowing out into the living room.

Brian shuffled through the acetates, most of which were unlabeled, identifying each by subtle differences in the patterns of the grooves. He had played them so often he knew the special look of each record the way you know the key to your front door by the shape of its teeth. Most were instrumental tracks, cut while the Beach Boys were in Europe, and for these Brian supplied the vocal in a high sound that seemed to come out of his head rather than his throat as he somehow managed to create complicated four and five part harmonies with only his own voice.

"Rock, rock, Plymouth rock roll over," Brian sang. "Bicycle rider, see what you done done to the church of the native American Indian . . . Over and over the crow cries uncover the cornfields . . . Who ran the Iron Horse . . . Out in the farmyard the cook is chopping lumber; out in the barnyard the chickens do their number . . . Bicycle rider see what you done done . . ."

A panorama of American history filled the room as the music shifted from theme to theme; the tinkling harpsichord-sounds of the bicycle rider pushed sad Indian sounds across the continent; the Iron Horse pounded across the plains in a wide-open rolling rhythm that summoned up visions of the old West; civilized chickens bobbed up and down in a tiny ballet of comic barnyard melody; the inexorable bicycle music, cold and charming as an infinitely talented music box, reappeared and faded away.

Like medieval choirboys, the voices of the Beach Boys pealed out in wordless prayer from the last acetate, thirty seconds of chorale that reached upward to the vaulted stone ceilings of an empty cathedral lit by thousands of tiny votive candles melting at last into one small, pure pool that whispered a universal *amen* in a sigh without words.

Brian's private radio show was finished. In the dining room a candle-lit table with a dark blue cloth was set for ten persons. In the kitchen, Marilyn Wilson was trying to get the meal organized and served, aided and hindered by the chattering suggestions of the guests' wives and girl friends. When everyone was seated and waiting for the food, Brian tapped his knife idly on a white china plate.

"Listen to that," he said. "That's really great!" Everybody listened as Brian played the plate. "Come on, let's get something going here," he ordered. "Michael—do this. David—you do this." A plate-and-spoon musicale began to develop as each guest played a distinctly different technique, rhythm and melody under Brian's enthusiastic direction.

"That's absolutely unbelievable!" said Brian. "Isn't that unbelievable?

That's so unbelievable I'm going to put it on the album. Michael, I want you to get a sound system up here tomorrow and I want everyone to be here tomorrow night. We're going to get this on tape."

Brian Wilson's plate-and-spoon musicale never did reach the public, but only because he forgot about it. Other sounds equally strange have found their way onto his records. On *Pet Sounds*, for example, on some tracks there is an odd, soft, hollow percussion effect that most musicians assume is some kind of electronically transmuted drum sound—a conga drum played with a stick perhaps, or an Indian tom-tom. Actually, it's drummer Hal Blaine playing the bottom of a plastic jug that once contained Sparklettes spring water. And, of course, at the end of the record there is the strangely affecting track of a train roaring through a lonely railroad crossing as a bell clangs and Brian's dogs, Banana, a beagle, and Louie, a dark brown weimaraner, bark after it.

More significant, perhaps, to those who that night heard the original instrumental tracks for both *Smile* and the Beach Boys' new single, "Heroes and Villains," is that entire sequences of extraordinary power and beauty are missing in the finished version of the single, and will undoubtedly be missing as well from *Smile*—victims of Brian's obsessive tinkering and, more importantly, sacrifices to the same strange combination of superstitious fear and God-like conviction of his own power he displayed when he destroyed the fire music.

The night of the dining-table concerto, it was the God-like confidence Brian must have been feeling as he put his guests on his trip, but the fear was soon to take over. At his house that night, he had assembled a new set of players to introduce into his life game, each of whom was to perform a specific role in the grander game he was playing with the world.

Earlier in the summer, Brian had hired Van Dyke Parks, a supersophisticated young songwriter and composer, to collaborate with him on the lyrics for *Smile*. With Van Dyke working for him, he had a fighting chance against John Lennon, whose literary skill and Liverpudlian wit had been one of the most important factors in making the Beatles the darlings of the hip intelligentsia.

With that flank covered, Brian was ready to deal with some of the other problems of trying to become hip, the most important of which was how was he going to get in touch with some really hip people. In effect, the dinner party at the house was his first hip social event, and the star of the evening, so far as Brian was concerned, was Van Dyke Parks' manager, David Anderle, who showed up with a whole group of very hip people.

Elegant, cool and impossibly cunning, Anderle was an artist who has somehow found himself in the record business as an executive for MGM Records, where he had earned himself a reputation as a genius by purportedly thinking up the million-dollar movie-TV-record offer that briefly lured Bob Dylan to MGM from Columbia until everybody had a change of heart and Dylan decided to go back home to Columbia.

Anderle had skipped back and forth between painting and the record business, with mixed results in both. Right now he was doing a little personal management and thinking about painting a lot. His appeal to Brian was simple: everybody recognized David Anderle as one of the hippest people in Los Angeles. In fact, he was something like the mayor of hipness as far as some people were concerned. And not only that, he was a genius.

Within six weeks, he was working for the Beach Boys; everything that Brian wanted seemed at last to be in reach. Like a magic genie, David Anderle produced miracles for him. A new Beach Boys record company was set up, Brother Records, with David Anderle at its head and, simultaneously, the Beach Boys sued Capitol Records in a move to force a renegotiation of their contract with the company.

The house was full of underground press writers. Anderle's friend Michael Vosse was on the Brother Records payroll out scouting TV contracts and performing other odd jobs. Another of Anderle's friends was writing the story on Brian for *The Saturday Evening Post* and a film crew from CBS-TV was up at the house for a documentary to be narrated by Leonard Bernstein. The Beach Boys were having meetings once or twice a week with teams of experts briefing them on corporate policy, drawing complicated chalk patterns as they described the millions of dollars everyone was going to earn out of all this.

As 1967 opened it seemed as though Brian and the Beach Boys were assured of a new world of success; yet something was going wrong. As the corporate activity reached a peak of intensity, Brian was becoming less and less productive and more and more erratic. *Smile*, which was to have been released for the Christmas season, remained unfinished. "Heroes and Villains," which was virtually complete, remained in the can, as Brian kept working out new little pieces and then scrapping them.

Van Dyke Parks had left and come back and would leave again, tired of being constantly dominated by Brian. Marilyn Wilson was having headaches and Dennis Wilson was leaving his wife. Session after session was canceled. One night a studio full of violinists waited while Brian tried to decide whether or not the vibrations were friendly or hostile. The answer was hostile and the session was canceled, at a cost of some $3,000. Everything seemed to be going wrong. Even the *Post* story fell through.

Brian seemed to be filled with secret fear. One night at the house, it began to surface. Marilyn sat nervously painting her fingernails as Brian stalked up and down, his face tight and his eyes small and red.

"What's the matter, Brian? You're really strung out," a friend asked.

"Yeah, I'm really strung out. Look, I mean I really feel strange. A really strange thing happened to me tonight. Did you see this picture, *Seconds*?"

"No, but I know what it's about; I read the book."

"Look, come into the kitchen; I really have to talk about this." In the kitchen they sat down in the black and white houndstooth-check wallpapered dinette area. A striped window shade clashed with the checks and the whole room vibrated like some kind of op art painting. Ordinarily, Brian wouldn't sit for more than a minute in it, but now he seemed to be unaware of anything except what he wanted to say.

"I walked into that movie," he said in a tense, high-pitched voice, "and the first thing that happened was a voice from the screen said 'Hello, Mr. Wilson.' It completely blew my mind. You've got to admit that's pretty spooky, right?"

"Maybe."

"That's not all. Then the whole thing was there. I mean my whole life. Birth and death and rebirth. The whole thing. Even the beach was in it, a whole thing about the beach. It was my whole life right there on the screen."

"It's just a coincidence, man. What are you getting all excited about?"

"Well, what if it isn't a coincidence? What if it's real? You know there's mind gangsters these days. There could be mind gangsters, couldn't there? I mean look at Spector, he could be involved in it, couldn't he? He's going into films. How hard would it be for him to set up something like that?"

"Brian, Phil Spector is not about to make a million-dollar movie just to scare you. Come on, stop trying to be so dramatic."

"All right, all right. I was just a little bit nervous about it," Brian said, after some more back and forth about the possibility that Phil Spector, the record producer, had somehow influenced the making of *Seconds* to disturb Brian Wilson's tranquillity. "I just had to get it out of my system. You can see where something like that could scare someone, can't you?"

They went into Brian's den, a small room papered in psychedelic orange, blue, yellow and red wall fabric with rounded corners. At the end of the room there was a juke box filled with Beach Boy singles and Phil Spector hits. Brian punched a button and Spector's "Be My Baby" began to pour out at top volume.

"Spector has always been a big thing with me, you know. I mean I heard that song three and a half years ago and I knew that it was between him and me. I knew exactly where he was at and now I've gone beyond him. You can understand how that movie might get someone upset under those circumstances, can't you?"

Brian sat down at his desk and began to draw a little diagram on a piece of printed stationery with his name at the top in the kind of large fat script printers of charitable dinner journals use when the customer asks for a hand-lettered look. With a felt-tipped pen, Brian drew a close approximation of a growth curve. "Spector started the whole thing," he said, dividing the curve into periods. "He was the first one to use the studio. But I've gone beyond him now. I'm doing the spiritual sound, a white spiritual sound. Religious music. Did you hear the Beatles album?

Religious, right? That's the whole movement. That's where I'm going. It's going to scare a lot of people.

"Yeah," Brain said, hitting his fist on the desk with a slap that sent the parakeets in the large cage facing him squalling and whistling. "Yeah," he said and smiled for the first time all evening. "That's where I'm going and it's going to scare a lot of people when I get there."

As the year drew deeper into winter, Brian's rate of activity grew more and more frantic, but nothing seemed to be accomplished. He tore the house apart and half redecorated it. One section of the living room was filled with a full-sized Arabian tent and the dining room, where the grand piano stood, was filled with sand to a depth of a foot or so and draped with nursery curtains. He had had his windows stained gray and put a sauna bath in the bedroom. He battled with his father and complained that his brothers weren't trying hard enough. He accused Mike Love of making too much money.

One by one, he canceled out the friends he had collected, sometimes for the strangest reasons. An acquaintance of several months who thought he had become extremely close with Brian showed up at a record session and found a guard barring the door. Michael Vosse came out to explain.

"Hey man, this is really terrible," said Vosse, smiling under a broad-brimmed straw hat. "It's not you, it's your chick. Brian says she's a witch and she's messing with his brain so bad by ESP that he can't work. It's like the Spector thing. You know how he is. Say, I'm really sorry." A couple of months later, Vosse was gone. Then, in the late spring, Anderle left. The game was over.

Several months later, the last move in Brian's attempt to win the hip community was played out. On July 15th, the Beach Boys were scheduled to appear at the Monterey International Pop Music Festival, a kind of summit of rock music with the emphasis on love, flowers and youth. Although Brian was a member of the board of this nonprofit event, the Beach Boys canceled their commitment to perform. The official reason was that their negotiations with Capitol Records were at a crucial stage and they had to get "Heroes and Villains" out right away. The second official reason was that Carl, who had been arrested for refusing to report for induction into the Army (he was later cleared in court), was so upset that he wouldn't be able to sing.

Whatever the merit in these reasons, the real one may have been closer to something John Phillips of the Mamas and Papas and a Monterey board member suggested: "Brian was afraid that the hippies from San Francisco would think the Beach Boys were square and boo them."

But maybe Brian was right. "Those candy-striped shirts just wouldn't have made it at Monterey, man," said David Anderle.

Whatever the case, at the end of the summer, "Heroes and Villains" was released in sharply edited form and *Smile* was reported to be on its way. In the meantime, however, the Beatles had released *Sergeant Pepper's Lonely Hearts Club Band* and John Lennon was riding about London in a bright yellow Phantom VII Rolls-Royce painted with flowers on the sides and his zodiac symbol on the top. In *Life* magazine, Paul McCartney came out openly for LSD and in the Haight-Ashbury district of San Francisco George Harrison walked through the streets blessing the hippies. Ringo was still collecting material for a Beatles museum. However good *Smile* might turn out to be, it seemed somehow that once more the Beatles had outdistanced the Beach Boys.

Back during that wonderful period in the fall of 1966 when everybody seemed to be his friend and plans were being laid for Brother Records and all kinds of fine things, Brian had gone on a brief visit to Michigan to hear a Beach Boys concert. The evening of his return, each of his friends and important acquaintances received a call asking everyone to please come to the airport to meet Brian, it was very important. When they gathered at the airport, Brian had a photographer on hand to take a series of group pictures. For a long time, a huge mounted blow-up of the best of the photographs hung on the living room wall, with some thirty people staring out—everyone from Van Dyke Parks and David Anderle to Michael Vosse and Terry Sachen. In the foreground was *The Saturday Evening Post* writer looking sourly out at the world.

The picture is no longer on Brian's wall and most of the people in it are no longer his friends. One by one each of them has either stepped out of the picture or been forced out of it. The whole cycle has returned to its beginning. Brian, who started out in Hawthorne, Calif., with his two brothers and a cousin, once more has surrounded himself with relatives. The house in Beverly Hills is empty. Brian and Marilyn are living in their new Spanish Mission estate in Bel-Air, cheek by jowl with the Mamas and Papas' Cass Elliott.

What remains, of course, is "Heroes and Villains." And there is also a spectacular peak, a song called "Surf's Up" that Brian recorded for the first time in December in Columbia Records Studio A for a CBS-TV pop music documentary. Earlier in the evening the film crew had covered a Beach Boys vocal session which had gone very badly. Now, at midnight, the Beach Boys had gone home and Brian was sitting in the back of his car, smoking a joint.

In the dark car, he breathed heavily, his hands in his lap, eyes staring nowhere.

"All right," he said at last. "Let's just sit here and see if we can get into something positive, but without any words. Let's just get into something quiet and positive on a nonverbal level." There was a long silence.

"OK, let's go," he said, and then, quickly, he was in the studio rehearsing, spotlighted in the center of the huge dark room, the cameramen moving about him invisibly outside the light.

"Let's do it," he announced, and the tape began to roll. In the control room no one moved. David Oppenheim, the TV producer, fortyish, handsome, usually studiously detached and professional, lay on the floor, hands behind his head, eyes closed. For three minutes and 27 seconds, Wilson played with delicate intensity, speaking moodily through the piano. Then he was finished. Oppenheim, whose last documentary had been a study of Stravinsky, lay motionless.

"That's it," Wilson said as the tape continued to whirl. The mood broke. As if awakening from heavy sleep the people stirred and shook their heads.

"I'd like to hear that," Wilson said. As his music replayed, he sang the lyrics in a high, almost falsetto voice, the cameras on him every second.

"The diamond necklace played the pawn," Wilson sang. ". . . A blind class aristocracy, back through the opera glass you see the pit and the pendulum drawn.

"Columnated ruins domino," his voice reached upward; the piano faltered a set of falling chords.

In a slow series of impressionistic images the song moved to its ending:

> *I heard the word:*
> *Wonderful thing!*
> *A children's song!*

On the last word Brian's voice rose and fell, like the ending of that prayer chorale he had played so many months before.

"That's really special," someone said.

"Special, that's right," said Wilson quietly. "Van Dyke and I really kind of thought we had done something special when we finished that one." He went back into the studio, put on the earphones and sang the song again for his audience in the control room, for the revolving tape recorder and for the cameras which relentlessly followed as he struggled to make manifest what still only existed as a perfect, incommunicable sound in his head.

At home, as the black acetate dub turned on his bedroom hi-fi set, Wilson tried to explain the words.

"It's a man at a concert," he said. "All around him there's the audience, playing their roles, dressed up in fancy clothes, looking through opera glasses, but so far away from the drama, from life—'Back through the opera glass you see the pit and the pendulum drawn.'

"The music begins to take over. 'Columnated ruins domino.' Empires, ideas, lives, institutions—everything has to fall, tumbling like dominoes.

"He begins to awaken to the music; sees the pretentiousness of everything. 'The music hall a costly bow.' Then even the music is gone, turned into a trumpeter swan, into what the music really is.

"'Canvas the town and brush the backdrop.' He's off in his vision, on a trip. Reality is gone; he's creating it like a dream. 'Dove-nested towers.' Europe, a long time ago. 'The laughs come hard in Auld Lang

Syne.' The poor people in the cellar taverns, trying to make themselves happy by singing.

"Then there's the parties, the drinking, trying to forget the wars, the battles at sea. 'While at port a do or die.' Ships in the harbor, battling it out. A kind of Roman Empire thing.

"'A choke of grief.' At his own sorrow and the emptiness of his life, because he can't even cry for the suffering in the world, for his own suffering.

"And then, hope. 'Surf's up! . . . Come about hard and join the once and often spring you gave.' Go back to the kids, to the beach, to childhood.

"'I heard the word'—of God; 'Wonderful thing'—the joy of enlightenment, of seeing God. And what is it? 'A children's song!' And then there's the song itself; the song of children; the song of the universe rising and falling in wave after wave, the song of God, hiding the love from us, but always letting us find it again, like a mother singing to her children."

The record was over. Wilson went into the kitchen and squirted Reddi-Whip direct from the can into his mouth; made himself a chocolate Great Shake, and ate a couple of candy bars.

"Of course that's a very intellectual explanation," he said. "But maybe sometimes you have to do an intellectual thing. If they don't get the words, they'll get the music. You can get hung up in words, you know. Maybe they work; I don't know." He fidgeted with a telescope.

"This thing is so bad," he complained. "So Mickey Mouse. It just won't work smoothly. I was really freaked out on astronomy when I was a kid. Baseball, too. I guess I went through a lot of phases. A lot of changes, too. But you can really get into things through the stars. And swimming. A lot of swimming. It's physical; really Zen, right? The whole spiritual thing is very physical. Swimming really does it sometimes." He sprawled on the couch and continued in a very small voice.

"So that's what I'm doing. Spiritual music."

"Brian," Marilyn called as she came into the room wearing a quilted bathrobe, "do you want me to get you anything, honey? I'm going to sleep."

"No, Mar," he answered, rising to kiss his wife goodnight. "You go on to bed. I want to work for a while."

"C'mon kids," Marilyn yelled to the dogs as she padded off to bed. "Time for bed. Louie! Banana! Come to bed. Goodnight, Brian. Goodnight, everybody."

Wilson paced. He went to the piano and began to play. His guests moved toward the door. From the piano, his feet shuffling in the sand, he called a perfunctory goodbye and continued to play, a melody beginning to take shape. Outside, the piano spoke from the house. Brian Wilson's guests stood for a moment, listening. As they got into their car, the melancholy piano moaned.

"Here's one that's really outasight from the fantabulous Beach Boys!" screamed a local early morning Top-40 DJ from the car radio on the way home, a little hysterical as usual, his voice drowning out the sobbing introduction to the song.

"We're sending this one out for Bob and Carol in Pomona. They've been going steady now for six months. Happy six months, kids, and dig! 'Good Vibrations!' *The Beach Boys! Outasight!*"

1967

Richard Goldstein

Richard Goldstein (b. 1944) figures prominently in the development of American rock writing. Upon leaving Columbia University's School of Journalism, he resolved to find a gig where he could "dance at the type-writer"—and in June 1966 became the nation's first full-time rock writer at *The Village Voice*. His style was characterized by a ready adoption of "hip" vocabulary and a deep, often personal, engagement with the musicians he wrote about. His profile pieces (like his brilliant 1967 interview with an about-to-debut Leonard Cohen or the Dick Clark profile included here) move artfully between the artist's own words and Goldstein's clear-eyed observations. Readers appreciated his honesty: his review of *Sgt. Pepper's* for *The New York Times*, for instance, dared to buck conventional wisdom and deem the album "spoiled . . . like an over-attended child." His reportorial instinct rendered him especially sensitive to the ways that the rock scene was losing its innocence; he sensed that the counterculture that had drawn him to music writing was quickly being taken over by cynical business interests and PR men in a phenomenon that he (echoing Robert Christgau) called "autohype." Early to the field, Goldstein was also one of its early apostates, leaving rock writing in early 1969 to "explore other, less trammeled areas of pop culture"—ultimately, gay and lesbian issues. His 2015 memoir, *Another Little Piece of My Heart: My Life of Rock and Revolution in the '60s*, provides valuable insight into rock writing's early years from the perspective of its vibrant East Village outpost.

Master of Mediocrity

WAY BACK there—in 1952—WFIL-TV in Philadelphia had a hassle on its hands. The disc jockey–host of its popular daytime "Bandstand" show had been charged with participating in "improper activities." That was a key phrase of the fifties. Just its utterance in tocsin tones, or its appearance in erect black headlines brought a not unpleasant chill to the nation's collective spine. Mouths salivated, ears perked up, and eyes read on.

Lest anybody wonder what sort of "improper activities" this broadcaster had indulged in, the authorities were holding in abeyance a member or two of the show's teen-age regulars, FEMALES! It was, in short, the kind of scandal everyone loved in those days—a vaguely plausible one.

As the story broke, WFIL found itself in the same boiling water that was later to solidify everything diverse in America into a hard-boiled egg. The station's brass scanned the industry for a replacement. They were looking for someone with a face like Bromo-Seltzer, whose very appearance would neutralize the doubts parents everywhere felt about their kids and their times. They wanted someone who could project, with utter certainty, the spinach culture of the fifties: it was hard to swallow, but good for you.

They found him on television, in Utica, New York. He had already made the big jump from a nearby radio station where he hosted a seven hour daily dose of pop music. He was—as one reporter later attested—"a solidly built square-shouldered lad, with an Arrow-collar profile and a deep portentous voice." There were no skeletons in his split-level closet, just a lot of two-button jackets and ties. At five, he had published a neighborhood gossip sheet; at six, he owned a sidewalk peanut-butter restaurant. President of his high-school class, he sold brushes door to door and built chicken crates at 52 cents an hour in college. His classmates at Syracuse University voted him "the man most likely to sell the Brooklyn Bridge."

Richard Augustus Clark II almost did!

They loved him from the start at WFIL. "To many mothers," wrote one copybopper, "the afternoon show has brought a sudden closer relationship with their children. 'He's sort of a big brother who sets a good example,' one father commented. 'Since Bandstand, kids have insisted on wearing jackets and girls have cooled it on too-tight sweaters.' Parents applauded."

So did the rating services. Shortly after Clark took over, Philadelphia's Bandstand became the highest-rated pre-dinner TV program in any major American city. Before you could say "Better buy Bird's Eye," the show was syndicated over the ABC network. At its peak, "American Bandstand" ran on 105 stations, reaching over 20 million teenagers. It became a springboard for variations on the stiffly stylized rite of adolescent dancing; it nurtured the Calypso, the Circle, the Stroll, and a bouffant ballet known in lingua franca as "Phillie style." It rocketed the southside Italian ghetto-dubbed "Brotherlylovesville" by the promo men—into national prominence. Superstars sat on their stoops combing their pompadours and waiting to be found. Under the knowing aegis of Dick Clark's associate, Bob Marcucci, they sometimes were.

Fabian (né Fabian Forte) was discovered at a record hop; he walked in and all the girls started screaming. "That was enough for us," explains Clark. "You don't look for a singer. The person who is the star has that magic thing, and that's all that matters. Fabian was always a far better actor than anything else."

In his leopard-skin shirt, very open at the throat, Fabian appeared on "American Bandstand" to grunt songs like "Tiger" and "Turn Me Loose." He was an echo-chamber Frankenstein, created in the recording studio. On TV, he merely mouthed the words to pre-recorded tracks. That Fabian couldn't sing was irrelevant; he worked in an image medium, and his audience squealed with a special delight when he fluffed his lines. Informality and ecstasy, the two pillars of teen culture in the fifties, had little to do with synchronization.

"American Bandstand" made superstars of a galaxy of tousled crooners from South Philadelphia, who dropped a few vowels from their names in a gesture of showbiz Americanization, and went on as Connie Francis, Frankie Avalon, or Bobby Rydell. While they sang or signed autographs, the Bandstand regulars strolled, bopped, and went steady. Their look was copied verbatim and Clark delighted in displaying a bulletin board filled with photos of studied look-alikes. That was the kind of rapport Bandstand thrived on. For the first time, after-school America was experiencing instant identity.

Books away and televisions on, they danced under the klieg lights or clapped their hands hypnotically. "We like Beechnut spearmint gum," they chanted in unison, fingering beads and badges inscribed with the holy word "IFIC." A skinny kid in a sequin-speckled suit bellowed into a dead mike; he looked like a cheap engagement ring but everyone screamed anyway. Old folks, busy conforming, called it "conformity." But a viable, visible sub-culture had been born on "American Bandstand" and Dick Clark—the guy in the plastic surgeon's mask—had shown us how easy a delivery it could be.

"I don't make culture," he insists today. "I sell it. A myth has grown up over the years that I have something to do with what becomes popular. Generally, I reflect what's going on early enough to make a profit on it. It's not my business to interpret."

He sits in a comfortably padded chair in his office on Sunset Boulevard. It is fifteen years after Dick Clark first climbed on the Bandstand bandwagon and over 2500 miles from Brotherlylovesville. He is pudgier now around the cheeks. There are off-camera wrinkles above his brow. But he still speaks like a disc jockey; in conversation, he announces each idea as though it were a new record. He seems to be wearing the same necktie he has used every day of his career. But he has worn the two-button wash-and-wear uniform well, and he is not about to part with it. All that distinguishes Dick Clark from the nice-guy mold are his fingernails—cut and polished to perfection. But who can deny a successful guy his manicure?

"I'm getting older and wiser, but I stay the same," he says. "My clothing changes according to the style for my age, but my relationship with kids doesn't. I was too old then to be a playmate, and too young to be a father. It's still that way. I'm constantly called upon to explain kids. It's a peculiar thing for me because I don't make believe I'm a kid. I'm an observer and a presenter." His eyes twinkle like a busy switchboard. "I've made a career out of being non-controversial."

Dick Clark gives an interview the way he runs his career. Everything he says is instantly screened. Opinions are followed by the inevitable warning, "You'd better not quote me on that." He is especially wary of the press. "People who write use me as a scapegoat," he confides.

Not always. When Clark first joined the panoply of television's host-celebrities, the fourth estate had nothing but praise. "He has become a symbol for all that is good in America's younger generation," burbled one writer. "Dick's acts of kindness are a legend," chortled another.

Legend they truly were. As the first man to achieve a nationwide audience of doting, solvent teenagers, Clark was the virtual dictator of Tin Pan Alley in 1959. While his patronage did not assure a hit, it helped many a gold record along the way. "When I recorded 'Venus,'" singer Frankie Avalon told one interviewer, "Dick got behind it and it sold 1.5 million copies. He's the greatest."

Frankie Avalon was not the only one to stand in awe. A congressional sub-committee then involved in probing graft within the record industry soon took a lively interest in Dick Clark's enterprises. To put it as tactfully as Richard Augustus II himself would, he was suspected of confusing aesthetic with financial judgment. In fact, it was not long after Frankie Avalon's tribute appeared that Rep. Peter F. Mack of Illinois called Clark "Top dog in the payola field."

With a press turned gleefully hostile, Dick Clark entered the halls of Congress to testify. As the Associated Press described it on April 29, 1960: "Dick Clark suavely swore today that his hands were never dirtied by payola." Soberly, he insisted his investments were neither improper nor uncommon, and staunchly accepted an ultimatum from ABC to divest himself of all outside interests. With a little soap and water behind the ears, Dick Clark was clean.

America acquitted, or at least forgave, Dick Clark. True, he was no longer the white knight riding off into a kinescopic sunset. But the scandals of the fifties had taught us not to demand propriety from our leaders, only cleverness and poise.

Dick Clark's calculated cool helped him survive. He developed a tough, arrogant honesty about his work. His interviews were peppered with knowing asides. "I don't think Hollywood knows any kids," he told the Los Angeles *Times*, "because, by the time they get here, they aren't kids anymore." When asked why he had decided to return to television as a dramatic actor, he forsook the stock answer about art and fulfillment, and quipped, "I decided if I wanted people to continue knowing who I am, I'd better figure out how many different ways I can poke my face on TV." And he added without a trace of the bashful elan which once accompanied such observations: "I always seem to play the nice, clean-cut fellow who turns out to be a louse."

Like Richard Nixon, Dick Clark had realized that the only humility we require from the defeated is pragmatism. We are able to accept idealism only from a winner. All-American boys who tarnish soon find themselves coming on as though innocence were a kind of virginity they have lost long ago, in some brothel of the soul. No longer quite clean-cut, Dick Clark's dignity had become that of the successful entrepreneur. It was his only remaining claim to grace and he has lived off it ever since.

He is anything but washed up today. Though he never left the periphery of the scene, there are signs that he is inching toward its center again. He says he has moved to Los Angeles because it is "the most youth-oriented city in the nation," and his camera crews can be seen canvassing the freeways and taco stands in search of the Now. Not long ago the Los Angeles *Free Press* discovered Clark's pop-squad shooting a film called "*Love in Haight*." If the hippy thing fails, there is always Country-Western music. (Clark owns a station and produces a show called "Swinging Country.") With the perennial success of patriotic monologues on records, Clark has a new single called "Open Letter To the Older Generation." And his partner of long standing, Bob Marcucci, is reactivating the old Chancellor label, which once showcased the brightest bellowers of "American Bandstand." To mark its grand re-entry, Marcucci plans to introduce a new singer from old South

Philadelphia called Bobby Jason. He makes his recording debut with an updated version of "Venus," the song Dick Clark once helped Frankie Avalon sell a million and a half copies of.

If Bobby Jason clicks, Clark can do it again. His production company is one of those showbiz complexes geared to thrive behind pasteboard properties. From a carpeted cottage on Sunset Boulevard, Clark runs the largest personal-appearance packaging agency in the world (it employs a staff of 40 and handles upwards of 300 one-night stands a year). Right now, its most important clients are the Monkees. Their association with Dick Clark seems inevitable. His genius has always been making gravy from raw meat, and convincing a hungry public that his gruel is healthier than the real thing.

"The name of the game is show business," Clark shrugs. His clients always play it well. The Monkees dab honesty make-up on their faces, and come on real. They wear musicianship like a tiara. "Their show is full of exuberance," Clark insists. "They do four or five costume changes, and it lasts a full hour. They don't do a fast fifteen minutes like our British friends."

Few subjects provoke as carping a response from Dick Clark as the English rock invasion. No wonder; what finally ended his pop dictatorship was not scandal or boredom, but the Beatles, with a little help from their friends. Though Clark goes easy on the Beatles ("Their major accomplishment," he thinks, "was getting the older generation interested in rock") he calls the folk-rockers who followed them "the greatest danger to pop music." What he objects to most is their repudiation of show business. "They get so involved in being admired by the people around them," he explains, "that they forget about the audience."

Clark's emphasis on commercialism (the audience first!) is understandable; he reigned in the age of the pop professional, who fit his personality to the function at hand. But the Beatles ushered in an era of the musician-idol, who sang and spoke his own thoughts. They were the first to prove that a rock performer could be his own image-maker. In the fifties, folk-rock singers Simon and Garfunkel found it necessary to call themselves Tom and Jerry, and act accordingly. But after the Beatles, they used their own names, and made it—as they felt it.

The new naturalness dethroned Dick Clark. The folk-rockers were amateurs in a sense which must have enraged him; they emphasized individuality over role, making their style impossible to assemble as a pop commodity. Dick Clark could create a celebrity, but not a Bob Dylan.

In 1965, with a galaxy of rock subversives carving up the world into fan clubs, Clark found himself in the same kind of situation that had spawned him ten years before. Rock 'n' roll was again a puzzling, even threatening, phenomenon to adults—so hairy that they sometimes had it banned. It is no accident that the Beatles and the Rolling Stones began in conscious imitation of pre-Bandstand rock idols whose black-and-blue sweat-music turned kids on and put adults uptight.

In the mid-fifties, teenagers occupied a prominent place in the headlines as hoodlums-saints not fit to be seen below the waist. The teen-hero had a lean and hungry look. His hair curled down over the bridge of his nose like a Sicilian grape arbor. His motorcycle jacket glittered with the reflected glory of a hundred brass studs. His parents thought he was a killer, but his girl knew he was a rebel without a cause, oppressed from all sides. If James Dean brought the teenage ethos of rumbling, bumbling sensuality to the screen, the hit parade was filled with its musical extensions: a yielding, yearning ecstasy that was almost antithetical to the Mickey Spillane adult culture of the time.

Dick Clark made his mark by castrating this teen hero. He substituted romance for sex, neckties for leather jackets, and swirling dance-curlicues for grinding. His music—with its Little League lushness—was accepted by adults as bad, but safe. Nobody ever banned Frankie Avalon. Even the fuzz approved. Said one official of the New York Police Department, "Dick Clark acts as a tranquilizing pill on youngsters."

He has been offering the same musical Miltown ever since. In the post-Bandstand years, his clients have maintained an uncanny sameness. Even when longhaired, they are happy, reverent kids with watermelon eyes and cantaloupe voices. Like Paul Revere and the Raiders, a cream-puff combo Clark found in the Pacific Northwest, they are costumed players, calculated to reassure everyone that the kids are all right (i.e. obedient).

For a while, repeated exposure on a daily pre-taped Clark package called "Where The Action Is" helped to establish the Raiders. In tight, taut britches and Revolutionary War frock coats which never hid their thighs, they romped and bounded past the cameras like the Three Stooges in Colonial drag. An early anti-drug sermon called "Kicks" brought them to the attention of disc jockeys during a spate of baffling psychedelic-code-songs. By once more exploiting the fears of adults, Dick Clark tried to sell the Raiders to the young as their own.

"We almost made it that time," he reflects today. But with the cancellation of "Where The Action Is," the group has all but faded, except on the vanity tables of pre-teens where they remain enshrined. Clark's other "Action" properties have met similar fates; we will probably never again get a chance to worship at the feet of Keith Allison (who was discovered when he happened by an "Action" set only because he looked like Paul McCartney. "Later," Clark explains, "we found out he could sing").

Later, we found out he couldn't!

Can Dick Clark do it again? Will we commission him to perform another hysterectomy? His scalpel is raised, his anesthesia ready for admission whenever we choose to breathe. If he does succeed in 1968, it will be because we need him. Dick Clark is a master of mediocrity, and Americans have a strange affection for the banal. It shows most during times of stress. In the prime spinach-years of "American Bandstand," we were all afraid of excellence. We wanted, more than anything, to be alike. Today, when that sameness had been smashed, we wonder if the center can hold together at all. If it cannot, Dick Clark will emerge in every field from pop to politics.

He leans back in his leather chair, feet firmly planted in California carpeting, and observes, "I'm one of the world's great finger-pointers." Then, with the grace of a man who knows when to be modest, he adds, "You'd better not quote me on that."

1968

PAUL WILLIAMS

Paul Williams (1948–2013) once wrote, "the only thing to do with rock and roll is to participate in it." As a teenager in 1966, from his Dartmouth dorm room, he virtually willed "rock criticism" into being with the mimeographed *Crawdaddy*, usually credited as the first national magazine in the United States devoted to rock music. Among the excited callers to his dorm's payphone were Paul Simon and Bob Dylan. Williams, perhaps needless to say, never finished college. His magazine became the first home for writers such as Richard Meltzer and Jon Landau, and for outpourings of Williams's trademark conversational style; he approached his analyses of artists such as The Beach Boys and Neil Young as an enthusiastic fan chatting with a group of friends. In the piece included here, for instance, his tone, especially when writing about the Rolling Stones' uneven *Their Satanic Majesties Request*, wobbles unnervingly between passionate engagement and self-parody. Williams lacked the instincts of a magazine publisher, and *Crawdaddy* was commercially lapped by *Rolling Stone*, and then sold. Williams preferred to participate informally in the social culture of the musicians, among whom he became a kind of Zelig figure: intimate witness to the aborted creation of Brian Wilson's *Smile* and to John Lennon and Yoko Ono's "Bed-In For Peace" in Toronto. Massively prolific, Williams was also a self-invented counterculture guru as the author of the best-selling *Das Energi*, the executor of Philip K. Dick's estate, and one of Bob Dylan's most thorough and patient explicators. He died from complications following a 1995 bicycle accident.

▼▼▼▼▼▼▼▼▼▼▼▼▼▼▼▼▼▼▼▼▼▼▼▼▼

Outlaw Blues

"I WISH I was on some Australian mountain range. . . ."

People who work in mass media are supposed to be half manipulator and half prophet; and all around the mulberry bush now producers, performers, and persons who just like to rap are wondering about the Future of Rock (and roll). They talk about stuff like the following:

During 1967 rock music, thanks to Beatles Doors Airplane etc., greatly expanded its audience to the point where maybe two-thirds of the people buying any records at all were buying rock albums. Meanwhile, also thanks to Beatles Doors Airplane etc., the number of creative musicians and groups within the field grew even faster. Situation: during the summer of 1967, by some awesome coincidence, the size and interests of the buying audience coincided nicely with the quantity and quality of rock albums newly available to them, and hence the considerable success of people like Jimi Hendrix, Country Joe & the Fish, the Doors, the Mothers, Moby Grape, and so on. Lots of creative people making it pretty big with creative stuff, and this in turn led to unrestrained enthusiasm on the part of large record companies, who've been spending unbelievable amounts to make sure that any group that sounds talented to them will in the future record on their label. In the same manner, successful groups have pushed and shoved their way into the studios, sparing no expense, taking as much time and using as many tools as might seem necessary to really Do What They Want To Do. Because it looks like the enthusiasm of the audience for good stuff will make it all worthwhile.

But already in December 1967 the difficulties are becoming apparent. For one thing, there are quite a number of good groups making records, and they all expect a slice of the pie. Can the same audience that—phenomenally—put the Beatles, the Doors, the Stones, and Jefferson Airplane in the top five on the lp charts at the same time, can they purchase enough records now to put Donovan, Love, Country Joe, Judy Collins, the Rolling Stones, the Beatles, the Beach Boys, Van Dyke Parks, the Hollies, Paul Butterfield, Jefferson Airplane, the Incredible

String Band, and Buffalo Springfield in the top five at the same time? All of the above have released new albums in the last month, as I write this, and the Who, the Kinks, Moby Grape, the Byrds, Jimi Hendrix, Randy Newman, the Grateful Dead, the Mothers, and the Velvet Underground have stuff scheduled for the immediate future. Elbow room! cried Dan'l Boone. Every one of these groups expects to be able to spend $50,000 or more recording an album, and if this much good stuff is going to be released every two months, who's going to pay for it?

The immediate answer is clear: expand the audience. But since we've already moved in on most of the existent music audience, this means a very heavy undertaking: we have to increase the number of people who are actually listening to and buying any music at all. We have to not only show why rock music is good music, but why Music Itself Is Good For You and so on and on. And maybe even the quantity of really good stuff being released nowadays will help us do it.

But there's one word back there you might have overlooked. *Coincidence.* What if it suddenly turns out that what Country Joe & the Fish (or even the Beatles) feel like doing with all that expensive recording-time freedom is not the same thing as what our dear expanding audience wants to listen to? What if good creative art is not always appreciated by huge numbers of people the instant it's available?

That's What People Are Talking About, folks. And it's all fairly relevant to the albums at hand. The Beach Boys, a group that class prejudice prevents many of us from appreciating, released in the summer of 1966 an album called *Pet Sounds*, to me one of the very finest rock albums of all time. It was not exactly Far*Out, but it was kinda subtle compared to the previous Beach Boys stuff; and partly for that reason, and mostly because of timing, *Pet Sounds* was the first Beach Boys album in several years *not* to be a million seller. The timing factor was one not unfamiliar to us in 1967—the big hit on the album, "Sloop John B," made it in December 1965, but because of the amount of studio time required to do the album right, *Pet Sounds* wasn't released till June and lost its impact as a result. And the mere fact that the record was really beautiful wasn't enough to salvage the situation. Fans don't always care about that.

But the fans *loved* the group's previous album, *Beach Boys Party*, a million-seller which most of us heavy rock listeners looked down upon as a sloppy, drunken recording of moldy oldies from 1961. Not even good (we thought then) in the context of the Beach Boys, let alone as a Rock Album. Yet the record sold terrifically, despite its dollar-extra price (a gala gatefold presentation) and the fact that there was another Beach Boys album, released just before it, competing for the fans' attention.

So maybe Beach Boys fans are stupid, and we can dismiss the whole thing. But maybe that's a pretty snotty attitude to take; maybe something is happening here that we just ought to know about. *Beach Boys Party* is an excellent album containing excellent music *that is easy to relate to*! And that's why the fans dug it, dug it more than that other excellent lp *Pet Sounds*, and that's the real reason people buy records—not because they're dupes, but because they like music, and the better it is the more they like it as long as they are still able to relate to what's good about it.

Not that I want to say that if lots of people like something, it's good. We all know what Humpty Dumpty said, and since I'm the one who's stuck with whatever definition of the word I care to accept, I'll feel more comfortable believing it's "good" if I feel it is rather than it's "good" if it wins the popularity polls. But we are talking about the relationship between what a performer feels like doing and what a large audience—large enough to pay for that performer's studio time—feels like listening to. So the extent to which large bunches of people are able to relate to things is pretty important.

I said the *Beach Boys Party* album is excellent, and I was talking about my own subjective response, of course. Yet that's an educated response—i.e., in 1965 I didn't like the record, I really put it down, and now after two more years of listening to rock intensively I feel that the album is a very good one. My opinion now is probably more valid than my opinion then—not because of any directionality of time but because I'm writing for an audience of people most of whom have also listened to a great deal of rock in the last two years. They can relate to my present point of view, at least in terms of common experience.

Let's drop this for a moment. Do you like the new Stones album?

I hope you do. I went through a period of about a week (after loving it initially) where I was really unsure if I liked it or not. I liked many parts of it, but I wasn't quite comfortable with the whole thing. I stuck with it, of course—there hasn't been a Rolling Stones album yet I've disliked, after giving it a little time to sink in—and pretty soon I lost my uneasiness, so that now I am quite convinced it's a great record, and I'm at a loss to explain my moments of doubt. Sometimes you have to listen to a record for a while before you can accept it on its own ground. And the *quantity* of good stuff coming out this month might have made me doubt my good judgment. Anyway, happy ending.

The Stones always come through. I didn't like *Flowers* at first, and now I realize how incredibly difficult it was to design an album so unpresuming that it could be released in June 1967 and not be compared to *Sergeant Pepper*. After the initial shock of seeing two songs on *Flowers* that were on the previous album, and realizing that the rest of the record was a chaotic assortment of rejects from *Buttons, Aftermath*, and *The Rolling Stones Sing Motown*, I now listen to the record with great pleasure, I feel that "Ride On Baby" is surely one of the great rock songs and that the Stones, faced with the problem (among others) of releasing some great 1966 songs in 1967, met the situation head-on with a thoroughly successful anachronistic album. And the fans didn't care (another million-seller). Only the critics were ruffled.

The Stones always come through. It's not a coincidence. I remember in 1965 I just assumed that you couldn't judge a song the first few times you heard it. "Satisfaction" felt great the first time through, but I couldn't *hear* anything at all. Piece by piece the structure of the song, as I listened again and again, came clear to me from all that confusion. "Get Off of My Cloud" sounded like pure noise the first ten times through on a transistor radio. The form of a song is something you see all at once. When it comes to you, you suddenly find a picture of the entire song in your head, and at any given point you're aware of the context, the whole thing. Until you get that picture, you just follow a line through the song—you hear something, you hear something else, finally the song is over. The more you listen, the more you begin to sense a shape replacing that line, until eventually the song is familiar to

you and you're not lost any more ("gestalt perception"—you can perceive a thing as part of a group, you can perceive a group as a collection
of things).

And it's not a coincidence. Because the one thing the Stones are
absolute masters of—and it certainly shows on the new album—is
structure. If you take the Rolling Stones and maroon them in the swirling vacuum of space, stranded with nothing but ether, that imponder-
able stuff of the universe, to play with, they'll take that ether and mold it
into a space ship and come chasing back after you, and they're the only
rock group that can do that.

Again and again, not just on this album but throughout their pro-
cession of not-quite-a-dozen albums, the Rolling Stones incorporate
chaos by creating entirely new structures out of it, and never are they
incoherent. If you listen to a Stones song long enough you'll *always*
see the picture, always perceive the whole and feel relaxed at the naturalness of it all . . . no matter how much of a struggle it was for you to
break through to that naturalness.

And the Stones love to fool around. They sound sloppy—they don't
want you to feel comfortable till you get there. They give the impression of incoherence so that their uptight listeners will buzz off and not
bother them, and so the people who care will not relax on the surface
but will continue to penetrate the song until they've really got to it.
"Open our minds let the pictures come. . . ."

This applies not only to songs, but to albums. *Their Satanic Majesties
Request* sounds like a wild assortment of stuff the first time you hear
it, and ends up being a monolith. Having a brand new Rolling Stones
album in your hands is like being a virgin, on the brink. The first rush
is ecstatic. And when you finally get *there*, you marvel at the Stones,
you can't believe they've really done it again, you're overcome with the
sense of wonder. Sure feels good.

And feeling good, let's wallow around in the album awhile, since
that's what's fun in a review. Take a song and notice some things about
it, petty pleasantries, universal truths, anything to give us that nice feeling that we're all listening to the same songs and hearing something
like the same sort of thing.

"Sing This All Together" is a nice idea. I don't want to get too involved in comparing it with the idea of *Sergeant Pepper*, because I really don't think they have much in common—on the surface they do (in fact, both concepts hark back to the end of *Between the Buttons*), but it's immediately apparent that the Lonely Hearts Club Band is a structural convenience, a cute outer shell, whereas "Sing This All Together" is a musical and emotional concept in which every track on the album is deeply involved. *Sergeant Pepper* isn't a very significant musical influence on *Satanic Majesties*—it's an experiential influence. That is, the Beatles took the Stones on a *Sergeant Pepper* trip, and the Stones returned and created this album. The audience, too, obviously listens to *Satanic Majesties* in the context of just having lived with *Sergeant Pepper* for lo, these several months, and thus the experience of the Beatles album is a strong influence on both the people who recorded the Stones lp, and the people who are listening to it. *Satanic Majesties* is influenced by but does not resemble *Sergeant Pepper*.

On page two of any British passport is a sentence which starts, "Her Britannic Majesty . . . requests and requires," etc.

And "Citadel" is about New York City. I read that in the *New Musical Express*. But it's really about Fritz Lang's *Metropolis*, a 1926 science-fiction flick envisioning City of the Future, with huge evil buildings run by steam, nightmare machines, and tiny people running every which way. The broken reentry in the middle of the song is kind of like the entire musical history of the Who in one half of a note; and maybe Candy and Taffy know that it can be pretty nice to live in a citadel. But if you've seen Mick stand there on stage after the girls have broken through the cop line, you know he doesn't want to be protected.

Oh, well, as Mick says toward the end of "Citadel." Bill Wyman is probably the only Stone who could have written a Gilbert (tarantara!) & Sullivan rock song. But the best thing about "In Another Land" is the tremendous sense of relief each time the sleeper wakes and finds himself surrounded by the Rolling Stones, drums, chorus, and all. In fact, no matter how far into the dim recesses of outer space this album may take you, you always get the comforting feeling that the Stones are right there beside you, and the situation's completely under control.

Things may seem to be getting out of hand—look at all that stuff on the front cover of the jacket—but the bored faces of the Stones remind you once again that it's all right.

And this certainly is a science-fiction album. While Bill Wyman, Jimi Hendrix, and Grace Slick were home reading each other's comic books, Mick and Keith must have been down at the movies, digging Robbie the Robot in *Forbidden Planet. Their Satanic Majesties Request* is full of ancient empires based on decimal computers, and monsters from behind the Id. Sandy Pearlman may think the Byrds sing about the way the earth turns, Bill Wyman in Wonderland accidentally wonders "Is this some kind of (cosmic) joke?" but Mick and Keith *know* that Old Sol (our mr. sun) is the best we can do for a local center of activity, and they never wonder where the yellow went. "Sun turning round with graceful motion." Solipsism is for the byrds. "Pictures of us spin the circling sun." Bill Wyman's probably afraid to close all his eyes together, by this time.

"2000 Man" is like the Incredible String Band's "Back in the 1960's." The structure of the song is breathtaking, a further step along the trail blazed by the Association with "Windy." And the phrase "don't you know I'm a 2000 man?" reflects an absolute mastery of rock lyrics.

A good thing, too, for the next track is an instrumental, sort of a "Now I've Got a Witness" (Stones album one, if your memory is failing) for "Sing This All Together"—a true Nanker Phelge creation. "Sing This All Together (See What Happens)" is my favorite track on an album that doesn't really have favorite tracks. Some people think it's silly, but they're wrong. It's even possible that "See What Happens" is influenced by "Goin' Home" via Love's "Revelation," which would be magnificent, but that's not important. What is important is that there's always something going on in this mosaic, and it's always not-quite-familiar and always worthwhile. See, the nice thing is not that they're doing "this kind of stuff"—any old Pink Floyd or John Fahey can do this kind of stuff, but in the case of the Stones the stuff itself is incredible. Brilliant raw music, the same stuff as very early rock and roll but without the words or much of the instrumentation. The same Music, though, don't you see? The Rolling Stones' instincts are absolutely musical, and that's one of the reasons they can't do anything wrong.

D. G. Hartwell points out that the reprise at the end of "See What Happens" is an electronic "We Wish You a Merry Christmas." And it's worth noting that in terms of timing and impact, this is the first Christmas album since *Rubber Soul*.

"She's a Rainbow" is a popular crowd-pleaser; and it's kind of relevant to our whole theme here to discuss how the Stones manage to keep turning out hit singles. Pretty melodies—this one reminds me of "Never on Sunday"—help, of course, but mostly I think they make it because they know how to knock people out and make them feel comfortable at the same time. "She's a Rainbow" *is* easy to relate to. It sounds like a song the very first time you hear it, and anyone can tell it's about how nice this girl is. So there aren't any obstacles to the casual listener's enjoyment of the song . . . but that doesn't mean it's superficial. Like "Paint It Black" or "Ruby Tuesday," "Rainbow" gets you deeper involved each time you hear it. And beneath that secure, surface feeling of order and accessibility, there's a lot of stuff happening here—much too much to immediately resolve and store away in some part of your mind, more than enough to make the song continually fresh and worthwhile. I don't want to pretend I've solved the mystery of what makes a hit record, but I think we can agree that "Rainbow" is the prettiest, and the most accessible, song on the album. That's interesting data.

"The Lantern" is another structural masterpiece, with those incredible sweeping transitions, perfectly placed feedback, echoes, guitar whispers and screams that never intrude, until you suddenly feel part of some exceedingly formal cosmic hopscotch game that has gone on for millennia. The song sounds absolutely right, without sounding like anything that ever was before. It's a Diogenes trip (and Bob Dylan said, "Don't ask me nothin' about nothin'; I just might tell you the truth." But the Stones aren't even afraid of being really serious).

"Gomper" (I'm reading the *New Musical Express* again) is supposed to be "the Tibetan term for the incredible journey some Tibetan monks make while under hypnosis." It sounds like a great outdoors trip to me—some kind of sexual encounter at the beginning, then lots of open meadows, afternoon sunshine, running and smiling, growing things and wildlife and a real sense of wonder. The music, which is just too good to describe, carries you further and further away, till all of a sudden you can't see the place you started from, and the music starts doing little fear things as the pleasure fades, and you're 2000 light-years from home. Which may sound contrived, but it works, over and over again. So the Stones can even create something completely open-ended, and give it that firm feeling of structure.

As for "2000 Light Years," it's really Twilight Zone stuff. Like Manzarek in "The End," the organist creates the whole song in the context of one note (another D. G. Hartwell revelation) while the bass and guitar go through some obscure variations on "Gloria." What you get is this sinuous, ethereal song that really feels like it could absorb dozens of adjectives like that with no trouble at all. And you learn all about the acceptance of alien surroundings. "Gomper"/"2000 Light Years" is really just a very subtle reworking of the theme of "Waterloo Sunset."

Each song on this album is different, but not really separate, from the others; the works are interconnected on almost every level. So you can apply your gestalt perception to the whole album, and this makes "On with the Show" a special pleasure simply because it's the final song. Everything is resolved, and you really feel good about it, like maybe you really did see, for a moment, where we all come from. And the other side of the coin is that "On with the Show" tells you you don't have to take it all too seriously ("Sergeant Pepper Reprise" told you you didn't have to take it all seriously *except* "A Day in the Life"). The way it works in the context of the Stones album is you can get as involved as you like while you're there, while you're listening to it, and you don't have to think about it at all once it's over. It's an experience we all have together, the Stones and us, and it's not meant to have any further significance. The Beatles say they'd "love to take you home with us"; the Stones aren't polite, but they'll "get you safely to your door." What more could you ask?

And the best thing about the cover is that they didn't spoil it by making it *too* good.

Two words are really significant to Jefferson Airplane's sound and appeal: complexity and kinetics. Familiar words, and fairly simple ones. Complexity: there's a lot going on, all the time. Kinetics: the listener is caught up in the motion of the songs. *After Bathing at Baxter's* is the best Jefferson Airplane album, in terms of both overall quality and the extent to which it captures the life style of the group. Had it been released in January 1967, I think it would have been generally recognized as the crowning achievement of the dawn of American rock, 1965–1966, just as *The Rolling Stones Now!* is the summation and peak of the young rock scene in Britain, 1963–1964. The mere fact that *Baxter's* arrived inappropriately in December 1967 does not take away its real importance. This is the album that all us young Byrds, Paul Butterfield, Lovin' Spoonful fans were waiting for.

Waves of "Pooneil," washing over the listener, carrying him back. It's always a nice transition into "Pooneil," from whatever album you were listening to, the cleansing feedback which is almost thematic in *Baxter's* and then that "Memphis" bass & drums opening which will outlive Chuck Berry and all the rest of us. The Stones album is nice to make noises to, blare at the brass parts and just be friendly with, but the Airplane lp is from the good ol' days when you'd move your whole body, or pretend you were playing along with the lead guitar. You can almost see Grace and Marty asking the audience to dance.

The complexity is apparent immediately. The Airplane don't have the inherent sense of structure that has blessed the Rolling Stones, but they know the rules, know them well enough to break them masterfully. "Watch Her Ride" and "Won't You Try/Saturday Afternoon" both take off from basic Byrds/Stones/Beatles concepts and then employ such daring and casually self-confident variations (watch what happens to the "watch you ride" phrase, for example) that it takes a while to realize what they're getting away with. Paul Kantner is on the verge of becoming a major rock architect. "Pooneil" is a stunning achievement, a five-minute song that flows as one line (with a loop) from beginning to end, never stopping long enough to let the listener see it as a static shape.

Complexity. In "Pooneil" Paul and Marty trade off lead vocals, sometimes sing together and sometimes sing together with Grace. Grace also has one brief solo moment, and may even act as a second voice to Paul or Marty. So you have vocals by A, B, A&B, A&B&C, C, A&C, and B&C. In addition to which Grace acts as a sort of shadow throughout the song, repeating what the lead voice sings in her own very special I-am-a-background-instrument style. Since the last album Grace has really gotten into the art of group vocals, and—like everyone else in the group she can't do the simplest thing without being clever and individualistic and creative about it—this really adds to the richness of the Airplane sound.

Complexity. So many personalities, and each completely independent of the others; each man integrating his music into the whole thing, but also using his instrument as a means to impose his personal style on whatever's going down. When the Stones do a song, there's some general feeling of "this is how it's gonna be," and while each musician's style is apparent and important, it's pretty well understood that the song should express whatever the songwriters had in mind. With the Airplane, the songwriter is considered just one of six group members, and so a song like "Wild Tyme" is created by a sort of committee consisting of one songwriter, three vocalists, a bass player, a drummer, a solo guitarist, a rhythm guitarist, and a guy with a tambourine. It sometimes takes a while to get all these heads together (seven months, in the case of this album), but in the end there is a real musical confluence, a feeling on the part of every group member that everything's in place.

But it wouldn't be very important *how* the music was created, were it not for the fact that you can hear the difference with your very own ears. A Stones song is listened to as a song, and you pretty much feel you hear the whole thing every time. Sometimes it doesn't hit you as hard as other times, but it's all there. With an Airplane song, it's very easy to hear different stuff each time you listen. Try it. Listen to "Wild Tyme," and then listen to it again concentrating just on what the lead guitar is doing. Then dig the rhythm guitar, the interaction between

Paul on rhythm and Jorma on lead and the huge differences between the two guitarists even when they're playing essentially the same part. The personalities of these musicians come through very clear in their playing—they aren't self-conscious, nothing is held back, it's all there for the listener to groove on. Pay attention to what the drums are doing. Try to feel the movement of the bass guitar, which is really buried on this track. Listen to the vocal very carefully, trying to pick out the quieter things that are happening. Listen for the separate personalities of the vocalists in the harmony parts. Pick up on the *way* each word is mouthed. There's a lot going on.

And you don't have to put in a lot of conscious effort to enjoy all this. One of the reasons the Airplane album is so fresh, so endlessly attractive, is that you do hear new stuff each time you listen. You can't help it—there are an awful lot of specifics on this album, crying out to be heard and appreciated, and they'll jump out at you no matter how you ignore them. Despite "Two Heads" being mostly Grace's song, with a heavy emphasis on her friend the percussionist, sooner or later you're sure to discover the sweetness of the bass part, the brilliance of what Jack is doing in there. The joy of complexity, when the music is good, is that every pleasure is pushed further by the constant discovery of yet *another* great thing going on, and there's just too much music, appreciable on too many levels, for it ever to grow tiresome. The sheer fun of the music is increased sixfold by the extent to which everyone's into it.

"Pooneil" is the masterpiece, every moment orchestrated, every musician loving it. And with all that activity, it's still just a Pooh trip: there wasn't That Much to learn out today, but it sure does feel better knowing it. Just another day, and who but the Airplane could get so much out of it? Who but JA would say "armadillo"?

"A Small Package of Value Will Come to You, Shortly" is great ad lib theatre, stretched and structured by the cleverness of the concertmaster and his tape recorder and his percussion collection. Spencer reaches out, grabs "Pooneil" with one hand, "Young Girl Sunday Blues" with the other, and ties them together with a wonderful word bath in concentric and overlapping circles, "Joy to the World" in the center for punctuation. The closer you listen to this, the more you like it; what makes the Airplane or the Stones more important than so many other clever people is that their cleverness holds up under inspection, in fact turns out to be real valid groovy music. And it's nice to be so careful without ever being too cautious.

"Young Girl Sunday Blues" is a pleasure: real Marty Balin lyrics, such as you don't hardly find anymore. Mick's great "Don't you know I'm a 2000 man?" is equaled and surpassed by Marty's "Don't you know [careful emphasis on each of the three words] what I have found—maybe you've found it too?" Not that either of these guys really wants to get into the social psychology of knowledge, or whatever; it's just that so much in rock depends on the singer's attitude toward the listener. Mick assumes absolutely nothing, so he can cheerfully pretend his audience knows everything, even things they might not know *how* to know. But Marty takes his listeners very seriously, and don't think "young and new" girls don't appreciate that. And what has Marty found? "Today is made up of yesterday and tomorrow—young girl Sunday blues and all her sorrow." Can you honestly say you didn't know *that*?

But I'm not kidding when I say I think Marty is the best lyricist in Airplane. Paul has a really nice feeling for words that don't mean very much, but Marty is just rational enough and just irrational enough to really set you free. "So much can be heard," he sings, and Jorma just goes right on playing "Get Out of My Life Woman" on his guitar.

Paul Kantner has David Crosby's rhythm and Gene Clark's mind. But none of these three guys is a member of the Byrds. "Martha she keeps her heart in a broken clock" ("she'll always be there, my love don't care about time"). "I didn't know you were the one for me, I couldn't see, but you were waiting" ("I have never been so far out in front that I could ask for what I want and have it any time"). John Kelehor told me about Crosby's incredible rhythm, and he should know (Byrd-for-a-day). But John also sat in for John Densmore in Portland recently; and Paul Rothchild and I both agree that Paul Kantner is one of the few people in the world who could be a Door. I only bring this up because Paul K. thinks *Crawdaddy* is too serious a magazine sometimes, and I wanted to show that we are.

And "Martha" is a pretty song. Unlike the Stones, the Airplane finds nothing mysterious in the great outdoors. Instead, they're comfortable enough to do verbal acrobatics ("she weeds a part through a token lock," very nice) and pull off a Lear Jet eggshell landing near the end. Everybody slows down, and Jorma is very careful; Paul recites, and the opening of "Wild Tyme" at that moment is about as perfect as anything on the album, or anywhere else.

"Wild Tyme" mostly borrows words from other songs on *Baxter's*, but that's okay for a genuine rave-up in the Yardbirds' "Strolling On" *Blow-Up* tradition. "I'm here for you any old time," and that's the Airplane—accessible.

Jorma's song is an assault, but it comes after so much other stuff that the listener is practically numb. I like the auto accident in the middle.

And there's more to the Airplane than accessibility. But their only air of mystery comes from their being so obvious on the surface (the words of the songs) and yet always so perceptibly better-than-obvious. It's always been a source of confusion to me that I get so much pleasure from the overfamiliar lyrics of "Today" or "Blues from an Airplane"—there must be more going on than the obvious, stereotyped stuff, or why do I like it so much? And Sandy's article on Jefferson Airplane's use of the cliché (*Crawdaddy* 9) by no means answers all my questions. Because Sandy doesn't really like Marty's lyrics; he only appreciates them.

Grace, in fact, sometimes suffers by seeming less obvious than the rest of the group. "White Rabbit" came on with an air of mystery, but was so utterly decipherable that, for me, it rapidly lost its impact. "Pooneil" pretends to no mystery at all, but the more you listen to it the more subtle it seems. Something's happening here. Grace's songs on this new album are both very good, easy to respect, but hard to really get into. There's no place to hide. When you wonder if "Two Heads" is about hypocrisy, the double standard, you do that on a very intellectual level. As you listen more, you don't get involved in the song; instead you get hung up in the very interesting, very exciting things that she does with her voice. Maybe you groove on the instrumentation. But you groove on its quality more than on any particular emotion it might inspire. Grace makes everyone, especially herself, a studio musician.

That isn't a put-down. But I think we're all aware of the good qualities of stuff like "rejoyce" and "Two Heads," and it's strange that the area in which Grace falls down is exactly that thing that the Airplane as a whole does best, the conjuring of emotions out of motion and involvement. Grace's stuff is not exactly static, but fluid—her singing has no real motion, since motion really cannot be divorced from the idea of movement in a direction, but rather flows from place to place without covering any ground to speak of. This is confusing. You can hear what I mean by listening to "rejoyce." ". . . I got his arm . . . I got his arm . . . I've had it for weeks . . . I got his arm Stephen won't give his arm to no gold-star mother's farm war's good business so give your son and I'd rather have my country die for me!" Even from the words you can see that she shifts from phrase to phrase without any apparent sense of overall direction. When you listen, you'll see that she also does it with absolutely no hesitation, shifting emotions timelessly from plea- sure and possessiveness to pride, a sort of stark innocence, warm female sensitivity, righteousness and derision and finally anger building to fury. If you tried to clock her speed in moving from one emotion to the next, you'd feel pretty silly, for she doesn't move in time in the sense that "Pooneil" or "Young Girl Sunday" moves. She merely shifts, now I'm here, now over here, now somewhere else, like that. In "Two Heads," toward the end, she flows like liquid on some nonabsorbent surface, splattering by sheer will power. This is the sort of thing we mortals can only sit back and watch, and maybe that's just as well. "Rejoyce," which used to be and should have been called "Ulysses," is a detached "work of art," not flawless but certainly impressive, and that's Grace doing all that fine piano and recorder stuff. The last line is regrettably unintelli- gible; reliable sources inform me she's saying "but somehow it all falls apart." She sure is cynical.

In opposition to this, we have Jefferson Airplane, including Grace as a harmony voice, with their incredible Airplane kineticism. Kineticism all started in rock 'n' roll with the basic desire to get the audience off their feet and dancing. So you employ every trick you know to make your listeners not just feel each beat, but feel the succession of beats, feel them more and more until they anticipate each beat and throw their bodies into it. And then you discover some simple devices that accent each movement even more than the audience expects, so that no matter how much they're moving, the song says, "Faster! Harder!" and pretty soon the people have forgotten all about the individual notes or beats and they're just moving with you, entirely caught up in the music.

There's a lot of technique that goes into kineticism, and none of the people who are best at it—the Who ("Anyway, Anyhow, Anywhere"), the Kinks ("Milk Cow Blues"), Them ("Mystic Eyes"), the Four Tops ("Reach Out, I'll Be There")—need to think about it very much. They strain to make the music move, and it moves. It moves because the singer holds back a little on the vocal while the music tries to plunge ahead, which is something like sitting on a ticking bomb. It moves because the bass and drums set up a powerful rhythmic constancy and then the rhythm guitar starts coming in on the beat, but just a tiny fraction late, pulling the listener ahead of the music. Tension is established. And once you've got a little tension, then you just make things a little louder and a little faster, harder, louder, faster, harder, faster, harder, louder, faster, faster, boom! More than one listener has had his head blown off by kinetic resolution.

Airplane kineticism won't blow your head off, but it should get you excited—it's high quality roller-coaster stuff. "Watch Her Ride" is high kinetics—the first two verses run along with Paul, Jack, and Spencer building it up nicely, Jorma hinting at better things to come with his truncated solo runs off to one side. Things break loose after "for me" in the second verse. Single guitar notes, punctuated by bass runs, are used as waves of sound, each wave rising from the crest of the one previous. Vocals break in on the fourth wave and sustain both the wave motion and the feeling of building intensity, while Jorma allows himself the luxury of three or even four notes to drive the vocals harder. The word phrases themselves are kinetic—"times don't change" moves into "times don't ever change"; "the only thing in my world, the only thing that my mind could find for love for love and peace of mind for me . . . for me." Grace's gliding solo on "for me" carries the force of this section nicely into the third verse of the song.

Kineticism is very much a group thing—if everyone in the band doesn't cooperate and work toward the same end, nothing will happen.

But the single most important contributor to the kineticism of the Airplane is the interaction between lead guitar and bass. Jack and Jorma have been playing together since long before the formation of the Airplane; they understand each other's music and work together with a closeness that is unusual to rock. They tie the group together, because the musical ground between bass and lead guitar is such that drums, rhythm guitar, and vocals can fit right into whatever motion is going on between them. The complexity of the group is likewise based on this bond; in the end, it is only the alliance between Jack and Jorma that allows one unified piece of music to emerge as the product of six highly individual minds.

The Casady-Kaukonen relationship is explored in depth on *Baxter's* in a jam guitar/bass/drums jam entitled "Spare Chaynge." Jefferson Airplane is fearless in a pleasantly insignificant way: they're not afraid of stuffing an album with good unaesthetic doodling (on the inside sleeve), photos that don't look like them (the centerfold), bad puns ("Spare Chaynge," "rejoyce," "How Suite It Is"), structureless nine-minute jam sessions, etc. Sometimes they really are ballsy in their pointless fearlessness. By making the "suites"—two or three songs segued together—look like single tracks, they make it extremely difficult for any dj to play individual songs off the album. This in spite of the fact that it is easy—the Rolling Stones did it—to link the songs with spiral grooves that will both make the music continuous and make the individual songs identifiable to anyone looking at the disk. In other words, the Airplane has the balls to stand up to dj's even for no reason at all.

The way to listen to the jam is position yourself before the speakers so that Jack is on one side, Jorma is on the other, and Spencer is somewhere in the middle. By consciously listening to what each guy is doing in relation to the others, you can really get at the heart of this track—it's a dance, a ballet interaction between three persons. And interpretation is entirely up to the listener. The piece starts—for me—with hesitation, not much music, kind of an uptight scene that has to be loosened for anything to happen. Jack assumes the burden of getting things going—he works at getting Jorma involved in the music, he hesitates, tries one tack, then another, never pushes too hard, plays very gently as he starts to get Jorma's interest, kindling the spark . . . Jorma loosens up under this foreplay, tries a run or two, still isn't quite comfortable—but he's coming alive. Spencer withdraws when he sees the tension of the situation, and the importance of leaving the two of them alone until Jack gets Jorma going. Jorma really starts to unwind, plays something nice, Jack coaxes him along, Jorma stops, comes back with a really satisfying thing, gets completely involved in his playing, almost immediately Jack lets loose for the first time, Spencer comes back in with dignity once the ice has been broken, and now, four minutes into the track, real music is happening. Music as an interaction, a conversation analogous to an intellectual or sexual meeting of minds, but separate from them, something that only musicians can experience. "Spare Chaynge" is, for me, a vicarious thrill, an exciting presentation of not music as external art, intended to reach some sort of audience, but music as personal, internal communication and understanding between three people. A jam like all others—but so clear, so easy-to-relate-to that it becomes one of the most important pieces of music in a long while.

Which leaves us with "Won't You Try," only one of the most optimistic performances in the history of rock and roll. The Airplane, despite everything, have absolute confidence in their audience. It's kind of like the early American preacher, in front of his congregation, looking out at the faces of every worst kind of sinner, and knowing that every last mother's son of them is going to be saved. It makes no difference at all that Paul Kantner said, in "Watch Her Ride," "Times don't ever change for me." Now the only truth—and it's noble, glorious, exultant—is this: "Times can change. It's what I say is true. All is real, and I'll come through for you." It doesn't even make much sense, but you know he means every word of it. They all do. You don't have to listen to the words—this song is the peak of the Airplane in terms of expressing pure emotion through complexity, loudness, movement. Every conceivable thing is going on, and it comes through as straightforward and plain as could be. If you're in any kind of good spirits, this song will raise them through the roof. And isn't that what we really want from rock music?

*　　*　　*

That's what we get from the Beach Boys. *Beach Boys Party* is a friendly, pleasant record, recorded by people who really understand the common ground between "Papa-Ooom-Mow-Mow," "Mountain of Love," and "The Times They Are A-Changin'." "It's *all* rock," as R. Meltzer or anybody would say, and the Beach Boys really know what that means. It means this is music that's "here for you any old time," and that means you if you're a performer pleasantly fooling around at a party, or you if you're a kid camping out at Big Sur with a baby phonograph and a copy of "Light My Fire."

And you've got to give the Beach Boys credit (especially if you don't want to). Because this album was recorded two and a half years ago, and it's full of the sort of understanding that most rock performers are just beginning to get into. Street noises were nice before John Cage put his signature on them; and what's the difference if the Beach Boys really *had* a party, and the Stones just pretended to have one?

I mean, I'm talking about the perception of things. It's all in how you see it. In *Crawdaddy* 11 we ran a centerfold of Jim Morrison, "Cancel My Subscription to the Resurrection." It was sort of designed as a poster, but we didn't indicate that in the magazine, because we thought it might sound silly. So a lot of people thought it was a paid ad. Then Jefferson Airplane sent us a thousand dollars, and a two-page ad of group doodling related to their new album. We ran it as a centerfold in number twelve, and naturally it looked like copy; it didn't look like an ad at all. But so what? Both spreads were quite attractive, and does it really matter *which one* brought in some cash to help put out the following issue?

What's important is that our readers enjoyed this stuff. Maybe even got something out of it, on a personal level. And what matters in music is what's there, what's audible and recognizable and "meaningful" in any way whatsoever to the person listening (and to the people playing). Intentions, motivations, circumstances . . . those are for historians. They're interesting, nice to know about, useful and even important, but they don't have to do with the music and the immediacy of listening to it.

And context notwithstanding, the thing that makes *Beach Boys Party* a good album (to me) is the fact that it's nice to listen to. But what makes it an excellent album is that while I'm listening to this record-that-is-nice-to-listen-to, I get a lot of extra stuff: I get moved on an emotional level, I get insight into the nature of rock music and the creative impulse itself, I get impressions of the world and the way people feel about it, I get a lot of just plain good reactions. Stuff that stays with me. And at no added cost, which kind of makes this record better than just any nice-to-listen-to album.

And the same is true of the Stones and Airplane albums, and lots of other stuff. The Beach Boys deserve historical credit for understanding and expressing something (a certain attitude toward music) first, but the value of the record *now* has nothing to do with when it came out. And it's obviously not necessary to read this review in order to appreciate any of these records. It might be nice to listen to some stuff after getting a really detailed look through another person's eyes (ears), but that's a different pleasure. I wrote a whole article in *Crawdaddy* 11 about the aspects of listening to rock in a particular environment, the extent to which the context can be part of the musical experience. Groovy. Now I want to make it clear as can be that the *creation* of the music is noncontextual, that we've gone beyond the days when rock was specifically designed for everybody's car radio. The musician, the performer, can*not* create music for people in other recording studios, who also have Altex 605 speakers, or whatever, to listen through. He can't become involved only in what his own ears perceive, at the moment of creation and the playback five minutes later.

Or rather, he certainly can. I correct myself. I'd be the last person to urge restrictions on anyone's freedom, and I sincerely believe that creating for an audience of ten, or one, or zero, is just as valid as anything else. Certainly the quality of something is not measured by multiplying it by the number of people who dig it.

But what I'm really talking about, of course, is that old coincidence. I'm talking about the performer who expects to spend as much money on recording time and engineers and instruments and whatever as is needed to do what he wants to do. No matter how you divide up the wealth of the world, there is not at the present time sufficient time-money-energy on Earth to give every person alive an engineer, a set of musicians, all the instruments he wants and five weeks of time in a well-equipped studio. So anyone who wants all those privileges had better either be a fascist, or a person who is creating for more than a half a dozen people. Because if people will pay for these records that cost so much to make, fine. If you want to spend all that money making the music, and they're willing to spend all that money to listen to it, nothing could be fairer.

But beware the coincidence. I've spent a lot of time in this article trying to get at some of the reasons *why* people are willing to buy what the Stones, the Airplane, and the Beach Boys are trying to do. Why people enjoy the stuff, what they get out of it. What makes it all worthwhile. There are a lot of records I couldn't justify as well. Some of these records cost a lot of money (and I'm not talking about dollars, I'm talking about people, and the time spent by people other than the artist on all the aspects of this process, including earning the "money" to support the process). And some of the artists who made these records are beginning to think they have a god-given right to take up as many people's time as they want in order to do their thing. Jabberwocky!

Beware the baldersnatch, my son. Beware the confusion that comes at the top, that comes from thousands of people waiting for your new album, that comes from record companies standing in line for the right to spend money on you, that comes from fourteen-page magazine articles about how great you are. Remember you are only you, remember that your prime concern should be doing what is most important to you, but that you have a responsibility, a very real responsibility to every person other than yourself who gets involved in the achieving of your personal goals.

That doesn't mean hey sing "White Rabbit" for us, Grace. No, the point is not to think that you have any responsibility to anybody because they've bought your records or whatever they did in the past. The point is to think about the present, think about whether what you're doing is worth whatever is going into it. Because, forgetting the morality of the thing, what happens to our creative artists if nobody buys their new albums and they have to go back to recording in a garage?

Rock music is the first good music in quite a while to achieve a mass acceptance. It is also one of the few really worthy side-effects of the current state of mass media in the Western world. Because many rock musicians, rock producers, rock etcetera do not appreciate the significance of this, we are in serious danger right now of blowing the whole bit. With the best intentions in the world, the ideal of serving pure art and pure individual creative instinct, we may drive ourselves out of the recording studio and the mass media and back into our garages and audiences of half a dozen friends. If we don't try our damndest to make music that is both of high quality *and* accessible to a fairly widespread audience, we may look pretty silly a year from now complaining that no one pays us any attention.

But I don't want to end on a polemical note. Why, it might cut down the pleasure value of my own creating! And anyway, I think Ray Davies must be the only man ever to have written a song entitled "There's Too Much on My Mind."

"I got no reason to be there, but I imagine it would be some kind of change."

December 1967

STANLEY BOOTH

After attending college in Memphis, Georgia-born Stanley Booth (b. 1942) pursued his desire to "become a writer, or die trying" by documenting Memphis soul and gospel musicians—notably the neglected bluesman Furry Lewis, in a celebrated 1970 profile for *Playboy* magazine. Booth inspired trust in musicians and had a talent for serendipitous proximity, exemplified in his attendance at the creation of "Dock of the Bay" by Otis Redding and Steve Cropper, the week before Redding's death, as recounted here. These same gifts found him a place as The Rolling Stones' designated confidant and "writer in residence"; he attended the infamous Altamont festival, at which the Hells Angels murdered a concertgoer. The resulting book, *Dance With the Devil* (1984, revised in 2000 as *The True Adventures of the Rolling Stones*), cost Booth fifteen torturous years and set standards for unimpeded access and unvarnished testimony in rock journalism. By his own account Booth became a participant in the Stones' traveling circus, experiencing both its hedonism and its hysteria firsthand. Booth has profiled musicians including Elvis Presley, B.B. King, Janis Joplin, Al Green, and James Brown for *GQ, Playboy, Esquire,* and *Rolling Stone*; many of these pieces were collected in *Rythm Oil*. He has also written a biography of Keith Richards, *Standing in the Shadows* (1996).

▼ ▼

The Memphis Soul Sound

BEFORE THE altar at the Clayborn Temple African Methodist Episcopal Church in Memphis, Tennessee, there are three white coffins. Outside, in a freezing drizzle, hundreds of people with umbrellas are trying to shove past the ones who have stopped at the church entrance to buy the glossy 8 × 10 photographs being sold there. The photographs show six teenaged boys, one of them white, the rest Negro, looking like a team of bright young pool hustlers in silk suits with short, double-breasted jackets and black shirts with long roll collars. The name of the group is printed at the bottom: THE BAR-KAYS.

The photographs cost a dollar, but inside you are given an eight-page illustrated Program. "OBSEQUIES," the cover announces in gothic print, "of the late Carl Cunningham, Jimmy Lee King, Matthew Kelly." Then there is another of the Bar-Kays' promotional pictures, with no indication which of them is which. Everybody knows that Carl is the one smiling in the center, and Jimmy is the one with glasses, kneeling down front. Matthew is not in the picture, because he was not a Bar-Kay, but the Bar-Kays' valet.

James Alexander, the plump boy standing at the left, was not on the plane that crashed a week earlier, killing several people, including the Bar-Kays' employer, singer Otis Redding. Ben Cauley, with a lip goatee, kneeling opposite Jimmy King, was the only survivor. The other two Bar-Kays are in Madison, Wisconsin. Phalon Jones, with the nicely processed hair, is at a local funeral parlor, and Ronnie Caldwell, the lanky white boy, is still in Lake Monona, where the crash occurred.

Inside the Program, on facing pages, there are individual photographs and biographical sketches of Jimmy King and Carl Cunningham. Jimmy, the group's guitarist and leader, "constantly sought to produce the degree of excellence in his performance that would bring kings to their feet and comfort and solace to men of lowest degree." Carl was a drummer, and "the music which poured from his soul reached the hearts of thousands of souls around the world. The rhythm of his drums still beats out a melody which lingers on and on." Matthew, the valet, is not pictured, but does receive his own, rather stark, biography: "His formal education began in the Memphis School System and continued until God moved in heaven and pronounced that his pilgrimage through life had ended."

The old-fashioned church, with tall stained-glass windows and an overhanging semicircular balcony, is packed to the walls with mourners. A very fat nurse is on duty, and pretty girls in ROTC uniforms are acting as ushers. As the white-gloved pallbearers come down the center aisle, the Booker T. Washington High School Band, seated up in the choirloft, begins a slow, shaking rendition of "When Day Is Done," and all the relatives, friends and fans of the Bar-Kays stand in silent tribute.

In a square on Beale Street, just a block away, the figure of W. C. Handy, molded in brass, stands in the rain. Since the Civil War there have been many funerals of young men who died in the pursuit of their music. In the old days they died of train wrecks, shooting scrapes, or unmentionable diseases. Now there are other hazards, but the ritual, the honor, remains the same. At the Clayborn Temple, an usher with creamed-coffee skin dabs at her long-lashed eyes, and somehow you cannot help thinking that the Bar-Kays might have lived out their lives and become old men without achieving anything to equal this glorious traditional celebration.

The official eulogy is presented by one of the church elders, a white-haired gentleman who speaks briefly and eloquently, and closes with a memory: "When I was a boy on Beale Street, we had no electric streetlamps. It was the era of the gaslight, and every evening towards dark the lamplighter would come along in his cart. Frequently night would overtake him as he proceeded slowly down the street, so that as you looked after him, he would vanish in the blackness, and you could not see where he was, but by the glowing light of the lamps, you could see where he had been.

"Now these boys have gone from us into the darkness where we can no longer see them. But when we hear a certain melody and rhythm, when we hear that *soul sound*—then we will remember, and we will know where they have been."

*   *   *

The early blues musicians were relatively unsophisticated performers, playing unamplified guitar, harmonica, and such primitive instruments as the jug and the tub bass. Professional songwriters, like W.C. Handy, and early recording companies, such as Vocalion and RCA Victor, capitalized on the initial popularity of the blues. But the Depression brought an end to the profits, and the Memphis music business did not revive until after World War Two, with another generation of blues men. They played amplified instruments and for the first time attracted a sizable white audience. A record producer has labelled the early blues "race" music, but the wider appeal and newly added heavy back beat caused the music of Muddy Waters, John Lee Hooker and Howlin' Wolf to be called rhythm and blues.

Elvis Presley in his earliest recordings combined the music of the country whites with rhythm and blues, and therefore probably deserves to be remembered as the first modern soul singer. As one contemporary soul musician has said, "Country and western music is the music of the white masses. Rhythm and blues is the music of the Negro masses. Today soul music is becoming the music of all the people."

Presley's reign was followed by a period of weak, derivative rock and roll, lasting from the late '50s through the early '60s, until the advent of the Beatles. The Beatles themselves, in the beginning, were not essentially different from the better white pop groups, such as Dion and the Belmonts. But the progress of their music toward greater complexity prepared the way for public acceptance of the candid lyrics and experimental techniques that have always been part of the Memphis sound.

The "new freedom" enjoyed by the pop community was present on the 1920s' recordings of Furry Lewis and Cannon's Jug Stompers; it was there on the early Sun records of Elvis Presley and Howlin' Wolf; and it exists now on the Stax/Volt recordings of Sam and Dave, Otis Redding, and the Mar-Keys. The Mar-Keys, whose rhythm section records alone under the name Booker T. and the MGs (Memphis Group) work as the Stax/Volt house band. The Bar-Kays were hired and trained by Stax to be the road band, because the Mar-Keys, almost constantly busy recording with the company's artists, limit their public engagements to weekends and special occasions, such as Otis Redding's appearance last summer at the Monterey Pop Festival.

At the festival, that celebration of the psychedelic/freak-out/blow-your-mind pop culture, it was sometimes difficult to tell the musicians from the dervishes. The Who exploded smoke bombs and demolished their instruments onstage. Jimi Hendrix, having made a variety of obscene overtures to his guitar, set fire to it, smashed it, and threw the fragments at the audience. But, as one journalist put it, "the most tumultuous reception of the Festival" went to Otis and the Mar-Keys, all of them conservatively dressed and groomed, succeeding with nothing more than musicianship and a sincere feeling for the roots of the blues.

These basic qualities have characterized Memphis music from the beginning, but they had never before raised it to such a position of leadership. In the next few months, Otis would be voted the world's leading male singer by the British pop music journal *Melody Maker.* The same poll would rate Steve Cropper, the Mar-Keys' guitarist, fifth among musicians. *Billboard* magazine named Booker T. and the MGs the top instrumental group of the year, as did the National Academy of Recording Arts and Sciences (NARAS), and the National Association of Radio Announcers, which also selected the MGs' hit single, "Hip Hug-Her," as the year's best instrumental recording. NARAS voted Carla Thomas, a Stax vocalist, the most promising female artist of the year. The US armed forces in Vietnam named her their favorite singer.

Earlier in the year, Otis, the Mar-Keys, Sam and Dave, Carla Thomas and other Stax/Volt artists had completed a successful European tour, out of which came a series of powerful live recordings. The Beatles wanted to record an album at the Stax/Volt studios, but security problems made it impossible. The album was to have been produced by guitarist Cropper, who, according to George Harrison, is "fahntahstic."

The technical ability possessed by the Memphis musicians can be acquired, but their feeling of affinity with the music seems to be inbred. The Memphis soul sound grows out of a very special environment.

* * *

The Mar-Keys, and Booker T. and the MGs, are listed as honorary pallbearers on the Programme, along with the Heat Waves, the Tornadoes and the Wild Cats. The Bar-Kays were protégés of the Mar-Keys, and the relationship was like that between older and younger brothers. Carl Cunningham had grown up at Stax, having been a fixture in the place since the day he came in off the street with his shoeshine kit. Stax bought him his first set of drums.

Now Booker and two of the MGs were sitting down front in a side pew, just behind the families of the dead Bar-Kays. I had seen none of them since the crash, and when the eulogy ended and the band began to play the recessional, I slipped down the aisle to where they were seated. Booker, at the end of the pew, saw me first. Booker has a college degree and drives a Buick. One gets the impression that he has never made any sort of mistake, not even an inappropriate gesture. As I approached, he extended his hand, the one nearest me and nearest his heart. We squeezed hands silently, and then he passed by, followed by Steve Cropper. Steve looks like a very young Gary Cooper. He produced the records of Otis Redding, who was to be buried the next day. Steve is an enigma. He shook my hand briefly but warmly and said, "How's it going?" He is white, as is bassist Donald "Duck" Dunn. Duck, short and plump, seems more of a good ole boy than anyone at Stax, but he is the only one who has been influenced by the hippies. When he came back from Monterey he let his red hair and beard grow, and now, with his little round belly and cherry-like lower lip, he looks like a blend of Sleepy, Happy and Dopey. We shook hands and walked together up the aisle. At the front door Duck reached into his pocket for a cigarette and said, in the manner of Southern country people who express their greatest sorrow as if it were an annoyance hardly worth mentioning, "Been to one today, got to get up and go to another one tomorrow."

Two weeks before, Otis Redding and Steve Cropper had been sitting on folding chairs, facing each other, in the dark cavern-like grey-and-pink studio at the Stax/Volt recording company. Stax is located in a converted movie theater in McLemore Street in Memphis, next to a housing project. The marquee is still there, with red plastic letters that spell "Soulsville, USA." The sign was changed once to read "Stay in School," but the kids from the project threw rocks at it, so it was changed back again.

Otis Redding grew up in a housing project and left school at fifteen, but now when he came to the studio he was in a chauffeured Continental. Still, he had not forgotten who he was, where he had come from. The boys from the project knew this, and called Otis their main man. When he got out of the long white car and started across the sidewalk, he took the time to say, "What's happening?" to the boys in bright pants, standing at the curb.

"I was born in Terrell County, Georgia, in a town called Dawson. After I was one year old we moved to Macon. I've stayed in Macon all my life. First we lived in a project house. We lived there for about fourteen years. Then we had to move out to the outskirts of the city. I was going to Ballard Hudson High School, and I kind of got unlucky. My old man got sick, so I had to come out of school and try to find some kind of gig to help my mother. I got a job drilling water wells in Macon. It's a pretty easy job, it sounds hard but it's pretty easy. The hardest thing about it is when you have to change bits. They have big iron bits that weigh 250 pounds, and we'd have to change them, put them on the stem so we could drill—that was the hardest thing about it.

"I was almost sixteen at this time, just getting started singing. I used to play gigs and not make any money. I wasn't looking for money out of it then. I just wanted to be a singer.

"I listened to Little Richard and Chuck Berry a lot. Little Richard is actually the guy that inspired me to start singing. He was from Macon, too. My favorite song of his was 'Heebie Jeebies.' I remember it went, 'My bad luck baby put the jinx on me.' That song really inspired me to start singing, because I won a talent show with it. This was at the Hillview Springs Social Club—it's not there any more—I won the talent show for fifteen Sunday nights straight with that song, and then they wouldn't let me sing no more, wouldn't let me win that five dollars any more. So that . . . really inspired me.

"Later on I started singing with a band called Johnnie Jenkins and the Pinetoppers. We played little night-club and college dates, played at the University of Georgia and Georgia Tech. Then in 1960 I went to California to cut a record, 'She's All Right.' It was with Lute Records, the label the Hollywood Argyles were on. It didn't do anything. I came back to Macon and recorded a song I wrote called 'Shout-bama-lama.' A fellow named Mickey Murray had a hit off the song recently, but it didn't sell when I did it. It kind of got me off to a start, though, and then I came to Memphis in November 1961.

"Johnnie Jenkins was going to record, and I came with him. I had this song, 'These Arms of Mine,' and I asked if I could record it. The musicians had been working with Johnnie all day, and they didn't have but twenty minutes before they went home. But they let me record 'These Arms of Mine.' I give John Richbourg at WLAC in Nashville a lot of credit for breaking that record, because he played it and kept playing it after everybody else had forgot about it. It took nine months to sell, but it sold real good, and—and I've just been going ever since."

Otis is playing a bright red dime-store guitar, strumming simple bar chords as he sings:

"Sittin' in the mornin' sun,
I'll be sittin' when the evenin' comes—"

The front of the guitar is cracked, as if someone has stepped on it. As he sings, Otis watches Steve, who nods and nods, bending almost double over his guitar, following Otis's chords with a shimmering electric response.

"Sittin' in the mornin' sun—"

"But I don't know why he's sittin'," Otis says, rocking back and forth as if he were still singing. "He's just sittin'. Got to be more to it than that." He pauses for a moment, shaking his head. Then he says, "Wait. Wait a minute," to Steve, who has been waiting patiently.

> "I left my home in Georgia,
> Headed for the Frisco bay—"

He pauses again, runs through the changes on his fractured guitar, then sings:

> "I had nothing to live for,
> Look like nothing's gonna come my way—"

"I write music everywhere, in motels, dressing rooms—I'll just play a song on the guitar and remember it. Then, usually, I come in the studio and Steve and I work it out. Sometimes I'll have just an idea, maybe for a bass line or some chord changes—maybe just a feeling—and we see what we can make out of it. We try to get everybody to groove together to the way a song feels."

When Steve and Otis have the outlines of a song, they are joined by the rest of the MGs. Booker and Duck come in first, followed by drummer Al Jackson. Duck is telling Booker about his new stereo record player. "I got me a nice one, man, with components. You can turn down one of the speakers and hear the words real clear. I been listening to the Beatles. Last night I played *Revolver*, and on 'Yellow Submarine,' you know what one of 'em says? I think it's Ringo, he says, 'Paul is a queer.' He really does, man. 'Paul-is-a-queer.' bigger'n shit."

Booker sits at the piano, Duck gets his bass, which has been lying in its case on the worn red rug, and they begin to pick up the chord patterns from Steve and Otis. Al stands by, listening, his head tilted to one side. Duck asks him a question about counting the rhythm, and Steve looks up to say, "In a minute he'll want to know what key we're in." Duck sticks out his lower lip. He plays bass as fluently as if it were guitar, plucking the stout steel strings with his first two fingers, holding a cigarette between the other two. Booker sits erect, his right hand playing short punctuating notes, his left hand resting on his left knee. Otis is standing now, moving around the room, waving his arms as he conducts these men, his friends, who are there to serve him. He looks like a swimmer, moving effortlessly underwater. Then something happens, a connection is made in Al Jackson's mind, and he goes to the drums, baffled on two sides with wallboard. "One, two," he announces. "One-two-three-four." And for the first time they are all together, everyone has found the groove.

The Mar-Keys drift into the studio and sit on folding chairs behind another baffle, one wall of which has a small window. They listen, sucking on reeds, blowing into mouthpieces, as Otis and the rhythm section rehearse the song. When Steve calls, "Hey, horns! Ready to record?" they are thrown into confusion, like a man waked in the middle of the night. They have nothing to record; there are, as yet, no horn parts. Steve and Otis develop them by singing to each other. "De-de-da-dee," Steve says. "De-de-da-*daaah*," says Otis, as if he were making a point in an argument. When they have the lines they want, they sing them to the Mar-Keys, starting with the verse part, which the Mar-Keys will forget while learning the parts for the chorus. After a few tries, however, they know both parts, and are ready to record. "That feels good, man, let's cut it."

During the rehearsal, one of the neighborhood kids, wearing blue jeans, an old cloth cap, and Congress basketball sneakers with one green and one yellow lace, has slipped into the studio. He sits behind a cluster of microphones, unnoticed by Otis, who passes directly by him on his way to the far corner of the room, where he strikes a wide, flat-footed stance facing a wallboard partition. Otis can hear but cannot see Al Jackson, holding one stick high as if it were a baton, counting four, then rolling his eyes toward the ceiling and starting to play.

After "Dock of the Bay" was recorded, Steve and Booker added guitar and piano fills. The song boomed into the studio from a speaker high on the rear wall, and Booker played precise little bop, bop-bop figures, while Steve followed the vocal with an almost quivering blues line. The speaker went dead, then the engineer's voice came: "Steve, one note's clashing."

"Sure it is," Steve tells him. "It was written to clash." Which, in point of fact, is not true, since nothing has been written down so far. "Let's do it once more," Steve says. "We can do that bridge better. I can. First part's a groove."

Inside the control room, Otis and Duck are talking. "I wish you all *could* go with me to the Fillmore on Christmas," Otis says.

"Man, so do I. I got some *good* fren's in San Francisco. We could rent one of them yachts."

"I *got* one already. Three bedrooms, two baths, sumbitch is nice, man."

"My ole lady's kill me," Duck says.

When the recording is finished, Steve and Booker come into the control room, followed after a moment by the little boy in Congress sneakers. The tape is played back at a painful volume level. Steve and Otis stare deep into each other's eyes, carrying a kind of telepathic communication. The little boy, looking up at the speaker the music is coming from, says, "I like that. That's good singin'. I'd like to be a singer myself."

"If you got the feelin', you can sing soul. You just sing from the heart, and—there's no difference between nobody's heart."

"That's it," Otis says when the record ends.

"That's a mother," says Booker.

Nearly every man at Stax dresses in a kind of uniform: narrow cuffless pants, Italian sweaters, shiny black slip-on shoes. But now, standing in the lobby, there is a tall young Negro man with a shaved head and full beard. He is wearing a Russian-style cap, a white pullover with green stripes, bright green pants, black nylon see-through socks with green ribs, and shiny green lizard shoes. In a paper sack he is carrying a few yards of imitation zebra material, which he intends to have made into a suit, to be worn with a white mohair overcoat. His name is Isaac Hayes. With his partner, David Porter, Hayes has written such hit songs as "Soul Man" and "Hold On, I'm Comin'" for Stax singers Sam and Dave. Porter, dressed less spectacularly in a beige sweater and corduroy Levis, is sitting at a desk in the foyer, not making a phone call.

"Come on," says Hayes. "Let's go next door and write. I'm hot."

"I can't go nowhere till I take care of this chick."

"Which chick is this?"

"You know which chick. You think I ought to call her?"

"What the hell do *I* care? I want to go write."

"Well, she's occupying my mind."

"Let's go, man, let's go. I'm hot."

Porter shrugs and follows Hayes to an office next door where there are three folding chairs, a table littered with old issues of *Billboard* and *Hit Parader*, and a baby grand piano with names and initials carved into it. Hayes sits down at the piano and immediately begins to play church chords, slow and earnest. As he plays he hums, whistles, sings. Porter hums along. He has brought with him a black attaché case, and now he opens it, takes out a ball-point pen and several sheets of white typing paper, and begins writing rapidly. After about three minutes he stops, takes a pair of shades from his pocket, puts them on, throws back his head, and sings: "You were raised from your cradle to be loved by only me—"

He begins the next line, then stops. "Don't fit, I'm sorry." He rewrites quickly and starts to sing again. Then Hayes stops playing, turns to Porter, and says, "You know what? That ain't exactly killing me right there. Couldn't we get something going like: 'You can run for so long, then you're tired, you can do so and so –'"

"Yeah," Porter says. "Got to get the message in."

The door opens, and a small man wearing a black suit, black hat and black mustache comes in, leading a very thin girl in an orange wig. "You got to hear this," the man says, nodding toward the girl, who is visibly shaking. "Are you nervous?" Hayes asks her. "Just relax and enjoy yourself. Don't worry about us. We just two cats off the street." The girl smiles weakly and sits down.

Porter is writing "Forever Wouldn't Be Too Long" across the top of the page. Then,

My love will last for you
Till the morning sun finds no dew
'Cause I'm not tired of loving you—

He stops, puts down the pen, and yawns: "Naw, I had something flowin' in my mind."

"How long you be working?" the man in the black suit asks.

"How do I know?" Hayes says. "We don't observe no time limits.

"Yes," says Porter, "Hayes will probably be here all night. He don't observe no time limits."

Hayes laughs, Porter stomps his right foot once, twice, Hayes strikes a chord, Porter closes his eyes and shouts: "Cross yo' fingers." He sings, bouncing, the chair squeaking, getting louder and faster, as if he were singing a song he had heard many times, and not one he was making up in an incredibly fluent improvisation. The girl smiles, then breaks into a giggle. When Porter stops, he groans. "Man, we should've had a tape-recorder, I'll never get that feeling again. Damn! That's a hit! 'Cross Yo' Fingers!' That's a hit title!" He turns back to his writing paper and begins to reconstruct the lyrics.

Hayes looks at the girl. "So you're a singer?" She gulps and nods. The wig, high heels, a tightly belted raincoat only make her seem thinner and more frightened. "Would you like to sing something for us?"

She swallows and nods again. They pick a song, a key (Hayes asks, "Can you sing that high?"), and she begins to sing. At first her voice trembles, but as she sings it grows stronger. She shuts her eyes and moves softly back and forth, as her voice fills the room. Porter stops writing to watch her. She is so frail looking that one expects her to miss the high notes, but she hits them perfectly each time, as her voice swells, blossoms. Finally she stops, on a long, mellow, vibrating note, opens her eyes, and gulps.

Porter applauds. "'Wasn't-that-beautiful," he says.

"Where did you go to high school?" Hayes asks the girl.

"Manassas."

"Man—I went to Manassas. How'd you escape the clutches— When did you graduate?"

She looks away and does not answer.

"Haven't you graduated? How old are you?"

The girl mumbles something.

"What?"

"Seventeen," she whispers.

"Seventeen? A voice like that at seventeen? Old Manassas. Damn, you can't beat it." Hayes begins singing the Manassas Alma Mater song. Porter joins in. They get up and start to dance. Porter takes the girl's hands, and she joins him, singing and dancing. They all whirl around the room, as the man with the mustache closes his eyes and smiles.

Stax's only current rival in success is American Studios, on Thomas Street in North Memphis. American has recorded hits by artists as various as Wilson Pickett, the soul singer; Sandy Posey, the country-pop singer; King Curtis, the funky tenor player; Patti La Belle and the Blue Belles, a girls' singing group; Paul Revere and the Raiders, a white rock group; and the Box Tops, a band of Memphis teenagers whose first record, "The Letter," outsold even the "Ode to Billy Joe" to become the year's number one pop single.

There is no sign outside American, but no one seeing the long sweep of charcoal-gray exterior would expect the place to be anything but a recording studio. American was created in 1962, when a Stax engineer, Lincoln "Chips" Moman, left and formed his own company with Donald Crews, a farmer from Lepanto, Arkansas. Moman, who started out as a house painter, has been described as "the living embodiment of the Memphis Sound." He has tattooed on his right arm the word "Memphis," on his left a big red heart. Although he produces most of the records cut at American, he has a reputation for never being at the studio. Donald Crews, who has never produced anything that could not be grown in rows, is almost always there, and he greeted me as I came in. "Used to be a receptionist around here," he said, "but she took to singin', and now we don't have one any more." With a wave he indicated two gold records on the wall. They had been awarded to Sandy Posey, the ex-receptionist, for her first two recordings, "Born a Woman" and "Single Girl."

I told Crews that I was writing about the current revival of the Memphis sound, and I wanted to understand it better. He told me that he wanted to, too. "The music business is a mystery to me," he said. "We've had good luck with it—had more than twenty records in the charts this year—but I don't know how we done it. Only thing I've noticed is, down here we're all independents. All the Memphis studios have been Memphis owned. In New York, or even Nashville, they're spending Warner Brothers' money, or CBS's money, but when we produce a record down here, it comes out of our own pockets. That makes a little difference. Who you ought to talk to is one of our producers. I believe Dan Penn is in his office upstairs."

I found Penn, a young blond man wearing blue jeans and bedroom slippers, at his desk playing a ukulele. He told me that he had come to Memphis from Vernon, Alabama, after working for a while as staff guitarist in a studio at Muscle Shoals, because he wanted to produce hit rock and roll records. One of his first was "The Letter."

"Dan," I said, "what is it about Memphis?"

"It ain't Memphis," he said. "It's the South."

"Well, what is it about the South?"

"People down here don't let nobody tell them what to do."

"But how does it happen that they know what to do?"

He twirled the ukulele by the neck, played two chords, and squinted at me across the desk. "I ain't any explanation for it," he said.

Downstairs, I was stopped by a little Negro boy wearing Congress basketball shoes. He looked even scruffier than the one who had been at Otis's session. "You Wilson?" he asked.

"What?"

"You name Wilson?"

"No," I said.

"I thought you was Wilson."

"Sorry," I said, and started out the door.

"Hey," the little boy said, "take this." It was a small grey business card, with an address and the inscription, "Charisma Project."

I was outside before I thought to wonder where the boy had gotten the card. It was a coincidence, because I was headed for the Charisma Project, but he could have found the card at any of a dozen places. James Dickinson, the Project's founder, has worked at nearly all the local studios. Under his direction the Project has created theater, recordings, and the annual Memphis Blues Festival, which in recent years has given work to some of the finest old Delta musicians. Dickinson alone in Memphis combines the talents of a musician, songwriter, producer and historian. And it was Dickinson who gave me, at last, a definition of soul.

The front office of the Charisma Project, located in an old white house on Yates Road in East Memphis, is crowded with sound equipment and antique instruments—a zither, a pump organ, a bass recorder, a drum with one head bearing a hand-painted view of Venice. Dickinson said that his involvement with Memphis music began after an incident which took place when he was twelve years old. "I was downtown with my father. We came out of the Falls Building into Whiskey Chute, and there it was—Will Shade, Memphis Willie B., Gus Cannon, and their jug band, playing 'Come On Down to My House, Honey, Ain't Nobody Home But Me.' I had had formal piano lessons since I was five years old, and all of a sudden here was this awful music. I loved it instantly. I had never known that music could make you feel so good. I started seeking out soul musicians, learning what I could from them. My first teachers were Piano Red, Butterfly Washington and, a little later, Mance Lipscomb." By his late teens Dickinson was fronting his own band, sharing billing with such early giants of rock as Bo Diddley.

He spent several years playing organ, guitar and piano at recording sessions in Memphis and Nashville, but since the formation of the Charisma Project he has concentrated on events such as the Blues Festival and on producing records. "Memphis is the center of American popular music," Dickinson said. "The market goes away at times, but it always comes back, because music that is honest will last. You hear soul music explained in terms of oppression and poverty, and that's certainly part of it—no soul musician was born rich—but it's more than that. It's being proud of your own people, what you come from. That's soul."

I'm a Soul Man
Got what I got the hard way
And I'll make it better each and every day
I'm a Soul Man

The Porter and Hayes song had just become the nation's number one hit, earning a gold record for Sam and Dave, who would be singing it in Memphis on Saturday night. With Carla Thomas, they were to headline the twentieth edition of the Goodwill Revue, a charity music concert sponsored annually by radio station WDIA.

In 1948 WDIA became the nation's first radio station with programming exclusively for Negroes. WDIA described itself then as "The Black Spot on Your Radio Dial—50,000 Watts of Black Power." Now the station has broadened its focus, and the word "Soul" has been substituted for "Black."

From the beginning WDIA has been involved with projects to aid the community it serves. Proceeds from such events as the Goodwill Revue help to provide and maintain boys' clubs and recreational centers in poverty areas, Goodwill Homes for juvenile court wards, and a school for handicapped Negro children. Perhaps because of its strictly philanthropic nature—many artists perform without pay, and all WDIA employees, even those who perform, must buy a ticket—the Goodwill Revue has become a sort of love feast of the soul community.

In an annual message to the station's friends, the general manager said, "In sponsoring these shows, WDIA is merely providing you with a means of expressing your own generosity." But this year the station was also providing the audience with an opportunity to enjoy its own music at a time when there was more reason than ever to be proud of it.

In previous years, the first half of the program, traditionally reserved for gospel music, has been at least as important as the latter, secular half. But the audience has grown steadily younger and less interested in the old-time religion, and now the gospel groups play to a half-empty house. The Revue was being held in the Mid-South Coliseum, and a scanty crowd, sitting on wooden folding chairs, their feet resting on cardboard matting laid out over an ice-hockey floor, listened coldly to the Evening Doves, the Harmonizing Four, the Gabriel Airs and the Spirit of Memphis Quartet. Only one group, the Jessy Dixon Singers, led by tall, handsome, white-gowned coloratura Aldrea Lenox, created much enthusiasm, with rousing, stomping choruses of "Long As I've Got King Jesus, Everything's All Right."

During the intermission, nine Negro policemen who had been sitting behind the big, roll-out stage took their folding chairs and went out front, where they could hear better. The Coliseum was nearly filled to its capacity of 14,000 for the opening acts (dancers, minor singing groups) of the Revue's second half, but the audience did not come to life until the appearance of a great figure in the history of soul music— Muddy Waters. Wearing an iridescent aquamarine/sapphire silk suit, huge green-and-white jewelled cuff-links, and matching pinky diamonds, Muddy walked onstage, sang the opening bars of one of his earliest recordings, and was greeted by a roar of welcoming applause.

> I got a black cat bone, I got a mojo tooth
> I got a John the Conqueror root, I'm gone mess with you
> I'm gone make all you girls lead me by the hand
> Then the world will know I'm a hoochie coochie man

The loudspeaker system crackled and spluttered while Muddy was on, but everyone knew the words. During the performance of the next singer, Bobby Bland, the first four rows to the right of the stage began to sway together and to sing, or hum, along with the music, long-held notes in four-part harmony, even anticipating the chord changes. The four rows were filled with the Teen Town Singers, a group of "about sixty talented youngsters" from high schools and junior colleges in the Memphis area, some of whom each year are given scholarships from Goodwill Revue revenues.

When Carla Thomas was eighteen, she was a Teen Town Singer. That year she wrote and recorded a song called "Gee Whiz," which made the top ten on the popularity charts, and made her a star. She has seldom been without a hit since, and now as a mature artist she is known as the "Queen of the Memphis Sound."

Her material has matured with her, but her first song at the Revue went back to the beginning. She stepped into a pink spot, a big, beautiful, brown girl wearing a white brocade dress flowered with pearly sequins, and sang one of her early successes, "B-A-B-Y." The Teen

Town Singers sang along on every note, inspired by the knowledge that any of them might become Royalty of Soul.

When Carla's father Rufus Thomas, a WDIA disc jockey with several record successes of his own (his hit, "Walking the Dog," created one of the dance crazes of the '60s), joined her for a duet, the atmosphere —was like that of a family reunion. Rufus and Carla sang, "'Cause I Love You," the first song Carla ever recorded, and the first hit, however small, to come out of the Stax/Volt studios. The audience loved it, clapping on the afterbeat, and they might not have allowed them to leave the stage if Sam and Dave had not been scheduled to appear next.

Sam Moore and Dave Prater, along with Carla and the other Stax artists, had taken soul around the world, and now they were bringing it back as number one, the world's most popular music. Their singing combines all the historical elements of soul music—gospel, blues, rhythm. "They'll go to church on you in a minute," a Stax executive has said, and it is an apt description of what they did at the Revue.

With their band, in black pants and turquoise balloon-sleeved shirts, strung out across the stage behind them, Sam and Dave, dressed all in white, singing, dancing, shouting, exhorting the congregation like old-fashioned preachers, created a sustained frenzy of near-religious ecstasy. "Now doggone it, I just want you to do what you want to do." "Put your hands together and give me some old soul clapping." "Little louder." "Little bit louder." "Do you like it?" "Well, do you like it?" "I said, Do you like it?" "Well, then, let me hear you say YEAH!"

It was nearly midnight when, with their coats off, shirts open and wringing with sweat, they got around to the song that seemed to say it all, for soul music's past, present and future.

> So honey, don't you fret
> 'Cause you ain't seen nothin' yet
> I'm a Soul Man

The next night, Otis Redding, the King of Memphis Soul Sound, and the Bar-Kays, who would have helped to shape its future, would be dead. It would be, as the Beatles called it, "a bitter tragedy." But the strength of soul music has always been the knowledge of how to survive tragedy. Remembering another great soul star, Otis Redding once said, "I want to fill the silent vacuum that was created when Sam Cooke died." Now Otis's death has left an even greater vacuum. But someone will come along to fill it. He may even be here already, walking down some street in Memphis, wearing Congress sneakers.

1969

Lillian Roxon

Lillian Roxon (1932–1973) came to rock writing by way of celebrity journalism, and to Max's Kansas City and New York by way of Sydney, Australia. Having entered the world of the tabloids after finishing college, her interest in the burgeoning rock scene in the United States spurred her to move to New York in 1959. Her roots as a gossip columnist informed the writing she would do for the rest of her life; in New York, she served as correspondent for the *Sydney Morning Herald*, but wrote for British and American audiences as well, including a column on sex, sexuality, and feminism for *Mademoiselle*. Her lasting contribution to rock writing is the monumental *Lillian Roxon's Rock Encyclopedia* (1969). Comprehensive (over 500 entries), discriminating, opinionated, witty, and compellingly readable, its ambition and insight remain impressive.

▼ ▼

from
Lillian Roxon's Rock Encyclopedia

THE DOORS / *Jim Morrison (vocals), Ray Manzarek (organ), Robbie Krieger (guitar), John Densmore (drums).*
More gloppy, pretentious, pseudosurrealistic, hyperliterary, quasimystical prose has been written about the Doors than about any rock group ever. Whenever the Doors are mentioned in print, the similes fly like shrapnel in an air raid. They are unendurable pleasure indefinitely

prolonged, they are the messengers of the devil, they are the patri-cide kids, the Los Angeles branch of the Oedipus Association, the boys next door (if you live next door to a penitentiary, a lunatic asylum or a leather shop). So say the metaphor makers anyway. The Doors seeped in through the underground early in 1967, a time when no one could possibly have predicted that a group that sang about the evil and the reptilian and the bloody was about to become not just the number one group in America, but the number one *teenybopper* group in America, which just shows what secret dreams of mayhem and vengeance and violent sexuality all those dear little suburban nymphets were harboring in the infant hearts beating under all those preteen bras.

Initially there was an album, *THE DOORS*, a growing reputation on the West Coast, and a ferocious single, "Break On Through," that defined their sound and image perfectly but got nowhere. The album, on the other hand, scored up the biggest underground following any local group had ever had—there was an organ *before* Procol Harum, images more grimly surreal than Dylan's; there was poetry, violence, mystery, suspense and terror. Wow, they were saying in those days when the Doors first came in from the West, this is *adult* rock, and the adults of the underground settled down smugly to keep this group to itself. At Ondine and then Steve Paul's The Scene, it became clear that theatre was a very important part of what the Doors were doing: Ray Manzarek played the organ as if he were on leave from a black mass engagement. In person, singer Jim Morrison was cold, insolent, evil, slightly mad and seemed to be in some sort of drugged or hypnotic trance. His shrieks as he killed that imaginary father in *The End* (which is an eleven-and-one-half minute piece) were straight out of Truman Capote's *In Cold Blood*. At that stage it was probably one of the most exciting rock performances ever.

Then several things happened. The second single, "Light My Fire," got on the charts and, as fire after fire was lit all over America, rocketed to number one. From that day on Morrison was lost to the under-ground forever. It's one thing to lick your lips and strain and sneer at Steve Paul's The Scene to a roomful of cognoscenti. It's another thing to do your thing, every nuance of it, not even bothering to change the order of each gesture, in front of five thousand screaming little girls. Jim Morrison's grimaces, Robbie Krieger's peasant-boy bewilderment, Ray Manzarek's satanic sweetness, John Densmore's wild drumming—they were all public property. As triumph piled on triumph for the Doors—packed auditoriums, television appearances, riots, hit after hit, albums in the top hundred, fees soaring and soaring—the underground drew back first in dismay, then in disgust. Incredible, incredible, the Doors, of all people, had sold out. First they sold out to *Sixteen* magazine, where Morrison allowed himself to be molded into a teeny idol. Then they sold out in performance by stereotyping all those seemingly spontaneous movements that had originally whacked half the underground out of its collective skull. It got so you couldn't go to a Doors concert because you'd seen it all before. An earthshaking second album might have saved the scene and allowed the Doors to win friends in both camps. But the second album was a repeat, a lesser repeat, of the first. And the third album, *WAITING FOR THE SUN,* strengthened dreadful suspicion that the Doors were in it just for the money (as did a single, "Hello I Love You," that seemed to be a straight cop from an early Kinks hit). Then a magical thing happened to the Doors, the big beautiful bust in New Haven, which to this day has not been matched for theatre and excitement. Morrison in tight leather pants or less embracing a beautiful young girl in the dressing room. Enter police. Morrison makes one violent movement and is Maced on the spot. He is allowed to go on stage and perform, but the "performance" is a monologue telling what has just happened. Police rush on, and there, in front of the paying customers, looking for all the world like a crucified angel or Saint Sebastian, Morrison is dragged off. It is no accident that the picture blown up to monster size now graces the walls of his recording company. Millions wouldn't have bought publicity like that. Later, Morrison made national headlines again when Miami, Florida police issued six warrants for his arrest on charges involving, "lewd and lascivious behavior in public by exposing his private parts and by simulating masturbation and oral copulation" and for alleged public profanity and drunkenness during a March 2, 1969 concert in Miami.

Things are looking up for The Doors. One more bust and they'll be back in favor with the underground.

JEFFERSON AIRPLANE / *Jorma Kaukonen (lead guitar), Jack Casady (bass), Spencer Dryden (replaced Skip Spence) (drums), Paul Kantner (rhythm guitar), Marty Balin (vocals), Grace Slick (replaced Signe Andersen) (bass & rhythm guitar, vocals).*

Jefferson Airplane was the first of the big San Francisco bands to make it, the first to snap up a big contract, the first to get big national promotion, the first with a big national hit ("Somebody to Love" in 1967). The implications of that are enormous. Until then, in spite of the minor eccentricities of the Byrds and the Lovin' Spoonful, the national rock scene was reasonably sedate. A Beatles cut here, a touch of Carnaby Street there, but little that was really freaky. The arrival of the Jefferson Airplane changed all that forever. Even the New York hippies had to do some serious readjusting when the Airplane first arrived (their first piece of promotion was the first of the psychedelic hippie-nouveau San Francisco style posters most New Yorkers had never seen). This was early 1967, when San Francisco and Haight-Ashbury and Flower Power were in full bloom, and the Airplane breezed into New York to plant those first seeds of love power in the East. Initially, the nation as a whole was a little suspicious, a little afraid of being taken in by a San Francisco hype. But you only had to hear Grace Slick and Marty Balin sing and Casady on bass and those incredible songs that told you, between the lines, swirling tales of chemical journeys and wondrous discoveries—and you knew it was real. After all those years of Frankie Avalon and Pat Boone, it was startling to hear Gracie singing about acid and drugs and pills on your friendly neighborhood station.

The commercial (as well as the artistic) success of the Airplane was immediate and enormous. Record companies rushed to sign up every other San Francisco band (after having completely ignored them). None ever equaled the Airplane in draw power, though Big Brother and the Holding Company, thanks only to Janis Joplin, was to get a number one album. In any case, we now had on a national level what

San Francisco had had all along since the golden days of the fall of 1965—the San Francisco sound. Apart from the goodtimey noises of the Spoonful and the Mamas and Papas, the San Francisco sound was the first original sound the United States had since the English invasion of 1964. (And the English loved it too.) It was a time of be-ins and bells and flowers and incense, and the oriental undertones of the San Francisco sound were the right background music for it all. There were bands that played good music and bands that were a total environment happening. The Jefferson Airplane hit you from all sides. They had Grace Slick, the first girl singer with a big band (she had, however, replaced another girl singer). Grace was an ex-model, a great beauty with a piercing voice. And though she tended to dominate, the band also had Marty Balin, one of the great singers of love songs in modern rock. They sang around each other and around the music like dancers.

The Airplane has a very wide musical range. In the beginning, when they were playing for dances at the Fillmore in San Francisco—where, if the participants weren't exactly zonked out of their minds, they at least wanted to feel that way—anything went. They could freak out all over the stage; they could get into jazz improvisations, into folk, into blues, into anything. There was no form in the usual rigid sense. There was no "audience" sitting rigidly with rigid expectations. Everything was flowing and free form, with just one important discipline, the usual one: give the customers what they came for. In this case, the customers came to be made one with the music. So there would be long instrumental passages, when everyone wanted to move and dance, and then the voices confirming for them what they knew already. "Triad" is about three people who all love one another, or at least, that's the only way out for them. "White Rabbit" reminds you that *Alice in Wonderland* was probably about drugs. In "Ulysses" you realize that James Joyce was ahead of his time and belongs to the age of McLuhan after all. And so on.

Away from the hot, heavy, sensual atmosphere of the San Francisco Fillmore (and do they ever miss it), the Jefferson Airplane has to come on like any other band. In a recording studio it was hard for them, since so much of their act was dependent upon their contact with their fans. And even in a concert hall without the feedback of that glazed, stoned Fillmore audience, without patterns and images swirling around them, it's very hard. Whenever possible they take Glenn McKay's Headlights with them, a light show that produces visually what the Airplane does with music. (Or is it the other way around?) But when they play, something does happen, even if it's not always their best. And Donovan sings "Fly Jefferson Airplane," not just because the band has the right name but because it is one of those bands you fly with. That's the whole thing about acid rock. Having experienced, as most San Francisco bands did (as most young San Francisco people did), the sometimes frightening, sometimes ecstatic but always overwhelming effects of lysergic acid diethylamide, the Airplane could not conceive of music in any other way. The group grew with San Francisco, with Timothy Leary's drug revolution, with everything that followed.

In 1965 Grace was with another group, the Great Society, which often appeared on the same bill as the Airplane. When the Airplane's girl singer left and the Great Society split, Grace moved in with the Airplane, taking a lot of her songs with her. (Grace says it was the Airplane that inspired her and her husband and brother-in-law to start their own group.) Since then a lot has happened. The magic went out of San Francisco. The San Francisco sound was imitated, cheapened and weakened, so that by 1968 it was stale. And the Airplane became America's top group anyway. This should have meant the kiss of death for the group—the usual death from overwork, overpromotion and too much money—and it's true that the hard core is unhappy about the Airplane's playing class gigs like the Whitney Museum and the Waldorf on New Year's Eve. Nevertheless, that mixture of jazz, folk, blues and surrealistic electronic tinkering works, and even when they're not performing well they never sound uptight. Years, or maybe centuries from now, someone will discover that there really was a music of the spheres, and it will sound not unlike the music the Airplane plays in the moments of its highest flight.

THE MONKEES / *Mickey Dolenz (guitar, lead vocals, drums), Davy Jones (vocals, tambourine), Michael Nesmith (bass).*
Previous Member: Peter Tork (guitar).
The cynicism with which it was done was incredible and created a lot of resentment. Four boys would be cast in Beatle-like roles, and each installment in the fall 1966 tv series would be done as much like *A Hard Day's Night* as humanly possible. Nobody really minded that the Monkees, as this new group was called, were manufactured entirely in cold blood and for bluntly commercial reasons. But when, never having played together before, their records hit the top of the charts on the strength of what seemed like nothing more than tv exposure and a good sound financial push, the bitterness from other struggling groups was overwhelming. The story went that they were being told what to play note by note, that it had all been worked out for them, and that half the time on the records *they* weren't playing but the Candy Store Prophets, experienced musicians (with Bobby Hart of the Hart and Boyce team which produced and wrote many of the Monkees' early hits), were. Today, merely to mention this possibility brings on the wrath of several million Monkee fans who regard even the suggestion as treason. But it really no longer matters whether the Monkees did play every note themselves on those early singles or not.

The four boys were brought together one way or another (the story that they all answered an ad in *Variety* is sometimes contradicted) and told they would star in a weekly tv series about a rock group. It was one of the Beatles who pointed out that just getting out that weekly episode was a full-time job and that it wasn't fair to expect the group to be monster musicians as well. And they said it too, that they were hired as *actors*, actors who would portray musicians, and that musical background would help but that that wasn't what it was about. So then why put out singles if they weren't musicians? The answer to that is why not? The public bought, didn't they? And in the beginning it was like that. The Monkees were treated as one big hype. It was very hard on the boys. Not so much on Davy, who was basically an actor (he'd been very big on Broadway as the Artful Dodger in *Oliver*). Not so much on Mickey, who also was a former child actor and had starred in the *Circus*

Boy tv series. But on Mike Nesmith and Peter Tork, who had paid a few dues in the music scene, it was rough. The point was in the beginning, with the series and the publicity, there hadn't been *time* to get together musically. But there was pressure to get a single out, so everyone did the best he could, and if that involved a little help from professional musicians, it wasn't the first time or the last time it had happened and with much more established groups than the poor old Monkees. Still, there was no doubt, and they were the first to admit it at the start, that they weren't four musical geniuses.

Mickey Dolenz had been a lead singer with a group called the Missing Links and he could play guitar and had started to play drums before he became a Monkee but, well, he was no Ginger Baker. Davy Jones played a little guitar and he'd sung in *Oliver* and Screen Gems had tried unsuccessfully to make him a solo singer before the Monkees. Peter Tork did that whole Greenwich Village coffeehouse circuit and had a lot of musical know-how. And Mike Nesmith was also performing professionally before the Monkees. After a while it got to be a matter of pride for the Monkees to master their own instruments, so when things were a little settled in the summer of 1967 they got together a live "act" with which they toured the country proving they could provide a pleasant evening's entertainment as well as anyone. The tour won them a lot of respect from people who had previously dismissed them as a non-group. It was not that they were so fantastic, though they certainly were entertaining and competent, but that they were willing to face an audience and be judged like any other group was to their credit. Somewhere in all this they got away from their plastic image into something a bit earthier. Individual personalities started to emerge. Nesmith's stint as a folk singer and comedian at Los Angeles' Troubadour stood him in good stead. (Later, when the Monkees were established, he wrote, produced and conducted an instrumental album of serious music, *THE WICHITA TRAIN WHISTLE.*) Dolenz did his James Brown imitation. Jones has Broadway ambitions. Tork is all gentleness and peace. It was the music people who first discovered that the Monkees were good guys. Everyone else followed. By 1968 it was distinctly *not done* to put down the Monkees. And to top things, they did a rather nice album that suggested there was more than tv exposure selling their singles for them. The end of 1968 saw their film *Head*, which finally established them as, if not exactly underground heroes, then underground pets. Early in 1969 Peter Tork left the group, but the Monkees decided to continue as a trio. Their latest album, *INSTANT REPLAY,* was recorded without Tork, and the group is supposedly much tighter now. Only time will tell if a barrel of three Monkees is as much fun as a barrel of four.

1969

LENNY KAYE

A number of rock musicians have dabbled in critical writing—Richard Hell and Robert Forster (of The Go-Betweens) are honorable examples—and a few critics, like Robert Palmer and Lester Bangs, have moonlighted in bands. But no precedent approaches the unique accomplishments of Lenny Kaye (b. 1946) in his multiple roles as sideman and co-songwriter in an epochal band, The Patti Smith Group; leader of his own band, The Lenny Kaye Connection; producer of albums by Kristin Hersh, Suzanne Vega, and Soul Asylum; and critic and author of liner notes. In the role of pop archivist, Kaye's legendary compilation *Nuggets: Original Artyfacts from the First Psychedelic Era* built a bridge between the "garage punk" of the '60s era and the punk revolution a decade later in which he was himself a participant. An expert taxonomist and celebrant of musical genres, Kaye had been a working musician before his life as a writer—even recording a single under the name Link Cromwell—but it was after distinguishing himself as a critic for *Crawdaddy*, *Creem*, and *Rolling Stone* that his seminal article on doowop, published in *Jazz and Pop* magazine, attracted the interest of his future collaborator, Patti Smith (she found him working at the counter of a record store). Kaye is the author of *You Call It Madness: The Sensuous Song of the Croon* and co-author of *Waylon*, the autobiography of Waylon Jennings.

▼ ▼

The Best of Acappella

IT USED to be that you could only find it in little, out of the way places. There was a cut on the first Captain Beefheart album, an Anglicized version by Them on their first effort, another on the Amboy Dukes' *Migration*. Or you might hear it in the midst of a jam session somewhere, flowing out amid laughter and shouts of hey-I-remember-*that*, a little I-IV-V progression and then into "Teen Angel." Frank Zappa once devoted an entire album to it (*Ruben and the Jets*), but fell prey to the too-easy temptation to parody.

But now the Rock and Roll revival is fully upon us. The music of the First Phase is all around; Chuck Berry is at the *Fillmore*, Fats Domino just recently had an almost-hit record, the Coasters are again recording and appearing. On another level, there was a Pachucho record hop at the *Family Dog* a while ago, Cat Mother is singing about Good Old Rock and Roll, and a group named Sha-Na-Na played oldies-but-goodies at the *Scene* to screaming crowds and rave reviews. We're almost back in 1958 again, with people starting to dig out their old 45's, immersing themselves in such as Dion and the Belmonts, the Big Bopper, the Earls and the Fascinations, doing the ol' hully-gully as they walk down the street.

It's nice to see rock nostalgia happening; more than that, it's nice to see something *past* nostalgia happening. The old values seem to be on their way back; as the decency rallies proliferate, we are slowly entering a new phase of the old outlaw days of rock and roll. The cycles are turning, my friend, around and around once more, and we're coming home at last. Goodbye, *Fillmore East*; hello, *Brooklyn Fox*.

But I don't really want to write a thing on late fifties/early sixties rock and roll: that topic deserves a book and (sadly) will probably get one in the near future. Rather, this is about a stream within a stream within a stream; a little thing that happened once a long time ago, something that began, went round in its own little circle, died after a time. Call it a movement if you will—art historians would like that term. Call it a sub-culture, or maybe a microcosm of a much larger rock society—sociologists would like that. Call it an "experiment with the polyphonic possibilities of the human voice within a set and limited structural framework"—musicologists would like that. Or call it a genre, or a style, or a fad. Anything your little heart desires.

But I call it Acappella music, which is what it was known as then, though all of us had to have the word explained at one time or another. "Hitting notes," in the language of the street, and this is probably the most fitting title, since it was born on the street, on the corners of the small cities and large metropolises. Somebody tried to make it a Star once; they almost succeeded, but it ultimately toppled over from its own weight, coming back, in the end, to the very place where it was born, the place where it probably still remains today.

This, as they used to say in the movies, is its story.

The formula was very simple. You would be at a dance (or a party or just sitting around on somebody's front stoop), and things were draggy so you would go in to the bathroom (or hallway or stay on the same old stoop) with four (or six or twenty) other guys and sing (and sing and sing). The songs were standards; there was "Gloria" (of course), and the lead singer's voice always cracked when he reached for the falsetto part. There was "Diamonds and Pearls," a must from the Paragons, then "Valerie" for the crying and melodrama, "What's Your Name" 'cause it had a boss bass part, finally into "Stormy Weather," that perennial old classic:

> *Don't know why*
> *(a-don't know why)*
> *There's no sun up in the sky*
> *It's Stormy Weather*
> *(Stormy wea-ther, wah-doo)...*

Acappella, not to be confused with the classical *a capella*, means "without music." We were told that on the first all-Acappella album ever released, called *The Best of Acappella, Vol. I.* (Relic 101). They weren't quite right, as it turned out—there was very definitely music involved.

What they really meant to say was that there was no musical accompaniment, no background instrumentation. Acappella groups had to rely solely on their voices (helped a bit at times by an echo chamber) using them to provide all the different parts of a song. This tended to put a greater emphasis on the role of the back-up part of the group, pushing the lead singer into a slightly less prestigous position. There was none of this limp Supremes background humming that is so prevalent today—Acappella groups really had to work, nearly scat-singing their way through the highs and lows of a song.

The movement began sometime in late 1962 or '63 with a group called the Zircons. The original Zircons (for there was a second, less creative group later) were probably together for about five days, at least long enough to cut a record which ultimately became the first big Acappella single. It was called "Lonely Way" (Mellomood GS-1000A), and sold somewhere above 3,000 records. In these days of the Big Huge, 3,000 really doesn't sound like much, but for an Acappella record, appealing to a limited audience in a limited area, the number was quite substantial. There had been a few other groups who preceded the Zircons (notably the Nutmegs who had made a lot of practice tapes in the style), but it was they who broke the initial ice, receiving some air play on AM stations and promptly breaking up over it.

"Lonely Way" was, and still remains, one of the finest Acappella songs produced throughout the entire history of the style. Many of the later productions had a tendency to be hollow; there were holes in the arrangements and you really missed the presence of the back-up music. Not so with "Lonely Way"—the harmonies were full and vibrant, the arrangement tight and tasteful, everything working together towards a melodious whole. I had the record for two weeks before I even realized they were singing alone.

After the Zircons, the Acappella movement went into full swing. In what surely must be a famous first, the style was not fostered by radio air play, by record companies, or even through personal appearances by the groups themselves. Instead, the driving forces behind Acappella, those who promoted, financed, and ultimately pushed it, were by and large *record stores*. And to fully understand this (though it occasionally will happen down South among specialty blues labels), we must do up a little background history.

Rock in the fifties, though it followed somewhat-national trends, was basically regional in nature. Southern California birthed a peculiar brand of pachucho-rock; Tex-Mex had the Buddys—Holly and Knox; Philadelphia gave the world dances, American Bandstand and Fabian; and New York had the groups. The groups, together for a day or a year, often recording under a variety of names, springing up at record hops or teen variety shows, here today and gone tomorrow. As a conservative estimate, I would say that close to 10,000 records by fly-by-night groups on similar fly-by-night labels were released in the late fifties and early sixties. And slowly, again mostly around New York, there grew up a little fandom around these groups, calling itself by various names—"oldies fans," "R 'n B lovers," etc.—who became really involved with the kind of music these groups were producing. In time, as the Top-40 began to play less and less of these combinations, the movement was pushed underground; groups like the Ravens, the Moonglows, the Five Satins, the Paragons slowly became the chief proponents of the older music. At a time when most radio stations were slowly sinking into the morass of Bobby Vee and Tony Orlando, groups like the Cadillacs and the Diablos were busily keeping the faith alive.

This fascination with groups has carried over to present-day rock and I've always been at a loss to figure out why. Even today, a group stands a better chance of being listened to than does a single artist; there is more glamour, more . . . well, *something* about a group that calls forth stronger loyalties. Whatever, this rock and roll underground, though it had no connection with the radical movements of the day and indeed was probably very hostile toward all outre forms of behavior, resembled very much the early days of progressive rock. There was the same sense of boosting involved, the same constant grumblings that the *radio* played *shit* and if *only* they would program some *good* groups . . . And if you can remember turning people on to the Airplane (or even grass) for the first time, you might be able to imagine what it was to turn someone on to Acappella records. ("Now here's this fine group," arm around shoulder, slowly leading toward the record player, a weird glint in the eye . . .) You were simply doing missionary work—taking care of God's business here on earth, and you just *knew* that He looked down and that He saw it was good.

In the true spirit of supply and demand, this group-oriented underground spawned record shops designed to meet their needs. Even at the height of their popularity, there were still only a few maybe one or two per city, sparsely spread in a ragged line from New York to Philadelphia. In New York there was Times Square records, later followed by the House of Oldies and Village Oldies on Bleecker St. In Hackensack, New Jersey (soon to be a major center of Acappella—no foolin') was the Relic Rack. Newark boasted Park Records, which gave away free coupons so that you stood to gain one record for every ten, and Plainfield had Brooks records, a store which had the dubious honor of having the dumbest salesgirls in existence. There were also a few in South Jersey, mostly around Trenton, one in Philadelphia whose name I can't remember, and maybe two or three others. The Acappella underground was not exactly a mass movement.

Times Square records, located in the 42nd St. subway arcade, was the biggest and best. It was run by Slim, a tall, gangling man who knew everything that there was to know about rock and roll, assisted by Harold, who knew nearly as much. Slim was a strange character, looking for all the world like a Midwestern con man, always ready to show you this or that little goodie which he had just gotten in. He used to write for some of the little hectographed magazines that sprang up around the movement, little rambling columns that talked about the health value of Benson and Hedges, his ex-wife, all the new records Times Square was going to find and sell at outrageous prices. In a sample column, from *Rhythm and Blues Train* # 5, he covered tapes that you could have made from the Times Square files, the fact that no one brought in "Saki-Laki-Waki" by the Viscounts on Vega label so that the cash price they would pay was now $200.00, a few upcoming inventions of his (including air-conditioned streets), and finally finished with a joke about the best thief in the world, who stole a tire off one of the wheels of his car when he was doing fifty.

Slim really came into his own when he had an FM radio show which appeared in odd corners of the dial on occasional Sunday afternoons. He used to play some fine music, new Acappella releases, also rarer records from the Times Square stock. "And now," he would say, "here's 'Sunday Kind of Love' by the Medievals, worth ten dollars at Times Square records." And then, "pop," there it would be, probably the first time it had ever been on a radio station, rescued from some dusty old file of DJ records. (This is all past now; Slim died a while ago, and maybe this could serve as a belated goodbye from at least one of his old fans.)

But if Slim was a world in himself, his store was a veritable universe. Records lined the walls, sparkling in all manners of color. One of the sneakier ways to make a record rare in those days was to release a limited amount in a red (or green, or yellow) plastic edition. Times Square had them all, Drifters 45s in purple, a copy of the long sought-after "Stormy Weather" by the Five Sharks in a full 5-color deluxe edition, others in varying hues and shades. Alongside the rows of hanging records were huge lists, detailing the prices Times Square would pay for rare records. Elvis Presley efforts on the Sun label went for ten dollars; "Darling, I'm Sorry" by the Ambassadors would bring the bearer a princely $200.00. The rarest record of all, which Slim never actually succeeded in obtaining, was the old 78 version of "Stormy Weather" by the Five Sharps, complete with sound effects of thunderstorms and rain. (In the end, he was forced to gather together a collection of drunks and name them the Five Sharks in order to re-cut re-release the record.) If you had the Five Sharps version, you could have made yourself an easy five hundred dollars.

The nicest thing about Times Square records, or any of the shops for that matter, was that they never minded if you just hung around the store, listening to records, rapping, trading and buying on your own. The clerks loved to talk, loved to show you obscure oldies, loved to find out if you could teach them anything in return. After a while, the stores became regular meeting halls, places where the groups hung out, where the kids brought their demos, where you could hear any number of versions of "Gloria," or "Pennies From Heaven," or "Ten Commandments of Love." It was a big club, and you could join if you had ever even remotely heard of Sonny Till and the Orioles.

But though Times Square was the headquarters, the Relic Rack actually started the whole thing off. Hackensack, New Jersey, is an unlikely spot for anything resembling a music center. It's dumpy, stodgily middle-class, right on the outskirts of the pleasant pastoral spots of Secaucus and Jersey City. Yet its one asset was that it had a fine record shop, one where you could find nearly anything you were looking for and one which had the same set of vibes as Times Square records.

The Rack, in the person of Eddie Gries, had experimented for a time with bringing out re-releases of some of their rare oldies on their own label, Relic. They had some success and so nearly simultaneously Times Square followed suit. After a time, there was an assortment of things out on these private labels, some Acappella and some not, all managing to do moderately well. The important thing here, though, was not so much in the labels themselves, but in the fact that when the Zircons proved Acappella could actually *sell*, at least in a limited circle, the labels were already in existence to push and provide a vehicle for the music. Which brings us, finally, to the Star itself.

Acappella music grew out of the fifties rock underground, which coalesced around an assortment of loosely-termed R 'n B groups all held together by this series of specialty record shops. The music itself was primarily more a style than anything else, using basically inter-changeable words and phrasing. Like blues, the thing was not in what you did, but rather how you did it. To generalize, we can divide the output into two main types, notably, the Fast song and the Slow song. The Fast song was up-tempo, lots of sharp vocal work in the back-ground, heavy emphasis on the bass, lead singer on top merely filling up the rest of the balance. In the context of Acappella music, it had more of a tendency to fall apart since even the most spirited singing could not usually make up for the loss of rhythm instruments. In these fast songs, all the holes could never really be filled adequately and the result, except in selected instances, was usually choppy, sounding weak and thin. Its good feature, however, was that it usually provided the most freaky vocal effects then present on record. In their push to clean up the loose ends, back-up vocalists were really hard pressed to find suitable accompaniment. Some of the results are like the Del-Stars' "Zoop Bop" (Mellomood GS-1001B), a song which is easily five years ahead of its time. Consisting of little more than a collection of indecipherable syllables, rhythmic effects and skillful use of the echo chamber, the record comes off as one of the first psychedelic golden oldies.

The Acappella form truly found itself however, in the Slow song. Essentially a ballad, it was soft, the background singers filling out the lead vocal, coming in over, under and through it at various times. When successful, the effect could be literally haunting in its starkness and purity. The Vi-Tones once made a record called "The Storm" (Times Square 105A) which is nothing less than unearthly, minor in mood, creating feelings I know I could never put down on paper. Acappella was really a true return to essentials, finding the emotions that could be represented by simple harmonies, using only the human voice as its instrument. When it was done well (something that often eluded the dozens of groups who relied on showy vocal pyrotechnics), it could be incredibly gripping and powerful.

We could get really hung up in drawing analogies to present-day rock here, but it's much too tempting to find any number of parallels in the rise and fall of Acappella and compare them with what has been happening over a like period of time in rock. Acappella began with a handful of groups, all highly polished in a crude sort of way, proud of their craft and creating a superior collection of recordings and performances. Then, as the movement's sense of self increased (much as in the curse of Marcuse's One-dimensional Man), the quality began regressing. It began to be self conscious of what had formerly been unconscious and the contrived results were hardly listenable. Pale imitations sprang up, filled with sloppy singing and off-key harmonies. Strangely, all this happened at a time when Acappella was actually increasing in popularity; the amount of good stuff simply decreased in a kind of inverse ratio. And Acappella, not having the numerical power nor the resiliency of rock, could not afford to have its strength so diluted—it literally *had* to keep being produced at a high level in order to survive. But once the downfall started, there was no stopping it. When Acappella finally died, there were few left around to mourn it.

But all that is much nearer the end of the story. Acappella's Great Groups come well at the beginning, and most managed to retain their high positions until the whole thing began to fade out of sight. We've already spoken about the Zircons; the newer group that sprang up to take their name was not nearly so good, producing one fine song ("Silver Bells," Cool Sound CS 1030A), and then concentrating on shlock versions of "Stormy Weather" and the like. This newer group actually got around to producing an album (on Cat-Time label), but it was significant only in the negative.

But the other large groups of Acappella managed to stay together, and several of them kept on producing more and better stuff. The Youngones, who became popular almost at the same time as the Zircons, were probably almost as well known, maintaining a high quality in their records (with resultant rise in reputation). The group was from Brooklyn, ranged in ages from 18 to 20 and managed to coalesce one of the truly unique sounds in Acappella, thanks to a lead singer who had the capacity to sound nearly *castrato* at certain times. Their first record, on the Yussels label, was called "Marie," a near-standard stereotypical Slow song:

> *He made the mountains*
> *He made a tree*
> *And He made a girl*
> *When He made Marie . . .*

But for whatever reason, the Youngones took this song and really did a Job on it, creating out of it one of the most moving records of the whole period. Though "Marie" contained some musical background, the Youngones soon moved over to Slim and the Times Square label and began producing Acappella records.

While there, they came up with several passable songs and two truly Great ones. The first of these was easily the finest version of "Gloria" (Times Square 28A) yet available, a tremendous reading of a song which had been done over and over and over, sometimes nearly to death, by some huge amount of groups. But even better than that was their Acappella version of "Sweeter Than" (Times Square 36A), a remake of the Passions' oldie of "This Is My Love." From the opening note to the final, bell-like harmonic rise at the end, the song had Classic written all over it.

If the Youngones represented some of the best that Acappella had to offer, the Camelots certainly showed the versatility of the style. For one, they produced the best up-tempo song, "Don't Leave Me Baby" (Aanko 1001), a record that featured a bottom line any present-day bass guitarist would be happy to make his own. The Camelots' success was mainly due to their incredibly rich harmony, a sound which brooked no faltering or loose moments; they were on top of their material at all times. Of all the groups, they made the best effort to go commercial, recording for both Laurie and Ember records, but, like the others, they have long since disappeared.

Underneath this top layer of groups were three or four secondary combinations, all of which had varying moments of excitement to them. I have a warm spot in my heart for the Savoys, hailing from Newark, who came out with some fine material on the Catamount label. They and a group called the Five Fashions were the literal stars of the best Acappella album ever put out. *I Dig Acappella* (Cat-Time LP 201A), featuring a cover photo of a plump girl in a bathing suit overseeing gravestones with the names of the groups on them (*I Dig* . . . get it?), contained some twenty cuts of sheer Acappella proficiency. There were the inevitable bummers, of course ("She Cried" by the Rue-Teens, the Zircons' "Unchained Melody"), but on the whole, it was the finest statement that the Acappella movement had yet made. It still *is*, by the way, and I can think of no better may to introduce anybody to music "without music" than to play them any one of half-a-dozen cuts from the album.

It would be nice to report that the other albums that came out were as consistent as *I Dig Acappella*. *The Best of Acappella* series on Relic only lived up to its name with the first volume and continued downward from there. Except for selected groups (The Citadels, a revival of the old Quotations, a few others), the series degenerated into a collection of poor imitations, flat harmonies and gimmick groups. They would feature Joey and the Majesties—"A twelve-year-old lead singer!"—songs done in barber shop harmony, the first Acappella song done in a foreign language, any number of other superficial hypes. My personal favorite from all of these winners was a group called Ginger and the Adorables, who appeared on the cover of Vol. IV, five chicks who really looked as if they could roll your back until it began to break. Unfortunately, they couldn't sing worth a damn. In the liner notes, we were told that

> Ginger and the Adorables (also known as the Lynettes) are from West Orange, New Jersey. They were discovered by Wayne Stierle while singing outside a local candy store. Lead singer is Ginger Scalione, 16; 1st tenor is Jill Tordell, 16; 2nd tenor is Gail Haberman, 14 . . .

The period of decadence was about to set in.

A group that was beyond decadence, though, indeed was beyond just about *anything* one could name, was a combination from New Jersey called the Velvet Angels. They released a few singles, had a few cuts on some of the anthologies, and were always rumored to be the pseudonym for a famous group currently slumming it. Whatever, the Angels' biggest claim to fame, aside from having the deepest bass in existence, was that their records always carried the notation that they were recorded in a Jersey City hotel room. It would say: "This Acappella recording was made in a Jersey City hotel room," and you would

listen and say, yup, it sure sounded like it. But they were good, one of
the better, and so above any sort of this petty teasing.

Withal, you could feel Acappella slowly fading away. It was losing steam,
fighting a weighted battle against a nearly overwhelming onslaught of
crap. But in November of 1965, as the whole thing was entering its twilight, Acappella had its finest moment. The occasion was the first Acappella show, sponsored by the Relic Rack, featuring all the groups that
we had heard but never seen, people like the Savoys, the Five Sharks,
the (new) Zircons. It was to be quite an Event; except within a small
home-town radius, Acappella groups almost never appeared anywhere.
They were simply much too esoteric and obscure. As the night drew
closer, it seemed as if a huge party was about to take place; good feelings were spread all around.

As it would, the night was fated: the entire East Coast was struck by
the Great Blackout. But Hackensack, for some unknown reason, was
one of the few remaining pockets of light. And it was exciting to be
at the theatre; a kind of community existed between the people who
came, a spiritual bond which said that there is one thing that binds us
all together—one thing that we have that the Others outside don't even
know about. There was a sense of belonging, of participation in a small
convention of your own personal friends. We were all together.

Now I suppose that it would be logical to describe a pseudo-mystical
experience at this point, complete with stars and flashing red lights. It
would bring things to a dramatic finale, tie together all the differing
streams of narrative we've started up and left hanging, round everything
off in a nice, warm ball. But I can't do that simply because it just didn't
happen. The groups came out; I remember seeing the Five Sharks, a
new group called the Meadowbrooks who did a few nice things, maybe
a couple of others, but the air was never charged with the feeling that
something Wonderful was taking place. The music was good, we all
liked it and applauded like mad, but the Magic simply wasn't there.

The reason that nothing like that could happen was because the
people on the stage were essentially no different than us. There was
no charismatic distance between us down here and them up there, no

feeling of the performer and his relation to the audience. These people weren't professionals; they were only doing the same things that we had been doing all along, leaning up against the wall, laughing a lot, trying to sing. They might have done it a little better than we could, but that was irrelevant.

It was fun. Like a sing-along, or a hootenanny. Like being in one of those 1890's rag-time places where people get drunk and sing the old songs. Like being home. And so, when it was over, we left and said it was fine, 'cause it was, especially when that big bass hit that riff, *damn* he had a low voice (trying it) *bah-doo bah-doo* and what about the falsetto from the Sharks *oo-whee-ee-oo-oo* yeah but remember . . .

There was another concert somewhere along the line, a lot more records, more groups, more everything. But toward the end, no one really cared very much. Acappella died because the confines of its own small world could not contain it when it became too large; it simply could not keep up enough quality per record. Toward its final days, when people like Stierle were producing Acappella's brand of bubble-gum music, when groups like the Autumns recorded limp versions of "Exodus," when it became nearly impossible to separate the good from the bad, many of the old fans began drifting away. And I was one of them, picking up on the Beatles, the Stones, on newer things with the vitality that Acappella once had, but somehow lost.

But because I still remembered, I went down to Times Square records the other day, just to check it out, to have some sides played, to find out what had happened in the years I had been away.

There was a sign on the door, saying the store was to be closed soon. It had moved from the old large location to a smaller, very cramped hole in the wall. Slim was gone, of course, and skinny little Harold was gone also. All that remained was a pale junkie behind the cash register who would doze off each time I would ask for a record. I wandered around inside, feeling fairly lost, remembering how things once were and irrationally wishing they might return again.

I asked the guy at the store what had happened. "Nobody likes the old music anymore," he told me. I said that was sad. He shrugged and dozed off again.

I left a little while after that. He was right, of course. Even the rock and roll revival will probably pass right over Acappella music, over the Five Satins, over the Orioles, even over the rainbow. Which is really too bad. In passing over all of them, it'll miss the heart of the whole thing, avoiding the meat and picking up some of the filler, bypassing a lot that might be nice to have in these days of giant festivals and supergroups.

Acappella was not the stuff of which you could make mountains. It was simple music, perhaps the simplest, easy to understand, easier to relate to, and so maybe it's not so bad that Acappella will be passed over after all. It would be lost at the *Fillmore* or the huge stadiums, swamped by the electrical energy that is so much a part of the contemporary scene. Acappella is meant to be personal, music for street corners and bathrooms, for happy memories and good times.

A stream within a stream within a stream. Folk music of a very special kind.

1969

RICHARD MELTZER

If rock & roll is "art"—as fully realized albums like *Pet Sounds* (1966) and *Sgt. Pepper's Lonely Hearts Club Band* (1967) began to suggest—then aesthetics, the philosophy of art, might seem the proper avenue of approach. Richard Meltzer (b. 1945) was singularly well prepared to find out: in the course of completing his bachelor's degree in philosophy (with a minor in art), he began delighting his professors with papers like "The Concept of the Synonym in the Dave Clark Five." (The faculty of his MA program at Yale were not as broad-minded: he was unceremoniously kicked out.) *The Aesthetics of Rock*, excerpted here, was Meltzer's grand attempt to bring the resources of philosophy to the matter of rock & roll. And grandiose: his tone sometimes seems a parody of academic rock criticism, and from the start (when excerpts were published in 1967 in *Crawdaddy*), some readers have suspected a put-on. Meltzer maintains that he was serious, though surely part of his aim was precisely to take the starch out of self-important rock writing that took itself too seriously. In *The Aesthetics of Rock*, he insists that the throwaway, ephemeral pop song has as much to teach us as the rock masterpiece. A selection of his magazine writing is presented in *A Whore Like the Rest* (2000).

▼ ▼

from
The Aesthetics of Rock

THIS IS a sequel, not a formulation of prolegomena.[1]

I seek to view philosophical inquiry (and everything else too), already itself an effete notion, as afterthought. Historically, multitudes have wailed that all knowledge has already been stated. Plato's *Meno* reveals that man's reason can penetrate all reality by memory of his immortal soul; Plato proceeds to render all truth himself and thus virtually closes the door, allowing for minor revision by such men as Kant. Bob Dylan is not moaning when he says, almost quotingly, "All the great books have been written," realizing that man can no longer open his mouth without seeming to quote. Zooey Glass of J. D. Salinger's *Franny and Zooey* sees as frightening the possibility of man knowing everything of his predecessors. But man must strive to order aesthetically[2] the knowledge available to him, knowing always that the entire system can become "played out" and crumble. I must begin this critique with the aesthetic notions presently composing the totality of my particular afterthought, realizing that they will quite likely be utterly different when I finish. "Tomorrow's Not Today," written by Sandy Fadin[3] of the obscure Tuckets, sets the tone for this procedure. The bulk of my writing itself will have affected my contemplative state, possibly quite vastly or minutely. In the course of my writing, objective changes in the face of rock 'n' roll have themselves taken place, and I began[4] dealing with "folk-rock" before the label ever achieved wide usage (and before rock 'n' roll became known nearly universally as rock). How I persist in my journey toward truth is inevitably dependent upon how bored I become before completing it.

1. Oh, you know, *prolegomena* (as in Kant's *Prolegomena to Any Future Metaphysics*)— sort of (clarification of) ground for future moves.
2. More grocery list is order too, etc.
3. Man Ray's grandson or grand-nephew or something like that.
4. In early 1965 or so.

One intention early in the explorations necessary for this work was the (athletic) struggle for neatly articulate scholarly summation of a thing-system-order-setup-stuff seemingly otherwise by itself; now at the end I am a former scholar who doesn't give much of a crap for any of that stuff,[5] and rock has been infiltrated by scholarship as insipid internal newly articulate reference to high art. It takes too many words to sum it all up except merely metaphorically, so sentence and paragraph length have served as inertial assurance of the elusiveness of the whole obviously elusively obvious standard whole thing. Part-whole articulateness has always been implicit in everything: in rock it is (for the first time ever—if that matters) the real-magical concrete-abstract explicit focal point of the explicitly explicit. Rock is the only possible future for philosophy and art (and finally philosophy and art are historically interchangeable). Warhol philosopherism and Warhol artiness have been the only major adjustments in terms of these fields proper, but rock is prior to (and more and less extensive than) Warhol, and Warhol has ended up within rock anyway. And *anyway* is a traditional final rock criterion. Etc. So. So. So *my* whole summation does whatever it does and does anyway too, but watch the anyway level. Preliminary Beatle reference: "Though she feels as though she's in a play, she is anyway." Summations of pretensions and a lot of things are pretentious anyway. Leaving only an inconsistent *present* finality.

John Dewey makes the mistake in *Experience and Nature* of tying a philosophy of art ultimately to experience without allowing for his own errors of observation of art itself, which precedes any of his discussion of it, to be part of the system common to both the artist and himself. The aesthetician, the philosopher of art and the art critic can never be epistemologically capable of describing art by thinking *at* being, but must think *from* and *within* being. I have thus deemed it a necessity to describe rock 'n' roll by allowing my description to be itself a parallel artistic effort. In choosing rock 'n' roll as my original totality I have selected something just as eligible for decay as my work, and I

5. And printed pages, black-on-white, are hot, stuffy prisons.

will probably embody this work with as much incoherency, incongruity, and downright self-contradiction as rock 'n' roll itself, and this is good. Philosophers and artists alike have erred in describing chaos, for their moment of apparent fixity is a negation of the eternal state. Nothing is cognitively eternal, nor is it consistent, nor parallel, but that's just an empirical sidelight. Art must inevitably strive, and has striven during this century, to produce creations eligible for the same corruption and decay as they represent in form and content. Jean Tinguely's self-destroying machines have sometimes not worked and have thus failed to fail. Boehme's or Berdyaev's ordered suggestions of primary chaos (or yours and mine) can therefore be viewed in the same light, as positive inconsistency. John Lennon, once apparently working toward D. Gerber's[6] highest conception of art, that of senseless masochism,[7] seemed once prolifically endeavoring to build a tooth-pick pyramid that would blow away overnight.[8] "Who'd want to listen to an eighty-year-old Beatle?" he has asked.[9] So far he too has failed to fail, and all the inherent personal inconsistencies of his system ambiguously relate to an ambiguous universe. My critique may be of value relevant to the positive garbage heap of philosophy and art which has preceded, or it may end up on a different, smaller garbage heap, eaten by worms and forgotten; either way I will deem it similarly futilely triumphant and triumphantly futile.

6. The great exhibitionistic Texan philosopher of science (1944–).
7. You know, *senseless masochism*. But that of Frank Zappa of the Mothers (of Invention) surpasses Lennon's, because the former seems to have missed (perhaps by having become *too old* for a while!) the whole sequence of English rock explosions. Consequently Zappa thinks he has to bother with empty parodies of early rock emptiness without realizing that the Beatles and everybody else have coped with that work problem (that is, senseless masochism especially when there's nothing else left from before to bother with) and gotten it well out of the way and/or internalized it as second-nature roughage (and he never parodies much of England except Donovan). Too much dues to pay to archaeology and art-as-imitation, so Frank ends up back in high school. And that's nice too.
8. Bob Dylan: "An evening's empire has re-turned into sand" ("Mr. Tambourine Man"). The Doors: "Try now we can only lose" ("Light My Fire"). The Beatles: "Love has a nasty habit of disappearing overnight" ("I'm Looking Through You").
9. And the Rolling Stones: "Who wants yesterday's papers?"

If all assumptions concerning the role of components of tragedy and comedy in the actualization of particular components of human emotion are placed aside for a while, one can still discover in any artistic event to be tested the range of components which will in some way relate to components in reacting man. Whatever it may fully entail, tragedy is at least (on first hack generalization) quite opposed to warmth and comfort, good fortune and unassailable yet impotent security; comedy, to a seriously considered mode of observing reality which emerges merely consistently boring. The combined antitragic-anticomic experience is thus blandly, numbly acceptable in its tedium. Tragedy and comedy are merely two escapes from this dulling state, in an aesthetic or ethical or metaphysical realm.

By and by a shift of emphasis thus can be labeled as the goal, as Milton Anderson (?) (!) has done. A high school teacher who, as *Life* has recounted, "had had his fill of the unmelodic grunts and groans from rock 'n' roll singing groups and decided to recruit a choral group composed of wholesome, handsome teen-agers with conventional haircuts," he has formed a group known as "The Young Americans" and has insured that "not a note of rock 'n' roll would pass their lips." Disabled of "all" commercial drive, this group of fifty simulated eunuchs has been using its profits to embark on a good-will tour.

This is one such aesthetic, moral and metaphysical solution, aiming directly at some acceptable model of Aristotle's golden mean writ large. Rock 'n' roll has quite understandably avoided such a direction. The fused rock 'n' roll experience is an overt avoidance of this abyss (used negatively). Rock 'n' roll's abyss (used positively) represents a solution in a realm in which all solutions are basically equal in their applicability and inapplicability to human reality.

Conventionally, all artists must deal with such separable problems as the correlation of the final creation to reality, the authenticity of the creative experience, and the manipulation of human reactions, and concentrate throughout the artistic process on formal unification, while also focusing on the possibility of introducing what in historical context will somehow contain novelty. Whether reality is rendered through imitation or is introduced anew, if it is to be measured for its viability, art is reduced to a dry empiricist epistemology.

Similarly, any judgment placed upon the authenticity of artistic experience is as meaningless as any other use of this intentional epistemological label. Marcello Mastroianni has noted the need to maintain an ambiguous laxity in the application of a label so potentially desiccating: "I am looking for myself in my roles. There is this synthesis between the roles and the real me, as if I'm trying out in them. Who knows which is more authentic? Each one seems so at the time."[10] Memphis Sam Pearlman has sarcastically noted the inadequacy of evaluating artistic experience in so limited a context; his response to the wildly exhibitionistic performance of James Brown in the TAMI Show was, "He's authentic!" Moreover, the validity of a mode of artistic expression in the integration of the total personality of the artist is currently an important question to the otherwise ignorant or unconcerned. A frequent afterthought towards a work of art that is otherwise abhorrent is, "But it's fine if you enjoy it."

Trapped by the rigors of art, the theater of the absurd is merely one particular solution other than tragedy, comedy, melodrama. Nikolai Gogol's *The Overcoat* focuses upon one avoidance of a dulling type of boredom, which his character is not sensitive enough to appreciate. But the context of experience must be carefully examined. Rock 'n' roll is at first essentially the creation of an "out" group (systematically, non-sociologically), baffling to art as it exists prior to it. As the latest perversions of "out," it may be harmed by either the *Time* or *Life* explanations of its being or by its reductionistic connection[11] (by jazz critic

10. *Playboy*, July 1965, p. 49.
11. Historical explanation is not necessarily "reductionist"—though it is, to be sure, when in the hands of boobs who think they can understand something merely by "placing" it in a "tradition." Historical reductionism is merely one facet of the general problem of analogy, which is a two-way relationship of both similarity and difference. The

Martin Williams or one-time folk singer John Hammond) to a crude developing form of the prior art. One seeking to analyze rock must realize that the context for experiencing it must be left intact. He must take the lesson of environment and happening, art forms which in their expanded use of spatio-temporality *contain the contexts for experiencing themselves.* All sorts of things are part of this context, as money, competition, survival, acceptance by adolescents, reaction by standard adults, peculiar reaction by the community of prior art. "In" and "out" are part of this broadened context of art in the world, both in its aesthetic and ethical toleration, not even in the camp sense of "in" and "out."

The sophistic objectification of evil out of context either weakens it directly, destroys it directly, or transforms it into something utterly benign. Profanity is never beheld for the exuberance of its direct experiential framework but is often reduced to a rather subdued quality of the (perverted) audience itself; one should cry "wow" to original profanity or it dies. Genet has slowly died through his literary acceptability, while Sonny Liston, as dealt with by Cassius Clay as "the big ugly bear," has flourished as a particularly (pseudo-) evil (hence lovable) figure.

The very possibility of judging a work of rock with no other response than "So what?" allows for its context to remain intact; "So what?" is thus a fine aesthetic judgment for two reasons, because it sums up a valid experience and leaves the work itself untarnished. Thus the tragic, comic, absurd are viewable as out-of-context considerations, while *The Overcoat* and rock 'n' roll in its uncontested uncontextualized uniqueness are still free.

In fact, why not judge art by its sheer stubbornness, defiance of any and all objectification? For art to appear cognitively graspable, assumed

---

great filmmaker and rock lights man David Flooke has regarded the Rolling Stones' *Between the Buttons* in its entirety as hinting that the Stones are on the verge of sounding like Paul Revere and the Raiders. This can be twisted around rightfully if anyone feels like it to provide an analogy that would make Paul Revere and the boys feel pretty good to sound like what the Stones just might be on the verge of sounding like. Or *dis*similarity, pushed to total difference, can be emphasized.

is an *a priori* willingness by the artist to follow a rationalizable (even if not wholly rational) course of creation. To rock 'n' roll any and all grids of objectification are totally acceptable and thus wrong on one level, and simultaneously significant and trivial on several levels. J. L. Austin, in "A Plea for Excuses,"[12] advocates the reconstruction of aesthetics by collecting all terms germane to the appreciation of art. A selection for the rock vocabulary might proceed as follows: incongruous, trivial, mediocre, banal, insipid, maudlin, abominable, trite, redundant, repulsive, ugly, innocuous, crass, incoherent, vulgar, tasteless, sour, boring. When it is seen that such expressions have allowed for such a widening of form and content to be considered, only then can the "in" terms (made out by their "alienation" from rock's "in") be brought near the rock context vocabulary: poignant, sincere, beautiful, etc.

Susan Sontag states in *Against Interpretation* that art today is to be judged by its sheer appearance, by how this appearance denies the critic ground for conventional analysis. Certainly a self-important lucid surface is to be desired, but why not esteem those elements in art which baffle the art critic, in other words generate a totality of art and art criticism with an internal chaos which serves as artistic self-nurture. Surely rock 'n' roll has achieved the most in this direction. One of the clearest indications of intent to cast asunder that previous structure which to Susan Sontag would allow for direct castigation is a scene in *A Hard Day's Night* full of explicit Freudian overtones (if you want them that way). The Beatles are in a compartment of a real/symbolic[13] train, symbolically encased with a middle-aged gentleman who refuses to allow them to reduce their symbolic intimacy by opening a window. John Lennon introduces "homosexuality" by asking the man, "Give us a kiss?" and "pervertedly" placing a soda bottle to each of his nostrils. Later Ringo turns away from the advances of a beautiful woman with

12. Austin's Presidential Address to the Aristotelian Society (1956), reprinted in *Classics of Analytic Philosophy*, McGraw Hill, New York 1965, pp. 379–98.
13. Reality fantasy symbol. Reality may easily be regarded as the most fantastic category, as the most crudely symbolic category. Symbol may be the realest, most accessible, etc. Etc.

the explanation, "She'll just reject me and I'll be frustrated," adding that he therefore must "compensate with me drums." Such intentional and obvious psychological references are so blatant as to *be* the surface appearance itself, supplying an explanation itself with no further need to reach below; yet this new type of self-explanatory surface is such an overstatement that it baffles the analytical critic far more than ordinarily. The sheer overstatement[14] of rock 'n' roll presents a front which escapes all criticism, but which leads to an interestingly absurd body of this attempted criticism.

One of the most frequent explanations back in its early days for the persistence of rock 'n' roll was that teen-agers, the original primary fans, have a tension/attention span not long enough to appreciate classical music; this attachment of value to the possession of that span which allows adults to appreciate "their" music is ludicrous. The explanation that rock fans would all be juvenile delinquents if it were not for the love with which they are imbued by the music is well worth noting. Just as noteworthy is Phil Spector's statement: "My job is to get that emotion into a record. We deal with the young generation, with people lacking identification, the disassociated, the kids who feel they don't belong, who are in the 'in between' period in their lives." The pseudo-hippy reliance on rock as folk is similarly sociological and (it happens) overly aware of explanation. Leonard Bernstein's comment that there is value in some rock, particularly that spark in the Beatles which in their "Love Me Do" is reminiscent of Hindu music, is an attempt to reduce rock to something other than itself in order to ascertain its validity. Frank Sinatra made his own reduction in the late 1950's in order to attack rock 'n' roll as being "dirty" and said that Elvis Presley might become a fair singer with the proper training.

14. That is, *systematic* (superstructural, meta-aesthetic) overstatement, as opposed to that involved in a mere content consideration, such as Ringo's overstatement, which is really mere protective device, but is, on a merely primary level, a *source* of paradigmatic multileveled overstatement. And source as genetic psychologism is here irrelevant (or mere additional accompanying data), it is the overstatement itself which is important. Cowboy "brag talk" is but one common old pop form of overstatement. And the Stones' "Jumpin' Jack Flash" is current overstatedly recontextualized brag talk.

Even those looking only at the commercial element at the surface and visible subsurface of rock have been both as futile and as artistically satisfying. You know, this kind of thing (just fill in the blanks): "While other groups were turning out carbon copies, each fighting the other for the same identical sound, the _____ decided to be different and daring. Then in August 1963 they cut their first record, _____. It was a sensation overnight, zooming straight into the English music charts where it stayed right on top for _____ consecutive weeks. The outcome was the first ballad-style record by a group ever to hit the top since the beat was beat."[15] Such analyses (of the obscure), appearing in the hit song magazines, are analyses by publications on the same level as rock and not seeking a reduction, and hence they are justifiably wrong in their art-critical triumphs.

Statements about rock by rock artists themselves are of the same character. Dave Clark's understanding of himself and his music was rendered through a serious interview appearing in a song hit magazine in which he was asked, among other things, whether he considered himself on the Beatle bandwagon or considered his group a separate entity. His answer: "Who are the Beatles?" And do they consider themselves mods or rockers? "Mods."[16] The Dave Clark Five produces music which is most often rock-like, but this misstatement of "truth" is beside the point.[17] Whenever a rock artist speaks of his own art, he is casually stating his observations, drenched in mere-preferential value judgment, about his art; and significantly there is little aesthetic difference between the casual snide remark and pure, coldly well-thought objective analysis.

The heterogeneity in the lists of the favorite performers of the Shangri-Las indicates, through their utter subjectivity (that is, prone to apparent inconsistency or whatever, which "subjectivity" used to imply in high-

15. Or _____ (anything written by a hack about novelty).
16. Lots more questions and answers, but the magazine won't let us reprint them.
17. And recent word from a random reliable English freak indicates that early D. C. Five material had been recorded by some defunct group well before the formation of the Five, with the boys just fronting it. Who knows? Truth-functionality is here irrelevant.

school English), the confusion[18] inherent in rock 'n' roll: "Betty's favorite singers are Dionne Warwick, Johnny Mathis, and Little Anthony and the Imperials. Mary Weiss likes Mary Wells, Jay and the Americans, and the Inkspots. Johnny Mathis, Dionne Warwick, and the Flamingos rate with Marge, and her sister Mary Ann digs Dusty Springfield, Johnny Mathis, and the Four Seasons."[19] Even without giving reasons couched in Freudian or Marxian (or even musical) terms, they have thereby implied an incoherency[20] to rock 'n' roll, of which they, bearing no direct relation to any of their favorites, are a distinct part.

Motown Marvin Gaye[21] has shown a similar lack of comprehension (and thus a higher instinctive comprehension) of the nature of rock in an interview with Don Paulsen:[22]

Don Paulsen: Who are some of your favorite singers?
Marvin Gaye: They all gas me.
Don Paulsen: Just name a couple.
Marvin Gaye: . . . Ray Charles, Frank Sinatra.
Don Paulsen: What do you think of the Beatles?
Marvin Gaye: I like them. I like their instrumentation. Being something of a drummer myself, I think Ringo plays good drums.

Announcer Bruce (Cousin Brucie) Morrow of WABC radio (New York) has displayed his similar inadvertent disdain for the lucidity of the rock question by asking the Beatles during their 1965 American tour such actually appropriate questions as how often they washed their hair.

18. Well, confusability, possible confusion, potential for confusion, etc.
19. *Rock and Roll Songs*, April 1965, p. 29.
20. Or, that which can easily generate apparent incoherency, sort of close to (if you really want it to be) brittle, unrecognized easy confusion.
21. A noted stylistic cripple who has *needed* (more than systematic choice) to enhance his own act (lots of self-perpetuation by self-feeding) by the addition of Broadway show material and, eventually, a nearly constant female partner, Tammi Terrell.
22. *Rock and Roll Songs*, April 1965, p. 10.

But perhaps the greatest source of public referential confusion is the attempt to objectify rock 'n' roll as an evolving art form, complete with all the inevitable reductions to more articulate units of analysis. The music of the Beatles has been compared to Carl Orff's "Carmina Burana," the Credo of Gounod's "St. Cecilia" Mass, as well as "Es fur ein pour gen holcz" from the "Locheimer Liederbuch" of the fifteenth century. George Harrison's reply to the suggestion that these and others have influenced the Beatles' style has been, "I don't know them." One really fine description of rock 'n' roll "confusedly" describes Bo Diddley as "the 26-year-old folk singer who is the rage of the rhythm and blues field." Duane Eddy, one of the founders of modern rock 'n' roll guitar twang, is similarly described: "Duane, quite naturally, favors Rock-A-Billy and Blues."[23]

To avoid the difficulty in using given terms to explain a rock phenomenon, Thomas Thompson created for *Life*[24] his own equally superficial terms, namely the Detroit (Motown) Sound, Nashville Sound, New York Sound, Chicago Sound, West Coast Sound, British Sound, and Phil Spector Sound. He has also contributed the finest interpretation/misinterpretation of the genesis of rock, in an illustrated chart (charts are always fun). It is too bad that the article did not appear a few months later, for new absurd connections of his branches became possible, with Ramsey Lewis demonstrating Thelonious Monk's direct influence[25] upon the mainstream of rock and Roger Miller doing the same by influencing the Fortunes. However I have never understood his exclusion of the Mormon Tabernacle Choir, for its impact on Jan and Dean is not too oblique, and this inclusion would have continued the influence of Thompson's religious branch.[26] A similar disappointment is

---

23. In a program from a 1957 Alan Freed show.
24. May 21, 1965, pp. 93–94.
25. "Influence" contradicts anti-historicism. "Influence" presupposes "history." But for object-expansionist rock, history is *part of the object* and not (particularly) a ground for the significance of the object.
26. Also, lots of real influence by pop Protestant music on some phases of rock and rhythm 'n' blues, as well as some direct appropriation (how about the Browns' "Three Bells" and that kind of stuff, or Wink Martindale's "A Deck of Cards"). Obviously some of the weakest gospel singing comes from non-sarcastic imitation of traditional respectable

his exclusion of the Pacific Ocean's effect on surfin' music, a connection which Trini Lopez has claimed to be evident in surf guitar imitations of the rolling of the surf.

1970

---

white church music, and (at least in rock) "weakness" is a groove. And there's Jew stuff too, with "Dance Everyone Dance" ("Hava Nageela") by Betty Somebody-or-other. And don't forget the Byrds' master-move into self-generating piety and generalized diffusely distinct sectarian non-sectarian religiosity. And, of course, the Cowsills are the wholeso-mely disguised familiar general religiosity move suffused with strong-as-weak-as-hell reli-gious music arrangements after-the-fact and even some Jan and Dean ("Indian Lake").

ELLEN SANDER

Ellen Sander (b. 1944) was *The Saturday Review*'s rock critic in the mid- to late sixties and also wrote on rock for *Vogue, The Realist, Cavalier, The L.A. Free Press*, the Sunday *New York Times* Arts & Leisure section, and many other venues. She is the author of *Trips: Rock Life in the Sixties* (1973), an important source for those seeking to understand the texture and allure of 1960s rock culture. A unique aspect of that culture was captured in Sander's piece "The Case of the Cock-Sure Groupies" (1968), a remarkably clear-eyed and nonjudgmental account of one of rock's less celebrated scenes. After her years of rock writing, Sander worked in various capacities in the software industry, from tech writing to computational linguistics. She then returned to her first love, poetry; most recently she served as the Poet Laureate of Belfast, Maine (2013–2014). Several collections of her rock journalism are available as Kindle ebooks.

▼ ▼

Inside the Cages of the Zoo

SOME YEARS later, a group called Led Zeppelin came to America to make it, taking a highly calculated risk. The group had been put together around Jimmy Page, who had a heavy personal following from his previous work with the Yardbirds, an immensely popular British group that generated a great deal of charisma in the States. They got a singer from another group, a knockabout band on the English club circuit, a raw ferocious guttersinger, Robert Plant.

John Paul Jones joined next, one of the foremost young sessions bass players in London, then drummer John Bonham, who had been working on a construction job to earn enough money to feed his family when he was asked to join the group. Jimmy Page and his guitar fame, together with Peter Grant, a burly ex-wrestler, ex-bouncer, a manager who knew the business from the tough side in, set out to put together the top group in the world. It is every musician's and manager's intention, but this band pulled it off. In 1970 they would knock the Beatles off the top of the Melody Maker popularity chart in England and would be the top touring group in the United States. It was a carefully laid-out strategy involving carefully chosen people, carefully made deals, carefully contrived music, all of which worked. A little luck, timing, and experience and a lot of talent pulled the troupe all the way to the undisputed top of the heap.

In the beginning they barely played England at all. The real money, they knew, was in the States. They had put together a first album, a spirited, crisp breath of freshness at a time when rock and roll was really getting bogged down. They released it in England, then in America, and followed it over the Atlantic to play.

The first tour just about broke even, a typical first tour; actually many first tours lose money. Jimmy and John Paul were stars starting all over again as relative unknowns with the new group and the generational leap in rock bands had yet to be proven. Bands had broken up and their key members re-formed that year (1969) and all the heavy blues musicians from London had a new group to tour with. This pattern would repeat itself with American musicians, but only months later.

With Led Zeppelin's first date at the Fillmore East in New York, they scored. The album had only been out a few weeks and the audience displayed a great deal of familiarity with the material. The reputation of Jimmy Page's guitar skill was enough to bring a full house out to hear the new band.

They began a second album back in England when they returned, rushing it a bit because they had no hit single, the express ticket to high concert prices. Rock and roll fans are easily distracted and notoriously fickle. Before the second album was even finished, it was time for another tour. They packed their gear and the unfinished tapes and set off for another five and a half weeks in America.

They opened in San Francisco, playing and drawing well for four consecutive days. Before the tour was over they would travel 14,000 miles, playing thirteen engagements to hundreds of thousands of people. They arrived healthy, rested, and well rehearsed. From San Francisco it was down to L.A. for almost two weeks of concerts, interviews, and raving. San Francisco had gone exceptionally well; concerts in L.A. were selling out.

They made such an impact on Los Angeles that the ringside clique of pop cognoscenti couldn't stop talking about it for weeks. Not that their performances were that overwhelming; the reviews had been quite mixed, a fact they hotly resented over the following weeks. It was their carryings-on that set the popvine aghast.

John Bonham had dressed up as a waiter and served little Jimmy Page up on a room service cart to a flock of girls. When the fracas was over in L.A., they traveled to British Columbia for two concerts. When they arrived there they found the dates to be five hundred miles and only one day apart. They had to drive the distance overnight. From B.C. they went down to Seattle and from there to Honolulu, where even a few days of sunshine and rest after a concert didn't get them back in good physical shape.

But it's make it, get there, play, and go on. The rock business is volatile, rapid, and dangerous. There's no backing out of a concert contract signed. If a musician gets sick, they shoot him up like a racehorse and send him on. If he gets crazy, they slap him into line long enough to finish the tour before they dump him. For alien dopers a bust is legal ostracism, deportation, locked out of the money pile in America for a rock group aiming determinedly for the top.

Exhaustion, anxiety, release, sex, drugs, traveling, and trying against incredible odds with their bare hearts and whatever managerial leverage they could muster.

At 7:00 A.M., having flown all night, the group straggled into a

Detroit motel and walked right into the aftermath of a murder. The body had been removed only moments before and steam was still rising from the blood on the floor. Nobody asked who, what, where, why, or when. "I only knew I'd spew if I looked at it another second," said Robert Plant, and he grabbed his baggage, his room key, and stumbled into Room 254 for some sleep.

For a rock and roll band on the road in this raw naked land, the trip is not entirely a barrel of yuks.

They lived and worked and struggled to survive from day to day, from place to place, through unspeakable nightmares just to play music. It was loud, hard, gutsy rock, violent and executed with a great deal of virtuosity. Robert Plant, woolly, handsome in an obscenely rugged way, sang as if the songs had to fight their way out of his throat. Jimmy Page, ethereal, effeminate, pale and frail, played physically melodic guitar, bowing it at times, augmenting it with electronic devices, completely energizing the peak of the ensemble's lead sound. John Bonham played ferocious drums, often shirtless and sweating like some gorilla on a rampage. John Paul Jones held the sound together at the bass with lines so surprising, tight, and facile but always recessive, leaving the dramatics to the other three who competed to outdo one another for the audience's favor.

No matter how miserably the group failed to keep their behavior up to a basic human level, they played well almost every night of the tour. If they were only one of the many British rock and roll groups touring at the time, they were also one of the finest. The stamina they found each night at curtain time was amazing, in the face of every conceivable kind of foul-up with equipment, timing, transportation, and organization at almost every date. They had that fire and musicianship going for them and a big burst of incentive; this time around, on their second tour, from the very beginning, they were almost stars.

While fans and the business staff were overjoyed, others were grudging. One of the managers of a rock and roll emporium they played was downright bitter. "They [Led Zeppelin] played here the first time around when they were nothing and we bent over backward to put them on. Now they're back for ten times the price and put on half the show. This isn't the sort of place where we make everyone leave after the first set, the kids are used to staying till we close." Because the group received a percentage of the gate receipts as part of their fee, their contract required the management to turn over the house after each set. "We're the ones the kids hold it against," complained the manager of the hall. "Now that they're getting big, they're getting away with it."

The group awoke to the Detroit late afternoon and munched on grilled cheese sandwiches in the motel snack shop, blocking out the next few hours before they'd have to play. Robert split for a brief walk and some shopping. As he crossed the street a motorist screeched to a stop beside him and spat in his face. He returned to the motel for a ride, all upset. "I'm white," he mused; "I can imagine how a spade feels here."

Detroit. The lowest.

He returned from the drugstore with shampoo, a comb, and some creme rinse for his copious mane, but no deodorant, which he needed regularly and badly.

During that evening's performance at the Grandee Ballroom, a converted mattress warehouse which was one of the country's oldest established rock halls, equipment failures plagued their music. The house was packed and restless, warmly appreciative, and relentlessly demanding. The vibes were heavy, the audience and crowd were infested with armed police who took a grim view of the scene. Even the groupies crowding the large dingy dressing room seemed particularly gross.

A pair of grotesquely painted, greasy-cheeked, overweight sex-bombs in their late twenties pushed their way through the young things to Robert Plant. One placed her hand on his thigh and brassily declared, "You're spending tonight with me." Robert grimaced and exploded. "Hey, wot, you bloody tart, old Robert's a married man!" The others tittered as he squirmed away, pausing to shoot them a leering wink.

The girls talked among themselves. The pair who had just accosted Robert bragged that they made their living boosting: shoplifting, and selling the merchandise off. They claimed to make between two and three hundred dollars a week from their efforts, a story their sleazy clothing belied.

The group huddled together and commiserated, discussing the girl situation. The two in question were dubbed the "ugly sisters," cursed down, and a scheme was cooked up to get them later on. The plot was to bring them back to the motel and pelt them with some cream-filled donuts, then gang bang them.

They seemed particularly delighted with the aspect of abuse in almost any situation regarding girls who sought them out. "Girls come around and pose like starlets, teasing and acting haughty," said Jimmy Page, by way of explanation, not excuse. "If you humiliate them a bit they tend to come on all right after that. Everybody knows what they come for and when they get here they act so special. I haven't got time to deal with it."

John Paul Jones appeared at the door, looked into the dressing room full of girls and hangers-on, and closed it. He sulked miserably outside where fans badgered him constantly. Jimmy Page, inside, with that febrile, forlorn look that brought out perversity in fifteen-year-olds, sat inside, chatting occasionally and quietly to whoever spoke to him, neither receiving nor giving any invitations.

Robert and John, Cockney sports at heart, continued to turn their uproariously vulgar sense of humor on the situation. It was unquestionably the low point of the tour, Detroit, a town as foul as exhaust fumes and as hard as cement.

The following morning as they met outside the motel before leaving Robert was livid. Apparently he'd had one of the ugly sisters, despite the fact that the donut scheme fell through (late at night on the way home there was nary a donut shop open it seems). He ranted and railed, cursing the girl out because she hadn't come once all night. "Can you believe that?" he fumed. "I was *embarrassed*!"

They were leaving for a concert at Ohio University on a two-stop flight from Detroit to Columbus. The sixty-mile drive from the airport to the campus in Athens, Ohio, was beautiful, lush in the height of springtime, but the group was too disoriented to enjoy it. Geography had been ripped past them at an unbelievable rate, so many time zones had been crossed and double crossed that the date, even the time, became irrelevant. The road manager kept it all together in between his own schedule of sexual sorties. He arranged reservations, arrival times, picking up money, waking the lads up in time. An equipment man was responsible for the thousands of pounds of instruments and sound equipment which had to be shipped, flown, expressed, driven, or otherwise transported from place to place intact. "How much time till the gig?" was the only question the group ever cared about at that point. Everything else was too fast, too complicated, or too troublesome to deal with. It got to the point by the time they got to Boston, where they asked a local disc jockey they knew to get girls for them, they didn't even want to bother wending their way through the groupies' come-hither games anymore.

Check into the hotel. A quick swim in the springtime chill. A bit of a drink at the hotel bar, crawling with conventioneers who pointed at them and guffawed. A sound check at the auditorium. Another nip at the bar. No supper.

They played a set, an encore, another. They were tired, keyed up, not knowing whether to shit or go blind, and they tumbled back to the hotel where they had to take pills to get to sleep. In the morning there was a mad, almost-missed-the-plane dash to the airport. It was a rainy Sunday morning in Hocking County, Ohio, as the cars hissed along the highway, skidding around wild curves on unfamiliar roads. The country music played soft. God's great word washed over God's great Midwest as country gospel quavered from the rentacar radio and the lads slumped in sleepy stupor through the careening drive, not knowing how dangerously fast the road manager was driving, seeming not to care. As the caravan of three cars turned into the airport the radio reported that John Wesley Smith had been shot in a fight in an eastside Cleveland bar.

Robert was first onto the plane, galloping down the aisle like a demented ape, his armpit hair hanging from his sleeveless open-knit shirt, yelling at the top of his lungs, "Toilets, TOILETS! *Toilets* for old Robert!" The dear little Middle America passengers went into a state of mild shock.

Nerves frayed when they reached Minneapolis and the driver kept losing his way to the Guthrie Memorial Theatre. They arrived some-what late; the performance nonetheless was spectacular, the audience laughing in polite embarrassment at Robert's orgasm sequence onstage, and applauding lustily afterward. It was a sit-down crowd, all natty and urban, country-club hip. Part of this particular engagement, it turned out, was the obligation to attend a party at the lady promoter's country house, full of young locals in blazers and party dresses who gaped at the group for several unbearably dull hours. Comparing notes afterward, other groups who had been through Minneapolis said that every group playing there had to go through the same lame scene.

The road manager called a meeting the next day. There was a deci-sion to be made. There were four days until Led Zeppelin were due to play in Chicago. Nobody liked Minneapolis very much so it was decided by Jimmy Page and the road manager that the group would fly to New York for a few days of rehearsals and interviews by day, record-ing sessions (the second album was only partially finished) by night. They were reminded that the second album should be out by their third tour to stack the cards in favor of their success.

Their success was built on a well-engineered promotional strategy. Recordings, airplay, personal appearances, and publicity have to be coordinated for the greatest impact. A constant flow of albums, the release of a new one timed with the dénouement of the current one is desirable. Their names must appear somewhere at all times in some sort of press, columns, fan magazines, critical journals, underground papers—no possible exposure is left untried. Their English manager, American lawyer, road manager, and publicity agency, one of Holly-wood's heaviest, conspired to pack the heaviest possible punch.

European performers are allowed only six months' working time in the States, for tax reasons. There is constant pressure to make every day, literally, pay. Little time for peace of mind or rest; play is nabbed on the run. Working into the early morning hours is the rule rather than the exception. Recording sessions in New York last until exhaustion overtakes each man by turn.

Groupies drop in on the session to check out the music and make sandwich runs. These are the accomplished groupies, the ones with the savvy to check the studio out during the day and get the particulars as to time and location of Led Zeppelin's sessions. Much to the group's dismay the girls simply show up, everywhere, as if informed by some freak's celebrity service of their every move. These are the socialite groupies, the *grandes dames* of the grapevine. Soon the word gets out (half of grouping is gossip) and the scuzzy second stringers arrive in unmanageable numbers, just when the group really wants to work.

The girls chat among themselves, catty, bragging, doing one another in. The group's reputation is ripe and they are by now considered heavy scores on the groupie roster. None of them luck into an invitation to come along on the tour, though. There is a fresh crop in every city and the group is getting blasé and annoyed with these girls; their nerves are about shot and they are exhausted; too tired to care and too bored to resist.

Once an outraged bridegroom followed his wife to a motel where she'd come to see Led Zeppelin. He beat her up on the street outside while the group ate dinner in the restaurant, completely unaware of the scene. Furious parents have broken down hotel doors to wrench their daughters from musicians' beds. A groupie following a group from city to city, bearing dope as several do, is an extremely dangerous situation. Often groupies plague performers with their neurotic fantasies. Once in New York Grace Slick opened the door to her hotel room to find a man in her bed hysterically claiming to be the father of the child she was at the time pregnant with. But for better or for worse, groupies provide most of the companionship and all of the sex on tour.

Hardly anyone provides a good meal. At 3:00 A.M. the cruise around town for an open diner is often fruitless. Parties offer only crackers and cheese and such. With strange girls in the car, in a strange city, both the hunger and the loneliness are gripping.

There was one groupie in New York, about the biggest absurdity on anyone's list. Well into her thirties, she claimed to be the ex-wife of a prominent producer and had researched the part to lie convincingly. She had dyed her hair pixie blonde (the roots showed only a little) and she wore high boots, a leather miniskirt, and a cowboy hat, the skirt just short enough to reveal a pair of well-shaped legs getting a little crepey at the thighs. She sauntered up to Jimmy Page, so in the know, dropping names, telling stories, talking English automobiles and pronouncing it Jag-you-are. She was cloying, enchanted with young Jimmy, a fellow Capricorn, brilliant, rich, ambitious, creative, just like her. And don't you know how Capricorns are vastly attracted to one another? And, she confided to the room at large (that being the control room of the recording studio), he was marvelous in bed last night, and in doing so, informs the mere teenage amateurs that Jimmy Page is her sexual territory. None of the other girls seemed particularly intimidated.

She had somehow got hold of the tour itinerary and she rang him up at weird hours of the morning to check him out on the road. When the group got back to New York, she appeared at the Fillmore East dressing room hovering over him. He'd scowl and move away but she was always—*there*—with some pretense at conversation with whoever would occupy her time and keep her from realizing that she was just beginning to be, generously speaking, unwanted there. At one point Jimmy left the room and came back cuddling the worst-looking girl, all sooty eyes, smeared lip gloss, and rotting teeth. He protectively led her over to the old babe and asked her to give the little wretch her seat. The lady clenched her teeth and finally left, standing up straight, her face crumpling under that tight mask. The following night she was out prowling for new blood in the Scene.

Led Zeppelin was on the way to Chicago. By that time word of their success on the tour was legend and they were very much in demand. The room was enormous, cavernous, packed; the enthusiasm was gen-uine and deafening. Members of the other band on the bill were old friends and everyone was happy before the show. Fired by the crowd the group outdid itself and the ovation was monumental. Ardent fans in Chicago, heavy Yardbirds' territory, were familiar with the group from a previous appearance. Jimmy Page was given a hero's welcome.

Fans attended by the tens of thousands, flamboyantly dressed and outrageously mannered. Call them hippies, heads, longhairs, freaks, praise or punish them, they alone knew who they were and why they were there. That same Chicago audience that cheered rock and roll into the night would have just as gleefully torn Mayor Daley limb from limb had he been there. Being a rock fan in 1969 was riding that edge.

There in Chicago, in the crucible of discontent, the city that became a metaphor for violent confrontation, these kids sought out a music that to them represented their desperation, anger, fear, and, more than anything, hope. Led Zeppelin is by no stretch of the imagination a politically oriented band, but what they do and how they catalyze their audience into a joyous, merging mass makes them a center for the mobilization of a power politicians haven't even found a name for. It is significant that the heroes of this age have not been statesmen or industrialists, scientists or generals, but poets, philosophers, satirists, and rock and roll stars who create out of their own personal torment the temper of the Sixties. They expressed their release through their art and embroiled their audience, who expressed their release through their lives.

Led Zeppelin were happy with their music. Jimmy Page fell seriously ill twice on the tour but played every night. "That's how you know you're a pro," he chirped on the plane.

Two nights in Chicago and one night in Columbia, Maryland. A day off? No, surprise, Atlantic Records was throwing them a party at the Plaza in New York. At the party they were informed that their album had to be ready in time for a marketing convention during the next few weeks. That meant another session that night and they dutifully trooped off to the studio.

Jimmy Page was getting snappy, ragged, and pathologically work-oriented. John Paul Jones seemed to let the bedlam bounce off a carefully cultivated hard shell. John Bonham was often bitterly silent and horribly homesick. Robert Plant who, much to the pique of Jimmy Page, was emerging as the star of the group, talked constantly about buying a christening gown for his infant daughter back home. Slugging down a glass of imitation orange drink one morning after a night of clowning around so loud the motel manager checked out his room to see what was happening, he sighed, "God, I miss my wife," to no one in particular.

But the depression never lasted very long. Conversations were livened by riotous accounts of the previous night's misadventures and the group developed a remarkable flair for irritating waitresses and airline hostesses who ogled over them. In flight they would collapse in their seats, their eyes dull, faces slack, finally falling into uncomfortable sleep. They were coming stars, but they looked like something the cat dragged in.

Everyone was wrecked, drained, moody, jet-shocked, and almost sick. They were advised that the tour was going extraordinarily well, better than even expected, but it did not seem to affect them, or perhaps they didn't realize the implications of what they'd been through. But each time they faced an audience (and they never disappointed an audience the whole time) they knew. This music they played, these people who loved them, no matter how gut-bustingly horrible that tour was, made it all worthwhile. In those few hours the boys would be transformed from tired carping brats into radiant gods. Whatever happened, it never took the joy out of playing and playing well.

The tour came off in the black that time around. In a fairly typical arrangement, the group traveled with a paid road crew. The money they earned had to support those salaries, transportation, lodging, food, repair or loss of equipment, and every other road expense incurred. They retained a publicity firm, lawyers in both countries, a manager, and an accountant. Managers' and booking agents' fees are deducted from the gross, and by the time the accounting was done they might have gotten to divide among themselves one-third of the more than $150,000 that tour grossed. The fees they were able to get, from a flat $5,000 a night to over $15,000 for the particularly successful two-day Chicago engagement, were good, but not top money in the field.

The scheme had worked. That tour was a setup for the next one, the superstar trip, where they would gross $350,000 to $400,000 for less time, fewer dates, and much more comfortable living and traveling arrangements.

When Herman's Hermits, for instance, were at the height of their career, they chartered a private jet for a month at a time, stocked it with their favorite food, and played poker with their agent, often betting their evening's earnings in the game. From airports they would charter helicopters to the city and limousines to the gigs, never rumpling their soft teddy suits on the way, always sending the road manager out to cull and deliver the right kinds of girls. For more sophisticated groups there are the world's finest hotels, chauffeurs, managers, agents, and local rock and roll bigwigs to squire them around town through pesty crowds of clawing fans into the most lavish of private homes with all their needs provided for. Past all this scuffling, it's clear sailing for the duration of rock and roll stardom. Get it while you can, pop is fast and fickle, and scorn for fallen stars is merciless.

"In this business," commented John Paul Jones, "it's not so much making it as fast as you can but making it fast *while* you can. The average life of a successful group is three years. You just have to get past that initial ordeal. The touring makes you into a different person. I realize that when I get home. It takes me weeks to recover after living like an animal for so long."

"But playing makes up for it," chimed in John Bonham. He had overheard the conversation and responded to the sadness in John Paul's voice. "Wait till we get to Boston," he enthused, as much for his own sagging spirits as for John Paul's. "That's the place! Remember when we were there the last time? They were banging their *heads* on the stage!"

The Boston Tea Party was alive with anticipation. The house was oversold, the group had broken the second attendance record of the tour. Grist for the press mill, ammunition sending future dates skyrocketing in price. Glee for the businessmen, all of whom flew up from New York to be with them. For the boys it was sweet justice. All those dues on the road the last tour and these last five weeks seemed to be coming in that night. It was beginning to really dawn on them just how big they had gotten. The magic of Led Zeppelin had culminated with this Boston stopover and everyone was there just to enjoy it, wallow in it, drink it in.

More importantly there was Tina, a twenty-year-old art student who shivered with excitement. There was Rusty, who drove all the way from Providence to see them. Jody said he'd drive all day to see Jimi Hendrix and Linda emphatically declared she would spend her last cent on a Jefferson Airplane album. Colored lights flashed on wall-to-wall people who cheered each member of the group as he stepped to the stage.

The Tea Party was formerly a synagogue, the stage sat in front of what was once the altar. Out of reverence or love or just plain joy the words "Praise Ye the Lord" were left on the altar wall and the celebration of togetherness buzzing through the room like current did the benediction justice. In its own funky way the Boston Tea Party and its counterparts around the country are houses of holy worship.

The room was jammed, dancing impossible, the music so loud that ovations were as much relief as they were appreciation. Long fluid notes pealed from Jimmy's guitar. John ripped into dazzling percussion acrobatics. John Paul Jones kept a bass line running through like a keel, stabilizing the music. Robert sang in an erotic howl and fans writhed with the changes in sound, interjecting hoots, groans, and whistles at each lull in the sound. The floor resounded with pounding feet when the set was over and the entire building shook rhythmically to its foundations. Three encores and they're still yelling for more. "Let's give 'em another," urges Robert backstage. "We don't know any others!" croaks Jimmy Page in a desperate whisper, laughing, gasping, sweating, heaving, totally overcome by delight.

Robert marches out to the stage anyway. The audience explodes in gratitude and approval. The group launches into a medley of Beatles and Stones songs to the crowd's delight. They are ecstatic, insatiable, and merciless. But the concert is over, there is just nothing left.

Afterward the dressing room was full of admirers, all competing for the group's attention. Though they sense they themselves are the substance of the magic that transpired, these people want to touch the source. John gulps a warm beer. Jimmy collapses in a corner. John Paul Jones wipes sweat from his face and his electric bass with the same towel, then tucks the towel and the instrument carefully into a plush-lined case, gazing down at it a moment before he folds the top down and clips the locks closed. Robert fumes, totally outraged because his favorite T-shirt has been stolen from the backstage area. "That's what it is," he splutters; "they love you and applaud you, you give them everything in your heart and they nick me T-shirt!"

Exhaustion, elation, and pride were all over the faces of Led Zeppelin. They exchanged congratulatory looks. It was late, very late. They had to play New York the next evening, the Fillmore East, the last date before going home. Everyone knew it was going to be a bummer after tonight but it was the last date. After Saturday, home to England. *Praise Ye the Lord.*

I had been covering this tour on assignment from *Life* magazine, living through the last three weeks of it with them, through the miles of exhaustion and undernourishment, suffering the company of the whiny groupies they attracted, the frazzled rush of arriving and departing, the uptightness at the airports, and the advances of their greasy road manager. I had been keeping a journal of our discomfort to document this unbelievably wearing and astoundingly exciting slice of professional life so germane to the rock and roll Sixties.

At the Fillmore East, on the last date of the tour, I stopped in to say good-bye and godspeed. Two members of the group attacked me, shrieking and grabbing at my clothes, totally over the edge. I fought them off until Peter Grant rescued me but not before they managed to tear my dress down the back. My young man of the evening took me home in a limousine borrowed from an agent friend and I trembled in exhaustion, anger, and bitterness all the way. Over the next week I tried to write the story. It was not about to happen. It took a whole year just to get back to my notes again with any kind of objectivity.

If you walk inside the cages of the zoo you get to see the animals close up, stroke the captive pelts, and mingle with the energy behind the mystique. You also get to smell the shit firsthand.

1973

Vince Aletti

For most of his readers, Vince Aletti (b. 1945) opened a window onto a new world with his 1973 *Rolling Stone* article "Discotheque Rock '72: Paaaaarty!" which, four years before *Saturday Night Fever*, detailed the existence of vibrant underground culture of DJs and dancers putting certain strains of then-contemporary funk and soul to singular cultural use. Aletti emerged as the disco scene's most informed and comprehensive chronicler, in a weekly column uniquely positioned in *Record World*. For five years Aletti's dispatches functioned both as trade chatter for working DJs, a listener's Consumer Guide in the vein of Robert Christgau, and a cumulative anthropology of clubland; the columns were later collected in *The Disco Files 1973–78*. During that same span Aletti continued to build mainstream awareness with coverage of disco's native terrain in *New York Magazine* and *The Village Voice*; he held the position of senior editor at the *Voice* for nearly twenty years. Aletti's subsequent career has been dedicated to the visual arts and photography, not only as a journalist for *The New Yorker* and other venues but as an exhibition curator, a prominent collector, and an editor of monographs.

▼ ▼

from
The Disco Files

APRIL 19, 1975

The Shape of Things To Come? A rather appalling little item appeared recently about a chain of steak restaurants that were turning themselves into discotheques. The chain's headquarters in Rockville, Maryland (disco central, right?), makes up a weekly list of 30 records which are supplied to DJs at each location, supplemented by basic collections of another 100 current "disco" records and 100 "oldie" dance cuts. The DJs, who are trained by the parent company, can play only those records on the lists and are expected to program the top 30 two or three times in the course of the night. Records by specially-spotlighted "artists of the month"—also chosen in Rockville—are programmed every 45 or 60 minutes in each of the locations in the chain. Clearly, disco DJing is the glamor, no-experience-necessary profession of the year, but is this what it's coming to? The best DJs—a number of whom were making record-to-record collages and brilliant musical connections years before the media discovered the disco phenomenon, years before many of us were ready to hear them—are artists, tastemakers, shaping the immediate environment with their music. God knows all those people out there at their double turntables are not cruising the same heights of creativity but, until now, they haven't been reduced to playlist automatons. With discotheques becoming Big Business, the "disco" chain, run like a fast-food empire or a string of laundromats, could be the next major move. If it is, count me out.

Michael Cappello points out that the version of Frankie Valli's "Swearin' To God" which appears on his list from Le Jardin is a disco re-mix by producer Bob Crewe which brings the cut up slightly, giving it a nicer, more attractive beat without changing the length substantially. Crewe left a few copies of this new mix with a number of New York DJs on his recent visit here—he was also sneak-previewing the new Disco Tex album, due out this month—but special promotional pressings should be generally available to clubs this week. Love Committee's "One Day Of Peace," also on Cappello's list, is another re-mix, this one almost doubling the length of the original Golden Fleece single but, as yet, not commercially released.

Louis Schneider and a few other New York DJs who have been given acetates, are excited about Bobbi Martin's "Man Was Made To Love Woman," an up-beat women's lib message with a Gloria Gaynor sound in spite of country-type vocals. Arrangement is by Harold Wheeler, production by Henry Jerome who is bringing it out this week on the Green Menu label and hoping it'll be snatched up by one of the majors. Schneider plays at New York's Casablanca, a Latin club on West 73rd Street which features live entertainment and disco, and should be distinguished from Club Casablanca downtown, from which Tom Savarese reported two weeks back for Disco File.

Our first Boston report comes this week from John Luongo who: plays at a club called Rhinoceros; runs a weekly disco program called "The Right Track" on Boston's WGBS-FM; produces occasional records (last effort: Leon Collins' "I Just Wanna Say I Love You" on the Elf label; coming up: a new version of Gentle Persuasion's "Dynamite Explodes") and has just started a bi-weekly disco newsletter called Night Fall, for which he compiles a top 12 from the Boston area (note: disco newsletters are proliferating like crazy—I'll have a report in an upcoming column). Luongo has this week's surprise tip: check out "Clap Your Hands" on the just-out Manhattan Transfer album (Atlantic), a terrific, high-spirited number as irresistible as anything I've heard this month.

The new essential albums: *Trammps* finally available (though copies have been floating around New York for the past few weeks, as prized as first-edition books) and including the familiar "Love Epidemic," "Where Do We Go From Here" and "Shout," plus the original, better version of "Trusting Heart" (previously only available on a one-sided promotional sampler of Philadelphia International material), "Trammps Disco Theme," "Stop And Think," "I Know That Feeling" and "Save

A Place"—all varying degrees of greatness; not a bad cut here and well worth the wait (on Golden Fleece). The O'Jays *Survival* (Philadelphia International) has just barely been absorbed here, but three cuts stand out immediately: "Give The People What They Want," also released as a 45, "Rich Get Richer" and "Survival," all tough, down-to-earth messages on the order of their own "For The Love Of Money" and Stevie Wonder's "You Haven't Done Nothing." With only one exception, the cuts on Hamilton Bohannon's *Insides Out* album (Dakar) are all over five minutes in length—the best, "Foot Stompin Music," runs 7:15—it's not as consistently danceable as his last album, but this is the best of the new mood music.

Also recommended: "Sign Of The Times," which blends with a version of Carole King's "Believe In Humanity," and "I Can't Move No Mountain" from Margie Joseph's excellent new album, *Margie*, produced by Arif Mardin (Atlantic). And these singles: a fiery "Super Kumba" by Manu Dibango (Atlantic); "Slippery When Wet" by the Commodores (Motown); Boby Franklin's "Whatever's Your Sign (You Got to Be Mine)" in a long version (4:51) which even this astrology cynic likes (Babylon); "Honey Baby Theme" with vocals by the Friends of Distinction and featuring Blood Hollins and Weldon Irvine (RCA), and, for a taste of nostalgia, an interesting version of Kim Weston's classic "Take Me In Your Arms (Rock Me a Little While)" by Charity Brown (A&M).

OCTOBER 2, 1976

Two trips this past week for sneak previews of two major fall releases. The first flight was to Los Angeles, where the new Donna Summer album was officially unveiled at a dinner party to celebrate Donna's return from Germany and the completion of her third album with producers Giorgio Moroder and Pete Bellotte. I heard the record first as background to a deliciously endless Chinese meal; then in an improvised after-dinner discotheque; then, the following day, in Neil Bogart's car and Neil Bogart's office, where Bogart, Casablanca Records' energetic president, impressed me with his real enthusiasm for disco, and his inside-out, no-nonsense understanding of the medium and the market; and finally, I heard the record at four different discotheques Saturday night when ace promotion man Marc Paul Simon took me and an acetate on a whirlwind tour. By the time I left LA the record had become so imprinted in my brain that I hardly needed my own copy, yet that was the first thing I put on the turntable once I got back home, and it's been there almost without interruption ever since.

The album's called *Four Seasons of Love* and it contains just four cuts, two to a side, with a short reprise at the end. The concept, as the title indicates, is the seasonal blossoming and dying of a love affair, giving each track its own mood: "Spring Affair" (8:32), the exhilarating opening, full of the bright, high excitement of falling in love; "Summer Fever" (8:08), celebrating the more intense passion of love at its peak, steamy and throbbing, with some terrific screams from Donna to send the temperature even higher; "Autumn Changes" (5:30), when the sound is ominous and the love fading and unsure, captured in the syncopation of a reggae steel drum beat; "Winter Melody," opening with an icy rush of wind and settling into a contemplative, lost-love song with vocals reminiscent of Dusty Springfield in her *Memphis* days. The final reprise cut brings the cycle back to Spring again and the flowering of a new affair. The Moroder-Bellotte production is, as usual, disco perfection: sharp, crisp, clear and full of brilliant changes; the transitions between the cuts are particularly fine and fluid, making the entire album not only a great disco concept, but one of the best executed concept lps since the theme format began. And wait 'til you see the cover! Release date is set for the first week in October and it's destined to be a record for all seasons.

The second trip was an excursion to a place called Long View Farm, a comfortable recording studio in a farmhouse outside of Worcester, Massachusetts, where a plane load of press people were given a first listen to Stevie Wonder's already-legendary *Songs In The Key Of Life* album. Stevie himself introduced the record, descending a staircase into a crush of photographers and cameramen, wearing a cream-colored cowboy suit and hat, complete with a special gun belt whose holsters held copies of his album cover and across whose back was printed "#1 WITH A BULLET." He also wore dark glasses with orange-bronze frames, short leather gloves, boots and a kerchief tied around his neck; in his hands he carried four boxes of tapes. But before they were played, he offered "a little background," to the album, his first in more than two years. Much of what he said sounded unusually self-conscious and stilted and he rambled nervously through serious platitudes and measured acknowledgements of help on the album before saying, "I hope that you all enjoy it but really doesn't matter so much because I know that I gave my all and all at this time to do the best that I can do."

Fortunately, his music spoke more forcefully, more fluidly. There are 17 songs on four sides of the album, plus four additional cuts that will be pressed on a seven-inch EP and included with the package. I won't venture to say whether or not the entire collection lived up to the great expectations that have built up over the long period of anticipation and constant rumor preceding its completion. One listening would hardly be enough, especially with the varied, complex group of tracks that Wonder has come up with. But, happily, I can report that there are at least two dance cuts so Stevie hasn't let the disco audience down. One is a long track called "Black Man" that is essentially a history lesson set to a percolating, popping rhythm and introducing various historical figures of different races who've made up the American melting pot. The chorus that unites these short sketches is one of Wonder's most powerful and direct and the song comes to a head with a break full of jumpy, snappy synthesizer. The end of the song turns into an aggressive question-and-answer quiz that is a strong rhetorical device but becomes undanceable. The second stunning cut is "Another Star," a love song with a big disco-style beginning that changes into a pounding Brazilian/Latin quick beat and a hard, heavy production fuller than most of the other material on the album. It's clinched by a long, instrumental break toward the end which jumps off with intense Latin drumming and includes a pretty lacing of flute and girls singing "la, la, la." Both are powerful and long. Two other disco possibilities are an engaging song called "As" and the second part of "Ordinary Pain," which features Shirley Brewer from Wonderlove on tough, gritty lead vocals. Offical release date: September 30; shipping, needless to say, as a gold album.

MARCH 11, 1978

Though the *USA-European Connection* album was only released this past week on TK's Marlin label, months of anticipation and a barrage of advance copies to key DJs have already zoomed it into the number five spot on the DISCO FILE Top 20, making it one of the strongest new disco albums of the moment (also red-hot: *Romeo & Juliet* and *Voyage*). To a certain extent, this is another confirmation of the strength of the Eurodisco sound—the format and musical vocabulary developed by Moroder, Bellotte, Cerrone and Costandinos have been freely borrowed from here—but what makes *USA-European* so interesting is the fact that it originated in Philadelphia and represents the first totally new disco sound from that city since the Gamble & Huff phenomenon. Composed, arranged, conducted and co-produced by Boris Midney, an Eastern-European emigre who has established his own recording studio (ALPHA International) in Philly, *USA-European Connection* is more than just the best American interpretation of the Eurodisco style to date—it's also original enough to stand on its own as one of the most exciting disco albums of the year. Each side is one long composition sustained by occasional vocals (by an excellent female trio) and stunning, constant orchestral movement: a series of breaks and changes that rivals the rhythmic ebb and flow of such masterpieces of this form as "I've Found Love" and "Give Me Love." The key line in "Come Into My Heart/Good Loving," the album's title track, sets the mood perfectly: "High winds of feeling tear me apart." The listener is caught up in the surge of the music and each wave of strings or eruption of synthesizers hits you with a distinctly emotional force. The sound here is somewhat sparer and more precise than on many European records, perhaps because Midney is working with a smaller

instrumental group, but the impact is incredible. Both sides are gloriously ecstatic, grand pieces of music that sweep you onto the dance
floor and keep you there. Overwhelmingly good and well worth the
wait. Boris Midney should also be added to everyone's list of producers
to watch; he's already at work on the second *USA-European* album, set
for release later in the year.

This week's other essential album is the second release by Jacques
Morali's Village People, titled *Macho Man*, on Casablanca. Basically a
re-run of "San Francisco" and "Fire Island" from the group's enormously successful first record, *Macho Man* makes few innovations
within the tough, hard-pounding style established for those tracks. The
music and the singing are appropriately, if unrelievedly, macho, from
the thumping, nearly brutal drumming to lead vocalist Victor Willis'
wonderfully gritty shouting—all best captured on the title cut and "I
Am What I Am," which together form an 11-minute medley that fills up
the album's first side. I find the glorification of macho dubious at best
(oppressive at worst, especially in a gay context, which this certainly is),
but its treatment by the Village People is comic enough not to be taken
seriously ("Body," the guys chant, "Wanna touch my body/Body—it's
too much, my body") and driving enough to be irresistible dance material: Following this shamelessly narcissistic number, "I Am What I Am"
extends the same sound to a rousing song, part plea, part demand for
tolerance, taking "I Was Born This Way" the necessary one step further: Willis and the chorus are especially powerful and convincing here.
Prime cut on side two is another stop on the Village People tour of gay
hot spots: "Key West" (5:42), an enthusiastic tribute to fun, fun, fun in
the sun with all the emotional and intellectual content of Jan & Dean's
"Surf City." The remainder of the album is filled by the inordinately
campy medley of "Just a Gigolo" and "I Ain't Got Nobody" and a song
called "Sodom and Gomorrah" whose cheerful retelling of the Biblical
story strikes an oddly discordant note in the midst of all this aggressive
hedonism. Still, everything here is undeniably catchy and entertaining—instant top 10 material, especially welcome at a time when there
are so few strong male vocal records around.

RECOMMENDED DISCO DISCS: "Rio De Janeiro" by Gary Criss (Salsoul) is a Philadelphia record—produced and written by Billy Terrel, arranged and conducted by John Davis—previously released only in Brazil and now available here with a "midnight mix" by New York DJ Richie Rivera that opens up the record beautifully. The song's first half is a pulsing, mostly vocal tribute to the attractions of Rio that is quite lovely and involving, but it's the soaring, spirited second half—chock full of changes, the orchestration vivid and glistening—that clinches the track. Excellent . . . Lucy Hawkins, who, it seems, was discovered as a worker in the Sam Records warehouse, now has a two-sided disco disc out on that label, both sides terrific: "Lady Of The Night" (5:30), an Evie Sands song that catches a warm, comfortable groove much like her often-covered "One Thing On My Mind," also has lyrics as memorable as those in "Native New Yorker" and Hawkins' fine, vibrant vocals; "Gotta Get Out Of Here" (5:50) has a funkier, chunkier beat (cf. "Up Jumped The Devil"), heftier vocals (sounds closer to Merry Clayton here) and quite a good break leading to a hot, rave-up ending. John Davis produced . . . The Larry Page Orchestra's "Slinky Thighs" (London) follows in the instrumental mold established with "Erotic Soul"—a sensuous meshing of the electronic and the acoustic—in a varied, alternately heavy and light composition, full of deep drums, ominous synthesizer or bursting with high strutting strings. A must for drum freaks.

A number of songs already reviewed here as album cuts have recently been made available as disco discs, most in substantially different versions, and are heartily re-recommended: "Street Dance" and "Music, Harmony And Rhythm" by Brooklyn Dreams (Millennium), both lengthened, the latter by about three minutes at the end which totally transforms the song and should give it a whole new appeal—terribly neglected on their original release, both cuts deserve a new hearing, especially since they're perhaps the best re-mixes Bobby Guttadaro did during his tenure with Casablanca . . . Al Green's fine "I Feel Good" (Hi), now running a hefty 7:30 with no major structural changes but some added riffing and a vastly improved sound quality . . . Peter Brown's

"Dance With Me" (TK), same length as the lp track that's already so successful, just spruced-up technically for a sharper edge . . . Chic's "Everybody Dance" (Atlantic), expanded to 8:25 in honor of its release as a single—minor revisions only . . . "My Man Is On His Way," the Retta Young record on All Platinum that became something of a cult favorite in New York, deserved better than merely being looped up to 6:45, but here it is . . . A 13:45 slice of Alec Costandinos & the Syncophonic Orchestra's "Romeo & Juliet" (Casablanca) isn't really satisfying—the jump-cut from material on side one to the beginning of side two is slightly jarring—but this music in any form is so exciting that this, too, is well worth having . . . Finally, Lonnie Smith's "Funk Reaction" (TK), same length as the album track and still sounding attractive.

DISCO FILE HERO OF THE MONTH: Leon Spinks, the heavyweight champion of the world, was photographed at Studio 54 recently and later told the *Times*, "I want to go out and see the people and talk to them and touch their hands. That's part of the reason I went to the discos." The other part? "I like the music. I jump rope, hit the bags, do my training to the music." Wonder what he listens to.

PAUL NELSON

With his friend Jon Pankake, Paul Nelson (1936–2006) created *The Little Sandy Review* in Minneapolis in 1959; a 'zine dedicated to folk music, it ran until 1965, and is one of the fanzines predating even *Crawdaddy* in offering a testing ground for early writing on rock & roll. While still in Minnesota, Nelson enjoyed a friendly rivalry in matters of folk expertise with Bob Dylan. After moving to New York City in 1963, Nelson became managing editor of *Sing Out!*, but broke with the magazine and the folk music orthodoxy in defending Dylan's shift to an electric band in 1965. In the early '70s, after writing for *The New York Times*, *The Village Voice*, *Circus*, and many other publications, Nelson detoured into the music business. As an A&R man at Mercury Records he assembled The Velvet Underground's *Live 1969/70*, worked with The Modern Lovers and Rod Stewart, and signed The New York Dolls, who became known as "Paul's Folly." Nelson returned to journalism as *Rolling Stone*'s record review editor, where his advocacy of acts like The Ramones and Joy Division ran at odds with the magazine's prevailing aesthetic. Nelson's later years included sporadic efforts on epic-length interviews with Warren Zevon, Clint Eastwood, and Ross Macdonald and an unproduced screenplay; as his writing career wound down, he spent his last years working as a clerk in a video store in Greenwich Village. A biography and posthumous anthology, *Everything Is an Afterthought: The Life and Writings of Paul Nelson*, was published in 2011.

▼ ▼

Valley of the New York Dolls

THE FIRST time I laid eyes on the New York Dolls, they were drunk in a Rolls-Royce Silver Wraith outside the terrace of the Dancers. David Johansen had lost the high heel from one of his shoes. He said, "I not only accept loss forever, I am made of loss," while, inside the club, the group's managerial brain trust planned the conquest of blue dawns over race tracks and kids from sweet Ioway. The rest of the band—Johnny Thunders, Sylvain Sylvain, Jerry Nolan, Arthur Harold Kane—talked happily about early days spent practicing in a bicycle shop near Central Park. And me? I'm a fool. My heart went out to the hopeful sounds. We all thought the group would achieve success through the purity of their rock 'n' roll art.

None of the above is true, of course—my apologies to Chandler and Kerouac—but some of it is, or could be. There was always a sense of American mythology about the Dolls, and those of us who spent three years of our lives working with them had to believe they were more than just another rock 'n' roll group, albeit the most misunderstood of recent times. We learned to measure our nights by Dolls concerts, spent even our holidays going to and from, and Mick Taylor's cryptic putdown—"They're the worst high school band I ever saw"—only further convinced us how right we were. Johansen shot back: "No—we're the best high school band you ever saw! The kids will love us!" and the point seemed settled. For, after all, the New York Dolls tried to hit the longest home run in American rock 'n' roll: they tried to impose themselves upon a nation's musical and cultural consciousness in much the same manner as had the Rolling Stones 10 years earlier.

*   *   *

Johansen: "In the beginning we weren't very good musically. That's why we put up with each other. We were all fabulous people. . . . We're a lot faster than the Stones." Laughter. "At least, younger."

* * *

For all their claim to being a band of and for kids, the Dolls rarely listened to Top 40 music—like them or not, no one could accuse them of creating that music industry euphemism for art, "product"—and their notions of technique mirrored more the tough sparseness of Hammett, the avant-garde fragmentation of Burroughs, and the cruel inward eye of Nathanael West than the easy flow of media favorites. The fact that AM radio reacted to their songs as if they had dropped from some alien sky was not, in the long run, surprising. Johansen-Thunders did not have the breadth of Jagger-Richards. While the Stones could have written "Bad Girl," the Dolls could never have brought about "Moonlight Mile": they lacked the smoke and duskiness, and their nocturnal sojourn through the desert took them far too close to a deli for the tastes of most of Middle America. Whereas the work of the Stones could encompass the broad human comedy of a Breughel or a Bosch, the Dolls proved to be subgenre miniaturists. They were unquestionably brilliant, but finally too spare, too restricted, to reach the hidden places in suburban, small-town hearts. In the end, they rode on real rather than symbolic subway trains to specific rather than universal places, played for an audience of intellectuals or kids even farther out than they were; and, when they eventually met the youth of the country, that youth seemed more confused than captivated by them, and could no more imagine itself a New York Doll than it could some exotic palm tree growing in Brooklyn. The Dolls appealed to an audience which had seen the end of the world, had in fact bought tickets for it but probably didn't attend because there was something even funnier on television that night.

Dave Marsh, who loved the group, put it best when he wrote: "The New York Dolls are the dead end of the '60s approach. They presume a closed community of rock fans, a limited field with common interests closely held. The new kind of rock singers are different. They know how much greater the stakes are, for a rock star who wants to count, but they also know there isn't any way to focus upon them, to make the meaning of having the whole world up for grabs come home."

*   *   *

Nolan: "I suppose everyone will be like the Dolls in a few years. Like a fad. The public and people in general always pick up things from leaders, rock groups especially."

*   *   *

To be the neo–Rolling Stones of the 1970s was to be a not-to-be, and, after two albums and much notoriety, the Dolls broke up in the final weeks of April, the legendary deserts having forever eluded them. If truth be known, the news of their death hardly produced a ripple throughout the nation they sought to win. Their demise was taken as inevitable. The dreams of rock 'n' roll's Dead End Kids burned out like a green light bulb on someone else's marquee, and nobody particularly noticed any loss of illumination. That must have been hard for the band to take, but perhaps no harder than some of the dates they had been forced to accept to remain even nominally solvent in the later stages of their existence. Somehow, everything had gone monstrously wrong; and, like characters in some tragicomic version of *Long Day's Journey Into Night*, everyone closely involved was innocent, everyone guilty. The only solution, finally, was to walk away from it, but none of us—musicians, managers (Marty Thau, Steve Leber, David Krebs), myself (the A&R man who signed the group to Mercury Records)— really could.

*   *   *

August 7, 1972: I see Dolls at Mercer Art Center, want to sign them to wary Mercury.

Late August: Dolls ask Merc for $250,000 deal. Merc blanches, sends in more scouts.

September 24. Merc VP Charlie Fach sees Dolls at Mercer. Dolls go on three hours late. Fach stays 15 minutes, says no. I persist.

October 1: Merc VP Lou Simon flies in from Chicago main office, sees Dolls at Mercer. Dolls go on two hours late. Simon loves them, says nothing until he checks the current political climate in Chi, then says no. I persist.

October 8: Merc A&R man Robin McBride flies in from Chi, sees Dolls at Mercer. Dolls go on one hour late. Thunders, wearing platform basketball shoes, kicks hole in stage. Kane's bass comes unplugged; he plays last four songs without making a sound. McBride says no. I persist.

Late October: Dolls, turned down by every major label, go to Europe. Merc President I. H. Steinberg and Fach see them in London, say no. I persist. Steinberg becomes enraged, calls Dolls worst band he has ever seen, says I must be crazy. Dolls original drummer Billy dies in England in what is usually referred to as a drug-related incident. Nolan replaces him.

Late 1972: I keep trying to convince very leery Merc.

* * *

The Dolls' first performance had been in July at the Diplomat Hotel in the seedy Times Square area ("You all know Times Square," Johansen used to chide his audience. "It's where we all met."), but it was at the Mercer they gained their reputation in a series of concerts which built in momentum until the nights one spent there with 600 similarly delirious people simply were not sane. Those vivacious evenings were like a benign *Clockwork Orange* filmed in a packed-to-the-rafters Hollywood Mutant High wired for massive sound. There was something marvelous about the band's all-out assault, fashioned as it was from wit, homage, honesty, self-parody, urban cunning, and the virtuosity of crudeness.

The Dolls and their early following were those kids who used to sneak into the Fillmore East every Saturday night; years later, when their musical time came, they couldn't wait to build their own home-made rocket ship and send it flying toward the moon on a return trip to innocence. If the fuel was more amateur energy than professional talent—well, one had to make do with what was at hand, surely the primary law of the streetwise. And it was a wondrous thing to see the group play rock 'n' roll with the enthusiasm of five people who felt and acted as if they had just invented it, hadn't quite worked out the kinks yet, but what matter?—it was raw flash, honest fun, erotically direct, and seemed to define them to, and make them inseparable from, their own kind. While they invented nothing, they did present a peculiar vision—lost youths roaming the nighttime city "looking for a kiss, not a fix," cosmic jet boys "flying around New York City so high," the teenager as group Frankenstein—and carried the music back to simpler times: there were almost no solos, and everybody played and sang as hard as they could until they got tired. Which wasn't often. Although some found their world dangerous and offensive—and not at all the dark side of sentimentality—it never seemed threatening to me. It must have been like this in London when people first heard the Stones, I kept thinking, secretly ruing the day when the Dolls would become stars and go public.

But when the Dolls left their milieu in New York City (the Mercer Art Center, Kenny's Castaways, et al.), something was lost. The many times I saw them in big halls in front of crowds of several thousand, the essence of their particular, insular magic somehow became diluted. Even at the Felt Forum, in their first "legitimate" concert before 5000 "normal" people (most of whom came to see Mott the Hoople), the band appeared nervous, ineffectual, and—how can one say it?—somewhat lost and harmless. Defanged. They never quite succeeded in finding a way to convey their intimacy and personal charm to a larger audience which oft times regarded them as technically inept, emotionally silly freaks—or worse. If there were ever to be a meeting between performer and potential fan, work needed to be done. The Dolls were something special. They required specific, sensitive handling and firm control. Unfortunately, they did not always get it.

*   *   *

January 30, 1973: Merc head of publicity Mike Gormley flies in from Chi, sees Dolls at Kenny's Castaways because he wants to, says yes. I am shocked. Gormley's memo reopens Dolls case.

March 20: Dolls and Merc agree to a deal.

Late June: Dolls finish first album with Todd Rundgren producing. Mixing takes less than six hours. Johansen calls Rundgren "an expert on second-rate rock 'n' roll."

July: Johansen falls asleep in Chi in front of Merc brass at special meeting to discuss Dolls. Steinberg isn't sure whether or not to wake him.

September: Dolls play Whiskey and Los Angeles for first time. Five hundred kids line up each night. Thunders falls in love with groupie queen Sable Starr; they become rock 'n' roll punkdom's Romeo and Juliet. Sylvain stays in biggest suite in hotel for week. How? I ask. "It was the room right next to mine," he says, "and it was empty so I just stayed there."

September 23: Johansen arrested in Memphis for stopping Dolls music while cops beat up a kid. He asks cops what they'd do if he were Elvis. "We'd love to get him!" cops reply.

Late 1973: Dolls named by *Creem* readers as Best New Group and Worst Group of Year. Despite Rundgren, the first album, *New York Dolls*, sells 100,000 copies.

* * *

"The Dolls are a vicious kick in the face to all that's careful, passive, and polished about today's popular music. The record companies, most of which have a great investment in exactly the kind of music the Dolls are rallying against, have naturally been turned off. . . ." (Bud Scoppa, *Penthouse*)

Kane, the shiest of the band, after having seen me for at least eight months: "Hi. I'm Arthur."

* * *

If the Dolls were difficult to work with at times, it was because they understood nothing of the music business and recording, seemed naive or unable to learn about either, and were rarely encouraged to exhibit any kind of self-control regarding the bankbook or the clock. To say that their record company thought them a mere critics' hype, did not understand them, and eventually grew to hate them would be an understatement; but, at the beginning, Mercury provided handsomely for the group's every whim. Management started well, too; Thau, the band's Napoleon, and Leber, their legal adviser and financial wizard, showed obvious devotion. As the months passed, trouble set in. The problems with Mercury rarely involved the Dolls personally, but had to do rather with mutual contempt among the men at the top on both sides, opposite viewpoints, management's apparent disdain for necessary budgets and deadlines, the record company's inability to get the group much AM or FM airplay, and—last but not least—money.

The clash between the Dolls and Mercury was finally a classic confrontation between two immovable objects: a company reluctant to spend any more money and a band that did not know how to stop spending it. Thau and Leber's penchant for potentiality required huge sums for bad-boy image-building and Stones-style high living, while Steinberg preferred to drop anchor until the bottom line told him when to raise it. A hot war was being waged. Further, Thau and Leber had begun to quarrel, a situation which proved very damaging at a time when the band needed all the outer stability they could get. The bills were piling up, and the hands at the controls had suddenly become fists.

One can learn much about the trouble among musicians, management, and record company in these excerpts from a confidential report written by Patrick Taton, a Mercury employee in Paris, concerning the group's 1973 French tour:

"November 28: Arrival at Orly. While camera went into action, Thunders got sick right on the airport floor and had to leave the scene for a minute to pull himself together and make a decent comeback. We spent the afternoon taking pictures at the hotel. The Dolls gave us a hint as to their drinking capacities, which we had to discover at our own expense. In the afternoon, Thunders got sick again and had to be replaced by one of the road managers for photo purposes.

"November 29: Press interviews began with the group, their friends, and managers gulping down champagne and cognac at an incredible speed, while we from Mercury were seated in the other corner of the bar. I was surprised when a not-so-sober Thau came up to us to remark that we weren't really interested in the Dolls because we weren't taking part in the interviews. When the interviews were over, I picked up the bill, which was incredibly high for so short a time. When I told Thau about it, he replied with utmost contempt, 'peanuts for a band like that!' and continued with some of the most insulting remarks I've ever heard about a record company and its executives.

"Next was a live concert at Radio Luxembourg. Although they had been requested for rehearsals at 17:30, the group were not ready before 19:00 and went to the studio in a frightening state of drunkenness—one of the most nerve-shattering experiences of my 'business' life.

"December 2: Olympia concert. Surprisingly enough, by the time we went to pick them up at their hotel, the Dolls had already set up their gear and rehearsed. The hall was nearly sold out, and the evening ended in a triumph with two encores. The band were then taken to a top restaurant. They invited their friends—over 50 people altogether—all of them lavishly drinking champagne and Cognac, making an incredible show of themselves, enraging patrons, and leaving us with a very nice bill.

"December 3: The day started with the news that Thau and Leber had gone back to America. The group were penniless and urgently requested an advance before they would fulfill their commitments: pure blackmail. The Dolls had to go to a TV studio for a very important show. Believe it or not, it took us over three hours to get them out of their rooms, while a frantic and irate producer was calling the hotel every five minutes, threatening to cancel the program and never again work with Mercury. Also, the band's equipment was set up five hours behind schedule. Finally, after a few minor incidents, the show was taped. It was a success from the first minute. The audience reacted very strongly to the storm of noise produced by the group. There was even a fight, a thing that pleased the Dolls very much, although they found French kids not so tough as those from New York.

"December 4: The band were ready to leave, but they had no money with which to pay their bill (rooms, drinks, numerous overseas telephone calls): over $3500. Stuck again. If I may offer a personal opinion, the New York Dolls are one of the worst examples of untogetherness I have ever seen. Johansen is a very intelligent guy, Sylvain is really clever and nice, the others are quite kind in their own way; but put them together, add their managers (each of them doing his own thing), mix with alcohol, and shake, and you've got a careless, selfish, vicious, and totally disorganized gang of New York hooligans—and I'm really sorry to say so.

"Despite all this, I believe we have managed to do good business."

* * *

Sylvain: "I want a Cadillac car. Or a Rolls. I don't care. I'm just dying for a car. I've had three cars, no license. I guess I'm a lucky person."

Johansen: "I used to be lucky. What happened? I grew up. It changed everything."

* * *

In 1974, the Dolls released a second LP, *Too Much, Too Soon*, produced by Shadow Morton. It sold about 55,000 copies and, like the first record, made the charts and appeared on almost every major critic's best-of-the-year list. Not bad for a new band, under the most convivial of circumstances; but the Dolls, unfortunately, were mired in the worst; Thau and Leber split, the group not talking much to either party; and Steinberg, all ire and ice, demanded the repayment of certain loans and a third album to be made only when management and monetary problems were rectified. They never were, of course. The band had no money, and their destructiveness and unpunctuality had alienated many promoters who no longer wanted to book them. Leber valiantly put together a lucrative tour of Europe and Japan. Krebs persuaded Jack Douglas to produce the third album, but the Dolls themselves—disillusioned and no longer trusting anyone—didn't take the offers seriously, and everything eventually fell apart. Legally, the group couldn't break free from any of their contracts. There was not much left to do but to go home and die.

The Dolls did make one small comeback, a series of concerts at the Little Hippodrome earlier this year, but even these did little but add to the misconceptions which had always surrounded the band. In the early days, they were constantly referred to as a glitter group, a fag band, five transvestites who played inexpedient rock 'n' roll and who were very offensive onstage. Needless to say, all of these "charges" were false. None of the group is homosexual, nor did the band ever dress as women. The infamous cover for their first LP was conceived as a deliberate eye-catcher—the ultimate satirical statement on makeup and glitter (the group appeared as they naturally look on the back of the jacket)—but somehow all too many people again failed to recognize the Dolls' nihilistic, riffraff sense of humor. At the Little Hippodrome, the band tailored their comeback around the comic conceit of what it would be like to see a rock 'n' roll concert in Red China, and, true to form, were quickly branded as Communists by many in the audience. With that maximum absurdity, perhaps it was indeed time to quit.

*   *   *

The dreams of so many good people died with the New York Dolls. I can still remember the night we finished the first album. Thau and I raced over to Mercury to have two acetates cut, and later we listened, the ghostly sounds of more than a year's worth of the group's concerts ringing in our ears. I put the dub on the turntable, sheer terror in my heart. Thau, who had discovered the band and had cared enough to spend the very best of himself and all of his money on the project, felt the same. It meant so much to us then. I think both of us suddenly realized that everything had, to some degree, passed out of our hands and into the hands of these kids from sweet Ioway whose legion ultimately said no! in thunder to the hopes of the New York Dolls. As Jean Renoir remarked: "You see, in this world, there is one awful thing, and that is that everyone has his reasons."

*   *   *

I think those kids from sweet Ioway were wrong, or rather perhaps that they never really had a chance to encounter the group on any significant level: on the radio or as part of a major tour. Instead, the band's philosophy of instant stardom and limited, headliner-only bookings proved to be the stuff of dreams. Even a cult favorite must eventually face the nation as a whole, but the Dolls never played by the rules of the game. Neither did the Velvet Underground, and their contributions will last. At times when I am feeling particularly perverse, I can't blame either of them.

The New York Dolls sang and played terrific rock 'n' roll—their own and other people's—and, in a better world, "Personality Crisis," "Trash," and "Stranded in the Jungle" would have been AM hits. (Perhaps two new songs, "Teenage News" and "Girls," will correct the deficit on some future Johansen LP.) Individually, each of the group will be heard from again—Thunders and Nolan have already formed a band called the Heartbreakers, Johansen and Sylvain have several plans, Kane is supposedly in California—but no matter. "Live fast, die young, and leave a good-looking corpse," someone once said. The Dolls went out with their high-heeled boots on.

They did it their way and got carried out dead, but with their pride intact. True, they did not grow old with the country, but that's probably the country's loss, not theirs. Corporation rock 'n' roll, wherein musicians like Bachman-Turner Overdrive are more gray-flanneled than the businessmen who kowtow to them, is so formularized, homogenized, and impersonal it must surely cause the death of anything that is at all out-of-bounds, mythopoeic, and rebellious. The Dolls were alive. Perhaps it killed them not to become stars, darkened their personalities, drove some of them into private worlds; but at least they had the courage to become figments of their own imaginations—and those creations were not altogether devoid of nobility. I will cherish always the friendship of each of them. Their last words on record were: "I'm a human being."

* * *

"Listen, bucko, these are the New York Dolls, the sweethearts of Babylon themselves, the band you're gonna love whether you like it or not. . . ." (*New Musical Express*)

* * *

I do not claim they were the best, but the New York Dolls are still my favorite rock 'n' roll group, although I will understand if you do not like them. I will understand, but deep down I will not want to know you.

1975

LESTER BANGS

The Romans had a saying, *nomen est omen*; the psychologist Carl Jung dubbed this phenomenon "the compulsion of the name." If any child was born to be a wild and boisterous and opinionated rock writer, it had to be Leslie Conway "Lester" Bangs (1948–1982). Throughout his career and following his untimely death, Bangs's writing and myth cut a wide swath through the world of rock writing. Influenced by Beat writers like Jack Kerouac and jazz improvisers like Miles Davis and John Coltrane, Bangs created for himself a version of the outlandish "gonzo" journalism pioneered by Hunter S. Thompson, whose *Fear and Loathing in Las Vegas* was serialized in the pages of *Rolling Stone* in 1971. Bangs wrote with the frenzy and abandon of a teenager discovering music, equally ebullient in his sometimes gushing praise and his scathing disparagement. Bangs himself first appeared in *Rolling Stone* after his voluminous correspondence wore down records editor Greil Marcus, who invited him to start reviewing for the magazine beginning with the first issue Marcus edited in July 1969. After being fired from *Rolling Stone* four years later for "disrespecting musicians," Bangs moved on to an editorial stint at *Creem* and freelance gigs for, among others, *The Village Voice* and Britain's *New Music Express*. Bangs's influence hasn't always been salutary; a legion of young men seem to mistake his calculated provocations for simple "mouthing off," and the Internet has given them plenty of space to do so. In "Where Were You When Elvis Died?" Bangs unleashes his trademark irreverence in the wake of The King's death, pointing a moral about artists who display contempt for their audience.

Some of his best pieces are collected in *Psychotic Reactions and Carburetor Dung* (1987) and *Main Lines, Blood Feasts, and Bad Taste* (2003).

▼ ▼

Where Were You When Elvis Died?

WHERE WERE *you* when Elvis died? What were you doing, and what did it give you an excuse to do with the rest of your day? That's what we'll be talking about in the future when we remember this grand occasion. Like Pearl Harbor or JFK's assassination, it boiled down to individual reminiscences, which is perhaps as it should be, because in spite of his greatness, etc., etc., Elvis had left us each as alone as he was; I mean, he wasn't exactly a Man of the People anymore, if you get my drift. If you don't I will drift even further, away from Elvis into the contemplation of why all our public heroes seem to reinforce our own solitude.

The ultimate sin of any performer is contempt for the audience. Those who indulge in it will ultimately reap the scorn of those they've dumped on, whether they live forever like Andy Paleface Warhol or die fashionably early like Lenny Bruce, Jimi Hendrix, Janis Joplin, Jim Morrison, Charlie Parker, Billie Holiday. The two things that distinguish those deaths from Elvis's (he and they having drug habits vaguely in common) were that all of them died on the outside looking in and none of them took their audience for granted. Which is why it's just a little bit harder for me to see Elvis as a tragic figure; I see him as being more like the Pentagon, a giant armored institution nobody knows anything about except that its power is legendary.

Obviously we all liked Elvis better than the Pentagon, but look at what a paltry statement that is. In the end, Elvis's scorn for his fans as manifested in "new" albums full of previously released material and one new song to make sure all us suckers would buy it was mirrored in the scorn we all secretly or not so secretly felt for a man who came closer to godhood than Carlos Castaneda until military conscription tamed and revealed him for the dumb lackey he always was in the first place. And ever since, for almost two decades now, we've been waiting for him to get wild again, fools that we are, and he probably knew better than any of us in his heart of hearts that it was never gonna happen, his heart of hearts so obviously not being our collective heart of hearts, he being so obviously just some poor dumb Southern boy with a Big Daddy manager to screen the world for him and filter out anything which might erode his status as big strapping baby bringing home the bucks, and finally being sort of perversely celebrated at least by rock critics for his utter contempt for whoever cared about him.

And Elvis was perverse; only a true pervert could put out something like *Having Fun with Elvis On Stage*, that album released three or so years back which consisted *entirely* of between-song onstage patter so redundant it would make both Willy Burroughs and Gert Stein blush. Elvis was into marketing boredom when Andy Warhol was still doing shoe ads, but Elvis's sin was his failure to realize that his fans were not perverse—they loved him without qualification, no matter what he dumped on them they loyally lapped it up, and that's why I feel a hell of a lot sorrier for all those poor jerks than for Elvis himself. I mean, who's left they can stand all night in the rain for? Nobody, and the true tragedy is the tragedy of an entire generation which refuses to give up its adolescence even as it feels its menopausal paunch begin to blossom and its hair recede over the horizon—along with Elvis and everything else they once thought they believed in. Will they care in five years what he's been doing for the last twenty?

Sure Elvis's death is a relatively minor ironic variant on the future-shock mazurka, and perhaps the most significant thing about Elvis's exit is that the entire history of the seventies has been retreads and brutal demystification; three of Elvis's ex-bodyguards recently got together with this hacker from the New York *Post* and whipped up a book which dosed us with all the dirt we'd yearned for for so long. Elvis was the last of our sacred cows to be publicly mutilated; everybody knows Keith Richard likes his junk, but when Elvis went onstage in a stupor nobody breathed a hint of "Quaalude. . . ." In a way, this was both good and bad, good because Elvis wasn't encouraging other people to think it was cool to be a walking *Physicians' Desk Reference*, bad because Elvis stood for that Nixonian Secrecy-as-Virtue which was passed off as the essence of Americanism for a few years there. In a sense he could be seen not only as a phenomenon that exploded in the fifties to help shape the psychic jailbreak of the sixties but ultimately as a perfect cultural expression of what the Nixon years were all about. Not that he prospered more then, but that his passion for the privacy of potentates allowed him to get away with almost literal murder, certainly with the symbolic rape of his fans, meaning that we might all do better to think about waving good-bye with one upraised finger.

I got the news of Elvis's death while drinking beer with a friend and fellow music journalist on his fire escape on 21st Street in Chelsea. Chelsea is a good neighborhood; in spite of the fact that the insane woman who lives upstairs keeps him awake all night every night with her rants at no one, my friend stays there because he likes the sense of community within diversity in that neighborhood: old-time card-carrying Communists live in his building alongside people of every persuasion popularly lumped as "ethnic." When we heard about Elvis we knew a wake was in order, so I went out to the deli for a case of beer. As I left the building I passed some Latin guys hanging out by the front door. "Heard the news? Elvis is dead!" I told them. They looked at me with contemptuous indifference. *So what.* Maybe if I had told them Donna Summer was dead I might have gotten a reaction; I do recall walking in this neighborhood wearing a T-shirt that said "Disco Sucks" with a vast unamused muttering in my wake, which only goes to show that not for everyone was Elvis the still-reigning King of Rock 'n' Roll, in fact not for everyone is rock 'n' roll the still-reigning music. By now, each citizen has found his own little obsessive corner to blast his brains in: as the sixties were supremely narcissistic, solipsism's what the seventies have been about, and nowhere is this better demonstrated than in the world of "pop" music. And Elvis may have been the greatest solipsist of all.

I asked for two six-packs at the deli and told the guy behind the counter the news. He looked fifty years old, greying, big belly, life still in his eyes, and he said: "Shit, that's too bad. I guess our only hope now is if the Beatles get back together."

Fifty years old.

I told him I thought that would be the biggest anticlimax in history and that the best thing the Stones could do now would be to break up and spare us all further embarrassments.

He laughed, and gave me directions to a meat market down the street. There I asked the counterman the same question I had been asking everyone. He was in his fifties too, and he said, "You know what? I don't *care* that bastard's dead. I took my wife to see him in Vegas in '73, we paid fourteen dollars a ticket, and he came out and sang for twenty minutes. Then he fell down. Then he stood up and sang a couple more songs, then he fell down again. Finally he said, 'Well, shit, I might as well sing sitting as standing.' So he squatted on the stage and asked the band what song they wanted to do next, but before they could answer he was complaining about the lights. 'They're too bright,' he says. 'They hurt my eyes. Put 'em out or I don't sing a note.' So they do. So me and my wife are sitting in total blackness listening to this guy sing songs we knew and loved, and I ain't just talking about his old goddam songs, but he totally *butchered* all of 'em. Fuck him. I'm not saying I'm glad he's dead, but I know one thing: I got taken when I went to see Elvis Presley."

I got taken too the one time I saw Elvis, but in a totally different way. It was the autumn of 1971, and two tickets to an Elvis show turned up at the offices of *Creem* magazine, where I was then employed. It was decided that those staff members who had never had the privilege of witnessing Elvis should get the tickets, which was how me and art director Charlie Auringer ended up in nearly the front row of the biggest arena in Detroit. Earlier Charlie had said, "Do you realize how much we could get if we sold these fucking things?" I didn't, but how precious they were became totally clear the instant Elvis sauntered onto the stage. He was the only male performer I have ever seen to whom I responded sexually; it wasn't real arousal, rather an erection of the heart, when I looked at him I went mad with desire and envy and worship and self-projection. I mean, Mick Jagger, whom I saw as far back as 1964 and twice in '65, never even came close.

There was Elvis, dressed up in this ridiculous white suit which looked like some studded Arthurian castle, and he was too fat, and the buckle on his belt was as big as your head except that your head is not made of solid gold, and any lesser man would have been the spittin' image of a Neil Diamond damfool in such a getup, but on Elvis it fit. What didn't? No matter how lousy his records ever got, no matter how intently he pursued mediocrity, there was still some hint, some flash left over from the days when . . . well, I wasn't there, so I won't presume to comment. But I will say this: Elvis Presley was the man who brought overt blatant vulgar sexual frenzy to the popular arts in America (and thereby to the nation itself, since putting "popular arts" and "America" in the same sentence seems almost redundant). It has been said that he was the first white to sing like a black person, which is untrue in terms of hard facts but totally true in terms of cultural impact. But what's more crucial is that when Elvis started wiggling his hips and Ed Sullivan refused to show it, the entire country went into a paroxysm of sexual frustration leading to abiding discontent which culminated in the explosion of psychedelic-militant folklore which was the sixties.

I mean, don't tell me about Lenny Bruce, man—Lenny Bruce said dirty words in public and obtained a kind of consensual martyrdom. Plus which Lenny Bruce was hip, too goddam hip if you ask me, which was his undoing, whereas Elvis was not hip at all, Elvis was a goddam truck driver who worshipped his mother and would never say shit or fuck around her, and Elvis alerted America to the fact that it had a groin with imperatives that had been stifled. Lenny Bruce demonstrated how far you could push a society as repressed as ours and how much you could get away with, but Elvis kicked "How Much Is That Doggie in the Window" *out* the window and replaced it with "Let's fuck." The rest of us are still reeling from the impact. Sexual chaos reigns currently, but out of chaos may flow true understanding and harmony, and either way Elvis almost singlehandedly opened the floodgates. That night in Detroit, a night I will never forget, he had but to ever so slightly move one shoulder muscle, not even a shrug, and the girls in the gallery hit by its ray screamed, fainted, howled in heat. Literally, every time this man moved any part of his body the slightest centimeter, tens or tens of thousands of people went berserk. Not Sinatra, not Jagger, not the Beatles, nobody you can come up with ever elicited such hysteria among so many. And this after a decade and a half of crappy records, of making a point of not trying.

If love truly is going out of fashion forever, which I do not believe, then along with our nurtured indifference to each other will be an even more contemptuous indifference to each others' objects of reverence. I thought it was Iggy Stooge, you thought it was Joni Mitchell or whoever else seemed to speak for your own private, entirely circumscribed situation's many pains and few ecstasies. We will continue to fragment in this manner, because solipsism holds all the cards at present; it is a king whose domain engulfs even Elvis's. But I can guarantee you one thing: we will never again agree on anything as we agreed on Elvis. So I won't bother saying good-bye to his corpse. I will say good-bye to you.

1977

Greg Shaw

More than a style of rock writing, Greg Shaw (1949–2004) helped develop a new medium: the 'zine. Though the two are intimately related, the informal feel of the 'zine synched up nicely with a chatty, participatory style of writing. His self-published *Mojo-Navigator Rock & Roll News* debuted in August 1966; during its one-year run, Shaw managed to turn a spotlight on the burgeoning Bay Area rock scene, and to inspire better-known successors like *Rolling Stone* and *Crawdaddy*. But it was his work on the formative DIY periodical *Who Put the Bomp* (later shortened to *Bomp!*) in the 1970s that inspired countless other fans of bands that were virtually ignored by mainstream publications to develop 'zines of their own. When punk broke, Shaw was ready for it, as his misleadingly titled "In Defense of Rock Theory" (1977) makes gloriously clear. *Bomp!* soon spawned a record label, issuing crucial releases from acts such as Devo, The Weirdos, and The Germs— bands that Shaw was among the first to champion in print. Shaw would go on to contribute to numerous other publications, but his most lasting legacy is his demonstration that a fan could become a critic with just two tools: a love of music and a copy machine.

▼ ▼

In Defense of Rock Theory

THERE'S SO much happening these days that it's all any of us can do to keep up with the news & events of the day, even with the hundreds of new magazines devoted to it. But with oceans of ink being spilled on punk coverage, the question of *why* all this is taking place, in this particular fashion, has been relatively overlooked. A few valuable 'think pieces' have appeared in the British pop weeklies, and over here in such wide-circulation papers as *The Village Voice* and *The New York Times* but no professional rock magazine, nor any fanzine, has run an analysis of recent events that was more than a superficial rehash of one of these.

Most articles of this nature have contained enough unique observations that I never tire of reading them, however it does seem to me that they all begin their arguments with a single unproven assumption: that rock & roll is coming back now because it *had* to, with the old stars getting lazy, a new generation coming up, sociological conditions, *bla bla bla*. It's all too easy to take one look at this dazzling spectacle and conclude that it was simply inevitable, but I think there's a lot more to it than that, and it's an important enough phenomenon to merit somewhat closer scrutiny . . .

Look, none of this just *happened*. A lot of *BOMP* readers have always held the belief that rock & roll would eventually have its day again, but we believed it back in the days when to do so made you an outcast, and I won't soon forget the 8 years I spent clinging to a conviction that might as well have been religious for all the foundation it had in observable reality. How can these critics, who only last year occupied their minds with devising elaborate theories to explain why rock & roll was dead forever, totally overlook the significance of what's happening, even as they rave about it?

When you contemplate the monstrous weight under which rock & roll has struggled, the multi-billion dollar music industry dedicated to keeping it down, the superstar system and its complete negation of new talent, the stranglehold of radio, the closed doors of the record and concert industries, the obscene wealth concentrated in the mechanisms of disco, arena rock, etc, and the self-protective instincts of the *mafioso* types who run it all—the fact that all this is being swept aside by a few kids with nothing going for them but an insane commitment to raw energy and total contempt for everything else . . . well it seems like a miracle to me, and one that's still taking place right in front of our eyes. The fascination of it is greater, for me, than any individual band or record could be. Not to mention that such a dramatic and literal answer to our prayers ought to inspire a little respectful humility in its presence.

The theme of this column is rock theory and how, in my view, its formulation over the last 4 or 5 years has played a central role in creating this revolution that so many are taking for granted. Although I've been typecast as one of the prime eggheads in this field and will admit to some inspirational responsibility for the excesses that have been committed in its name, I've always tried to draw the line between real bullshit—trying to "justify" rock in terms of modern art, film critique, literary tradition, "auteur theory," etc—and the kind of questions that any rock & roll fan who cares about the music, has a brain, and doesn't mind using it, is gonna want answers to.

I don't think there's any great Meaning in rock & roll . . . and I have little patience with those who seek it in Dylan lyrics or the lost chords of the Moody Blues. To me, rock theory has always started from the fact that this music, when it's done right, has an amazing power to make me (and a lot of other people too, presumably) feel great in a way that nothing else can. The *experience* of hearing a great record or seeing a great concert or just participating in an active pop culture is what we all crave and keep coming back for, and I think the goal of rock theory, if we're gonna have such a thing at all, should be to figure out how and why it achieves these effects, and thereby maybe make it possible for us to have more & greater such experiences. "Experience" is really the key word here—I'm convinced that the only "meaningful" way to relate to and get the most from rock & roll is to let its spirit of youth, strength, exuberance, independence, rebellion, honesty, hipness/awareness, sensuality, etc., penetrate and reinforce these qualities in ourselves, which we then display in our lives in our method of speaking, dressing, acting, and dealing with the world.

I'm convinced the *real* reason so many British kids have jumped into the punk scene has a lot less to do with their intellectual reaction to the conditions around them than with their gut reaction. Very few of them are punks because of the ideas they read in the massive treatises in *NME*, etc—they leave that kind of thing to the scribes who must seek explanations. The kids are into it because they value the fact that the pop culture of punk and their involvement in it provides a central focus in their lives that gives them more satisfaction than the life they had without it.

Getting back to where we started, I believe that something extremely significant is taking place, of which punk rock is only the first symptom, namely the assertion of rock & roll, on its own terms, supported actively and consciously by the people who care about it—us, the fans. This is a point worth stressing if only because all the pundits have ignored it. None of this is happening accidentally. It has been the activities of people like us, writing in fanzines, forming groups to play the kind of music we believe in regardless its commercial potential, collecting records and learning rock history and by discovering the great music of the past, turning our friends on to it, etc, in ever widening circles, raising the general awareness of the record-buying public to the point where it can make educated decisions largely based on ideas derived from fanzine writers . . . If it weren't for this trend, which has been growing steadily since about 1973 when fanzines first started to proliferate and has now begun to snowball, I see no reason why anti-rock shouldn't have been lapped up forever by the same audiences that have accepted it since 1968 (and still largely do).

Despite the impression we receive from all the press that's been devoted to the New Wave, in reality we're a long way from home free. Aesthetically, sure, the old has been proven superfluous and all the cultural nabobs have heralded the new age, but the Eagles still sell 10,000,000 albums each time out and the Ramones are lucky to pay their rent each month . . . So it's important now that we (as readers of this magazine, I suppose you may all consider yourselves members of, in Robert Christgau's phrase, the "vanguard audience.") really understand the forces at work promoting the rock & roll renaissance so we can do our best to support them.

Let's get back to some rock theory. My reputation in this area stems from the days in 1972 (and '73 and '74 and '75 . . .) when I was going on and on in the pages of *Creem* and *PRM* about some invisible-but-imminent Pop Revival, which convinced a lot of people (including the editors of the aforementioned *Creem*, who expelled me from its pages as a result) that I had become completely unbalanced and no longer capable of "serious rock criticism." There was, then, no evidence that any such thing was taking shape or any sane reason for assuming it might—all the weight of the music industry and prevailing cultural trends was against it.

I felt, along with a lot of people, that some kind of rock & roll revival (and not the Richard Nader kind) *had* to happen sooner or later, because I just couldn't accept that a thing which had been the most dynamic artform of our time could fizzle out into complete decadence in less than 10 years. So, starting from this emotional/intuitional position, I looked for avenues by which the desired results could be reached with the resources at hand. This, for me was the beginning of rock theory, and its development has preoccupied me ever since.

In the first place, this approach to rock theory seems valid because it cuts through the bullshit and gets right to the central problem of why we don't have enough great music or a decent pop culture, and finds the answers. Secondly, the ideas that have evolved from this type of theory are important because they have been proven correct almost to the tiniest detail by events of the past 2 years. If anyone had stood up before the assembled Rock Writers of the World at the abortive 1973 convention in Memphis and suggested that within 4 years the Presidents of companies like Warner Bros and Columbia would be scrambling to sign the latest "Punk Rock" groups, every last one of them would have rolled on the floor with laughter. Punk Rock in those days was a quaint fanzine term for a transient form of mid-'60s music considered so bad (by the standards of the time) that it was a joke to the "critics" who made their livings analyzing the neuroses of Joni Mitchell. If you had predicted furthermore that people like Sky Saxon, Roky Erickson, Patti Smith and Iggy would become culture heroes and that the music press would be made obsolete by millions of swarming fanzines writing about bands doing songs like "Surfin' Bird" . . . you might well have been taken away to a rubber room! And yet, in this short time, it's just about come to that. The megalithic world of Led Zep and Elton John is tottering before the slings of a vocal minority *who owe their existence to the collective efforts of what was, a few years ago, a lunatic fringe of surf nuts, Beatlemaniacs, punk rockers, discophiles and fanzine writers—ie,* rock fandom.

None of this had to happen the way it did. The time was ripe for a change; logically, it should've been a change to the heavy metal "kick ass" rock of Kiss, Nugent, Rex, Thin Lizzy, Starz, etc. That's the new trend the record companies and magazines like *Creem* were pushing. This punk rock stuff was *not* inevitable! Everything that's happened in the New Wave can be traced back directly to the efforts of rock fandom—acting under a common philosophy and in accordance with the principles that I refer to here as rock theory. Just in case anyone fails to see the connection, let me trace how it developed in my own writings and thoughts over the past few years.

Previously, "rock theory" had consisted of the notion that some mystical "Ten Year Cycle" was at work. When ten years and more had passed and the '70s had not repeated the pattern of the '60s, it was time to stop taking it on faith and start looking for the source of the changes that were necessary. It seemed to me, in formulating my "Pop Revival" essays of 1973, that the root of the problem lay back in 1967, when the "vanguard audience" threw its weight behind the progressive/ underground rock built on eclecticism, extended pieces, long jams—in short, abandonment of form and structure. (The influential force of this vanguard audience, incidentally, has been dramatically proven by the now-enormous mass acceptance of free-form rock, a style essentially *un*commercial by virtue of its lack of memorable hooks & melodies—if *that* stuff is selling millions today because a few hip people liked it in '67, just imagine what 10 years from now will be like . . . !) Although it was producing some interesting music at the time, the seeds of later damage were sown in the creation of a schism between this music, which found its outlet in concerts and the new FM stations, and the former mainstream of rock, AM radio and its attendant industries. As a result, AM pop lost most of its rock element and became more sterile than ever, while rock lost its sense of pop and went to the extremes of "heaviness." Not only the music, but the audience and everything else seemed permanently fragmented.

In light of this, I thought the only hope was to unite rock and pop, since in my view the best records had always contained strong elements of both. Therefore I got excited about and threw my support behind anything that seemed part of a move in this direction. So in saying that "Good Grief Christina" by Chicory Tip was the most important single of '73, above "Ramblin' Man," I was correct according to my theory, but deranged by any other criterion . . .

With nothing else to go on, I took the attitude that it was better to try and get people excited about stuff that would lead to better things than to concentrate on what was bad.

As I developed this theory, I began to dream that if enough people were only exposed to fanzines and the writing of people who had been inspired by the great rock of the '50s and '60s, maybe through mail-order channels the readers of all these fanzines could collectively form enough of a minority power bloc to begin demanding the music they liked from the industry, and directly supporting those who were making it. Not only did this prove true, but the size of this educated, rock-history-oriented audience grew vastly beyond anything I had envisioned. A handful of fanzines became scores, then hundreds, and in turn spawned powerful, widely distributed regional music & entertainment magazines that, following *BOMP*'s lead and writing exhaustive histories of their local music roots, inspired countless kids in cities around the country to start building up their local scenes as they had once been.

The other idea I always clung to as an article of faith was the hypothesis that rock had to periodically renew itself by going back to the roots, or more precisely, to the high mark of the previous peak era, for direct inspiration. Thus the Beatles started as a Chuck Berry revival band, and any '70s phenomenon would have to start by mining the mid-'60s. This idea lay behind my unwavering belief that bands like the Raspberries and the Flamin' Groovies were on the right track, and there were always enough people moving in the right direction throughout the early '70s to keep all of us hoping. Despite that, I never dreamed how far it would go, with bands who had started as fanzine readers, with the idea of doing 13th Floor Elevators and Count Five songs for the sheer fun of it, being hailed in '76 as the leaders of a new avant-garde movement!

What it boils down to is the fact that my wildest fantasies of 3 years ago have been totally dwarfed by the reality of what *applied* rock theory has accomplished. I sort of figured we'd have 5 years or so of imitation punk and Merseybeat records on odd independent labels sold thru fanzines, then maybe there'd be enough buyers out there to petition the industry to let one or two of these groups put out albums, as a public service perhaps. The principles on which we, as fans, based our efforts to promote the early stages of what they now call the New Wave have been proven not only correct but rock-solid. This means, I think, something truly revolutionary. Where all the radical rhetoric of the '60s failed to accomplish anything, a few logical deductions in the '70s have given us (rock fandom) the keys to the music industry, the power to keep the music on the right track and make sure it just keeps getting better and better. Always before, when things just started getting good, it somehow ended, slipped away or turned into something else. Eight years were lost because nobody knew what to do about it. Now that we're beginning to understand what makes this whole world of pop music, pop culture and the music industry tick; the mere first inklings of power (power of the press, power of the dollar, opinion-making power through the people we influence as the acknowledged "experts") has already resulted in changes of incalculable proportions.

All this was accomplished through a primitive, shaky, groping form of rock theory. Now that various premises are being tested and proven by events, there's no reason our understanding of the process can't become firm enough to give us—the fans—absolute control over the direction of rock & roll. In my view of rock theory, that has always been the goal, and it's closer than a lot of people may think.

1977

ROBERT CHRISTGAU

Over five decades of work, Robert Christgau (b. 1942) has placed himself at the rhetorical center of pop criticism as a serious enterprise. His writing has justified that place, with its inexhaustible curiosity and combative verve, and a range of reference and dynamic syntax that allies his voice with the New Journalism movement. His terse, letter-graded *Consumer Guide* columns—which began running in *The Village Voice* in 1969—provided a template for album assessments that has been inescapably influential, even for his doubters. Christgau's métier has always been short-form writing: terse, opinionated, short-deadline work that manages to be both timely and seemingly timeless. In the wake of Prince's unexpected early death, Christgau's reviews of Prince's albums provide both a wonderful overview of a remarkable musician's work and a fascinating cross section of the writing career of one of the country's most influential working critics. Christgau's editorial stewardship of younger writers and his creation of the *Voice*'s "Pazz and Jop Poll," a survey of year-end critical averages from hundreds of fellow critics, both consolidated and extended that influence; the 2002 festschrift *Don't Stop 'til You Get Enough* provides eloquent testimony from many of those whose careers he has nurtured. Born in Queens, Christgau's vantage as a resolute New Yorker granted him a front-row seat for the evolution of punk, disco, and hip-hop; his alertness to developments in black popular music after '60s soul was unusually prescient. If his self-appointment as "the Dean of American Rock Critics" was always partly a joke, no one but Christgau could have borne the title so credibly.

▼ ▼

Prince

1970s

Prince: *For You* (Warner Bros. '78). Like most in-studio one-man bands, the nineteen-year-old kid who pieced this disco-rock-pop-funk concoction together has a weakness for the programmatic—lots of chops, not much challenge. But I like "Baby," about making one, and "Soft and Wet," ditto only he doesn't know it yet. And his falsetto beats Stevie Wonder's, not to mention Emitt Rhodes's.   **B–**

Prince: *Prince* (Warner Bros. '79). This boy is going to be a big star, and he deserves it—he's got a great line, "I want to come inside you" is good enough, but (in a different song) the simple "I'm physically attracted to you" sets new standards of "naive," winning candor. The vulnerable teen-macho falsetto idea is pretty good too. But he does leave something to be desired in the depth-of-feeling department—you know, soul.   **B+**

1980s

Prince: *Dirty Mind* (Warner Bros. '80). After going gold in 1979 as an utterly uncrossed over falsetto love man, he takes care of the song-writing, transmutes the persona, revs up the guitar, muscles into the vocals, leans down hard on a rock-steady, funk-tinged four-four, and conceptualizes—about sex, mostly. Thus he becomes the first commercially viable artist in a decade to claim the visionary high ground of Lennon and Dylan and Hendrix (and Jim Morrison), whose rebel turf has been ceded to such marginal heroes-by-fiat as Patti Smith and John Rotten-Lydon. Brashly lubricious where the typical love man plays the lead in "He's So Shy," he specializes here in full-fledged fuckbook fantasies—the kid sleeps with his sister and digs it, sleeps with his girlfriend's boyfriend and doesn't, stops a wedding by gamahuching the bride on her way to church. Mick Jagger should fold up his penis and go home.   **A**

Prince: *Controversy* (Warner Bros. '81). Maybe *Dirty Mind* wasn't a
tour de force after all; maybe it was dumb luck. The socially conscious songs are catchy enough, but they spring from the mind of a
rather confused young fellow, and while his politics get better when
he sticks to his favorite subject, which is s-e-x, nothing here is as
far-out and on-the-money as "Head" or "Sister" or the magnificent
"When You Were Mine." In fact, for a while I thought the best new
song was "Jack U Off," an utter throwaway. But that was before
the confused young fellow climbed onto the sofa with me and my
sweetie during "Do Me, Baby."   **A–**

Prince: *1999* (Warner Bros. '82). Like every black pop auteur, Prince
commands his own personal groove, and by stretching his flat funk
forcebeat onto two discs worth of deeply useful dance tracks he
makes his most convincing political statement to date—about race,
the one subject where his instincts always serve him reliably. I mean,
you don't hang on his every word in re sex or the end of the world,
now do you?   **A–**

Prince and the Revolution: *Purple Rain* (Paisley Park '84). Like the
cocky high speed of the brazenly redundant "Baby I'm a Star," the
demurely complaisant "Thank you" that answers "You're sheer perfection" signals an artist in full formal flower, and he's got something to say. Maybe even a structure: the frantic self-indulgence
of "Let's Go Crazy" gives way to a bitter on-again-off-again affair
that climaxes in the loving resignation of the title song—from in-
this-life-you're-on-your-own to in-this-life-heaven-is-other-people
(and-you're-still-on-your-own). But insofar as his messages are the
same old outrageous ones, they've lost steam: "1999" is a more irresistible dance lesson for the edge of the apocalyse than "Let's Go
Crazy," "Head" and "Jack U Off" more salacious than the ground-
out "Darling Nikki." He may have gained maturity, but like many
grown-ups before him, he gets a little blocked making rebel-rock
out of it.   **A–**

Prince and the Revolution: *Around the World in a Day* (Warner Bros. '85). It's pretty strange, given that he looked like a visionary not long ago. But this arrested adolescent obviously don't know nuthin about nuthin—except maybe his own life, which for all practical purposes ended in his adolescence, since even for a pop star he does his damnedest to keep the world out. So while his sexual fantasies are outrageous only in their callous predictability and his ballads compelling only as shows of technique, they sure beat his reflexive antinomianism and dim politics. Which suggests why the solid if decidedly unpsychedelic musical pleasures our young craftsman makes available here don't wash. Only the crass "Raspberry Beret" and maybe the crooning "Condition of the Heart" are worth your time.   **B–**

Prince and the Revolution: *Parade* (Paisley Park '86). Musically, this anything but retro fusion of *Fresh*'s foundation and *Sgt. Pepper*'s filigrees is nothing short of amazing. Only the tin-eared will overlook the unkiltered wit of its pop-baroque inventions, only the lead-assed deny its lean, quirky grooves, both of which are so arresting that at first you don't take in the equally spectacular assurance with which the singer skips from mood to mood and register to register. I just wish the thing weren't such a damn kaleidoscope: far from unifying its multifarious parts, its soundtrack function destroys what little chance the lyrics have of bringing it together. Christopher is Prince, I guess, but nothing here tempts me to make sure. I'd much rather find out whether the former Rogers Nelson really takes all this trouble just so he can die and/or make love underneath whatever kind of moon, or if he has something less banal in mind.   **A–**

Prince: *Sign 'o' the Times* (Paisley Park '87). No formal breakthrough, and despite the title/lead/debut single, no social relevance move either, which given the message of "The Cross" (guess, just guess) suits me fine. Merely the most gifted pop musician of his generation proving what a motherfucker he is for two discs start to finish. With helpmate turns from Camille, Susannah, Sheila E., Sheena

Easton, he's back to his one-man-band tricks, so collective creation
fans should be grateful that at least the second-hottest groove here,
after the galvanic "U Got the Look," is Revolution live. Elsewhere
Prince-the-rhythm-section works on his r&b so Prince-the-harmony-
group can show off vocal chops that make Stevie Wonder sound like
a struggling ventriloquist. Yet the voices put over real emotions—
studio solitude hasn't reactivated his solipsism. The objects of his
desire are also objects of interest, affection, and respect. Some of
them he may not even fuck. Original grade: A.   **A+**

Prince: *The Black Album* (unlabeled cassette '88). Uncle Jam's sonic
wallop and communal craziness are the project's obvious starting
point, though Prince will never be as funny. Even better, they're
also its finish line. Except for "When 2 R in Love," easily the lamest
thing on two otherwise distinct records, the bassy murk never lets
up, and at its weirdest—an unpleasant impersonation of a dumbfuck
B-boy that's no lost masterpiece and far more arresting than anything on the official product—it's as dark as "Cosmic Slop." With
retail sources drying up (I have a fourth-generation dub from a relatively inside source myself), those who pine for heavy funk should
nag their local dealers. This is capitalism, so supply'll meet demand,
right? [Available on CD in Japan, rumor has it.]   **A–**

Prince: *Lovesexy* (Paisley Park '88). He's a talented little guy, and this
has plenty of pizzazz. But I'll take *The Black Album*'s fat-bottomed
whomp over its attention-grabbing beats and halfway decent tunes
any day, and despite appearances it sure ain't where he explains why
sexiness is next to godliness—lyrically it's sloppy if not pseudo if not
stupid. This is doubly bothersome because added religious content is
what it's supposed to have over its not terribly shocking alternative.
Leading one to the obvious conclusion that the real reason the little
guy made the switch was that he was scared to reveal how, shall we
say, unpop he could be.   **B+**

1990s

Prince: *Graffiti Bridge* (Paisley Park '90). On his third studio double in a decade, he's definitely cheating. Half the music isn't really his, and the other half is overly subtle if not rehashed or just weak: title track, generational anthem, and lead single all reprise familiar themes, and the ballads fall short of the exquisite vocalese that can make his slow ones sing. But some of the subtle stuff—"Tick, Tick, Bang"'s PE-style electrobeats, say—is pretty out, most of the received stuff is pretty surefire, and from unknowns to old pros, his cameos earn their billings. Also, there's half a great Time album here—did he steal it or just conceive it? **B+**

Prince and the New Power Generation: *Diamonds and Pearls* (Paisley Park/Warner Bros. '91). Doesn't know his own new power ("Willing and Able," "Jug-head," "Cream"). ******

Prince and the New Power Generation: *[File Under Prince]* (Paisley Park '92). Designed to prove his utter inexhaustibility in the wake of *Diamonds and Pearls,* by some stroke of commerce his best-selling album since *Purple Rain,* this absurdly designated "rock soap opera" (is he serious? is he ever? is he ever not?) proves mainly that he's got the funk. I confess I'm too square to regale the guests at my all-ages dance party with "Sexy M.F.," a title extended to six syllables in its recorded version. But "My Name Is Prince" clears up a question posed by the title, a rune available on floppy disc to any publication willing to take his guff. And "Blue Light," a ballad that's got the reggae, is a sexy motherfucker. **A−**

Prince: *The Hits/The B-Sides* (Paisley Park/Warner Bros. '93). Take as a given that this is an overpriced exploitation or indulgence, depending on your point of view—that is, whether you're Prince or not. The two discs of A sides are indeed choice, but most come from albums that yield more choice (not to say choicer) stuff, and their recontextualization isn't as jaw-dropping as an admirer of our greatest popular musician might hope. Whether the duplications merit the tariff you can decide for yourself. So would the B sides justify purchase on their own were the little man so generous as to make them available as such (or were the world to end, whichever comes first)? And the answer is: maybe. The porny stuff—especially "Irresistible Bitch," "Scarlet Pussy," the wicked "Feel U Up," and the absolutely classic "Erotic City"—is must-hear for any sex fan. The funky stuff is fonky. The dog bit is like bow-wow. And the ballads are of every description, including godawful.   **B+**

Prince: *Come* (Warner Bros. '94). Porn now an annoyance, funk still a surprise ("Loose!" "Pheromone").   *******

[File Under Prince]: *The Gold Experience* (Warner Bros./NPG '95). After two or three plays, convinced that "P Control" and "Endorphinmachine" slam harder than any hip hop I've heard in years, I shrugged and recalled that, after all, I already knew he was the most gifted recording artist of the era. But this album documents more than professional genius rampant—all of them do that. This album is a renewal. It's as sex-obsessed as ever, only with more juice—"Shhh" and "319" especially pack the kind of jolt sexy music seldom gets near and hard music never does. And you'd best believe "Shhh" and "319" are hard—not for years has the auteur (as opposed to some hired gat) sounded so black, and not for years has the guitarist sounded so rock. As for the ballads, they suffer only by their failure to dominate. One of them has already stormed the radio—and another, good for him, takes too many risks to follow.   **A**

Prince: *"Don't Talk 2 Strangers," "Girl 6"* (*Girl 6* [ST], Warner Bros. '96)   **Choice Cut**

[File Under Prince]: *Chaos and Disorder* (Warner Bros. '96). Always a slippery devil, he's damn near vaporized commercially over the past few years, as has his promotional budget, basically because he's reached that certain age—way too familiar for ye olde shock of the new, way too boyish for intimations of immortality. So it's understandable that what's sworn to be "the last original material recorded by [File Under Prince] 4 warner brothers records" has been ignored all around. But anybody expecting a kissoff or a throwaway radically underestimates his irrepressible musicality. Apropos of nothing, here's a guitar album for your earhole, enhanced by a fresh if not shocking array of voices and trick sounds and cluttered now and then by horns. Theme song: "I Rock, Therefore I Am." And right, WEA, it wouldn't have been a hit even with some muscle behind it.   **A–**

[File Under Prince]: *Emancipation* (NPG '96). Writing the book for the young turks of a reborn, historically hip r&b—three disks and hours of liberation, hubris, divine superfluity, and proof that he can come all night even if by six in the morning it takes too long and he never actually gets hard. Yet although there's not a bad track in the 36, I bet he himself would have trouble remembering them all, and hear nothing that tops the Delfonics and Stylistics covers, which latter wasn't the debut single for nothing and flopped anyway. Great grooves abound, however. As does great singing. Harmonies too. Did I mention that the horns are surprisingly cool? And hey, the little guy has a sense of humor.   **A–**

[File Under Prince]: *Rave Un2 the Joy Fantastic* (Arista '99). Put it this way—two decades after "What'd I Say," Ray Charles's shtick was a lot tireder ("Hot Wit U," "Undisputed").   **

2000s

Prince: *Musicology* (Columbia 2004). The title track he provides his fourth major label since 1996 states this entry's noticeably spare and controlled m.o. It's a straight James Brown rip—Jimmy Nolen guitar, understated bass curlicue, syncopated tom, daubs of organ and faux horn, irregular backup vocals, with every sound, presumably including the thugs and munchkins, provided by Prince himself. The back-in-the-day lyric claiming JB, Sly, Earth, Wind & Fire, old-school rap, and bands-not-turntables might render all this unspontaneous multitracking a contradiction, but hell—he contains multitudes, and he loves playing with himself. "Illusion, Coma, Pimp & Circumstance" is just as lean and more out; the requisite "Life 'O' the Party" adds femme vox and femme sax to Prince's one-man singing group and ersatz horn charts. And then, having gotten our attention with an uptempo trifecta, this lifelong tease slows the pace, permanently—without wrecking the record. Pleasant shocks lurk near the surface and go against the flow of the quality material, and almost everything packs payback: apt rock guitar turning into apt tasty guitar (lick me); vocal calculations that could only have been improvised (right?); godfathered horn charts, some live (Maceo!). **A–**

Prince: *3121* (Universal 2006). It could be argued that music this masterful waives all claim to the sound of surprise—until you pay attention. Sure "Love" and "Satisfied" and "Fury" constitute a standard sequence, key funk to torch r&b to u-got-the-rock—but only by genius standards. Sure he overdubs all the time, but he risks letting the Other play bass and drums on the over-under-sideways-down title tune—and then immediately prefabs the cockeyed "Lolita" by himself. The dubiosities he induces NPG fans to collect prove only that geniuses know who their friends are. I'm back to suspecting that, at 47, the Abstemious One can keep laying top-shelf stuff on the public for as long as he's in the mood. Even if he gets on your nerves, treat him nice. **A–**

Prince: *Planet Earth* (NPG/Columbia 2007). Viva Las Vegas and later for Viagra—but not never ("Guitar," "The One U Wanna C"). *******

Prince: *Art Official Age* (Warner Bros./NPG 2014). Our greatest composer-performer of romantic nu-funk erotica wakes up 40 years later wishing he was Janelle Monae ("Breakfast Can Wait," "Funknroll"). *****

JON PARELES

No critic's career could better describe pop music's steady trajectory toward institutional recognition than that of Jon Pareles (b. 1953). After graduating with a degree in classical music from Yale—where he also played in rock bands and was a disc jockey and station manager at the college radio station—Pareles began sending his earliest pieces to *Crawdaddy*. He moved to New York City to become that magazine's managing editor, and soon shifted to *Rolling Stone*, where he both wrote and edited; in 1983, with Patricia Romanowski, he edited *Rolling Stone's Encyclopedia of Rock*. After filling in for Robert Christgau as music editor of *The Village Voice* during his yearlong absence, in 1982 Pareles was hired by Robert Palmer at *The New York Times*. By the end of the decade he had succeeded Palmer as the *Times*' chief critic and assigning editor for popular music. In that position he has established himself as the consummate "professional" rock critic, a tutor to innumerable younger writers, and a newspaperman by disposition and preference, one who has stated his preference for the "instant gratification" of daily publication. In an interview with Rockcritics.com Pareles said, "If pop culture is society's id, music is the fastest, most polymorphous, least compromised vision of that id."

▼ ▼

The Cars' Power Steering

For some reason, when we're on tour all our dressing rooms have
blackboards. So we chalk up New Laws of the Universe like,
"What is not there, will be," and "All roads lead to other roads."
—GREG HAWKES, *KEYBOARDIST, THE CARS*

YOUNG RICHARD OTCASEK pulled the mysterious little dashboard
lever and the car *roared*. Nice. And no small accomplishment. He'd
been working secretly on his father's Mercury Comet every day after
school, getting it ready for the nights when anybody could enter the
races at Thompson's drag strip in Cleveland. Lots of kids brought their
family cars, souped up or not, just to try the track. Richard had done
that too, but his heap was a loser, a bomb—no torque, no speed, no
damned fun. Richard knew automobiles, and he was confident the
Comet would never lead the pack.

So he'd "customized" the car's exhaust pipe. Clandestinely, he'd
installed one extra lever on the dashboard—nah, his father wouldn't
notice—that controlled the muffler. One simple tug and he'd be wide
open; the putt-putt would turn into a dynamo. *Vrooom.* Maybe he'd
never burn rubber in the straightaway, but now he'd at least be able
to make as much noise as any hot rod in the lineup. Screaming down
Thompson's track, not quite in last place, young Richard Otcasek would
be enveloped in the full, rich roar he'd always desired. . . .

A few days later, when the Comet's muffler broke, there was hell to
pay at the Otcasek household. Richard's father was unforgiving. As he
tells the story now, Ric Ocasek (he dropped the *t* for verbal stream-
lining) seems quizzical, his azure eyes clouding over as he recalls his
father's reaction. "You know," he muses somberly, "he *never* understood why I did it."

OCASEK DRIVES FAST, with one hand on the radio. Along Cambridge's
Massachusetts Avenue, which extends from Harvard Square to the Massachusetts Institute of Technology (MIT) and into Boston's Back Bay,

the traffic and pedestrians are, as usual, moving in flagrant violation of both law and common sense. Yet Ocasek, leader and songwriter for the Cars, steers his white Volvo with none of the typical flinching or hasty maneuvering typical of Boston drivers. We pause as a brigade armed with slide rules occupies a crosswalk; Ocasek groans when I mention the Beantown college circuit, but obligingly points out the MIT building in which the Cars played mixers just over a year ago.

Meanwhile, his slim fingers dance upon the radio buttons. Each song gets about seven seconds to prove itself, and if it doesn't pass scrutiny, Ric punches it into oblivion. After nixing five songs in less than a minute, he shoots a troubled glance my way. "Have you ever noticed?" he ventures, sending the needle one notch further across the dial. "Sometimes they *all* sound the same."

I'd been waiting for a Cars song to pop out of the Volvo's speakers. Ever since their debut on December 31st, 1976, at Pease Air Force Base in New Hampshire, the Cars have been the very model of a modern regional band. They quickly gained a core following at the Rat, a.k.a. the Rathskeller, downtown Boston's prime New Wave club. In March 1977, a sudden cancellation and some fast talking by Cars manager Fred Lewis netted them the opening slot in a Bob Seger concert at Boston's 4200-seat Music Hall. By summer, a demo tape that included "Just What I Needed" was heard regularly on local FM stations and the lines for the band's Rat gigs stretched from Kenmore Square out to Fenway Park. (Well, *almost.*)

Elektra Records signed the Cars in November and set up a six-week recording schedule for February and March 1978. But it took only twenty-one days in London (twelve to record, nine to mix) to complete their debut LP. Released in June, *The Cars* will probably be platinum by the time you read this story. Everybody liked it: New Wavers recognized Ocasek's Velvet Underground debts and the cunning ambivalence of his lyrics, while rock fans and radio programmers picked up on the catchy tunes and meticulous arrangements. The album has produced two exhilarating hit singles, "Just What I Needed" and "My Best Friend's Girl," both propelled by punchy rhythms and Ocasek's poutful foghorn vocals. Less than two years after their first performance, the

Cars have headlined at such New England arenas as the 14,000-seat Providence Civic Center and the even larger Boston Garden. With characteristic terseness, Ocasek sums up: "We were ready."

Indeed, it seems the Cars *were* ready—and not by accident. But what is most intriguing about the band is that its enthusiasm is not apparent. On a personal level, a curious kind of wariness reigns, while musically and in performance, a great deal of careful preparation is in evidence. Just as leader Ric Ocasek once took pains to make his father's old Comet at least sound like a winner, his group demonstrates a passion for form, while its interest in substance remains undefined. Ocasek's detached demeanor appears to have rubbed off on the rest of the guys; on- and offstage, emotions are kept in check. But aren't emotions, and content, what rock is all about?

OCASEK CASUALLY leans his rangy frame against a wall of Boston's Paradise Theater while an opening act drones inside the music room. The place might as well be his, considering that his band sold out six shows in a row last time it played here, headlining what is usually a showcase club. On this weekend night, latecomers straggling through the entrance can't help gawking at the snazzy outlandishness of Ric's badge-festooned, black-and-white leather jacket, pleated tan pants and white satin sneakers. College students in down parkas file by until one stops, sizes up Ocasek and inquires, "Are you a *Car*?" Ric nods. Another devotee. There are 5000 unopened fan letters at the Cars' Carlisle, Massachusetts, post office box.

The Cars' smooth ascent followed a decade-long countdown. Ocasek, who claims to be twenty-nine but looks a few years older, says he was in his early twenties when he met Cars bassist and vocalist Benjamin Orr (formerly Orzechowski) in the Columbus, Ohio, office of a now-defunct booking agency where they both worked.

Ocasek was born into a Polish Catholic family in Baltimore, the son of a computer systems analyst, and attended a parochial elementary school. He was kicked out in fifth grade for offenses he insists he doesn't remember. "I wasn't feeling too good about being pushed around or having to believe in spirits and things," he minimizes. "There were a lot of fears, a lot of restrictions that people built into your mind."

Ocasek preferred to hang out with the drakes. "In Baltimore, if you were a drake you were a hardass," he explains. "Kids would start little gangs and they'd all get matching jackets. Gangs were named after fraternities, for some reason, like Sigma Chi, Phi Delta. . . . It was rampant, it was fun. You'd have BB guns, shoot pigeons. Nothing really heavy."

Ocasek's grandmother gave him a guitar when he was about ten because he was enraptured by the Crickets' "That'll Be the Day" (which, if his recollections are accurate, would put his age at about thirty-one), but he gave it up after three months of lessons. As a teenager, Ric prized his independence and rapidly grew estranged from his parents; he'd organize expeditions from Baltimore to Ocean City, Maryland, and hang out on the boardwalk there for weeks at a time. When he was sixteen, his father was transferred in his job and the family moved to Cleveland. During his last two years of high school, Ocasek decided he'd need good grades if he wanted to go to college—so he became a bookworm and got them.

Neither Antioch College nor Bowling Green State University held Ocasek's interest for long. When he dropped out for good, he returned to guitar, which he approached in typically pragmatic fashion: "I started immediately writing; I thought that was the thing to do. In fact, the first song I ever wrote, I copyrighted. After I started writing songs I figured it would be good to start a band. Sometimes I'd put together a band just to hear my songs. If a person couldn't play that well, there'd be fewer outside ideas to incorporate."

Ben Orr's approach to rock & roll was a bit more sophisticated. The teenage Orzechowski had fronted the house band on the Cleveland TV rock show *Upbeat*, which featured British invaders like the Rolling Stones, Peter and Gordon and the Dave Clark Five. As a child Ben had entertained his parents' friends by miming Elvis Presley records: "I always knew I had something special," he says, straight-faced. He dropped out of high school and became involved in Cleveland's then-modest music scene, writing songs, doing studio production, playing sessions on drums, bass, guitar, keyboards. Three weeks after he met Ocasek, Orr worked on one of Ric's demos, inaugurating their partnership.

Physically they make an unlikely pair. Ocasek is lanky, obsidian haired, with high, angular cheekbones; Orr is stocky and a bleached blond (including his eyebrows), with a Slavic jack-o'-lantern face punctuated by a cleft chin. Married since 1972, Ocasek is diffident, soft-spoken, while Orr takes pains to be cordial. Onstage, Ocasek hides behind his shades as Orr smiles down at the front rows. Yet Orr, who once rebelled because *Upbeat*'s producers habitually told him what to do, is for the moment content to be Ocasek's accomplice. "I like singing Ric's stuff," he says.

Ocasek seems to be strangely persuasive. And there's something in his presence—his deep-set eyes framed by midnight-black hair, perhaps, or his pallor and elongation—that is almost spectral. Even five-year-old Eron Ocasek treats his father like some supernatural being; when Ric tells Eron one night at home about which guitar is inside a certain closed case, an awed Eron assumes his daddy has X-ray eyes. When Ocasek first started putting together bands, he'd tell the musicians *which* instrument to play, albeit gently, and each would always go along. He once convinced a friend to quit a solid job and join one of his tentative groups. And while Ocasek insists—correctly—that "all the [musical] parts are what make the Cars the Cars," his subtle authority centers the group.

"We got along famously," Orr says of the early days. "It's one of those things where you have to say nothing—it's just there. And we just went on, kept going from state to state, doing our thing."

"I was attracted by Ben's voice the first night I met him," says Ocasek. "He was singing Beatles songs, and I thought he had the greatest voice. By now, we know each other so well I hardly talk to him."

Ocasek and Orr traveled from Cleveland to New York City to Woodstock, New York, to Ann Arbor, Michigan, singing Buddy Holly songs as a duo, playing hard rock as an opening act for the MC5. They'd lie to club owners and do their own songs after contracting to pump out the Top Forty. In band after band, the Ocasek/Orr axis tightened—a defense against drunken frat kids, poverty, the grind of the road. At one point, Ric was so broke he pawned Ben's guitar and Orr redeemed it without complaint.

"Once we got run out of town with guns," Ocasek recounts. "Up in Alpena, Michigan, we were doing a gig in a bar, a deer-hunters' hangout. After we played a few songs a couple of guys with rifles came up and said, 'We're hunting deer up here, but we ain't looking for you *dears*. You guys get out!' They made us leave town that night."

From the unenlightened Midwest, Ocasek and later Orr worked their way East again. This time they gravitated to the Boston area, with its promise of mental stimulation and plentiful gigs. Ocasek settled in Cambridge, Massachusetts, near Harvard Square, intrigued by the proximity of the famed university. Sometimes he dropped in on lectures for entertainment's sake. "I knew I was out of place," he chuckles, "but I enjoyed it."

Cambridge clubs preferred quiet, thoughtful fare over hard rock, and, casually adopting the prevailing local sound, Ocasek and Orr soon found themselves in a folk trio called Milkwood. "We were playing around town and somebody asked us if we wanted to make a record," Ocasek relates. "In two weeks we recorded that Milkwood thing."

Although Ocasek would prefer to forget it, Milkwood's sole album (1972, Paramount, long unavailable) is merely naive, the product of a Cambridge ethos that encouraged fingerpicking and such spacey songs as "Timetrain Wonderwheel." Nonetheless, the project had salutary effects: Ocasek learned not to stumble into business deals, and he and Orr were introduced to a future Car—keyboardist/saxophonist/arranger Greg Hawkes. "He had the simplicity concept," says Ocasek, "but he wasn't afraid to do interesting things. I knew he'd be the keyboard player I wanted."

Hawkes joined one early Ocasek/Orr group, then drifted toward steadier work: Martin Mull's "Fabulous Furniture" band, studio jobs, a local country-rock outfit called Orphan. He'd sometimes join Ric and Ben for late-night demo sessions at Northern Studios— the struggling band paying for its studio time by doing carpentry work for owner Bill Riseman.

Ocasek became a father in December of 1973, further straining his finances; he and Ben worked in clothing stores to stay solvent. But whenever he came close to bottoming out, Ocasek says, "I'd just break up the band I was in and start working on the next one."

And he was getting better at assembling them. Ocasek's early 1976 model, Cap'n Swing, thoroughly impressed Boston DJ Maxanne Sartori. In her two p.m. to six p.m. shift on WBCN-FM, Sartori had helped break Aerosmith, and she consistently boosted area bands. In this case, she was swayed when she heard Cap'n Swing at a station-sponsored Newbury Street Music Fair. "They were amazing!" she recalls. "Here was this band I'd never heard of, that sounded like a cross between Roxy Music and Steely Dan." Sartori began to play Cap'n Swing demos on her show; the local press was also enthusiastic. Buoyed by such support, Cap'n Swing subsequently showcased for management companies in New York City—and got blown out of the water.

"We took it back to Boston with our tails between our legs," says Elliot Easton, lead guitarist for both Cap'n Swing and the Cars. Sartori, until recently working in A&R for Island Records in New York, played me a Cap'n Swing tape, and it's apparent what was wrong: the musicians were overly clever at the expense of the songs; the arrangements weren't focused.

"Ric made the decision that we were gonna fix it, get rid of people," says Easton evenly. "When the smoke cleared, it was just me and Ric and Ben, and we got Greg back again."

The new band still needed a drummer; Sartori says she recommended that Ocasek contact David Robinson, the erstwhile backbone of Boston's legendary Jonathan Richman and the Modern Lovers, and who was then playing with psycho-punk band DMZ. Ocasek played Robinson a tape. "I figured it was worth a try," Robinson shrugs in retrospect. "It was going to be my last band."

THE BASEMENT OF RIC Ocasek's Newton, Massachusetts, carriage house is tiny: an open trapezoid, maybe eight feet wide at the narrow end, with fifteen-foot sides fanning out. Plastered everywhere are black-and-white photos clipped from fashion magazines—one of Sissy

Spacck, a few stark Helmut Newtons—and those of an array of futuristic fantasy cars. The pipes are painted black, and the boiler is embla-
zoned with a psychedelic crescent moon design that Ric reluctantly
admits he rendered. Here is where the Cars assembled their hit-bound
material during the fall and winter of 1976.

"It was beautiful to put that first bunch of songs together," Easton
says with a grin. "It was the first time it was so easy in any band I'd been
in. We knew we wanted to stick it out. The way it worked was, it would
either be on a cassette, or Ric would pick up his guitar and perform the
song for us. We'd all watch his hands and listen to the lyrics and talk
about it. We knew enough about music, so we just built the songs up.
When there was a space for a hook or a line—or a sinker—we put it in."

Roy Thomas Baker, who produced their debut LP and is scheduled
to produce their second, marvels at their attention to detail. "They
were all very logical," he says. "They were always thinking ahead. Ric
was very, very sober and very down to earth, which is rare."

"Probably all the songs on the album were worked out down there. I
was in the basement all the time," Ocasek remembers fondly. "I mean,
twelve hours a day—make coffee, go back down, just working."

It wasn't his first stint underground. In seventh grade, Ocasek had
backed off from abusive schoolteachers and immersed himself in photography, particularly the dark, solitary rituals of print-making. For
three years, he was fascinated—until electronics became his next obsession: down in the cool, musty air he'd construct transmitters and ampli-
fiers, just as he would later piece together songs and arrangements.

"I remember staying in a basement in Ohio for four months, going
through piano chords three notes at a time to see if they worked.
Nobody knew theory, but there were sounds there. . . ." He trails off
for a moment. "I must have lived half my life in basements! You know,
darkroom in the basement, electronics in the basement, arranging
songs in the basement, basements—I must love basements! In high
school, when it was almost time for me to leave home anyway, my
father told me that I was taking up too much room—in the basement."

When the Cars finally climbed out of Ocasek's cellar, they were confident. "We knew we were good before we did our first gig," David

Robinson assures me. Solid tunes and arrangements weren't enough, however. Robinson, who had supplied the band's name, was determined to give the Cars a strong visual image as well.

"We played real good," he explains, "but we looked real funny: tall guys, short guys. Elliot, you would not recognize. Ben used to wear striped bell-bottom pants. They looked like college dudes. When I saw Greg I thought, 'Another weird-looking guy to deal with.' He really looked like a hippie—he used to wear corduroy pants and Earth shoes. I'd be showing up in my shag haircut trying to put everything together. Miraculously, it worked."

Robinson coordinated a red, white and black Cars color scheme "because everybody had a lot of black and white clothes." Later he and a friend, Jerome Higgins, fashioned an album cover that Elektra's art department shunted onto the inner sleeve in altered form. (The band reportedly dislikes the LP's cover art.) Robinson also fabricated stage backdrops and intro tapes, and he encouraged the other Cars to flaunt some stage presence.

"I wanted everybody's character to be more animated," he explains. "Greg was little and funny—he should be littler and funnier. Ben was going to be like a sex-symbol-type guy, he should really get into that. Elliot is one of the best guitarists anywhere, so when he does his solo he should play it right in the people's faces. Ric's so tall, he just has to stand there and it's pretty much of a show. Me, I'm just in the back."

When they played for an audience of fans at a recent Boston press party, the Cars' strategically heightened contrasts were striking. Orr went all out to ingratiate himself with the dancing women in the front rows, while Ocasek, private even onstage, swayed and waved around his mike like a bare tree in a head wind. Their red, white and black motif *is* flashy, and they stress the symmetry of Easton's left-handed guitar against Ric's right-hander or Ben's bass (just like the Beatles, Elliot eagerly points out).

In a less-friendly hall like New York's Palladium, however, the Cars can seem stiff. Ocasek doesn't want to look "ridiculous" with exaggerated gestures, and he sometimes fails to reflect the band's energy. (Conveniently, stiffness also suits the Cars' music; their songs of distanced emotion make an ironic delivery appropriate.)

As we talk in his apartment, Robinson orchestrates an assortment of hit-and-split singles by Old and New Wave acts like the Easybeats, the Critters, Mud, Gruppo Sportivo, Radio Stars, the Merry-Go-Round and Boston legends Barry and the Remains. Inevitably, discussion of the Beantown scene of the last ten years invokes the Rat—a basement to end all basements.

"Once I saw a rat running around out front" says the owlish Hawkes. "Really—they'd go in under the stage. Pretty treacherous territory, the Rat."

The Rat is certainly no place to be at midnight on a Sunday. I follow Robinson downstairs—he has to meet a girl about a haircut—to where some twenty regulars are ignoring the band onstage. Two rouged, bottle-blonds dance listlessly near each other; a student couple deliberates leaving; a gaunt, androgynous, Teutonic-looking girl in a half-length blue velvet jacket with studded leather bracelets improvises a jaded slouch. The dust of centuries is clumped on the exposed pipes, and the concrete floor is carpeted with cigarette butts. Most of the singles in the jukebox are local products, with "Just What I Needed" occupying a strategic central position at number 133. Robinson's entrance—he's decked out in leopard-patterned pants and a black leather jacket—causes no great stir. He circulates, lets people shout above the music into his ear, studiously ignores the girl in blue velvet, talks to the band's guitarist after the set. When we reemerge from this Dissipation Row, he mutters: "*It's still there.*"

Early in 1977 the Rat had a different aura. Boston's newspapers were giving the club extensive coverage, Maxanne Sartori was regularly playing tapes by Rat groups on WBCN, and there was a feeling that Reddy Teddy, Real Kids, Thundertrain, DMZ and Willie "Loco" Alexander would promulgate a new Boston sound. The Cars' attention to musical detail and to image made them the standard-bearers. Riding everybody's high hopes, their demo tape made the crucial breakthrough to "heavy airplay" on both WBCN and WCOZ. Their initial following—"slutty girls and strippers from the Combat Zone [Boston's porno house district]," according to Ocasek—swiftly snowballed. And Sartori is convinced their groundswell success can, and should, happen again.

"There are no regional records anymore," she argues, "but there are plenty of regional tapes. If every radio station took its FCC license seriously—that part about serving the community—then every town would have a Cars."

Sadly, rock & roll is increasingly dominated by the business of producing platinum records. New artists with a good marketing sense and a flair for calculation have become the big winners, while the rest often get short shrift or even the heave-ho. The Cars and driver Ric Ocasek sometimes seem to fit very neatly into the former slot, being a band that obviously knows how to package itself—and leave out a lot of the noncommercial quirks and wrinkles that lend charm and personality to popular music. While the band's sound has an undeniable freshness, much of it is owing to their shrewd amalgam of many late Seventies pop, rock and New Wave styles. And they have handily sidestepped the punk-label pitfalls that might have undermined their cause, keeping the energy on a short leash, presenting themselves as mysterious without seeming aloof or arcane, and demonstrating taste without an off-putting air of artiness. As for content, they maintain that their songs are just songs, with little or no background.

Maybe they're simply scared, but in a genre once characterized by youthful abandon, the Cars exude caution and control, while their management and record company refuse to divulge the band members' real ages. As one Boston writer put it, "Like Athena, the Cars were born mature and fully armed."

OCASEK AND I HEAD into Boston to check out a guitar store. Strictly business. "I don't go out looking for fun," Ric tells me, his voice dropping. "I think fun's almost a false sense of ecstasy that people go out looking for. What is fun? I think it's different for everybody. I just don't think there's a general kind of fun. I had fun in the studio, I had fun working things out. . . . I don't play cards or board games, don't see any need."

Instead, he has his little "projects." When Ocasek and Orr were down to a duo briefly in 1976, Ric and illustrator Laurie Paradise published a fifteen-page booklet of poems and pictures, *Freely Sing and Paradise*. He left five copies at Grolier Book Shop in Harvard Square on consignment, "just to see if anyone would take it. I never even went back to collect any money—that's not what I did it for."

Songwriting also is a project: once undertaken, it must be realized with efficiency. "I never give up on something halfway through," says Ocasek. "I can feel when it's coming—the solitude, the speediness. Sometimes I'll lay down five, seven songs one after the other without stopping to hear them, and then I'll play them all back to see what they were."

We park—Ric ignores the expired meter—and walk about half a block before we meet Robinson, who agrees to assist in the deliberations. Inside the guitar shop, a Cars promo photo is posted prominently among the announcements of local club gigs. A white, sleekly futuristic Dean Elite guitar catches Ocasek's eye; the now image-conscious Ric earlier confided that he chooses an axe "primarily on the basis of how it looks." The knowing salesman beckons him toward a back room where he unveils a mirror-bright chrome guitar with a wickedly curved, pointed top. "You could take out someone's eye with that," Robinson grumbles admiringly, but the chrome guitar plays like tin. No sale.

Afterward, Robinson wants to say hello to a waitress friend, so on the way to the nearby coffee shop where she works, we wander through the sci-fi corridors of the landmark Prudential/Sheraton commercial complex. On display at F.A.O. Schwarz is a half-scale model of a yellow Corvette Sting Ray, complete with gasoline engine. Robinson points to it excitedly.

"It's the perfect car to drive around Boston!" he exults with a laugh. "When somebody crashes into it and destroys it, you could walk away and say, 'What the hell! It was only a *toy.*'"

1979

ELLEN WILLIS

Rock writing, especially in its early years, was a boys' club: the near-invisibility of women performers found a troublingly precise mirror in those who wrote about the scene. But in 1967, Ellen Willis (1941–2006) announced her arrival in one of the most stunning debuts in rock writing history. Her piece in the short-lived counterculture magazine *Cheetah*, simply titled "Dylan," set a new mark for what rock writing might do and be. On the strength of that piece, Willis was hired in 1968 as *The New Yorker*'s first rock writer; her "Rock, etc." pieces ranged widely across the spectrum of contemporary popular music, combining dazzlingly broad synthetic powers with a gift for the aperçu: "Though Lou Reed rejected optimism, he was enough of his time to crave transcendence." Readers valued Willis's writing for the window it opened onto the spectacle of a brilliant mind at work. Rather than marching lockstep toward conclusions arrived at in advance, her essays feel as if anything might happen; she always assumed the music was strong enough and important enough to face the truth about itself. With her partner Robert Christgau, she formulated an approach to pop summed up in the opening to a review of late 1968 albums by the Beatles and the Stones: "It's my theory that rock and roll happens between fans and stars, rather than between listeners and musicians." In 1975 she effectively left rock writing to focus on feminist issues; at the time of her death, she was the head of NYU's Center for Cultural Reporting and Criticism. A collection of her music writing was published in 2011 as *Out of the Vinyl Deeps*.

▼ ▼

Janis Joplin

Janis Joplin was born in 1943 and grew up in Port Arthur, Texas. She began singing in bars and coffeehouses, first locally, then in Austin, where she spent most of a year at the University of Texas. In 1966, she went to San Francisco and got together with a rock band in search of a singer, Big Brother and the Holding Company. The following summer Big Brother performed at the Monterey Pop Festival; Janis got raves from the fans and the critics and from then on she was a star. Cheap Thrills, *Big Brother's first major album (there had been an early record on a small-time label), came out in July 1968. By then there were tensions between Janis and the group, and she left soon afterward.*

With her new backup band she made another album, I Got Dem Ol' Kozmic Blues Again Mama! *But the band never quite jelled, and in the spring of 1970, Janis formed another, Full-Tilt Boogie. They spent most of the summer touring, then went to Los Angeles to record an album,* Pearl. *It was Janis's last. On October 4th, 1970, she died of an overdose of heroin.*

The hippie rock stars of the late Sixties merged two versions of that hardy American myth, the free individual. They were stars, which meant achieving liberation by becoming rich and famous *on their own terms*; and they were, or purported to be, apostles of cultural revolution, a considerably more ambitious and romantic vision of freedom that nevertheless had a similar economic foundation. Young Americans were in a sense the stars of the world, drawing on an overblown prosperity that could afford to indulge all manner of rebellious and experimental behavior. The combination was inherently unstable— Whitman's open road is not, finally, the Hollywood Freeway, and in any case neither stardom nor prosperity could deliver what it seemed to promise. For a fragile historical moment rock transcended those contradictions; in its aftermath our pop heroes found themselves grappling, like the rest of us, with what are probably enduring changes in the white American consciousness—changes that have to do with something very like an awareness of tragedy. It is in this context that Janis

Joplin developed as an artist, a celebrity, a rebel, a woman, and it is in this context that she died.

Joplin belonged to that select group of pop figures who mattered as much for themselves as for their music; among American rock performers she was second only to Bob Dylan in importance as a creator/recorder/embodiment of her generation's history and mythology. She was also the only woman to achieve that kind of stature in what was basically a male club, the only Sixties culture hero to make visible and public women's experience of the quest for individual liberation, which was very different from men's. If Janis's favorite metaphors—singing as fucking (a first principle of rock and roll) and fucking as liberation (a first principle of the cultural revolution)—were equally approved by her male peers, the congruence was only on the surface. Underneath—just barely—lurked a feminist (or prefeminist) paradox.

The male-dominated counterculture defined freedom for women almost exclusively in sexual terms. As a result, women endowed the idea of sexual liberation with immense symbolic importance; it became charged with all the secret energy of an as yet suppressed larger rebellion. Yet to express one's rebellion in that limited way was a painfully literal form of submission. Whether or not Janis understood that, her dual persona—lusty hedonist and suffering victim—suggested that she felt it. Dope, another term in her metaphorical equation (getting high as singing as fucking as liberation) was, in its more sinister aspect, a pain-killer and finally a killer. Which is not to say that the good times weren't real, as far as they went. Whatever the limitations of hippie/rock star life, it was better than being a provincial matron—or a lonely weirdo.

For Janis, as for others of us who suffered the worst fate that can befall an adolescent girl in America—*unpopularity*—a crucial aspect of the cultural revolution was its assault on the rigid sexual styles of the Fifties. Joplin's metamorphosis from the ugly duckling of Port Arthur to the peacock of Haight-Ashbury meant, among other things, that a woman who was not conventionally pretty, who had acne and an intermittent weight problem and hair that stuck out, could not only invent her own beauty (just as she invented her wonderful sleazofreak costumes) out of sheer energy, soul, sweetness, arrogance, and a sense of humor, but have that beauty appreciated. Not that Janis merely took advantage of changes in our notions of attractiveness; she herself changed them. It was seeing Janis Joplin that made me resolve, once and for all, not to get my hair straightened. And there was a direct line from that sort of response to those apocryphal burned bras and all that followed.

Direct, but not simple. Janis once crowed, "They're paying me $50,000 a year to be like me." But the truth was that they were paying her to be a personality, and the relation of public personality to private self—something every popular artist has to work out—is especially problematic for a woman. Men are used to playing roles and projecting images in order to compete and succeed. Male celebrities tend to identify with their mask-making, to see it as creative and—more or less—to control it. In contrast, women need images simply to survive. A woman is usually aware, on some level, that men do not allow her to be her "real self," and worse, that the acceptable masks represent men's fantasies, not her own. She can choose the most interesting image available, present it dramatically, individualize it with small elaborations, undercut it with irony. But ultimately she must serve some male fantasy to be loved—and then it will be only the fantasy that is loved anyway. The female celebrity is confronted with this dilemma in its starkest form. Joplin's revolt against conventional femininity was brave and imaginative, but it also dovetailed with a stereotype—the ballsy, one-of-the-guys chick who is a needy, vulnerable cream puff underneath—cherished by her legions of hip male fans. It may be that she could have pushed beyond it and taken the audience with her; that was one of the possibilities that made her death an artistic as well as human calamity. There is, for instance, the question of her bisexuality. People who knew Janis differ on whether sexual relationships with women were an important part of her life, and I don't know the facts. In any case, a public acknowledgment of bisexual proclivities would not necessarily have contradicted her image; it could easily have been passed off as more pull-out-the-stops hedonism or another manifestation of her all-encompassing need for love. On the other hand, she could have used it to say something new about women and liberation. What makes me wonder is something I always noticed and liked about Janis: unlike most female performers whose act is intensely erotic, she never made me feel as if I were crashing an orgy that consisted of her and the men in the audience. When she got it on at a concert, she got it on with everybody.

Still, the songs she sang assumed heterosexual romance; it was men who made her hurt, who took another little piece of her heart. Watching men groove on Janis, I began to appreciate the resentment many black people feel toward whites who are blues freaks. Janis sang out of her pain as a woman, and men dug it. Yet it was men who caused the pain, and if they stopped causing it they would not have her to dig. In a way, their adulation was the cruelest insult of all. And Janis's response—to sing harder, get higher, be worshiped more—was rebellious, acquiescent, bewildered all at once. When she said, "Onstage I make love to 25,000 people, then I go home alone," she was not merely repeating the cliché of the sad clown or the poor little rich girl. She was noting that the more she gave the less she got, and that honey, it ain't fair.

Like most women singers, Joplin did not write many songs; she mostly interpreted other people's. But she made them her own in a way few singers dare to do. She did not sing them so much as struggle with them, assault them. Some critics complained, not always unfairly, that she strangled them to death, but at her best she whipped them to new life. She had an analogous adversary relationship with the musical form that dominated her imagination—the blues. Blues represented another external structure, one with its own contradictory tradition of sexual affirmation and sexist conservatism. But Janis used blues conventions to reject blues sensibility. To sing the blues is a way of transcending pain by confronting it with dignity, but Janis wanted nothing less than to scream it out of existence. Big Mama Thornton's classic rendition of "Ball and Chain" carefully balances defiance and resignation, toughness and vulnerability. She almost pities her oppressor. Her singing conveys, above all, her determination to survive abuse. Janis makes the song into one long frenzied, despairing protest. Why, why, *why*, she asks over and over, like a child unable to comprehend injustice. The pain is overwhelming her. There are similar differences between her recording of "Piece of My Heart" and Erma Franklin's. When Franklin sings it, it is a challenge: no matter what you do to me, I will not let you destroy my ability to be human, to love. Joplin seems rather to be saying, surely if I keep taking this, if I keep setting an example of love and forgiveness, surely he has to understand, change, give me back what I have given.

Her pursuit of pleasure had the same driven quality; what it amounted to was refusal to admit of any limits that would not finally yield to the virtue of persistence—*try just a little bit harder*—and the magic of extremes. This war against limits was largely responsible for the electrifying power of Joplin's early performances; it was what made *Cheap Thrills* a classic, in spite of unevenness and the impossibility of duplicating on a record the excitement of her concerts. After the split with Big Brother, Janis retrenched considerably, perhaps because she simply couldn't maintain that level of intensity, perhaps for other reasons that would have become clear if she had lived. My uncertainty on this point makes me hesitate to be too dogmatic about my conviction that leaving Big Brother was a mistake.

I was a Big Brother fan. I thought they were better musicians than their detractors claimed, but more to the point, technical accomplishment, in itself, was not something I cared about. I thought it was an ominous sign that so many people did care—including Janis. It was, in fact, a sign that the tenuous alliance between mass culture and bohemianism—or, in my original formulation, the fantasy of stardom and the fantasy of cultural revolution—was breaking down. But the breakdown was not as neat as it might appear. For the elitist concept of "good musicianship" was as alien to the holistic, egalitarian spirit of rock and roll as the act of leaving one's group the better to pursue one's individual ambition was alien to the holistic, egalitarian pretensions of the cultural revolutionaries. If Joplin's decision to go it alone was influenced by all the obvious professional/commercial pressures, it also reflected a conflict of values within the counterculture itself—a conflict that foreshadowed its imminent disintegration. And again, Janis's femaleness complicated the issues, raised the stakes. She had less room to maneuver than a man in her position, fewer alternatives to fall back on if she blew it. If she had to choose between fantasies, it made sense for her to go with stardom as far as it would take her.

But I wonder if she really had to choose, if her choice was not in some sense a failure of nerve and therefore of greatness. Janis was afraid Big Brother would hold her back, but if she had thought it was important enough, she might have been able to carry them along, make them transcend their limitations. There is more than a semantic difference between a group and a backup band. Janis had to relate to the members of Big Brother as spiritual (not to mention financial) equals even though she had more talent than they, and I can't help suspecting that that was good for her not only emotionally and socially but aesthetically. Committed to the hippie ethic of music-for-the-hell-of-it—if only because there was no possibility of their becoming stars on their own—Big Brother helped Janis sustain the amateur quality that was an integral part of her effect. Their zaniness was a salutary reminder that good times meant silly fun—remember "Caterpillar"?—as well as Dionysiac abandon; it was a relief from Janis's extremism and at the same time a foil for it. At their best moments Big Brother made me think of the Beatles, who weren't (at least in the beginning) such terrific musicians either. Though I'm not quite softheaded enough to imagine that by keeping her group intact Janis Joplin could somehow have prevented or delayed the end of an era, or even saved her own life, it would have been an impressive act of faith. And acts of faith by public figures always have reverberations, one way or another.

Such speculation is of course complicated by the fact that Janis died before she really had a chance to define her post-San Francisco, post-Big Brother self. Her last two albums, like her performances with the ill-fated Kozmic Blues band, had a tentative, transitional feel. She was obviously going through important changes; the best evidence of that was "Me and Bobby McGee," which could be considered her "Dear Landlord." Both formally—as a low-keyed, soft, folkie tune—and substantively—as a lyric that spoke of choices made, regretted and survived, with the distinct implication that compromise could be a positive act—what it expressed would have been heresy to the Janis Joplin of *Cheap Thrills*. "Freedom's just another word for nothing left to lose" is as good an epitaph for the counterculture as any; we'll never know how—or if—Janis meant to go on from there.

Janis Joplin's death, like that of a fighter in the ring, was not exactly an accident. Yet it's too easy to label it either suicide or murder, though it involved elements of both. Call it rather an inherent risk of the game she was playing, a game whose often frivolous rules both hid and revealed a deadly serious struggle. The form that struggle took was incomplete, shortsighted, egotistical, self-destructive. But survivors who give in to the temptation to feel superior to all that are in the end no better than those who romanticize it. Janis was not so much a victim as a casualty. The difference matters.

1980

Carola Dibbell

A native of New York City, Carola Dibbell (b. 1946) came of age as a leftist and feminist activist before forging a place as one of the earliest and most formidable female voices in music writing. An early champion of punk rock, like that made by the British band The Slits, whose early performance she documents here, Dibbell explored the fellowship of the female musicians who anchored several of the genre's key bands in her piece "Inside Was Us: Women in American Punk," included in *Trouble Girls: The Rolling Stone Book of Women in Rock*. Dibbell was a contributor to *The Village Voice* for several years; her work has been widely anthologized. Her first novel, *The Only Ones*, was published in 2015.

▼ ▼

The Slits Go Native

IF THE best thing the Slits ever did were to pose in mud and loincloths for the *Cut* cover, I'd be satisfied. What courage to bare the multitude of sins that clothes are designed to hide: the thick waist and big bust of bassist Tessa; poking through dreadlocks, the teeny breasts and giant nipples, like walnuts, of singer Arri Up; and, dead center, Viv Albertine's pride, a torso of nearly cartoonish perfection—as unsuspected under sloppy petticoats as Tessa's breadth under T-shirts. Nuder than the average *Oui* model, the image stakes out the female body as female territory better than anything this side of Judy Chicago's "The Dinner

Party": solid, varied, flawed, defiant, and irreverent. Women are creatures of mystery, yuk, yuk, yuk.

Seventies feminism left a mess of open questions about sexuality—it was nothing to be ashamed of, but was it something to be proud of? It was owing as much to these questions as to punk's puritanism and chauvinism that the women who helped make punk, from Patti Smith on, tended to keep their sexuality androgynous or tongue-in-cheek. But though playing sex object takes its toll in authenticity, the effort not to can take its toll in animation, just like in the real world. For the Slits—maybe because they were so young when, opening for the Clash tour of 1977, they became the first all-female punk band—things were a bit different. They were theatrical. They liked gym skirts and old white underwear more than Spandex or death, giggled when their instruments failed, and were bored silly by masochism or even stoicism. The music they managed to make was bottom-light, multi-layered, thin, the instrumentals scratchy and choked, the vocals husky, abstract, the lyrics associative and playful. They opposed consumerism and vapidity rather than injustice. Even without mud they looked dirty and pudgy, and Arri Up's animal-style vocals and aery dances were like seizures. Their first performances (with drummer Palmolive and a 15-year-old Arri!) were the pits, but their skeptical interview in Caroline Coon's book on punk (*1988*) made me think, and their 1979 New Year's Eve appearance in New York, a miracle of incompetence, made me cry. Last week's belated Boston debut, on the other hand, made me wonder.

I don't live in Boston, so it took a local to tell me the crowd at the Bradford was unusually varied and happy. There were straight people, student types, and degrees of punk, with high proportions of unaccompanied women and writers. Like a Clash concert, the evening would include openers by an area band (the Scientific Americans) and a nonwhite performer, reggae singer Earl Zero, who briefly fronted the Offs. The Offs I took to be examples of a new breed, punk professionals, playing creditably but without any discernible personality.

When Viv Albertine walked onstage, she looked surprisingly clean in a short white dress and white Indian-style boots, but she came on tough: "Turn off this slow music, I want to play." The others finally wandered out, Tessa in her usual T-shirt and shyness, Arri severe in black modern governess suit, modern Oxfords, and her trademark derby (from which she would spring her dreadlocks), Bruce Smith to the drums, and Tony Wafter and Dave Lewis to assorted instruments on the side.

Later in the set, Arri would explain: "Our drum and bass are primitive because everything's too technical." Which is perhaps the other joke of the Slits' go-native cover. Their playing has to be primitive, yuk, yuk, yuk—a year ago they still had trouble holding their instruments. As we all know, primitivism was one of punk's founding principles. The idea was that with sophistication rock had lost its soul and that by investing brutally simple forms with feeling (or energy) some kind of magic would occur, and it did. But the structure's limited, so where do you go when you start repeating yourself? The Sex Pistols dissolved. The Clash got better, and it didn't hurt. Bands like the Gang of Four or the Feelies exploit technical simplicity with increasingly canny conceptual foundations. What the Slits did, I think, was to pursue the spirit of primitivism—or what they took that to be—rather than the form. Rather than build formally on the idea of freedom-within-limits, they pursued the venerable bohemian ideal of pure self-expression.

The set opened with "Newtown" in a fairly subdued rendition, but Arri did get out her first scream of the night, a glass-shatterer. There is no one really like her. Her voice has no clear center, equally at home with the piercing, the guttural, the conversational. Her physical presence is hard to pin down, too: she's thin, but fat; lovely, but ugly, with doe-eyes, Lucille Ball lips, all-elbows clumsiness, and no-gravity grace. As the set went on, she looked and acted more and more like a bird— cockatoo, maybe, or crow. Van Morrison looked for the lion in his soul, and animalism is one way home. Arri's flights of voice and body seem effortless, accidental, and perfectly sincere.

There was a bit of a wait between flights, though. There was a wait, too, for the next recognizable song. Most—disproportionately unfamiliar—involved quasi-African influences, reggae-mike effects, Rasta talk, native-American guttural, and one lyric went, "Weekend warrior, bread-and-butter hunter." Get it? Today primitive, tomorrow—tribal.

Did I hear this right? Arri saying: "We're in a meditation." Moments later: "Our songs are based on weightlessness and space." A heckler: "Bullshit!"

"I wonder what we're thinking of each other." This is Viv being coy. Answers: "Rip-off"; "You're perfect"; or, more to the point, "Grapevine!" There were calls for the band's great cover of the Motown classic all night, but it never came. Nor did their hookier material, except for "In the Beginning There Was Rhythm" and "Typical Girls"—which after 20 minutes of the other shit sounded like "Let's Spend the Night Together." Viv sang lead on an awful, completely abstract number. One bit had her and Arri doing pseudo-languages, including Arri's Crazy Eddie commercial. By the end we certainly had earned "Grapevine." Instead we got Earl Zero banally exhorting, "I wanna see you reggae with the Slits . . . rock with the Slits . . . listen to the bass" (played by Arri). The set closed to screams of pleasure, cries of rip-off, bemused applause, and stony silence.

Punk's gotten depressingly institutionalized with dress and behavior codes that it's a treat to see the Slits defy; they're not cool. But they seem to be taking some pretty silly things seriously: the road to self-expression is full of unmarked forks. Why do wrong turns so often lead straight to the exotic? Isn't this where we came in?

1980

▼

DEBRA RAE COHEN

After stints as a DJ at Yale University's radio station WYBC, executive editor of the *Yale Daily News*, and arts editor of the short-lived *Connecticut Eagle*, Debra Rae Cohen (b. 1955) started moonlighting as a rock critic in 1977 while working days as a junior editor for *Psychology Today*. She made a living freelancing for *Rolling Stone*, *The Village Voice*, *Soho Weekly News*, and a host of other publications before joining the *Voice* staff in 1981 to help launch its literary supplement, *VLS*. Cohen completed a PhD in English in 2000, and is currently an associate professor of English at the University of South Carolina.

▼ ▼

David Bowie Eats His Young

IN NICHOLAS Roeg's movie *The Man Who Fell to Earth*, there's a scene in which David Bowie, playing a vulnerable extraterrestrial visitor, intently watches the ritualized, larger-than-life violence of a Kabuki performance. That scene—the way Bowie is at first transfixed and then darts abruptly away, as if repulsed, satiated and sufficiently instructed— keeps coming to mind while listening to *Scary Monsters*. Like the character in *The Man Who Fell to Earth*, Bowie has been continually fascinated by the use of stylized postures (i.e., tropisms ballooned to human scale) as a means of objectifying horror. On *Scary Monsters*, he deals with the greater horror of letting such postures pass for people.

On his early albums, Bowie changed ironic manifestations like a man running a magnifying glass through his own body—liver, genitals, spleen—in order to mimic the excesses of the body politic. His was an aesthetic that involved distance, subverted from within by its very ambitiousness and from without by a rush toward spectacle that blurred the distinctions between purposeful distortion and simple hyperbole. Aided by the artist's collaboration with his own legend, his often coy self-congratulation and his refusal to disclose the crucial machinery, it was easy for people to mistake his shifts of persona for meaningful internal dialogue or, worse, to take them all literally.

Scary Monsters clarifies the David Bowie/Brian Eno *Low*-*"Heroes"*-*Lodger* experiments. They were reeducational projects: deliberate, short-term consolidations of the singer's skills and audience. While the Devos of this world forged his dramas into dogma, lampooning and literalizing his heritage, Bowie toiled in the training camp of the musical avant-garde, acquiring yet another synthetic vocabulary and releasing miniaturistic exercises that, stripped of their pretensions, turned out to be some of his finest work.

On *Scary Monsters*, he comes out fighting. Fusing the sheet-metal textures of the Eno trilogy into something darker and more dense, Bowie focuses his attention on a world he helped create. *Lodger*, with its sardonic gambol through "the hinterland," was the final serving—and sendup—of the old pose of evasive escapism. *Scary Monsters* presents David Bowie riveted to life's passing parade: streamlined moderns, trendies and sycophants in 360 degrees of stark, scarifying Panavision. With its nervous voyeurism, *Scary Monsters* is more like *Aladdin Sane* (probably Bowie's best record) than anything else. But because the bleakness that Bowie now witnesses is partially of his own devising, it gives the new LP a heavy, stricken pall. If there's condescension in the artist's stance (Prometheus aghast at what mortals have made of his gift?), there's also genuine concern. Bowie has the air of a superhero who's shrugged off his powers and thus volunteered himself to a reality from which he can't quick-change away.

Claustrophobia descends immediately in the opening "It's No Game (Part 1)," which clanks and jerks its way into a lumbering, robotic dance. Bowie's vocal—a long, distorted yowl of pain—is intercut with a harsh, rapid-fire Japanese translation. With its blunt rhythms, discordant accents and cautionary lyrics ("Throw the rock against the road and / It breaks into pieces . . . / It's no game"), the song is meant to jolt and distress. The end is particularly disturbing. As the tune falls away, Robert Fripp's stair-stepping guitar riff continues until the singer's screams of "Shut up!" snap it to a halt—and you realize it was just a tape loop: mechanical companionship. It's an ugly, disorienting moment. *Scary Monsters* is full of them.

Throughout the album, the beat is so jackbooted, the pressure so intense, you find yourself casting about for relief. Yet each hint of help (the ice-crystal space walk of "Ashes to Ashes," the crooner's catch to Bowie's vocal in "Because You're Young," his failed leaps at a romantic falsetto in "Teenage Wildlife") pulls you back into the same gray nightmare. The freeze-dried Bo Diddley riff that begins "Up the Hill Backwards" slashes into the middle of a bunch of swaying, arm-linked half-wits, who coo with the blank contentment of *Brave New World* soma addicts: "More idols than realities / Oooh / I'm O.K.—you're so-so / Oooh / It's got nothing to do with you / If one can grasp it."

David Bowie has always utilized distance for self-preservation, but now he's shuddering at the results—at what happens when estrangement becomes not only an illustrative concept but a code to live by. The wraiths who inhabit *Scary Monsters* are all either running scared with their eyes closed or too wasted to notice what's in front of them. They're antiromantic, half-dead, disposable. "I love the little girl and I'll love her till the day she dies," Bowie leers in the title track, his exaggerated London accent a garish caricature of maudlin sentiment.

"Ashes to Ashes," a sequel to "Space Oddity," is Bowie's most explicit self-indictment. Mirroring the malaise of the times, Major Tom—the escapist hero—has metamorphosed into a space-bound junkie, clinging hard to his pride and the fantasy that he'll "stay clean tonight." Though the image is chilling, it's difficult to see "Ashes to Ashes," with its reference to "a guy that's been / In such an early song," as anything but perverse self-aggrandizement. More successful is "Fashion," a heavy-handed, irony-laden parody of stylistic fascism ("We are the

goon squad / And we're coming to town / Beep beep"), complete
with handclaps and trendy buzz-and-whir accents. Hollow to the core,
the tune is infectious enough to be a dance-floor hit, which will merely
prove its point.

Terse, rocky and often didactic, David Bowie's compositions cut away
all illusions of dignity in isolation, of comfort in crowds. Even Bowie's
cover version of "Kingdom Come," Tom Verlaine's anthem about strife
and salvation, is dark. He changes the heart-stopping shimmer of the
original into a strained lock step. Verlaine's affirming call-and-response
("I'll be breaking these rocks / Until the kingdom comes") is treated as
a deadly joke. Bowie sings "Kingdom Come" in a flat, fake-naive drawl,
and each line is answered—not with a promise but with a mock-gospel
echo—by the lobotomized choir of "Up the Hill Backwards." Since
every last knee slap has been preplanned, it's like a revival meeting in
which nobody is transfigured. Any chance for redemption is out.

No one breaks through on *Scary Monsters*. No one is saved. Major
Tom is left unrescued. The tortured, reprocessed gays of "Scream
Like a Baby" can't save their friends—or their badge of difference.
The human mannequins of "Fashion" can't stop marching. Indeed,
the kids in "Because You're Young" can't even tell each other apart.
Instead, beguiled by the hope of hope, they track the wasted remnants
of romance ("A million dreams / A million scars") until youth, too, is
wasted.

Where do you go when hope is gone? Bowie's enervated, meditative, half-speed reprise of "It's No Game" leaves the question—and the
record—hanging. The artist's next album may see him questing, but
on *Scary Monsters*, he's settling old scores. Slowly, brutally and with a
savage, satisfying crunch, David Bowie eats his young.

1980

NICK TOSCHES

Nick Tosches was born in 1949 in Newark, New Jersey; he worked as a porter and a snake-hunter before turning to writing. Beginning as a chronicler of country music and the earliest rock & roll, Tosches distinguished himself for the force of implication in his style, and an interest in underworlds and conspiracies of power. His incisive biographical studies defy category: boxer Sonny Liston (*The Devil and Sonny Liston*), crooner Dean Martin (*Dino: Living High in the Dirty Business of Dreams*), country singer Emmett Miller (*Where Dead Voices Gather*), gangster Arnold Rothstein (*King of the Jews*), and his 1982 study of Jerry Lee Lewis, *Hellfire*, called "the best rock n' roll biography ever written" by *Rolling Stone*. In each, Tosches analyzes his subjects from their darkest corners as a means of bringing them into the light. His most recent foray into rock's often murky past was *Save the Last Dance for Satan* (2011); he is also the author of four novels, including *In the Hand of Dante*, and a children's book, *Johnny's First Cigarette*.

▼ ▼

from
Hellfire

THE MOMENT he heard it, the very moment he heard himself make that song like he had been trying to make it—and he had been trying to make something that was fine; not just something that would seem fine coming from an eight-year-old boy with freckles and stuck-out ears, which he knew he was, but something that would seem fine coming from the nickel machine in one of those drunk-morning juke joints, or from his daddy's Victrola, or from a radio; something that would seem fine coming from any of these, and yet had not, because it was different—the moment he heard it, he abruptly spun around, as if a door had just slammed shut behind him in an empty room, and he looked straight at Uncle Lee Calhoun, who was sitting there in that big chair of his with his potbelly sticking out, looking right straight back at him, and they sat there like that, the two of them, peering at each other from opposite ends of lifelong stubbornness, and they broke into grinning and laughing, each in his own way.

The first song that Jerry Lee could play straight through the way he wanted was the nineteenth-century Christmas carol "Silent Night," and he played it in a boogie-woogie style. Elmo was so proud of his son that he borrowed money against what worldly possessions he had, and he drove to Monroe, that place of tales, and he purchased a used Starck upright piano, and he hauled it back down to Ferriday in his pickup truck, and he dragged it into his home and set it before Jerry Lee.

This was in early 1945. The Mississippi flooded that year, and it was the worst flood since 1927. Downtown Ferriday was inundated, and many of the townsfolk had to evacuate their homes and take refuge in a tent camp at the Lake Concordia levee. The war ended that year, too, just a few weeks before Jerry Lee's tenth birthday. As Lee Calhoun had predicted, cotton prices rose to more than thirty cents on the pound during the following year.

Now that Jerry Lee had a piano, he attended school even less frequently than he had in the past, and he suffered less at home for his poor grades. Both Elmo and Mamie were confident that their son would be a great music-maker, though from the very beginning Mamie hoped and prayed that Jerry Lee would dedicate his talent to the Holy Spirit.

In the summer of 1945, Mamie's elder sister Fannie Sue and her family came to visit from Pine Bluff, Arkansas. At the age of fifteen, Fannie Sue had married a nineteen-year-old man named John Glasscock, who became a Pentecostal preacher not long after the marriage. They had a fourteen-year-old son named Carl, who had been born in Epps,

Louisiana, on January 3, 1931. Like most preachers' sons, Carl played piano, and this interested his younger cousin Jerry Lee a great deal. Carl told Jerry Lee that he performed regularly at his daddy's church, but once in a while he leaned a little bit on the boogie and that made his daddy madder than hell. He sat down at Jerry Lee's Starck upright and began to hit some Holy Ghost boogie, and sure enough his daddy shot him a nasty glance from across the room.

"They'd bought an old piano," Carl recalled many years later, after he had become known by a different name, "and moved it in that old shotgun house. It was the sort of piano you'd have trouble giving away. I came in there and played the fire out of the thing. Jerry couldn't play too well then. When we left, he came back to Pine Bluff, Arkansas, with us for the summer. He stayed with us about a month and a half, and he made me play the piano every day. When he left to go home, he could do everything I could do. He just had that knack. He didn't have those big fingers yet—he couldn't hit those octaves—but he knew the boogie. It was great."

Jerry Lee sat at his Starck upright every day for hours at a time. He practiced what some people called boogie-woogie and others called the Devil's music. Two of his favorites in these early years were "Down the Road a Piece," which had been a hit boogie-woogie record in 1940, and "House of Blue Lights," which Jerry Lee learned from a record of piano player Freddie Slack right after it came out, in 1946. He practiced both these songs continuously, and from them he learned to keep a fast, heavy rhythm going with his left hand while he played melody with his right. The more he practiced, the surer the left hand and the wilder the right hand became. Jerry Lee also practiced Jimmie Rodgers songs and Al Jolson songs, which he learned from his parents' records; but these, in Jerry Lee's mind, were more for singing than for the fingers. From the Jimmie Rodgers records Jerry Lee learned to blue-yodel, and from the Al Jolson records he learned the power of vocal audacity. (His favorite Jolson record was "Down Among the Sheltering Palms.") He played old Tin Pan Alley tunes, too, such as "In a Shanty in Old Shanty Town," which had been one of the most popular songs of the Depression; but he took a whip to these tunes and shook them down to boogie-woogie, as he had done with "Silent Night." And he always learned the latest Gene Autry songs, such as "You're the Only Star (In My Blue Heaven)," which also became a reconstructed boogie-woogie song in the hands of young Jerry Lee.

In the autumn of 1946, Mamie Lewis became pregnant for the last time. On July 18, 1947, she gave birth to another dark-haired daughter, whom she and Elmo named Linda Gail. By this time, Elmo had installed electrical wiring in his house. (For water, however, the Lewises still had to go outside to the well.) He purchased a radio, from which Jerry Lee absorbed music of every sort. He listened to the popular dance bands that were broadcast by WWL in New Orleans. He listened to the Mississippi bluesmen whose records were played by WMIS, right across the river in Natchez. On Saturday nights he heard "The Grand Ole Opry," routed from Nashville by way of WSMB in New Orleans. Whatever he heard, he swallowed it, then he spat it out on that old Starck upright.

On the first Saturday night of April, 1948, KWKH in Shreveport, the most powerful Louisiana radio station north of New Orleans, introduced a country-music program called "The Louisiana Hayride," which was patterned after, and in competition with, "The Grand Ole Opry." Jerry Lee was listening to the "Hayride" one Saturday night the following August when a twenty-four-year-old man from Alabama named Hank Williams made his debut. Hank's voice grabbed Jerry Lee and sent shivers through him, as the Holy Ghost had sent shivers through others he knew. He had already made up his mind that Jimmie Rodgers and Al Jolson were the two greatest singers who ever were. Now he placed this new Hank Williams fellow right up there with them. Hank became the most celebrated singer on "The Louisiana Hayride," and Jerry Lee listened for him every Saturday night, wondering what he looked like and resolving that he must someday meet him. Occasionally Hank Williams would get drunk and out of hand. Horace Logan, the man in charge of the program, would fire him. Jerry Lee would listen to the show for Saturday night upon Saturday night, wondering where Hank had gone to; then, always, Hank Williams would return, saying, "Howdy, neighbors, it's mighty good to be back." Jerry Lee went to the Starck upright and practiced whatever songs he heard Hank sing. The best one of all, he thought, was "Lovesick Blues," which Hank first sang on the "Hayride" sometime after Christmas. It was an old song, copyrighted in the spring of 1922. The lyrics had been written by Irving Mills, a Jewish immigrant from Russia, and the music had been composed by a vaudeville pianist named Cliff Friend. The song had been recorded several times in the twenties, and in 1939 it was cut by an Alabama-born country singer named Rex Griffin, from whose record Hank Williams had learned the song. But Hank let everyone believe that the song was his. To Jerry Lee's thinking, it was a perfect song, a song that both Jimmie Rodgers and Al Jolson might have recorded. Listening to Hank sing it, Jerry Lee knew that he must ask Hank, on that day when they met, where he stood on Jimmie and Al. Eventually Hank's fame grew too large for the "Hayride" to contain him, and in the spring of 1949 he moved north to the "Opry." Jerry Lee followed him with a turn of the dial.

Jerry Lee's cousins Jimmy Lee Swaggart and Mickey Gilley had also been working at the piano. All three boys now performed occasionally at the Assembly of God meetings, as Brother Culbreth had once said they would. Of the three boys, Jerry Lee was by far the best, but Jimmy Lee showed a prodigious gift as well. Unlike Jerry Lee, however, Jimmy Lee devoted most of his talent to the Lord, who had claimed him as a vessel, and did not spend much time practicing worldly music (although, if you took the words away, there were more than a few Pentecostal hymns that would not sound foreign coming from the nickel machine in the wildest juke joint). But, sometime after his thirteenth birthday, Jimmy Lee began to backslide, and he and Jerry Lee began to make forays into the slow river of dark night.

On Fourth Street, in the black part of Ferriday, there was a wooden nightclub called Haney's Big House. It was owned and operated by a colored man named Big Will Haney. In those days segregation in the Deep South was a two-way street, and whites were no more welcome in black clubs than blacks were in white clubs. At Haney's Big House the only whitefolk allowed were the disc jockeys from WMIS in Natchez, and they were set off and restricted to a table at the side of the stage.

The finest bluesmen in the South came to Haney's Big House. There were old, established piano players, such as Sunnyland Slim and Big Maceo. There were younger men who had just begun to make names for themselves, men like Muddy Waters, who just a few years back had been working in the cotton fields across the river. There were wild new dance bands, such as Roy Milton and His Solid Senders, Memphis Slim and His House Rockers. Then there were some very young men in their teens and twenties whom no one had yet heard of—men such as Ray Charles, Bobby Bland, and Blues Boy King. The late forties were the most exciting years of black music, for it was then that rock 'n' roll was being born. Old rhythms merged with new, and the ancient raw power of the country blues begat a fierce new creature in sharkskin britches, a creature delivered by the men, old and young, who wrought their wicked music, night after dark night, at Haney's Big House and a hundred other places like it in the colored parts of a hundred other Deep South towns. The creature was to grow to great majesty, then be devoured by another, paler, new creature.

It was to Haney's that Jerry Lee and Jimmy Lee, blond and pubescent, did sneak. In the *Concordia Sentinel*, the weekly newspaper published in Ferriday, there was a column called "Among the Colored," which Jerry Lee examined every Friday when the paper came out to see who would be coming to Haney's Big House the following week. He and Jimmy would steal away from their homes and bicycle down to the bad part of Fourth Street.

"We'd go down there," Jerry Lee recalled years later, after the Big House had fallen. "We'd go down there and sell newspapers and shine shoes and everything, and we'd keep on doin' it until nobody was lookin', and then we'd work our way through the door, y'know. And them cats is so drunk they couldn't walk. And, man, we'd sneak in there and old Haney, he'd catch us. He'd say, 'Boy, yo' Uncle Lee come down heah and *kill* me and you both!' And he'd throw us out. But I sure heard a lot of good piano playin' down there. Man, these old black cats come through in them old buses, feet stickin' out the windows, eatin' sardines. But I tell you, they could really play some music—that's a guaranteed fact."

On some nights Jerry Lee and Jimmy Lee snuck out but did not go to Haney's. They broke into stores downtown and robbed them. Whenever they did this, they would stop by the police station the next day and ask Police Chief Harrison if there was any news about the thieves. "Well, boys," he would say, "we ain't got 'em yet, but we're on their trail." They would ask the chief how many men he figured were involved. "It's a gang of 'em," he would say.

The boys began scheming a big heist as they went about their night thieving. Under one full moon they stole some scrap iron from Lee Calhoun's backyard. They later sold it back to him, and this may have been the only time Uncle Lee was taken in a transaction. Another night they busted into a warehouse at the edge of town, expecting to find all manner of worldly spoil. Instead they found more rolls of barbed wire than they had ever imagined to exist—nothing but rolls and rolls of barbed wire. Jimmy Lee took a roll of it, but discarded it on the way home.

Then one night Jerry Lee went off into the dark without his cousin, and he busted into a store and took some jewelry, and he got caught. This cost Elmo and Uncle Lee a few hundred dollars to straighten out, and it convinced Jimmy Lee that the Holy Ghost was giving him one last chance to vessel-up.

Not long after this incident, Elmo moved his family out of Concordia Parish, south to West Feliciana Parish, where he had been offered a good-paying construction job in Angola, at the state penitentiary.

Angola had once been a great cotton plantation. In 1869 it was purchased by Major Samuel Lawrence James, who transformed the plantation into a brutal, profit-making prison, which he personally operated until his death in 1894. At the turn of the century, the state of Louisiana purchased the Angola prison from the Major's heirs, running it in much the same cruel way as the old Major himself had. Prisoners were shackled, underfed, horsewhipped, and forced to slave-farm cotton on the prison's rich bottomland. In 1946 Governor Jimmie H. Davis, who had been elected to office two years before largely on the basis of his song "You Are My Sunshine," instituted a long-range program to modernize and humanize Angola. Part of this plan called for the removal of all women prisoners from the penitentiary. Another part called for the construction of a new receiving station, classification center, and hospital; and this was the part of Governor Davis's program that brought Elmo Lewis and his family to Angola in 1948.

The Lewises moved into wooden quarters outside the walls of the penitentiary. Jerry Lee and his little sister Frankie Jean attended a slat-patched old school along with the children of the other laborers. It was at this school that Frankie Jean learned to read and write. On the few occasions when Jerry Lee showed up for class, he was relieved to hear no mention of Columbus and his loathsome ball.

Now, Jerry Lee at this time had neither use nor liking for any girl-creature too young to wear an undershirt, and he regarded his sisters not so much as kin or even flesh, but rather as dark-haired, wailing thorns. Frankie Jean was the greater of the thorns, for she was larger than baby Linda Gail and she not only wailed but also spoke. One afternoon Jerry Lee had him an idea. It was the finest idea he had devised since the invention of the great compromise.

His mother had been pleading with him all day to take Frankie Jean outside and play with her. Finally he inhaled through his teeth and dragged the thorn from the house, letting the screen door slam weakly behind him. Frankie Jean climbed into her baby sister's stroller and commanded Jerry Lee to take her for a ride. It was then that he had his idea.

He pushed Frankie Jean for a long while, across dirt and grass and stones, toward a hill that dynamite and steam shovels and bulldozers had recently cleft in twain to make way for a new road. He pushed her to the top of this progress-ravaged hill, to the edge of this barren cliff that God never made. He peered into the chasm, to the moved-mountain rubble many feet below. Then he gave the stroller one final push and heard the scream of the thorn.

The stroller teetered, then plummeted from the cliff. It smashed against a jutting rock and burst into a noisy shower of flesh and hardware. Chrome, cheap wood, and pink tatters sprayed outward and

downward in myriad wild trajectories. And in the middle of this crash-
ing, splintering tumblement: the spinning, wailing thorn. It was a glorious sight, and Jerry Lee beheld it.

When he returned home alone, his mother asked where Frankie Jean
was. He did not reply, so she asked him again.

"A chicken hawk," he answered. He unscrewed the lid from a jar of
peanut butter and stuck in the two longest fingers he had. "Biggest one
I ever seen. Snatched her up like a poor little chicklin' hen and carried
her off." He squinted upward and raised his hand, the one with the peanut butter on it—raised it toward the heavens and moved it in a long,
slow arc, like an Indian in a movie. "Stroller and all."

Frankie Jean entered the house, bleeding and bruised and wailing
from the abyss. Mamie grabbed a broom handle and took it to her son
until he, too, was bruised; but he would not wail. Frankie Jean did not
smile again until she was twelve years old, when she was married.

For a long time after this, there was enmity between Jerry Lee and
Frankie Jean. One day Jerry Lee brought home a grasshopper with
a broken leg. He fashioned a splint from a match stick and tied it to
the insect's leg with black thread. Then he set the grasshopper on the
floor—and out leaped Frankie Jean, upon it with one small foot, reduc-
ing the creature to an unholy stain.

On a certain night Jerry Lee pretended an armistice and offered to
tell Frankie Jean a bedtime story. Frankie Jean lay in bed, and Jerry Lee
leaned back beside her and folded his hands behind his head. He closed
his eyes.

"Once upon a time, there was this little girl and she was comin' after
me." Then he was silent. Then he said, "She's comin' after me." Then
he was silent. Then he said, "She's comin' after me." He continued
this for some time in the darkness. Frankie Jean was frightened and
she pleaded with him to stop, to tell the story right. But all he said
was, "She's comin' after me." Frankie Jean knew that Jerry Lee had
nosebleed problems, so she drove her little fist straight into his nose
and made it spurt blood—made it spurt blood all down his shirt, all
over the bed, all over the floor of that little wooden house. They came
together like pit dogs, and Elmo separated them.

Some girls, older girls, were not thorns. At Angola thirteen-year-old Jerry Lee discovered romance, and their names were Nell and Ruth. He never forgot those first girl friends, as he never forgot that Starck upright.

Elmo had hauled the piano to Angola, and Jerry Lee continued to make his boogie every day. But here Jerry Lee encountered new distractions: Nell and Ruth, of course, and football. The boys at the slat-patched school in Angola formed a team, and Jerry Lee, who was small but fast and a good receiver, became a running-back and the star of the team. The girls idolized him, and he did too. He loved to watch them press their knees together, watch their eyes cloud like hothouse grapes when they talked to him after the games. One afternoon Jerry Lee was running with the ball toward the thirty-yard line. A *big* sonofabitch came at him, and Jerry Lee leaped sideways into the wintry air. When he came down, he busted his hip and tore his thighbone from his pelvis.

The doctor at Angola put him in a cast from the waist down, and Jerry Lee cursed the hog that ball had been made from. For two months he had to be carried to and from the Starck upright. Because of the cast on his right leg, he was forced to play the piano with that leg stuck out at an angle. He became so used to playing like this, with that leg stuck out, that he continued to sit at the piano in this odd way for the rest of his life. Frankie Jean was assigned the chore of placing a pillow beneath Jerry Lee's busted leg after Elmo had deposited him on the piano stool. She sometimes raised his leg higher than she had to, until he screamed with pain. "I'll kill you, girl, I'll kill you," he would say, then wince into his boogie with wrath.

Elmo packed his family and left Angola in the summer of 1949, returning to Ferriday, to a bigger house, on the Black River. By the end of that summer Jerry Lee knew that he could make music as fine and wild as anything he had heard at Haney's Big House. He was ready to turn professional, and he did.

1982

ARIEL SWARTLEY

Raised in Boston then educated in Philadelphia, Ariel Swartley (b. 1947) was, at the *Boston Phoenix,* one of the first regularly employed female rock critics. She moved to New York in the 1970s, and Los Angeles in the '80s, never living, in her own words, "much more than an hour from the ocean." Further writing appeared in *Rolling Stone, Mother Jones,* and *The Village Voice.* Her witty and acerbic essay here on the phenomenon she dubs "boyrock" is an obvious forebear of Jessica Hopper's "Emo: Where the Girls Aren't." In Los Angeles, Swartley turned her attention to photography, drawing upon the region's hidden topography, while expanding her writing to subjects including art, ecology, food, architecture, and media, for publications including *LA Weekly* and *The New York Times;* her commentary on music appeared on NPR. At *Los Angeles* magazine she contributed a regular column on books, and she was included in the inaugural class of USC's Getty-Annenberg Fellows in Arts Journalism. Swartley's photography has been displayed in galleries in New York, California, and Massachusetts, and is included as part of an evolving multimedia installation on her website, *The Last Seacoast.*

▼ ▼ ▼ ▼ ▼ ▼ ▼ ▼ ▼ ▼ ▼ ▼ ▼ ▼ ▼ ▼ ▼ ▼ ▼ ▼

Boys' Night Out:
Aztec Camera Clicks

WHAT IS boyrock? Briefly, the guitars ring, the voices ache, and the lyrics yearn. Specifically, it is a genre born of the self-consciousness that rock and roll acquired during its coming of age in the '70s; a genre predicated on the idea that there's a new generation every six years and that the Clash, no matter how newly arrived to the charts, are old enough to have fathered musical sons; a genre nurtured on earnestness, passion and some romance—but not to the total exclusion of wit. Next question.

Does this mean that Fabian and Paul Anka were proto-boys?

No. They were old boys—or, possibly, young maître d's.

Who then are the boys of, say, the last few summers?

Well, there are the Shoes, of course, and the Cure—before they got arty and long before they got dancy. The dB's—yeah, the dB's are great, and the Jam . . .

Do boyrockers ever grow up?

Not often. The Jam came close, but then did you really want them to? The Ramones have actually grown down.

Is Jonathan Richman a boy?

Compared to what?

Can girls be boys?

Natch. Look at Chrissie Hynde. Of course, she raises a whole other question: What happens to boyish admiration when you set up house with your former guitar hero?

Is anyone ever too old to be a boy?

Certainly. The Eagles were overripe at six. Jackson Browne throbs with as much surging passion as a hardened artery. After a certain age innocence seems like stupidity.

So why bother?

Because, at its best, boyrock holds its heart in its hand and its tongue ever so slightly in its cheek (one nifty acrobatic feat that). The performers' dedication is that of a fan's; their world view is deliberately parochial. The Clash, who were brash but never really young, turned London's districts into metaphors and claimed the entire Third World as their province, but the boyrockers set their sights closer to home. See, they seem to be saying, this is what it's like growing up in my neighborhood with the radio on. And whether that neighborhood is Jonathan Richman's 128 or the dBs' Manhattan, where you go to see a girl and have to talk to her doorman, there's a lurking sense that rock and roll's romance is capable of wearing thin. The ache in their voices suggests that the lights were never so bright as the guitars imply and that no one was ever quite so innocent as those high harmonies—but never mind. Turn up the treble and dream on.

Recently, boyrock's best has been Aztec Camera, four young Scots led by singer/songwriter/guitarist Roddy Frame who have arrived here with Elvis Costello's imprimatur (they opened for him on his summer tour) and a knockout debut album, *high land, hard rain* (Sire). They appeared among the costumed deca-debs at Spit recently looking spruce and almost callow. Ruddy cheeked and ruffle haired, they were wearing buttoned-to-the-neck Western shirts complete with silver collar tips and bolo ties, and they were armed with enough acoustic, hollow-body, and F-hole guitars to outfit Bob Wills. But if Santa Fe is their latest flame, Scotland's still their mother. The landscape of Frame's songs is wintry and industrial. Walls, gates, and tunnels—all, you imagine, built of sooty 17th-century brick—outnumber the occasional loch or ben. The scenario is the by now familiar one of British unemployment—breadlines and ballrooms and broken glass, only more vividly described. "You burn in the breadlines in ribbons and all" ("Walk out to Winter"). "Bottle merchants both of us, overdosed on Keats, we smashed them all / And watched them fall like magic in the streets." ("Release"). There's a Gaelic lilt to Frame's sorrows as well as a down-to-earth streak that can't help puncturing the euphoria of a rock anthem ("A different drum is playing a different kind of beat") with a moment of self-deprecating frankness: "I want to kill your friends" ("Oblivious").

The frills of *high land, hard rain* were missing at Spit a week ago. No handclaps and football cheers in "The Boy Wonders." No roller-rink organ—though live, Frame's voice has a tremulousness all its own—and no multi-tracked oohs rising into the stratosphere. No matter: Frame wears his skeptical innocence, his hedged romanticism, on his face; in fact, his eyes are a whole lot bigger than his mouth. What did matter at Spit were the broken strings and guitar trouble the band kept having, since Frame's songs are so guitar-centered. Like the finest boyrock, his songs seem very much the products of hours spent alone in his room. I don't mean that they sound studied, only that in the various vamps and picking styles you can hear Frame's efforts to translate every record that ever came his way—folk, jazz, rock, pop—into acoustic-guitar terms. A person could spend an entire adolescence on the project. Perhaps he did, but now his songs segue neatly out of a boppy Brazilian beat and into cocktail jazz. "Lost Outside the Tunnel" blends '60s harmonies with a flamenco finger roll. "Back on Board" begins with a leisurely echo of Major Lance's sweet soul-monkey strut. In the midst of his Caledonian gothic landscapes, Frame's guitar speaks of warm winds and faraway places, of sambas on a beach, or drinks in a smoky piano bar. He uses his guitar as if it were a one-way ticket anywhere else, and yet even as he's flying you down to Rio, he's remembering the old neighborhood in crystalline detail. But there's no time for nostalgia; the chord changes themselves hurry you along. One verse, bridge, or chorus drives into the next, eager for resolution—which often doesn't arrive until the melody has doubled back on itself. In the end Frame's guitar becomes as seductive as a movie soundtrack, and all his great escapes only bring him back more firmly to the home he's trying to leave.

The most poignant moment in Aztec Camera's performance was the last encore. In case there was any doubt that they do believe in anthems, they dedicated their final song to Mick Jones on the occasion of his being fired by the Clash, and, accompanied by two members of the visiting Violent Femmes, gave him a loving, outraged sendoff with "Garageland." Six or seven years ago, Jones, too, was trying to play his way out of somewhere and toasting disbanded mentors like the Dolls. Six years is how long it takes to get from puberty to the drinking age. And even now as Aztec Camera are beginning to see the world, there's a whole new generation "digging through those dustbins, giving things new names." As definitions of youth culture go, that's one of the best I've heard.

1983

▼

NELSON GEORGE

Nelson George (b. 1957), one of his generation's most acute observers of African American culture, boasts an impressive and wide-ranging résumé as author, editor, screenwriter, television producer, and filmmaker. After college George worked briefly as black music editor at *Record World* before moving to *Billboard* in 1982, where he served as music editor until 1989. A lifelong resident of Brooklyn, George's "Native Son" column for *The Village Voice* (1988–92) and his memoir *City Kid* (2009) used the borough as a laboratory in which to fuse experience and criticism to celebrate contemporary urban pop culture. To date he has published fifteen books—among them the award-winning *Where Did Our Love Go: The Rise and Fall of the Motown Sound* (1986), *The Death of Rhythm & Blues* (1988), and *Hip Hop America* (1998). Despite the demands of projects in other media, George never strays too far from the musical foundation of his work: his most recent book, *The Hippest Trip in America: Soul Train and the Evolution of Culture & Style*, was published in 2014.

▼ ▼

The Power and the Glory

MARCH 1983—In the motel's living room two women in their late thirties, wearing much too much makeup, and clothes too tight covering too much flesh, hovered over a hot plate, concerned that everything would taste right "for him." In the bedroom, behind closed doors, dressed in a robe and stocking cap, his face covered with a facial mask, Marvin Gaye accompanied by three biceped roadies (bodyguards?) watched a fight on *Wide World of Sports*. Marvin and I sat next to each other in tacky motel chairs, his attention wandering from our conversation to the fight.

I anticipated an upbeat conversation full of the self-righteous I-told you-so fervor so many performers, back from commercial death, inflict upon interviewers and the public. After all, Gaye was in the midst of one of the most thrilling comebacks in pop music history. "Sexual Healing," some freedom from the IRS, CBS's mammoth music machine in high gear for him, and adoration from two generations of fans, were all part of a wave of prosperity. Even his stage act, in the past marked by a palpable diffidence, had been spellbinding. The night before, at San Mateo's Circle Star Theater, he had been brilliant, performing all the good stuff, and even reviving Mary Wells's "Two Lovers," one of Smokey's best early songs, about a total schizophrenic, a man who was both lovingly faithful and totally amoral.

Gaye's voice was soft, relaxed, and strangely monotonous (he spoke with almost no inflection). His precise elocution was reminiscent of your stereotypical English gentleman, but he spoke of a world far removed from delicacy and style. These were words of isolation, alienation, and downright confusion. His reviewed acclaim had in no way silenced the demons that made his last Motown album *In Our Lifetime* (despite its premature release by Motown) an explicit battle between the devil and the Lord for his heart, soul, and future.

I said to him, "The times seem to call for the kind of social commentary you provided on "What's Going On."

"It seems to me I have to do some soul searching to see what I want to say," he said. "You can say something. Or you can say something profound. It calls for fasting, feeling, praying, lots of prayer, and maybe we can come up with a more spiritual social statement, to give people more food for thought."

"I take it this process hasn't been going on within you in quite some time."

"I have been apathetic, because I know the end is near. Sometimes

I feel like going off and taking a vacation and enjoying the last 10 or 15 years and forgetting about my message, which I feel is in a form of being a true messenger of God."

"What about doing like Al Green and turn your back on the whole thing?"

"That's his role. My role is not necessarily his. That doesn't make me a devil. It's just that my role is different, you see. If he wants to turn to God and become without sin and have his reputation become that, then that is what it should be. I am not concerned with what my role should be. I am only concerned with completing my mission here on Earth. My mission is what it is and I think I'm presenting it in a proper way. What people think about me is their business."

"What is your mission?"

Without a moment's hesitation he responded, "My mission is to tell the world and the people about the upcoming holocaust and to find all those of higher consciousness who can be saved. Those who can't can be left alone."

A year later I reflected on those words while reading the comments of Rev. Marvin Gaye, Sr., Marvin's father, from his Los Angeles jail cell. It had all gone wrong for Marvin since our talk. The physical assaults on others, including his 70 year old father, Marvin's self-inflicted psychological degradation of himself with his "sniffing," and the lack of creative energy it all suggested, meant Marvin's unrest was real. Still, to me, the most frightening comment was Rev. Gaye's response to whether he loved his son or not: "Let's say that I didn't dislike him."

SUMMER 1958—Stardom was taking its toll on the Moonglows, one of the 1950s top vocal groups. One member had been hospitalized for drug abuse. Another was tripping on the glamour and the friendly little girls. Harvey Fuqua, the Moonglows' founder and most level-headed member, was disturbed to see how the Moonglows were not profiting from their fame. It was during this period of growing disillusionment that four Washington, D.C. teens, called the Marquees, finally talked Fuqua into listening to them in his hotel room. Well Fuqua was "freaked out" by them, particularly the lanky kid in the back named

Marvin Gaye. By the winter of 1959 two editions of the Moonglows had come and gone when Fuqua accepted an offer to move to Detroit as a partner in Gwen Gordy and Billy Davis's Anna records.

That Fuqua kept Marvin with him is testimony to his eye for talent and the growth of a friendship that, in many ways, would parallel that of future Motown coworkers Smokey Robinson and Berry Gordy. On the surface Marvin was this seemingly calm, tall, smooth-skinned charmer whom the ladies found most seductive. Marvin was cool. Yet there was an insecurity and a spirituality in his soul that overwhelmed his worldly desire, causing great inner turmoil. This conflict could be traced to his often strained relationship with his father, a well-known minister in Washington, D.C. Rev. Gaye was flamboyant, persuasive, and yet disquieting as well. There was a strange, repressed sexuality about him that caused whispers in the nation's capital. His son, so sensitive and so clearly possessed of his father's spiritual determination and his own special musical gifts (he sang, played piano and drums), sought to establish his own identity.

So he pursued a career singing "the devil's music" and in Fuqua found a strong, masculine figure who respected his talent. Together they'd sit for hours at the piano, Fuqua showing Marvin chord progressions. Marvin took instruction well, but his rebel's edge would flash when something conflicted with his views. His combination of sex and spirituality, malleability and conviction, made Fuqua feel Marvin was something special. Marvin, not crazy about returning to D.C., accepted Fuqua's invitation.

Marvin never recorded for Anna records. But he sure met the label's namesake, Gwen's sister Anna. "Right away Anna snatched him," Fuqua told Aaron Fuchs, "just snatched him immediately." Anna was something. She was 17 years older than Marvin, but folks in Detroit thought she was more than a match for most men. Ambitious, shrewd, and quite "fine," she introduced Marvin to brother Berry, leading to session work as a pianist and drummer. Later, after Berry had established Motown as an independent label, Marvin cut *The Soulful Moods of Marvin Gaye*, a collection of MOR standards done with a bit of jazz flavor. It was an effort, the first of several by Motown, to reach the supper club audience that supported black crooners Nat King Cole, Johnny Mathis, and Sam Cooke. It flopped and some were doubtful he'd get another chance. Yeah, he was Berry's brother-in-law (that's the reason some figured he got the shot in the first place), but Berry was cold-blooded about business.

Then in July Stevenson and Berry's brother George had an idea for a dance record. Marvin wasn't crazy about singing hardcore r&b. But Anna was used to being pampered and Marvin's pretty face didn't pay bills. Neither did a drummer's salary. With Marvin's songwriting aid "Stubborn Kind of Fellow" was recorded late in the month. "You could hear the man screaming on that tune, you could tell he was hungry," says Dave Hamilton who played guitar on it. "If you listen to that song you'll say, 'Hey, man, he was trying to make it because he was on his last leg.'" Despite "Stubborn" cracking the r&b top ten Marvin's future at Motown was in no way assured. He was already getting a reputation for being "moody" and "difficult." It wasn't until December that he cut anything else with hit potential. "Hitch Hike," a thumping boogie turn that again called for a rougher style than Gaye enjoyed, was produced by Stevenson and his bright young assistant Clarence Paul. "Stubborn"'s groove wears better than "Hitch Hike"'s twenty years later, yet his second hit was probably more important to his career. Gaye proved he wasn't a one-hit wonder. He proved too that the intangible "thing" some heard in Gaye's performance of "Stubborn" was no fluke. The man had sex appeal. "I never wanted to sing the hot stuff," he would later tell David Ritz in *Essence*. "With a great deal of bucking, I did it because . . . well I wanted the money and the glory. So I worked with all the producers. But I wanted to be a pop singer—like Nat Cole or Sinatra or Tony Bennett. I wanted to be a pop singer Sam Cooke, proving that our kind of music and our kind of feeling could work in the context of pop ballads. Motown never gave me the push I needed."

Cholly Atkins, Motown's choreographer during the glory years, remembers things differently. "Marvin had the greatest opportunity in the world and we were grooming him for it," Atkins says. "He almost had first choice to replace Sam Cooke when Sam passed away. He had his foot in the door. He was playing smart supper clubs and doing excellent, but it wasn't his bag. He wanted to go on not shaving with a skull cap on and old dungarees, you know what I mean, instead of the tuxedo and stuff. That's what he felt comfortable doing. . . . But he has his own thoughts about where he wants to go or what he wants to do with his life. And he doesn't like anybody influencing him otherwise."

Beans Bowles, a road manager and Motown executive in the mid-60s, remembers Marvin as a "very disturbed young man . . . because of what he wanted to do and the frustrations that he had trying to do them. He wanted to play football. He tried to join the Detroit Lions."

In 1970, at 31, Marvin tried to get Detroit's local NFL franchise to let him attend rookie camp. This was the period after Tammi Terrell's death when he was, against Motown's wishes, working on *What's Going On*. Yet he was willing to stop all that for the opportunity to play pro football. Why?

"My father was a minister and he wanted me in church most of the time," he told the *Detroit Free Press*. "I played very little sandlot football and I got me a few whippin's for staying after school watching the team practice." This parental discipline only ignited Marvin's contrary nature and his fantasies. "I don't want to be known as the black George Plimpton," he said, somewhat insulted by the comparison. "I have no ulterior motive . . . I'm not writing a book. I just love football. I love the glory of it . . . there's an ego thing involved . . . and the glory is with the pros."

The Lions, not surprisingly, turned him down flat. Marvin's attempt didn't surprise those who knew him then either. At Motown picnics he always played all out, trying to outshine his contemporaries at every opportunity. One time he severely strained an ankle running a pass pattern. In Los Angeles in the early 1970s he developed quite a reputation as a treacherous half-court basketball player. He even tried to buy a piece of a WFL franchise in the mid-70s.

There were two levels to Marvin's often fanatical attachment to sports. One was a deep seated desire to prove his manhood, his strength, his macho, in a world where brute power met delicate grace in physical celebration. For all his sex appeal and interest in sexuality ("you make a person think you're going to do something, but never do until you're ready"), Gaye wanted to assert his physical superiority over other men.

Linked to this was a need for teamwork, a need to enjoy the fruits of collaboration. All his best work, be it some early hits with Micky Stevenson, *Let's Get It On* with Ed Townsend, *What's Going On* with Alfred Cleveland or *Midnight Love* with Harvey Fuqua were done in tandem with others. For all his self-conscious artistic arrogance, he was a team player. In the '60s Marvin bent his voice to the wishes of Motown, but he did so his way, vocally if not musically. He claimed he had three different voices, a falsetto, a gritty gospel shout, and a smooth midrange close to his speaking voice. Depending on the tune's key, tone and intention he was able to accommodate it, becoming a creative slave to the music's will. On the early hits ("Ain't That Peculiar," "Hitch-Hike") Gaye is rough, ready, and willing. His glide through the opening verse of "Ain't No Mountain High Enough" is the riff Nick Ashford, the song's co-writer and producer, has been reaching for all these years. On Berry Gordy's "Try It Baby" Marvin's coolly slick delivery reminds us of the Harlem bars I visited with my father as a child. His version of "Grapevine" is so intense, so pretty, so god-damn black in spirit, it seems to catalogue that world of black male emotions Charles Fuller evokes in his insightful *Soldier's Play*. Listening to Marvin's three-record *Anthology* LP will confirm that no Motown artist gave as much to the music as he did. If he had never made another record after December 31, 1969 his contributions to the company would have given a lasting fame even greater than that reserved for Levi Stubbs and Martha Reeves. But, as Marvin often tried to tell them, he had even more to offer.

In 1971, Motown released *What's Going On*, a landmark that, forgive the heresy, is as important and as successfully ambitious as *Sergeant Pepper*. What?! I said this before Gaye's demise and I still say it. Stanley Crouch, in a well-reasoned analysis of *What's Going On*, explains it better than anyone ever has.

"His is a talent for which the studio must have been invented. Through overdubbing, Gaye imparted lyric, rhythmic, and emotional counterpoint to his material. The result was a swirling stream-of-consciousness that enabled him to protest, show allegiance, love, hate, dismiss, and desire in one proverbial fell swoop. In his way, what Gaye did was reiterate electronically the polyrhythmic African underpinnings of black American music and reassess the domestic polyphony which is its linear extension."

Furthermore, Crouch asserted, "the upshot of his genius was the ease and power with which he could pivot from a superficially simple but virtuosic use of rests and accents to a multilinear layered density. In fact, if one were to say that James Brown could be the Fletcher Henderson and Count Basie of rhythm and blues, then Marvin Gaye is obviously its Ellington and Miles Davis."

Though lyrically Marvin never again reached as far outside his personal experience for material, the musical ambience of *What's Going On* was refined with varying degrees of effectiveness for the rest of his career.

Part of the reason for Gaye's introspection was a series of personal dramas—a costly divorce from Anna, a tempestuous marriage to a woman 17 years *his* junior, constant creative hassles with Motown and antagonism with his father over religion, money, and his mother. Drugs became his escape hatch and his prison. As his *In Our Lifetime* so brazenly articulates, the devil was after his soul and damned if he wasn't determined to win.

APRIL 1983—Any purchaser of other Rupert Murdoch newstock publications knows the details of Marvin Gaye's death. I expect the trial, if his father isn't declared insane, to be an evil spectacle, full of drugs, sex, and interfamily conflicts. It won't be fun. What was, and will always be my favorite memory of Marvin, was his performance of the National Anthem at the 1983 NBA Allstar Game. Dressed as dapperly as any nightclub star, standing before an audience of die-hard sports fans, and some of the world's greatest athletes, Gaye turned out our nation's most confusing melody, asserting an aesthetic and intellectual power that rocked the house. I play it over and over now. CBS was going to release it as a single. Don't you think they should now?

1984

PETER GURALNICK

A member of the founding generation of popular music writers, Peter Guralnick (b. 1943) is less a journalist or critic than a documentary scholar. He
stands slightly apart from his peers in having studied creative writing and
published two collections of short fiction before entering the field. Guralnick's early portraits and profiles of country, R&B, and blues musicians, collected in *Feel Like Going Home* (1971) and *Lost Highways* (1979), stand out
for their narrative eloquence and self-effacing grace. A transubstantiating
sympathy for his subjects, combined with an archivist's belief in the value of
the comprehensive array of detail, characterizes his seminal biographies of
Elvis Presley, Sam Cooke, and Sun Records founder Sam Phillips. Guralnick
has written screenplays for the television documentary *Sam Cooke—Legend*
and for Martin Scorsese's adaptation of his *Feel Like Going Home*, and was
awarded a Grammy for his liner notes to *Sam Cooke: Live at the Harlem
Square Club*. A novel, *Nighthawk Blues*, was published in 1988.

▼ ▼

King Solomon: The Throne in Exile

"WHEN I was on Atlantic, it was a real record company, it was a family.
Now I hear Jerry and Ahmet don't even get along—that's a shame,
that's a shame. Maybe it's their oil wells. Hey, hey, hey. Maybe it's Jerry's oil wells in Iran and Ahmet's oil wells in Saudi Arabia—that would
cause you, you know, to fall out. That'll do it every time."

Everyone has their favorite soul singer. To Phil Walden and many critics Otis Redding was without peer; Sam Cooke and Ray Charles are cited as the unquestionable originators, James Brown was the greatest showman of them all, and even Wilson Pickett has his partisans. For Jerry Wexler, on the other hand, there are different orders of choice. "I was talking with Jimmy Bishop once, who used to be a very big DJ in the Philadelphia area, and we were sitting around talking about who was the best soul singer of that time. People were saying Otis Redding, Wilson Pickett, Ben E. King. Jimmy said, 'No way. The best soul singer of all time is Solomon Burke. With a borrowed band.' Which I agree with. Both parts."

I remember the first time I saw Solomon Burke myself, in 1964. He was wearing a gold tuxedo with a gold cummerbund and was headlining a show that included Joe Tex, Otis Redding, and Garnet Mimms. Solomon had no competition. There has never been a warmer, more charismatic presence on stage, and when he stretched out his arms to the audience, when he declared at the outset, "There's a song that I sing, and I believe if everybody was to sing this song, it would save the whole world," there was scarcely anyone in that frenzied crowd who could resist either the message or the conviction that seemingly lay behind it. When I first met him some fifteen years later, he was just the same, only bigger. His 200-plus pounds had swelled to 300-plus pounds; his congregation, on the other hand, had diminished from a theater full of secular parishioners ready to testify to a small club in New York City whose sparse audience was made up mostly of white faces and a few curious Japanese tourists. He was no longer hailed as King of Rock 'n' Soul, or, if he was, it was evident his kingdom was in disarray. And yet the voice was still there, as smooth as silk, as capable of swelling to an impassioned, effortless crescendo, as likely to soar to a thrilling high note or drop to a confidential whisper. The talent was intact, and so was the charm. Solomon Burke remained king.

There has never been any doubt in Solomon's mind of his lineage. Everywhere that I have gone with him in the last few years, whether to the filming of a television pilot in Nashville, a revival in Bedford-Stuyvesant, his own church in Los Angeles (Solomon is an ordained minister and bishop of the faith), or a restaurant on Broadway, Solomon has remained centerstage; he has created a drama, or several—it's like a royal roadshow in which waiters, deacons, family, reporters, and always women, countless pretty women, make up his traveling court. Everywhere he goes he picks up an entourage of men and women both (though women certainly predominate) who become his supporting cast in a shifting drama which can turn in an instant from moments of high comedy to passages of the utmost depth and profundity without so much as the blinking of an eye. Throughout it all Solomon maintains the poise of the master showman, animating all, orchestrating all, a storyteller who spins tales of the past, his own and the planet's, which hold his audience spellbound until the punch line—which as often as not turns out to be a joke. He is that rare spirit, a "character" who is also a serious artist. Everyone I spoke to for this book remembers Solomon (he is so much larger than life, who could ever forget him?), some as "a big liar," one as "crazy as a damn loon," almost all with fondness and something close to awe for his outsized spirit and outsized talent. You can't spend time with Solomon Burke and not begin to wonder, not so much because of the improbability of the stories he tells but because so many of them are confirmed as the characters he is speaking about walk right in the door.

Father of twenty-one, grandfather of fourteen ("I got lost on one of the Bible verses that said, 'Be fruitful and multiply.' I didn't read no further"), spiritual head of a church that Solomon says has 40,000 parishioners across the country (there are 168 allied churches in all, with outposts in Jamaica and Canada), Solomon has survived a career that saw him begin preaching at the age of seven, reach worldly heights in his twenties, survive what he describes as at least two descents into "the pits of hell," only to emerge with a best-selling gospel album and a gospel Grammy nomination in the early '80s. The two elements that have sustained him throughout this heady rise and fall and rise again are his resourcefulness and his talent: a quick-wittedness that very likely would have made him a success in any field that he chose to enter and might very well have brought him down again (because Solomon has always found it next to impossible to resist a laugh); and a talent that sets him apart from almost any other performer that I have ever known, both because it is so inspired and because he can turn it on and off so easily, seemingly at will, rouse a whole hall or congregation and then come back to earth again, without missing a beat, after the performance is over. Solomon Burke—the Bishop, the King of Rock 'n' Soul, the man who would once again be king ("Here's to the throne," he declared one time, raising a jar of honey. "We in exile trying to get it back"), with a biography as singular as anything else about him.

He was born in Philadelphia in either 1936 (the commonly cited date) or 1940, the confusion arising, Solomon says, because he came to his grandmother in a dream twelve years before his actual birth. It was on the basis of that dream that the grandmother, Eleanora A. Moore, founded a church, Solomon's Temple: The House of God for All People, in anticipation of the arrival of its spiritual head. His father, Vince, a native of Kingston, Jamaica, was a chicken plucker in a kosher market and (again according to Solomon) a black Jew. Solomon was the oldest of seven children and obviously the cynosure of every eye. "It was such a big deal when he was born," says his mother, Josephine, herself an ordained preacher. To his grandmother he was the confirmation of a long-held faith, and with his uncle, Harry R. Moore, who was seven years older, he undertook spiritual leadership of the church at a very early age. At seven he delivered his first sermon; at nine he was widely known as the Wonder Boy Preacher; at twelve he was conducting a radio ministry and traveling on weekends, with a truck and tent, to Maryland, Virginia, and the Carolinas to carry on the spiritual crusade.

According to Solomon none of this was anything to turn a young boy's head, and in a sense, looking at Solomon conduct affairs of church and state today with nearly imperturbable good humor, you can almost believe it. Solomon has described his House of God for All People in a less serious vein as the church of Let It All Hang Out, and he points to basic differences with his uncle, who died in 1982 and did not believe, as Solomon does, in miracle healing, liberal interpretation of the Bible, or informal dress. "My ministry was totally different than his, still is. We still stand under the same things, teach basically the same philosophy, but mine is a little more open and a little more flamboyant than my uncle's. God, money, and women, hey, hey, hey; truth, love, peace, and get it on. It never bothered me, because I was in the world but not of it. Part of my belief is to be able to serve God anywhere at any time and still come out saved, so I could be around people with cocaine, pot, booze, and it wouldn't mean a thing to me, even as a kid. My leadership was beyond question."

In 1954 his life took a turn. "I wrote a song for my grandmother for a Christmas present. God gave me the song on December 10, I finished the song on December 17, and on the eighteenth she said that she wanted to speak to me. She said, 'I want you to see your Christmas present.' And I said, 'Now?' She said, 'Yes, look under my bed.' And I looked under her bed, and there was a guitar wrapped in a pillow case. And then I sang my little song that I had written for her, called 'Christmas Presents From Heaven,' not knowing that it was a prophecy for me, to alert me to the future. Then on the morning of the nineteenth my grandmother passed in her sleep, so she only heard the song one day—but that whole day she was briefing me and telling me the different things that were going to happen and all the children that I would have, the loves in my life, just laying it out: 'You'll have big homes, fancy cars'—but I'll never forget the most exciting thing she said to me, and then the most depressing thing, too. The most exciting thing was that I would be able to reach out and touch people and help them spiritually, thousands of people, millions of people, and then she said to me that I would go down to the pits of hell and submerge at will, and I've been there a couple of times, Pete, I've been there, you know."

Just months after his grandmother died there was a gospel talent show down at the Liberty Baptist Church, and Solomon tried to get his group, the Gospel Cavaliers, to enter. One of them had just gotten a TV, though, and another had tickets to a football game, so Solomon went down alone in his uncle's pants and father's too-small pepperpot jacket, borrowed a guitar from one of the other groups, entered, and sang "The Old Ship of Zion." He must have been a big success, because Viola Williams, wife of Kae Williams, a prominent Philadelphia DJ, spotted him there and introduced him to Bess Berman, the owner of the New York independent label Apollo. It was for Apollo that he made his first records in early 1955.

Like so many of his contemporaries who came out of the church, Solomon was clearly in the process of change. These early sides are very much based on the big-voiced gospel-laden style that Roy Hamilton had recently pioneered (ambiguous words, inspirational setting). The genre, and indeed many of the songs, are clearly modeled on Hamilton's 1954 best-seller, the improbably authored Rodgers and Hammerstein collaboration "You'll Never Walk Alone," and there are definite bows to other popular artists of the day (including one of Roy Hamilton's most devoted admirers, Elvis Presley). What stood out most clearly, though, even in these tentative stylistic ventures, was the protean Solomon Burke voice, distinguished, whether at the age of fifteen or nineteen, by its control, range, and astonishing variety of textures and hues. Surprisingly, for a singer who was to become so strongly identified with the foundation of soul, there was almost no racial inflection, none of the broader accents of the church. Nor did there appear to be any interest on Apollo's part in recording him strictly as a gospel artist. But then, by all appearances Solomon wasn't much interested in that route either, having discovered, as he says, "a new avenue, a new dimension to spread the gospel." He appeared frequently at the Apollo Theatre, where he met rising stars like Joe Tex and Little Willie John, and he traveled all over the country in the next couple of years with a piano player named Slim Howard as his accompanist. He played shows with Wynonie Harris and Amos Milburn and recalls singing "One Scotch, One Bourbon, One Beer" without realizing it was Milburn's hit. "The people all went wild, and I thought, I'm gonna kill him, I'm gonna kill him—I didn't know he'd made the record, I was into my church thing, man. I'll never forget, I finally ran into Lottie the Body's dressing room, because I didn't know if he was going to murder me or not. She was just standing there with her body, and I says, 'Lady, oh, lady, I'm so sorry.' And she says, 'Stay, honey.' I say, 'Right!'"

His biggest success came with a song called "You Can Run (But You Can't Hide)," for which cowriting credit was assigned to ex-heavyweight champion Joe Louis, who had used the saying as his boxing slogan.

Louis helped promote the song in exchange for the credit, even appearing on *The Steve Allen Show* with his young protégé but unfortunately forgetting Solomon's name. "Steve says, 'You know. Solomon Burke.' And Joe says, 'Oh, yeah. And Dick Haymes has the same song out on Decca Records.' My poor little record company must have had a heart attack. Here we are on national television, and the guy's plugging a record by somebody else. Those were funny days, man."

They were funny days and ended as oddly as they had begun, as Solomon came to the conclusion around 1957 that neither his manager nor the Apollo label had been paying him all the money that he felt was his due. His reaction was to withdraw not just from the record business but from the world as well. It was his first descent into the pits of hell. "My manager told me that I could not record for anyone, that I would be blackballed all over the world. So I became a bum, because I was just really terrified, I thought my whole little world had crumbled. Well, it had. And I'll never forget, I asked a guy standing on the corner of Sixteenth and Ridge in Philadelphia in the summertime to loan me fifty cents, and he took fifty cents out of his pocket and kind of tossed it to me. Well, in Philadelphia we have grates on the sewers, and the fifty cents landed right on one of those grates, and you had to be very careful how you picked it up, 'cause otherwise it would fall down the sewer. So I got down on my knees and very gently tried to get that fifty cents from the sewer grate, and all of a sudden something came over me spiritually that said, 'If you pick up that fifty cents now, you'll be picking up change for the rest of your life.' I made the decision, and I kicked the fifty cents in the sewer. And the guy said, 'You gotta be crazy. You crazy nut.' Well, he went to run after me, and I run out in the street, and a lady hit me with her car, and when she hit me with her car, she got out and offered to take me to the hospital and come to find out she knew me (her name was Lathella Thompson), because I had been dating her niece. Well, she took me home with her, and that whole cycle of my life was over. That's when I went back to school and became a mortician."

An unlikely twist, perhaps—but then, that's the way things always seem to have happened for Solomon. With the encouragement of his aunt, Anna, who owned and operated the A. V. Berkley Funeral Home in Philadelphia, Solomon went off to Eccles Mortuary College, where he became a Doctor of Mortuary Science and then rejoined the family firm. Very successfully, too, by all accounts, as Solomon's funeral homes became a significant pillar of his burgeoning financial edifice, which in later years would include a limousine service, a chain of drugstores, an unsuccessful restaurant or two, and a whole string of "nonprofit" ventures ("they're nonprofit as far as I'm concerned") that have gotten him involved in feeding programs, academies for the performing arts, and other enterprises of varying degrees of improbability. As Solomon has said, "You know, the beauty of America is that you can try anything, and if people go for it, you can keep on doing it."

The funeral business led him, indirectly as always, back into the record business. "I was very content to become a successful mortician and build an empire of funeral homes," he declares, but then a man named Babe Shivian came along and said, "'You got to be out there singing. Baby, can I manage you?' Well, I wasn't into singing at all at this point—I had the churches, I had the funeral home—but he convinced me by giving me this red Lincoln limousine; he kept it sitting in front of the funeral home, and there was no way we could let this red Lincoln convertible sit in front of the funeral home—it was just the wrong place for it. So the family talked to him, and he said, 'Man, you need to make a record.' Well, we went back in and made a few records for him and Artie Singer, Singular Records, and the next thing you know we had a deal with Atlantic."

Almost from the beginning it was a very different situation with Atlantic. Whether by happenstance or because of Jerry Wexler's perception of the enormous potential that Solomon possessed, Atlantic from the beginning seemed to have much more grandiose plans for its artist than either Singular or Apollo. After a lushly orchestrated first outing that didn't go anywhere, in the summer of 1961 Atlantic finally put out the c&w number that *Billboard* editor Paul Ackerman had presented to Wexler for the first session, a bathetic ballad that had been a recent country release for Billy Brown on Republic and did as little for Brown as it had previously done for Faron Young, Patsy Cline, and T. Texas

Tyler. Solomon doesn't claim any more credit than Wexler for the song choice. "I liked country music," he says, "but I don't think it was deliberate. I think it was something we just accidentally happened onto. By my being versatile. By my being able to sing different songs—being able to change my tone quality, having the different octaves. You must remember, I was capable of singing anything."

Indeed he was, as he proved during his Atlantic stay, covering everything from the smoothest of ballads to the roughest of soul imprecations, often in the course of the same song. He turned out to have a real predilection for country, too, whether because of his diction or because of his feeling for the more exalted emotions or because of the ability, which he shared in part with Elvis Presley, to descend from the purest of tenors to the most thrilling of bass notes, and then rise back up again. None of it seemed like such a big deal at the time, though. According to Jerry Wexler, "When the session was over and we started to listen to it, Solomon cut out; he wasn't going to listen. I said, 'Where are you going?' He said, 'I'm going back to Philadelphia. I'm on a snow-removal gig at $3.50 an hour.' He had eight children to support!" According to Solomon, who remembers the incident vividly, "I had to split because they were telling me, 'Well, uh, hey, man, let's do one more song.' So I say, 'Well, man, this is hurting my income.' Hey, hey, those were the days. And I got a lot of assistance from Jerry. Being there, he gave me a lot of freedom—to do whatever I wanted to do. He would sit there and say, 'That's great, that's great, do that again.' Or just the encouragement of 'Do you want a sandwich? Let's send out for some sandwiches.' Or 'What are we going to do about the publishing? What about the writers?' Hey, he's a genius!"

"Just Out of Reach" was an r&b and pop smash. So was the follow-up, "Cry to Me," which was written and coproduced by Bert Berns, a vastly underrated composer and producer (he shared writing credits for "Twist and Shout," "Piece of My Heart," "Cry Baby," and "Hang On Sloopy," as well as producing such diverse artists as the Drifters, Neil Diamond, Van Morrison, and Aretha Franklin's sister Erma), who more or less took over Solomon's recording career at this point. Under Berns (with Wexler's executive supervision) he recorded transcendent versions of "Down in the Valley," the Eddy Arnold ballad "I Really Don't Want to Know," Jim Reeves's classic "He'll Have to Go," as well as the Wilson Pickett–composed "If You Need Me." Even more compelling were his own "Everybody Needs Somebody to Love" with its inspired and inspirational message and "The Price" with its no less extraordinary sermon, improvised one night at the Apollo Theatre, which declares: "You cost me my mother / The love of my father / Sister / My brother, too. . . ."

It was a remarkable run and a remarkable four-year string of hits. According to Jerry Wexler, Solomon practically kept Atlantic alive between 1961 and 1964, and even allowing for some degree of poetic license, one still feels that there was an undeniable spirit of creative involvement, a sense of high drama that couldn't have failed to capture the imagination of anyone caught up in the life and work of Solomon Burke at this stage of his development. Each of the songs achieved a climax of feeling, each of the songs was a masterpiece of emotional orchestration. The country-oriented numbers showed off the breathtaking range of Solomon's voice, the ballads throbbed with a seething undercurrent, and when Solomon shifted to a blacker emphasis, the barely latent accents of the church—the broader diction, the impassioned preaching, the abandoned transport—all emerged. The force of his voice in songs like "The Price" is almost frightening. It sounds sometimes as if he is addressing a congregation right there in the studio, and indeed singer Don Covay, who wrote or cowrote some of Solomon's biggest hits and has been close to him over the years, has said, "Solomon wouldn't record without his pulpit in the studio. We'd dim the lights. Solomon would stand up there in front of that pulpit, and we'd have church." Not surprisingly Solomon reinterprets the story, saying, "All I had to do was be there. Just show up. There was no need for any special atmosphere. All these songs were part of my life, things I lived."

Recording was probably only a very incidental part of his life in any case. Recording was the straw that stirred the drink, the promotional device that supported his touring. The road was where you made your money and met the public that could sustain your career. Sometimes,

though, the public could surprise you, and sometimes you could surprise the public. When he first went out behind "Just Out of Reach,"
says Solomon, there was considerable confusion about the racial identity of the singer; in those days, before mass television exposure—particularly for an r&b or country singer—people just flocked to see the
person who had made the hit, without much idea of who it might be.
Solomon has lots of stories of that innocent era when "I was just about
the most popular singer in the South," but perhaps the funniest has to
do with a Friday night booking down in Mississippi.

"This was in some little place in Mississippi, between Tupelo and
Philadelphia, and we had everything we could ask for. They had those
big flatbed trucks with the loudspeakers hooked up, and the black people was just bringing us fried chicken and ribs. Oh, my God, they got
corn on the cob, they making cakes and pies, they got hot bread, barbecued ribs, they barbecuing the whole hog—oh, man, they got ten
whole hogs over there, sides of beef, looked like they were going to
feed about 20,000. Oh, man, I can't even begin to tell you—it looked
like the festival of the year!

"My band come up to me, they say, 'Man, this is the greatest job we
ever played.' I said, 'See? Don't it pay to get here early? These guys got
tents set up for us, they got sleeping cots, they got a portable toilet,
what more can we ask for?' Well, round about seven o'clock this man
says, 'You boys got enough to eat?' Then they had some girls come
over and entertain us. Then a little later this guy comes and says [nasal
peckerwood accent], 'I'm Sheriff Stanleyhoop, and my name's on the
contract, and I want you to know I'm forced to give you seventy-five
hundred dollars, and here's your money.' I say, 'Great! This is a fantastic
gig we got. Seventy-five hundred dollars for the one show, and we got
another gig on the same night for the same amount. In other words,
black people paying fifteen thousand dollars for me to perform on a
Friday night—in Mississippi. This is heavy!'

"So he paid us, and he said, 'Now I want you boys to hit the bandstand at eight-fifteen sharp. It's going to start to get dark, and they
hooking up the lights, and I don't want you boys to worry about a
thing. When you get ready to leave tonight, we going to escort you

all the way to the main highway. Y'all going to Jackson, right?' 'That's right.' 'Well, don't y'all worry about a thing. You got police protection. In fact I'm going to make you an honorary deputy sheriff tonight. Would you like that?' I said, 'Yes, sir, that'd be great! Yes, sir. Right!'

"Five of eight, I told the band, 'Come on, you guys, we got our money, get ready, I want you to hit the stand at eight-fifteen, just like the man said. Don't forget, we got two shows tonight.'

"Man, ten after eight came, the drummer, he's out there, testing, testing. It's really getting dark now, right? Man, about eight-fifteen they start playing. I'm just relaxing, enjoying myself—the chicken legs and chicken wings, homemade sausages and stuff. I said, 'Lord, this is ridiculous.' Big old jug of lemonade, just push the button and it come out. It was great.

"Well, it come time for me to go on at about quarter of nine, I walked out there and noticed—man, I was singing and trying to see what was going on—all the way as far as your eye could see was lights, like people holding a blowtorch, coming, they was just coming slowly, they was coming towards the stage. And I started singing, 'I'm so happy to be here tonight, I'm so glad-glad-glad . . .' They got closer and closer. Man, they was 30,000 Ku Klux Klanners in their sheets—it was their annual rally. The whole time we played that show those people kept coming. With their sheets on. Little kids with little sheets, ladies, man, everybody just coming up, just moving under the lights, everyone dancing and having a good time. I'll tell you, we did a forty-five-minute show like this. Frozen. Man, my band was so scared that when I told them to pack up, the drummer just picked up his drums, didn't break down the set, just picked up the whole kit, man; the guitarist picked up his Fender amp, no problem, no problem. They escorted us right out onto the main highway, and we played our other show."

Another time, Solomon insists, a local promoter hired him, not knowing he was black, and then, when he showed up, he was made to go on with his face all covered with bandages so that the audience didn't get out of hand. Obviously taken with the idea, Solomon feels his face for tape and pokes a hole for his mouth and nose through the imagined mask.

You wonder how fanciful the story might be, but then you come up against someone else's depiction of the same scene, you run into other participants who instantly recall many of the same tableaux, if not all of the little fillips, that Solomon has so vividly conjured up. They may not remember the details as colorfully, they may not tell the tale as well (no one tells a story like Solomon), but there is no story that Solomon has told me that does not appear to have a basis in fact. The musicians at Muscle Shoals remember him interrupting a session to confer with a parishioner come to seek spiritual solace. "He said, 'Wait a minute, guys, I got to go make a witness.' And there was a sister out in the hall, and he went out there and prayed for her. She gave him $500, and he walked back in and fanned himself with it, said, 'Okay, let's go.'" Everyone remembers him selling concessions on the crowded tour bus, offering orange juice, tomato juice, sandwiches, and ice water at prices that started out low and, by the end of a long, hot bus ride, had appreciated considerably. "Solomon," says Rodgers Redding, Otis's brother, "always carried stuff like ice water, cookies, candy, gum; even though he didn't drink at all, you'd go into his room at the hotel and see all this Courvoisier, different kinds of wine, the whole room would be full of booze. He'd have a hot plate, frying pan, flowers, roses, everything, just for his guests, whoever would come by. I remember one tour, I think it was Dionne Warwick who was the headliner, and Solomon was selling his ice water for ten cents, sandwiches for a dollar—everybody just laughed at him. By the time they got about halfway there, he was selling that water for a dollar, sandwiches for $7.50!"

"Solomon had so many side gigs," recalls Jerry Wexler, not without asperity. "The game between me and Solomon was how much jive he could lay on me before I would set him down. He had his mortician's license, which I think he got by mail order. Also at one time he was an herbal doctor, he had a beautiful fitted case of herbal extracts, you know, root medicines—every kind of mojo juice and conjure, peppermint and all of those kinds of things. He had a drugstore, too, but it was a jive drugstore because it didn't have a prescription department. You'd have someone in a white coat take the prescriptions, and then at the end of the day he'd get on his bike and go down to a real drugstore and have them all filled. I once had this idea to have a sign made for the drugstore: Dr. Solomon Burke, Notions, Lotions, and Potions, Roots, Fruits, and Snoots."

And, of course, no one will ever forget the time he played the Apollo Theatre at the height of his popularity and demanded the right to sell concessions. Which was fine with owner Frank Schiffman, since it was not unusual for singers to sell their pictures and records, and Solomon was known for marching up and down the aisles during intermission to sell souvenirs. This time, however, Solomon had something else in mind. Somewhere or other he had gotten hold of a truckload of popcorn. When he started selling it, Frank Schiffman was outraged. Here's the official story.

"Who'd want to sell popcorn when he's pulling down four grand for a week's engagement?" declared Bobby Schiffman, in his brother Jack's *Uptown: The Story of Harlem's Apollo Theatre.* "But Solomon arrived . . . with a cooker on which he fried pork chops to sell the gang backstage, and a carton of candy. . . . I decided to humor him—until the truck pulled up. The truck was loaded with popcorn. I put my foot down, but Solomon said, 'It's in the contract. Read your contract.' . . . I finally made a deal with him. I bought all that goddamned popcorn from him for fifty bucks."

Here's Solomon's story, abbreviated, and unpunctuated by the guffaws and imitations, the takeoffs of uncanny accuracy and comic diversity that will simply have to be imagined.

"The truth of the whole story was that I was in Miami Beach at the Holland House Hotel on vacation with my family, and Bob Schiffman calls me from the Apollo and says, 'Man, I really need you.' Well, I'd just gotten involved with my drugstores (Notions, lotions, and potions, roots, fruits, and snoots), and I'd just bought the popcorn business, and I was supplying popcorn for all the theaters in Philadelphia, and I had the Mountain Dew franchise for Philadelphia, too, first one. But I had bought too much popcorn, and I had like a whole house stacked with popcorn that was already popped. Would you go for 15,000 twenty-five-pound bags? And I had deals going on with my popcorn, jack, any of my stores you get free popcorn, just bring the box back for a refill!

So I had to do something, and I agreed to play the Apollo under one condition: that I have the concessions. Bob Schiffman thought about it for about a minute and said, 'Okay. You got it.' And I said, 'Send me a telegram to that effect, I must have a telegram today that I have *all* the concessions, because I must get everything ready.'

"Now back in those days a black man who had the concessions meant that you would come in and sell your pictures, your records, and those felt hats that you take some glue and write your name over it with sprinkles. But *my* idea of concessions was the hot dogs, the hamburgers, the candy (I had three drugstores, right?). *And* the popcorn. I didn't really care about the candy, the hot dogs, the hamburgs, not even the sodas, but I want to unload that popcorn, jack. I even brought a trailer along with me to Florida, man, and I was giving popcorn to the people along the highway. Bags of it. Anything to get rid of that popcorn.

"Well, anyway, I had about 10,000 stickers printed up to go on the boxes of popcorn saying, 'Thank you for coming to the Apollo Theatre from Solomon Burke, Atlantic Records Recording Artist. Your Box of Soul Popcorn.' I ordered a tractor-trailer truck with union personnel to roll in immediately. I had my people stack that tractor-trailer with candy, sodas, pretzels, potato chips, and I had my people loading up 10,000 boxes already packed—with popcorn. Well, everything was cool, I got to the Apollo, I said, 'Hey, what's happening? The concessions are set up, my people are here to go to work.' They said, 'What are you talking about? You can set up out on the sidewalk.' I said, 'No. No, man, ain't setting up on no sidewalk, brother, *we* got the concessions.' Said, 'I have a contract here. What it say? Man, I can't read it. I'm dumb, I went to Catholic school. It say concessions? It say *all* concessions? The word *all* is very important. That means I *can* put a meter on the toilets, but we're not gonna do that, y'understand, we gonna be a nice guy.' The regular concession people from ABC say, 'Do you believe this? Man, I gotta sell my stuff.' I said, 'Well, jack, you gonna sell it across the street. It's in my contract.'

"Then Bobby Schiffman came down and said, 'What are you doing to my father? Do you want to give him a heart attack?' I said, 'What's the problem, man? You gave me the concessions.' He says, 'What's wrong with you, fool, don't you know what concessions mean?' I said, 'No, you tell me.' He said, 'You know, you sell your pictures and your hats and your feathers.' I said, 'No, let me tell you what concessions mean. It means anything that you sell here. Food, beverages, *all*, the word *all* means programs, books, magazines, hot dogs, popcorn. *Popcorn*—very important.'

"Then Mr. Schiffman comes down, and he was a little upset, he's screaming, 'Who does he think he is, Nat King Cole, Ray Charles? Let him take the damn theater.' I said, 'No, just the concessions, man.'

"Well, we finally bargained down to a figure because ABC did have a legitimate contract on the concessions, but I agreed to the deal on one condition only: that I give the popcorn away. I said, 'I won't sell it. I'll take a loss on the candy, the Baby Ruths, the Snickers bars, Oh Henrys, Hersheys, and the Mounds. I'll take a loss on the peanuts. I'll even take a loss on the pretzels and the Mountain Dews. But the popcorn must go.'

"By the end of that week everybody in New York had popcorn. Bob Schiffman, Honi Coles, everybody was out there in the street handing it out. The next week, when I came up to Atlantic Records, there was boxes of popcorn on everybody's desk. Everybody was telling me the story of the popcorn.

"To this day they never let me back in the Apollo Theatre. I wanted to buy it and make a church out of it, but they wouldn't even sell it to me. That's been my problem my whole life in entertainment: I utilize my educational background, and maybe that makes me a little too smart for my britches. They assumed that my intelligence was limited, that my ability to supply a demand was limited. I wasn't even thinking about singing that week. My biggest shot was: *get rid of that popcorn.* But it was the greatest publicity thing that I ever did."

Everywhere that he went Solomon employed his ingenuity to challenge the ways of the world, and maybe even to test its love for him a little, too. To Solomon it was all a trip, and when he says that he thrived on it, delighted in it all, you can believe that he did, the con as much as the material rewards, the contact with people as much as the stardom, the transcendent, almost religious experience of his art as much as the accumulation of transitory riches and temporal wealth.

"We played places no one else could, because we had the hits, and we had the manners, and we had the reputation. We had our own security, we moved in and out like that. I paid top dollar, and we had twenty-six people on our payroll. I loved those little country towns down South, I wouldn't take nothing for 'em. They brought out them old beat-up albums, you know what I mean, them old ladies bring food around to you, say, 'Son, you looking a little peak-ed. Son, you got to eat.' After a while I told my band, 'Don't eat nothing. Don't you be going to no restaurants.' 'Cause I couldn't eat everything them old ladies would be bringing me. I couldn't handle it. We'd get to the next town sometime in the morning after the night of a show, and I'd start looking for dogs. We'd be cruising back alleys, looking for dogs. Well-fed dogs, 'cause they're always a sure sign. Then them old ladies would come out with their biscuits and fresh-baked pies, they'd say, 'Here's some fresh milk for you, son, just be sure and bring back my thermos.' Fried chicken, barbecued ribs, ham hocks, collard greens, man, it was great. Then one of them old ladies would say, 'Son, would you drive my granddaughter out to the main highway? Don't you worry none, she can find her own way back.' No sooner do we get in the car and pull away from her grandmother than up come the dress—she isn't wearing no underwear—and she say, 'I'm sorry, I can't go back to the hotel with you, but I can give you something right here.' 'Okay, great!' 'What can I do for you?' 'Are you kidding? What have you got in mind?' Half the time they were so quick, man, I wasn't even ready."

"The first time he played Chicago," says Jerry Wexler, "he ordered a chicken dinner, and the chef, it was a black chef, heard it was Solomon Burke and brought the dinner out himself. He said, 'Is there anything I can do for you?' Solomon said, 'Just one thing. Can I get fifteen of these dinners and wrap them in wax paper and put them on the bus?' Sometimes when they were traveling in the South and they'd come to a crossroads, Solomon would turn his collar around and walk into a crossroads store and say, 'Man, I've got some hungry boys out there,' and con the guy out of Swiss cheese and ham, you know. You've got to remember, this was the South."

It all sounds like a lot of fun, and Solomon relished every minute of it. The food. The women. The games. Today, in his more meditative moments, he will say, "I'm a homebody. It's no life living in hotels. I like TV and home and fireplaces—and lawns, you must not forget the lawns," but in his heyday I doubt that he would even have been capable of so disingenuous a statement. He loved the crowd, he loved the adulation—there was no singer who responded more generously to the outstretched arms of his audience, and Solomon would typically conclude his act by turning over the microphone to a frenzied fan or get so deep into the message of a song like "The Price" or "Cry to Me" that it would become an extended sermonette, a small show in itself.

But music, as should be evident by now, took up only a small portion of the day. On the package shows each singer was allotted no more than fifteen minutes to a half hour of time, and even if there were two shows a day—or, at a sit-down gig like the Apollo, as many as five or six, in a continuous loop—more time was spent making contacts than making music. There was more dead time than live, and for many artists this was the real dark night of the soul, when the question arose and re-arose: What am I doing out here? This was the time when so many artists, major and otherwise, got themselves into trouble. For Solomon Burke, who is nothing if not creative in his use of everything, from spiritual resources to the telephone, there was scarcely enough time even to begin to fulfill all the roles in which he had cast himself.

"I'd go to the radio station and see the disc jockeys, go to the church and, of course, have prayer, go to the homes and bless the homes and babies, and then maybe baptize a few people. My schedule, you see, has always been a three-way personality. There's the artist, the religious leader, and just plain old Solomon Burke, who had his problems, who had his love life problems. Sometimes that's another movie, you know, God help us, Jesus."

Through the church he had contacts in every town. Even his peripheral interests exposed him to out-of-the-way places and experiences. One time as he was driving through Little Rock he was speaking to the members of the band about his background in mortuary science, and they disbelieved his estimate of the price of caskets. Piqued, he stopped the bus in front of a funeral home. "They're saying, 'Doc, there's no way that a casket can cost $2000.' I say, 'Are you kidding?' So we walk into this funeral home, and the guy's in there struggling with this body, he's using too much formaldehyde, he doesn't know what to do with it, you know. He says, 'Oh, God, it's too dark.' I'm saying, 'Wait a minute. Hold it.' And I wind up forgetting what we come in there for, I'm in there embalming. The cats are saying, 'What are you doing, man? We got a gig.' I say, 'I'm working on a gig right now.'" If it wasn't one thing, says Solomon uncomplainingly, it was another. There were always the old ladies to charm, and their young daughters, grand-daughters, or perhaps even the ladies themselves to satisfy. And satisfy them he undoubtedly did—because Solomon is nothing if not consid-erate in his apportionment of attention and energies, and he never likes to let an audience go away calling for more.

And then, of course, there were his fellow artists, whom Solomon appreciated to the same degree that he appreciates anyone else of strik-ing or eccentric individuality. He tended to gravitate, he says, toward the more "serious" members of the tour, singers for the most part who lacked a drug or alcohol problem and took a somewhat disciplined approach to their careers. He idolized Sam Cooke, as well he might, not only for Cooke's contributions to his musical style but also as some-one who was canny enough to beat the man at his own game. Don Covay, whose songs Solomon admired and who in turn admires "Big Sol" extravagantly himself, was a particular friend, and so were Otis Redding—only then emerging from the shadow of singers like Solo-mon and Cooke—and Joe Tex, whom he had met at an amateur show at the Apollo (Solomon won, they both agree) soon after they both arrived in New York. "We'd always hang out together, ride in each oth-er's limousines, stay in the same hotels—we interlocked ourselves, so to speak. You got to remember that the Otis Reddings, Joe Texes were never alcoholics or dope addicts; we never had a problem with booze or drugs, we just had fun. Real fun."

To other singers like Little Willie John, less disciplined in their personal conduct, Solomon was something of a father figure. "I think they had respect for me. For example, if the guys were all drinking and gambling, and I'd be coming into the room, they'd say, 'Oh, Doc's coming, Bishop's coming.' And everybody'd stop gambling and say, 'Hey, yeah, how's it going? Yeah, hey.' And I'd begin to catch on, you know, and one time Bobby 'Blue' Bland walked in and said, 'Hey, you're holding up the game, baby.' Which is cute—but to me it made me feel good, because it said, 'Hey, they're giving you the respect.' Or they'd come to me and say, 'Hey, I've got a bet on so and so, I'm betting $500, you hold the money.'

"Okay. I remember one night when Sam Cooke was playing with Jerry Butler, Little Willie John, Dee Clark, and a guy named Lotsa Poppa. Lotsa was a big guy, two times as big as me. You've probably seen him on the show with me—he sings all my songs. I found him in Atlanta, and I'm crazy about the guy. Every time I'd see him, I'd call him up on stage 'cause he was bigger than me and he made me look small. And when he got up there, he could barely move around, and I could just dance all around him, it really made me look good. I *loved* to have the guy around.

"Okay, Lotsa was the smallest act on the show, he didn't even have a record, you know what I mean, and this particular night he took $5000 off of Sam, he walked away with a ring of Jerry's, he had a diamond stickpin of Dee Clark's, maybe about $6000 more he won from that crap game. I said, 'Lotsa, you had a successful night.' He said, 'What should I do with it, Doc?' I said, 'What you should do now is send some money home, buy yourself a house.' He says, 'I'm gonna get me a Cadillac.' I say, 'Get you a nice house. Call your wife. Let *her* buy the house.' You could get a nice house down in Georgia for three or four thousand dollars then.

"Lotsa wouldn't listen. Lotsa went out the next day and bought this and that. That night we were some other place, some other city, and he wanted to start the crap game again, and I said, 'Lotsa, don't get into that crap game, you can't never win again.' Lotsa says, 'Thousand dollars a roll.' They wiped out poor Lotsa that night. Sam was throwing, he got like a streak, I want to say he made eleven straight passes with the craps, sevens and elevens eleven times straight. He must have gotten those guys for twelve grand, and he come to me and says, 'Doc, you hold it.' And I said, 'Where's J.W.? Where's your manager?' Hey, hey, hey, poor Lotsa Poppa."

In 1964, after a dozen straight hits, Solomon was crowned King of Rock 'n' Soul by Rockin' Robin of radio station WEBB in Baltimore. Needless to say, he took the title seriously. From this point on, it seems, at least for the next decade, he never performed without a robe and a crown and all the trappings (which occasionally included midgets strewing flowers) of royalty. In England, he claims, perhaps a little fancifully, he was almost deported for practicing religion without a license, and his shows at their peak did take on all the air of a religious revival. "People fainted, people would break out into fights on certain songs, whenever I'd sing, 'I'm throwing away my little black book' in the song 'I'm Hanging Up My Heart for You,' some lady would scream out, 'How come you didn't throw it away already?' 'Tonight's the Night' always created problems in certain cities. Yeah, people took it seriously. One time in Atlanta this lady committed suicide. A very weird and troubling experience."

There were sour notes, to be sure, and there were disappointments along the way, but Solomon was unquestioned king in his day, his popularity rivaling that even of the legendary James Brown, who was known not so much for his royal aspirations as for his reputation as "the hardest-working man in show business." Brown is virtually the only one of his former colleagues about whom Solomon has less than kind words to say, but even James is dismissed with relative equanimity, as Solomon makes it clear that their differences were one-sided only and Brown is more to be pitied (for his monomania and humorlessness) than scorned.

"Well, there was no rivalry," Solomon declares. "The only problem we ever had, and it wasn't really a problem—I thought it was very amusing—you see, being the King of Rock 'n' Soul was not a situation where I had to fight for it, but a James Brown, who was the only other person with a cape out there, felt at one point after he had 'Papa's Got a Brand New Bag' and a few other songs that *he* should be the King of Soul. Now he hired me to perform with him one time in Chicago. And he paid me $10,000 for the one night, great date, because it was an early Wednesday show, we were off anyway, and when we got there, we come to find out he didn't even want the band to work, his band was going to play. So I said, 'Great!' 'Cause he had a bigger band. I was only carrying seven or eight pieces at the time, and he had a big sixteen-piece orchestra. So I said, 'Fantastic. No problem.'

"Well, we got out there, and his man comes up and says, 'Mr. Brown would like to know if you have your robe and your crown.' I say, 'Yes, I do.' And he says, 'Mr. Brown would like for you to wear it.' I say, 'No problem.' The other guy comes and says, 'Mr. Brown would like to know if you have your carpet.' I say, 'Yes, I do.' He says, 'Fine. Mr. Brown would like for you to use it.' Fine. The other guy comes out and says, 'Mr. Brown requires that you be ready to go on in five minutes.' I say, 'Okay, no problem, great.' I say, 'Could you do me one favor, though? Could you tell Mr. Brown I'd like to take care of the contract.' So another little guy comes over with a briefcase and says, 'Mr. Brown never pays the artist till after the artist performs.' I say, 'My contract requires that Mr. Brown, Mr. Blue, Mr. Black, Mr. White pays before I perform.' So it goes back and forth, it was not for real. Next thing I know James come over with all the money and threw it on the table and says, 'I got your money, I got your money, you just be out there.' He says, 'I'm gonna show you something tonight.' So this guy says, 'Mr. Brown is going to show you something tonight.' Okay, great.

"It came time for me to go on, and they had my carpet brought up to the stage and everything, and the guy says, 'Ladies and gentlemens'—a big fat guy—'the man you've all been waiting for'—and they rolled my carpet out. And I say, 'Sounds like they gonna introduce me just like they do James.' And I'm standing in the wings, you know, with my robe and my crown on. 'The man that had million sellers,' and so on and so forth. '"You Can Make It If You Try '—and I say, 'What is this?'—'"Please, Please, Please"'—I say, 'What?'—'"Papa's Got a Brand New Bag," James,'—dadedadeda—'Brown, the new King of Soul!' And James came on with his cape, dancing on the carpet. That was funny, man. He says, 'Your job, just watch me. Watch the real king.' And they kept trying to tell me, 'Mr. Brown wants you to go out now and take your crown off and put it on him.' I say, 'Man, you're crazy! Y'all are crazy.' They *would* not let me go on. He did the whole show, and the people holler, 'Solomon, Solomon, Solomon,' and he says, 'Solomon Burke cannot perform because he's been decrowned.' I never did find out what 'decrowned' meant. But it was, as I say, very amusing, and the one thing I said to James after that, I said, 'James, I want to tell you something. I enjoyed watching you perform. Really great. If you got another little job for us to do tomorrow night, we'll do it. And for only $8000. Providing we do the same thing we did tonight.'

"Oh, there were so many great times," says Solomon, who has just as many great times today and who, as we flip through a book on the Harlem Renaissance, lights up as he spies a picture of one of his idols, Father Divine. "Now that's a great image," he says. "Don't you think that would make a great image for me, Peter? Just get rid of some of the jokes."

1986

DONNA GAINES

Donna Gaines (b. 1951) earned her reputation as one of the best informed and most insightful voices in her field through decades of pop culture reportage, the pioneering texts *Teenage Wasteland: Suburbia's Dead End Kids* (1991) and *A Misfit's Manifesto: The Sociological Memoir of a Rock & Roll Heart* (2007), and her continued devotion to understanding the misunderstood as both a social worker and a sought-after lecturer on youth issues. She spent much of her adolescence and young adulthood in the vicinity of Rockaway Beach, immersing herself in the scene that bands like The Ramones would soon immortalize and learning firsthand about music's ability to "obliterate pain, transform experience, reinvent meaning . . . [and] change personal identity." In "Sylvia's Husband" she explores her own and her friends' responses to Lou Reed, and along the way learns something about the idiosyncratic ways listeners use pop music. Gaines went on to earn a master's in social work and a PhD in sociology, while establishing herself as an authority on punk and metal sound and culture with contributions to publications such as *Rolling Stone, Spin, Newsday, Salon, The Village Voice*, and numerous 'zines. She has taught sociology at Barnard College and The New School.

▼ ▼

Sylvia's Husband

THIS IS a story about Lou Reed. But it has very little to do with Reed or his wife, Sylvia Morales. Lou Reed remains unrevealed, just like any other mass-mediated icon. Madonna, for example—is she really Tom Ward's "capitalist slut," or is she Barry Walters's "pro-sex feminist," or Vince Aletti's "prokie"? We don't know and some of us don't care. So I'm not concerned with deconstructing Mr. Reed's oeuvre, in finding its telos, or in figuring out if he fucked us over by "selling out." I don't care whether Lou Reed is a legend, or a has-been grasping at maximum video revenue. What does it matter if he prefers Hondas to Harleys or if he's just putting us on? These are his problems, not mine. I'm not even one of his many obsessive fans. Some of my best friends are, though, and they've already warned me to watch what I say about Him.

First there was the Bible, then Marx, and then there was rock & roll. When things get ugly I guess I *should* invoke the psalms or Marcuse or de Beauvoir. I should be calling on them to help me understand living in the world. I mean, how else can we explain the everyday excrement where animals endure Auschwitz for human vanity and progress, where the only hold on life that teenagers feel they have left is suicide (ending it) or procreation (starting it). And then there are the betrayals: friends who die too young, lovers who turn out to be assholes, people we believe in who stick it to us. In the minutes that lie between the hurt, anger, and confusion and finding the guts to call a friend, what do I do? You got it—I stick my head inside my speakers.

But Lou Reed was never my patron saint. The thing that stood between me and mass murder was always a buzz-saw guitar. Thanks to Jimi Hendrix, somebody's life was saved by rock & roll, but not mine. As a general rule I'd rather dish it out than take it—but please, don't play an album like *Berlin* around me on a bad day. My mother was a band vocalist who sang beautiful, sad songs like "Tenderly" and "Solitude." But she was a widow in mourning. My favorite lullaby was "Summertime." It still makes me cry. I feel helpless and hopeless until I can get angry—if daddy is not "standing by," well, I want to know who is responsible. I want blood and I need noise.

Unfortunately, Lou Reed isn't loud enough to make my ears bleed. But the biggest strain in my relationship with him is that he's always seemed too smooth, too distant, too hard, too "male." Almost every obsessive female Reed fan thinks he's sexy, and has desires and fantasies about him. Not me. My great dark man has a big nose, high cheekbones, droopy eyelids and pops a rooster in the center of his crown. He's raw, loose, sloppy, and unprofessional: Johnny Thunders. But I'm not interested in having sexual fantasies about Thunderella, or Keith Richards, or even Chuck Berry. Look, it's not that simple.

Consciously, Lou Reed doesn't interest me that much. The only reason I think about him is because my friends constantly annoy me about him. (They are compelled to give me tapes of his newest albums and periodically force me to go see him live. In turn they must go with me to see Thunders, and if I am really pissed, I even make them sit through one of his annoying acoustic sets. We aren't *totally* retro, we do like to see all the new, now bands. But I'm not talking about music here, this is religion.) Unconsciously, I think I've internalized Lou Reed more than anyone else. Like everyone else I loved the Velvets. And at least one song on every solo album has broken off some of the ice around my heart. In the gut level moment of anger, pain, hatred, horror, passion, or despair it's Lou I turn to. He says all the creepy things I can't put into words. Often I'll say something wise to myself. Then I'll realize it's a Lou Reed proverb I've picked up off my turntable. I'm talking, but it's his voice.

It's now 20 years after the Velvets' first album, and people get fixated at different phases of Reed's career. Some know him only from "Heroin." Other people remember the Rock & Roll Animal boy. But my Lou Reed is the wretch who found salvation, the one who became whole. Lou Reed After Sylvia.

Some people are offended by Reed's "misogyny"—his cold mistrust of women or his glass menagerie treatment of them. At the very least, women have been problematic in Reed's work. This never bothered me, since I felt the same way about men. Reed as faggot junkie was another peacock, just like all the young dudes of that era. This "pop transvestism" revolutionized nothing much in the world of genital politics but it was fun. Anyway, the brutal feelings of fear, rage and disgust that Reed expressed never seemed gender specific to me. Whether the loved one is the other or the same sex, the roles of power and submission don't really change. There is always a struggle, always some permutation of ecstasy, trust, pain, and confusion.

From the beginning I could handle Reed's surface anger and strut, but stayed happily immune to his ever-present vulnerability. In his earlier albums there were some possibilities for getting close. But there was always a buffer zone, some escape valve that protected him from us, and us from him. For example, the bitterness and cold resolve of his "universal truth" that the dead "bitch" in "Street Hassle" will "never fuck again" is quickly betrayed by a pathetic whine that "love is gone." Here, the whiner just slips away, sha la la la, so easy to forget.

A year later, in 1979, Reed gives us the song of songs. "The Bells" is the "Kol Nidre" of rock & roll. The wedding march of the mutant bride down the aisle of some bizarro-world Brooklyn catering hall. Rococo-bop. Ave Maria, baby. Here we are as usual, waiting for something: the Messiah, the man, the beloved, the "show of shows." Meantime, we get *King Crimson Live at The Yiddish Theater*. In nine minutes and 18 seconds we have the good old wavering flame of truth, a flicker of hope for our redemption. But it's just a good drunken cry. Reed's shaky goat voice is shrouded in so much pissy schmaltz, we can laugh it off and sneak quietly out the back door.

In *Growing Up in Public*, the moth flies dangerously close to the flame. First Lou has to drag us through the mud of the human condition in "How Do You Speak to an Angel?" It's getting pretty hot, but we are not at all prepared. Our clothes are off, but we leave our shades on. We're playing it safe again in "So Alone," we're on for one last hustle.

And then the sop goes and gets married on Valentine's Day!

Two years later, in 1982, he came out with *The Blue Mask*. For no apparent reason, my friend bought it for me. I listened to "Heavenly

Arms." This is very creepy, I thought. This is too pure. The goat voice is steady and he sounds like he means it. No apology, no bravado, and no gimmicks? I waited for the punch line, but it never came.

I wondered, is Lou Reed serious—all this talk about women on the album, "only a woman can love a man"? Why? Because *they're* so disgusting and *we're* so degraded that we'll put up with them? Or is it because women are angels of mercy, not human beings? Or because only we *really* know how to give love? Even worse, was Reed just like all the other boys in the glitter bands of the 70s now asserting an orthodox heterosexuality to advance the career in Reagan's homophobe '80s? So, he "loves women"? Was he reading Ashley Montagu? Was he for real or what? Was this born-again feminism a knee-jerk reaction or a true-blue confession? In the title song, he was really baiting me—"take the Blue Mask down from my face and look me in the eye." Fuck off!

This was too much. I was confused. After the years of fancy approach-avoidance footwork, how could I trust him not to laugh at me for believing that this time he really meant it? What *was* Lou Reed's angle anyway? And what would a man be able to tell me, a woman, about emotions? How dare he intrude on female turf, to try and teach me something about feelings? No way could icy Lou be this open. Was salvation finally to be found in romantic, hetero love—the premier ideological weapon of the patriarchy? No way would I fall into that trap, and how could *he*, of all people, buy into it? He was supposed to be so smart. What about god, the movies, revolution, the purge (writing), alcohol, and noise—those more trusted saviors? Where did this leave me? I had to consult the panel of experts, among them some of my best friends.

My best friend Anthony says that Lou Reed is someone to grow old with. Reed is an organic intellectual of New York. Every region has a few, and sometimes these mentors reach out to people in other places. Anthony was brought up in rural Northwest Florida, about 30 miles south of the Alabama border. He was raised a Christian, a member of The Popular Head Free Will Baptist Church. He claims that he *was* an atheist, but now he "believes in Lou Reed." Anthony's mother has "never traveled north of the Mason-Dixon line, and has no intention of doing so." She does not like Yankees, but every Christmas she sends me Tupperware. In high school, Anthony overdosed from recreational Thorazine. The next week he was voted president of the school's honor society. He tells me that if it were not for Lou Reed, he would have done himself in long ago. Like many people, Anthony is a lonely genius. He was hard to get close to at first. But once we became friends, he was the kindest and most giving of all.

Anthony got involved with Lou through the mail. The album came rural delivery. Sometime in the early '70s he picked up a fanzine at a local convenience store. Some distributor from New York was advertising an album that looked "ultra-hip." Anthony ordered it and embraced Lou after hearing this, the Velvet Underground's third album. Anthony admits that a skinny middle-class Jewish boy from a suburb of New York is not a likely sage for a 315-pound biker from Bonifay, Florida. Anthony's obsessions should have included Lynyrd Skynyrd, Hank Williams Jr., or Molly Hatchet. He could care less if he ever meets Lou Reed. Some people have a friend in Jesus, Anthony has one in Lou. Anthony has at least five copies of everything ever issued by or about Lou Reed. This includes legitimate and bootleg albums and tapes, books, interviews, and videos, although he does not own a VCR. He has an inventory written to computer disk, consisting of five pages of text in need of chronic updating. So far Anthony has three elaborate tattoos inspired by Lou Reed, and inscribed for eternity with Reed titles—"Berlin," "Venus in Furs," and "Rock & Roll Heart."

Anthony's idea of a blissful New Year's Eve is to sit alone in the woods of his Florida plantation, with a bottle of Johnny Walker Black and a tape of *Berlin*. He finds this cathartic. Anthony admits that his relationship with Lou Reed is a little psychotic. It even drove him to violate me by dragging me to a poetry reading by Lou Reed and Jim Carroll, at the West Side YMCA a few years back. I hate poetry. Anthony never refers to Lou Reed as Lou or as Reed. Only as Lou Reed. He owns about 86 black T-shirts, many of which are Reed memorabilia, some of them in triplicate. This obsessive collecting behavior spilled over into my life when he bought me seven copies of *L.A.M.F.*, the Heartbreakers' classic album. *L.A.M.F.* has my favorite Thunders back-room pleasure hymn, "Pirate Love." Once, when I got Anthony the "Berlin" tattoo for his birthday, I almost got drunk enough to get "Pirate Love" tattooed on my forearm. But I didn't—I still hope to be buried in a Jewish cemetery, in Israel.

Anthony admires Ellen Willis, since she shares his obsession with Lou Reed. When he taught sociology at Big Science University out on Eastern Long Island, Willis's book *Beginning To See the Light* was required reading for his course. He perpetrated several abuses against the youth of America in the name of Lou Reed, like making the kids listen to *Metal Machine Music*. They were also expected to write a critique of Diana Clapton's book on Reed, drawing on sociological theories of deviance. Anthony got very good teacher evaluations, one from the Vice Provost of Undergraduate Studies himself.

Anthony does respect that Thunders is my guiding light—the principle behind my haircut and everything else that really matters—but he is a true believer. He sincerely wants to help me develop my relationship with Lou Reed. Since Ellen Willis is a feminist, Anthony figures he can use her arguments to spread Lou's word to me. In her essay about the Velvets, Willis says that listening to "Heroin" she feels "simultaneously impelled" to save Lou from the needle *and* to take it herself. Anthony twists this around to argue that men mainly identify with Lou, whereas women want to save him. I think about this. I hate heroin as much as poetry, so yeah, maybe I wouldn't identify with Lou. But the idea of saving some man, even my beloved St. John of the gutter guitar, does not move me. In rock & roll's hetero discourse of romantic love, women save men. For the man, Love is Salvation. For the woman, it's just another burden to bear. The idea of symbiosis is appealing, and some men do save women, but a chemically dependent lover of any sex is just a pain in the ass. No way. Johnny Thunders puts out hard chord in a blues field—just the thing I need to feel better. Transcendence for the moment. There's no feminist theory generated in his brilliant dick-for-brains lyrics. But that's okay, I'm just using him, I don't want to marry him.

After "Heavenly Arms" Anthony and I began using the name of Lou Reed's wife Sylvia metaphorically, to signify the most committed form of nurture. "Sylvia" was the one who would always love you, believe in you, tell you how great you were. The lover as one big pep talk. Again, this is a concept and probably has nothing much to do with Ms. Morales and her husband. If one of our friends was depressed, Anthony would say I should call him and "be Sylvia." Forget Yoko, she had an ego of her own, "Sylvia" represented the purest form of unconditional positive regard.

Anthony's reading of Willis on Reed was convincing until I got a phone call from California. My friend Vicki said she was coming to New York for a few days. I asked her how things were going between her and Lou. Vicki comes from Brighton Beach, and her father is an accountant, just like Lou's, she says. Brighton is right next to Coney Island. And so when Lou sings "Coney Island Baby" she knows he wrote it for her, even if it is dedicated to Rachel. In the summer of 1970 Vicki and I hitchhiked into New York City to see the Velvet Underground at Max's. It was the first time either of us saw Lou. I think I was a hippie then, since I remember wearing a cotton, Indian print tablecloth that I had made into a dress. I had gotten the tablecloth from Babs's father, who owned a schlock store in Brooklyn. Babs had moved to New York City and opened a boutique with a guy named Richard. Richard was an artist, and he was gorgeous. He wore antique clothes and old ladies' orthopedic shoes and streaked his long brown hair with blue and red vegetable dyes. They lived on Second Avenue with Holly Woodlawn and *Warhol* was the word. Babs was glitter and dressed very hot and vampy. Vicki and I didn't know what the fuck, but that night at Max's we were sure that Lou was singing to us. Babs is now retired and living in Florida with her three children. Vicki went on to the wild life, then marriage, divorce, and now a brilliant career in microchip.

Vicki says that Lou is still the great love of her life, and thinks he's really sexy. She'd love to "fuck his brains out" and "could give a shit about saving him." Vicki is about 10 years younger than Lou Reed, and believes that Reed makes an impressive adult role model. For Anthony, Lou Reed is the men's liberation movement. He helps Anthony to allow and understand feelings like "the violent rage that turns inward."

He "knows" he will never be "like most people," or ever "be happy."
Lou understands why, so it's all right. I feel that way too a lot, but I
just blame it on monopoly capitalism. Unfortunately this insight isn't
much help to the atomized, in those moments of pain when we all feel
so alone.

Two years ago Anthony drove out to Freeport, Long Island, to find a
certain high school. He walked across the football field trying to understand Lou's relationship with the coach he did it for in "Coney Island
Baby." Anthony didn't care if this was the same high school football
field where the real Lou Reed and his coach had a moment or if it all
happened in Coney Island near Vicki's house or off the back of Lou
Reed's eyelids one night. We've never seen god except in pictures. People have always needed something to believe in. The rock & roll sage
is there for us, the message is inscribed in vinyl, to guide us in sickness
and in health.

Now I'm real tough and Anthony's groovy. Lou is a reptile. He's cold
and hard and distant, he's so "male." Lou Reed has always played both
sides of the fence: too cool, and too deep. Reed the trickster explores
the things we won't 'fess up to. Then, just when it gets scary, he lets
us off the hook. Except sometimes he makes us sweat and that's good
for us, and for him. I remember hanging out at Max's back then, with
Babs and Vicki; everyone is trying to be so cool that nobody will make
eye contact. People are high and sneer at anyone they aren't cruising.
By 1987 we are mature, even bored, thinking about alienation. We have
our lovely lives. We're beyond these questions. But Lou Reed knows
better, like the way he cautions the pained and frustrated to "spit it
out" on *Mistrial.*

There are political explanations for the personal things that Lou Reed
has articulated all these years. We know all the reasons why we protect
and pretend the self, and about how order is served by "self-control."
We're wise to how we get burned in the name of the things we hold
sacred. Lou Reed's naked embrace of "Sylvia" in "Heavenly Arms" was
the most subversive move he's made so far. And whatever the hell he
"really" had in mind, I don't know. And where he's gone from there, I

don't care. 'Cause when I heard that, I could not deny the possibilities he held out. And though this embarrassed me, it made a few of my friends very happy.

1987

DAVE MARSH

Whether devoting an entire book to one track (*Louie Louie: The History and Mythology of the World's Most Famous Rock 'n' Roll Song*) or a thousand of them (*The Heart of Rock & Soul: The 1001 Greatest Singles Ever Made*), Dave Marsh's writing gives free rein to his obsession with rock and pop music. A founding editor of *Creem*, Marsh (b. 1950) may have coined the term "punk rock" in a 1971 piece on ? and the Mysterians. To date, he has written more than twenty books, including studies of stars ranging from Elvis Presley to The Who to Michael Jackson to Bruce Springsteen. He has frequently spoken out against the censorship of music and regularly exercises his own right to speak freely in his writing—especially his album reviews, in which he often seems to take unbecoming glee in lacerating his subject. His uncensored commentary has not won him any friends in the Bay Area bands Journey or the Grateful Dead ("the worst band in creation"), but it has fueled over four decades of contributions to *Rolling Stone*, *Newsday*, *The Village Voice*, and *Playboy*, among others. His most recent book, *360 Sound: The Columbia Records Story, Legends and Legacy* (2012), chronicles the 264 greatest songs from Columbia Records, from John Philip Sousa's "Washington Post March" (1890) to Adele's "Rolling in the Deep" (2011). His encyclopedic proclivities and confident assertions of taste combine gloriously in the entries from *The Heart of Rock & Soul* included here.

▼ ▼

from
The Heart of Rock & Soul: The 1001 Greatest Singles Ever Made

189 DEDICATED TO THE ONE I LOVE, The Shirelles
Produced by Luther Dixon; written by Lowman Pauling and Ralph Bass
Scepter 1203   1959   *Billboard*: #3

"Dedicated to the One I Love" may be the key record in the development of contemporary black vocal group harmony, the clearest single example of what happened as the sounds of Southern Negroes migrated to the industrialized North. The "5" Royales version reflects tough, Southern R&B in the waning days of its power. Although the disc's signature moment comes at the top, with Johnny Tanner's ragged a cappella cry, "This is dedicated to the one I-ay-I love!" the record's center is Lowman Pauling's stinging guitar lick, and the solo that he builds from it.

That's not to say that the record is crude. In fact, the Royales were perhaps the most sophisticated of all the R&B groups, and their arrangement of "Dedicated" is no exception. In this version, the song was an adult's statement of devotion despite physical separation, and Tanner sings it in a style closer to jump band vocalists like Wynonie Harris and Roy Brown than to any street corner doo-wopper.

Luther Dixon picked "Dedicated to the One I Love" for his first production with what became the first great girl group. The Shirelles were four high school kids from Passaic, New Jersey: Shirley Owens, Beverly Lee, Doris Kenner, and Mickey Harris. In early 1958, they scored a minor hit on Decca (originally, Tiara) with "I Met Him on a Sunday." When Decca, one of the industry "majors" and thus still oriented to blues-less white pop, couldn't provide a follow-up hit, their manager, Florence Greenberg started Scepter as a vehicle for the girls and a main chance for herself.

Luther Dixon's career began in the Four Buddies, a first-rate R&B quartet. By the time he hooked up with these girls, he'd had a good deal of experience as a songwriter and publisher, contributing smooth crooner ballads to the likes of Pat Boone and Perry Como. Even after the Shirelles started to click, Dixon was the most in-demand demo singer in New York. Dixon's importance on the New York pop scene was great enough that Greenberg had to give him substantial incentives to work with the Shirelles: He obtained both a piece of the action (in the form of song publishing rights and an ownership position in Scepter) and the right to produce the group to his own specifications.

"Dedicated to the One I Love" became Dixon's first production with the girls. His arrangement smoothed over much of the original grit. The guitar lick disappeared, replaced by a wordless soprano obligato, and the female chorus that had been a minor accoutrement was brought front and center. Tanner's stop-time vocal effects were replaced by straight vocal group harmonizing.

The result was as stunning in its own right as the original. At the time, female black harmony groups were all but unknown; besides "I Met Him on a Sunday," only the Chantels' "Maybe" had ever made much of a commercial or creative impression. Kenner's initial "This is dedicated to the one I love" was less melismatic but more plaintive than Tanner's, and the girls' harmonies conveyed not the story of two mature lovers trying to cope with a pragmatic dislocation but the story of two teenagers separated by social convention rather than great distance. (The boy and girl in this song might well be living next door to one another.) There's a kind of knowing innocence in the Shirelles' version of "Dedicated to the One I Love" that would thereafter become part of the common stock of rock and roll but was nowhere to be found before it. No adult singer could have given the song this implied subtext.

"Dedicated to the One I Love" brought the Shirelles back to the pop charts but not for long; the record peaked at Number 83 and dropped off the pop chart after only four weeks. But it gave Dixon a sense of direction and he focused all the group's subsequent releases around the same idea, edging into the Top 40 in September 1960 with "Tonight's the Night" and hitting the jackpot at the end of the year with "Will You Still Love Me Tomorrow," in which the subtext—female teenage sexual activity—became as overt as contemporary radio could cope with. That record went all the way to Number One, and it had a lot to do with initiating both the doo-wop revival and the dawning of the great age of the girl groups.

"Will You Still Love Me Tomorrow" was so massive, in fact, that it dragged "Dedicated to the One I Love" back to the charts. In late February 1961, "Dedicated" cracked the *Billboard* Top Ten. ("Will You Still Love Me Tomorrow" was still there, too.) It eventually reached the Top Three, and its own drawing power was so great that the "5" Royales's reissued original was pulled onto the pop charts for the first time.

For the past quarter century, "Dedicated to the One I Love" has been almost continually revived: The Mamas and Papas steam-cleaned the harmonies and took it to Number Two in 1967, and it's charted twice more since then. But in the context of today's more sexually open society, the *song's* innocence isn't really anything more than an opportunity to play nostalgic games with its contextual incongruity. These *records*, however, are stamped with the sense of daring and innovation with which they were made.

247 CRUISIN', Smokey Robinson
Produced by Smokey Robinson; written by Smokey Robinson and Marvin Tarplin
Tamla 54306   1979   *Billboard*: #4

Sometimes I feel that Smokey Robinson raised me from a pup. Surely, it was his voice that first beckoned me from the radio to a world outside my house and neighborhood that was unimaginably larger than anything I'd dreamed. And though these days he's ofttimes too slick and bland for his own good, his early music—not only the records he led with the Miracles but the songs he wrote and produced for the Temptations and Marvin Gaye and other subjects of the Motown empire—remains central to my definition of what's important in pop. And though he's defined earlier in this volume as a non-soul singer, that just shows you the limitation of taking such an elastic term and giving it a purely musical definition (not that you don't have to do just that, sometimes).

When I was a kid, Smokey's voice called to me as an exemplar of smooth cool, a surface unrippled even though heartbreak lurked just beneath. It took me years to understand why the *really* dangerous aspect of what Smokey (and the singers like him) were selling was the romantic stuff, not because it represents an inadequate dream (it may represent the only adequate one, since it posits grace and gentleness and giving and love transcending lust as the greatest of all human and sexual virtues) but because it proffers an impossible reality. So there's simply no reason to feel all that abject in the moments when you don't have those things . . . or all that triumphant in the moments when, quite temporarily, you think you do. Nevertheless the ideas the records expressed were what counted, and they were both complex and transformative.

Fifteen years after our first encounter, I was cruising through Hollywood in somebody else's Cadillac when "Cruisin'" came on the radio. I'd already heard it on a Robinson album called *Where There's Smoke*, but there it was suffocated by the songs and arrangements that surrounded it.

Tooling that massive hunk of Detroit luxury iron down Sunset Strip, caught by surprise through the mysteries of the airwaves, "Cruisin'" revealed itself as something better and finer than anything else Smokey had done in his solo career. The singing absolutely glided on a bed of strings, the rhythm popped along gently, driven by nothing more forceful than conga and tambourine and the restless tug of Marvin Tarplin's soft electric guitar. He kept the tone restful and sensuous, like an airier "Let's Get It On." The result was a call to seduction so persuasive that it nearly (nearly) overrode the ambiguities raised by his selection of a gay term as the central metaphor.

A decade later, none of that seems as consequential as the thrillingly high "Aah" to which Smokey twice drives himself during the final choruses. As with "Let's Get It On," the record can't entirely conceal a predatory male perspective. (I mean, none of this breathless "Baby, tonight belongs to us" shit would really work if you said it to somebody in a bar, or even in bed. Would it?) So there's grave danger in taking it too seriously. But even if you—or rather, I—feel a little duped and entrapped by the philosophy behind those seductive phrases, there's no point in bearing a grudge. Beauty carries its own prejudices, and this is one hell of a beautiful record.

385 RUNNING ON EMPTY, Jackson Browne
Written and produced by Jackson Browne
Asylum 45460   1978   *Billboard*: #11

386 ROLL ME AWAY, Bob Seger
Produced by Jimmy Iovine; written by Bob Seger
Capitol 5235   1983   *Billboard*: #27

"Running on Empty" and "Roll Me Away" serve as generational anthems for a whole crowd of people who found the seventies and early eighties increasing both their material riches and spiritual impoverishment. They meet in the middle of mainstream (nonpunk) rock trends of the period, Browne appearing as the most fecund California singer/songwriter, Seger as the anguished embodiment of Midwestern rock. What makes the dialogue between these records more arresting is that each appeared at a moment of transition for its creator, a time when populist Seger was heading for ultraprivate concerns and the comparatively cloistered singer/songwriter Browne began to test the social limits of his personal vision.

I feel this connection strongly because it was Bob Seger who clued me in to "Running on Empty"'s finest line: "I look around for the friends that I used to turn to to pull me through / Lookin' into their eyes, I see them runnin' too." And though Waddy Wachtel's excessively wailing guitar seems more dated every year, it's hard to think of another record that speaks so forthrightly to and about a world that was disintegrating before its own eyes in a cycle of denial and repression that took the shape of rampant hedonism. "Running on Empty" is the title track of an album that winds down with a tribute to cocaine. Today, hearing the lyric that Seger's acute ear picked up so quickly, I think of a roster of Browne's friends that might include Lowell George, who overdosed and died, Warren Zevon, rehabbed and rehabbed and held together with main human strength and raw talent, and David Crosby, surviv-

ing massive cocaine addiction through a period of imprisonment but
ballooned to three hundred pounds in compensation. In that crowd,
"Running on Empty" was less a metaphor than a prophesy, a post-
Woodstock "Dead Man's Curve."

"Everyone I know, everywhere I go / People need some reason to
believe," Browne sings. And then, in the most pained voice he's ever
used, he stops and shouts: "I don't know about anyone but me!" It's a
cry that defines the period and Browne has spent the rest of his career
trying to resolve the contradiction it expresses.

When the Selfish Seventies drew to a close, things got worse, not
better. For a performer as devoted to both craft and populist insight as
Bob Seger, the situation was worse than confusing. Beyond what was
happening in a world run by Reagans and Thatchers and in a music
scene overpopulated with art students perfectly comfortable in their
contempt for the mass audience, there was a purely personal level on
which it grew ever harder to walk the line between high energy Detroit
rock and roll and the facts of a fortyish existence.

"Roll Me Away" speaks to all these things through the story of a
cross-country motorcycle trip, rumbling from Mackinac City, the
Hiawatha village where Lake Michigan converges with Lake Huron, to
the Continental Divide. Along the way, Seger finds a love and lets it dis-
sipate, turns alone into the cold winds of the Rockies and lets his frustrations and confusion congeal into one sad cry that dissolves his fate
into what has happened to the whole crazy mess of a world in which he
lives. He vows to keep moving, rolling away, rolling away, promises that
he can straighten everything out so long as the search never ceases—so
long as he never rests. And then pulls the trigger on the joke. "And as
the sunset faded I spoke to the famous first starlight," Seger sings, in a
perfect parody of the Saturday afternoon westerns that inspired him, "I
said next time—next time—we'll get it right."

It's Roy Bittan's elegiac piano chords that tell the bitter truth. The
time for roving is over. It's time to settle in, time for America to abandon its gluttonous expansionism, time for the wild boys of rock and roll
to come indoors and call what they find there home. (It's what happens
after the last scene of John Ford's *The Searchers*.)

Seger's more recent records have been bland, the lyrics glossing over issues he used to penetrate, the music too often nothing more than highly crafted country-pop. Browne has thrown himself into a virtually full-time commitment to opposing U.S. intervention in Central America; his more recent songs abandon psychological complexities for agitprop that, no matter how highly polished, lacks the reach of his best personal material. So neither Seger nor Browne has resolved the contradiction at the heart of their best singles. But then, neither have many of the people to whom their songs most clearly speak.

510 TIME AFTER TIME, Cyndi Lauper

Produced by Rick Chertoff; written by Cyndi Lauper and Rob Hyman
Portrait 04432   1984   *Billboard*: #1 (2 weeks)

Lying in bed, a young woman stares up at the ceiling and sees the stars beyond the grime. Unable to sleep, she dreams of changing worlds, not least or just her own. The ticking of a clock counts the score.

Cyndi Lauper perhaps wrote "Time After Time" as a parable of her own life as a misfit artiste but she scored with it by capturing the wee hours heebie-jeebies of just about any old body. The music—mainly a wash of synthesizer, a heartbeat bass drum, metronomic snare shots and a growly guitar—resonates at exactly the right frequency to put her mood across, but it's the gently desperate singing that clinches the deal. If she let that misfit metaphor slide over into a reincarnation fantasy, she'd have confirmed her bubblehead surface. Instead, she totally subverted it by making her most mystical-sounding line into a ferocious cry of fidelity. "*I* will be waiting," Cyndi shouts, and everybody in earshot wakes up.

1989

CHUCK EDDY

Like Lester Bangs before him, Chuck Eddy (b. 1960) is a controversialist. He's a man with strong opinions, and he tosses them about like small grenades, goading his readers (and sometimes his subjects) into response; he's a provocateur, seeking to upset rock writing's pieties and to declare that the emperor has no clothes (as he did in his infamous posthumous takedown of Kurt Cobain). Or the 1990 assessment of The Ramones' career included here: The Ramones prove useful to a point in understanding the cultural significance of punk—but their recent work shows they've lost their edge, and Eddy seems to feel an ethical obligation to say so. None of this is surprising, perhaps, in a critic who got his start by writing a letter to *The Village Voice* deriding the state of popular music criticism. Besides working as editor and writer at the *Voice*, Eddy has written for *Creem*, *Rolling Stone*, *Spin*, *Entertainment Weekly*, and other national magazines. Much of the energy of his writing derives from the uncertain register of his authorial voice, which teeters uncertainly between earnestness and facetiousness (again evoking Bangs). Did he really believe the Osmonds belonged in *Stairway to Hell: The 500 Best Heavy Metal Albums in the Universe*? That the hair-metal band Poison was better than The Beatles? The simple fact is, he does make us wonder. In 2011, Duke University Press collected some of his best pieces in *Rock and Roll Always Forgets: A Quarter Century of Music Criticism.*

▼ ▼

The Ramones

THE APRIL 1977 issue of *16* magazine had the teen icons the Bay City Rollers on the cover. But inside, in her "Music Makers" column—amid textual analysis of the Sylvers and David Soul—a writer named Mandy answered the question "What is Punk Rock?" This was, no doubt, the first time many young Americans had heard this curious phrase. "Punk Rock is a term being applied to lots of different groups!" wrote Mandy. "Most Punk Rock groups have one thing in common—a good, loud, exciting hard rock sound, and a tendency to keep songs fairly short." Actually, that's *two* things they have in common. Regardless, nobody has explained it better since.

Two months earlier Mandy had gushed over "I Wanna Be Your Boyfriend," the new Ramones single, calling it "super romantic and sexy." "I Wanna Be Your Boyfriend," like another Ramones song called "Now I Wanna Sniff Some Glue," was in the grand tradition of "I wanna" records, dating back through the Stooges' "I Wanna Be Your Dog" to the Beatles' "I Want to Hold Your Hand." Like other punk bands, the Ramones presented themselves as a return to what had once made rock & roll great, before it became soggy and serious and slick and stagnant. Punk set out to revive what it saw as simplicity, chaos, danger, irony, fun. So, throughout the middle Seventies, at such New York venues as the Mercer Arts Center and Max's Kansas City and CBGB, bar bands and art bands full of dropouts and prep-school misfits and failed poets from Forest Hills and Rhode Island and Detroit ruled the roost, often glorifying being down and out, a condition that more than a few such scenesters consciously selected. They wore unusual haircuts and jumped up and down a lot. Most of these groups—the Mumps, Tuff Darts, Psychotic Frogs, Laughing Dogs—aren't even footnotes anymore.

In 1976 the Ramones, one of the best and most famous of these New York bands, toured England and instigated an explosion. The Sex Pistols—vermin that had found their artistic calling while killing time at a respected bondage-and-rubber outlet called Sex, owned by a Situationist huckster named Malcolm McLaren—had played their first show in November 1975; a year later, their singer, snarling as though he were burning himself at the stake, they issued "Anarchy in the UK," their first single. Within months it seemed every other disgruntled resident of the United Kingdom under the age of twenty had joined a band and released a punk single of his or her own. (The *her* was important—like no rock before, punk inspired women to develop their own voices.)

The New York bands had sung with their tongues in their cheeks, but in the U.K., punk was played as if far more were at stake than the future of rock & roll—the future of their nation, perhaps, or the human race. England, then, was where most of the enduring punk recordings —the early Pistols singles, the first Clash album, the Vibrators' *Pure Mania*, the Adverts' *Crossing the Red Sea*, X-ray Spex' "Oh Bondage Up Yours!"—came from.

In 1977 people thought this stuff might take over the world, or at least the Top Forty. In England, at least for a while, it did. Back in the U.S.A., it didn't even come close. But in both countries bands playing original material appeared in every borough, suburb and hamlet, having learned from the Ramones and Pistols that "anyone could do it" (which turned out to be a baldfaced lie, but what the heck).

Every town had its own punk-rock club; in 1982, *Volume: International Discography of the New Wave* listed more than 16,000 records by more than 7500 bands on 3000 labels, as well as 1300 fanzines. Eventually, the music split into scores of factions, encompassing everything from Marxist avant-funk to revivalist rockabilly to power pop and techno-disco. But one congregation of stubborn souls insisted on remaining true to punk as it was played in 1977, and in 1990 the Ramones are still among them.

"There's some of us here today that still fuckin' *remembuh rock & roll radio*," shouts Joey Ramone from the concrete stage, lamenting the passing of the Animals and Murray the K, beating a horse that's been dead for decades. With the rest of his band, Joey is wrapping up the Cincinnati installment of Escape From New York, a summer package tour also starring Debbie Harry, Tom Tom Club and Jerry Harrison (the last two units billing themselves collectively as Shrunken Heads), graduates all of the Bowery punk milieu of the mid-Seventies.

Joey, still a string bean, exudes a warped charisma none of the thousand punk frontmen he inspired can touch. But it's 1990, and it's really hard to care. Behind him, bedecked with that classic Ramones emblem—an American eagle clutching a baseball bat in one talon and an apple-tree branch in the other—is a canvas sheet painted to look like a brick wall. The canvas could represent the urban hell from which this band supposedly sprang, or the Phil Spector Wall of Sound they electrocuted into a wall of noise, or the wall whose collapse they celebrated in their beloved Germany last year. Or what it may represent is the wall that's held the Ramones at square 1, the wall that's kept them, and so very much of the music they fathered and grandfathered, safe.

To Joey's left is C.J. Ramone, a bassist who these days moves around more than any of his proud pinhead siblings; onstage he is the new king of the Ramones leg-spread stance. C.J. wasn't born till 1965, so he's too young to remember rock & roll radio. Instead, he grew up on the Ramones and the Dead Kennedys and Metallica; he knew only one other punk rocker at his high school. When Dee Dee Ramone defected to rap, C.J. figured he'd never attend a Ramones show again, but then the band hired him to take Dee Dee's place. C.J. was AWOL from the marines at the time. Joey says C.J. had the right attitude, but guitarist Johnny Ramone says he makes the band look young. That was a priority.

As he finishes breakfast at a Bob Evans restaurant in Lafayette, Indiana, C.J. realizes this is the hometown of another early Ramones fan by the name of Axl Rose. Which figures—with his torsoful of tattoos, C.J. is the only Ramone who'd look right in Guns n' Roses. Later that day, in Cincinnati, Robin Frantz, the seven-year-old son of Chris Frantz and Tina Weymouth of Tom Tom Club and Talking Heads, is running around wearing a Guns n' Roses T-shirt. Robin says he likes G n' R "the same" as Tom Tom Club; says most heavy metal is just good for pumping your fist but "Welcome to the Jungle" is good for dancing; says Donatello is his favorite Teenage Mutant Ninja Turtle "'cause he can hit things from far away"; says he doesn't have a favorite Tom Tom or T-Heads song, but his favorite G n' R tune is "Sweet Child o' Mine"; and says his mom doesn't like G n' R, because "Axl's voice goes too high." Tina Weymouth says she thinks Axl is cute and tells me she's "sick of boring pseudo-intellectuals like David Byrne."

Escape From New York is *not*, the principals will assure you, a nostalgia tour, but when ? and the Mysterians played Bookie's Club 870 in Detroit in 1980, *that* was certainly nostalgia, and ? was a punk before CBGB punks were punks, and "96 Tears" came out in 1966, and *The Ramones* came out in 1976, and fourteen years is fourteen years, right? Johnny, clad in the band's best shag and a U.S. Army Special Forces T-shirt, insists the Ramones aren't relics, because "we never stopped putting out records, and when I watch us on videotapes from five or ten years ago, I find out we're better now than we were then."

And they've got a point—to a point. Though there are a few well-bred waistline casualties who look as if they had closed up the office early for the day, the Cincy crowd isn't mostly old New Wavers out for memories; it's kids out for kicks, scrubbed suburban brats in Smiths and 7 Seconds and Faster Pussycat T-shirts. The teenybopper girls in Cure and Depeche Mode T's are way more lively than the rad boys in Misfits and Danzig T's, but every last member of the crowd is involved, screaming at lung tops while standing on seat tops.

The Ramones have a very loyal audience, and all the way back to "Sheena Is a Punk Rocker," Joey's songs have suggested that he loves his disciples as much as they love him. "They know that we care about them," he says. Their audience has evolved over the years, from post-Warhol art students in the early days to gobbing mohawk-wearers of yore to postmetal high-school students today, but all along it's been a self-classified community of misfits—"Gabba gabba we accept you we accept you one of us," goes the Ramones anthem "Pinhead."

An obvious comparison is to the Grateful Dead (an analogy C.J. likes, though Johnny can't stomach it), with Joey as the punk Jerry Garcia. Could be. The extent to which these original punks are still children of the Sixties at heart—greasers and hippies—is surprising. Tina Weymouth uses the word *Zen* a lot; the Ramones stay tuned to the oldies stations. Still, it's easy to understand why teenage newcomers keep joining the Ramones army—take the guns-on-automatic part, the five or six straight crash-bangs, at the end of their set. In concert the Ramones play the "hits," like "I Wanna Be Sedated," because that's what the fans scream for. They play them like seasoned pros; the problem is, standing against seasoned professionalism is what once made this a great band.

And an important one, too, obviously. British punk can be read as a reaction to the dole queue and impending Thatcherism, but inasmuch as Ameripunk meant anything, it meant putting a generation of old farts out to pasture. At least that's what it meant if you're to believe most of the zillion words that have been written about it since—that the music had grown overblown and impersonal and corporate and soft, that the stars were all either blow-dried bores or black-tied jet-setters sniffing powder in the back seats of limos, blah blah blah. Punks defined themselves, or were defined, as the opposition; the New Wave audience identified itself as an "alternative." Drummer Marky Ramone, all Brooklyn biceps beneath his *War of the Worlds* shirt, says how "in those days there were a lot of stuffy people who took rock way too seriously." So punk rock, starting with the Ramones, changed the rules. It redefined "success."

What does this formulation ignore? First, punk rock didn't just "happen." In New York, at least, it was a direct offshoot of glitter rock as typified by the New York Dolls, who were inspired by the British glitter of David Bowie, who was inspired in turn by New York's Velvet Underground, which also largely inspired mid-Seventies Cleveland bands like Rocket From the Tombs and the Electric Eels, both of which also drew on late-Sixties Detroit bands like the Stooges and MC5, which were inspired by the Stones and the Doors . . . and so on.

Yet in the early Seventies, while Joey Ramone was biding time at Slade and Black Sabbath shows and not finding them impersonal in any way he can remember, Marky Ramone was still Marc Bell, drumming for a street-level speed-metal band named Dust. And as late as 1975 and 1976, AC/DC's *High Voltage* and Aerosmith's *Toys in the Attic* and Ted Nugent's "Free for All" were uniting punk volumes with punk tempos with punk attitudes with better-than-punk rhythm sections. And unlike the bands the Gotham media were falling in love with at the time, these bands were selling records—to high-school kids, of all people!

So was punk rock really new? Who knows! The Ramones combined old stuff, mainly power chords and bubblegum-surfboard harmonies, but they did it in a brand-new way. "Our music was structured like nothing else was ever structured before it," says Johnny. "Ballroom Blitz," by the Sweet, had gone Top Five the year before the suspiciously similar "Blitzkrieg Bop" hit the racks, but the Sweet never had the Ramones' singleness of purpose. In Ramones rock, there was no respite, no letup; the slightest change—a hand clap, a falsetto, an echo, a three-second Farfisa or a twenty-second guitar solo—felt cataclysmic.

And nobody else had ever celebrated the fuck-up-at-life disease the way the Ramones did—nobody ever sang anything like "Sitting here in Queens / Eating refried beans / We're in all the magazines / Gulping down Thorazines" before. "We always had this trademark," Joey says. "I just figured it was some kind of chemical imbalance." They gave a voice to the junk-food anomie of postaffluent American adolescence— like Chuck Berry or *MAD* magazine, only sicker.

The Ramones still don't understand how this linked them with Blondie and Talking Heads and Television and Patti Smith. "I never thought we had anything in common with those bands," says Joey. "We were the only hard-rock group there." But Tina Weymouth claims that all the bands were making music that hadn't been made before, that "the Ramones were an art band too, in their own way." To be that "spontaneous" in 1976, to record your album in a week for $6400, to adopt a common last name and common leather-jacket-and-ripped-jeans uniform, to create such cartoonish personas—to do all these things required a degree of meticulous thought unheard of in the land of AC/DC and Nugent and even Kiss. "What set the Ramones apart from all the hardcore bands that came later was their discipline," says Weymouth. They chose to be primitive.

And, boy, did the idea ever catch on. "I bet the Ramones influenced more bands than anybody else on the scene today," says C.J. Between speed metal and the Sex Pistols and hardcore and the whole idea of do-it-yourself, which spawned the whole idea of local scenes, which spawned the whole idea of postpunk independent labels, C.J. may be right. Consider, too, all the onetime punk rockers who wound up as stars, invariably playing something other than punk rock—Billy Idol, the Beastie Boys, Belinda Carlisle, Neneh Cherry, Debbie Harry, Joan Jett, various members of Guns n' Roses. And then think of the Ramones T-shirts you'll find on the chests of guys in Def Leppard and Poison; then the Megadeth and Skid Row covers of the Pistols—sometimes it seems heavy metal simply absorbed punk outright.

But that hasn't stopped the Ramones from rolling. They're now into their fifth van in umpteen years (it's a Chevy with transmission problems). Their twelfth album, *Brain Drain*, released in 1989, has a song about not fighting on Christmas, a Freddy Cannon cover, some leaden playing, some heartfelt crap, even some bubble-headed rock poetry in "Punishment Fits the Crime." Like every Ramones recording after their uncharacteristically scary "Bonzo Goes to Bitburg," in 1985, *Brain Drain* is impossible to get excited about. Maybe they should try house music or something. As Johnny says, "In this ever-changing world the Ramones stay the same." (Or as their tour manager, Monte Melnick, puts it, "The song Ramones the same.") Only the Ramones don't see it as a problem.

"We try to maintain what the Ramones are known for—hard, fast, crazy music," says Joey. Unfortunately, in 1990, hard, fast, crazy, three-chord, two-minute alienation feels like old hat. Johnny says he plans to retire after twenty years, which means 1994, since this combo dates to 1974. Until then, he says, "we just have to keep doing what we do well, even though there's no way we're gonna shake the world like we did with that first record." Sounds a bit like he's surrendering, doesn't it?

Instead of learning from Bon Jovi or New Kids on the Block, the way they once learned from the Ohio Express and the Trashmen, all the Ramones can do now is dismiss today's teenyboppers as kids who "don't know anything about real music and who just get suckered in by the radio" (according to Johnny) or who "buy records just because they like how the band looks" (according to C.J.). These nice guys are missing the boat, missing the joke, missing what's fun, pretending the world has stopped turning. Discussing the contradictions inherent in Ramones-on-CD, Marky says: "You can't fight progress." These days punk rock is trying its damnedest to do just that.

1990

Eve Babitz

Eve Babitz's hoard of indelible experiences ensured her legend. Her brilliance in documenting the bohemian excess in which she participated made her a key witness to her era in the Southern California counterculture. Born in 1943 in Los Angeles to a family of musicians, Babitz began her artistic career in visual mediums, modeling for one of the decade's most iconic photographs—a nude chess match against artist Marcel Duchamp—and later working at Atlantic Records designing album covers for The Byrds and Buffalo Springfield. Her 1974 book, *Eve's Hollywood*, itemized her romantic entanglements with a number of prominent musicians and screen stars, in an imperishable voice that made it an outspoken declaration of sexual independence. Her subsequent books include *Slow Days, Fast Company: The World, The Flesh, and L.A.*; and *Sex and Rage: Advice to Young Ladies Eager for a Good Time*. Babitz contributed to publications such as *Cosmopolitan*, *Esquire*, *Vogue*, and *Rolling Stone*. Her piece here on The Doors' lead singer Jim Morrison is representative in the way it combines intimate knowledge of its subject with a coolly critical eye. Injuries suffered in a 1997 fire precipitated a partial retreat from public life. *Eve's Hollywood* was reissued, to great acclaim, by New York Review Books in 2015.

▼ ▼

Jim Morrison Is Dead and Living in Hollywood

J.D. SOUTHER once told me he spent his first years in L.A. learning how to stand. Jim knew how to stand from the start. He stood pigeon-toed, filled with poetry against a mike with that honky-tonk Berlin organ in the background, and sang about "another kiss."

And there is something to be said for singing in tune. Jim not only sang in tune, he sang intimately—as Doors producer Paul Rothchild once pointed out to me, "Jim was the greatest crooner since Bing Crosby."

He was Bing Crosby from hell.

In those days, in the '60s, people in L.A. with romantic streaks who knew music went for the Byrds, Buffalo Springfield, Paul Butterfield—and for clubs like the Troubadour and the Trip and the Ash Grove. The Whiskey, where the Doors flourished, was the kind of place where the headliner would be Johnny Rivers, a white boy who covered Chuck Berry's "Memphis." By the '60s, white boys weren't supposed to cover soul anymore, but at the Whiskey it was still groovy. The Carpenters played the Whiskey.

At the Whiskey, the bouncers were bouncers, the management was from New York City, and the women wore beehive hairdos long after it was cool.

Rock groups who went to college and actually got degrees were not only uncool, they were unheard-of.

Jim went to college and he graduated. My friend Judy Raphael, who went to film school, too, remembers Jim as this pudgy guy with a marine haircut who worked in the library at UCLA and who was supposed to help her with her documentary term paper one night but ended up talking drunkenly and endlessly about Oedipus, which meant she had to take the course over that summer.

The Doors were embarrassing, like their name. I dragged Jim into bed before they'd decided on the name and tried to dissuade him; it was so corny naming yourself after something Aldous Huxley wrote.

I mean, *The Doors of Perception* . . . what an Ojai-geeky-too-L.A.-pottery-glazer kind of uncool idea.

The Beatles were desperate criminals compared with them. The Beatles only had one leg to stand on—rock 'n' roll. The Doors, though, were film majors. Being a film major in the '60s was hopelessly square. If you wanted to make a movie, even if you went to UCLA like Francis Coppola and then to the Roger Corman School of Never Lost a Dime Pictures, you *still* weren't cool. Even Jack Nicholson wasn't cool in the '60s. Being an actor wasn't cool in the '60s, because all movies did was get everything *all wrong*. At least until *Easy Rider*, being in the movie business was a horrible thing to admit.

Of course, Oliver Stone was *so* uncool he voluntarily went to Vietnam instead of prowling around the Sunset Strip with the rest of his generation. Oliver Stone was such a nerd he became a soldier, a Real Man. He didn't understand that in the '60s real men were not soldiers. A real man was Mick Jagger in *Performance*, in bed with two women, wearing eye makeup and kimonos. Or John Phillip Law, with wings, in *Barbarella*. Of course, Bob Dylan was even cooler than Mick Jagger, so cool he couldn't sing. He didn't bother, and he was so skinny, with those narrow little East Coast shoulders and that face. And he was mean.

Like everyone back then, Jim hated his parents, hated home, hated it all. If he could have gotten away with it, Jim would have been an orphan. He tried lying about having parents, creating his life anew—about what you'd expect from someone who'd lost thirty pounds in one summer (the summer of '65, from taking drugs instead of eating, and hanging out on the Venice boardwalk). I mean, he awoke one morning and was *so* cute, how *could* he have parents?

According to some health statistics I recently heard about, the '50s was the decade when the American diet contained its highest percentage of fat—over 50 percent. And these '50s children, overfed, repressed, and indignant, waited in the wings, lurking and praying to get big enough to get the fuck out. Jim Morrison had it worse than a lot of kids. He was fat. And his father was a naval officer.

Then the ultimate dream of everyone who weighs too much and gets thin happened to Jim. He lost the weight and turned into the Prince.

Into John, Paul, George, and Ringo.

Into Mick.

I met Jim early in '66, when he'd just lost the weight and wore a suit made of gray suede, lashed together at the seams with lanyards, and no shirt. It was the best outfit he ever had, and he was so cute that no woman was safe. He was twenty-two, a few months younger than I.

He had the freshness and humility of someone who had been fat all his life and was now suddenly a morning glory.

I met Jim and propositioned him in three minutes, even *before* he so much as opened his mouth to sing. This great event took place not at the Whiskey but at a now-forgotten club just down on the Strip called the London Fog, the first bar there the Doors played. And there were only about seven people in the room anyway.

"Take me home," I demurely offered when we were introduced. "You're not really going to stay here playing, are you?"

"Uh," he replied, "we don't play. We work."

I suggested the next night. And that's when it happened (finally!). Naturally, I dressed my part—black eye makeup out to there, a mini-skirt up to here—but the truth was that I did, in fact, have parents. On our first date I even confessed to Jim that my ridiculous father was on that very night playing violin in a program of music by Palestrina. To my tremendous dismay, Jim immediately expressed his desire to drive to Pasadena. I packed him into my '52 Cadillac and off we went, but by intermission I had had enough. He whined that he wanted to stay for the second half, but I put my foot down.

"You just can't be here," I said. "Listening to this. You just can't."

Being in bed with Jim was like being in bed with Michelangelo's *David*, only with blue eyes. His skin was so white, his muscles were so pure, he was so innocent. The last time I saw him with no shirt on, at a party up in Coldwater, his body was so ravaged by scars, toxins, and puffy pudginess, I wanted to kill him.

He never really stopped being a fat kid. He used to suggest, "Let's go to Ships and get blueberry pancakes with blueberry syrup."

"It's so fattening," I would point out.

I mean, really.

Jim was embarrassing because he wasn't cool, but I still loved him. It was his mouth, of course, which was so edible. Just so long as he didn't smile and reveal his too-Irish teeth, just so long as he kept his James Dean smolder, it worked. But it takes a lot of downers to achieve that on a full-time basis. And no fat.

Just so long as he stood there in the leather clothes my sister had hand-made for him, the ones lined with turquoise satin, trimmed with snakeskin and lizard. The black leather pants, the leather jackets. My sister never thought Jim was that cute, but then my sister was one of his girlfriend Pamela's friends, and it was in her best interest to ignore Jim, even though, for a month, my sister and her boyfriend lived with Jim and Pamela, and it was almost impossible. "He was always a very dark presence in a room," she said. "In fact, if you asked me today the feeling I got, I'd say it was of a person who was severely depressed. Clinically depressed." She's now a psychologist, so she knows.

"He thought he was ugly," she said. "He'd look at himself in the mirror trying on those clothes, but he hated looking at himself, because he thought he was ugly."

My sister and Pamela had to fight to persuade him to leave his hair long, because left to his own devices he'd get it cut preppy-short and break everyone's heart.

Even his voice was embarrassing, sounding so sudden and personal and uttering such hogwash in a time when, if you were going to say words, they were to be ironic and a little off-center. Jim just blurted things the fuck out. My artist friends found him excruciating, too, but my movie friends (who were, by definition, out of it and behind the times and got everything all wrong) loved him. He said what they meant. They might not have understood Dylan—they thought he couldn't sing—but in Hollywood they loved Jim.

Jim as a sex object and the Doors as a group were two entirely different stories. The whole audience would put up with long, tortured silences and humiliation and just awful schmuck stuff Jim did during performances. He could get away with it because his audience was all college kids who thought the Doors were cool because they had lyrics you could understand about stuff they learned in Psychology 101 and Art History. The kids who liked the Doors were so misguided they thought "Crystal Ship" was for intellectuals.

Jim as a sex object lasted for about two years.

In fact, once he and Pamela became entangled in their fantastic killing struggle—once he finally found someone who, when he said, "Let's drive over this cliff," actually *would*—he became more of a death object than a sex object. Which was even sexier.

When Pamela Courson met Jim, he began putting his money where his mouth was. Whereas all he had previously brought to the moment was morbid romantic excess, he now had someone looking at him and saying, "Well, are you going to drive off this cliff, or what?"

She was someone with red hair and a heart embroidered on her pants over the place her anus would be. He was a backdoor man, and Pamela was the door. Pamela was the cool one.

Everything a nerd could possibly wish to be, Pamela *was*. She had guns, took heroin, and was fearless in every situation. Socially she didn't care, emotionally she was shockproof, and as for her eating disorders— her idea of the diet to be on while Jim was in Miami going to court was ten days of heroin. Every time she awoke she did some, so she just sort of slept through her fast. Once, when she did wake up, she went with some friends to the Beverly Hills Hotel to see Ahmet Ertegun and fainted. Voilà, there she was back at UCLA, diagnosed as dying of malnutrition.

Good old Pamela, what a sport.

She would take Jim's favorite vest and write FAG in giant letters on the back in india ink. She would go through Rodeo Drive's Yves Saint Laurent Rive Gauche, piling her arms higher and higher with more stuff, muttering under her breath, "He owes it to me, he owes it to me, he owes it to me."

Pamela was mean and she was cool. She liked to scare people. Pamela had control over Jim in real life. He made his audience suffer for that.

And I mean, he was so cute, you *would*.

Pamela looked sunny and sweet and cute—she had freckles and red hair and the greenest eyes and just the country-girl glow. It was hard to believe her purse was stuffed with Thorazine (that horrible drug they used to give acid freak-outs). She wore mauve, and large, soft, expensive suede boots and large shawls, but even her laugh was mean.

She was so mean, she told Ray Manzarek (the worst nerd worldwide, known to his friends as Ray of the Desert) that Jim's last words were, "Pam, are you out there?" even though he actually left a note. And she *knew* that the note would establish forever the literature-movie myth of Jim's Lizard King image. Everyone hated Pam except Jim.

A friend of mine once said, "You can say anything about a woman a man marries, but I'll tell you one thing—it's *always* his mother."

"Mother," Jim sang, "I want to . . . *aggghh.*" Pamela was more than happy to supply the lip back: "Oh, you would, would you? Well, fuck *you*!"

I couldn't be mean to him. If the phone rang at night and there was a long pause after I said hello, I knew it was Jim. He and I had a lot of ESP in some kind of laser-twisted, wish-fulfillment kind of way. I *always* wished he were there, and every so often, he zoomed in.

"The thing that really made people mad at him," my sister reminds me, "was that he drank. And it wasn't cool to drink in those days."

"Yeah," I say, "he *did* drink."

Of course, I drank, but I tried to keep my drinking within the psychedelia-prescribed boundaries of okayness. I drank Dos Equis, wine, and tequila. Jim drank Scotch.

Scotches.

Adults drank and got drunk and were uncool. I myself drank, got drunk, and was uncool. But I myself didn't drink, get drunk, and become *so* uncool I flashed an audience in the South. I myself didn't drink, get drunk, and then jump out of windows, get busted, stick my fist through plate glass, show up three days late for an interview with Joan Didion from *Life* magazine, drunk, unshaven, and throwing lit matches in her lap.

But Jim did.

Jim drank, got drunk, and woke up bloated and miserable and had to apologize and say he loved you, the alcoholic's ancient saving grace. Jim drank and got drunk and then was so uncool he had to walk home.

I never saw him drive—he was always on foot in L.A. He didn't dare drive himself anywhere. He *knew* in his worst blackouts not to drive. Just as I knew in my worst blackouts to put my diaphragm in and take my contact lenses out.

Jim drank, got drunk, and wanted to be shown the way to the Next Whiskey Bar. Whereas the Rolling Stones were ripping off Otis and Robert Johnson and Chuck Berry, and the cool and hip Buffalo Springfield were riffling through Woody Guthrie and Hank Williams with folkie touches or else trying to achieve soul, Jim was ripping off Kurt Weill, Bertolt Brecht, Jean Cocteau, and Lawrence Durrell. While the Rolling Stones were making it cool to be black and folk rockers were making it cool to be white trash, Jim was making it cool to be a poet. If Jim had lived in another era, he would have had a schoolteacher wife to support him while he sat home writing "brilliant" poetry.

One night I was in the bungalow of Ahmet Ertegun (this was when I wised up and quit aiming at rock stars and went for record-company presidents instead—but *cool* ones, not Clive Davis). It was the night of the 1971 moon landing, and when I came in wearing my divine little black velvet dress, my tan, my blond art-nouveau hair, and my one pair of high heels I used for whenever Ahmet was in town, who should be sitting in front of the TV watching the moon landing but Jim, a Scotch and Coke (no ice) in his hand.

Ahmet proceeded to tell a rather gross story about midgets in India, and when he was through, Jim rose to his feet and bellowed, "You think you're going to *win*, don't you?! Well, you're not, you're not going to win. We're going to win, *us*—the artists. Not you capitalist pigs!"

You could have heard a pin drop in this roomful of Ahmet's fashionable friends, architects from France, artists, English lords, *W*-type women. Of course, Ahmet *was* a capitalist pig, but still, he did write some Drifters lyrics and produce records and his acts sang in tune. Anyway, everybody was silent (except for the moon-landing reporter on the TV) until I stood up and heard myself say, "But Ahmet *is* an artist, Jim!"

I became so embarrassed by how uncool *I* was, I ran down the hallway and into the bathroom, where I stood looking at myself in the mirror and wondering why I didn't get married and move to Orange County and what was I doing there.

There was a knock on the door.

I opened it and Jim came in and shut the door behind him.

"You know," he said, staring straight into my eyes, "I've always loved you."

Later that night he came back and apologized to Ahmet. But it was too late; by then he was too fat to get away with it. The people who were there refused to remember that it had happened. It was one of those tricky nights when Ahmet was trying to make up his mind whether he was going to seduce Jim away from Elektra Records (whose contract was nearly up). Ahmet had lured Mick away from *his* label the year before, Ahmet bespoke elegance, Côte d'Azur loafers with no socks, Bentleys and Rolls-Royces. Ahmet knew everybody. Jac Holzman of Elektra was an awkward bumpkin compared with Ahmet. Jac was a Virgo, Ahmet the world's most sophisticated Leo. Ahmet had Magrittes in his living room in New York, his wife was on the Ten Best Dressed list, he'd been everywhere, done everything, and spoke all these languages. Jac liked camping.

Of course, today Ahmet might deny this was going on, but at that time Ahmet never saw a rock star who made money whom he didn't want. Especially if he could sing in tune. Jim might also have denied anything was going on, or maybe he did notice he was being seduced, maybe that's why he was on about the capitalist pigs not winning. But then, Jim was drunk and uncool, so maybe what he said wasn't about anything. That's the thing with alcoholics: Their resentments are a condition of their disease and not really political at all. A condition of their allergy to alcohol—and allergies mean if you're allergic to strawberries and eat them, you break out in hives. If Jim drank Scotch, he broke out in fuckups.

But as long as Jim was on foot in L.A.—as long as he was signed to Elektra and in a world where if he fell, it would be into the arms of emergency rooms or girls who knew and loved him—he was, if not okay, at least not dead. There was always somebody around who would break down the door. He could never get away with killing himself in L.A.

Someone in Paris told me that when she met Jim at a party after he had moved there, he looked into her face and said, "Would you mind scratching my back? It itches." Her arm went around him, their bodies facing as she scratched. Then Jim said, "You know what? I can't feel a thing." Which was really humiliating to her, since having your arm around someone who says he can't feel it is . . . well, it sounds like one of Pamela's tricks.

Jim burned his bridges in Paris. He got fatter and fatter, drank more and more, sampled Pamela's heroin, and piled up suicide notes on a table in their rooms. Since Jim had rheumatic fever in his youth, his heart was not in condition for what he did to it there—combining insult with fuckups until finally one day Pamela came into the bathroom and Jim wasn't kidding.

She pulled him out of the tub and there she was—stuck in Paris in early July, forced to put him into a too-small coffin wearing a too-large suit. (Since no one in those days had suits, she had to buy one for him. She didn't know his size.)

Pamela told me she fled to Morocco with an eighteen-year-old French count, a junkie who also OD'd on her and died. And then, having worn out her stay abroad, she returned to the West Coast and sued for her share of Jim's estate until she got it and then, since three years had passed and she was now the same age Jim was when he died, she, too, OD'd and died.

She left behind a VW Bug, two fur coats, and Sage, Jim's dog. A quarter of the group's estate was split between her family and his, and her father saved Jim's "poems" and put them in a safe place in Orange County. The wonderful Julia Densmore Negron, who had divorced the drummer, John, was given royalties as a settlement because, as she said, "By 1971 they were worth practically nothing. But they've gone up more than 1,500 percent in the past eleven years." Since she was only married to John during the last two years of the Doors, when their records didn't sell much anyway, sales must have really gone up, but *why*?

Because Francis Ford Coppola used the song "The End" to make Jim a star in *Apocalypse Now*, which came out in 1979. And now Vietnam's about to do it for Jim again.

If, in the '60s, you were white and political and had noblesse oblige drummed into you (Yale's big selling point), you might have gone to Vietnam as a soldier, as Oliver Stone did, so you could come home and write a book the way Kennedy did and then be elected president.

Being Kennedy was not entirely uncool, but I knew a guy who went to Yale and then officer school at Annapolis and then Guam and then a ship in the harbor at Saigon (if it has a harbor, I don't know; it was someplace with a harbor). And all he did there was drink, and when he got home and went into seclusion to write his book like Kennedy, he couldn't write it. It was one thing being a World War II hero and writing a book. In Vietnam there weren't any heroes.

In *Salvador* (one of the last Oliver Stone movies I'm ever going to see), he created two sleazeballs who can't handle women, who are so incapable of having a real life in a real place that they have to slop down to hell, where they are the richest and most powerful people around. And *still* these guys manage to make victims out of themselves. Stone's heroes always wind up as victims, no matter how sleazy they are.

It has been rumored around L.A. that Oliver Stone is asking everyone in connection with the Doors movie if Jim was impotent, and it makes you think Oliver Stone doesn't know much about Jim's main disease. You'd think he'd at least read up on the symptoms that show up in a person who takes depressants as a cure for depression. Taking Seconal and Tuinal and drinking brandy will bring your sex life to a grinding halt.

But what I want to know about Oliver Stone is not whether he can get it up or not, but why anyone in the '60s would *join* the Army, would *go* to Vietnam and become part of the war and murder and atrocity, when the action for Real Men was on Sunset Strip, the Lower East Side, and in San Francisco. Why did he join them, and why is he now in love with our Jim?

The thing is, we in Los Angeles have always been willing to give a lot of slack for looks—for beauty—but Oliver Stone doesn't have any. He doesn't even like it. His movies are always about horrible men doing awful stuff, horrible men who are too far into their vileness to look beautiful. It's as though everything he's done is against the very premise of looks; he can't even show Daryl Hannah and understand what she's about. His idea of a good thing is a man bellowing about how being stupid is not that bad. (But it is.)

If being stupid is not that bad, then Jim's poetry would be okay, but it's not. Fortunately Jim had looks.

Maybe like Jim's other nerdy fans, Oliver Stone really believes that Jim was "serious" about breaking on through to the other side. But what does that *mean*—death, the way it sounds? It meant death to Jim personally, if what Pamela told her neighbor Diane Gardiner is to be believed, if he really died in Paris, his suicide note against a lamp, "Last Words, Last Words, Out."

By the time Jim left L.A., everyone thought he was a fool; he was fat, getting fatter, and even his fans were unwilling to look at his cock. He didn't have enough ideas in his head to keep people interested any longer.

Underneath his mask, he was dead.

But then, by 1971, who wasn't?

I certainly had washed ashore, without illusions. Everyone was afraid of Manson (Jim looked like him in his obit picture in the *Los Angeles Times*), acid had suffered a defeat, and cocaine was up for a long, ugly ride. Until Jim died, I had made a living doing album covers—psychedelic valentines for groups I loved, like Buffalo Springfield. I was in France in 1962 when Marilyn Monroe died, and now Jim was in France, dead, and I was nearly twenty-eight, unmarried, no future, no going forth in glory, only waking up at 3:00 A.M. with free-floating anxiety (which someone said was "the only thing floating around free anymore").

Someone said the '60s was drugs and the '70s was sex, but for me the '70s was staying home.

It was a time when I began to write for a living, and though I never wrote movies, they began seeming not that bad to me. Actors suddenly became okay (at least from afar). I began running into women who kept Jim alive—as did I—because something about him began seeming great compared with everything else that was going on. He may have been a film-school poet, but at least he wasn't disco.

People began trying to make a movie about Jim, and everyone I ran into who tried either died or wound up in AA. They wanted . . . John Travolta! Casting *anyone* to play Jim was just totally ridiculous to me.

My incredibly beautiful neighbor, Enid Karl, had two children by Donovan in the '60s, and their son, also Donovan, worked as an extra in the Doors movie (the daughter, Ione Skye, is an actress, too, but she was in a play in New York during the filming). The experience left Donovan thrilled, excited, and completely on Oliver Stone's side. (Everyone I talked to who worked on the movie—wardrobe women, actors—was on Oliver Stone's side. *Le tout* L.A.)

"In the first scene at the Whiskey, I played my father—because I asked. There were four hundred extras, but I got to sit in front and wear a caftan like my father wore. I thought I was going to end up lost in the crowd with an A.D. in front of me and not in the movie, but Oliver saw me and called out from the stage, 'Donovan! Donovan!' and suddenly they put me in the front row."

Then they gave Donovan a blond wig to wear as an extra in the Ray Manzarek wedding scene, and once he added muttonchops and a moustache he looked so much like Ray's brother that they let him sit with the wedding party.

"The extras were all too young to have been around in the '60s," young Donovan reports, "but really, it felt like everyone loved the Doors, and it was a happening. You didn't feel you were on a movie set."

I heard that once shooting began, Val Kilmer sent around a memo demanding that no one speak to him except as Jim. And that no one was allowed to come within ten feet of him. Plus, he wore a sweat shirt with a hood so he could hide his face. Not at all like Jim, who was all things to all people, like Marilyn, but how else can a boy stay in character if he's not actually Jim? (When Dustin Hoffman arrived on the set of *Marathon Man* looking worn and exhausted because he had deliberately avoided sleep for two nights, Laurence Olivier remarked,

"Dear boy, you look absolutely awful. Why don't you try *acting*? It's so much easier.")

According to everyone, Val Kilmer is supposed to have gotten Jim's looks exactly right, but what can Val Kilmer know of having been fat all of his life and suddenly one summer taking so much LSD and waking up a prince? Val Kilmer has *always* been a prince, so he can't have the glow; when you've never been a mud lark it's just not the same. And people these days, they don't know what it was to suddenly possess the power to fuck every single person you even idly fancied, they don't know the physical glamour of *that*—back when rock 'n' roll was in flower and movies were hopelessly square. And we were all so young.

1991

▼

GINA ARNOLD

Regina "Gina" Arnold's debut as a rock writer didn't come with a paycheck. Annoyed with *The San Francisco Chronicle*'s obtuse coverage of The Sex Pistols' epochal Winterland gig in January 1978, Arnold (b. 1961) fired off a fiery letter to the paper—and they published it. They followed up with an assignment, then another, then another; for two decades she wrote for the most prominent magazines in rock writing, including *Spin, Rolling Stone, Entertainment Weekly, The Los Angeles Times*, and *The Village Voice*. Her passionately intelligent writing about the indie and punk rock scenes, culminating in the books *Route 666: On the Road to Nirvana* (1993) and *Kiss This: Punk in the Present Tense* (1997), won her legions of fans. They also attracted the venom of scores of fanboys who resented a woman's incursion into the boys' club of rock writing; for years, "Kill Gina Arnold" graffiti and T-shirts were disturbingly common around the Bay Area. In 2011 Arnold earned a PhD from the program in modern thought and literature at Stanford; she now teaches at both Stanford and the University of San Francisco. Her powerful 2014 study of Liz Phair's *Exile in Guyville* was greeted as one of the finest entries in Bloomsbury's critically acclaimed 33⅓ book series.

▼ ▼

from
Route 666

HONOLULU: "I hope you have good health insurance," Debbie says anxiously. We're standing in a back alley in Honolulu, getting ready to go into the Nirvana show at Pink's Garage. All around us the surfer boys are standing by their cars, changing their karate slippers for Mexican army boots. The two of us look down at our legs apprehensively. Two minutes later we are jammed into the club so tight we can't even sway. There's water coming off the walls—wood sweats, don't you know—and as for our faces, they've just poured out every ounce of moisture in our bodies and then dried off immediately from the heat. I catch a glimpse of my forearm, on which, earlier in the day, I'd drawn the K shield symbol in indelible ink on the same spot as Kurt Cobain's tattoo: now both it and the club's stamp have completely disappeared from my flesh. I feel like I'm on the planet in *Dune*.

Then the room roars. Nirvana is onstage. I can just see the tippy tops of their pointed little heads. They begin with the song "Aneurysm," there's a quick lurch left, and I'm lifted off my feet, carried forward on an exoskeletal tide, as the entire room starts shrieking and stomping martially in unison along with the band. The beat slows down, and Kurt approaches the mike, by which time, along with everyone else, I think I'm actually holding my breath. *Come on over and do the twist.* He cracks the hard *t* like a bullet—ping!—and the audience moans. "Aaaahhh-ow!" *Overdo it and have a fit!*

"Aaaaah-ow."

Love you so much, it makes me sick . . .

"Aaaaah-ow."

Come on over and shoot the shit . . .

"Aaaah-ow . . ." And this time the whole room pauses, as if with the beat. There's a palpable gasp as our lungs expand with his. Then: "*Beat me out of it!*" we bellow altogether. "*Beat me out of it.*" For the tiniest second, we stand rock still, catching what breath we have. Then BOOM; BOOM! The band begins the verse, and we leap heavenward again. My

feet don't find the ground for a full minute and a half, and by the time
they do I've been carried away on a tide of flesh. Everyone's bumping
heedlessly into one another, skin slapping sinew and then—schwack!—
sticking. And yet our bodies have suddenly lost all sexual properties and
have become mere tissue. It has happened at last: we are finally free of
suggestion.

An hour later we burst out on the pavement, sopping wet. Nirvana
fans were pouring out all around us. The alley was full of hefty boys
in backward ball caps, all shirtless, their faces glowing red with the
mysterious exertions inside. Many of them had no shoes on; my own
legs were mud-spattered, and my green frock had somehow acquired
a big hole nowhere near a seam. We milled about dazedly in the warm
Hawaiian night—almost satiated, almost postcoital. Quickly, Debbie
and I ran across the bigger boulevards to the ocean, where we plunged
into the surf.

And then, I remember—I will always remember—looking up at the
lights of the high-rise Hilton Hawaiian Village and thinking: Somewhere
behind one of those cubelike balconies, Kurt and Courtney were anticipating their imminent wedding, while all around them, surrounded
and confusing, Middle America in its rawest, ugliest, newlywed state
slept peacefully, entirely unaware of the monster in its midst. I looked
up at that hotel that night from my secret offshore vantage point and
thought blissfully of kings and queens and conquering heroes, of the
Trojan Horse and the French Revolution and that part of the Bible
where it says that the meek shall inherit the earth. I floated on my back
and stared at the shoreline, and as I did so my mind turned idly on the
thought of nearby Pearl Harbor. I felt like an explosion had gone off a
long, long way away and now we were bathing placidly in the warmth
of its rays. If war were cathartic, if war were a happy thing, if war were
like the Special Olympics and everyone went home the winner, then
this is what it would be like when it was over. You know how the Eski-
mos have three hundred words for snow because it's the most important facet of their life? In America, there should be more synonyms for
violence, including one that does not imply either injury or rage. There
should be more words for success.

                                                                    1993

ANN POWERS

Since the early 1980s Ann Powers (b. 1964) has been a constant presence in rock writing, serving variously as music editor for *The Village Voice* and pop critic for *The New York Times, Spin, Rolling Stone, The Los Angeles Times,* and *Blender*. Her writing consistently spotlights the vexed position of women in the music industry. At her best, she connects with her subject in a distinctive and energetic prose, as in the piece reprinted here, where she memorably writes of Polly Jean Harvey: "She's a drag king from the inside out." From 2001 until May 2005, Powers was senior curator at the Experience Music Project, an interactive music museum in Seattle. She has reached her widest audience as a frequent contributor to National Public Radio, where she has also been writing for the music blog *The Record* since 2011. Her books include *Piece by Piece* (2005), cowritten with singer-songwriter Tori Amos; a volume in the 33⅓ series on Kate Bush's *The Dreaming* (2008); and *Weird Like Us: My Bohemian America* (1999). She is the coeditor, with Evelyn McDonnell, of the influential anthology *Rock She Wrote: Women Write About Rock, Pop, and Rap* (1995). A study of the intersections of love, sex, race, and the spirit throughout the history of American popular music is forthcoming from Dey Street Books.

▼ ▼

Houses of the Holy

"LOVE AND inestimable satiety, which, although it is satiated, generated an insatiable hunger, so that all her members were unstrung. . . ."
So an Italian woman of the fourteenth century described the passion
that had claimed her soul. A modern lover may argue the benefits of
independence, but sometimes, caught up in the magnetism of her
own desire, she can understand the sensual chaos behind her ances-
tor's words. Even as the mind dissects the chocolate-box semiotics of
romance, the body can feel lovesickness as sickness unto death.

Polly Jean Harvey takes for granted that eroticism hurts, that nothing pretty comes of giving over to love's irrational pull. Listening to
her band's new *Rid of Me* (Island) is like holding the shoulders of a
friend as she fights back nausea; every calm moment holds the menace of a new outburst. With the symbiotic tie between Harvey, bassist
Steve Vaughan, and drummer Robert Ellis so tight that their playing
seems generated by her unkempt vocal rhythms, *Rid of Me* magnifies
the skintight discomfort of last year's debut album *Dry* until it takes
on mystical proportions. And that's the point, because Polly Harvey's
seduction tales bespeak no ordinary love: she's telling us how she was
taken by a god.

That's what the Christian adept Angela of Foligno did when she
chronicled the love that made her so ravenous. Holy women of the
Middle Ages typically experienced their faith in terms of bodily transformation, partly self-induced, but ultimately mysterious. Stigmata,
elongation or enlargement of body parts, levitations, and catatonic
seizures proved the union with Christ that these women attained,
although such symptoms rarely visited men. Accounts of these miracles, like the testimony of Angela that historian Caroline Walker Bynum
has uncovered, suggest that women could actually change form, if only
momentarily, and so push through the limitations of their traditionally
scorned and feared female bodies.

Polly Harvey cultivates that same shape-changing power. Throughout *Rid of Me,* she characterizes her rapture in terms of thirst, dismem-

berment, and grotesque bodily shifts. Following the mystical tradition, Harvey goes inside the myths she attempts to reconstruct and simultaneously lets them swallow her. In "Snake," the band screams and clatters as Harvey, inhabiting Eve, pushes her voice to a limit that touches utter panic. "Missed," which could be about Mary Magdalene finding Jesus's empty grave, epitomizes faith as desperate yearning. As Harvey's guitar and Ellis's bass weave a heavy bed of muddy noise, she pleads for a visitation: "Show yourself to me, and I'd believe, I'd moan and I'd weep . . . I'd burst in, full to the brim." By the song's cymbal-crash crescendo, it's clear the vision she seeks won't come. But Harvey's found new resolve in her divine lover's absence. "I've missed him!" she wails, and this defiant refrain transforms the search into her new addiction.

Harvey paints carnal desire as inevitably mystical as well, going beyond sense into self-destructive experiences of union and absence. The title track insinuates a threat of undying, obsessive love—"don't you wish you'd never, never met her?" she spits at the unwitting owner of her heart, but the song's secret lies in a background vocal reproducing true abandon. In animal rage and desperate need, someone screams, "Lick my legs, I'm on fire!" The phrase boils over, overcoming both words and music until it's the only sound left. Only after many rounds may the listener realize that this plea comes not from Harvey's mouth but from Ellis's, voicing a lust that confounds expectations.

Such moments release a furious energy, as PJ Harvey calls forth the mythic power of eroticism to move beyond biological constraints. It's there in her mummery of familiar temptresses and mad lovers but it's also in the music. Harvey, Ellis, and Vaughan invoke classic rock forms (power ballad, three-minute thrash, acid overdrive, postpunk discombobulation), blow them out of proportion, then shred them to pieces. Short songs move sickeningly fast; ballads drag and bolt as if they're afflicted with manic depression. From Ellis's willfully misplaced cymbal crashes to Harvey's gutter yowls, the performances tear apart the structures they're supposed to fit. Steve Albini's production makes sense of this jones for excess through wild dynamic shifts: inaudible passages give way to earsplitting cacophony, effects smother Harvey's words and then she's pressed up against the vocal mike, enunciating

334 %. SHAKE IT UP

for her life. On the first few listens—and by the way, it's impossible on the Walkman—his hand seems mortally heavy, pushing the music in all the wrong directions. Eventually, though, the material's emotional depth and the strength of Harvey's performance cuts through Albini's attempt to match this power with his own will.

On the surface Harvey's tales of growing huge or cutting off her lover's legs seem linked to raging feminist rhetoric—the castrating bitch, she's out to devour us (or, if you're on her side, the Amazon's gonna show those boys). But *Rid of Me* exudes too much terror to work as dogma; instead of critiquing or even documenting the struggle to be sexually whole in a misogynist and body-fearing society, Harvey means to create that fight's sonic equivalent. And although Harvey may herself believe in the fight for women's rights, it's not the point of her art. *Rid of Me* envisions a subject between sexes, empowered by the possibilities and entrapped by the limits of both masculine and feminine. Throughout "Rid of Me," she switches sexual identities like a runaway darting from one blind alley to another. Woman-loving woman on "Yuri G," woman-prizing dude in "Man-Size," self-proclaimed king of the world in "50FT Queenie," Harvey refuses not only to speak for her gender, but to believe in its solidity. She's a drag king from the inside out. It's a trait she shares with ecstatics from the Eleusinian priestesses and St. Joan to Little Richard, Prince, and Prince Be.

The disconcerting union of sex and spirituality plays a role in virtually every religious tradition, and it's just as common for rock music to explicitly unite the two. PJ Harvey's traditionalism lies precisely in the band's constant striving for such grand moments. (The cover of Dylan's *Highway 61 Revisited* does away with the original's B-movie sarcasm, instead using the accumulation of details as momentum on a highway ride toward hell.) The point of making rock so big eludes today's zeitgeist, which prefers the small miracles and accidental triumphs of acerbic do-it-yourselfers. If Polly Harvey weren't a woman, PJ Harvey very well could be U2, trying to save souls. If she tried to take an explicit political stance, she'd probably resemble Sinéad O'Connor, letting her flair for drama drag her down.

Turned on by punk's nasty streak, though, Harvey's sound comes closer to the perversity of Nick Cave and Mark E. Smith of the Fall, or the oblique cataloging of relics that Black Francis made his business in the Pixies. The inevitable Patti Smith comparison's not *completely* inaccurate, either, although Smith was more sure of her own ability to articulate. Diamanda Galas may make more sense as a foremother. Like Harvey, she's compelled toward the language of physical pain, and she claws the ground of ancient wisdom, looking for stories enormous enough to fit realities that confound today's usual means of expression. Galas's testimonies about the AIDS epidemic and the degradation of women can't be restrained within the usual parameters of the avant garde. Nor does Harvey's breakdown of the flesh settle within the bounds of a typical rock record.

PJ Harvey dismantles the customary arrangements of guitar flash, bass groove, and drum bottom to reach some essence of rock that precedes the familiar. The god that Harvey moans to wed is rock itself, in its role as source of divine power in a secular age. She wants to make that noise in order to believe in it. On "Dry," the debaucher who can't make her come touches her from a stage, not in bed; as she churns out the catchiest, most expendable riff on *Rid of Me*, she offers her immense hunger as inspiration. "I'm sucking on the well, I'm sucking till I'm white," she wails. She's trying to overcome history's dull weight by going to the source. Once there, she finds it has no place for her; trying to fit, she risks obliteration. That's the cost in any supernatural union; mystics are forever trying to rid themselves of ego. Harvey's miraculous accomplishment is to get there and live to tell.

1993

ROBERT PALMER

Robert Palmer (1945–1997) was rock writing's great polymath. Another music writer once described the tone of Palmer's writing as "Don't worry, I know everything." In addition to his impressive body of written work, Palmer earned recognition as a talented musician (most notably in the late '60s outfit The Insect Trust, darlings of underground rock fans and treasure-seeking record collectors alike), producer (overseeing critically acclaimed releases by Junior Kimbrough and R. L. Burnside), and professor of ethnomusicology and American music studies. Born in Little Rock, Arkansas, Palmer developed an early love for the blues, drawn to both its emotional potency and its cultural heritage. That genre would provide the inspiration for his most influential work, 1982's *Deep Blues*, which was adapted into a well-received documentary. In 1995 he served as chief consultant on the PBS/BBC documentary *Rock & Roll: An Unruly History*, for which he also wrote the companion volume. Palmer was a regular contributor to *Rolling Stone* and the first full-time rock writer on staff at *The New York Times*. His deep knowledge of his subject matter was regularly on display in his writing about a wide range of popular music, from jazz and blues to soul, R&B, rock & roll, and what we've learned to call "world music." Palmer once said, "I do continue to believe in the transformative power of rock and roll"; this belief shone through in his work and transformed his readers into believers too.

▼ ▼

Sam Cooke's *Night Beat*

I COULD tell from all the way across the local newspaper's marbled lobby that something was wrong with my friend who worked in the coffee shop. She was going about her usual business, wearing the uniform dress and disposable apron our Little Rock newspaper deemed appropriate for "kitchen help," but there was a look of profound sadness on her face instead of her usual radiant smile, and her eyes were brimming with tears. And there was something else about her, something she'd never let me see before: maximum anger, held in check under maximum pressure. I thought of a song, Sam Cooke's "Laughin' and Cryin'." "I keep on trying to hide my feelings," he sang, "trying to hide my soul." My friend was trying hard.

It was the winter of 1964, my friend and I were both in our teens, but in certain ways we were strangers. She was, as far as I knew, the newspaper's only black employee; I worked part-time after school, moving immense rolls of newsprint around the basement. What we had in common, the whole basis of our friendship, really, was music. It was all we talked about when we got together on coffee breaks or after work. We each had our individual heroes and solid senders, our "wait-till-you-hear-this" discoveries, but when it came to naming the greatest of them all, we were in complete agreement: Sam Cooke ruled.

And now my friend was telling me, "They shot Sam." Who shot him, I asked, knowing there was only one Sam that meant that much to her, or to me. "I don't know," she said, no longer able to hold back her tears. "They said—who cares what they said. SAM COOKE IS DEAD." And with that she straightened her dress, wiped away the tears, and went back to work, serving hamburgers and Cokes to people who were utterly unaware that anyone of importance had passed. Most people who grew up in the 1960s remember exactly where they were and what they were doing when they heard of the Kennedy assassination; the day I recall with preternatural clarity is the day we lost Sam Cooke.

Cooke meant many things to many people. To some, he was the most gifted pop vocalist of his time; no more, no less. He was a spellbinding performer; my friend and I had seen him play in Little Rock a few short months before his death, and we weren't just captivated, we were utterly entranced and illuminated, along with everyone else. It was the gritty, soulful sort of show captured on *Live at the Harlem Square Club*, chock full of hits, most of which Cooke himself had written, arranged, and in effect produced. But seeing him that night was more like going to church than going to an R&B show.

I didn't realize at the time that from 1950 to 1957, before he'd ever made a pop or R&B record, Sam Cooke was already a star in the world of black gospel music as lead singer with the Soul Stirrers, one of the most popular and respected groups of its time. Many of his earlier pop fans, after he made the switch to secular music with his spectacular first hit, "You Send Me," had seen him sing in their own church or town hall; some resented his abandoning gospel for the more lucrative world of pop, but many more cheered him on. Whether the text was addressed to "my Lord" or "my baby," people continued to attend Sam Cooke shows expecting to "have church," and church, at its most inspirational and transcendent, is what he gave them.

His music was so spiritually resonant and nurturing, it preached so eloquently and prayed for a better day with such contagious fervor, that it could penetrate the deepest despair, find a glimmer of hope even in the heart of darkness. After far too many disappointments and casual indignities had bruised the spirit and sapped the will, Sam Cooke's music could actually make life seem worth living again.

And he was inspirational in other ways. While paying his bills playing R&B shows on the "chitlin circuit," he was slowly and methodically working up a more "uptown" presentation he could take into a Las Vegas hotel or a major club like New York's Copacabana. His first attempt at playing the Copa was a disaster. Cooke learned from the experience and returned to the Copa in triumph. Similarly, he started his own record label, SAR, as another step in the crossover of pop and gospel music—a crossover Cooke first conceptualized, then worked to make a reality. He was one of the first popular artists to take a firm stand against the segregation of concert audiences by race—and the first with enough earning power, determination, and sheer charisma to have his way and make it stick.

White record buyers were largely unaware of this side of Sam Cooke, but to many black musicians and would-be record-business tycoons, Cooke was a hero and a role model. The battles he fought were their battles as well, and he opened doors many more black Americans would walk through in the coming years.

Much of what Sam Cooke meant during his tragically foreshortened career is history now. Thankfully, the music remains. The best of his singles, collected on *The Man and His Music*, are as original and virtuosic as one could wish. He wrote most of them, gave his arranger Rene Hall specific rhythm section, horn, and string parts to orchestrate, and served as de facto producer at all his sessions, whether for his own records or for releases by other artists on his SAR roster. The problem with the best of Cooke's own recordings is simply that there aren't enough of them. There are the singles; his earlier gospel recordings with the Soul Stirrers (Cooke at his very best, according to many aficionados); and two splendid live albums, one from the Copa and one, considerably more muscular, from a black dance hall in Miami, the Harlem Square Club.

But when Cooke was making records, singles were the name of the game. Even the Harlem Square album went unreleased until more than twenty years after Cooke's death. In those days, an "album" was usually one of several hit singles and a lot of "filler." In Cooke's case, the "filler" was often Broadway-style tunes and standards for which he seemed to have little natural affinity. He could certainly hit the note, as the more carefully chosen and sympathetically arranged standards on the albums handily demonstrate. What is lacking in the less successful album tracks is some evident emotional connection between the singer and his material. What isn't lacking—but should be—is overdone orchestrations and chirpy "pop" vocal choruses, which only made matters worse.

This brings us to *Night Beat*, an anomaly in the Cooke discography. Backed by a superbly supple and attentive soul combo, Cooke sang his heart out on these informal, late-night recording sessions from winter

1963. There isn't even a hint of filler. The result is a vocal tour de force, and just under the music's gracefully melodious surface, the emotional waters run deep.

The remarkably consistent mood of the album is a 2 A.M., last-call sort of feeling. It's a blues mood, but the diversity of the songs—from spirituals to bluesy ballads to Cooke's sophisticated gospel-rooted originals—and the singer's ability to make every song his own, regardless of genre, keep it from becoming a "blues album."

Above all, this is a *Sam Cooke* album—his greatest, according to many. Of all his records, it's the one you'd put on to show the uninitiated what an extraordinary vocal musician and communicator the man was. It's also by far Cooke's most intimate album, sounding for all the world like you're sitting in a dark, late-night bar listening to a man pour his heart out. Even as he worries and embellishes the lines about "trying to hide my feelings, trying to hide my soul," he's revealing, not hiding. We can only speculate as to what masterworks Cooke might have given us if he'd had the time and the opportunity to make more of his own albums in his own way, with only himself to satisfy. Thankfully, we do have one such album, this one, and a glorious album it is.

Even Rene Hall, the bandleader, arranger, and session musician from New Orleans who worked with Cooke throughout the singer's career, speaks for his former associate in tones bordering on awe. "I rate him as being a genius," says Hall, "as a person who was able to create as he did with no formal musical training whatsoever. He could hum a part to you, and what he would hum would be in perfect sequence with the orchestrational concept. Or Sam would tell me, 'I want the bass to play this,' and hum the part, and he was never musically incorrect. I never had to say, 'Sam, this isn't the right note for the bass'; it just never happened. He could hear the entire orchestra, the string lines, the bass lines, the horn lines, the backing singers' lines. And as a spiritual singer, he had never dealt with these things before. Cliff White [Cooke's long-time guitarist] would hear Sam do things and think they'd never work, like the way he went from major to minor chords in his version of 'Summertime.' Things like that, Cliff was going, 'Jesus Christ!' and then he'd do what Sam asked for, not believing that it would work, and when he tried it, it did. Even at the beginning of his career, just before he left the Soul Stirrers, he was trying to cut his first pop session, but he said he didn't get the feel of the songs. Then he told me that if I showed him a few chords on the guitar, he said, 'Maybe I can come up with a tune.' So I showed him three chords, and on the three chords he learned, he composed 'You Send Me.' He said, 'Man, this is gold; I can write a lot of these things.' I consider something like that a gift, a special talent."

Cooke was such a protean musical figure that even though he can legitimately be considered the original soul singer, the first successful gospel artist to understand and effectively utilize hard gospel elements in a deliberately "pop" context, this reputation rests on a relatively small part of his recorded output. Certainly his training and his most enduring stylistic orientation were in gospel, and Cooke-penned singles like "Shake," "Another Saturday Night," "Soothe Me," and "Bring It on Home to Me" were among the first and deepest soul hits.

But as Rene Hall observes, "Sam had a very strange ear, different from even gospel singers. Because most gospel singers deal in sevenths—like blues-type changes—and Sam dealt in sixths. Like you hear him do his yoo-hoo-hoo, that's sixths. I had played jazz, and we did a lot of sixths and ninths and so on, but it was strange for me to hear that from a gospel singer . . . because Sam wasn't actually singing proper gospel, he was singing a pop concept of his own. The entire concept or approach to melody that Sam used was completely original. Even when he did a standard tune, and he did quite a few standards in his day, he would approach them with his original version of the melody."

Cooke altered melodies the way a jazz musician will, as a way of personalizing a tune. He drew on gospel, blues, and related idioms for his basic stylistic orientation, but while his melodic embellishments had a gospelish fluidity and timing, the intervals he sang were more common in jazz than in gospel or blues—more sixths than sevenths, as Rene Hall put it.

What does it all add up to? None of our tired old genre clichés is inclusive enough to describe, let alone contain, the artistry of Sam Cooke. It's great American music—Sam Cooke music, a genre in itself.

It may not have the special emotional relevance for you that it has for me, but I'm sure it will get to you, too, in its own way. Because as soon as you put on *Night Beat* and hear Cooke's first mellifluous tones, riding nothing but a light bass, an occasional tap on the snare drum, and his own sovereign command of rhythm and inflection, something magical begins to happen. Cooke and his musicians—who include pianist Ray Johnson, organist Billy Preston, lead guitarist Barney Kessell, alternating drummers Hal Blaine and Ed Hall, bassist Cliff Hils, and Cliff White and probably Rene Hall on rhythm guitar—are going to take you to church.

Just stand back and let the man sing.

1995

GERALD EARLY

Gerald Early (b. 1952) is a scholarly critic of American and African American popular culture, in essays on subjects spanning Miles Davis, Ralph Ellison, and Sammy Davis, Jr. His monograph *One Nation Under a Groove: Motown and American Culture* (1995) gains its authority not through a broad aggregation of facts but by the eloquence of his telling details and unique perspective. Early has also written on the subject of his life as a father and citizen, and on race in American sports. His collection *The Culture of Bruising: Essays on Prizefighting, Literature, and Modern American Culture* won the National Book Critics Circle award in 1994, and he has received Grammy Awards for his liner notes for *Yes I Can! The Sammy Davis Jr. Story* and *Rhapsodies in Black: Music and Words from the Harlem Renaissance.*

▼ ▼

from
One Nation Under a Groove

IT IS one of the least recognized facts of American popular culture that the Middle West—an area that runs from, say, Cincinnati to Kansas City, from Detroit to Oklahoma City, from Chicago to St. Louis, from Alton, Illinois, to Little Rock, Arkansas—is responsible for most black popular music in America. From Scott Joplin to Miles Davis, from Charlie Parker to Jimmy Rushing, from Curtis Mayfield to Sam Cooke, from Jimmy Blanton to Donny Hathaway, from the Isley Brothers to

Brother Joe May, the Gospel Thunderbolt of the Midwest, this area was pivotal in the development of virtually every style of black music. The Middle West is where jazz came in the 1920s when King Oliver and Louis Armstrong migrated to Chicago. It is where blues became a formalized 12-bar musical pattern at the turn of the century, in places like St. Louis and Evanston, and where it became electric with the coming of the great post–World War II bluesmen like Muddy Waters, Howling Wolf, Buddy Guy, Elmore James, B. B. King, and Little Walter. It is where jazz redeveloped and redefined itself as swing in Kansas City in the 1930s and it is where Charlie Parker emerged from the Jay McShann band to reshape jazz as bebop in the 1940s. Illinois native Miles Davis made jazz cool in the 1950s, and Missourian Chuck Berry reinvented Rhythm and Blues as a youth music that a white deejay from Cleveland, Alan Freed, was to call Rock and Roll. From Coleman Hawkins to Screamin' Jay Hawkins, from Joe Turner to Tina Turner, from Milt Jackson to Michael Jackson, from Roland Kirk to Bobby Watson, the Middle West has been a central, even mythological, location for black popular culture and black popular music. And the three principal musical cities in this area have been Detroit, Chicago, and Kansas City.

From Detroit alone, after World War II, came such talents as Yusef Lateef, Thad, Hank, and Elvin Jones, Della Reese, Little Willie John, Tommy Flanagan, Kenny Burrell, Jackie Wilson, Barry Harris, Donald Byrd, Aretha Franklin, Paul Chambers, Roland Hanna, Alice Coltrane, and Charles McPherson, as well as, of course, the talent that came out of Motown after 1959. Why did Detroit become such a hothouse of musical talent after the war? It is difficult to pinpoint a precise answer but part of it lies in the intense emphasis on musical education among Detroit blacks. It is a common myth that blacks learn about music in their churches and like all myths it has a considerable amount of truth. Yet black secular music education provides as much, if not more, training for blacks who seek a music career than churches do. For instance, Ralph Ellison, in writing about jazz guitarist Charlie Christian, describes music education in the black Oklahoma school he attended: ". . . harmony was taught from the ninth through the twelfth grades; there was an extensive and compulsory music-appreciation program, and . . . a concert band and orchestra and several vocal organizations."

At the turn of the century, E. Azalia Hackley, a light-skinned black woman from Detroit who was trained as a soprano, adopted the musical education of black youth as her mission; she was called "Our National Voice Teacher" in the black press and was wont to stop for 15 minutes during her recitals and give her audiences lessons in musical appreciation and voice training. From Hackley's instructorship to that of such storied black Detroit public-school music teachers as Ernest Rodgers, Orville Lawrence, and James Tatum, Detroit black youth have been reared in a vibrant musical atmosphere in their public schools. The annual E. Azalia Hackley Program featuring black composers and black classical performers started in 1943, and such noted black Detroit performers as Rogie Clark, Robert A. Harris, and Charles Coleman (also music critic for Detroit's black newspaper, the *Michigan Chronicle*) have been featured in various years. Indeed, an aspect of black music education that is not as written about as it should be is how much blacks, in their schools, are exposed to classical European music, marching-band music, and pseudo-classical show tunes, and how much these forms of music have been traditionally enjoyed in the black community and not necessarily by the black bourgeoisie only. Blacks have often found some of these forms as attractive, as much a part of their cultural language— as they rightly should—as the musical forms that are more expressive of their own African-derived aesthetics and sensibilities, and this has influenced overall the shaping of their popular music.

Consider this fact about Motown: The three major early groups of the company—the Supremes, the Temptations, and the Miracles—were put together and rehearsed at their high schools. They were not church groups; in fact, the members did not attend the same church, and in various autobiographies there is little talk about the influence of the black church in their music. For instance, Smokey Robinson speaks about the influence of Sarah Vaughn, and Mary Wilson singles out the McGuire sisters, Doris Day, and Patti Page as her personal favorites when she was growing up (an indication, among other things, that the popular-culture broadcasting devices—radio and television—not only exposed white audiences to black music but, just as important, exposed black audiences to white music, and that black musical taste could be just as pedestrian as the white mainstream or that white mainstream tastes ought not to be routinely stereotyped and dismissed more so than black tastes are subject to be). Black music has been equally a product of secular and sacred forces and impulses. One finds this is true equally of Ray Charles, who became closely tied with the secularization of black gospel although he never learned his craft in a black church but rather at the school for the blind he attended and on gigs, and of Michael Jackson who, true to his Motown roots, also put a great deal of gospel fervor into his music but who had "music class and band in the Gary [Indiana] schools" where he grew up.

Here are two undeniable facts: First, Motown could not have happened without a strong public-school music-education program in Detroit, even if many of its performers were musically illiterate. The session musicians, the arrangers, and often the producers were not, and nearly all of them were trained in the public schools of Detroit. Moreover, the performers themselves received some musical training and exposure to music in school, which in many instances turned out to be highly influential. Second, Motown could not have happened anywhere else but in the Middle West, despite the fact that the greatest number of R and B independent labels were located in Los Angeles. (This is not where the greatest number of black artists originated or honed their craft, and as blacks were mostly shut out of both the movie industry and Las Vegas during the Cold War period of 1945 through 1960, Los Angeles was not an especially supportive environment in many respects.) For it was in the Middle West, finally, until 1970, despite New York doo-wop and the Brill Building, Philadelphia with the Twist, the Italian teen idols, and Kenny Gamble's record store at 15th and South Streets, or the proliferation of record labels in Los Angeles and a bopping Central Avenue down South Central Way, where the creative crucible of black music existed.

But Motown would not have succeeded without a crossover rise in the interest in black music, particularly in postwar Rhythm and Blues.

Several factors conjoined to make this possible: First, after the war, big bands and swing were passé, particularly because big bands were no longer economically feasible. Ellington and Basie, veritable institutions and the most important big bands in American music history, continued to produce new and exciting music, but most black bands disappeared, and those white swing bands that continued, with the exceptions of Stan Kenton, Buddy Rich, and Woody Herman, became, in effect, fossilized "oldie" acts.

Second, the invention and growing popularity of the electric bass changed entirely how popular music was conceived; contemporary popular dance music eventually was built around the sonic phenomenon of the electric bass. Electric instruments generally tended to find their first practitioners among black musicians because they were usually regarded in white mainstream circles as being freakish, novelty items. After blacks have created a system of playing these instruments the better to reinvent their own music, white musicians will then begin to use them extensively and create further innovations.

Third, the popularity of white covers of black Rhythm and Blues in the 1950s conferred a kind of respectability and mystique on the black versions, which led many white teenagers to seek out the real thing in curiosity and in quest of hipness (as was shown in Alan Freed's *Mister Rock and Roll*, for instance). These same white teenagers helped fuel the entire youth culture movement and many of them wound up figuring in the civil rights movement, in part because of their exposure to this music. Teens, with more expendable money, became a real presence in the mass marketplace in the 1950s. What made Motown possible was not that Elvis Presley covered R and B but that Fats Domino, in the end a more significant artist, not only crossed over with R and B hits in 1955 but with a Country and Western tune, "Blueberry Hill."

What was indeed far more radical than the Presley success in the mid- and late-1950s was the prominence of three black male romantic balladeers and show-tune singers—Johnny Mathis, Nat King Cole, and Sammy Davis, Jr., by the end of the decade. Davis made it big in the 1956 Broadway show *Mr. Wonderful*, which was specifically written for him by Jule Styne. Cole, enjoying many years of crossover success

since 1948 with "Nature Boy" and "Mona Lisa," had a short-lived television variety show in 1956 (although the show was unable to find a
single national sponsor). By then he had become one of the most successful ballad singers in American popular-music history. Mathis broke
big with "Wonderful, Wonderful," in 1958, made an album of standard
romantic ballads in 1959 entitled *Open Fire, Two Guitars*, and became
not simply a successful singer but, with youthful good looks and slick
hair making him appear, to white and black taste, a bit exotic like an
Indian, he was, in short order, a teenage heartthrob among both black
and white girls. He appeared on his album covers more in idealized and
stylized drawings and photographs than virtually any other black male
artist of the period. Indeed, in *Life Magazine*'s 1958 feature on Rock
and Roll, whose "most numerous fans are girls aged 8 to 16"—an article, in effect, about teen idols—Johnny Mathis is the only black singer
mentioned, and with an accompanying photograph, especially surprising as Mathis's singing style was not remotely Rock and Roll.

Black male singers found it difficult to make it in romantic balladry
because of the open sexual appeal needed for the music to go over with
women listeners. The entire white commercial music establishment
frowned upon, and felt great unease about, making a black male a legitimate sex symbol. Indeed, the fear of miscegenated sex appeal explains,
in part, why such true black Rock and Roll artists as Chuck Berry, Fats
Domino, or Little Richard were not promoted as were lesser white
teen idols. The other factor was age, as many black male artists associated with Rock and Roll, like Berry and Domino, were considerably
older than the white girls who were crazy about their records. But the
success of Mathis, Cole, and Davis—which came about in part because
the black male as sex symbol was making his presence felt in popular
culture in the 1950s—was an enormous breakthrough that helped ease
the way for Motown artists, although the first genuine black male Rock
and Roll teen idol would be Twist King Chubby Checker, who did not
record for Motown. (Interestingly, Checker, in an emergency for Dick
Clark's "American Bandstand" show, covered R and B performer Hank
Ballard's "The Twist" for a huge crossover hit in 1960, the first time a
black crossed over by covering a black R and B tune, creating a dance

craze in the process. Checker's youth and manner, and his lack of reputation as an aggressively sexual R and B artist, put the song over for
white mainstream audiences, including adults. Gordy had never been
a fan of Ballard's more salacious material, such as the mid-1950s hits,
"Work with Me, Annie" and "Annie Had a Baby," and with his unerring
sense for cultural trends, starting with the comic book industry's self-
imposed, self-regulatory code of 1954 to rid itself of exposed breasts
and horrific violence in the name of protecting America's youth, he
made sure that in crossing over, Motown's music never brought with
it R and B's more debauched element of good-timing jungle bunnies
in the ghetto.)

The fourth factor that made crossover possible was the breakup of
the music entertainment industry, caused by the decline of big bands
and of the power of the Hollywood film in the 1950s due to the growth
of television. New York Tin Pan Alley composers no longer reigned
supreme. The major record labels—Columbia, RCA Victor, and Decca
(soon to be MCA)—were being challenged by trend-setting small
independent labels. Most R and B was recorded for small independent
labels, as was a good deal of early Rock and Roll, bebop and soul jazz.
Specialty in Los Angeles, King/Federal in Cincinnati, National and
Atlantic Records, both in New York, Sun Records in Memphis, Apollo
Records in New York, Chess Records in Chicago, Modern Records and
Imperial Records in Los Angeles, and Savoy Records of Newark, New
Jersey, are just a few of the companies that proliferated like mushrooms
in the dark seeking local black music after World War II. As Arnold
Shaw pointed out near the end of his book, *The Rocking 50s*, a compar-
ison of the top pop songs of 1939 and 1959 found that in 1939, the Top
Ten pop discs were made by only three companies—all located in New
York—whereas in 1959, 39 companies produced Top Ten records and
these were located in ten states. Popular music in America was truly
becoming regionalized and more open. Moreover, the music that was
most likely to attract adventuresome kids, the music that the majors had
white artists covering, was the music of the small independent label.

By the time Gordy started Motown in 1959, he was not thinking,
as many indies owners were, that having a white cover of their own R

and B was the ultimate mark of success. Gordy was thinking not only that the Motown publishing catalogue would be covered—which it has been much to Gordy's fabulous enrichment—but that Motown recordings would stand up as pop hits on their own, without benefit of covers, which has turned out to be true as well. This is how Motown changed American culture: by Gordy's insistence that *his* performers be able to sell the company's songs to whites and that *his* performers be able to play at the better-playing white venues. Gordy's objective always was to reconfigure what was meant by pop music, to reiterate in his approach that pop was as black as it was white. In this regard, perhaps the most remarkable album the Supremes made was the 1967 issue *The Supremes Sing Holland, Dozier, Holland,* wherein the group sang the songs of their producers, who happened to be, at that time, the hottest songwriting team in America. A black pop group legitimated the music of a black pop writing team and HDH's songs legitimated the Supremes. Nothing quite like this had ever happened in American popular culture before. (Ella Fitzgerald's 1957 *Duke Ellington Songbook* comes close.) And to emphasize the point, four months later Motown released the next Supremes album: *The Supremes Sing Rodgers and Hart.* They had been authenticated as a significant interpretative and stylistic group of singers, and HDH was on par with the great songwriters of Tin Pan Alley and the American musical theater.

Regarding Gordy's vision of reshaping and exploding the racial underpinnings of pop music, he took advantage of his time and place: From the early 1960s fascination with folk music, to the mid- and late-1960s quest to acknowledge the sources of popular music in urban electric blues and early forms of 1950s doo-wop, R and B, and rockabilly, there was a search for authentication and authenticity in pop music despite (or perhaps because of) its contrivance and its falsity—the sheer artistic and emotional vacuity of much of it. This "authenticity" is a service that blacks have learned to provide for American popular culture, though what was really being authenticated was the separation of black music as "race records," which was largely a political act to keep black music (and black artistic expression, generally) understood popularly as a marginal phenomenon. Motown changed this with its huge success, moving black music, largely on its own terms, within the popular-music mainstream, negotiating, with considerable aplomb, the enterprise of authenticating itself as youth music, while acknowledging, even celebrating, the R and B sources of African-American music, reaffirming, in an astonishing cultural wave, the innovative power of R and B as a pop music. The deep complexity of the quest for authentication in popular music lies in the extraordinary happenstance that all cultural innovations are subject to cooptation by a mainstream that tends to "normalize" or nonspecialize the innovations for mass consumption. These societal instances of reenforcing marginality while thwarting it by erasing its existence as a threat produces, ultimately, in differing ways, among both the elites and the masses, an urge for more authentication and innovation. This is the elementary dynamic of creation in a capitalist culture. Within a little more than a decade, from 1945 to 1959, from, say, Louis Jordan to Ray Charles, the first wash of "authentic" black music, R and B, began beneath bourgeois moral (this is dirty music), political (this music promotes race mixing and disturbs the status quo) and commercial pressures (this independent music is undercutting the power of the major record companies) to experience its own dilution and decadence, moving from a marginalized but artistically rigorous avant-gardism into an orthodoxy of mediocrity. That, as much as anything, made possible the success of Motown (and to a lesser degree its rivals Atlantic and Stax) in the 1960s era of renewed authentication, and the quest for authentication was made all the more vigorous because black people—with a revitalized political consciousness and momentous political agenda that for the first time in American history had a huge impact on the culture at large—desired it so very much.

In the 1960s the only other force in black American popular music that rivaled Motown as an authenticator was James Brown, the Godfather of Soul himself. As Bruce Tucker, coauthor of Brown's autobiography, points out, Brown was not a product of Stax, Atlantic, or Motown, but a sort of freelance presence in black music in the 1960s; and after 1965, when he became a pioneer in funk—or a kind of extremely rhythm-based, almost antisong, rifflike dance tune, he began to undermine Motown's "crossover" influence through new groups like Sly and the Family Stone and through his influence on a wide variety of established black artists, including Miles Davis, Jimi Hendrix (during his Band of Gypsies phase), Herbie Hancock, and Motown's own producer Norman Whitfield, who all began to formulate tunes in the studio based on musicians playing counterriffs on an improvised bass riff. In other words, in the late 1960s, and certainly by the early 1970s, during the height of the black power and black pride movement, many younger blacks thought Motown sounded too "white," too crossover, and not authentically "black" enough, but this was not actually a realization that grew from Motown's "sound" as much as from its marketing success and the growing tendency for young whites to co-opt Motown as their own cultural authentication. Young blacks felt simply that this music "cannot authenticate them and us, too and still be our music," as one black collegian told me back in 1972. Interestingly, Hendrix, Davis (in his electric phase from 1970 to 1975), and Sly Stone—mentioned above as three artists influenced by the funk innovations of Brown—were also influenced by the pop crossover innovation of Motown, and each had a large crossover audience. And each, in his distinct way, became entangled in the limitations of both funk and crossover, in ways that both Brown and Motown avoided, becoming in the end hideously costumed minstrels unable to escape the cultural entrapment of black "rhythm" as a stigma of stereotyped black male sexuality and clownish showmanship that became an artistic cul-de-sac. (Black life and music in America has been sullied by its two most striking characteristics: rhythm and fervor, two musical and psychic features that whites have convinced themselves that they intrinsically lack, so much the better that they might have a neurotic need for the Negroes in their midst who supply them in abundance! Motown and Brown built their music on both rhythm and fervor, but Motown managed to transcend them so that both became in Gordy's vision assertions of Negro soul and adumbrations of the American pulse of creative "force," while Brown monopolized them as blatant individual expressions of American entrepreneurial energy and drive. For both Motown and Brown, rhythm and fervor became new versions of multiplicity, of the dynamo.) That all three men—Davis, Hendrix, and Stone—in different ways, despite their remarkable success commercially and artistically, were destroyed by drugs by the mid-1970s was not surprising, even, in some ways, predictable.

1995

ED WARD

Ed Ward (b. 1946) has been active on the rock writing scene for more than half a century, a record that more than qualifies him for the title "rock-and-roll historian" attached to his name during his regular appearances on National Public Radio's arts and culture program *Fresh Air*. Ward has long been a fixture in the Austin, Texas, music scene, providing insider coverage for the *Austin American-Statesman* and the *Austin Chronicle* as well as chronicling the formative years of the annual South by Southwest Music Festival. His writing has appeared in *Creem, Crawdaddy*, and *Rolling Stone*, and he continues to contribute to numerous publications, including *The Wall Street Journal* and *The New York Times*. Ward also maintains a blog, *City on a Hill*, that weaves together memoir, travelogue, historical anecdotes, and—of course—music reportage. Ward is co-author (with Geoffrey Stokes and Ken Tucker) of *Rock of Ages: The Rolling Stone History of Rock & Roll* (1986). In this piece, Ward uses the occasion of the twentieth anniversary of Bruce Springsteen's *Born to Run* to think about the rock industry's mythmaking machinery and his own collaboration with it. The first volume of his ambitious two-volume history of rock & roll appeared in the fall of 2016.

Bruce Springsteen: *Born To Run*

LORD, WHAT did I *ever* see in Bruce Springsteen? But I did once see something, and even went on record as having seen it. In fact, I remember being hurt when Columbia put out that famous ad for his second album, *The Wild, The Innocent, & The E-Street Shuffle*, headlined with Jon Landau's epochal I-have-seen-the-future quote, and my rave review from *Creem* was, it seemed, the only one not quoted in it. Hell, Springsteen was a Rock Critic Consensus Artist, like Bowie and Roxy Music (and, in the first half of the '70s, precious few American artists), and I wanted to be part of the crowd.

Not that I was particularly looking for a New Dylan, as some people were; I was just starved for something I could listen to twice, a singer-songwriter who dealt in something other than cocaine-etiolated solipsism, something that rocked. And here one came along, and then there was this silence. Only a year, but a year can be crucial to building momentum the way Springsteen was. There were reasons, all having to do with behind-the-scenes manoeuvring by Mike Appel, his about-to-be-former manager, and, of all people, Jon Landau, who was—get this—producing the next Springsteen album!

This news, gleefully transmitted by my colleagues over long-distance telephone calls, didn't particularly make me look forward to this next, make-or-break LP. I believed, and still do, that artists are artists and critics are critics, and when artists start making records for critics, they're short-circuiting their art. Critics get records for free. They have nothing invested in what's on the wax. You have to please the audience, and whether the critics like it or not usually has no real impact on the public's opinion. Not to mention that critics (do I really have to say this in a *British* magazine, for heaven's sake?) can be fickle.

So, on September 6, 1975, *Born To Run* came out. Within a month and a half, the hype machine had gone bazootie: *Time* and *Newsweek* put Springsteen on simultaneous covers, and the verbiage coming from Columbia could have caused one to think that this boy from the Jersey Shore might not only have made a darn good record, but made the lame to walk and the blind to see. I saw the tour. The first time, I was amazed at the spontaneity and pacing, the stories Springsteen spun about his life and music. The tour came back again, and I got fifth-row seats with friends who were a bit closer to Landau than I. This time, it dawned on me that it was about as spontaneous as Noh theatre, and seemed to go on for about as long. I thought Springsteen's onstage use of Clarence Clemons was patronising, bordering on racist.

Afterwards, we went backstage, where Landau and Springsteen were holding court. I finally had to ask my friends for the keys to their car, and went outside to wait for them. My love affair with Bruce Spring-steen was over, and, I later realized, so was my wanting to be part of the consensus.

Born To Run, though, became a classic. It must have: Columbia's given it the 24-carat-gold CD, 20-bit digital SBM re-mastering treat-ment. But really . . . do I want to listen to it again? Yes, thunders the Editor, and . . .

And I realize that this is Springsteen on the Divide, one foot in the innocent myth-making that made us love him to start with, one in a future of portentous statements backed by rock pomp that'll lead us straight to fellow New Jerseyan Jon Bon Jovi. This is a moment that couldn't last, in which the naive equations made of girls, guitars and cars reach a baroque interplay that can't go any further. It's Springsteen about to grow up, about to make some choices that will leave me, at least, disappointed and lead him to acceptance by a mass audience that doesn't even pay attention to what he's saying. Listening to songs like "Thunder Road" and "Born To Run," I can still marvel at the way he caught the mystery of life on the edge and mythologised it perfectly in a way that one can only do if one doesn't examine or understand it too deeply, which can make for great pop music, if lousy literature. Nor is *Born To Run* a perfect album: "Night" and "Meeting Across The River" are as unmemorable today as they were when they were new, the former because it just doesn't have music and lyrics that go any-where, the latter because the story's strength is sapped by a forgettable tune. And the nine-minute-plus epic album-closer, "Jungleland," is still too much, a mess that ends with Springsteen bellowing wordlessly and faux-operatically almost as if, in retrospect, he knew that a moment was ending forever.

What followed, of course, was a tale of Good Intentions, two auteurs (Springsteen and Landau) making records on which Great Rock supported Deep Ideas by a People's Artist. *Born To Run* remains a thrilling moment, a cautionary tale reminding us of the fragility of youthful perception. (It was also, from a technical standpoint, one of the worst-mastered records ever, and this reconstruction clarifies the muddy mess brilliantly, although who's to say that a regular ol' silver CD might not be just as good for the average Joe, the kind of guy who drives a Springsteenian beater Chevy instead of a Lexus or whatever Bruce drives these days.)

I once thought of *Born To Run* as a statement of optimism against insuperable odds. It turns out, instead, to be a lament, a song of regret. As another songwriter familiar with cars and guitars once said, it goes to show you never can tell.

1995

Camden Joy

"Camden Joy" was created by the writer Tom Adelman (b. 1964) as something more than a pseudonym: Joy functions as a versatile conceptual art gesture, appearing as both protagonist and the ostensible author of various pop music–themed fictions, including *Liz Phair: The Last Rockstar Book* (1998) and *Boy Island* (2000). Joy's earliest public role was as a guerrilla critic on the streets of New York City, in the form of a series of wheat-pasted posters containing rants and manifestos offering oblique surrealist commentary on then-current pop music, film, and writing. These artifacts were collected in 2002 in the volume *Lost Joy*. As Tom Adelman, he is the author of several books about major-league baseball.

▼ ▼

Total Systems Failure

SPOON
"The Agony of Laffitte"/
"Laffitte Don't Fail Me Now"   Saddle Creek

As ANYBODY who has flipped past *Rolling Stone*'s editorial page to read their business section recently can attest, popular music is undergoing what those in the know like to call "really something." All the record company people who signed the good indie bands and orchestrated bringing us the very best music of the '90s are being put on ice in favor of rootless meanies who favor brand-name ballads, dance crazes, and tits. It's perhaps true when people paraphrase the Clash these days that "even if the Beatles flew in today, they'd send no limousine anyway" (although people declaring such usually forget that the Beatles seemed harmless at the start, which is how they got so big; they began as Backstreets and became Beasties). So far, in my debatably short life, I've been lucky enough to see punk fall out of fashion not once but twice (it was better the second time because effects pedals caught up with the theory, and deadpan wit entered the rhetoric; at long last, wiseasses got the girls!). We had some good times, didn't we, back when smart, sloppy groups had their shiny moment, back when the paying public seemed to've come over (at last!) to our way of thinking. Then the record companies ran out of Nirvana specialty reissues and Sonic Youth did not make another *Daydream Nation* and stupid Mark E. Smith assaulted his girlfriend while Elvis Costello forfeited his place in the pantheon and generation-defining classics were on the tips of the Breeders' and Uncle Tupelo's tongues when the band members turned on one another as Nick Cave and Morrissey became jokes and Bob Mould and Mike Watt continued on cluelessly and the gifted pop band Christmas came back as the utterly irrelevant smug swingers Combustible Edison and traditionally deserving dues-paying types like Vic Chesnutt and the Fastbacks could not get a commercial purchase on the popular imagination as everybody from the Posies to Pearl Jam to Archers of Loaf never figured out how to make an album entirely important from start to finish, forgetting the point of pop stardom is to bring together huge clumps of otherwise unaffiliated folks, and Pavement couldn't follow up the *Pacific Trim* EP with the requisite jubilant breakthrough (their *Let It Be*) and Cat Power and the Mountain Goats defiantly clung to Dylan pre-'65 and Tom Waits was too late with *The Black Rider* and Yo La Tengo were inexplicably overlooked (how does that begin to happen?) and the fetish for releasing crappy home demos—whose very lack of finish lent them the steady hiss of a gradually disappointed public—succeeded only in stealing mid-decade credibility from keenly perfectionist pop stars like Robyn Hitchcock and Nick Lowe and They Might Be Giants precisely when they issued their masterpieces.

What a decade of sleights-of-hand and comic mistimings this has been, as we emerge with none of our alt-spokesmen standing, and their industry support utterly squeezed out between urban enthusiasts and country-western fans. Only a few years back you'd catch major-label A&R kids speaking like mature individuals who'd survived relationship counseling, saying that certain acts had to be nurtured, talking about honesty and commitment, that audiences required respect, that expectations had to be patiently shaped. . . . Well, such talkers are no more, replaced now by bottom-dwellers dwelling on the bottom line who treat imaginative singers and songwriters with contempt like one-night stands. As a side consequence, not only have I been purged from the demographic that once used to nourish me, but also my demographic itself has been purged. People assure me the future is online and the underground will rise yet again, but lately my legs are cramping up, I'd like to sit down, so fuck you, how long am I supposed to wait? Should I be satisfied that Ween is nearly a household name? Am I to feel gleeful that Elliott Smith played the Oscars while resting in Celine Dion's bosom and that the money we paid for the song "Man on the Moon" now brings it back to us in movie form? I can march up and down my aisle of favorite '90s records and almost all I see are artists who guaranteed something they didn't deliver or just got screwed (the one exception, I can be persuaded, is the Beastie Boys), or wonderful acts like the Lilys and Lambchop who would've significantly altered our beloved revolutionary popscape had they been promoted, or musicmakers in possession of Dylan's head-full-of-ideas-that're-driving-them-insane like Very Pleasant Neighbor and Death Cab for Cutie who couldn't even get their discs into shops.

All of which is to say I like this band called Spoon. They're three fellows from Texas who in 1998—after a record and a half on a smallish label—made *A Series of Sneaks* for Elektra. *Sneaks* has all the sounds of crushed fury and longing I love, thick-tongued words that appear supersignificant but once deciphered make sense only in a found-object sorta way, songs of a minute or two in length. It's a record that stinks to high heaven of unbridled ambition (remember ambition?), reminiscent of Bruce Sterling—or some similarly pirate-minded attackist author person—assuring the *Times* that he wasn't TRYING to do ANYTHING with CULTURE except to TAKE IT OVER. But would the takeover be worth celebrating? Despite *Sneaks*'s old-fashioned enthusiasm about itself, Spoon were quite cognizant of all the ways '90s rock was supposed to bring us together but hadn't, because the breakthroughs didn't break through, or the geniuses croaked or choked.

I listened to *Sneaks* mostly to imagine the singer guy's face, a face I heard as resembling the young Joe Strummer, the young Paul Westerberg. The sneer, the hopefulness, the clouded gaze lit with fiery dawn. In truth, there lives no face not beautiful when painted in colors of passion and pride. Behind the brow furrowed in suspicion, in back of the scowl and the fed-up stubbornness, he sings as if understanding all we have riding on him, wanting more than anything to honor that.

By now you're assuming I've made up this record because (1) you've never heard of it, and (2) things that're that good get heard. They don't, though. A lot of good bands don't get signed, even more good bands make bad records, still more good bands make good records that're distributed or promoted badly. Out of nowhere our tastes change and we confound the moneymen. The music market is just the dance of so many random intangibles. The record companies alertly stand to the side, conducting polls and dictating memos as baffled as anyone about why we're sick of Alanis now but not yet over Britney, why we fickle folks like what we like. It's akin to the stock exchange, really, a scene of bluffing gamblers, or a bunker full of addictive liars or con men guessing at the dreams of the customers—as Joseph did with Pharaoh—to thereby establish a wise reputation. Case in point, something went wrong, terribly wrong, with Spoon: Before their imminent classic *Sneaks* ever had its chance to be "worked," some god gave them the finger. They were cut from Elektra's roster only four months after *Sneaks* came out. (*Four months!* Jello pudding snacks have a longer shelf life.) Of course, it's not just Spoon: that's what I'm saying—everyone who looked or sounded "alternative" suddenly couldn't summon up enough sales to make big the eyes of the bigwigs. Spoon, for one, were not surprised, but that doesn't mean they weren't hurt.

Their response was a two-song CD—a "concept single"—addressed

362 // SHAKE IT UP

to Ron Laffitte (their former A&R guy at Elektra). Lacking any context, I assumed, when first I heard how these songs hovered between sobbing and spitting, that they were telling about a cruel ex, or possibly an elected official who broke our hearts. *Are you ever honest with anyone?* "It's like I knew two of you, man," goes the vocalist, discouraged, disgusted, "one before and after we shook hands." The songs—"The Agony of Laffitte" and "Laffitte Don't Fail Me Now"—manage to say things that no band, to my knowledge, has ever sung to a former record company. They're not exercises in bratty name-calling and bellyaching. Whether people like Elektra chairman Sylvia Rhone—who repeatedly assured Spoon she wouldn't drop them until she did exactly that—deserve our pity or not, Spoon apparently think so. These songs do not lack sympathy. The singer sings as one who is intimate with betrayal, even expects it, for he himself has gotten through life—as Spoon's only major-label title admitted—using a series of sneaks. This new release's balance of compassion and blame and fury and guilt and impatience sounds creepily like Kurt Cobain will—once he's dug up and unplugged again.

2000

CHUCK KLOSTERMAN

"What we have loved," William Wordsworth wrote in *The Prelude* (1798), "others will love, and we will teach them how." It's a pithy description of the motive for a certain kind of critical writing. And though he's no Romantic poet, it's also a surprisingly apt description of Chuck Klosterman's breakthrough memoir–cum–critical study *Fargo Rock City: A Heavy Metal Odyssey in Rural Nörth Daköta* (2001). Born in Minnesota and raised in North Dakota, Klosterman (b. 1972) has written for *Spin, GQ, Esquire, The Believer, The Guardian,* and *The Washington Post.* It was *Fargo Rock City,* though, that announced the arrival of an important (and disarmingly clever) new voice in popular-culture journalism. At the turn of the millennium, no pop music was so universally despised as glam metal; and no one would have been thought less well positioned to treat it seriously than an alcoholic headbanger from "flyover country." Yet through its winning mix of self-deprecating humor and unaffected intelligence, *Fargo Rock City* managed to demonstrate why this music, regularly dismissed by the rock critical establishment, meant so much to so very many. Klosterman's crisp, accessible voice—"homespun," sometimes teetering on the brink of "cloying"—has propelled his writing into wide circulation: for a time, he even wrote *The New York Times Magazine* advice column "The Ethicist." In recent years he has been writing more and more about sports—an impressively wide variety of sports—for ESPN, among other outlets. In addition to *Fargo Rock City,* Klosterman has published another memoir, *Killing Yourself to Live: 85% of a True Story* (2005), a critical study, *I Wear the Black Hat: Grappling with Villains (Real and Imagined)* (2013), and *But What If We're Wrong: Thinking*

About the Present As If It Were the Past (2016), along with three collections of critical essays and two novels.

▼ ▼

from
Fargo Rock City

YOU KNOW, I've never had long hair.

I don't think there has ever been a day when the back of my neck wasn't visible. In fact, I think I've had pretty much the same Richie Cunningham haircut for the past twenty-seven years (excluding a three-year stretch from 1985 to 1988, when I parted my hair down the middle and feathered it back). It seems like I spent half my life arguing with my parents over this issue, and it was a debate I obviously lost every single time. As a ninth-grader, I once became so enraged about the length of my hair that I actually spit on our kitchen floor. Remarkably, that clever gesture did not seem to influence my mother's aesthetics.

What my mom failed to understand was that I didn't even want long hair—I *needed* long hair. And my desire for protracted, flowing locks had virtually nothing to do with fashion, nor was it a form of protest against the constructions of mainstream society. My motivation was far more philosophical.

I wanted to rock.

To me, rocking was everything. As a skinny white kid on a family farm in North Dakota, it seemed to be the answer to all the problems I thought I had. I couldn't sing and I played no instruments, but I knew I had the potential to rock. All night long I slapped Mötley Crüe and Ratt cassettes into my boom box (which we called a "ghetto blaster," which I suppose would now be considered racist) and rocked out in my bedroom while I read *Hit Parader* and played one-on-none Nerf hoop basketball. Clearly, I was always ready to rock—*but I needed the hair.* I didn't care if it was blond and severe like Vince Neil's or black and explosive like Nikki Sixx's—I just needed *more* of it. It would have been my singular conduit to greatness, and it was the only part of my life that had a hope of mirroring the world of the Crüe: They lived in L.A., they banged porn stars, they drank Jack Daniel's for breakfast, and they could spit on their kitchen floor with no repercussions whatsoever. They were like gods on Mount Olympus, and it's all because they understood the awe-inspiring majesty of rock. Compared to Nikki and Vince, Zeus was a total poseur.

Sadly, the Crüe proved to be ephemeral, coke-addled deities. Rock critics spent an entire decade waiting for heavy metal to crash like a lead zeppelin, and—seemingly seconds after Kurt Cobain wore a dress on MTV's *Headbanger's Ball*—they all got their shovels and began pouring dirt on the graves of Faster Pussycat, Winger, Tesla, Kix, and every other band that experimented with spandex, hairspray, and flash pots. Metal had always been a little stupid; now it wasn't even cool. This was the end. Yngwie Malmsteen, we hardly knew ye.

I became a cultural exile; I wandered the 1990s in search of pyrotechnic riffs and lukewarm Budweiser. It didn't matter how much I pretended to like Sub Pop or hip-hop—I was an indisputable fossil from a musical bronze age, and everybody knew it. My street cred was always in question. Like a mutant species of metal morlocks, my fellow headbangers and I went into hiding, praying that the cute alternachick who worked at the local coffeehouse would not suss out our love for Krokus.

But that era of darkness is going to end.

It is time for all of us to embrace our heavy metal past. It is time to admit that we used to rock like hurricanes. It is time to run for the hills and go round and round. It is time for us to *Shout at the Devil*. We've got the right to choose it, there ain't no way we'll lose it, and we're not gonna take it anymore.

Quite simply, that's why I wrote this book: to recognize that all that poofy, sexist, shallow glam rock *was* important (at least to the kids who loved it). I'm not necessarily claiming that the metal genre was intellectually underrated, but I feel compelled to insist it's been unjustifiably ignored.

In 1998, I was in a Borders bookstore, browsing through the music section. Chain bookstores always amaze me, because it seems like some-one has written a book about absolutely everything. I think that's why bookstores have become the hot place for single adults to hook up—bookstores have a built-in pickup line that always fits the situation. You simply walk up to any desirable person in the place, look at whatever section they're in, and you say (with a certain sense of endearing bewil-derment), "Isn't it insane how many books there are about _____?" Fill in the blank with whatever subject at which the individual happens to be looking, and you will always seem perceptive. *Of course* there's going to be a ridiculous number of books on draft horses (or David Berkowitz, or the pipe organ renaissance, or theories about the mating habits of the Sasquatch, or whatever), and you will both enjoy a chuckle over the concept of literary overkill. The best part of this scheme is that it actually seems spontaneous. Bookstores have always been a great place for liars and sexual predators.

ANYWAY, I was shocked to realize this phenomenon does not apply to heavy metal. There are plenty of books about every other pop sub-culture—grunge, disco, techno, rap, punk, alt country—but virtually nothing about 1980s hard rock. All you find are a few rock encyclope-dias, a handful of "serious" metal examinations, and maybe something by Chuck Eddy.

At first blush, that shouldn't seem altogether surprising. I mean, nobody literate cares about metal, right? But then something else occurred to me: I like metal, and I'm at least semiliterate. In fact, a lot of the most intelligent people I knew at college grew up on metal, just like me. And we were obviously not alone.

Let's say you walked into the average American record store on a typical summer day in 1987 (and for sake of argument, let's say it was June 20). What was selling? Well, U2's *The Joshua Tree* was No. 1 on the charts—but Whitesnake was No. 2. Mötley Crüe's *Girls Girls Girls* was No. 3. Bon Jovi's commercial monster *Slippery When Wet* was still No. 4 (in fact, three Bon Jovi records were in the Top 200). Poison was No. 5. Ozzy Osbourne's live *Tribute* to Randy Rhoads was No. 6. Cinderella's *Night Songs* was a year old, but it was hanging on at No. 27. Ace Frehley was showing his windshield-scarred face at No. 43.

Tesla's *Mechanical Resonance* was outperforming R.E.M.'s *Dead Letter Office* by eleven spots (and—perhaps even more telling—*Dead Letter Office* featured a cover of Aerosmith's "Toys in the Attic"). Christ, even Stryper's *To Hell with the Devil* was at No. 74.

There were between twenty and twenty-five metal bands on the *Billboard* Top 200 album chart that week (depending on your definition of "heavy metal"), and—in reality—there almost certainly should have been more. Remember, this was before Soundscan, and metal acts were faced with the same problem that plagued rappers and country artists: They were often ignored by the record store owners who reported the sales, usually by pure estimation. This was clearly illustrated in the summer of 1991, when Soundscan was finally introduced and Skid Row's *Slave to the Grind* immediately debuted at No. 1. The Skid's eponymous first record sold three times as many units as its follow-up, but *Billboard* had never placed *Skid Row* higher than No. 7 and forced it to crawl up the chart, one position per week. It almost certainly flew off shelves far faster (and far more often).

In the 1980s, heavy metal *was* pop (and I say that to mean it was "*pop*ular"). Growing up, it was the soundtrack for my life, and for the life of pretty much everyone I cared about. We didn't necessarily dress in leather chaps and we didn't wear makeup to school, but this stuff touched our minds. Regardless of its artistic merit, Guns N' Roses' 1987 *Appetite for Destruction* affected the guys in my shop class the same way teens in 1967 were touched by Paul McCartney and John Lennon. Commercial success does not legitimize musical consequence, but it does legitimize cultural consequence. And this shit was everywhere.

I walked out of that Borders bookstore thinking that someone needed to write a book about the cultural impact of heavy metal from a *fan's* perspective (Deena Weinstein's *Heavy Metal: A Cultural Sociology* is arguably brilliant, but Deena never reminded me of anyone I ever hung out with). As I drove home, the classic rock station on my car radio played Thin Lizzy's "Cowboy Song." I was struck by how much it reminded me of "Wanted Dead or Alive," the best Bon Jovi song there ever was. Obviously, my youth makes this process work in reverse; members of the generation that came before me were more likely reminded of Phil Lynott when they first heard Jon Bon Jovi talk about riding his steel horse. However, I don't think historical sequence matters when you're talking about being personally affected. I'd like to think my memories count for *something*.

You know, if someone wrote an essay insisting Thin Lizzy provided the backbone for his teen experience in the mid 1970s, every rock critic in America would nod their head in agreement. A serious discussion on the metaphorical significance of *Jailbreak* would be totally acceptable. I just happen to think the same dialogue can be had about *Slippery When Wet*.

Whenever social pundits try to explain why glam metal died, they usually insist that "It wasn't real" or that "It didn't say anything." Well, it was certainly real to me and all my friends. And more importantly, it *did* say something.

It said something about us.

October 26, 1983
The worldwide release of Mötley Crüe's *Shout at the Devil*.

It's easy for me to recall the morning I was absorbed into the cult of heavy metal. As is so often the case with this sort of thing, it was all my brother's fault.

As a painfully typical fifth-grader living in the rural Midwest, my life was boring, just like it was supposed to be. I lived five miles south of a tiny town called Wyndmere, where I spent a lot of time drinking Pepsi in the basement and watching syndicated episodes of *Laverne & Shirley* and *Diff'rent Strokes*. I killed the rest of my free time listening to Y-94, the lone Top 40 radio station transmitted out of Fargo, sixty-five miles to the north (in the horizontal wasteland of North Dakota, radio waves travel forever). This was 1983, which—at least in Fargo—was the era of mainstream "new wave" pop (although it seems the phrase "new wave" was only used by people who never actually listened to that kind of music). The artists who appear exclusively on today's "Best of the '80s" compilations were the dominant attractions: Madness, Culture Club, Falco, the Stray Cats, German songstress Nena, and—of course—

Duran Duran (the economic backbone of *Friday Night Videos'* cultural economy). The most popular song in my elementary school was Eddy Grant's "Electric Avenue," but that was destined to be replaced by Prince's "Let's Go Crazy" (which would subsequently be replaced by "Raspberry Beret").

Obviously, popular music was not in a state of revolution, or turbulence, or even contrived horror. The only exposure anyone in Wyndmere had to punk rock was an episode of *Quincy* that focused on the rising danger of slam dancing (later, we found out that Courtney Love had made a cameo appearance in that particular program, but that kind of trivia wouldn't be worth knowing until college). There were five hundred people in my hometown, and exactly zero of them knew about Motorhead, Judas Priest, or anything loud and British. Rock historians typically describe this as the period where hard rock moved "underground," and that's the perfect metaphor; the magma of heavy metal was thousands of miles below the snow-packed surface of Wyndmere, North Dakota.

Was this some kind of unadulterated tranquillity? Certainly not. As I look back, nothing seems retroactively utopian about Rick Springfield, even though others might try to tell you differently. Whenever people look back on their grammar school days, they inevitably insist that they remember feeling "safe" or "pure" or "hungry for discovery." Of course, the people who say those things are lying (or stupid, or both). It's revisionist history; it's someone trying to describe how it felt to be eleven by comparing it to how it feels to be thirty-one, and it has nothing to do with how things really were. When you actually *are* eleven, your life always feels exhaustively normal, because your definition of "normal" is whatever is going on at the moment. You view the entire concept of "life" as *your* life, because you have nothing else to measure it against. Unless your mom dies or you get your foot caught in the family lawn mower, every part of childhood happens exactly as it should. It's the only way things *can* happen.

That changed when my older brother returned from the army. He was on leave from Fort Benning in Georgia, and he had two cassettes in his duffel bag (both of which he would forget to take back with him when he returned to his base). The first, *Sports*, by Huey Lewis and the News, was already a known quantity ("I Want a New Drug" happened to be the song of the moment on Y-94). However, the second cassette would redirect the path of my life: *Shout at the Devil* by Mötley Crüe.

As cliché as it now seems, I was wholly disturbed by the *Shout at the Devil* cover. I clearly remember thinking, Who the fuck *are* these guys? Who *the fuck* are these guys? And—more importantly—Are these guys even *guys?* The blond one looked like a chick, and one of the members was named "Nikki." Fortunately, my sister broached this issue seconds after seeing the album cover, and my brother (eleven years my senior) said, "No, they're all guys. They're really twisted, but it's pretty good music." When my brother was a senior in high school, he used to drive me to school; I remembered that he always listened to 8-tracks featuring Meat Loaf, Molly Hatchet, and what I later recognized to be old Van Halen. Using that memory as my reference point, I assumed I had a vague idea what Mötley Crüe might sound like.

Still, I didn't listen to it. I put Huey Lewis into my brother's trendy Walkman (another first) and fast-forwarded to all the songs I already knew. Meanwhile, I read the liner notes to *Shout at the Devil*. It was like stumbling across a copy of Anton LaVey's *Satanic Bible* (which—of course—was a book I had never heard of or could even imagine existing). The band insisted that "This album was recorded on Foster's Lager, Budweiser, Bombay Gin, lots of Jack Daniel's, Kahlua and Brandy, Quakers and Krell, and Wild Women!" And they even included an advisory: *Caution: This record may contain backwards messages.* What the hell did that mean? Why would anyone do that? I wondered if my brother (or anyone in the world, for that matter) had a tape player that played cassettes backward.

The day before I actually listened to the album, I told my friends about this awesome new band I had discovered. Eleven years later I would become a rock critic and do that sort of thing all the time, so maybe this was like vocational training. Everyone seemed mildly impressed that the Crüe had a song named "Bastard." "God Bless the Children of the Beast" also seemed promising.

Clearly, this was a cool band. Clearly, I was an idiot and so were all my friends. It's incredible to look back and realize how effectively the Mötley image machine operated. It didn't occur to anyone that we were going to listen to Mötley Crüe for the same reason we all watched *KISS Meets the Phantom of the Park* in 1978, when we were first-graders who liked Ace Frehley for the same reasons we liked Spider-Man.

Yet I would be lying if I said the only thing we dug about Mötley Crüe was their persona. Without a doubt, their image was the catalyst for the attraction—but that wasn't the entire equation. I say this because I also remember sitting on my bed on a Sunday afternoon and playing *Shout at the Devil* for the first time. This may make a sad statement about my generation (or perhaps just myself), but *Shout at the Devil* was my *Sgt. Pepper's*.

The LP opens with a spoken-word piece called "In the Beginning." The track doesn't make a whole lot of sense and would seem laughable on any record made after 1992, but I was predictably (and stereotypically) bewitched. The next three songs would forever define my image of what glam metal was supposed to sound like: "Shout at the Devil," "Looks That Kill," and the seminal "Bastard." Although the instrumental "God Bless the Children of the Beast" kind of wasted my precious time, the last song on side one was "Helter Skelter," which I immediately decided was the catchiest tune on the record (fortunately, I was still a decade away from understanding irony). I was possessed, just as Tipper Gore always feared; I had no choice but to listen to these songs again. And again. And again.

It was three months before I took the time to listen to side two.

It can safely be said that few rock historians consider *Shout at the Devil* a "concept album." In fact, few rock historians have ever considered *Shout at the Devil* in any way whatsoever (the only exception might be when J. D. Considine reviewed it for *Rolling Stone* and compared it to disco-era KISS). Bassist Nikki Sixx wrote virtually every song on *Shout*, and he probably didn't see it as a concept record either. But for someone (read: me) who had never really listened to albums before—I had only been exposed to singles on the radio—*Shout at the Devil* took on a conceptual quality that Yes would have castrated themselves to achieve. Like all great '80s music, it was inadvertently post-modern: The significance of *Shout at the Devil* had nothing to do with the concepts it introduced; its significance was the concept of what it literally *was*.

I realize this argument could be made by anyone when they discuss their first favorite album. My sister probably saw epic ideas in the Thompson Twins. That's the nature of an adolescent's relationship with rock 'n' roll. Sixx himself has described Aerosmith as "my Beatles." Using that logic, Mötley Crüe was "my Aerosmith," who (along these same lines) would still ultimately be "my Beatles."

Yet this personal relationship is only half the story, and not even the half that matters. There is another reason to look at the Crüe with slightly more seriousness (the operative word here being "slightly"). As we all know, '80s glam metal came from predictable sources: the aforementioned Aerosmith (seemingly every glam artist's favorite band), early and midperiod KISS (duh), Alice Cooper (but not so much musically), Slade (at least according to Quiet Riot), T. Rex (more than logic would dictate), Blue Cheer (supposedly), and—of course—Black Sabbath and Led Zeppelin (although those two bands had just as much effect on Pearl Jam, Soundgarden, and all the Sasquatch Rockers who would rise from the Pacific Northwest when metal started to flounder). In other words, this wasn't groundbreaking stuff, and no one is trying to argue otherwise. Sonically and visually, heavy metal was (and is) an unabashedly derivative art form.

But those sonic thefts are only half the equation, and maybe even less than that. We have to consider when this happened. The decade of the 1980s is constantly misrepresented by writers who obviously did not have the typical teen experience. If you believe unofficial Gen X spokesman Douglas Coupland (a title I realize he never asked for), every kid in the 1980s laid awake at night and worried about nuclear war. I don't recall the fear of nuclear apocalypse being an issue for me, for anyone I knew, or for any kid who wasn't trying to win an essay contest. The imprint Ronald Reagan placed on Children of the '80s had nothing to do with the escalation of the Cold War; it had more to do with the fact that he was the only president any of us could really remember (most of my information on Jimmy Carter had been learned through *Real People*, and—in retrospect—I suspect a bias in its news reporting).

In the attempt to paint the 1980s as some glossy, capitalistic wasteland, contemporary writers tend to ignore how unremarkable things actually were. John Hughes movies like *The Breakfast Club* and *Sixteen Candles* were perfect period pieces for their era—all his characters were obsessed with overwrought, self-centered personal problems, exactly like the rest of us. I suppose all the '80s films about the raging arms race are culturally relevant, much in the same way that Godzilla films are interesting reflections on the atomic age. But those films certainly weren't unsettling to anyone who didn't know better. *WarGames* and the TV movie *The Day After* were more plausible than something like *Planet of the Apes*, but—quite frankly—*every* new movie seemed a little more plausible than the stuff made before we were born. Anything could happen and probably would (sooner or later), but nothing would really change. Nobody seemed too shocked over the abundance of nuclear warheads the Soviets pointed at us; as far as I could tell, we were supposed to be on the brink of war 24/7. That was part of being an American. I remember when *Newsweek* ran a cover story introducing a new breed of adults called "Yuppies," a class of people who wore Nikes to the office and were money-hungry egomaniacs. No fifteen-year-old saw anything unusual about this. I mean, wouldn't that be normal behavior? The single biggest influence on our lives was the inescapable *sameness* of everything, which is probably true for most generations.

Jefferson Morley makes a brilliant point about inflation in his 1988 essay "Twentysomething": "For us, everything seemed normal. I remember wondering why people were surprised that prices were going up. I thought, That's what prices did." Consider that those sentiments come from a guy who was already in high school during Watergate—roughly the same year I was born. To be honest, I don't know if I've ever been legitimately *shocked* by anything, even as a third-grader in 1981. That was the year John Hinckley shot Ronald Reagan, and I wasn't surprised at all (in fact, it seemed to me that presidential assassinations didn't happen nearly as often as one would expect). From what I could tell, the world had always been a deeply underwhelming place;

my generation inherited this paradigm, and it was perfectly fine with me (both then and now).

Mötley Crüe was made to live in this kind of world. *Shout at the Devil* injected itself into a social vortex of jaded pragmatism; subsequently, it was the best album my friends and I had ever heard. We never scoffed at the content as "contrived shock rock." By 1983, that idea was the norm. Elvis Costello has questioned whether or not '80s glam metal should even be considered rock 'n' roll, because he thinks it's a "facsimile" of what legitimate artists already did in the past. What he fails to realize is that no one born after 1970 can possibly appreciate any creative element in rock 'n' roll: By 1980, there was no creativity left. The freshest ideas in pop music's past twenty years have come out of rap, and that genre is totally based on recycled, bastardized riffs. Clever facsimiles are all we really expect.

The problem with the current generation of rock academics is that they remember when rock music seemed new. It's impossible for them to relate to those of us who have never known a world where rock 'n' roll wasn't *everywhere*, all the time. They remind me of my eleventh-grade history teacher—a guy who simply could not fathom why nobody in my class seemed impressed by the *Apollo* moon landing. As long as I can remember, all good rock bands told lies about themselves and dressed like freaks; that was part of what defined being a "rock star." Mötley Crüe was a little more overt about following this criterion, but that only made me like them *immediately*.

In fact, I loved Mötley Crüe with such reckless abandon that I didn't waste my time learning much about the band. I consistently mispronounced Sixx's name wrong (I usually called him "Nikki Stixx"), and I got Tommy Lee and Mick Mars mixed up for almost a year.

Until 1992, I didn't even know that the cover art for the vinyl version of *Shout at the Devil* was a singular, bad-ass pentagram that was only visible when the album was held at a forty-five-degree angle. The reason this slipped under my radar was because *Shout at the Devil* was released in 1983, a period when the only people who were still buying vinyl were serious music fans. Obviously, serious music fans weren't buying Mötley Crüe. I've never even *seen* Mötley Crüe on vinyl; I used to buy most of my music at a Pamida in Wahpeton, ND—the only town within a half hour's drive that sold rock 'n' roll—and the last piece of vinyl I recall noticing in the racks was the soundtrack to *Grease*. The rest of us got *Shout at the Devil* on tape. The cassette's jacket featured the four band members in four different photographs, apparently taken on the set for the "Looks That Kill" video (which is probably the most ridiculous video ever made, unless you count videos made in Canada). By the look of the photographs, the band is supposed to be in either (a) hell, or (b) a realm that is remarkably similar to hell, only less expensive to decorate.

Like a conceptual album of the proper variety, *Shout at the Devil* opens with the aforementioned spoken-word piece "In the Beginning." It describes an evil force (the devil?) who devastated society, thereby forcing the "youth" to join forces and destroy it (apparently by shouting in its general direction). This intro leads directly into "Shout . . . shout . . . shout . . . shout . . . shout . . . shout . . . shout at the Devil," a textbook metal anthem if there ever was one.

Humorless Jesus freaks always accused Mötley Crüe of satanism, and mostly because of this record. But—if taken literally (a practice that only seems to happen to rock music when it shouldn't)—the lyrics actually suggest an anti-Satan sentiment, which means Mötley Crüe released the most popular Christian rock record of the 1980s. They're not shouting *with* the devil or *for* the devil: They're shouting *at* the devil. Exactly what they're shouting remains open to interpretation; a cynic might speculate Tommy Lee was shouting, "In exchange for letting me sleep with some of the sexiest women in television history, I will act like a goddamn moron in every social situation for the rest of my life." However, I suspect Sixx had more high-minded ideas. In fact, as I reconsider the mood and message of these songs, I'm starting to think he really *did* intend this to be a concept album, and I'm merely the first person insane enough to notice.

There are two ways to look at the messages in *Shout at the Devil*. The first is to say "It's elementary antiauthority language, like every other rock record that was geared toward a teen audience. Don't ignore the obvious." But that kind of dismissive language suggests there's no reason to look for significance in *anything*. It's one thing to realize that something is goofy, but it's quite another to suggest that goofiness disqualifies its significance. If anything, it *expands* the significance, because the product becomes accessible to a wider audience (and to the kind of audience who would never look for symbolism on its own). I think it was Brian Eno who said, "Only a thousand people bought the first Velvet Underground album, but every one of them became a musician." Well, millions of people bought *Shout at the Devil*, and every single one of them remained a person (excluding the kids who moved on to Judas Priest and decided to shoot themselves in the face).

Fifteen years later, I am not embarrassed by my boyhood idolization of Mötley Crüe. The fact that I once put a Mötley Crüe bumper sticker on the headboard of my bed seems vaguely endearing. And if I hadn't been so obsessed with shouting at the devil, the cultural context of heavy metal might not seem as clear (or as real) as it does for me today.

Through the circumstances of my profession (and without really trying), I've ended up interviewing many of the poofy-haired metal stars I used to mimic against the reflection of my old bedroom windows. But in 1983, the idea of talking with Nikki Sixx or Vince Neil wasn't my dream or even my fantasy—it was something that never crossed my mind. Nikki and Vince did not seem like people you talked to. I was a myopic white kid who had never drank, never had sex, had never seen drugs, and had never even been in a fight. Judging from the content of *Shout at the Devil*, those were apparently the *only* things the guys in Mötley Crüe did. As far as I could deduce, getting wasted with strippers and beating up cops was their full-time job, so we really had nothing to talk about.

2001

GEOFFREY O'BRIEN

Geoffrey O'Brien (b. 1948) applies his poet's instincts for compression, allusion, and lyrical evocation to essays and more extended reflections on cinema, popular music, and the reading life in *The Phantom Empire, Sonata for Jukebox: An Autobiography of My Ears*, and *The Browser's Ecstasy*. His essay-memoir of the '60s, *Dream Time*, exemplifies O'Brien's special capacity for evoking collective cultural life as a compilation of intuitions and associations. A regular contributor to *The New York Review of Books*, O'Brien is also the author of *The Times Square Story* and *Hardboiled America: Lurid Paperbacks and the Masters of Noir* as well as seven volumes of poetry. He was named editor-in-chief of Library of America in 1998.

▼ ▼

Seven Years in the Life

The Beatles Anthology
by the Beatles.
Chronicle Books, 368 pp., $60.00

1
by the Beatles.
EMI, compact disc, $18.99

On a summer afternoon in 1964 I went to a neighborhood movie theater to see the Beatles in *A Hard Day's Night*. It was less than a year since John F. Kennedy had been assassinated. Kennedy's death, and its aftermath of ceremonial grief and unscheduled violence, had if nothing else given younger observers an inkling of what it meant to be part of an immense audience. We had been brought together in horrified spectatorship, and the sense of shared spectatorship outlasted the horror. The period of private shock and public mourning seemed to go on forever, yet it was only a matter of weeks before the phenomenally swift rise of a pop group from Liverpool became so pervasive a concern that Kennedy seemed already relegated to an archaic period in which the Beatles had not existed. The New York DJs who promised their listeners "all Beatles all the time" were not so much shaping as reflecting an emergence that seemed almost an eruption of collective will. The Beatles had come, as if on occult summons, to drive away darkness and embody public desire on a scale not previously imagined.

Before the Christmas recess—just as "I Want to Hold Your Hand" was finally breaking through to a US market that had resisted earlier releases by the Beatles—girls in my tenth-grade class began coming to school with Beatles albums and pictures of individual Beatles, discussing in tones appropriate to a secret religion the relative attractions of John or Paul or Ringo or even the underappreciated George. A month or so later the Beatles arrived in New York to appear on *The Ed Sullivan Show* and were duly ratified as the show business wonder of the age. Everybody liked them, from the Queen of England and *The New York Times* on down.

Even bystanders with no emotional or generational stake in the Beatles could appreciate the adrenaline rush of computing just how much this particular success story surpassed all previous ones in terms of money and media and market penetration. It was all moving too fast even for the so-called professionals. The Beatles were such a fresh product that those looking for ways to exploit it—from Ed Sullivan to the aging news photographers and press agents who seemed holdovers from the Walter Winchell era—stood revealed as anachronisms as they flanked a group who moved and thought too fast for them.[1]

* * *

1. Or so it seemed at the time. The anachronisms worried about it, of course, all the way

And what was the product? Four young men who seemed more alive than their handlers and more knowing than their fans; aware of their own capacity to please more or less everybody, yet apparently savoring among themselves a joke too rich for the general public; professional in so unobtrusive a fashion that it looked like inspired amateurism. The songs had no preambles or buildups: the opening phrase—"Well, she was just seventeen" or "Close your eyes and I'll kiss you"—was a plunge into movement, a celebration of its own anthemic impetus. Sheer enthusiasm, yet tempered by a suggestion of knowledge held in reserve, a distancing that was cool without malice. When you looked at them they looked back; when they were interviewed, it was the interviewers who ended up on the spot.

That the Beatles excited young girls—mobs of them—made them an unavoidable subject of interest for young boys, even if the boys might have preferred more familiar local products like Dion and the Belmonts or Freddy Cannon to a group that was foreign and long-haired and too cute not to be a little androgynous. The near-riots that accompanied the Beatles' arrival in New York, bringing about something like martial law in the vicinity of the Warwick Hotel, were an epic demonstration of nascent female desire. The spectacle was not tender but warlike. The oscillation between glassy-eyed entrancement and emotional explosion, the screams that sounded like chants and bouts of weeping that were like acts of aggression, the aura of impending upheaval that promised the breaking down of doors and the shattering of glass: this was love that could tear apart its object.

Idols who needed to be protected under armed guard from their own worshippers acquired even greater fascination, especially when they carried themselves with such cool comic grace. To become involved with the Beatles, even as a fan among millions of others, carried with it the possibility of meddling with ferocious energies. Spectatorship here became participation. There were no longer to be any bystanders, only sharers. We were all going to give way to the temptation not just to gawk at the girl in Ed Sullivan's audience—the one who repeatedly

---

to the bank, while the Beatles ultimately did their own computing to figure out just how badly they had been shortchanged by the industry pros.

bounced straight up out of her seat during "All My Loving" as if pulled by a radar-controlled anti-gravity device—but to become her.

I emerged from *A Hard Day's Night* as from a conversion experience. Having walked into the theater as a solitary observer with more or less random musical tastes, I came out as a member of a generation, sharing a common repertoire with a sea of contemporaries. The four albums already released by the Beatles would soon be known down to every hesitation, every intake of breath; even the moments of flawed pitch and vocal exhaustion could be savored as part of what amounted to an emotional continuum, an almost embarrassingly comforting sonic environment summed up, naturally, in a Beatles lyric:

> *There's a place*
> *Where I can go*
> *When I feel low . . .*
> *And it's my mind,*
> *And there's no time.*

Listening to Beatles records turned out to be an excellent cure for too much thinking. It was even better that the sense of refreshment was shared by so many others; the world became, with very little effort, a more companionable place. Effortlessness—the effortlessness of, say, the Beatles leaping with goofy freedom around a meadow in *A Hard Day's Night*—began to seem a fundamental value. That's what they were there for: to have fun, and allow us to watch them having it. That this was a myth—that even *A Hard Day's Night*, with its evocation of the impossible pressure and isolation of the Beatles as hostages of their fame, acknowledged it as a myth—mattered, curiously, not at all. The converted choose the leap into faith over rational argument. It was enough to believe that they were taking over the world on our behalf.

A few weeks later, at dusk in a suburban park, I sat with old friends as one of our number, a girl who had learned guitar in emulation of Joan Baez, led us in song. She had never found much of an audience for her folksinging, but she won our enthusiastic admiration for having mastered the chord changes of all the songs in *A Hard Day's Night*. We sang for hours. If we had sung together before, the songs had probably been those of Woody Guthrie or the New Lost City Ramblers, mementos of a legendary folk past. This time there was the altogether different sensation of participating in a new venture, a world-changing enterprise that indiscriminately mingled aesthetic, social, and sexual possibilities.

An illusion of intimacy, of companionship, made the Beatles characters in everyone's private drama. We thought we knew them, or more precisely, and eerily, thought that they knew us. We imagined a give-and-take of communication between the singers in their sealed-off dome and the rest of us listening in on their every thought and musical reverie. It is hard to remember now how familiarly people came to speak of the Beatles toward the end of the Sixties, as if they were close associates whose reactions and shifts of thought could be gauged intuitively. They were the invisible guests at the party, or the relatives whose momentary absence provided an occasion to dissect their temperament and proclivities.

That intimacy owed everything to an intimate knowledge of every record they had made, every facial variation gleaned from movies and countless photographs. The knowledge was not necessarily sought; it was merely unavoidable. The knowledge became complex when the Beatles' rapid public evolution (they were after all releasing an album every six months or so, laying down tracks in a couple of weeks in between the tours and the interviews and the press conferences) turned their cozily monolithic identity into a maze of alternate personas. Which John were we talking about, which Paul? Each song had its own personality, further elaborated or distorted by each of its listeners. Many came to feel that the Beatles enjoyed some kind of privileged wisdom—the evidence was their capacity to extend their impossible string of successes while continuing to find new styles, new techniques, new personalities—but what exactly might it consist of? The songs were bulletins, necessarily cryptic, always surprising, from within their hermetic dome at the center of the world, the seat of cultural power.

Outside the dome, millions of internalized Johns and Pauls and

Georges and Ringos stalked the globe. What had at first seemed a har-monious surface dissolved gradually into its components, to reveal a chaos of conflicting impulses. Then, all too often, came the recrimi-nations, the absurd discussions of what the Beatles ought to do with their money or how they had failed to make proper use of their poten-tial political influence, as if they owed a debt for having been placed in a position of odd and untenable centrality. All that energy, all that authority: toward what end might it not have been harnessed?

At the end of the seven-year run, after the group finally broke up, the fragments of those songs and images would continue to intersect with the scenes of one's own life, so that the miseries of high school love were permanently imbued with the strains of "No Reply" and "I'm a Loser," and a hundred varieties of psychic fracturing acquired a com-mon soundtrack stitched together from "She Said She Said" ("I know what it's like to be dead") or the tornado-like crescendo in the middle of "A Day in the Life." Only that unnaturally close identification could account for the way in which the breakup of the Beatles functioned as a token for every frustrated wish or curdled aspiration of the era. Their seven fat years went from a point where everything was possible—hair-cuts, love affairs, initiatives toward world peace—to a point where only silence remained open for exploration.

All of this long since settled into material for biographies and made-for-TV biopics. Even as the newly released CD of their number one hits breaks all previous sales records, the number of books on the Beatles begins to approach the plateau where Jesus, Shakespeare, Lincoln, and Napoleon enjoy their bibliographic afterlife. If *The Beatles Anthology* has any claim, it is as "The Beatles' Own Story," an oral history patched together from past and present interviews, with the ghost of John Len-non sitting in for an impossible reunion at which all the old anecdotes are told one more time, and occasion is provided for a last word in edgewise about everything from LSD and the Maharishi to Allen Klein and the corporate misfortunes of Apple.

The book, which reads something like a *Rolling Stone* interview that

unaccountably goes on for hundreds of pages, is heavy enough to challenge the carrying capacity of some coffee tables and is spread over
multicolored page layouts that seem like dutifully hard-to-read tributes
to the golden age of psychedelia. It is the final installment of a protracted multimedia project whose most interesting component was a
six-CD compilation of outtakes, alternates, and rarities released under
the same title in 1995.

Those rarities—from a crude tape of McCartney, Lennon, and Harrison performing Buddy Holly's "That'll Be the Day" in Liverpool in
1958 to John Lennon's original 1968 recording of "Across the Universe"
without Phil Spector's subsequently added orchestral excrescences—
were revealing and often moving, and left no question at all that the
Beatles were no mirage. Indeed, even the most minor differences in
some of the alternate versions served the valuable function of making
audible again songs whose impact had worn away through overexpo-
sure. In the print-version *Anthology*, the Beatles are limited to words,
words whose frequent banality and inadequacy only increase one's
admiration for the expressiveness of their art. People who can make
things like *With the Beatles* or *Rubber Soul* or *The White Album* should
not really be required also to comment on what they have done.

The most interesting words come early. Before *Love Me Do* and Beatlemania and the first American tour, the Beatles actually lived in the same
world as the rest of us, and it is their memories of that world—from
Liverpool to Hamburg to the dance clubs of northern England—that
are the most suggestive. The earliest memories are most often of a
generalized boredom and sense of deprivation. A postwar Liverpool
barely out of the rationing card era, with bombsites for parks (Paul
recalls "going down the bombie" to play) and not much in the way of
excitement, figures mostly as the blank backdrop against which movies and music (almost exclusively American) could make themselves
felt all the more powerfully. "We were just desperate to get anything,"
George remarks. "Whatever film came out, we'd try to see it. Whatever
record was being played, we'd try to listen to, because there was very

little of anything. . . . You couldn't even get a cup of sugar, let alone a rock'n'roll record."

Fitfully a secret history of childhood music takes form: Paul listening to his pianist father play "Lullaby of the Leaves" and "Stairway to Paradise," George discovering Hoagy Carmichael songs and Josh White's "One Meatball," and Ringo (the most unassuming and therefore often the most eloquent speaker here) recalling his moment of illumination:

> My first musical memory was when I was about eight: Gene Autry singing "South of the Border." That was the first time I really got shivers down my backbone, as they say. He had his three compadres singing, "Ai, ai, ai, ai," and it was just a thrill to me. Gene Autry has been my hero ever since.

Only John—indifferent to folk ("college students with big scarfs and a pint of beer in their hands singing in la-di-da voices") and jazz ("it's always the same, and all they do is drink pints of beer")—seems to have reserved his enthusiasm until the advent of Elvis and Jerry Lee Lewis and Little Richard: "It was Elvis who really got me out of Liverpool. Once I heard it and got into it, that was life, there was no other thing." If one can imagine Paul playing piano for local weddings and dances, George driving a bus like his old man, and Ringo perhaps falling into the life of crime his teenage gang exploits seemed to promise, it is inconceivable that John could have settled into any of the choices he was being offered in his youth.

None of them ever did much except prepare themselves to be the Beatles. Their youths were devoid of incident (at least of incident that anyone cared to write into the record) and largely of education. John, the eldest, had a bit of art school training, but for all of them real education consisted more of repeated exposure to Carl Perkins, Chuck Berry, and Frank Tashlin's Cinemascope rock'n'roll extravaganza *The Girl Can't Help It.* On the British side, they steeped themselves in the surreal BBC radio comedy *The Goon Show*—echoes of Spike Milligan and Peter Sellers's non sequiturs are an abiding presence in their work—and in the skiffle band craze of the late Fifties (a renewal of old-fashioned jug band styles) they found a point of entry into the world of actual bands and actual gigs.

"I would often sag off school for the afternoon," writes Paul, "and John would get off art college, and we would sit down with our two guitars and plonk away." Along with the younger George, they formed a band that played skiffle, country, and rock, and played local dances, and after some changes in personnel officially became, around 1960, the Beatles, in allusion to the "beat music" that was England's term for what was left of a rock'n'roll at that point almost moribund. Hard up for jobs, they found themselves in Hamburg, in a series of Reeper-bahn beer joints, and by their own account were pretty much forced to become adequate musicians by the discipline of eight-hour sets and demanding, unruly audiences. Amid the amiable chaos of whores, gangsters, and endless amphetamine-fueled jamming—"it was pretty vicious," remarks Ringo, who joined the group during this period, "but on the other hand the hookers loved us"—they transformed themselves into an anarchic rock band, "wild men in leather suits." Back in the UK they blew away the local competition: "There were all these acts going 'dum de dum' and suddenly we'd come on, jumping and stomping," in George's account. "In those days, when we were rocking on, becoming popular in the little clubs where there was no big deal about The Beatles, it was fun."

Once the group gets back to England, the days of "sagging off" and "plonking away" are numbered. As their ascent swiftly takes shape—within a year of a Decca executive dismissing them with the comment that "guitar groups are on the way out" they have dropped the "wild man" act and are already awash in Beatlemania—the reminiscences have less and less to do with anything other than the day-to-day business of recording and performing. Once within the universe of EMI, life becomes something of a controlled experiment, with the Beatles subjected to unfamiliar sorts of corporate oversight:

> PAUL: . . . We weren't even allowed into the control room, then. It was Us and Them. They had white shirts and ties in

the control room, they were grown-ups. In the corridors and back rooms there were guys in full-length lab coats, maintenance men and engineers, and then there was us, the tradesmen. . . . We gradually became the workmen who took over the factory.

If they took over, though, it was at the cost of working at a killing pace, churning out songs, touring and making public appearances as instructed, keeping the merchandise coming. It can of course be wondered whether this forced production didn't have a positive effect on their work, simply because the work they were then turning out—everything from "Love Me Do" and "Please Please Me" to *Rubber Soul* was produced virtually without a break from performing or recording—could hardly be improved.

It is the paradox of such a life that it precludes the sort of experience on which art usually nurtures itself. The latter-day reminiscences evoke the crew members on a prolonged interstellar flight, thrown back on each other and on their increasingly abstract memories of Earth, and livening the journey with whatever drugs or therapies promise something like the terrestrial environment they have left behind. In this context marijuana and LSD are not passing episodes but central events, the true subject matter of the later Beatles records. In the inner storms of the bubble world, dreams and private portents take the place of the comings and goings of a street life that has become remote.

The isolation becomes glaring in, say, Paul's recollections of 1967: "I've got memories of bombing around London to all the clubs and the shops. . . . It always seemed to be sunny and we wore the far-out clothes and the far-out little sunglasses. The rest of it was just music." One can be sure that the "bombing around" took place within a well-protected perimeter. It is around this time that we find the Beatles pondering the possibility of buying a Greek island in order to build four separate residences linked by tunnels to a central dome, like something out of *Dr. No* or *Modesty Blaise*, with John commenting blithely that "I'm not worried about the political situation in Greece, as long as it doesn't affect us. I don't care if the government is all fascist, or commu-nist. . . . They're all as bad as here."

The conviction grows that the Beatles are in no better position than anyone else to get a clear view of their own career. "The moral of the story," says George, "is that if you accept the high points you're going to have to go through the lows. . . . So, basically, it's all good." They know what it was to have been a Beatle, but not really—or only by inference—what it all looked like to everybody else. This leads to odd distortions in tone, as if after all they had not really grasped the singu-larity of their fate. From inside the rocket was not necessarily the best vantage point for charting its trajectory.

Paul's comments on how certain famous songs actually got to be written are amiably vague: "'Oh, you can drive my car.' What is it? What's he doing? Is he offering a job as a chauffeur, or what? And then it became much more ambiguous, which we liked." As much in the dark as the rest of us as to the ultimate significance of what they were doing, the Beatles were all the more free to follow their usually impec-cable instincts. So if John Lennon chose to describe "Rain" as "a song I wrote about people moaning about the weather all the time," and Paul sees the lyrics of "A Day in the Life" as "a little poetic jumble that sounded nice," it confirms the inadvisability of seeking enlightenment other than by just listening to the records. (John, again: "What does it really mean, 'I am the eggman'? It could have been the pudding basin, for all I care.") The band doesn't know, they just write them.

In the end it was not the music that wore out but the drama, the personalities, the weight of expectation and identity. By the time the Beatles felt obliged to make exhortations like "all you need is love" and "you know it's gonna be all right," it was already time to bail out. How nice it would be to clear away the mass of history and personal associ-ation and just hear the records for the notes and words. Sometimes it's necessary to wait twenty years to be able to hear it again, the formal beauty that begins as far back as "Ask Me Why" and "There's a Place" and is sustained for years without ever settling into formula. Nothing really explains how or why musicians who spent years jamming on "Be Bop a Lula" and "Long Tall Sally" turned to writing songs like "Not a Second Time" and "If I Fell" and "Things We Said Today," so altogether different in structure and harmony. Before the addition of all the sitars and tape loops and symphony orchestras, before the lyrical turn toward eggmen and floating downstream, Lennon and McCartney (and, on occasion, Harrison) were already making musical objects of such elegant simplicity, such unhectoring emotional force, that if they had quit after *Help!* (their last "conventional" album) the work would still persist.

Paul McCartney recollects that when the Beatles heard the first playbacks at EMI it was the first time they'd really heard what they sounded like: "Oh, that sounds just like a record! Let's do this again and again and again!" The workmen taking over the factory were also the children taking over the playroom, determined to find effects that no one had thought of pulling out of the drawer before. They went from being performers to being songwriters, but didn't make the final leap until they became makers of records. Beyond all echoes of yesterday's mythologized excitement, the records—whether "The Night Before" or "Drive My Car" or "I'm Only Sleeping" or any of the dozens of others—lose nothing of a beauty so singular it might almost be called underrated.

2001

DEVIN MCKINNEY

Devin McKinney (b. 1966) is an archivist at Gettysburg College in Pennsylvania. His debut book, *Magic Circles: The Beatles in Dream and History* (2003), from which the following excerpt is taken, managed to say something new about the most written-about band in rock history, precisely by turning to out-of-the-way corners in the Beatles' dense and brief career. "Everything the Beatles did meant something," he writes, "because there was no way for it to mean nothing." In 2012 he published *The Man Who Saw a Ghost: The Life and Work of Henry Fonda* (2012). His work has appeared in *The American Prospect*, *The Village Voice*, *The Boston Globe*, *The Believer*, *Film Quarterly*, *Bookforum*, *The Oxford American*, and *Black Clock*; he contributes regularly to the websites Critics at Large and Hi Lobrow.

▼▼▼▼▼▼▼▼▼▼▼▼▼▼▼▼▼▼▼▼▼▼▼

from
O.P.D. / *Deus Est Vivus*:
The Beatles and the Death Cults

To reason about holes seems to involve reasoning about the shape of
an object, but also about its dispositions to interact with other objects;
about the way in which a hole is or can be generated, modified, used,
destroyed; and, finally, about the ways in which it is or can be per-
ceived, identified, re-identified. We will track all of these clues.
—ROBERTO CASATI AND ACHILLE C. VARZI,
HOLES AND OTHER SUPERFICIALITIES (1994)

IN THE beginning was the Word; and the Word was *you.*

Fair notice: at this point, the Beatles—not "the Beatles" but the four
men themselves—pretty much disappear from the story.

And a prefatory word to those readers who may not know or might
not believe: aside from speculations on the part of myself or other individuals—always clearly marked—everything described in this chapter
actually happened.

We are never content with mere deductive explanations for traumatic
shifts in the lives of entire generations. Plagues, assassinations—reality and causality are not enough to deal with them: they frustrate our
instinct for proportion. So we invent the crime to fit the punishment,
the myth to justify the monument. It is the only way of assigning meaning—however creative, crackpot, or plain crazy—to something that
defies reason: a search for truth in which the search becomes the truth,
and endings have purpose.

Artists, like the Beatles, search by means of their art. The rest of us
use myths and legends—instruments in one way more limited than art,
in another far more powerful. Myth has been described as a waking
dream, and dreaming on a mass scale may be most effective when an era

is freest in its potentials, when none of its possibilities or limits is quite nailed down. Myth takes over when those potentials are realized, and tremors become quakes. The time comes when we must *speak* our fears by making stories of them: what was unrecognized in its dream form takes the shape of narrative. The volatile, far-flung community becomes a campfire; frightening times become the darkness surrounding it; and unity, if we're lucky, is a result.

1969 was the moment for such myths. Few would say it, but nearly everyone felt it: the end was near. The end of that world which a generation had worked to build for itself, in the process compelling the generations on either side to respond to what that world contained and implied. And many people, eager to cluster into tight, fanatical groups of like minds—cults, in the soon-to-be-common designation—made myths to prepare for and even welcome the end, but mostly to master it by writing their own scenario upon it.

Most of the myths had an element of religion to them—for religions have always rejoiced in detailing how the end will come and who will suffer hardest by it. That the ragged end of the 1960s produced such an apocalyptic impulse is easy to fathom. The most traumatic year in recent U.S. memory had just passed; heroes were dead, and to all appearances the same forces of darkness were in power and only growing stronger. Death was already eating at the heart of this generation's common body, in its music, its political confrontations, its dwindling store of viable leaders. Unable just yet to deal with defeat and death as looming realities, many of this generation recast them in the terms of myth.

The myths were, in one way or another, all about death—also a subject that religion was invented to deal with. What the Beatles had lately been attempting to cover up, successfully with *Sgt. Pepper*, less so with the White Album—that history was turning, and death was coming— was an anxiety which had always found release in religious myth: in religion death is meaningful, never random, its causes noble and divine. But there's no God without some sense of the devil. So it came to pass that midway into the year 1969, the holy and the profane were made to fuse. The angel and the demon of this generation, the good and evil of the time it had defined, came together for the End. And in the End, it fell again to the Beatles to midwife a mutation born of needs and desperations. It fell to them because in their unity the Beatles contained, and in their music expressed, the best of their generation's spirit—its most transformative values, its largest visions. It fell to them also because they had been, for some time, prophesying the compromise of those values, and the dimming of those visions.

Late 1969: the chronology of these few months is so irretrievably bizarre, so cosmically screwy with synchronicities and scattered insanities, that one is now tempted to reconceive of it as a mammoth conspiracy fiction handed down as historical fact. The substance of these few months was itself constructed of parallel fictions—the fictions around which two groups of people, far removed in space, circumstance, and ideology (or lack thereof), chose, for a time, to structure their lives in whole or in part. These community fictions made sacred truths of the most gruesome fantasies; they were equal parts Holy Bible and *National Enquirer*. For both groups, the wildest flights of Beatle-sparked imagination became both the stuff of life and the rationale for death. And though both fictions had everything to do with the Beatles, neither required the participation, consent, or acknowledgement of the Beatles themselves to rise and thrive.

Why do we make myths? We might as well ask why we make wars, or why we build gods. It is simply something we have always done: apparently we've had no choice. The other thing we've had no choice in is dying; and surely we make myths for the same reason we make wars and gods, or write books, or preserve our songs and paintings, or in some other manner mark our spot of earth in ways that will reach into the lives of those we'll never know: to defer as long as possible the certainty that one day, fairly soon, we'll be only another set of bones in the boneyard.

We have got to leave a trace behind.

> Attempting to classify holes is an important part of our work.
> It is convenient to have a general idea of what holes look like
> and of the various forms they can come in.
> —CASATI AND VARZI, *HOLES AND OTHER SUPERFICIALITIES*

Suddenly everyone was looking for a hole. Once there had been any number of circles to join; now, in 1969, a hole was the spatial metaphor of choice. In some ways a hole was the same as a circle: a space in the imagination. In other ways holes and circles were opposites. Circles were large, round, and flat against the earth; holes were deep, dark, and narrow. A circle was for inclusion; a hole was for keeping other people out.

That is how this theory of holes in the late '60s begins. But it doesn't end so simply. A taxonomy of 1969 holes is called for—an inquiry into types, methods, functions.

The Beatles, seeking a hole in their fame, began the year by going underground. They spent all of January rehearsing and recording songs for their next album, an album advertised with the tag-line "The Beatles as Nature Intended." *Get Back* was its symbolic title: the songs would be rock and roll primitive, free of overdubs and post-psychedelic fairy dust. By so stripping their music, they obviously hoped to renew their unity—but also to cleanse themselves of the mythic barnacles history and fantasy had placed upon them. It was both a search for the bog and another late-'60s escape attempt: the Beatles needed a hole for shelter, but, as always, their own needs had to be justified in terms of music and audience. In earlier passages their penchant for exotica had resulted in rich and strange diversities of sound; now their psychic need for the clean and simple would be channeled through music whose populist ethic was its basicness.

And *basic* meant *basic*. Even the White Album songs hadn't gotten back far enough. Those had been hard rock, often incredibly simple, but laden with a mature sense of doom and bewilderment. *Get Back* was meant as unadorned, head-in-the-sand rock and roll. Among the songs they focused on, performing it dozens of times in search of its essence, was "One after 909," a number John and Paul had written as teenagers, and first recorded in Paul's living room.

Meanwhile, thousands of miles away in southern California, Charles Manson was dreaming of a hole in the desert. The Hopi Indians of that region had for centuries retold a myth about the hole, which they believed lay hidden somewhere in the vast floor of Death Valley. Manson was obsessed with finding the hole, and at a certain point this jailhouse prophet and flower-power fascist began to tell people he had found it. He described the hole as an underground paradise where water cascaded and the very dirt was made of gold; and his plan was that he and his followers would descend into the hole, there to live until the apocalypse had come and gone and the band of underworld-dwelling gypsies would emerge to assume control of what was left.

"I found a hole in the desert," Manson is reported to have said. "I covered it up and I hid it. I called it . . . The Devil's Hole."[1]

Meanwhile, two thousand miles away in the American Midwest, another group of young people was searching for another kind of hole. Like a lot of holes, this one came in the shape of an O. This group kept searching for the O on the covers of Beatle albums, where, if you could find it, it was damaged, and if you couldn't, it was notable in its absence.

O was a letter you needed to form the word "love." And Paul McCartney, people now realized, was the only Beatle without an O in his name.

> How do you describe what you see? A spot in the wall, darker than the rest, filled with shadow, that goes deep inside (though you cannot really tell how deep). It looks unitary and complete, compact, though less dense than the wall. A thing, perhaps, but a bit mysterious.
> —CASATI AND VARZI, *HOLES AND OTHER SUPERFICIALITIES*

Most Americans first heard of a bizarre rumor involving Paul McCartney in the latter days of October 1969, when brief items began to appear at the margins of major newspapers.

1. Ed Sanders, *The Family: The Manson Group and Its Aftermath* (New York: Signet, 1989 [1971], p. 101.

It was a rumor like other rumors: no one knew quite where it had begun. But it began for the same reason that rumors always begin: someone, somewhere, dreamed up a notion. The myth of Paul McCartney's death materialized out of nothing because that someone, in whatever manner or measure, wanted it to be the truth. It then gathered force, turned nothing into something, because a large number of people found they *liked* the idea of its being the truth. At the time, some truly believed that Paul was dead, and that the Beatles were subtly and systematically revealing this fact in words and pictures. Many others suspected that Paul was as alive as you or me, but felt the clues were nonetheless there, planted by mischievous Beatles for no goal grander than their private amusement. Still others bypassed the factual question of death altogether, caring only to hunt up new clues. The rumor allowed all to take part, whatever their belief; it enabled fun from any position.

But that's too flippant, because in another way this was *not* a rumor like other rumors. Quickly, and mostly quietly—away from conventional media, passed by mouth, in the smoke and hush of dormitory rooms after midnight—it accrued a wealth of arcana, explanation, elaboration, mystification, and solemnization which put it well past the league of any other rumor one can name. Obviously it was not only fun the rumormongers were after. It was also a sense of involvement, being in on the creation of something excitingly bigger than any of them, which was nonetheless theirs. *All* theirs, since one didn't actually need the Beatles to play the game. You had no more need of the Beatles than the authors of the Gospels had needed Jesus: you needed only their artifacts, and the creative faculty to make narrative of them.

The death rumor, I like to believe, was the unconscious pursuit of a mystery—a historical mystery that was unfolding as it was being investigated. Unlike other rumors, it was a trivial exercise with a profound impulse. The conscious, articulated mysteries—Is Paul dead? If so, how did he die? How have the Beatles been telling us this?—were manageable, ostensibly answerable (and yes, fun) surrogates for other, deeper mysteries. Is our time, our moment in history, dead? If so, how did it die? How have the Beatles been telling us this? The rumormongers were generational detectives working on a case that had not been named. The crime scene, where traces would be sifted and fingerprints lifted, was the Beatles' post-1966 art. The corpse was the world their generation had dreamed, and so very nearly fought into being.

But who was the murderer?

The identity of a hole over time will have to be traced to some delicate interplay between the identity of the host and the identity of the filler.
—CASATI AND VARZI, *HOLES AND OTHER SUPERFICIALITIES*

Like most Americans, Charles Manson discovered the Beatles in the spring of 1964. Unlike most Americans, he was in prison—specifically the U.S. Penitentiary at McNeil Island, Washington State, where he'd been incarcerated since June 1961. He may have seen the Beatles' pictures in *Life* magazine, or heard their voices coming from a transistor radio. Instantly, he was excited by them. Some said obsessed. One of his friends, the legendary Alvin "Creepy" Karpis—in the '30s a member of Ma Barker's gang, now the fellow inmate who taught Manson guitar—said later, "He was constantly telling people he could come on like the Beatles, if he got the chance."[2]

The intensity of Manson's reaction was not unusual in that feverish spring; the precise quality of that reaction was. Manson's urgent response to what the Beatles were setting off was more akin to jealousy than joy—the sense not that something had been given him, but that something had been stolen. Those screams, he was implying to whoever would listen, were rightfully *his*. The Beatles seem to have awakened a latent sense of entitlement in this 29-year-old petty crook. Suddenly, with Alvin Karpis' guitar in his hands and the Beatles' music in his head, he had a purpose.

But where did it come from, this fierce certainty, unprecedented given Manson's record as an inveterate small-timer, that he had some-

---

2. Ibid., p. 19. See also Vincent Bugliosi with Curt Gentry, *Helter Skelter: The True Story of the Manson Murders* (New York: Bantam, 1994 [1974]), pp. 195–198.

thing to say that was worthy of being attended to by those awed millions? From what interior palette did this determinedly insignificant man—who had spent more than half his life in juvenile institutions and prisons, who had never aimed at any success higher than the next stolen car or forged check, and whose musical tastes ran to Perry Como and away from Elvis Presley—draw such a grand rock and roll vision of himself? What self-discipline enabled him to do honest time for the next three years, earn release in early 1967, and methodically recruit a cluster of fanatical followers over the next two years, all the while constructing an elaborate personal cosmology *and* staying clear of prison longer than he had since reaching his majority, long enough to orchestrate crimes that would place him near Hitler as a madman of the age?

Perhaps he drew the discipline from the dimensions of his prison cell. Unlike those experiencing the Beatles on the outside, those who could *do* something with their excitement, Manson found himself imprisoned with a burgeoning sense of possibility: torture, of a kind, to know that there is something out there to be done, and have no arms or legs with which to do it. But probably the sense of mission was most attributable to the fact that nothing like the Beatles had occurred in his lifetime. If they were truly something new, it was obvious that, as a result, other *somethings* would take shape; and that in among all the *somethings* wholesome and harmless there would be coiled others which were cruel, diseased, fixed on destruction.

So it's quite possible that Manson, wavering always between lucidity and psychosis, gifted equally in cool calculation and mystical fancy, was turned on by the Beatles because he knew instantly that something had changed: a hole had opened. It's quite possible that he saw as deeply into the potential of the Beatle phenomenon as anyone, far deeper than any objective newsman or social commentator, and knew that a universe of potentials, dormant the day before, had now come to trembling life. And it's quite possible that he took that opening as the personal cue which he, like the fifteen-year-old girl, had been waiting for his whole life. His chance to make a mark on his time, to influence mass consciousness. His time to go insane.

2003

JESSICA HOPPER

"I'm really all about reclaiming the fangirl," Jessica Hopper (b. 1976) suggested in a 2015 interview for Salon.com. The manifesto-like piece that opens her defiantly titled collection *The First Collection of Criticism by a Living Female Rock Critic* describes her posture as "an inextricable soul-entanglement with music that is insular, boundless, devoted, celebratory, and willfully pathetic." That nicely captures the "fan" piece: Hopper's is a distinctive voice in contemporary rock and pop writing in part because she refuses to divorce the role of critic from that of fan. And the stakes of the music are very different for a fangirl than a fanboy: a woman is often forced to confront the ways that the music she loves promotes self-loathing. Emerging from 'zine culture, Hopper has been working as a professional writer since age sixteen; she has worked as a senior editor at *Pitchfork* and is currently editorial director of music for MTV News.

▼ ▼

Emo: Where the Girls Aren't

A FEW months back, I was at a Strike Anywhere show. The band launched into "Refusal," a song that offers solidarity with the feminist movement and bears witness to the struggles inherent to women's lives. It is not a song of protection, there is no romantic undertow, it's just about all people being equally important. Everyone was dancing, fanboys and girls at the lip of the stage screaming along—like so many shows at the Fireside. By the first chorus of the song, I was in tears with a sudden awareness: I've been going to three shows a week for the last decade and the number of times I've heard women's reality acknowledged or portrayed in a song sung by a male-fronted band was at zero and holding. This song was the first.

It's no wonder why my girlfriends and I have grown increasingly alienated and distanced from the scene, or have begun taking shelter from emo's pervasive stronghold in the recesses of electronic, DJ or experimental music. No wonder girls I know are feeling dismissive and faithless towards music. No wonder I feel much more allegiance to MOP's "Ante Up" than any song by an all-dude band about the singer's romantic holocaust. Because as it stands in 2003 I simply cannot substantiate the effort it takes to give a flying fuck about the genre/plague that we know as emo or myopic songs that don't consider the world beyond boy bodies, their broken hearts or their vans. Meanwhile, we're left wondering—how did we get here?

As hardcore and political punk's charged sentiments became more cliché towards the end of the '80s and we all began slipping into the armchair comfort of the Clinton era—punk stopped looking outward and began stripping off its tough skin only and examined its squishy heart instead, forsaking songs about the impact of trickle down economics for ones about elusive kisses. Mixtapes across America became laden with relational eulogies—hopeful boys with their hearts masted to sleeves, their pillows soaked in tears. Punk's songs became personal, often myopically so.

Perhaps we lost the map, or simply stopped consulting it. There was a time when emo seemed reasonable, encouraging, exciting—revivifying in its earnestness and personal stakes. These new bands modeled themselves on bands we all liked: Jawbox, Jawbreaker, Sunny Day Real Estate. The difference was, in those bands' songs about women, the girls had names, details to their lives. Jawbox's most popular song, "Savory," was about recognizing male normative privilege, about the weight of objectification on a woman ("See you feign surprise / That

I'm all eyes"). In Jawbreaker songs, women had leverage, had life, had animus and agency to them. Sometimes they were friends, or a sister, not always a girl to be bedded or dumped by. They were unidealized, realistic characters.

And then something broke—and not just Mr. Dashboard's sensitive heart. Records by a legion of romantically-wronged boys suddenly lined the record store shelves. Every record was seemingly a concept album about a breakup, damning the girl on the other side. Emo's contentious monologues—these balled-fist, Peter Pan mash-note dilemmas—have now gone from being descriptive to being prescriptive. Emo has become another forum where women were locked out, observing ourselves through the eyes of others.

Girls in emo songs today do not have names. We are not identified beyond our absence, our shape drawn by the pain we've caused. Our lives, our day-to-day-to-day does not exist, we do not get colored in. Our actions are portrayed solely through the detailing of neurotic self-entanglement of the boy singer—our region of personal power, simply, is our impact on his romantic life. We're vessels redeemed in the light of boy-love. On a pedestal, on our backs. Muses at best. Cum rags or invisible at worst. Check out our pictures on the covers of records—we are sad-eyed and winsome and comely (thank you Hot Rod Circuit, The Crush, Cursive, Something Corporate, et al.)—the fantasy girl you could take home and comfort.

It's evident from these bands' lyrics and shared aesthetic that their knowledge of actual living, breathing women is notional at best. Emo's characteristic vulnerable front is limited to self-sensitivity, every song a high-stakes game of control that involves "winning" or "losing" possession of the girl (see Dashboard Confessional, Brand New, New Found Glory and Glassjaw albums for prime examples). Yet, in the vulnerability there is no empathy, no peerage or parallelism. Emo's yearning doesn't connect it with women—it omits them.

As Andy Greenwald notes in his book about emo culture, *Nothing Feels Good: Punk Rock, Teenagers and Emo*, lyrically, emo singers "revel in their misery and suffering to an almost ecstatic degree, but with a limited use of subtlety and language. It tends to come off like Rimbaud relocated to the Food Court." Women in emo songs are denied the dignity of humanization through both the language and narratives, we are omnipresent yet chimerical, only of consequence in romantic settings.

On a dance floor in Seattle, a boy I know decides to plumb the topic:
"I heard you're writing a column about how emo is sexist."
"I am."
"What do you mean '*emo is sexist*'? Emo songs are no different than all of rock history, than Rolling Stones or Led Zeppelin."
"I know—I'd rather not get into it right now."
"How are songs about breaking up sexist though? Everyone breaks up. If you have a problem with emo, you have a problem with all of rock history!"
"I know. I do."
To paraphrase Nixon sidekick H.R. Haldeman, "History is wack."
There must be some discussion, at least for context, about the well-worn narrative of the boy rebel's broken heart, as exemplified by the last fifty-plus years of blues-based music, that there are songs about loving and losing women; that *men writing songs about women* is practically the definition of rock 'n' roll. And as a woman, as a music critic, as someone who lives and dies for music, there is a rift within, a struggle of how much deference you can afford, and how much you are willing to ignore what happens in these songs simply because you like the music.

Can you ignore the lyrical content of the Stones' "Under My Thumb" because you like the song? Are you willing to? Or the heaping pile of dead or brutalized women that amasses in Big Black's discography? Is emo exceptional in the scope of the rock canon either in terms of treatment of women or in its continual rubbing salute to its own trouble-boy cliché image? Is there anything that separates Dashboard Confessional's condemnation of his bed-hopping betrayer and makes it any more egregious than any woman/mother/whore/ex-girlfriend showing up in songs of Jane's Addiction, Nick Cave, The Animals or Justin Timberlake? Can you forgo judgment woe to women in the recorded catalog of Zeppelin because the first eight bars of "Communication Breakdown" is total fucking godhead? Where do you split? Do you even bother to care, because if you're going to try and kick against it, you, as my dancing friend says, "have a problem with all of rock history," and because who, other than a petty, too-serious bitch dismisses Zeppelin?! Do you accept the sexism and phallocentricity of the last few decades of popular music and in your punk rock community as just how it is?

Who do you excuse and why? Do you check your politics at the door and just dance or just rock or just let side A spin out? Can you ignore the marginalization of women's lives on the records that line your record shelves in hopes that feigned ignorance will bridge the gulf, because it's either that or purge your collection of everything but free jazz, micro house 12"s and the Mr. Lady Records catalog?

It's almost too big of a question to ask. I start to ask this of myself, to really start investigating, and stop, realizing full well that if I get an answer I might just have to retire to an adobe hut in the Italian countryside and not take any visitors for a long time. Or turn into the rock critical Andrea Dworkin, and report with resignation that all music made by men propagates the continual oppression and domination of women. Sometimes I feel like every rock song I hear is a sucker punch towards us. And I feel like no one takes that impact seriously, let alone notices it. It is "just" music.

My deepest concerns about the lingering effects of emo is not so much for myself or for my friends—we have refuge in our personal-political platforms and deep-crated record collections—but rather for the teenage girls I see crowding front and center at emo shows. The ones for whom this is their inaugural introduction to the underground, whose gateway may have been through Weezer or the Vagrant America tour or maybe Dashboard Confessional's *Unplugged*. The ones who are seeking music out, who are wanting to stake some claim to punk rock, or an underground avenue, for a way out, a way under, to sate the seemingly unquenchable, nameless need—the same need I know I came to punk rock with. Emo is the province of the young, their foundation is fresh-laid, my concern is for people who have no other previous acquaintance with the underground, save for these bands and their songs.

When I was that age, I too had a hunger for a music that spoke a language I was just starting to decipher, music that affirmed my ninth grade fuck-you values—music that encouraged me to not allow my budding feminist ways to be bludgeoned by the weight of mainstream, patriarchal culture—I was lucky I was met at the door with things like the Bikini Kill demo, Fugazi and the first Kill Rock Stars comp. I was met with polemics and respectful address; I heard my life and concerns in those songs. I was met with girl heroes deep in guitar squall, kicking out the jams under the stage lights. I was being hurtled towards deeper rewards. Records and bands were triggering ideas and inspiration. I acknowledge the importance of all of that because I know I would not be who I am now, doing what I do, 12 years down the line, if I had not gotten those fundamentals, been presented with those big ideas about what music and, moreover, what life, can be about.

So now I watch these girls at emo shows more than I ever do the band. I watch them sing along, to see what parts they freak out over. I wonder if this does it for them, if seeing these bands, these dudes on stage, resonates and inspires them to want to pick up a guitar or drum sticks. Or if they just see this as something dudes do, since there are no girls, there is no *them* up there. I wonder if they see themselves as participants, or only as consumers or—if we reference the songs directly— the consumed. I wonder if this is where music will begin and end for them. If they can be radicalized in spite of this. If being denied keys to the clubhouse is enough to spur them into action.

I know that, for me, even as a teenage autodidact who thought her every idea was worthy of expression and an audience, it did not occur to me to start a band until I saw other women in one. It took seeing Babes in Toyland and Bikini Kill to truly throw on the lights, to show me that there was more than one place, one role, for women to occupy, and that our participation was important and vital—it was YOU MAT TER writ large.

I don't want these front row girls to miss that. I don't want girls leaving clubs denied of encouragement and potential. As lame as punk rock can be, as hollow as all of our self-serving claims ring—that the culture of punk is truly different somehow than that of median society—at its gnarled foundations still exists the possibilities for connection. There is still the possibility for exposure to radical notions, for punk rock to match up to what many kids dream, or hope for punk DIY to mean. But much of that hinges on the continual presence of radicalized women within the leagues, and those women being encouraged—given reasons to stay, to want to belong—rather than diminished by the music which glues the community together.

Us girls deserve more than one song. We deserve more than one pledge of solidarity. We deserve better songs than any boy will ever write about us.

2003

DOUGLAS WOLK

Whether writing tight, astute album reviews, page-by-page analyses of individual comic book issues, or a book-length exploration of a single LP, Douglas Wolk (b. 1970) immerses himself in his subjects with the fervor of an obsessive fan and the detachment of a seasoned critic—perhaps because he is both. His infectious enthusiasm for comics and music as both art and entertainment makes his voice equally authoritative whether he's assessing the latest "complete" Velvet Underground boxed set or dissecting the panels of the latest issue of *Judge Dredd*. Wolk is the author of *Reading Comics: How Graphic Novels Work and What They Mean* (2007), a landmark study that considers comics as an artistically vital form of literature. His meditations on popular culture have appeared in a wide variety of venues, including *Rolling Stone*, *The New York Times*, *The New Republic*, *The Nation*, *The Believer*, and *Pitchfork*. His volume in the 33⅓ series on James Brown's *Live at the Apollo*, from which the following excerpt is taken, weaves a high-tension bridge between Brown's stage show, as captured on the album, and the potentially cataclysmic events taking place on the world stage beyond those theater walls.

▼▼▼▼▼▼▼▼▼▼▼▼▼▼▼▼▼▼▼▼▼▼▼▼▼

from
Live at the Apollo

TODD GITLIN, ON THE WEEK OF OCTOBER 24, 1962, IN HIS BOOK *THE SIXTIES*

"Time was deformed, everyday life suddenly dwarfed and illuminated, as if by the glare of an explosion that had not yet taken place."

DIONYSUS LIVE AT THE APOLLO

In the fall of 1962, the Apollo Theater's stage area appeared to its audience as a box, twice as wide as it was tall. The worn-down wooden planks of the stage floor were perpendicular to the audience. Originally a burlesque house, Hurtig & Seamon's Music Hall, the Apollo had "turned black" in 1934, as risqué stage shows fell to a city crackdown and vaudeville lost the last of its territory to the talkies. Located "in the heart of friendly Harlem," as its ads said, at 125th Street off Eighth Avenue in Manhattan, it booked star acts to play for a solid week, in front of the toughest and most devoted crowds they'd ever face. By the early '60s, the Apollo was well established as the crown jewel of the "chitlin circuit"—the network of small and large halls, mostly in the South and on the East Coast, where black artists would play to black audiences, touring as hard as they could bear.

Standing on the stage of the Apollo at a sold-out show on the night of October 24, 1962, screaming, James Brown would have looked out and seen 1500 people screaming back at him in the audience, split between the floor and the balconies. The walls behind them were a dark crimson; the balconies were decorated with the laurel wreaths that are the emblem of Apollo the god, recalling Daphne, who became a laurel tree to escape his lust. Most of the audience thought there was a good chance they'd be dead within the week.

That night, on stage at the Apollo, James Brown made a new kind of pop record, based on the force of a single, superhuman will, and built around performance itself, even more than performances of particular songs. *Live at the Apollo* is one of the most *charged* albums ever made—electrical arcs fly between Brown and his terrified, ecstatic, howling audience.

Brown has built the structures of the album around himself, so that he can break free of them. Every word and note that *doesn't* come from him, beginning with the opening incantation and ending with the chorus that ends the record, is ritualized, precise, formally scripted; his own performance is unrestricted and overwhelming, an explosion about to take place at the intersection of lust and terror. The moment of sexual abandonment (and erotic abandon) was the subject of all of James Brown's great songs in those days. He sings as if his lover leaving him would be the end of the world, which is also a way of singing about the end of the world. The song ceases to be the song, and becomes James Brown. "Supernatural sounds emanate from him," as Friedrich Nietzsche wrote about man under the charm of the Dionysian. "He is no longer an artist; he has become a work of art."

It cost two dollars to get into the Apollo, and you could stay all day if you wanted to.

WHAT MIKHAIL POLONIK, THE SOVIET PRESS OFFICER AT THE UNITED NATIONS, TOLD AN AMERICAN OFFICIAL THE EVENING BEFORE THE EVENTS RELATED IN THIS BOOK

"This could well be our last conversation. New York will be blown up tomorrow by Soviet nuclear weapons."

THE ALBUM

Live at the Apollo doesn't say "Live at the Apollo" anywhere on its front cover. The cover painting, by Dan Quest, is an indistinct, chunky watercolor of a crowd clustering around a marquee that looks a little like the Apollo's, framed by a white border; the only other sharp lines belong to something that's presumably a car passing by the front. The type on the marquee says "The Apollo Theatre (*sic*) Presents—In

Person! The James Brown ···"Show"···." The marquee's side panel adds "James Brown" and, below that, "Voted No. 1 R&B Star of 1962." The back cover explains that the vote came from a national poll of disc jockeys, although which national poll has never been clear.

On the original front cover, a King Records logo bulges out of the top right-hand corner of the painting. "Vivid Sound," declares a banner within the car shape down at the bottom—a tag-line that King put on many of its LPs in 1963 and 1964. ("That was just advertising," King's former chief engineer Chuck Seitz says. "Matter of fact, we were doing a lot of stuff with primitive equipment. Our main console was handmade.") The back cover's banner type reads "James Brown 'Live' at the Apollo," which is the title that caught on.

The title of the album has never quite stabilized, actually. When the Solid Smoke label reissued it in 1980, it was retitled *Live and Lowdown at the Apollo, Vol. 1*. (The Solid Smoke version is a real oddity, if you can track a copy down: unlike most stereo copies, which let the vocals and instruments overlap, it was mixed with the vocals all the way on one side and the instrumental parts all the way on the other. The company also released a DJ edition, which keeps "Lost Someone" in one piece on side 2, and displaces the long medley to the first side.) And where did that "lowdown" come from? Possibly from Marva Whitney's JB-produced 1969 album, *Live and Lowdown at the Apollo*. The Polydor CD that came out in 1990 is *James Brown Live at the Apollo, 1962*, to distinguish it from his three later *Apollo* albums. At least that's what it says on the spine—the disc itself is labeled as *The Apollo Theater Presents, In Person, The James Brown Show*. The 2004 edition is *James Brown Live at the Apollo (1962)*. For the purposes of this book, it's *Live at the Apollo* or LATA, but call it what you like.

HOW IT HAPPENED

In 1962, you could've gathered from James Brown's record sales that he was a reasonably successful R&B act—no Ray Charles or Jackie Wilson, certainly, but a solid, dependable singles artist, along the lines of, say,

Bobby Bland. Where Brown really shone, though, was in performance. Constantly on the road and a scenery-chewing showman, he'd built up a huge following as a live act; for a few years, he'd been traveling with a full band and a supporting revue.

Brown got the notion in the fall of 1962 that a recording of his live show, along the lines of Ray Charles's 1959 LP *In Person*, would be a good idea. King Records president Syd Nathan, in one of a string of legendarily awful judgment calls that his business miraculously survived, thought it was a terrible idea, and declared that nobody would ever buy it; he refused to fund a recording. King wasn't one of those big East Coast labels with a big promotional budget, it was an independent operation based in Cincinnati. It was in the business of putting out hit singles, and as far as Nathan was concerned the only reason anybody bought R&B albums was to get the singles, which of course wouldn't appear on a live album.

So Brown made his own arrangements to turn his show into a record. He spent $5700 recording the album; instead of going for the usual deal with the Apollo where he would be paid a percentage of the door after expenses, he rented out the theater, and arranged for its employees to wear uniforms for his weeklong engagement there—the ushers wore tuxedos. The James Brown Revue opened at the Apollo on Friday, October 19, and ran through the following Thursday, October 25.

GETTING READY

On the night of October 22, President Kennedy had made a televised appearance announcing a U.S. naval blockade of Cuba, which began at 10 A.M. on the 24th: the Atlantic Fleet was told to shoot, if necessary, at Russian cargo ships bound for Cuba. Defense Secretary Robert McNamara had predicted on the evening of the 23rd that some sort of "challenge" might well happen within 24 hours. American stores, that week, were full of panic buyers, stockpiling food and supplies, but also buying appliances: they were not ready to have their lives end without a dishwasher or a television.

WHAT THEY WERE STOCKING UP ON IN THE RECORD STORES

According to the local Top 40 station WMCA, the best-selling record in New York City stores the week of October 24, 1962, was the Contours' "Do You Love Me." Nationally, it was Bobby "Boris" Pickett's "Monster Mash."

THE NO. 1 HIT ON RADIO MOSCOW

That would be the statement, repeated every half-hour on October 24, that the naval blockade would "unleash nuclear war."

WEDNESDAY MORNING

John F. Kennedy held a meeting with his cabinet at 10 A.M. Robert McNamara told him that the Navy's procedure upon encountering Russian submarines would be to drop "practice depth charges" to get them to surface. Robert Kennedy wrote, later that day, that his brother's "hand went up to his face & covered his mouth and he closed his fist. His eyes were tense, almost gray."

In a flat in London, Sylvia Plath wrote her poem "Cut," with its images of a thumb wound transformed into a military nightmare: "Out of a gap / A million soldiers run / Redcoats, every one."

At the Apollo, Hal Neely, the coordinator of the Brown recording project and James Brown's longtime business partner, possibly assisted by Tom Nola, set up microphones to tape that day's performances on a big rented AMPEX tape machine.

WEDNESDAY AFTERNOON

October 24, 1962, was U.N. Day, and at 3:00 in the afternoon, as the James Brown revue was already well underway, there was a gala concert in the United Nations General Assembly Hall, about four miles southeast of the Apollo. Yevgeni Mravinsky conducted the Leningrad Philharmonic with violinist David Oistrakh, and a gala reception was held for the musicians afterwards, or at least as gala as possible under the circumstances. Secretary-General U Thant, meanwhile, was desperately trying to convince the American and Soviet governments to cool down their aggression for a few weeks; he made a statement to the Security Council that "the very fate of mankind" was at stake.

The Manchurian Candidate played in theaters for the first time.

The Soviet Union launched Sputnik 22, a space probe intended to fly past Mars. As it was going into Earth orbit, it exploded. American "early warning" radar systems in Alaska detected the debris; for a few minutes, NORAD observers thought it was the start of a nuclear ICBM attack. NORAD's Command Post logs for the day are still classified.

WEDNESDAY EVENING

CBS showed a special at 7:30: The Other Face of Dixie, about public-school integration in the South. At the Countee Cullen Library at 138th and Lenox in Manhattan, a documentary on lunchroom sit-in demonstrations was screened at 8:00.

In Cambridge, Massachusetts, Rev. Martin Luther King, Jr., spoke at Harvard Law School's Forum on "The Future of Integration." Across the street from him, Todd Gitlin and the Harvard peace group Tocsin organized a rally with Stuart Hughes and Barrington Moore, Jr.; both drew over a thousand spectators. "Until the news was broadcast [on Saturday the 27th] that Khrushchev was backing down," Gitlin wrote in The Sixties, "the country lived out the awe and truculence and simmering near-panic always implicit in the thermonuclear age."

AMATEUR NIGHT

The crowds to get into James Brown's show at the Apollo stretched around the block, by all reports. Wednesday nights were, and still generally are, amateur nights at the Apollo; the amateurs were always featured at the beginning of the 11:00 show. You'd rub the stump of the "Tree of Hope," someone would announce what song you'd be performing, and you'd have a cruel and hungry audience waiting for you. If you were less than stellar, it was the hook for you—the comedy "stagehand" Porto Rico would chase you off the stage. If you were Sarah Vaughan or Ruth Brown, winning at amateur night was the first step to stardom. If you weren't, it didn't generally make much of a difference. But the amateur night audiences were screamers—the final show Wednesday would have the most enthusiastic audience response, and the most warmed-up band, of the week.

(There is a long-circulating tale that James Brown competed in amateur night sometime in the '50s, in a shirt and shoes that stage manager Sandman Sims lent him. Brown vehemently denies it in his autobiography, *The Godfather of Soul*, and it does sound like one of those stories that's way too good to be true.)

Immediately before the amateur-night show, at 10:52 P.M., President Kennedy's staff read him a cable from Premier Khrushchev, to the effect that the American blockade was "an act of aggression which pushes mankind toward the abyss of a world nuclear-missile war," and that he would not tell Soviet ships to comply with it. Meanwhile, the Strategic Air Command went to DEFCON 2, the highest level of military alert it had ever reached; DEFCON 1 would have been nuclear war.

STAR TIME

Live at the Apollo begins *in medias res*, cutting into the middle of a speech. "So now ladiesangennamen it is *star time* are you ready for STAR *TIME?*" announces Lucas "Fats" Gonder, the James Brown Orchestra's organist and the show's emcee. At this point, the show has already been going on for a good hour or so. "Star time" doesn't mean "seeing James Brown for the first time"—he's already spent quite a bit of time on stage—it means the part of the show where he comes up front and sings.

Here's what probably happened in that night's late show between the amateur-night feature and Star Time (suggested by Alan Leeds' copious notes):

The James Brown Orchestra almost certainly opened the show with a short instrumental set—songs like "Suds" (a composition credited to drummer Nat Kendrick, featuring a ringing guitar hook from Les Buie) and "Night Flying." Sometimes Brown played on the band's instrumental recordings, sometimes he didn't, but they tended to appear on albums with titles like *James Brown Presents His Band and Five Other Great Artists*. The opening set, though, would have been the band playing without Brown, which they still do even now. The band was on a riser at the back of the stage, in two tiers. The front of the riser was decorated with a musical staff, with notes running all the way across it; the horn section (trumpeters Lewis Hamlin, Jr., Roscoe Patrick and Teddy Washington, saxophonists William Burgess, Al "Brisco" Clark, Clifford "Ace King" MacMillan and St. Clair Pinckney, and trombonist Dicky Wells) stood behind waist-high music stands with pictures of saxophones on them. Hamlin, who was celebrating his 32nd birthday that day, was the musical director of the band in those days—the 1990 CD of LATA misspells his name as "Louis Hamblin."

The Orchestra was followed by the Brownies, a dancing chorus who'd joined the revue in September 1961, before which they'd been called the Hortense Allen Dancers. At the time of the Apollo show, they included Helen Riley, Rusty Williams and Pat Perkins, and probably a couple of others; there's a publicity photo of them wearing feathered headdresses, feathered right (but not left) wristbands, feathered bikini bottoms and feathered boots, along with bikini tops that are some kind of advanced (but featherless) sartorial disaster. They're posed in front of a Mondrian-style geometrical backdrop, grinning like they're in on a secret. The picture is captioned in awkward Letraset lettering: "THE BROWN IES DANCING DOLLS FEAT WITH JAMES BROWN SHOW." (The Brownies don't appear to be the same people as the Brownettes, who recorded a JB-produced single a few years later.)

Then James Brown himself came on and sat in for a few instrumentals with the band, first on organ (starting with "Mashed Potatoes U.S.A.," a single that had been released earlier in October), then on drums ("Doin' the Limbo" and "Choo-Choo (Locomotion)"). The Apollo held a dance contest during this segment of the show; there exists a single, blurry photograph of it, with three sharply dressed teenagers doing the mashed potatoes at the front of the stage, while the rhythm section grooves and the horn players look expectantly at Brown, who's sitting at the organ.

Several hundred miles away, President Kennedy called Robert McNamara, who assured him that U.S. armed forces would be ready to invade Cuba in seven days.

2004

DAVID HAJDU

David Hajdu (b. 1955) is a New York–based writer on rock, pop, and jazz. His criticism on a wide array of popular music ran in *The New Republic* from 2002 until 2014, when he joined the staff of *The Nation*. He is best known for his thickly textured music biographies: *Lush Life: A Biography of Billy Strayhorn* (1996), and his group biography of the early '60s folk-rock scene, *Positively 4th Street: The Lives and Times of Joan Baez, Bob Dylan, Mimi Baez Fariña and Richard Fariña* (2001), which argued for the neglected genius of Joan Baez's sister Mimi and her husband Richard Fariña. He is also the author of *The Ten-Cent Plague: The Great Comic Book Scare and How It Changed America* (2008) and the essay collection *Heroes and Villains: Essays on Music, Movies, Comics, and Culture* (2009), in which this piece on Ray Charles appears. He is a professor at the Columbia University Graduate School of Journalism.

▼ ▼

Ray Charles

IN MARCH 1962, Atco Records issued a harbinger of the 2004 winter movie season: the album *Bobby Darin Sings Ray Charles*, in which one of two popular singers famous for crossing multiple genre lines paid homage to the other. Hollywood delivered Jamie Foxx as Charles in Taylor Hackford's screen biography *Ray* (which was called *Unchain My Heart* prior to its release), followed by Kevin Spacey in a self-directed

Darin bio called *Beyond the Sea* (which should have been titled *Bobby*). In the former, we see Charles, early in his career, imitating both Nat "King" Cole and the suave blues singer Charles Brown. "I can mimic anybody I hear," he explains in the film. Of course, Ray Charles found a genuinely distinctive and profoundly influential voice of his own, and he employed it to monumental effect for decades, as the absence of a record called *Ray Charles Sings Bobby Darin* reminds us. When Darin took up rock 'n' roll, abandoned it for swing, and then dropped that for folk and country, he subordinated himself to each type of music; he shrank to fit every style he tried. Charles, by contrast, drew from all those genres and others, subsuming them into his own musical personality; he grew with every genre he absorbed.

The muscular and sensual music of Ray Charles was in the air again, in part because of the new movie and all the talk about Foxx's uncanny performance, and also because Charles's last album, *Genius Loves Company*, a collection of duets with contemporary pop stars and other big-name singers released not long after Charles's death from liver disease that June, proved to have enough of the intended crossover appeal to become a bigger hit than Charles had had in many years. Suddenly nostalgic for Charles, I bought a small pile of CD re-issues of his early albums on Atlantic, which I had only on vinyl LP. (Some of his best output, recorded for ABC Records between 1960 and 1973, is not available on CD; Charles retained ownership of the masters and always focused on touring and making new recordings, rather than on his past work.) "He's really popular lately," the thirtyish man at the checkout counter said as he rang up my sale. Noticing that one of the CDs in the stack was titled *The Genius of Ray Charles*, he asked earnestly, "Is that true? Was he really a genius?"

If the Atlantic marketing people were the first to say so, no one except Charles himself ever came forth to argue otherwise. Frank Sinatra called Ray Charles "the only true genius in our business" and demonstrated his admiration by emulating Charles on the gutsier recordings he started making in the mid-1960s. If not for Charles, we would surely not have "That's Life" and its ilk. (Whatever the merits of that music, it is striking for Charles's effect on the generally impenetrable Sinatra.)

Nor would we have the countless rock artists, from Mick Jagger to Bruce Springsteen, who have aimed to convey an earthy authenticity by singing in a raw, volatile growl. Nor, arguably, would we have the very art of soul music, which Ray Charles virtually invented by combining traditional gospel music with postwar rhythm and blues.

Charles, who had been raised in merciless poverty in the rural South, would always take pride in his status as "raw-ass country." He was far too humble about his musical achievements and uncomfortable with his longtime sobriquet. As he told David Ritz, the co-author of his memoir, *Brother Ray: Ray Charles' Own Story*, which appeared in 1978, "I never came up with that 'genius' tag. Someone else did. I don't like the genius business. It's not me. Erroll Garner was a genius. Art Tatum. Oscar Peterson. Charlie Parker. Artie Shaw. Dizzy [Gillespie] was the genius. . . . I learned it all from others."

Before he went blind at the age of seven (from an undiagnosed disease that he later believed was glaucoma), Charles had had a bit of musical coaching from a boogie-woogie piano player who ran an all-purpose shop near his saltbox house in the backwoods of northern Florida. His sole formal training came at the state-run St. Augustine School for the Deaf and the Blind, where he learned to read and to write music in Braille and to play classical studies on the piano and the clarinet. Upon the death of his mother when he was fifteen, Charles quit school and started pursuing work as a jazz pianist. After a few years of apprenticeship, he headed for the city by bus, making Seattle his destination of choice because it was the farthest city from his hometown in the continental United States.

All the pianists Charles said he admired most—Garner, Tatum, and Peterson—had an orchestral approach to the keyboard. Their conceptions are epic, layered with ornament and intensely dynamic. That's not the way Charles played (at least not on record, nor in his known performances); to the contrary, he was a forceful but disciplined pianist who tended to limit himself to laying down a rhythmic foundation for his own vocals. His contrapuntal work was mainly chordal, and the obbligato lines that he would play were imaginative but sparse, like those of Nat Cole or Hank Jones. Even on instrumentals, such as "Doodlin'" and "'Deed I Do" on his non-vocal jazz albums, Charles played with the discretion of a sympathetic accompanist.

It's his singing that was orchestral. The proof of Charles's genius lies not in the breadth of his influence but in the depth of his music, and he was a singer of almost otherworldly originality and emotive power. His phrasing was naturalistic and seemingly spontaneous, yet the lyrics invariably swung to a pulse. Verses exploded with surprise: he might stop dead and then whisper a few words or break into a whoop. Apparently lost in ecstasy, he would burst into a giddy falsetto or interject a conspiratorial aside: "Looky here. . . ." Although the gravelly texture of his voice is immediately recognizable and has been widely imitated, he could conjure a considerable range of timbres, and he used them commandingly, often playfully. On his familiar rendition of "America the Beautiful," from 1972, he begins the second chorus like a choirboy, crooning in a sweet tenor, and then appears to change characters: now a preacher, he hurls out the words in fiery bursts.

Charles's vocal intonation was so complex and nuanced that he could make a world out of a note. He rarely sang any note dead on pitch, but preferred to work in shades of microtones around the center. Often he would sing near the top end of notes—almost sharp but not quite, to conjure a sense of yearning or, when he pushed the effect, a feeling of teetering on the emotional brink. At other times he would hang toward the bottom of a note to evoke melancholy or to set the listener up for a subtly uplifting glissando at the end of a phrase.

One of the secrets of Charles's potency as a singer is the extraordinary sensitivity under the powerhouse surface of his presentation. A brawny, square-jawed man from the backcountry with a rough-hewn voice, Charles was also a person of delicate temperament, prone to crying jags. He generally drank milk because his stomach was too sensitive to tolerate tap water. "I know that men ain't supposed to cry, but I think that's wrong," he said in his book. "Crying's always been a way for me to get things out which are buried deep, deep down. When I sing, I often cry. Crying is feeling, and feeling is only human. Oh yes, I cry." When, in 1979, the state of Georgia proclaimed his recording of Hoagy Carmichael's "Georgia on My Mind" the official state song,

Charles stood in the chamber of the state legislature and bawled. "I felt kind of stupid standing there crying," Charles later recalled, "but I couldn't help it."

The same unfettered emotionality permeates his music, not only ballads such as "What'll I Do," "You Don't Know Me," and "Born to Lose," but also many up-tempo numbers such as "Just for a Thrill" and "Let the Good Times Roll," which have something—a gentleness at their heart—that prevents their essential bravura from seeming overly aggressive. Country singers such as George Jones and Italian American crooners such as Frank Sinatra and Tony Bennett share this counterbalancing combination of conspicuous tenderness and conspicuous toughness, though few, perhaps none, to the extremes of Ray Charles.

The tension between elements in opposition also informs Charles's lasting creation as a composer and arranger: the union of sacred music and carnal sensibility that came to be known as soul music. An interpretive artist by inclination, Charles became a songwriter (of sorts) by necessity when, in the early 1950s, he began recording in earnest and had trouble finding material that suited his impulses. (Bob Dylan, about a decade later, took up songwriting for a similar reason: as he once observed, no one else was creating the kind of songs he wanted to sing.) Charles, who recalled the fervor of gospel music from his youth, sought a musical vehicle with the capacity to express the roiling passions of adulthood and decided to adapt the former to the latter purpose. (Thomas A. Dorsey, the father of gospel music, composed bawdy secular songs as well as hymns, but his two sets of works are largely unrelated, musically and lyrically.) Charles took gospel pieces, presumably in the public domain, and modified the lyrics: "This Little Light of Mine" became "This Little Girl of Mine"; "Talkin' 'Bout Jesus" became "Talkin' 'Bout You"; "You Better Leave That Liar Alone" became "You Better Leave That Woman Alone," and so forth. Even "What'd I Say" and "Hit the Road, Jack," while not derived from specific sacred tunes, drew expressly upon the call-and-response tradition of the gospel style.

Charles's method offended traditionalists, including the blues singer Big Bill Broonzy, who groused that "he's mixing the blues with spirituals. I know that's wrong. . . . He should be singing in church." Some radio stations banned "What'd I Say" for the sexual suggestion in Charles's groans, but the music rang true because it was utterly true to its singer, who was far more interested in matters of the flesh than in matters of the spirit. It carried no ethical compromise for Charles. "If Mama gave me religion, the religion said, 'Believe in yourself,'" he told David Ritz. "Jesus was Jewish, and if he couldn't convince his own people he was the messiah, why should I be convinced?" The musical amalgam that Charles created had the passion of gospel, but no piety— indeed, no reverence for anything but the earthliest sort of love. In this regard, it was an inspiration to generations of soul singers profoundly concerned with the body, from Marvin Gaye to Prince (who has conflated the divine with the hardcore throughout his career).

In the 1950s, few African American men dared to present the overtly sexual package that Charles offered to black and white men and women. Billy Eckstine, the boyishly handsome singer and bandleader who had outdrawn Sinatra at the Paramount and outsold him on records for a time, was nearly banished from show business in 1950 after a photograph in *Life* magazine showed him surrounded by worshipful fans—all of them young, white females. (Prior to Charles and Eckstine, most African American singers who appealed to white audiences survived by playing "cute," like Louis Armstrong and Fats Waller, or exuded the sex appeal of a Sunday-school teacher, like Nat Cole; either way, they appeared unthreatening to women of any color.) Charles prevailed, no doubt, because of his blindness; his Ray-Bans shielded him. Had he had the same chiseled good looks, swayed his body in time with the same intensity, sung the same licentious songs, and made eye contact with the white women in his audiences, his obituaries might have been published fifty years sooner.

Oddly, though, the dark-glass barrier between Charles's eyes and ours always made the experience of seeing him uncommonly intimate. We are accustomed to watching performers' eyes for innumerable signals. How can we tell what the person is thinking and feeling when the window to the soul is closed? We turn to the body. I saw Charles in concert half a dozen times, once from the distance of a few feet at the Blue Note in New York. My memories are of his shoulders, bobbing from side to side; his hands and arms, locked in place as he blocked chords on the piano; and his right leg, kicking out from under the piano in time. Rarely does one attend so closely to the body of someone other than a lover, apart from when watching dance performances, during which one can also see the dancers' eyes.

Charles ended up having two careers: one prior to his arrest in Boston in 1964 for heroin possession, and one beginning the following year, when he voluntarily detoxed in a Los Angeles hospital. To acknowledge the higher level of innovation and greater vitality in the first period is neither to endorse hard drugs nor to deny the occasional spikes of glory in Charles's last four decades. His commercials for both Coke and Pepsi ("Uh huh") were delightful; his uncharacteristically lugubrious reading of "America the Beautiful" at the Republican Convention in 1984 was less so. His recording of *Porgy and Bess* with Cleo Laine in 1976 had enough fine moments—particularly Charles's singing on "Summertime"—to excuse the project's mimicry of the landmark Louis Armstrong–Ella Fitzgerald version. Five of the six country albums that he made in the 1980s are embarrassments, though the one of duets with George Jones, Merle Haggard, Johnny Cash, Willie Nelson, and others is spirited and shows Charles in far stronger form than *Genius Loves Company*.

As for the latter album, Charles's whispered good-bye from behind the shadows of some friends (and some lessers), it has a couple of lovely, poignant tracks: "Sinner's Prayer," a salty blues Charles used to do fifty years earlier, which he and B. B. King pull off with old-rascal wile; and "It Was a Very Good Year," Ervin Drake's bittersweet lament to aging, done with Willie Nelson, who sounds more than ever as if he were singing to himself in his car. Last works are often just occasions for mourning, beyond the scope of criticism, and in this instance I say so be it. Ray Charles made two hundred fifty other recordings, and they are much more than relics.

2004

▼

LUC SANTE

Luc Sante was born in Belgium in 1954, and has lived in Paris and New York. A cartographer of urban cultural geographies, Sante's body of writing traces a transcontinental immersion in literature, music, film, and photography. His first book, *Low Life: Lures and Snares of Old New York* (1991), is a definitive chronicle of New York's forgotten underworlds, and his recent *The Other Paris* undertakes a parallel survey of Paris. Sante has been a professor in the Columbia University MFA writing program and currently teaches writing and photography courses at Bard College; other books include *The Factory of Facts* (1998), *Evidence: NYPD Crime Scene Photographs: 1914–1918* (1992), and *Folk Photography* (2009). Sante's writing appears frequently in *The New York Review of Books* and *Bookforum*; a selection from this work has been published as *Kill All Your Darlings: Pieces 1990–2005*. He received a Grammy for his album note contributions to the Smithsonian Folkways *Anthology of American Folk Music*. Using the publication of Bob Dylan's *Chronicles: Volume 1* as an opportunity to discuss the career, Sante, in the piece reprinted here, argues that "Dylan remains a mystery" and proceeds to describe the contours of that mystery, without succumbing to the temptation to decode it.

▼ ▼

I Is Somebody Else

BE CAREFUL what you wish for, the cliché goes. Having aspired from early youth to become stars, people who achieve that status suddenly find themselves imprisoned, unable to walk down the street without being importuned by strangers. The higher their name floats, the greater the levy imposed, the less of ordinary life they can enjoy. In his memoir, Bob Dylan never precisely articulates the ambition that brought him to New York City from northern Minnesota in 1961, maybe because it felt improbable even to him at the time. Nominally, he was angling for Leading Young Folksinger, which was a plausible goal then, when every college town had three or four coffeehouses and each one had its Hootenanny Night, and when performers who wowed the crowds on that circuit went on to make records that sometimes sold in the thousands. But from the beginning Dylan had his sights set much higher: the world, glory, eternity—ambitions laughably incommensurate with the modest confines of American folk music. He got his wish, in spades. He achieved leading young folksinger status almost immediately, then was quickly promoted to poet, oracle, conscience of his generation, and, in a lateral move, pop star.

Each promotion was heavily taxed. On "Positively Fourth Street" you can hear his half of a recrimination match with one or more former Greenwich Village competitors, once resentful and now obsequious. ("Fame opens up, first, every irony back onto one's past; one is abruptly *valued* by one's *friends*. Then actual envy and malice are hard to ignore. It is difficult just to be watched. There is injury to one's sense of rebellion . . ."—John Berryman on Stephen Crane.) The year of booing he endured after he started going onstage with an amplified band in 1965 is a familiar tale. In *Chronicles*, which is apparently the first installment of a memoir told in chronologically shuffled vignettes, he revisits the period after his motorcycle crash in 1966, after he had withdrawn from live performance and had only issued one, rather enigmatic record, *John Wesley Harding*, a year and a half later. His silence contributed to his mystique, and that in turn became the focus of a craving for direction and guidance on the part of beleaguered youth in that time of failed revolution. As a result:

> Moochers showed up from as far away as California on pilgrimages. Goons were breaking into our place all hours of the night. At first, it was merely the nomadic homeless making illegal entry—seemed harmless enough, but then rogue radicals looking for the Prince of Protest began to arrive. . . .

And a person named A. J. Weberman began going through the Dylan family's garbage and subjecting it to talmudic analysis. ("One night I went over D's garbage just for old time's sake and in an envelope separate from the rest of the trash there were five toothbrushes of various sizes and an unused tube of toothpaste wrapped in a plastic bag. 'Tooth' means 'electric guitar' in D's symbology. . . .") Dylan was doubly consumable by his audience, at once the star on whose image any fantasy could be projected and the sage whose gnomic utterances could be interpreted to justify any feverish scheme. He had become a floating signifier of the greatest order of magnitude.

Overwhelmed by the situation he had semi-wittingly created, Dylan tried various means to escape it. In *Chronicles* he accounts for what seemed at the time to be eccentricities or missteps; they were, he says, intended to bore, mystify, or disgust his admirers so that they would leave him alone. He recorded a country & western album "and made sure it sounded pretty bridled and housebroken," employing a crooner's voice cleansed of all his lye and vinegar; had himself photographed wearing a yarmulke at the Western Wall in Jerusalem ("quickly all the great rags changed me overnight into a Zionist"); started a rumor that he was enrolling in the Rhode Island School of Design; failed to show up at any of the major counterculture festivals. All the while he dreamed of "a nine-to-five existence, a house on a tree-lined block with a white picket fence, pink roses in the backyard." This sounds suspiciously like a line of dialogue from the second act of an MGM musical, begging a question—is this candor, hindsight, irony, spin, rhetorical flight, or some combination thereof?—not unlike those that attend virtually everything else Dylan has written. He can't seem to help putting forth vivid images equipped with yawning ambiguities. That means that even when he has been at pains to make himself transparent, he has given grist to the interpretation mills, which have rarely been idle in forty years.

It is perfectly possible that the succession of odd choices he made in the late 1960s and early '70s were meant as deliberate roadblocks to set in the way of overeager fans. It is equally credible, though, that crooning, Zionism, returning to college, cornball self-parody (aspects of the 1970 album *Self-Portrait*) and, later, born-again Christianity and a range of variously slick show-biz moves were matters he considered quite seriously, if only for a week or a year, as ways of escaping from the burden of himself. What seems to have happened is that he lost or at least misplaced parts of his power and inspiration without actually achieving serenity. Speaking to David Gates in the *Newsweek* interview that heralded the release of *Chronicles*, he went so far as to claim that his artistic drought lasted from sometime in the early '70s until 1998, when he issued his record *Time Out of Mind*. Gates bit his tongue: "He's talking about the twenty-five years that produced *Blood on the Tracks, Slow Train Coming, Shot of Love, Infidels* and its sublime out-takes, and—no. Let's not argue with the man who's in possession of what really matters." Everyone who paid attention to Dylan in that period will have a greater or lesser number of reservations about the quality of the work he did then, but his sweeping assessment is not altogether wrong. A majority of the songs from then are in some way at odds with themselves—compelling words hitched to perfunctory music, or strong ideas clumsily executed, or misfires caused by dunning self-consciousness, or well-conceived pieces sabotaged by their arrange-ment or production. Everywhere there is evidence of crippling internal struggle, of conflicting intentions that have arrived at a deadlock. It is telling that many of his best songs from that era were officially cast off and not released until much later, if at all.

It's not easy to identify with Dylan's predicament, since so few people have had the experience of finding themselves appointed prophet, and not having the assignment quickly washed away by the tides of fashion.

And fame, although significant, is only part of the story. (Berryman on Crane, again: "One's sense of self-reliance is disturbed. Under the special new conditions one behaves—at best—at first as before; but this is not adequate. Also the burden of confidence in oneself is to some extent assumed by *others*; and the sudden lightness inclines to overset one.") An even greater burden comes from being ceaselessly analyzed, as if one were the reviewing lineup at a May Day parade and the rest of the world was composed of Kremlinologists. And Dylan's audience does not merely appreciate him; it wants things from him, particular things: insights, instructions, answers to questions, a flattering reflection of itself, a mind it can pretend to inhabit. The responses to *Chronicles* include the common complaint that Dylan evades telling us what we want to know. He doesn't explain how he wrote "Visions of Johanna," for example, or what his emotions were during the process— he fails to conduct a tour of his peak moments, and he does not specify how he unbottles his genie. He doesn't discuss such major works as *Highway 61 Revisited* or *Blonde on Blonde* or the huge, only partly issued body of work known in aggregate as *The Basement Tapes*. He doesn't mention *Blood on the Tracks*, either, although when he writes, "Eventually I would even record an entire album based on Chekhov short stories—critics thought it was autobiographical," it would seem, by process of elimination, to be the record he is referring to. But is he serious?

The way *Chronicles* is structured suggests that it is primarily about the interstices in Dylan's life so far, periods when he was attempting to find or retrieve his own voice. The third chapter describes that period around 1969 and 1970 when pressure on him was greatest and his wish to escape from it at its most acute. It reaches a non-climax with the recording of *New Morning*, which was a perfectly decent job of work, neither brilliant nor disastrous. The fourth chapter is concerned with the recording in New Orleans in 1989 of *Oh Mercy*, also a middling performance. Frustration and confusion are palpable there, too: he can't control the recording process; the songs come out sounding very different from what he had intended; he can have anything he wishes, and yet he is uncertain and adrift. The other three chapters, which bracket the work and comprise nearly two-thirds of it, are a very differ-ent proposition, because they focus on the period between his arrival in New York City in 1961 and the issuing of his first record just over a year later. Even if Dylan had not been thrust so quickly into a position of unwanted responsibility, and even if his most fecund period—the years 1965 and 1966—had not been an epic blur of such intensity and speed (in both senses of the term) that it was sure to end in some sort of crack-up, the eve of success, a sweet and achingly distant time, might well appear to him a career peak. Everything seemed possible then; no options had been used up and nothing had yet been sacrificed.

What Dylan describes in chapters one, two, and five is his education. For all the structural oddity of *Chronicles*, it is in many ways a very traditional sort of memoir, and nowhere more than in those chapters. We see the young man arrive in the city from the provinces, stumble around chasms and into opportunities, sit at the feet of the mighty, acquire necessary tools and skills, begin to be noticed, find a home, fall in love, and then we leave him on the eve of success, full of expectancy but serenely unaware of what is about to befall him. The young Dylan makes an appealing nineteenth-century junior hero: crafty but ingen-uous, wide-eyed but nobody's fool, an eager sponge for every sort of experience and information. As in the equivalent *Bildungsroman*, we are given a set piece, a soiree at which are gathered all the leading lights of the world he is poised to enter.

The occasion is a going-away party for Cisco Houston, a handsome ("looked like a riverboat gambler, like Errol Flynn") singer of cowboy and lumberjack and railroad songs and friend of Woody Guthrie, so mature and gracious and imposing that he does not let on that he is going off to die of cancer. The party is held in a "Romanesque man-sion" on Fifth Avenue, in a top-floor apartment with Victorian furnish-ings and a roaring fireplace. Pete Seeger is there, and the manager of the Weavers, and Moe Asch (founder of Folkways Records), and Theo-dore Bikel, and Irwin Silber (editor of *Sing Out!*), and sundry cowboy artists, labor organizers, underground filmmakers, ex–Martha Graham dancers, Off-Broadway actors, and a passel of folk singers of greater and lesser importance. Dylan takes us around the room supplying thumbnail sketches of the cast, like a moving camera focusing briefly and then tracking on. He is able to look hard at them all because he is largely invisible to them, and he can provide details of their biographies because he is somewhat in awe of everyone. If this were a nineteenth-century novel, or its 1930s film adaptation, we might later be treated to a succession of scenes in which the hero conquers, supplants, wins over, or silences all the worthies in the room that night. That isn't necessary here.

Dylan isn't out to gloat or settle scores, for which it is far too late anyway. On the contrary, he is keen to record his debts and apprecia-tions, an accounting that takes in a wide range of personalities from the entertainment world of the early 1960s, including such unlikely names as Bobby Vee (for whom he briefly played piano when Vee was on his way up and Dylan was unknown), Tiny Tim (with whom he shared stages and meals in the coffeehouse days), Frank Sinatra, Jr. (for whose unenviable career as a shadow he feels tactful sympathy), and Gorgeous George (who fleetingly but memorably offered encouragement when the very young Dylan performed on a makeshift stage in the lobby of the armory in his Minnesota hometown). He knows that it will confuse his more literal-minded fans that he loves the songs of Harold Arlen ("In Harold's songs, I could hear rural blues and folk music"), polkas, Franz Liszt, "Moon River," Neil Sedaka, as much as he admires Thu-cydides, Clausewitz, Leopardi, Tolstoy, Thaddeus Stevens. He is proud that he has one foot in a vanished world:

> If you were born around this time [1941] or were living and alive, you could feel the old world go and the new one begin-ning. It was like putting the clock back to when B.C. became A.D. Everybody born around my time was a part of both.

Dylan's preoccupation with the past isn't only an incipient codger's gambol down memory lane. While he caused a big splash in the mid-'60s for his dramatic break with folk tradition as it was then understood, the ways in which he has always kept faith with tradition look arguably more radical today. In an interview, considering younger musicians, he

once noted, "They weren't there to see the end of the traditional people. But I was." Like his contemporaries, he witnessed the reappearance
of various blues and country performers—Skip James, Dock Boggs,
Son House, Clarence Ashley, among others—who had recorded in the
late 1920s and had returned to obscurity when the Depression all but
killed the recording of rural music, and who were tracked down by
diligent young fans in the early 1960s and enjoyed a few years in the
limelight of Northern stages at the sunset of their lives. Those people
were embodiments of a past so far removed by technological and societal changes that they might as well have emerged from Civil War graves.
While folk music had taken on a new, confrontational stance toward the
world by then—a development for which Dylan was partly responsible—involvement in folk music still entailed an active engagement with
the past. This meant that young performers, from the scholarly and
meticulous New Lost City Ramblers to the slick and broadly popular
Kingston Trio, saw themselves as carrying on a set of skills and themes
and concerns and melodies and lyrics that had come down at least from
the nineteenth century—even from the Middle Ages, with the earlier
Child ballads.

The young Dylan believed fervently in the passing of the torch,
the laying on of hands—he learned blues chord changes from Lonnie
Johnson and Victoria Spivey, visited the paralytic Woody Guthrie in
the hospital and played him his own songs (he doesn't mention here a
more purely magical transference, when Buddy Holly looked directly
at him from the stage of the Duluth Armory, a few days before his
death in a plane crash in Clear Lake, Iowa). And while he was never
as extreme as the folk purists—who were so involved with the past
that they lived there, like Civil War reenactors who become experts
on nineteenth-century underwear—Dylan treated history in a way that
was not uncommon then but is sufficiently rare now that some critics
of this book have professed their suspicions. In 1961 the past was alive
not just in the songs but in the city itself—everybody who played at
the Café Bizarre on MacDougal Street knew the place had once been
Aaron Burr's livery stable. Dylan tells us he made regular trips to the
microfilm room of the New York Public Library, to read newspapers

from the 1850s and '60s. "I wasn't so much interested in the issues as intrigued by the language and rhetoric of the times," he writes. But also: "The godawful truth of [the Civil War] would become the all-encompassing template behind everything that I would write."

The songs of the folk-lyric tradition were half truism, half enigma. The key to the latter could perhaps be found in the past.

> All of these songs were originally sung by singers who seemed to be groping for words, almost in an alien tongue. I was beginning to feel that maybe the language had something to do with causes and ideals that were tied to the circumstances and blood of what happened over a hundred years ago. . . . All of a sudden, it didn't seem that far back.

Folk songs, no matter how distant or exotic, spoke with bare-bones candor and deployed blunt imagery much more immediate than the froth that came over the radio, telling of "debauched bootleggers, mothers that drowned their own children, Cadillacs that only got five miles to the gallon, floods, union hall fires, darkness and cadavers at the bottom of rivers. . . ." For a long time it didn't occur to him to write his own songs (his first album only contains two, or maybe one-and-a-half: "Song to Woody" and "Talking New York"—the latter is more recitation than song). Few did so then, because the gravity of tradition had been created by the implacable, burning-eyed Anon. and not by tenderfeet from the suburbs. And anyway,

> It's not like you see songs approaching and you invite them in. It's not that easy. You want to write songs that are bigger than life. . . . You have to know and understand something and then go past the vernacular. The chilling precision that these old-timers used in coming up with their songs was no small thing.

When he did start writing, "I rattled off lines and verses based on the stuff I knew—'Cumberland Gap,' 'Fire on the Mountain,' 'Shady

Grove,' 'Hard, Ain't It Hard.' I changed words around and added something of my own here and there. . . . You could write twenty or more songs off . . . one melody by slightly altering it. I could slip in verses or lines from old spirituals or blues. That was okay; others did it all the time." That is, in fact, a fairly exact description of the folk-lyric process as it was enacted until about seventy years ago by the fearsome and remote Anon.

Once Dylan got started writing songs, other influences were not slow in coming. There was Red Grooms, his girlfriend's favorite artist:

> He incorporated every living thing into something and made it scream—everything side by side created equal—old tennis shoes, vending machines, alligators that crawled through sewers. . . . Brahman bulls, cowgirls, rodeo queens and Mickey Mouse heads, castle turrets and Mrs. O'Leary's cow, creeps and greasers and weirdos and grinning, bejeweled nude models. . . . Subconsciously, I was wondering if it was possible to write songs like that.

The same girlfriend, Suze Rotolo, worked backstage at a "presentation of songs" by Kurt Weill and Bertolt Brecht. "I . . . was aroused straight away by the raw intensity of the songs. . . . They were erratic, unrhythmical and herky-jerky—weird visions. . . . Every song seemed to come from some obscure tradition, seemed to have a pistol in its hip pocket, a club or a brickbat and they came at you in crutches, braces and wheelchairs." And John Hammond, who signed Dylan to his first recording contract, was then about to reissue the neglected songs of the great Delta blues artist Robert Johnson, whose

> words made my nerves quiver like piano wires. They were so elemental in meaning and feeling and gave you so much of the inside picture. It's not that you could sort out every moment carefully, because you can't. There are too many missing terms and too much dual existence. . . . There's no guarantee that any of his lines . . . happened, were said, or

even imagined. . . . You have to wonder if Johnson was playing for an audience that only he could see, one off in the
future.

Around the same time, Suze Rotolo introduced him to the works of
Rimbaud. "I came across one of his letters called 'Je est un autre,'
which translates as 'I is somebody else.' When I read those words the
bells went off. It made perfect sense. I wished someone would have
mentioned that to me earlier." Dylan was now armed.

Of Dylan's many achievements, the most fundamental was his hitch-
ing together of the folk-lyric tradition and Western modernism, connecting them at the point where their expressive ambiguities met. The
merger was not entirely unprecedented, maybe—there are glimmers in
The Waste Land of Eliot's St. Louis–bred acquaintance with the world
of "Frankie and Johnnie," and Robert Johnson can certainly sound
like a modernist, especially, as Dylan suggests, by virtue of how much
he omits. But no one had previously planted a firm foot in each and
assumed an equivalence between them. Dylan did not do this to prove
a point; he was naturally omnivorous, and he intuited the connection
without worrying about pedigree. As a songwriter, he knew what played
to the ear, and disregarded the fact that such effects don't always work
on the page. His primary gambit was to take the blues or ballad form
and some of its vocabulary and then expand it, or slash it, or smudge
it, or make the literal figurative, or the figurative literal. He could, as in
"A Hard Rain's A-Gonna Fall," take the ancient ballad "Lord Randal"
and transform it into a Symbolist catalog of apocalyptic images, or he
could, as in "From a Buick 6," take Sleepy John Estes's "Milk Cow
Blues" and employ it as the frame for a collage of blues-lyric fragments
that makes perfect emotional sense even as it resists parsing ("Well, you
know I need a steam shovel mama to keep away the dead / I need a
dump truck mama to unload my head").

In a revealing interview for a book called *Songwriters on Songwriting*,
Dylan talks about the "unconscious frame of mind," the state of sus-
pension he uses to bypass literal thinking:

[I]n the unconscious state of mind, you can pull yourself out and throw out two rhymes first and work it back. You get the rhymes first and work it back and then see if you can make it make sense in another kind of way. You can still stay in the unconscious frame of mind to pull it off, which is the state of mind you have to be in anyway.

In other words, his use of rhymes is not unlike a Surrealist game or an Oulipo exercise, a way to outsmart front-brain thinking, and the same is true of his employment of folk-lyric readymades. When Dylan hit mid-career, though, exhaustion and self-consciousness and the weight of his own reputation pushed him into self-impersonation, and he began to write songs that laboriously strove for effects. He knows the difference. In the same interview he is asked about a line from "Slow Train": "But that line . . . is an intellectual line. It's a line, 'Well, the enemy I see wears a cloak of decency,' that could be a lie. It could just be. Whereas 'Standing under your yellow railroad,' that's not a lie." The former makes sense, in a stilted and poetistic way, while the latter apparently makes no sense, but in context it is inarguable (he misquotes it slightly): "And now I stand here lookin' at your yellow railroad / In the ruins of your balcony / Wond'ring where you are tonight, sweet Marie." The blanket dismissal of a quarter century's work that Dylan offered to David Gates is of course an overstatement, but it is a gauge of his realization that he had long mistaken or overlooked his greatest strengths. The ability to hatch an epigram—the way "To live outside the law you must be honest" emerges right in the middle of "Absolutely Sweet Marie," between two lines twisted from Blind Lemon Jefferson's "See That My Grave Is Kept Clean" and the refrain—is a function of that unconscious frame of mind, that willed trance state, that educated lurching, not of the wish to construct an epigram.

Among the four-fifths of the Basement Tapes material that remains officially unreleased is a song called "I'm Not There (1956)." It is glaringly unfinished. Dylan mumbles unintelligibly through parts of it, and throws together fragments of lyrics apparently at random—and yet it is one of his greatest songs. The hymn-like melody, rising from mournful to exalted, is certainly one reason for this, and another is the perfect accompaniment by three members of the Band, but the very discontinuity of the lyrics, in combination with Dylan's unflagging intensity, creates a powerful, tantalizing indeterminacy that is suddenly if provisionally resolved by every return of the refrain.

> Now when I [*unintelligible*] I was born to love her
> But she knows that the kingdom weighs so high above her
> And I run but I race but it's not too fast or soon [?]
> But I don't perceive her, I'm not there, I'm gone.

The third line is clearly filler; what can be made out of the first probably contains an echo of a Stevie Wonder song played on the radio that same summer; the second, for all that it does not lend itself to reasonable interpretation, rings the bell, and it pulls the previous and succeeding lines along with it into relief and down to the last line, which includes the refrain. Every verse is crowned by one or more such glowing fragments, which materialize, linger briefly, and then vanish, like urgent dispatches transmitted by a spirit medium. The song evades the intellect to address the emotions through underground passageways of memory and association—biblical, in the case of that second line—and it is a document of the artist in the very midst of the act of creation.

The song gives a sense of how Dylan works when he is tapping his richest vein: the form presents him with a container—a blues basket, a ballad box—which he fills with lines the shapes of which he can discern before he knows their specific content. Such a shape is not simply a measurement determined by meter—it is a ghost outline, maybe a half-heard utterance in which he can make out an emphasis here, a compressed cluster of syllables there, now and again an entire word, which he can use as a dowsing rod for the content. If the shape is not forthcoming, he can fill the space with a folk-lyric readymade. That he has been tapping this vein again is shown by every song on his most recent release, "*Love and Theft*" (2001). "Bye and Bye," for example, has a melody derived from "Blue Moon" ("You could write twenty or more songs off . . . one melody by slightly altering it"); its final verse is:

> Papa gone mad, mamma, she's feeling sad
> I'm gonna baptize you in fire so you can sin no more
> I'm gonna establish my rule through civil war
> Gonna make you see just how loyal and true a man can be.

The first and last lines are brazenly drawn from the common well, while the middle lines had to have been dispatched straight from the unconscious. The song's atmosphere is breezy and menacing; the first and last lines of each verse supply the breeziness, the middle two the menace. The printed lyrics do not, of course, account for Dylan's vocal performance, which, of a piece with the white suits and riverboat-gambler hats he has been affecting lately, renders uncannily credible the grandiose rhetoric of the middle lines; nor do they convey the insouciant creepiness of Augie Meyers's roller-rink organ. Treating Dylan as merely a writer is like judging a movie on its screenplay alone.

Blood on the Tracks (1974) is cited by many as their favorite Dylan record—Rick Moody calls it "the truest, most honest account of a love affair from tip to stern ever put down on magnetic tape." It is, to be sure, quite an achievement, with a wealth of lived experience in its dense, intricately plotted songs. And yet, in comparison to the songs on *Blonde on Blonde* or *The Basement Tapes*—which are genuine, sphinx-like, irreducible, hard-shell poems whether or not the words can ever be usefully divorced from the music—such numbers as "Tangled Up in Blue" and "Idiot Wind" are prose. They are driven by their narratives, and their imagery is determined by its function.

> I ran into the fortune-teller, who said beware of lightning that
>   might strike
> I haven't known peace and quiet for so long I can't remember
>   what it's like

> There's a lone soldier on the cross, smoke pourin' out of
>   a boxcar door
> You didn't know it, you didn't think it could be done, in the
>   final end he won the wars
> After losin' every battle.

The smoke issuing from the boxcar door, which is there only to fill
out the line and supply an end-rhyme, does come out of nowhere, but
everything else seems cooked—the palmist is from central casting and
her warning is generic; the soldier on the cross is on loan from an anti-
war poster (he seems to be wearing a gas mask); the connecting lines
are rhetorical and flat; it could, after all, be a lie. This is not to say that
the song is bad, merely purpose-driven, with every verse hastening us
along to the point, which is "We're idiots, babe / It's a wonder we
can even feed ourselves." And that, in turn, is a great line from a note
left on a pillow at dawn. Nothing on *Blood on the Tracks* hobbles in on
crutches or speaks to the future or appears on the wall in letters of fire.
It is a brilliant account of the vicissitudes of a love affair, an exemplary
specimen of the confessional culture of the period, a remarkable work
of emotional intelligence. It is so many people's favorite Dylan album
in large part because it is the one that people can imagine themselves
creating, were the muse to tap them on the forehead with a nine-pound
hammer.

But who, on the other hand, could imagine coming up with "John
Wesley Harding / Was a friend to the poor / He trav'led with a gun
in ev'ry hand"? The outlaw looks like Shiva, a brace of guns in a brace
of hands, the apotheosis of Western legend by way of an apparent awk-
wardness of syntax, and the impression endures even if we know that
Dylan lifted those five words from Woody Guthrie's "Ludlow Massacre," in which the striking miners' women sell their potatoes and with
the proceeds "put a gun in every hand." It takes an unusual mind to
pick that unremarkable scrap from Guthrie's pocket and paste it athwart
a completely different sort of genre piece, like Kurt Schwitters inserting
a bus ticket into a landscape.[1] Dylan drives critics mad, because while his

1. It is possible that the disguised quote, coming right after "was a friend to the poor,"

vast range of sources can be endlessly itemized and dissected, the ways
in which he puts things together tease rational explication before finally
betraying it. (Stephen Crane quoted by Berryman: "An artist, I think,
is nothing but a powerful memory that can move itself through certain
experiences sideways and every artist must be in some things powerless
as a dead snake.")

You can find almost anything in Dylan's lyrics, employ them as balm
for heartbreak or call to riot, engage in bibliomancy by sticking a knife
between the pages of *Lyrics* and divining fortune from the line the tip
has come to rest upon. You can find Dylan's rhythms and word choices
and as it were his fingerprints in literature that predates him. Michael
Gray, who is probably Dylan's single most assiduous critic, turns up a
quatrain by Robert Browning that the mind's ear has no trouble hearing in Dylan's voice, and not only because the end-rhymes prefigure
"Subterranean Homesick Blues":

> Look, two and two go the priests, then the monks with cowls
>   and sandals
> And the penitents dressed in white shirts, a-holding the yellow
>   candles
> One, he carries a flag up straight, and another a cross with
>   handles,
> And the Duke's guard brings up the rear, for the better preven-
>   tion of scandals.

Dylan himself, in the *Songwriters* interview, cites a Byron couplet that
is equally convincing: "What is it you buy so dear / With your pain and
with your fear?" But then, as he told Robert Hilburn of the *Los Angeles
Times*, "It's like a ghost is writing [the] song. . . . It gives you the song
and it goes away. You don't know what it means. Except the ghost
picked me to write the song."

---

combines with it to form a subliminal image of popular insurgency. The album came
out early in 1968, after all, and the most memorable and hotly debated critical line concerning it has always been Jon Landau's contention that, although it takes place entirely
within the folk-lyric universe, it "manifests a profound awareness of the war and how it
is affecting all of us."

Dylan is a mystery, as he has been since his first record, made when he was twenty, established his eerie prerogative to inhabit songs written long before his birth by people with lifetimes of bitter experience. The mystery has endured ever since, through fallow as well as fecund periods, through miscellaneous errors and embarrassments and other demonstrations of common humanity as well as unbelievable runs of consecutive masterpieces. It has survived through candid and guarded and put-on interviews, various appearances on film, and the roughly two hundred concert appearances he has put in every year for the last couple of decades. It is if anything enhanced by Dylan's most astute critics (Greil Marcus, Sean Wilentz, Christopher Ricks, Michael Gray) and untouched by the legions of nit-collectors and communicants in the church of whangdoodle who unstoppably issue treatises and skeleton keys. It will survive his disarmingly unaffected memoir, too. The playwright Sam Shepard noted after observing Dylan for months during the 1974 Rolling Thunder tour that

> If a mystery is solved, the case is dropped. In this case, in the case of Dylan, the mystery is never solved, so the case keeps on. It keeps coming up again. Over and over the years. Who is this character anyway?

Dylan is a complex, mercurial human being of astounding gifts, whose purposes are usually ambiguous, frequently elusive, and sometimes downright unguessable. At the same time he is a sort of communicating vessel, open to currents that run up and down the ages quite outside the confines of the popular culture of any given period. That he is able to tune his radio to those long waves in a time of increasingly short memories and ever more rapid fashion cycles is not the least of his achievements.

Chronicles, which would appear to have been printed without editorial intervention,[2] is so fluid in its prose and alive in its observations that Dylan looks like a natural at the book game, although his previous expe-

2. This guess is based primarily on the fact that it doesn't seem to have been proofread,

rience was not so happy. *Tarantula* was the result of a much-trumpeted contract for a novel that Dylan signed with Macmillan in 1966. The book was not published until 1970, having in the meantime been boot-legged in several different versions. Nearly everyone was disappointed in the final product, which arrived behind the prow of a carefully hedged and rather condescending preface by its editor, Bob Markel. Ever since, the phrase "famously unreadable" has been attached to it, and persons who have wished to demonstrate that Dylan's vaunted verbal mastery was just so much hype have used it as a handy chair-leg with which to beat its author. It is, in fact, a mess, but it's a fascinating mess—it's what Dylan's automatic writing looks like when it doesn't have formal containers to shape it. The population of Dylan's world (Homer the Slut, Popeye Squirm, "Phil, who has now turned into an inexpensive Protestant ambassador from Nebraska & who speaks with a marvelous accent," etc.) hurtles hectically through a landscape of tanktowns and drunk tanks, all of the action telegraphically alluded to, at best, as if the book were a compilation of gossip columns from whatever newspaper Smokey Stover subscribed to. Although it is easily more entertaining than any of the automatic productions of the Parisian Surrealist crowd, it only clicks at odd intervals, when Dylan briefly finds a model for parody, such as the interspersed letters, which have something of Ring Lardner about them:

> cant you figure out all this commie business for yourself? you know, like how long can car thieves terrify the nation? gotta go. there's a fire engine chasing me. see you when i get my degree. i'm going crazy without you. cant see enough movies
>
> your crippled lover,
> benjamin turtle

Its one moment of transcendence is the only thing in the book that could have been a song, an ode to Aretha Franklin.

---

to judge by the presence of misspellings and inconsistencies in proper nouns, which a spell-checking program does not catch.

> aretha—known in gallup as number 69—in wheeling as the
> cat's in heat—in pittsburgh as number 5—in brownsville as the
> left road, the lonesome sound—in atlanta as dont dance, lis-
> ten—in bowling green as oh no, no, not again—she's known
> as horse chick up in cheyenne—in new york city she's known
> as just plain aretha . . . i shall play her as my trump card

Here he's hit on a pair of riffs—the urban-hotspot shout-out of '60s
soul anthems such as Martha and the Vandellas' "Dancing in the
Street" and the shifting-name trope familiar from both cowboy movies
and doo-wop (e.g. the Cadillacs' "You know they often call me Speedo
but my real name is Mister Earl")—that he can set to play off each
other, arriving at a propulsive litany.

Chronicles works so well in part because in writing it he apparently
found a formal model to adhere to or violate at will, and if he did
not have in mind any specific nineteenth-century account of callowness
and ambition, maybe he conjured up a cumulative memory of dusty
volumes found on friends' bookshelves in Greenwich Village or in the
basement of the bookshop in Dinkytown he worked in as a student. He
also found an outlet for his inclination to counter his audience's expectations. Readers, guessing on the basis of interviews and movies as well
as the hydra-headed mythic image that has grown around Dylan over
the decades, might have expected his memoir to be variously inscru-
table, gnomic, bilious, confused, preening, recriminatory, impersonal,
defensive, perfunctory, smug, or even ghost-written. Instead Dylan had
to outflank them by exercising candor, warmth, diligence, humor, and
vulnerability. If there is ever a second volume, he may have to contra-
dict himself yet again.

2004

JOHN JEREMIAH SULLIVAN

A native of Louisville, Kentucky, John Jeremiah Sullivan (b. 1974) first came to public attention with the publication of *Blood Horses: Notes of a Sportswriter's Son* (2004). His subsequent writing for *New York Magazine*, *The New York Times Magazine*, *GQ*, *Harper's*, *The Paris Review*, and *Oxford American* has ranged from memoir to rock writing to politics to the family business, sports coverage. His essay collection *Pulphead* (2011) brings together fourteen pieces ranging widely over American culture, including essays on Christian rock, Michael Jackson, and the following piece on Axl Rose. Sullivan avoids the pitfalls and clichés of the celebrity profile through meticulous evocation of his subject's world, and through channeling the words of those who create our celebrities—including the author himself. His cultural journalism has won both a National Magazine Award and a Pushcart Prize.

▼ ▼

The Final Comeback of Axl Rose

1.

He is from nowhere.

That sounds coyly rhetorical in this day and age, it's even a boast: socioeconomic code for "I went to a second-tier school and had no connections and made all this money myself."

I don't mean it that way. I mean he is from nowhere. Given the relevant maps and a pointer, I know I could convince even the most exacting minds that when the vast and blood-soaked jigsaw puzzle that is this country's regional scheme coalesced into more or less its present configuration after the Civil War, somebody dropped a piece, which left a void, and they called the void "central Indiana." I'm not trying to say there's no there there. I'm trying to say there's no there. Think about it; get systematic on it. What's the most nowhere part of America? The Midwest, right? But once you get into the Midwest, you find that each of the different nowherenesses has laid claim to its own somewhereness. There are the lonely plains in Iowa. In Michigan there's a Gordon Lightfoot song. Ohio has its very blandness and averageness, faintly comical, to cling to. All of them have something. But now I invite you to close your eyes, and when I say "Indiana" . . . blue screen, no? And we are speaking only of Indiana generally, which includes southern Indiana, where I grew up, and northern Indiana, which touches a Great Lake. We have not even narrowed it down to central Indiana. Central Indiana? That's like, "Where are you?" I'm nowhere. "Go there."

When I asked Jeff Strange, a morning-rock DJ in Lafayette, how he thought about this part of the world—for instance, did he think of it as the South? After all, it's a Klan hot spot (which can be read as a somewhat desperate affectation); or did he think of it as the Midwest, or what—you know what he told me? He said, "Some people here would call it 'the region.'"

William Bruce Rose, Jr.; William Bruce Bailey; Bill Bailey; William Rose; Axl Rose; W. Axl Rose.

That's where he's from. Bear that in mind.

2.

On May 15, he came out in jeans and a black leather jacket and giant black sunglasses, all lens, that made him look like a wasp-man. We had been waiting so long, in both years and hours. It was the third of the four comeback shows in New York, at the Hammerstein Ballroom. It was after eleven o'clock. The doors had opened at seven o'clock. The opening act had been off by eight-thirty. There'd already been fights on the floor, and it didn't feel like the room could get any more wound up without some type of event. I was next to a really nice woman from New Jersey, a hairdresser, who told me her husband "did pyro" for Bon Jovi. She kept texting one of her husband's friends, who was "doing pyro" for this show, and asking him, "When's it gonna start?" And he'd text back, "We haven't even gone inside." I said to her at one point, "Have you ever seen a crowd this pumped up before a show?" She goes, "Yeah, they get this pumped up every night before Bon Jovi."

Then he was there. And apologies to the nice woman, but people do not go that nuts when Bon Jovi appears. People were: Going. Nuts. He is not a tall man—I doubt even the heels of his boots (red leather) put him over five feet ten. He walked toward us with stalking, cartoonish pugnaciousness.

All anybody talks about with Axl anymore is his strange new appearance, but it is hard to get past the unusual impression he makes. To me he looks like he's wearing an Axl Rose mask. He looks like a man I saw eating by himself at a truck stop in Monteagle, Tennessee, at two o'clock in the morning about twelve years ago. He looks increasingly like the albino reggae legend Yellowman. His mane evokes a gathering of strawberry-red intricately braided hempen fibers, the sharply twisted ends of which have been punched, individually, a half inch into his scalp. His chest hair is the color of a new penny. With the wasp-man sunglasses and the braids and the goatee, he reminds one of the monster in *Predator*, or of that monster's wife on its home planet. When he first came onto the scene, he often looked, in photographs, like a beautiful, slender, redheaded twenty-year-old girl. Now he has thickened through the middle—muscly thickness, not the lard-ass thickness of some years back. He grabs his package tightly, and his package is huge. Only reporting. Now he plants his feet apart. "You know where you are?" he asks, and we bellow that we do, we do know, but he tells us anyway. "You're in the jungle, baby," he says, and then he tells us that we are going to die.

He must be pleased, not only at the extreme way that we are freaking out to see him but also at the age range on view: there are hipsters who were probably born around the time *Appetite* got released, all the way up to aging heads who've handed in their giant rock hair for grizzled rattails, with plenty of microgenerations in between. But why should I even find this worth remarking? The readers of *Teen* magazine, less than one year ago, put him at number two (behind "Grandparents") on the list of the "100 Coolest Old People" . . . Axl Rose, who hasn't released a legitimate recording in thirteen years and who, during that time, turned into an almost Howard Hughes–like character—only ordering in, transmitting sporadic promises that a new album, titled *Chinese Democracy*, was about to drop, making occasional startling appearances at sporting events and fashion shows, stuff like that—looking a little feral, a little lost, looking not unlike a man who's been given his first day's unsupervised leave from a state facility. Now he has returned. The guitarists dig in, the drummer starts his I-Am-BUil-DINg-UP-TO-THE!-*VERSE!* pounding section, and at the risk of revealing certain weaknesses of taste on my own part, I have to say, the sinister perfection of that opening riff has aged not a day.

There's only one thing to do, and you can feel everybody doing it: comparing this with the MTV thing in 2002. If you've seen that, you may find a recounting here of its grotesqueries tedious, but to that I say, never forget. About the guitar player Buckethead. About the other guitar player. About Axl's billowing tentlike football jersey or the heartbreaking way he aborted his snaky slide-foot dance after only a few seconds on the stage projection, like, "You wanna see my snaky dance? Here, I'll do my snaky dance. Oh, no, I think I just had a small stroke. Run away." The audible gasp for oxygen on the second "knees" in Sh-na-na-na-na-na-na-na-na-na-na-na knees, kn[gasp!]ees. The running and singing that came more and more to resemble stumbling and squawking as the interminable minutes groaned by. The constant, geriatric-seeming messing with the earpiece monitor.

My point is, it's different tonight. For one thing, these guys can handle or choose to handle Slash's parts. They aren't fake-booking, like happened on MTV. Buckethead has been replaced by a guy called Bumblefoot, and Bumblefoot can shred. So can Robin Finck, formerly of Nine Inch Nails. Everything's note for note. And although we could get into the whole problem of virtuosity as it applies to popular music—namely, that for some reason people who can play anything will, nine times out of ten, when asked to make something up, play something terrible—still, if you mean to replace your entire band one instrument at a time and tell them, "Do it like this," you'll be wanting to find some monster players.

The whole arc of the show has this very straightforward plot. Crudity is in the service of truth-telling here: it's a battle between the dissonance of seeing all these guys who were not in Guns N' Roses jumping around with Axl and playing Guns N' Roses songs—between the off-putting and even disturbing uncanny dissonance of that—and the enduring qualities of the songs themselves. The outcome will determine whether tonight was badass or "Sort of sad, but hey, it's Axl." For what it's worth, I thought he won. His voice is back, for starters. He was inhabiting the notes. And his dancing—I don't quite know how else to say this. It has matured. From the beginning, he's been the only indispensable white male rock dancer of his generation, the only one worth imitating in mockery. I consider the moment in the "Patience" video when he does the slow-motion snaky slide-foot dance while letting his hands float down as if they were feathers in a draftless room—one fleeting near-pause in their descent for each note that Slash emphasizes in his transition to the coda—the greatest white male rock dance moment of the video age. What Axl does is lovely, I'm sorry. If I could, I would be doing that as I walk to the store. I would wake up and dance every morning like William Byrd of Westover, and that would be my dance. And while I cannot say Axl is dancing as well tonight as he used to, that so fluidly are his heels gliding out and away from his center they look each to have been tapped with a wand that absolved them of resistance and weight, and although he does at particular moments remind one of one's wasted redneck uncle trying to "do his Axl Rose" after a Super Bowl party, he is nevertheless acquitting himself honorably. He is doing "dammit just dropped a bowling ball on my foot spin-with-mike-stand" dance; he is doing "prance sideways with mike stand like an attacking staff-wielding ritual warrior" between-verses dance. And after each line he is gazing at the crowd with those strangely startled yet fearless eyes, as though we had just surprised him in his den, tearing into some carrion.

3.

Conversation with wife, Mariana, June 27, 2006:

ME: Oh, my God.

HER: What?

ME: Axl just bit a security guard's leg in Sweden. He's in jail.

HER: Is that gonna affect your interview with him?

ME: No, I don't think they ever really considered letting me talk to him . . . Biting somebody on the leg, though—it forces you to picture him in such a, like a, disgraced position.

HER: Does anybody help Axl when that happens?

4.

I'd been shuffling around a surprisingly pretty, sunny, newly renovated downtown Lafayette for a couple of days, scraping at whatever I could find. I saw the house where he grew up. I looked at his old yearbook pictures in the public library. Everyone had his or her Axl story. He stole a TV from that house there. Here's where he tried to ride his skateboard on the back of a car and fell and got road rash all up his arm. He came out of this motel with a half-naked woman and some older guys were looking at her and one of 'em threw down a cigarette, not meaning anything by it, but Axl freaked out and flipped 'em off and they beat the crap out of him. Hard to document any of this stuff. Still, enough Wanted On Warrant reports exist for Axl's Indiana years to lend credence to the claim that the city cops and county troopers pretty much felt justified, and technically speaking were justified, in picking him up and hassling him whenever they spotted him out. One doubts he left the house much that they didn't spot him, what with the long, fine, flowing red hair. Not always fun to be Axl.

I went to the city cops. They've mellowed with the town. In fact, they were friendly. They found and processed the negatives of some never-before-seen mug shots for me, from '80 and '82, the former of which (where he's only eighteen) is an unknown American masterpiece of the saddest, crappiest kind. The ladies in the records department rummaged some and came back with the report connected to that picture, as well, which I'd never seen mentioned in any of the bios or online or anything. It's written by an officer signing himself "1–4." I took it back to the Holiday Inn and spent the rest of the afternoon reading. Call it the Sheidler Incident. It begins:

FULL NAME: BAILEY, WILLIAM BRUCE . . .
ALIASES: BILL BAILEY . . .
CURRENT PLACE OF EMPLOYMENT: SELF
 EMPLOYED—BAND
CHARGE: W[ANTED]O[N]W[ARRANT] BATTERY . . .
AGE: 18; HEIGHT: 5'9"; WEIGHT: 149; HAIR: RED; EYES:
 GRN; BUILD: SLENDER; COMPLEXION: FAIR . . .

Here's how it went down that day—"allegedly" (I'll cherry-pick the good bits for you). A little kid named Scott Sheidler was riding his bike in front of the house of an older kid named Dana Gregory. Scott made skid marks on the sidewalk. Dana Gregory ran out, picked Scott up under the armpits, kicked over his bike, and ordered the boy TO GET ON HIS HANDS AND KNEES AND SCRUB THE SKID MARKS OFF THE SIDEWALK. The kid went squealing to his old man, Tom Sheidler. Tom Sheidler went to young Dana Gregory and asked if it was true, what Scotty had said. Dana Gregory said, "YES AND I'M GOING TO BEAT THE FUCK OUT OF YOU." The mom, Marleen, then ran up to the scene and began to shout. Around the same time, BILL BAILEY appeared, red, green, slender, and fair. And here I need to let the report take over, if only temporarily, as I can't begin to simulate its succinctness or authority:

M. Sheidler stated that BAILEY was also arguing with SHEIDLER and that he was using the "F" WORD in front of her kids. M. SHEIDLER stated that she went up to BAILEY and pointed her finger at BAILEY and told him not to use the "F" WORD in front of her kids. M. SHEIDLER stated that BAILEY, who has a SPLINT ON HIS ARM, then struck her on the arm and neck with the splint. I looked at M. SHEIDLER and could see some RED MARKS on her ARM and NECK which could have been made by being struck.

This matter of which hand it was takes over the narrative for a stretch. Marleen Sheidler says "with the SPLINT," and little Scott says "with a SPLINT," but Dana Gregory's younger brother CHRIS 15 says "with the opposite hand that his SPLINT is on" (adding that Bailey struck Sheidler in response to "SHEIDLER STRIKEING [*sic*]" him). Bill Bailey himself then goes on to say that he "struck M. SHEIDLER in the FACE with his LEFT HAND the hand with out the SPLINT." Once again, this only after "MARLEEN SHEIDLER struck him in the face" (though seconds earlier, by his own admission, he'd told her "to keep her fucking brats at home"). The story ends with a strangely affecting suddenness: "BAILEY stated SHEIDLER then jumped at him and fell on his face, he then left and went home . . ."

The thing I couldn't stop wondering as I read it over was: Why were they so freaked out about the skid marks? Is making skid marks on the sidewalk a bad thing to do? It makes me think I spent half my childhood inadvertently infuriating my entire neighborhood.

The local Lafayette morning-rock DJ Jeff Strange, on Axl's extremely brief but much-reported fisticuffs with the diminutive and seemingly gentle designer of mall clothes Tommy Hilfiger; actually, "fisticuffs" is strong—accounts suggest that the fight consisted mostly of Hilfiger slapping Axl on the arm many times, and photos show Axl staring at Hilfiger with an improbable fifty-fifty mixture of rage and amused disbelief, like, "Should I . . . hurt it?":

"Man, I saw that, and I thought, That is straight Lafayette."

5.

I found Dana Gregory. I called his stepmom. He's Axl's oldest friend and worked for him at one time in L.A., after Guns had gotten big. When I sat down at the table in the back-patio area of a pub-type place called Sgt. Preston's, he had sunglasses on. When he pushed them up into his bushy gray hair, he had unnervingly pale mineral-blue eyes that had seen plenty of sunrises. He'd been there. You knew it before he even spoke. He'd done a spectacular amount of crazy shit in his life, and the rest of his life would be spent remembering and reflecting on that shit and focusing on taking it day by day. The metamorphosis of Bill, the friend of his youth, in whose mother's kitchen he ate breakfast every morning, his Cub Scouts buddy (a coin was tossed: Bill would be Raggedy Ann in the parade; Dana, Raggedy Andy), into—for a while—the biggest rock star on the planet, a man who started riots in more than one country and dumped a supermodel and duetted with Mick Jagger and then did even stranger shit like telling *Rolling Stone* he'd recovered memories of being sodomized by his stepfather at the age of two, a man who took as his legal name and made into a household word the name of a band (Axl) that Gregory was once in, on bass, and that Bill was never even in, man . . . This event had appeared in Gregory's life like a supernova to a prescientific culture. What was he supposed to do with it?

I said, "Do you call him Bill or Axl?"

He smiled: "I call him Ax."

"Still talk to him much?"

"Haven't talked to him since 1992. We had sort of a falling-out."

"Over what?"

He looked away. "Bullshit." Then, after a few pulls and drags, "It might have been over a woman."

He was nervous, but nervous in the way that any decent person is when you sit down in front of him with a notebook and are basically like, "I have to make a two thirty flight. Can you tell me about the heaviest things in your life? Order more spinach-'n'-artichoke dip, I can expense it."

He finished beers quickly. He used, repeatedly, without the slight-est self-consciousness, an idiom I've always loved—"*Right* on," spoken quickly and with the intonation a half octave higher on "Right," to mean not "That's correct" or "Exactly" but simply "Yes," as in "Hey, you like to party?" *Right* on.

"Tell me about L.A.," I said. "You said you were working for him out there. What kind of stuff?"

"Fixing shit that he broke," Gregory said.

"Did he break a lot of shit?" I said.

"His condo had these giant mirrors going all around it. And every now and then, he'd take that spaceman statue they give you when you win an award on MTV and smash up the mirrors with it. Well, he slept till four o'clock in the afternoon every day. Somebody had to let the guy in when he came to fix the mirrors. Shit like that."

He told me another L.A. story, about the time Axl picked up Slash's beloved albino boa constrictor and it shat all over Axl. And Axl had on some expensive clothes. He got so mad he wanted to hurt the snake. He was cussing at it. But Slash picked up his guitar—here Dana imi-tated a tree-chopping backswing pose—and said, "Don't. Hurt. My. Snake." Axl backed off.

I guess we sat there a pretty long time. Dana has four children and four grandchildren. When I said he seemed young for that (can you imagine Axl with four grandchildren?), he said, "Started young. Like I was saying, there was a lot of experimentation." His ex-wife, Monica Gregory, also knew Axl. She gave him his first PA. Gregory said he talks to her only once a year, "when I have to." He said what he wants is to lower the level of dysfunction for the next generation. He told me about how he and Axl and Monica and their group of friends used to go to a park in Lafayette after dark, Columbian Park—"We ruled that place at night"—and pick the lock on the piano case that was built into the outdoor stage and play for themselves till the small hours. I'd wandered around Columbian Park. It's more or less across the street from where those boys grew up. Not twenty feet from the stage, there's a memorial to the sons of Lafayette who "made the supreme sacrifice in defense of our country," and it includes the name of William Rose, probably Axl's great-great-great-grandpa, killed in the Civil War, which I suppose was fought in defense of our country in some not quite precise way. And now, as Gregory talked, I thought about how weird it was, all those years of Axl probably reading that name a hundred times, not making anything of it, not knowing that it was his own name—he who one day, having discovered his original name while going through some of his mother's papers and taking it as his own, would sing, "I don't need your Civil War," and ask the still-unanswered question, "What's so civil about war, anyway?"

Back then, Gregory said, Axl played all kinds of stuff. He mentioned Thin Lizzy. "But the only time I ever really heard him sing was in the bathroom. He'd be in there for an hour doing God knows what. Prancing around like a woman, for all I know."

"So, what is there of Lafayette in his music, do you think?"

"The anger, man. I'd say he got that here."

"He used to get beat up a lot, right?" (More than one person had told me this since I'd come to town.)

"I beat him up a lot," Gregory said. "Well, I'd win one year, he'd win the next. One time we was fighting in his backyard, and I was winning. My dad saw what was going on and tried to stop it, but his mom said, 'No, let 'em fight it out.' We always hashed it out, though. When you get older, it takes longer to heal."

It was awkward, trying incessantly to steer the conversation back toward the Sheidler business without being too obvious about it. Did Dana honestly have no memory of the fracas? He kept answering elliptically. "I remember the cops wanted to know who'd spray-painted all over the street," he said, smiling.

"The night Axl left for L.A., he wrote, 'Kiss my ass, Lafayette. I'm out of here.' I wish I'd taken a picture of that."

Finally, I grew impatient and said, "Mr. Gregory, you can't possibly not remember this. Listen: You. A kid with a bike. Axl and a woman got into a fight. He had a splint on his arm."

"I can tell you how he got the splint," he said. "It was from holding on to an M-80 too long. We thought they were pretty harmless, but I guess they weren't, 'cause it 'bout blew his fucking hand off."

"But why were you so mad about the skid marks in the first place?"
I asked.

"My dad was in construction. Still is. That's what I do. It's Gregory
and Sons—me and my brother are the sons. Mostly residential concrete. My brother, he's dead now. He was thirty-nine. A heart thing.
My dad still can't bring himself to get rid of the 'Sons.' Anyway, see,
we poured that sidewalk. He'd get so pissed if he saw it was scuffed
up—'Goddamm it, you know how hard it is to get that off?' He'd think
we done it and beat our ass. So, I saw [little Scott Sheidler's handi-
work], and I said, 'No, I don't think that's gonna do.'"

That was all. I couldn't get too many beats into any particular topic
with Gregory before his gaze would drift off, before he'd get pensive. I
started to get the feeling that this—his being here, his decision to meet
with me—was about something, that we had not yet gotten around to
the subject he was here to discuss.

"You know," he said, "I've never talked to a reporter before. I've
always turned down requests."

"Why'd you agree to this one?" I asked.

"I wasn't going to call you back, but my dad said I should. You
oughta thank my dad. My son said, 'Tell him what an asshole that guy
was, Dad.' I said, 'Ah, he knows all that shit, son.'"

"Is it that you feel it's been long enough, and now you can talk about
all that stuff?"

"Shit, I don't know. I figure maybe he'll see the article and give me a
call. It's been a long time. I'd really love just to talk to him and find out
what he's really been into."

"Do you still consider him a friend?" I said.

"I don't know. I miss the guy. I love him."

We were quiet for a minute, and then Gregory leaned to the side
and pulled out his wallet. He opened it and withdrew a folded piece of
white notepaper. He placed it into my hand, still folded. "Put that in
your story," he said. "He'll know what it means." I went straight to the
car after the interview and remembered about the note only when I was
already on the plane. Written on it in pencil were a couple of lines from
"Estranged," off *Use Your Illusion II*:

But everything we've ever known's here.
I never wanted it to die.

6.

Axl has said, "I sing in five or six different voices that are all part of me. It's not contrived." I agree. One of them is an unexpectedly competent baritone. The most important of the voices, though, is Devil Woman. Devil Woman comes from a deeper part of Axl than do any of the other voices. Often she will not enter until nearer the end of a song. In fact, the dramatic conflict between Devil Woman and her sweet, melodic yang—the Axl who sings such lines as "Her hair reminds me of a warm, safe place" and "If you want to love me, then darling, don't refrain"—is precisely what resulted in Guns N' Roses' greatest songs. Take "Sweet Child o' Mine." It's not that you don't love it from the beginning, what with the killer riffs and the oddly antiquated-sounding chorus, yet a sword hangs over it. You think: This can't be everything. Come on, I mean, "Now and then when I see her face / It takes me away to that special place"? What is that?

Then, around 5:04, she arrives. The song has veered minor-key by then, the clouds have begun to gather, and I never hear that awesome, intelligent solo that I don't imagine Axl's gone off somewhere at the start of it, to be by himself while his body undergoes certain changes. What I love is how when he comes back in, he comes in on top of himself ("five or six different voices that are all part of me"); he's not yet all the way finished with I, I, I, I, I, I, I, I when that fearsome timbre tears itself open. And what does she say, this Devil Woman? What does she always say, for that matter? Have you ever thought about it? I hadn't. "Sweet Child," "Paradise City," "November Rain," "Patience," they all come down to codas—Axl was a poet of the dark, unresolved coda—and to what do these codas themselves come down? "Everybody needs somebody." "Don't you think that you need someone?" "I need you. Oh, I need you." "Where do we go? Where do we go now?" "I wanna go." "Oh, won't you please take me home?"

7.

When I was about seventeen, I drove back to Indiana with my oldest friend, Trent. We'd grown up in the same small river town there and both went off to school elsewhere at about the same time, so we romanticized our childhood haunts and playmates a little, the way you do. The summer before our senior year of high school, we made a sentimental journey home to drop in on everybody and see how each had fared. This is 1991, when *Use Your Illusion* came out. "Don't Cry" was on the radio all the time and fun to imitate. Still, that turned out to be one of the more colossally bleak afternoons of my life.

To a man, our old chums divided along class lines. Those of us who'd grown up in Silver Hills, where kids were raised to finish high school and go to college, were finishing high school and applying to colleges. Those who hadn't, weren't. They weren't doing anything. There were these two guys from our old gang, Brad Hope and Rick Sissy. Their fathers were working-class—one drove a bus and the other a concrete truck; the latter couldn't read or write. But the public elementary where we met them was mixed in every sense. And there's something about that age, from nine to eleven—your personality has appeared, but if you're lucky you haven't internalized yet the idea that you're any different from anyone else, that there's a ladder in life.

We stopped by Ricky's house first. Ricky had been a kind of white-trash genius, into everything. You know those ads in the back of comics that say you can make a hovercraft out of vacuum-cleaner parts? Ricky was the kid who made the hovercraft. And souped it up. He was taller and chubbier than the rest of us and had a high-pitched voice and used some kind of oil in his hair. Trent would eventually get into the University of Chicago and wind up writing a two-hundred-page thesis on the Munich Conference, and even he would tell you: Ricky was the smartest. One time Ricky and I were shooting pellet guns at cars in the small junkyard his father maintained as a sort of sideline. We were spider-webbing the glass. Suddenly Ricky's dad, who had just been woken up from one of his epic diurnal naps between shifts, hollered from the window of his bedroom, "Ricky, you'd better not be shooting at that orange truck! I done sold the windshield on that."

I'll never forget; Ricky didn't even look at me first. He just ran. Dropping the pistol at his feet, he ran into the forest. I followed. We spent the whole rest of the day up there. We found an old grave in the middle of a field. We climbed to the top of Slate Hill, the highest knob in our town, and Ricky gave me a whole talk on how slate formed, how it was and was not shale. I'll never forget the scared, ecstatic freedom of those hours in the woods.

When Trent and I rediscovered Ricky, he was sitting alone in a darkened room watching a porn movie of a woman doing herself with a peeled banana. He said, "What the fuck is that thing on your head?" I was in a bandanna-wearing phase. This one was yellow. He said, "When I saw you get out of the car, I thought, Who the fuck is that? I 'bout shot you for a faggot." We asked him what was going on. He said he'd just been expelled from school, for trying to destroy one of the boys' restrooms by flushing lit waterproof M-8os down the toilets. Also, he'd just been in a bad jeep accident; his shoulder was messed up somehow. All scabbed over, maybe? This entire conversation unfolded as the woman with the banana worked away. Ricky's dad was asleep in the next room. Retired now. We told him we were headed over to Brad's next. He said, "I haven't seen Brad in a while. Did you hear he dorked a spook?" That's what he said: "dorked a spook."

We were quiet on the way to Brad's. He had a real mustache already. He'd always been an early bloomer. When we knew him well, he was constantly exposing himself. Once I watched him run around the perimeter of a campsite with his underpants at his ankles going, "Does this look like the penis of an eleven-year-old?" It did not. Brad used to plead with his mom to sing "Birmingham Sunday" for us, which she'd do, a cappella, in the kitchen. Now he was all nigger this, nigger that. Trent was dating a black girl in Louisville at the time. Neither of us knew how to behave. Brad must have noticed us squirming, because he looked at me at one point and said, "Ah, y'all probably got some good niggers in Ohio." That's where I was living. "We're fixin' to have a race war with the ones we got here." He had dropped out of high school. It had been only four years since we'd been sleeping over at his house, doing séances and whatnot, and now we had no way to reach each other. A gulf had appeared. It opened the first day of seventh grade when some of us went into the "accelerated" program and others went into the "standard" program. By sheerest coincidence, I'm sure, this division ran perfectly parallel to the one between our respective parents' income brackets. I remember Ricky and me running into each other in the hallway the first day of seventh grade and with a confusion that we were far too young to handle, both being like, "Why aren't you in any of my classes?" When I think about it, I never saw those boys again, not after that day.

Axl got away.

8.

There were hundreds of blue flags draped along the south bank of the Nervión in Bilbao, and across the top of each it said GUNS N' ROSES. The flags were of Moorish blue, and they shook against a spotless sky that was only barely more pale than that. Late that night, in the hills over the city, the band would begin headlining a three-day festival, and the river valley echoed the sound so clearly, so helplessly, people in the old part of town would be able, if they understood English, to make out the individual words, but for now Bilbao retained its slightly buttoned-up tranquillity and charm. There's a fountain next to the Guggenheim that fires bursts of water every four or five seconds, and the olive-skinned kids jump up and down in it. They just strip to their underpants and go wild, male and female, and to watch them at it was lovely. Can you imagine, in the center of some major American city, a bunch of twelve-year-old girls in their panties capering in the water, their lank hair flinging arcs of droplets? Hard to say which would be greater: the level of parental paranoia or the actual volume of loitering pervs. Here things seemed so sane. Axl and the boys hadn't landed yet. They were still in the air.

The district where they played is called Kobetamendi. It's high up, and from there you could see the city, the river, the spires, the flashing titanium scales of the museum. When it got dark, you could see the lights. When there aren't stages set up at Kobetamendi, it's just a large empty field with a road and, across the road, some modest farmhouses.

As I reached the crest of the hill, a rap-rock band was playing. The justification for rap rock seems to be that if you take really bad rock and put really bad rap over it, the result is somehow good, provided the raps are being barked by an overweight white guy with cropped hair and forearm tattoos. The women from those few little farmhouses had gathered at their fence; they leaned and mumbled and dangled their canes. One of them was one of the oldest-looking old people I have ever seen, with stiff white hair and that face, like the inside of a walnut shell, that only truly ancient women get. She and her friends were actually listening to the rap rock, and part of me wanted to run over to them and assure them that after they died, there would still be people left in the world who knew how horrifying this music was, and that these people would transmit their knowledge to carefully chosen members of future generations, but the ladies did not appear worried. They were even laughing. I'm sure they remembered traveling circuses in that field in eighteen ninety something, and what was the difference, really?

That night I wheedled my way backstage by doing a small favor for the bassist's Portuguese model girlfriend (I gave her buddy from home a spare media pass they'd accidentally given me). When the security guard on the back ramp leading up to the stage, who did not even make eye contact with the Portuguese model as she floated past him, put his palm against my chest, as if to say, "Whoa, that's a little much," she turned around briefly and said, "*Está conmigo.*" She said this with about the level of nervousness and uncertainty with which you might say, to a maître d', "Smoking." Before I could thank her, I was watching Axl dance from such an inconceivable propinquity that if I'd bent my knees, thrust my hands forward, and leapt, I'd have been on the front page of the entertainment section of *El País* the next day for assaulting him in front of twenty-five thousand people.

I've been a part of virtual seas of screaming sweaty kids before, but to see one from the stage, from just above, to see that many thousand people shaping with their mouths some words you made up in your head one time while you were brushing your teeth (needless to say, I was trying to imagine I'd written them), that was heady. "Guns and RO-SES, Guns and RO-SES" . . . Axl was pounding with the base of his mike stand on the stage in time to the chant. A kid with a beard looked at us, me and the model and her friend, every ten minutes or so, put his hands on his ears, and mouthed the word *pyro*. Then we were supposed to put our hands on our ears, because the explosion was about to take place ten feet away. Sometimes the kid would forget—he was busy—and then everyone would go, "Aaaarrrgh!" and clutch their head.

There was a sort of shambling older dude next to me in a newsboy cap, with a guitar in his hands—a tech, I figured. Then he ran out onto the stage, and I was like, "That's Izzy Stradlin" (founding Guns N' Roses guitarist).

Izzy, I know, is the reason the band sounds so much better tonight than they did two months ago in New York. He started joining them on three or four songs the very next night, after the debut, and has been showing up periodically ever since. His presence—or to put it more accurately, the presence of another original member of the band—seems to have made the other guys feel more like they are Guns N' Roses and less like, as *El Diario Vasco* will put it tomorrow, "*una bullanguera formación de mercenarios al servicio del ego del vocalista*," which means "a noisy bunch of mercenaries in the service of the vocalist's ego."

The Spanish press—they weren't kind. They said Axl was a "grotesque spectacle"; they called him "*el divo*"; they talked about the endless, Nigel Tufnel–esque "*solos absurdos*" that he makes each of the band members play, in an effort to get the audience to invest emotionally in the new lineup (it's true that these are fairly ill-advised, as has been the rock solo generally since Jimi died). One article says, "*Las fotos de Axl dan miedo*," which translates literally and, I think, evocatively as "Pictures of Axl give fear," with his "goatee that gives him the look of a Texas millionaire." In a crowning moment, they say that he has "the voice of a priapic rooster." They say he demands his room be covered in Oriental carpets and that he not be required to interact with the other band members. That he arrived on a separate plane. They say security guards have been ordered never to look him in the eye. They say the other band members also hate one another and demand to be placed on different floors of the hotel. They say he's traveling with a tiny Asian guru named Sharon Maynard, "alias Yoda," and that he does nothing without her guidance, that she chooses the people he should hire by examining their faces. But mostly the Spaniards are fixated, as have been all the European media gangs on this tour, with the secret oxygen chamber into which he supposedly disappears during the shows and from which he emerges "*más fresco que una lechuga*"—fresher than a head of lettuce.

I can't confirm or deny the oxygen thing, and it's hard to say whether the constant mentions of it in the press are evidence of its being real or just a sign that people are recycling the same rumor. The manager of a Hungarian band called Sex Action, which opened for G N' R, claims to have seen the device itself, but Hungarians make up tales like that for entertainment.

What I can tell you, based on my model-side vantage, is that there is a square cell entirely covered in black curtains just to the rear of stage left. You cannot see as much as a crack of light through the curtains, and I tried. Axl runs into this thing about fifteen times during the course of a show. Sometimes he emerges with a new costume on—makes sense—but sometimes he doesn't. Sometimes he goes in there when one of the guys is soloing or something—makes sense—but sometimes he goes in there at a moment when it's really distracting not to have him onstage. I do not know whether Sharon Maynard is in this cell. I do not know what he does in there. If he's huffing reconstituted gas, I don't know whether it's in a Michael Jackson "This is good for me" sort of way or if he has a legitimate lung problem. I don't know anything about what goes on in the cell, only that it exists and that being in there is important to Axl.

Overall, I can't agree with my fellow ink-stained wretches in the Old World about this show. Axl is sounding fuller and fuller. Every now and then the sound guy, just to make sure the board is calibrated, pushes the vocal mike way up in the mix, and we hear nothing but Axl, and the notes are on. Nor is he fat at all. In fact, he looks pretty lithe. At one point, he puts on a rather skimpy T-shirt and sprints from one end of the stage to the other, and it's the sprint of the cross-country runner he used to be. Dana Gregory told me Axl used to run everywhere. Just run and run. Dana Gregory said there was one time out west when G N' R played in a stadium that had a track around it, and Axl just started sprinting around the track during a song. When a security guard, believing him to be a crazed fan, tried to tackle him, Axl kicked the guy in the face. "That happened ten feet in front of me," Gregory said. And now here the bastard was, ten feet in front of me. The moon looked like she was yelling for help because some dark power was erasing her side. They brought out a piano so that he could do "November Rain," and the way they positioned the piano, he was facing me directly. Like we were sitting across a table from each other. This is as close as I ever got to him. And what I noticed at this almost nonexistent remove was the peace in his features as he tinkled out the intro. Absolute peace. A warm slackness to the facial muscles way beyond what Botox can do, though I'm not saying it didn't contribute. His face was for now beyond the reach of whatever it is that makes him crazy.

After the final encore, he and the rest of the band ran down a ramp, into the open door of a waiting van. Heavy men in black ran alongside them like drill instructors. The van squealed away, taking the model with it. Big, heavy black cars pulled out alongside the van. And then it was quiet. The Basque country. Next morning the flags were still flying by the river, the press was preparing the scathing reviews, but Axl was gone.

They were the last great rock band that didn't think there was something a bit embarrassing about being in a rock band. There are thousands of bands around at any given time that don't think rock is the least bit funny, but rarely is one of them good. With G N' R, no matter how sophisticated you felt yourself to be about pop music (leaving aside for now the paradoxical nature of that very social category), you couldn't entirely deny them. They were the first band I got to be right about with my older brother. It was that way for a lot of people in my generation. All my youth, my brother had been force-feeding me my musical taste—"Def Leppard is shit; listen to the Jam"—and now there was finally one band I wouldn't have to live down; and I recall the tiny glow of triumph, blended with fraternity, that I felt when one day he said, "Dude, you were right about Guns N' Roses. That's a good record." That was *Appetite*, of course. Things got strange after that.

You read things that say Nirvana made Guns N' Roses obsolete. But Guns N' Roses were never made obsolete. They just sort of disintegrated.

Closer to the case is that G N' R made Nirvana possible. When you think about the niche that Nirvana supposedly created and per-fected—a megaband that indie snobs couldn't entirely disavow, no mat-ter how badly they wanted to—G N' R got there first. Or almost there. They dressed silly. They didn't seem to know the difference between their good songs and their crap songs. But we have to remember, too, how they came along at a time when bands with singers who looked like Axl and thrust their hips unironically, and lead players who spread their legs and reeled off guitar-god noodling weren't supposed to be interesting, melodically or culturally or in any other way. G N' R were. They were also grotesque and crass and stupid sometimes, even most of the time. Even almost all of the time. But you always knew you were seeing something when you saw them.

Shouldn't the band just get back together? Don't they know how huge that'd be? Dana Gregory told me Slash and Izzy will never play full-time with Axl again: "They know him too well."

I don't know him at all. Maybe if his people had let me talk to him, he'd have bitten and struck me and told me to leave my fucking brats at home, and I could transcend these feelings. As it is, I'm left listening to "Patience" again. I don't know how it is where you are, but in the South, where I live, they still play it all the time. And I whistle along and wait for that voice, toward the end, when he goes, *Ooooooo, I need you. OOOOOOO, I need you.* And on the first *Ooooooo,* he finds this tissue-shredding note. It conjures the image of someone peeling his own scalp back, like the skin of a grape. I have to be careful not to attempt to sing along with this part, because it can make you sort of choke and almost throw up a little bit. And on the second *OOOOOOO*, you picture just a naked glowing green skull that hangs there vibrating gape-mouthed in a prison cell.

Or whatever it is you picture.

2006

GREG TATE

Greg Tate first dreamed of writing about popular music when he read Amiri Baraka's *Black Music* and *Rolling Stone* magazine as a teenager. He attended Howard University, learned to play guitar, and moved to New York City, where in 1985 he founded the Black Music Coalition with Living Colour guitarist Vernon Reid and producer Konda Mason. Tate was a staff writer at *The Village Voice* from 1987 to 2003. His writing has also been published in *The New York Times, The Washington Post, Artforum, Rolling Stone, VIBE,* and *Downbeat.* He moves with unusual ease among rock & roll, hip-hop, and jazz; in the review of Kanye West and 50 Cent included here, Tate deploys his distinctive voice to render the indefensible indispensable. His books include *Flyboy in the Buttermilk: Essays on Contemporary America* (1992), *Everything but the Burden: What White People Are Taking from Black Culture* (2003), *Midnight Lightning: Jimi Hendrix and the Black Experience* (2003), and *Flyboy 2: The Greg Tate Reader* (2016).

▼ ▼

In Praise of Assholes

Kanye West and 50 Cent are the two biggest drama queens to hit pop music since Alice Cooper and Iggy Pop, and that's not a bad thing. Hiphop, still the voice of Young Black America, is only going to get louder and prouder as it goes along, if only because that demographic's voice is so hushed elsewhere. Barack Obama's campaign manager claims his candidate's currently muted campaign voice is the product of his belief that America isn't ready for a fire-breathing Black man, and our nation's prisons and graveyards are full of the proof. But nature abhorring a vacuum, Kanye and 50 have rushed in to fill the void in that last safe space left for such characters. A sister I know once told me she had no respect for a Black man who wasn't arrogant. Maybe the advent of Mr. West and Mr. Cent warms her heart, maybe not. Regardless, there is, of course, that bothersome question: loud and proud and arrogant in the name of what? Wealth, fame, and gossip? Hmmm. While traveling about the country speaking in the 19th century, Sojourner Truth, our beloved godmother of The Struggle, used to sell postcards of herself, rationalizing this enterprise thus: "I use the shadow to support the substance."

These are the days when we ask whether there's anything but shade being served up as Black Popular Culture. With respect to West's new *Graduation* and 50's new *Curtis*, one could easily come to feel that hype is being sold to support hype, so please don't believe the hype. But as Melville, another 19th-century godmother of truth, set forth in *The Confidence Man*, America is nothing if not a land where hustlers, grifters, con artists, and slicksters grease the wheel of populism, where the shadow often is the substance and where even those who've come to peddle the righteous Truth realize they need to get some hustle up in their game, too. On a recent PBS report about Europe's love-hate relationship with America, a bizarre sidebar hustled us into the studio apartment of two French rappers of Arabic descent. Dudes wore fat gold chains, shined diamond grills, and gushed repeatedly about how they viewed both American MCs and Herr Bush as idols because their "game was so tight," repeatedly and ferociously invoking that phrase. They believe the hype, conflating Bushology and bling-ology as the new-model American Dream. Mr. Cent has also spoken admiringly of Herr Bush's aggression. Real knows real.

Mr. West and Mr. Cent are both now as well-known for inciting beef as for recording and performing. You could think they both make records just to sell hype as opposed to the other way around, but they're also both formidable, state-of-the-art 21st-century pop tunesmiths who take the job of writing delectable hits as seriously as any Brill or Motown scrivener ever did. One old-school hiphop maven recently lamented how she can't believe she lives in a world where "Kanye is even a factor," largely because he can't really rap. (Mr. Cent she loves, reminding those of us less titillated that the man does have charms to stir the distaff breast.) But while it's true that Mr. West will probably never end up on anybody's list of even the 100 greatest MCs of all time, he's clearly got an exceptional ear for hooks, both musical and lyrical. Furthermore, he's got stuff to say that isn't the standard fare, stuff that still has undeniable mass-ass appeal. He also has a unique personality and a confidently outsized opinion of same—that combined with moxie will still get you somewhere in this country.

Mr. West and Mr. Cent share in being two of the most unrepentantly obnoxious figures to arrive in American pop culture since Cheney and Rumsfeld. The difference between them being, Mr. West is loud, bratty, obnoxious, but seemingly harmless, while Mr. Cent is laconic, bratty, obnoxious, but genuinely sinister. His now-legendary Hot 97 interview, calmly warning a histrionic, hyperventilating Cam'ron about the dangers of his mouth writing checks his ass couldn't cash, was as surgical, chilling, and devastating a threat as you've heard since Pacino played Corleone. But somewhere during 2005's *The Massacre*, Mr. Cent realized he didn't have to make records for gangsters, wanksters, or even guys anymore, that he could just be the lone NY kingpin who made records strictly for the ladies. Those with truly savage breasts and literal *cojones* would have to find their high-testosterone hiphop elsewhere—Mr. Cent could care less for your love anymore. Certainly not after cashing in those Glaceau stock options; if hiphop is now more defined by the corporate game than the street game, that lucrative little coup just might be the definitive hiphop act of 2007.

After all, brothers like Mr. West and Mr. Cent can sell hype to support hype and thus generate as much personal wealth as many African nations can with all the diamonds, gold, and titanium in their sovereign ground. African-American entertainment is our De Beers, our Nokia, our Lockheed—the only bloodsucking industry we (sorta) (symbolically, at least) got, and likely the only nation-state (figuratively, at least) we'll ever have as well. Meaning that in some perverse Black Nationalist way, you have to admire the loot Mr. Cent, Mr. Combs, Mr. Simmons, and Mr. Carter have hustled out of corporate America by wearing little more than their well-hyped shadows. Meanwhile, back in the real jungle, real Africans—Rwandans, no less—are slaughtering one another to corner the market on the colombite-tantalite-laced mud (known as coltan) that keeps your cell phone ringing. (For more on this, see Black Brit artist Steve McQueen's upcoming exhibition *Gravesend*.) Mr. West and Mr. Cent may indeed be assholes, but they're symbolic assholes who remind us that American Darwinism has produced a species of Negro Male who can now exploit his fetishized vernacular aura as profitably as multinational corporations can the minerals in your whole damn ancestral homeland. Mr. Cent will never win the NAACP Image Award he deserves for this achievement, mainly because that lot's more interested in "burying" the word *nigga* or "redeeming" Michael Vick's dog-mangling ass than applauding or even analyzing it.

Oh yes, BTW, FYI, Mr. Cent and Mr. West both have new albums out. Of course, Mr. West's previous effort, 2005's *Late Registration*, belongs in the pantheon of superlative hiphop albums, despite his being a mere step or three above Mr. Combs in the "least enchanting rhymers of all time" category. To his credit, though, he's far wittier than Diddy, with reams of jokes and edgy one-liners ("I'm like the Malcolm X of fly/Buy any jeans necessary"), and something like a social conscience, too—see his blood-diamond confessions on *Registration*'s "Diamonds from Sierra Leone." What he lacks in ferocious flow, he makes up for in plaintive verbal harassment—he's kinda like the guy who will beg his way into your panties if he has to, the one who will simply not shut up or back off until your ears give him the equivalent of sympathy punani. He's the Rodney Dangerfield of rap, in other words, and fortunately for us, what he lacks in MC finesse he makes up for in musical panache. *Registration* had a jillion snappy ideas about what a hiphop song could be—from show tunes to power ballads, from symphonic airs to Curtis Mayfield elegies—and mucho ear candy to burn. Mr. West proved he knew a ripe, juicy hook when he stole, borrowed, or chipmunked one, and he knew how to attach himself to it like a writhing, self-aggrandizing barnacle to boot. *Graduation* builds on this formula, even if this time around his lyric conceits prove less galvanizing than his purely musical snatches.

Let's take "Drunk and Hot Girls," for starters. Ostensibly *Graduation*'s "Gold Digger," its similarly breezy girl-bashing never achieves the deadpan hilarity of that *Registration* highlight because, like too many other moments this time, Mr. West presumes our sympathy for his rock-star pain—here, specifically, the downside of being entangled with intoxicated hotties. (The track does, however, prove he can mire himself in lounge music as seedy as any Tom Waits has trawled in.) The folly of his pathos, though, reaches its nadir on "Big Brother," a song about how much he loves and owes his big bruh Jay-Z, and how little love and respect lil' bruh Kanye feels he gets in return. Not exactly Cain and Abel drama here.

Now, if there's anything Kanye and 50 both want and will never, ever have, it's the genuine Vito Corleone–Muhammad Ali love and respect Mr. Shawn Carter has out here on these streets, a love I never truly appreciated until around December 4 of last year, when I was on Harlem's 145th Street A-train platform and overheard a young sister, about 17 or so, tell her homegirl she was on her way home to bake a birthday cake, like she always did for her "big brother" Jayhova. Both these guys could give away every dime they make from now until perdition to homeless orphans and not get that kind of unabashed 'hood love in return. Of all the things Mr. Carter has that other high-rolling hiphop brothers might covet, the thing they covet the most can't be bought or sold: his "big man on campus" affability. In recognition of this lack, Mr. West and Mr. Cent take an opposite tack, seeing how far they can push straight-faced arrogance as an icebreaker, if not a virtue.

When Mr. West's braggadocio turns whiny, *Graduation* proves why he's so easy to loathe, but also why he's so easy to applaud as the most genuinely confessional MC in hiphop today. (Some would say "narcissistic," but c'mon, this is hiphop, not emo, yo.) On "The Glory," he congratulates himself for raising the thematic bar in hiphop, and also for buying clothes with haute logos. On "Everything I Am," he congratulates himself for not being more gangsta, notes the number of caskets in Chicago last year (600), and speaks up for the down-and-out brother in the 'hood who can't even get the church to give his depression the time of day. And grating bouts of narcissism aside, *Graduation* contains killer pieces of production: "Stronger" uses Daft Punk's "Harder, Better, Faster, Stronger" to practically revive Euro-disco, while "Champion" snarkily snatches its hook from Steely Dan's "Kid Charlemagne" and allows Mr. West to declare how much he's an idol for the kids, if not the ages.

For Mr. Cent's part, he and his *Curtis* co-producers continue to per-fect a style of lean, sleek, bubbly, robo-industrial hiphop that nearly qualifies as a modern form of visual design, each track the equivalent of watching a Maserati roll off the assembly line. We're talking a form as sleek, dark, and aerodynamic in form as a Mirage fighter—one that allows Mr. Cent to shadily blend and disappear into the music like a grinning, evil Cheshire cat and thus maintain his Zen profile as the anti-Kanye: the least excitable prime-time rapper this side of Snoop. An extremely limited thematic palette of sex, money, and dissing still wets his whistle, even if, on "Straight to the Bank," he reminds us that he's so rich he doesn't have to rap anymore. But even if you have no ears for his lyrical swagger (I don't have much), can't anybody say he makes indifferent, lazy albums. *Curtis* is stuffed with tightly wound 21st-century pop songwriting, full of that invisible craft and flow that renders a thing eminently listenable even if it's gratuitously raunchy, politically reprehensible, and sexually retrograde. America wouldn't be America if pro-capitalist assholes and con men couldn't run roughshod over the body politic, and the day there's no room for two full-time careerist drama queens like Mr. West and Mr. Cent will be the day the revolution comes, the day of al-Kebulan, the Taliban, the tsunami, the asteroid, the omega, man.

2007

ELIJAH WALD

Elijah Wald (b. 1959) is one of rock writing's most meticulous historians. He specializes in investigating and retelling the story that "everyone knows" already, from the myth of Robert Johnson selling his soul to the devil at the crossroads in order to play guitar (*Escaping the Delta*, 2004) to Bob Dylan's selling out at the Newport Folk Festival in 1965 by plugging in an electric guitar (*Dylan Goes Electric*, 2015). *How the Beatles Destroyed Rock 'n' Roll*, excerpted here, is probably the most influential book to date in Wald's prolific career. Invariably, Wald's research demonstrates that the stories we think we know aren't nearly as simple as we'd thought. A gifted folk performer in his own right, Wald is especially strong on the folk musics of the United States and North America, as illustrated in *Narcocorrido: A Journey into the Music of Drugs, Guns and Guerrillas* (2002). The memoir he cowrote with Dave van Ronk, *The Mayor of MacDougal Street* (2005), provided the basis for the Coen Brothers' 2013 film *Inside Llewyn Davis*.

▼ ▼

Say You Want a Revolution . . .

[The Beatles] are leading an evolution in which the best of current post-rock sounds are becoming something that pop music has never been before: an art form.

TIME MAGAZINE, 1967

I'm sick and tired of British-accented youths ripping off
black American artists and, because they're white,
being accepted by the American audience.
MITCH MILLER

ALL OF this happened a long time ago. A half century has passed since
a group of young Liverpudlians got together and named themselves the
Beatles, and their triumphant arrival in New York is now as distant from
us as the arrival of the Original Dixieland Jazz Band was then. Those
of us who grew up on their music may take pleasure in the fact that it
is still widely heard, but we need to remember that our parents' and
grandparents' music also held on through their lifetimes: In the first
months of 1964, the record that pushed the Beatles off the top of the
singles charts was Louis Armstrong's "Hello, Dolly!" and the album
right below them on the LP charts was by the Dixieland revivalist Al
Hirt. Armstrong was sixty-two years old—younger than Bob Dylan or
Paul McCartney is now. And the youth of the 1960s was as familiar with
older stars as kids are today. Dean Martin and Frank Sinatra were television and radio regulars, and although McCartney was joking when he
referred to Sophie Tucker, whose career reached back to 1911, as "our
favorite American group" at the 1963 Royal Variety Performance, he
wasn't pulling her name from the distant past; she had been the highest-
billed singer on the previous year's show.[1]

For the youth of the 1960s, the "generation gap" between our elders
and us was an article of faith, and rock music was its most potent symbol. Even ten years seemed to us a cultural eternity, and it was typical that when John Lennon, in 1968, named Little Richard and Elvis
Presley as influences, the interviewer responded by asking, "Anyone
contemporary?"

Lennon, well aware of the difficulties of maintaining a place in the
pop pantheon, coyly replied, "Are they dead?"[2]

1. Royal Variety Performance programs, http://www.richardmmills.com (accessed 18
May 2008).
2. Jonathan Cott, "John Lennon Interview," *Rolling Stone*, 23 Nov. 1968, http://
dmbeatles.com/interviews.php?interview=67 (accessed 21 Mar. 2008).

The Beatles, along with Bob Dylan and a long list of other names, were hailed as spokesmen for a generation that was rebelling against the past, and that made it easy for their fans to see them as separate from that past. But it is telling that Lennon, while granting that the Beatles provided the soundtrack of their time, would say "I don't think they were more important than Glenn Miller or Woody Herman or Bessie Smith."[3] If one accepts the conventional wisdom that "the '60s" began around 1964 or 1965 and lasted into the early 1970s, the Beatles are an obvious symbol of that decade, and it was a unique and exciting time— for one thing, 1964 was the peak of the "baby boom," with 45 percent of the population under twenty-five and seventeen-year-olds the largest age group. But looking back from the vantage point of thirty years of hip-hop and rap, it makes as much sense to see the Beatles as signaling the end of a musical era as the beginning of one. Like the musicians before them, they had started out as a live band, playing covers of other people's songs for audiences of young dancers, and on their early records they simply went into the studio and performed the selections the same way they would do them onstage, as most bands had done since the 'teens. That was already a fairly old-fashioned approach in pop music terms, and by *Rubber Soul* and *Revolver* they were thinking like record makers rather than live performers, but they never lost their attachment to and affection for that past.

Indeed, one could see the early Beatles as a summation of all the trends of the previous few years wrapped in a particularly attractive package. "I Want to Hold Your Hand," their first hit in the United States, had the hand-claps of the girl groups, the melodic sophistication of the best Brill Building compositions, a rhythm perfectly suited to the new dances, and the loose energy of the surf bands—one reviewer tagged it "Surf on the Thames."[4] The fanzines quickly adopted the "fab four" as ideal boyfriends, with the advantage that readers didn't have to choose between buying records by Elvis, Ricky, Frankie, or one of

3. David Sheff, *All We Are Saying: The Last Major Interview with John Lennon and Yoko Ono* (New York: St. Martin's Griffin, 2000), 93.
4. Michael Bryan Kelly, *The Beatle Myth: The British Invasion of American Popular Music, 1959–1969* (Jefferson, NC: McFarland, 1991), 22.

the various Bobbys, because all tastes could be accommodated in one group. As Roy Orbison noted, "It's not completely a sexy thing either. Guys are interested, too. They might get a chance to chat with Ringo."⁵ Older fans recognized a sophistication that the previous teen idols had lacked—not so much in the music, in those first months, but in the cool, absurdist intelligence of the press conferences and soon in the anarchic *nouvelle vague* artiness of *A Hard Day's Night*.

It all happened very fast: Beatlemania arrived before the Beatles did, primed by reports of mobs chasing them around England and the coup of getting booked for three appearances on the *Ed Sullivan Show* before having their first American hit—a happy accident, sparked by Sullivan's being delayed on a London airport runway by hordes of Beatle fans. When they made their U.S. debut in February 1964 the *New York Times* noted that they had "simply followed their fame across the Atlantic."⁶ Capitol Records had initially passed on its option to release the group's recordings, allowing several other American labels to get early Beatles singles, but it now provided a barrage of publicity, and the fact that there were competing singles on five different labels meant that the radio was deluged with Beatles material. To the surprise of almost everyone, the band's talent lived up to this craziness, though at live shows that was more a matter of infectious energy than musical skill, as the screaming girls rendered them all but inaudible.

The startling thing was how quickly the Beatles transcended that initial image. It took Sinatra more than a dozen years to get over being typed as the bobby-soxers' dreamboat, but the Beatles managed the same feat almost instantaneously. It helped that they were British. Even if their remarks had been less witty, their accents would have made them seem smart and cosmopolitan to American ears, and they arrived at a particularly anglophilic moment. A year earlier, the *New York Times* had announced a "British invasion" of Broadway,⁷ and their fellow acts on that first *Ed Sullivan* appearance included the British stars of *The*

---

5. Roy Orbison, "Roy Orbison's Own Rock History, Part 2," *Hit Parader*, Jan. 1968, 64.
6. McCandlish Phillips, "Publicitywise," *New York Times*, 17 Feb. 1964, 20.
7. Howard Taubman, "British a Fixture along Broadway," *New York Times*, 14 Feb. 1963, 5.

Girl Who Came to Supper and *Oliver!* (including future Monkee Davy Jones). It was also a moment when Americans desperately needed a dash of escapism: President Kennedy had been assassinated two months earlier, and though it is simplistic to talk of a "national mood," it is easy to understand how a bevy of cheery Brits contrasted with the way a lot of Americans were feeling.[8]

The mix of jangling guitars with jet-set sophistication fit neatly into the romance between rock 'n' roll and high society that had started with the twist, and the British Invasion overlapped the discothèque craze, which likewise was marketed as rock 'n' roll *à l'européen*. In May of 1964, *Life* magazine opened its feature on discothèques with a photo of young dancers at New Jimmy's in Paris doing the saint (it involved throwing your arms in the air as if at a revival meeting), followed by a shot of the club's owner, Regine, doing the surf with Omar Sharif, then "lively young aristocrats" in London doing the woodpecker. By page three the magazine was in Los Angeles, but the featured club was named for a Paris disco, the Whisky à Go-Go, and by 1965 there were Whisky (or Whiskey) à Go-Gos in Milwaukee, Chicago, Washington, San Francisco, and Atlanta, as well as a Frisky à Go-Go in San Antonio, a Champagne à Go-Go in Madison, Wisconsin, and so on.[9] As the liner notes to Arthur Murray's *Discothèque Dance Party* put it:

> Who but the frugal French would have hit on the idea that the fanciest dance joints don't really need a band. Play records instead. Gives you a wider choice of musical styles. Besides, a small place with just a phonograph is a lot more *intime* than a ballroom. So the most fashionable dancing places in Paris these days are Discothèques—tiny little spots with just a record player and lots of atmosphere.[10]

8. Lester Bangs stressed this point in "The British Invasion" in Jim Miller, *Rolling Stone Illustrated History* (New York: Rolling Stone Press; Random House, 1976), 164.
9. "Discothèque Dancing," *Life*, 22 May 1964, 97-99; "The Sound of the Sixties," *Time*, 21 May 1965, http://www.time.com/time/magazine/article/0,9171,901728,00.html (accessed 6 June 2008).
10. Francis Traun, *Arthur Murray Presents Discothèque Dance Party*, RCA LP-2998, 1964, LP notes.

Both discothèques and guitar-based groups on the Beatles model succeeded in a large part for economic reasons. They were far cheaper than
live music and larger bands, and earlier equivalents had been making
inroads on the music scene for twenty years. But the appeal of London
and Paris was quite different from the appeal of an R&B or rockabilly
combo, a soda fountain jukebox or a deejayed sock hop, and the effort
to associate discothèques with Continental chic was sometimes taken
to ridiculous lengths. The producers of *Hullabaloo*, a prime-time network TV show that appeared early in 1965, claimed in their *Discothèque
Dance Book* that "All the Discothèque Dances are imported, mostly
from Europe," though its only steps with even faintly foreign roots
were the bossa nova and the ska, and the rest were rehashes of old
Bandstand favorites.[11]

One obvious effect of this European glamour was to separate rock 'n'
roll from its associations with juvenile delinquency and, more endur-
ingly, with black Americans. Another was to smooth the path to its
acceptance as art. In the long run, the discothèque craze did not much
influence either of those trends: Record-propelled dance clubs were
relatively cheap to run, so they quickly lost their aristocratic, European associations, and black recording artists by and large held onto
the dance-floor primacy they had won during the twist era. As for art,
it seems to be a given that any music intended primarily for dancing is,
ipso facto, not accepted as serious art.

By contrast, classical music—even mediocre classical music—is the
quintessence of seriousness for most pop listeners, and by the fall of
1965 the number one song in the United States was "Yesterday," featuring Paul McCartney accompanied by a string quartet. Like Whiteman's
first "jazz classique" discs, this did not excite the interest of many highbrow critics, but it was immediately greeted with enthusiasm by older
pop musicians and Tin Pan Alley tunesmiths. The Beatles themselves
had some ambivalence about this—McCartney recalled, "we didn't
release 'Yesterday' as a single in England at all, because we were a lit-

11. *Hullabaloo Discothèque Dance Book*, (New York: Parallax, 1966) 7.

tle embarrassed about it; we were a rock 'n' roll band."[12] But with its romantically world-weary lyric, soothing melody, and mild variation of the conventional thirty-two-bar song structure, it was accepted as an olive branch across the generation gap.[13] The song was quickly covered by every old-line orchestra leader and vocalist who dreamed of being more than a nostalgia act, and by August 1966 *Billboard* proclaimed it a modern standard, noting that there were already over 175 versions on the market, including recordings by Lawrence Welk, Xavier Cugat, and Mantovani, as well as by country singers, cabaret artists, and the Supremes. The only comparably covered recent compositions were "The Girl from Ipanema," popularized by Stan Getz and Astrud Gilberto, and "A Taste of Honey," which had its greatest success in a pseudo-mariachi version by Herb Alpert.[14] The Beatles, as it happens, had recorded "A Taste of Honey" on their first album, an apt reminder that from the beginning they showed a breadth of taste that would allow them to capture not only young rock 'n' rollers but also the sort of listeners who enjoyed the perky trumpets of the Tijuana Brass and the gentle lilt of bossa nova.[15]

That breadth of appeal was what set the Beatles apart from their contemporaries. They got the teenage girls, the rock 'n' rollers, the easy listening fans, and a good part of the folk audience, and they soon were making inroads with devotees of jazz and classical music. It took a while, but as they followed the string quartet of "Yesterday" with the string octet of "Eleanor Rigby," the brass, strings, and woodwinds of "Strawberry Fields" and "Penny Lane," and finally *Sgt. Pepper*, they found themselves hailed as kindred spirits by the likes of Leonard Bernstein

12. The Beatles, *The Beatles Anthology* (San Francisco: Chronicle Books, 2000), 175.
13. Rather than three eight-bar A sections and an eight-bar bridge—the standard Tin Pan Alley form—"Yesterday" has three seven-bar A sections and an eight-bar bridge, for a total of twenty-nine bars.
14. Hank Fox, "An Age-Old Rule Broken as New Tunes Become Instant Standards," *Billboard*, 13 Aug. 1966, 3, 14.
15. The Beatles recorded "A Taste of Honey" in 1963, two years before Alpert did. The song was inspired by a play about British working-class life that had been made into a 1961 movie starring the young Liverpudlian Rita Tushingham (though the song was not included in the film), and first hit in 1962 in an instrumental version by Martin Denny.

(who compared them to Schumann) and the avant-garde composer and diarist Ned Rorem (who threw in Chopin, Monteverdi, and Poulenc).[16] And that conquest had a value far beyond the classical market, because it made all the other listeners feel as if they were joining the cultural elite. The only major audiences the Beatles lost as they became more serious were the little sisters of their first fans, who had loved them as cuddly mop-tops and transferred this affection to the Monkees, and the dancers. (There were also some hard-core rock 'n' rollers who sheared off in favor of the Rolling Stones, but though they grumbled about pretentiousness and slack rhythms, they still bought *Rubber Soul*, *Revolver*, and *Sgt. Pepper.*) From 1964 through 1970 the Beatles had fourteen number-one albums, and unlike Sinatra's run in the 1950s, those albums were outselling most hit singles. No other group or artist even came close, and not since Whiteman in the 1920s had any band so completely overshadowed an era's popular mainstream.

In the mid-1950s Whiteman had prophesied that rock 'n' roll would go through the same evolution as jazz, saying "they'll get tired of that one- or two-guitar sound, and eventually they'll add fiddles and saxes and brass, like we did when we started the big-band business."[17] In the Beatles' case, the connection was relatively direct: McCartney traced his love of old-fashioned pop melodies to hearing his father play Whiteman's music on the piano, and George Martin, the group's producer and arranger, was an admirer of Gershwin and Ferde Grofé and saw his work with the band as an extension of that tradition.[18] Even the British cachet had been part of Whiteman's story: "I had seen, as everybody must see, the American adoration for the European," he

16. "The Messengers," *Time*, 22 Sept. 1967, http://www.time.com/time/magazine/article/0,9171,837319,00.html; Ned Rorem, "The Music of the Beatles," *New York Reiew of Books*, 18 Jan. 1968, http://www.nybooks.com/articles/11829.

17. Thomas A. DeLong, *Pops: Paul Whiteman, King of Jazz* (Piscataway, NJ: New Century, 1983), 307.

18. McCartney recalled "lovely childhood memories of . . . listening to my dad play . . . music from the Paul Whiteman era (Paul Whiteman was one of his favourites)"; Beatles, *Beatles Anthology*, 18. Martin wrote, "The Beatles couldn't have existed without the Gershwins"; Ron Cowen, "George Gershwin: He Got Rhythm," http://www.washingtonpost.com/wp-srv/national/horizon/nov98/gershwin.htm.

recalled, so he took his orchestra to London in 1923 and began work on the Aeolian Hall concert only after returning with the English nobility's seal of approval, "as if we'd been distinguished foreigners."[19]

There were also striking similarities in the ways the two groups were treated by their eras' respective critics. The reception was not universally laudatory in either case, with plenty of classical gatekeepers moaning about lowered standards and some purist rock 'n' roll fans echoing the complaints of Roger Pryor Dodge that the music they loved was being emasculated by middlebrow pretension. To the English writer Nik Cohn, the evolutions from *Rubber Soul* through *Sgt. Pepper* each represented "a big step forward in ingenuity, and . . . a big step back in guts," and he accused the Beatles of becoming "updated George Gershwins . . . the posh Sundays called them Art, as Gershwin was once called Art for *Rhapsody in Blue* . . . but what, by definition, is so great about Art?"[20]

In general, though, there was agreement that for better or worse Whiteman and the Beatles represented the future of their respective styles and a previously unrealized rapprochement between high and low culture. Carl Belz, whose groundbreaking *Story of Rock* opened with the declaration that it would "consider the music *as* art and *in terms* of art,"[21] even provided a parallel to George Seldes's statement contrasting the general superiority of black bands with the specific superiority of Whiteman: "Negro Rhythm and Blues has possessed a consistency which is not present in the white music of the 1960s," Belz wrote in 1969. "And a listener hears a higher percentage of *good* records on the soul stations than on white or integrated programs, although he does not hear anything as artistically advanced as the Beatles."[22]

I want to take a moment to place those statements in the context

19. Paul Whiteman and Margaret McBride, *Jazz* (New York: J. H. Sears and Company, 1926), 70, 84.
20. Nik Cohn, *Rock: From the Beginning* (New York: Stein and Day, 1969), 157; Nik Cohn, *Awopbopaloobop Alopbamboom: The Golden Age of Rock* (New York: Grove Press, 1996), 144-145. (The latter is a revision of the former, which had compared the Beatles to Cole Porter rather than to Gershwin.)
21. Carl Belz, *Story of Rock* (New York: Oxford University Press, 1969), ix.
22. Ibid., 188.

of their times, because the civil rights movement and rock 'n' roll had dramatically changed the status of black music in white America. So it is a profound irony that the attempt to make highbrow art out of jazz in the 1920s (which put white artists at the forefront of the movement) is generally recalled by historians as an embarrassing wrong turn, whereas the attempt to make highbrow art out of rock 'n' roll in the 1960s (again putting white artists in the forefront of the movement) is generally viewed as a step forward for the genre, which has been led by white artists ever since.

For one thing, the idea of art itself had changed. In the 1920s, jazz was widely compared to Picasso's cubism and the abstractions of Piet Mondrian—that is, popular dance music was being equated with the personal creations of academically trained high modernists. In the 1960s, rock was compared to Roy Lichtenstein's comic book paintings and Andy Warhol's Brillo boxes—that is, "pop art," a name that denied any primacy to individual creation over the mass products of the marketplace and allied the visual arts with what was happening on radios and television screens. And that difference signaled not only shifting fashions but also a shifting balance of power. The combination of technologies of mass reproduction and dissemination—movies, phonographs, radio, television, glossy color printing—with a new degree of economic and educational equality and the intellectual and moral weight of democratic, socialist, and communist ideals had made "popular culture" a potent force in the academic and critical mainstream. In Whiteman's day, almost everyone took it for granted that popular music gained something by being compared to high modern art, but by the 1960s a lot of people were dismissing high art as elitist and irrelevant. As Bob Dylan put it, "Museums are cemeteries. Paintings should be on the walls of restaurants, in dime stores, in gas stations, in men's rooms. . . . Music is the only thing that's in tune with what's happening . . . . All this art they've been talking about is nonexistent."[23] Linking pop art to pop music did more for the painters than it did for the musicians, many of whom—Lennon, Pete Townshend, Eric Clap-

23. Nora Ephron and Susan Edmiston, "Bob Dylan Interview," in Jonathan Eisen, ed., *Age of Rock* 2 (New York: Vintage Books, 1970), 71.

ton, Jimmy Page, and Keith Richards among them—had, as it happens, attended art school.

At the other extreme, some critics in the 1920s had hailed jazz as a modern folk music, but in those days that was another way of saying that it was raw material for high art, bearing the same relationship to the *Rhapsody in Blue* that an African mask bore to Picasso's *Demoiselles d'Avignon*. By the mid-1960s, folk music was overtaking classical music as the favored listening for serious young intellectuals, so when rock 'n' roll was described as a folk style (by Belz, among others), that was a claim of roots and authenticity, not an invitation to transform it into something more elevated. As it happened, the Beatles made their New York concert debut at Carnegie Hall, but they emphasized their lack of respect for the venue by opening with "Roll Over, Beethoven." And when they wanted to have their music taken more seriously, they did not attempt to get more bookings in classical concert halls—which, in any case, were by then far too small for them—they just made it more varied and complex, and less dance-oriented.[24] By *Rubber Soul* (their ninth American LP in less than two years[25]) they had added elements of French *chanson* and North Indian sitar, along with a potent dose of American folk and country, and by *Revolver* they were experimenting with tape loops and electronic noise, and McCartney was citing the influence of Karlheinz Stockhausen. (In hindsight, George Harrison would jokingly refer to this as their "'avant garde a clue' music."[26]) With *Sgt. Pepper* they imposed a new aesthetic by refusing to release a single, forcing fans to view the mélange of musical styles from ragtime to raga as a long-form sonic equivalent of the photographic collage on the album's cover.

In terms of their own creations, the Beatles' work was both more daring and more enduring than what Whiteman's crew produced, but that was in part because they had a freedom that would have been

24. Jonathan Gould, *Can't Buy Me Love: The Beatles, Britain, and America* (New York: Harmony Books, 2007), 6.
25. *Rubber Soul* was released in December 1965. I'm leaving out two documentary LPs and counting VeeJay's *Introducing the Beatles* and Capitol's *The Early Beatles* as one LP, because they have roughly the same songs.
26. Beatles, *Beatles Anthology*, 210.

unimaginable in earlier eras: The fact that they could retire from performing and make their whole artistic statement on records meant
that they could ignore the day-to-day concert and dance business. The
later Beatles records were not a take-home equivalent or even a studio-
enhanced improvement of live performances. They were, after 1966,
the entirety of the group's musical oeuvre: fully conceived, finished
objects in the same way that a book or a painting is a fully conceived,
finished object. There was a precedent of sorts in previous studio pop
productions, but although Brian Wilson and his critical soulmates
hailed Phil Spector's "Be My Baby" as a three-minute pop symphony,
most fans heard it as a girl-group hit, dancing to it and enjoying it
not as a unique work of genius but as part of the commercial collage
of Top 40 radio. The later Beatles LPs, by contrast, were treated as
musical novels, designed for individual contemplation in their entirety.
Although the band continued to release singles that got plenty of radio
play, both they and their fans thought of their primary work as a series
of albums, and that became the defining form for any band that hoped
for its work to be viewed as art rather than disposable commercial pop.
It was the age of Marshall McLuhan, and the medium was the message:
Musicians who had big ideas made big records.

In retrospect, the critic Robert Hilburn expressed a widespread
verdict when he wrote, "Bob Dylan and the Beatles had turned the
primitive energy of teen-oriented '50s rock into an art form that could
express adult themes and emotions."[27] Looked at another way, the Beatles had joined Dylan in a format that had never been associated with
either teen or rock energy. Since the mid-1950s, folk, classical, and jazz
musicians had been known for albums rather than singles, and pop
performers from Ray Charles to Connie Francis had turned to the LP
form when they wanted to record adult material. In the past, though,
it had been taken for granted that Charles's and Francis's albums of
jazz, country, and Tin Pan Alley standards were aimed at different audiences than the teens who danced to their singles. The Beatles, by con-

27. Robert Hilburn, "A Backstage Pass to Intimate Moments in Rock's Odyssey," *Los
Angeles Times*, 22 July 2006, 1.

trast, were seen as expanding their genre rather than stepping outside it, and *Sgt. Pepper* as a maturation of their youthful style rather than as an extension of the adult pop they had dabbled in with "A Taste of Honey" and "Till There Was You."

Which is to say that, as usual, the genre labels had more to do with the audience than with the music. Though the Beatles' fan base had changed (screaming teenyboppers ceased to be their core constituency even before the lads grew beards and moustaches) and though they now were hiring symphony musicians as a backing band, the older teens and twenty-somethings who put them at the forefront of a musical movement that included Dylan, the Byrds, the Rolling Stones, the San Francisco psychedelic groups, and soon such phenomenal album-sellers as Simon and Garfunkel and Crosby, Stills, and Nash did not choose to think of themselves or their musical heroes as abandoning youth styles. By the later 1960s, there had clearly been a major change in orientation, and some people were beginning to make a semantic distinction between rock 'n' roll (the earlier, teen-oriented music) and rock (its myriad post-Beatles offshoots). But even the most intellectual rock fans held fast to the notion that the music they now loved was an evolution of the style pioneered by Chuck Berry, Little Richard, and the Coasters rather than an adult style for which they had forsaken the heroes of their adolescence.

It was true that the Beatles and their peers continued to play a lot of music that had links to early rock 'n' roll and, with the exception of a few songs, their work was very different from what was being played and sung by older pop performers. There was a cultural revolution going on, and though in retrospect one can argue that a lot of the changes were more a matter of fashion than of substance, they were grounded in solid and harsh realities. First among these was the Vietnam War, and more particularly the military draft, which threatened a generation of young men with being shipped off to die for a cause that to many of them seemed at best pointless and at worst evil. From early childhood that generation had been threatened with nuclear annihilation, wondering if their world would explode before they had a chance to experience it, and their elders had done little to assuage their fears.

So as they reached their twenties, they did not see the obvious paths to security that their parents had followed after World War II. Add to that the contraceptive pill, which meant that sex did not have to lead to babies and thence families. And stir into the mix a new range of drugs, which offered a more interesting escape from those fears than alcohol did, but also could land you in jail. There has been a lot of sneering in later years about '60s-era, antiestablishment hippies settling down to traditional families and careers, but the reality is that during that time a lot of them doubted they would make it to age thirty—and when they did, the world naturally looked different.

Rock also set itself apart from other teen and adult styles by creating new radio, print, and concert scenes. Since the mid-1950s, commercial radio stations had been experimenting with variations of the Top 40 format, in which the same few hits were played over and over, and the payola scandal pushed more broadcasters to take musical choice out of the hands of deejays in favor of restricted committee- and chart-determined playlists. This meant that chart positions ceased to be just measures of popularity and became self-fulfilling prophecies: On Top 40 stations, the top-charting records were pretty much all that were played, day in and day out. (Repetitive as this was, it was a far cry from the genre-specific commercial format of later years, as a typical Top 40 playlist would mingle the Beatles and Herman's Hermits with Motown, Frank and Nancy Sinatra, Herb Alpert, and Dionne Warwick.) By the later 1960s, though, FM stations in many cities were letting young deejays program free-form mixes that included album cuts and leaned heavily to the new rock styles. Meanwhile, a new kind of music magazine was appearing, first *Crawdaddy* in January 1966, then *Rolling Stone* in November 1967 and a host of short- and occasionally longer-lived competitors, which focused on rock not simply as music but as the voice of a generation. And in San Francisco a new kind of concert scene emerged, bringing the bohemian attitude of college-town coffeehouses to huge, free outdoor performances and ballroom gatherings that mixed the music with light shows, hallucinogenic drugs, and a spirit of community that captured the imaginations of young people across the country.

It is easy, and was easy even then, to regard 1967's "summer of love" with cynicism, and all the critiques have elements of truth to them. But so did the romantic myths, and it was natural to counter the nightmare of planetary destruction with the utopian dream of building a new world in the shell of the old. Nor was it all airy dreaming. San Francisco was full of young people who just wanted to "turn on, tune in, and drop out," but there were also plenty of young activists who had traveled to Mississippi to register voters, who would travel to Chicago to protest at the Democratic convention, and who were working with the Black Panthers or the United Farm Workers—and both hippies and activists were growing their hair, smoking dope, and listening to rock bands.

In terms of the broad history of popular music, though, something odd was happening. As rock was vested with more and more importance, both as an art form and as the voice of a young counterculture, its acolytes began to be bothered by the blatantly commercial, dance-hit mentality that had been taken for granted in the music's early days. And, with increasing frequency, that meant that rock was being separated from black music. Or, more accurately, from recent black styles, since blues bands, white and black, were a bigger part of the rock scene than ever before. Indeed, in an odd twist, many writers have described the British Invasion as a discovery of black music, applauding the Beatles, Stones, and Animals for introducing European Americans to African-American masters from Muddy Waters and Howlin' Wolf to Bo Diddley and Chuck Berry. The British stars certainly distinguished themselves from previous rockers by focusing attention on their early idols, and gave a vital boost to some important and deserving artists, but this was part of a larger process in which black music was being recast as the roots of rock 'n' roll rather than as part of its evolving present. Venues like the Fillmore West booked Waters, John Lee Hooker, and B. B. King, along with the racially mixed Butterfield Blues Band and a new generation of white blues-rockers that included Janis Joplin, the Blues Project, and Canned Heat, and at times they added gospel-infused soul singers like Otis Redding and Aretha Franklin to that mix. But it was in much the same spirit that the 1965 Newport Folk Festival—at which

Dylan famously went electric—presented Butterfield, Wolf, and Berry alongside acoustic elders like Mississippi John Hurt, Son House, and the Reverend Gary Davis.

Until the mid-1960s, white and black rock 'n' roll styles had evolved more or less in tandem, whether it was Little Richard and Jerry Lee Lewis, the Drifters and the Belmonts, Hank Ballard and Joey Dee, Ray Charles and Bobby Darin, or the Crystals and the Shangri-Las. The black artists may have pioneered more new styles than the white ones, and their share of the rewards was frequently incommensurate with their talents, but they were competing for the same radio and record audiences and appearing in a lot of the same clubs, concert packages, and TV showcases. The pop music world had been becoming less segregated with every passing year, and by 1964 *Billboard* stopped publishing separate pop and R&B charts, apparently deeming the division both politically and musically untenable. The big success stories on the rock 'n' roll scene that year were the British Invasion and Motown, and the Beatles and Berry Gordy both took pains to emphasize that, in Gordy's words, "They're creating the same type of music as we are and we're part of the same stream."[28] As a friend of mine who was then a Midwestern teenager recalls, "we all dreamed of being a Supreme and of dating a Beatle."

That blend of musical and racial integration had defined rock 'n' roll since Alan Freed's time, but the stream divided with the arrival of "folk rock" (or "rock folk," as it was often called at first), which stressed poetic or socially conscious lyrics over dance rhythms, and the sonic explorations of the Beatles, the Byrds, the Beach Boys, and the San Francisco groups. To an audience caught up in these developments, contemporary black artists seemed to be lagging behind, still focusing on dance beats and AM hits. As *Crawdaddy*'s founder, Paul Williams, wrote in a review of a new Temptations LP, "One of the curious things

28. Gerri Hirshey, *Nowhere to Run: The Story of Soul Music* (London: Southbank, 2006), 185. In Paul McCartney's words, "For us, Motown artists were taking the place of [Little] Richard. We loved the black artists so much; and it was the greatest accolade to have somebody with one of those *real* voices, as we saw it, sing our own songs (we'd certainly been doing theirs)"; Beatles, *Beatles Anthology*, 198.

about the year 1966 is that for the first time in the history of America, the best contemporary music is not being made by the American Negro."[29]

It was inescapably true that black performers, by and large, were thinking in different terms from the new rock groups. When Michael Lydon interviewed Smokey Robinson for *Rolling Stone* in 1968, Robinson made no bones about Motown editing his records to fit Top-40 programming strictures. Of one recent hit, "I Second That Emotion," he said:

> It was 3:15 when it was done and Berry—who has an ingenious sense of knowing hit records, it's uncanny—he heard it, he told us, 'It's a great tune, but it's too long, so I want you to cut that other verse down and come right out of the solo and go back into the chorus and on out.' So we did and the record was a smash. . . . The shorter a record is these days, the more it's gonna be played, you dig? If you have a record that's 2:15 long it's definitely gonna get more play than one that's 3:15, *at first*, which is *very* important.

That logic would have made perfect sense to the Beatles circa 1964, but by 1968 it was not at all the *Rolling Stone* aesthetic, and Lydon responded by suggesting that Robinson "was not aware that for many people in rock and roll, the Top-40 has become an irrelevant concern." Robinson wasn't buying it, though: "Everybody who approaches this, approaches it with the idea of being in the Top Ten," he insisted, "because . . . let's face it, this is the record *industry*, one of the biggest industries going nowadays."[30]

The idea that music should be treated as an industry was exactly what the new rock fans rejected. Gordy had patterned Motown's production process on the Ford assembly line, and when he wasn't stamping out hits, he was putting his artists through intensive training in dance

---

29. Paul Williams, "Getting Ready: The Temptations," *Crawdaddy* 5 (Sept. 1966), 29.
30. Michael Lydon, "Smokey Robinson," *Rolling Stone*, 28 Sept. 1968, 21.

and deportment and planning the conquest of the Copacabana and Las Vegas. Both his methods and his aspirations exemplified everything that the counterculture despised—but he and his artists were coming from a very different place. They were not convinced by the Beatles' assurances that all they needed was love and everything would be all right if they could free their minds.[31] As a member of the Fifth Dimension, a pop-oriented black group from Los Angeles that ran up a string of hits in the late 1960s, told an interviewer:

> When you start talking about the fact that the black man is still hung up with status symbols, man, don't forget that he's trying to grab on to exactly the things that the white kids are trying to give up. Drop out? Wow, man, what we got to drop out of, anyway? You don't want your fancy house or your good job? Shit, let me have it, man, 'cause I've been trying to get something like that all my miserable life.[32]

Beyond that cultural disconnect, and despite all the changes in the music scene, Robinson was right that top ten hits continued to drive record sales. Even Dylan, the prototypical modern album artist, got very different sales when one of his LPs spawned a hit single. Clive Davis, the head of Columbia Records' pop division during the late 1960s, recalled, "*John Wesley Harding* sold 500,000 albums without a single; but *Nashville Skyline*, with 'Lay Lady Lay's AM-radio help, sold 1.2 million."[33] For Dylan's fans, of course, that was irrelevant. His enduring victory is not that he sold a lot of records but that he forever changed popular songwriting, and everyone from the Beatles and

31. John Lennon and Paul McCartney, "All You Need Is Love," 1967, and "Revolution," 1968. The latter song was a flashpoint of contention from the moment it appeared. As Ellen Willis wrote, "It takes a lot of chutzpah for a millionaire to assure the rest of us, 'You know it's gonna be alright.' And Lennon's 'Change your head' line is just an up-to-date version of 'Let them eat cake'; anyone in a position to follow such advice doesn't need it." Ellen Willis, "Records: Rock, Etc.: The Big Ones," *New Yorker*, 1 Feb. 1969, 61.
32. J. Marks, *Rock and Other Four-Letter Words* (New York: Bantam Books, 1968), 19. The group member is not specified.
33. Clive Davis, *Clive: Inside the Record Business* (New York: Morrow, 1975), 63.

Stones to Marvin Gaye, Stevie Wonder, and the Brill Building pros rethought their styles in response to his work.

But it was no accident that most of the early Dylan hits were for other singers—Peter, Paul, and Mary, the Byrds, and Johnny Cash all charted with his compositions before he did, and they were soon joined by the Turtles and Cher. His nasal voice and aggressively unpolished instrumental backings won him a uniquely devoted following but also turned a lot of listeners off. And that polarization meant not only that his record sales were incommensurate with his influence but that they were even lower than the charts suggest: "His cult besieged record stores when a new album arrived," Davis recalled. "The charts always reflect a concentrated buying spree, so any new Dylan album immediately zoomed to the top. Ray Conniff [an easy-listening arranger], by contrast, might have sold three times as many albums over a longer period of time, but nobody was rushing into the stores to buy him, so his chart action was relatively minimal."[34] A good example of this pattern is Dylan's 1967 *Greatest Hits* package, which charted lower than his previous few records because his fans didn't need it, but was his first million-selling LP because it sold to the larger, less fervent audience (my father, for example) that had become aware that he was important and wanted a representative sample of his work.

As for *Nashville Skyline*, although its hit single undoubtedly helped, it was also a very different sort of album from Dylan's previous work, and its broader acceptance is a reminder that in some ways the world had not changed all that much since the days of Mitch Miller. As at the end of the swing era, the shift away from dance music led to a partial rapprochement between urban pop and country and western. So in 1969 Bobbie Gentry and Jeannie C. Riley had country ballads on top of the pop charts, and Dylan's disc featured Nashville studio backing and a guest appearance and liner notes by Johnny Cash. New Yorkers and San Franciscans associated folk music with leftist politics, but a lot of people between the coasts had welcomed the Weavers, the Kingston Trio, and Peter, Paul, and Mary as wholesome alternatives to jazz or rock 'n'

34. Ibid., 53.

roll, and shifting technologies extended country music's popularity to a broader audience than ever before. In Miller's day, pop singers reliably outsold country artists when they did the same songs, but in 1969, thanks to the success of his weekly TV program and live recordings at Folsom and San Quentin prisons, Cash sold 6.5 million albums, more than any previous solo performer in any genre.[35]

The youth market was huge, and rock was getting most of the headlines, but there were still plenty of older and more conservative listeners, and, as in the past, the biggest-selling artists were those who appealed across the widest range of generational and cultural boundaries. The Rolling Stones were rock's most celebrated live band, and within that world were often placed on a level near or equal to the Beatles, but they didn't sell as well as the mellower folk-rock stars whose songs were played not only on FM rock and Top 40 radio but also on middle-of-the-road (MOR) stations. In a 1972 *Rolling Stone* interview, Paul Simon expressed disappointment that his first solo album had sold only 850,000 units, and when the interviewer pointed out that this was more than any Stones LP except *Sticky Fingers*, Simon's response was "Yeah, but, permit me my arrogance. . . . I always was aware that S&G was a much bigger phenomenon in general, to the general public, than the Rolling Stones."[36] Indeed, with the exception of their acoustic debut, all the Simon and Garfunkel LPs had sold at least two million units, and a couple were already over three million, because they appealed not only to rock fans but also to fans of Cash, Joan Baez, and Barbra Streisand.

Those were incredible numbers, and the rewards that Simon and the Beatles were reaping not only for themselves but also for their record and publishing companies were changing the music business. There had been popular performer-songwriters before, from Duke Ellington and Johnny Mercer to Chuck Berry and Paul Anka, but they had always been a minority, and in any case the money one earned from writ-

35. Ibid., 134.
36. Ben Fong-Torres, ed., *The Rolling Stone Interviews, Vol. 2* (New York: Warner Paperback Library, 1973), 429.

ing and recording even a million-selling single was peanuts compared with what one got for writing and recording every song on a string of million-selling albums. The combination of prestige and wealth was irresistible, and by the later 1960s it was taken for granted that any serious rock group would create its own material.

What is more, although Lennon and McCartney had started out as fairly traditional songwriters, their later albums were not just written but produced and directed with a degree of effort and thought that had previously been reserved for filmmaking—in George Martin's words, they were "making little movies in sound."[37] After they devoted a fabled 700 hours to recording *Sgt. Pepper* and it was acclaimed a masterpiece, studio experimentation became the order of the day even for a lot of unproven groups, and bands and songwriters came to see themselves less as musicians than as sonic auteurs.[38] Records seemed to emerge from the inspired mind of a single artist or small groups of artists in a communal process, and Judy Collins expressed a widespread belief when she imagined a future in which "we will have pop song cycles like classical *Lieder*, but we will create our own words, music, and orchestrations, because we are a generation of whole people."[39]

Some of the top African-American singers were also writing their own material, and a few were arranging and producing their own records. James Brown had taken full control of his work in the early 1960s, and his *Live at the Apollo* LP, which made it to number two on the *Billboard* album chart in 1963, had proved that his talents were not limited to dance beats and hit singles. But no one was comparing his music—or Robinson's, or Aretha Franklin's—to classical *Lieder*, and white listeners and critics, if they knew him at all, celebrated him as a gritty shouter and phenomenal showman, not as a sonic auteur.

It was not that white rock fans necessarily were unaware of the inno-

---

37. George Martin, *With a Little Help from My Friends: The Making of Sgt. Pepper* (Boston: Little, Brown, 1994), 139.
38. Jonathan Gould, *Can't Buy Me Love: The Beatles, Britain, and America* (New York: Harmony Books, 2007), 387, reports that in fact the *Sgt. Pepper* sessions took roughly half the reported 700-hour figure, but the legend persists.
39. Marks, J., *Rock and Other Four Letter Words*, (New York: Bantam Books, 1968) 15.

vations in recent African-American styles or disrespected the current black stars. But as Robert Christgau noted in his review of the Monterey Pop Festival, by 1967 the relationship was very different from what it had been just three or four years earlier:

> White rock performers seem uncomfortable with contemporary black music. Most of them like the best of it or think they do, but they don't want to imitate it, especially since they know how pallid their imitation is likely to be. So they hone their lyrics and develop their instrumental chops and experiment with their equipment and come to regard artists like Martha & the Vandellas, say, as some wondrous breed of porpoise, very talented, but somehow . . . different. And their audience concurs.[40]

By that time, there was also a new genre name to express that difference. In January 1965, recognizing that the British Invasion and folk-rock trends had reopened the gap between white and black styles, *Billboard* had reinstituted its R&B chart, but there were obvious problems with maintaining the old rubric of segregation. So by 1967 the magazine was running an annual *World of Soul* section, and in 1969 the black music chart was renamed "Best-Selling Soul Singles." What "soul" meant was a bit vague: The first *World of Soul* was largely devoted to older blues styles, including articles on 78-rpm record collecting, on John Hammond's role as a blues promoter, and on Billie Holiday; and just as with R&B there was always some question of whether it was a musical or simply a racial designation. But at least it acknowledged that black artists were playing a modern style—indeed, the name change was accompanied by the claim that soul was "the most meaningful development in the broad mass music market within the last decade"— while at the same time separating that style from rock.[41]

40. Robert Christgau, "Anatomy of a Love Festival," *Esquire*, Jan. 1968, in Robert Christgau, *Any Old Way You Choose It: Rock and Other Pop Music, 1967–1973* (Baltimore: Penguin Books, 1973), 17.
41. "R&B Now Soul," *Billboard*, 23 Aug. 1969, 3; *Billboard World of Soul*, 24 June 1967.

There were genuine musical differences between the styles favored by white and black groups in the later 1960s, but the problem, as always, was that the categories were neither distinct nor homogeneous. In the continuum of singers, Janis Joplin was a lot closer to Tina Turner and James Brown than she was to Grace Slick or Mick Jagger, so the choice to regard her as a rocker rather than a porpoise was not made on musical grounds. Nor was it true that white players couldn't master the new soul sounds: The records that Otis Redding, Aretha Franklin, and Wilson Pickett cut at Stax and Muscle Shoals were considered even funkier than what was coming out of Motown, and the Stax house band was racially mixed, while the Muscle Shoals musicians were all white. If the spectrum of pop now ranged from James Brown to Simon and Garfunkel rather than from Count Basie to Guy Lombardo, there was still a lot of middle ground, and Booker T and the MGs could potentially have been a unifying force on the order of the Benny Goodman Quartet—indeed, Otis Redding and the MGs' Steve Cropper created a perfect fusion of the folk-rock and soul sensibilities with their acoustic-guitar-backed "Dock of the Bay."

But if the victories of the civil rights movement were dismantling de jure segregation, the de facto segregation of American culture was in some ways growing stronger. On the black side, there were radical voices calling for racial separatism and many more promoting self-determination and a fairer share of power—in 1969, only five of the country's 528 soul stations were black-owned, and listeners were bringing pressure on the others to hire not only more black deejays but also more black program directors and executives[42]—and a lot of white people, liberals included, were beginning to realize that the racial divide went much deeper than separate schools and drinking fountains. It was easy for sympathetic Euro-Americans to sing along with "We Shall Overcome," but "Say It Loud, I'm Black and I'm Proud" was another story, even though James Brown's ferociously danceable anthem made

---

"Rock" and "rock 'n' roll" continued to be used interchangeably by many writers, even in rock publications, at least into the early 1970s, and many people still fail to make a distinction between the terms.

42. Thomas Barry, "The Importance of Being Mr. James Brown," *Look*, 18 Feb. 1969, 56.

Billboard's pop top ten in 1968. As Jonathan Eisen put it, explaining the absence of current black styles from his 1969 anthology, *The Age of Rock*:

> In recent years, young black musicians on the whole have been involved within an entirely different milieu, both social and musical, most of them concentrating on developing greater nationalistic self-consciousness. The electronic music "bag" has been primarily confined to white musicians, with most of the blacks working in the area of jazz and soul . . . speaking to different constituencies in different idioms and with different meaning—though with equal infectiousness and intensity.[43]

Some black artists would have echoed Eisen's statement, but it was also a handy way to excuse the fact that rock books, magazines, radio stations, and festivals were including only a token selection of black performers and, however complimentary the language, white formulations of "separate but equal" had never been anything but a trap. Black stars were getting behind the pride movement and singing about "Respect," but as Marvin Gaye bluntly put it, "Everyone wanted to sell [to] whites, 'cause whites got the most money."[44] So, far from isolating themselves in a separate world of soul, most of them were doing their best to maintain the racial overlap that had defined the earlier rock 'n' roll scene, recording songs by the Beatles, the Stones, Simon and Garfunkel, Dylan, the Band, the Doors—even the Archies. Motown hired white guitarists in "the electronic music bag" to give a contemporary rock feel to the Temptations' "Psychedelic Shack," and Atlantic used Eric Clapton and Duane Allman on recordings by Franklin and Pickett. But it was becoming increasingly difficult to overcome the rock-soul division. In 1961, Ike and Tina Turner's "It's Gonna Work Out Fine" had been one of three records by black artists among the five nominees

---

43. Jonathan Eisen, *The Age of Rock* (New York: Random House, 1969), xv–xvi.
44. David Ritz, *Divided Soul: The Life of Marvin Gaye* (Cambridge, MA: Da Capo Press, 1991), 73.

for the first rock & roll Grammy. By 1966, the Grammys had three "contemporary (rock & roll)" performance categories, but there was not one black name among the sixteen nominees, an omission made more galling for the Turners by the fact that Tina had teamed up with Phil Spector that year to make "River Deep—Mountain High." As Ike pointed out:

> [That]'s not a groove record for dancin' . . . it's the same kind of record "Good Vibrations" was . . . but right away when they see Tina Turner on the record they name it r&b . . . and it would have to go number one r&b before the Top 40 station would play it, well man I don't think this is fair . . . Negroes not going to buy that record . . . it's strictly . . . for the white market.[45]

The Turners would eventually become one of the few black acts to break into the rock scene, but only after touring and appearing in a movie with the Rolling Stones and recording covers of the Beatles' "Come Together" and Creedence Clearwater Revival's "Proud Mary."

In hindsight, it is striking to watch *The T.A.M.I. Show*, a concert filmed in Santa Monica in 1964, and see the Beach Boys, Chuck Berry, Lesley Gore, the Supremes, Smokey Robinson and the Miracles, Gerry and the Pacemakers, James Brown, and the Rolling Stones all greeted with equally fervent screams by an overwhelmingly white, female audience, then to watch the effort Otis Redding had to make just three years later to connect with the audience of white hippies in Monterey. By the most generous count, Monterey Pop presented six acts featuring black artists out of a total of thirty-two—and that includes the MGs, the Electric Flag (a white band led by Mike Bloomfield, but with Buddy Miles on drums and vocals), and the Jimi Hendrix Experience, which was arriving from London on Paul McCartney's recommendation, had a white, British rhythm section, and was introduced by the Stones' Brian Jones. Still, that was better than Woodstock two years

45. "Ike and Tina Are Double Dynamite," *Hit Parader*, July 1970, 12–13.

later, where, out of thirty-three acts, the only featured black performers were Hendrix, Richie Havens, and Sly and the Family Stone. And the decline was more than numeric: In 1964, rock 'n' roll was still a completely biracial genre; in 1967, Monterey booked Redding, the MGs, and Lou Rawls specifically to include a taste of contemporary black music; at Woodstock, Hendrix and Havens were both primarily associated with the white market, while Sly Stone had carved out a unique position as a bridge builder between ghetto funk and the hippie scene, becoming, in the words of *Rolling Stone*'s Jon Landau, "the only major rock figure who has a deep following with both whites and blacks."[46]

Some people in the rock world were clearly troubled by this split. Bill Graham experimented with bills at the Fillmore West in which white stars introduced their black peers, pairing the Al Kooper–Mike Bloomfield Super Session with Sam and Dave, and Janis Joplin with Mavis Staples. Landau and Christgau both pushed their readers to keep on top of what was happening in black music and on AM radio. The Stones frequently toured with black groups, helping both the Turners and Stevie Wonder to cross over to a larger white audience, and they also made some effort to keep up with current dance rhythms, getting their last number-one hit in 1978 with the disco-inflected "Miss You." The Young Rascals (later just the Rascals) took a particularly explicit stand against the racial divide: Three of the band's members had worked in Joey Dee's Starliters, and they carried on Dee's attempt to be part of the R&B scene, evolving along with Brown and the Southern soul artists and becoming one of the few white acts to get regular play on black radio. (The two names mentioned most often by black deejays as examples of their integrated playlist in the later 1960s were the Rascals and, oddly enough, Frank Sinatra.) Though rarely remembered in the same breath with the Beatles and Stones, the Rascals earned seven gold records in 1968 alone—including one for "People Got to Be Free," an ode to racial harmony—and in 1969 they announced that they would

46. Jon Landau, "Rock 1970—It's Too Late to Stop Now," *Rolling Stone*, 2 Dec. 1970, in Charles Nanry, ed., *American Music: From Storyville to Woodstock* (New Brunswick, NJ: Transaction Books, 1972), 250.

no longer appear on programs that were not racially balanced. "We can't control the audience, guaranteeing it will be integrated, and you better believe they're still segregated, if only by psychological forces," said the group's organist and main composer, Felix Cavaliere. "But we can control the show. So from now on . . . all our major concerts will be half black, half white, or we stay home."[47]

It is worth noting that, whereas the Starliters of 1962 had been racially mixed and that fact had excited little comment, the Rascals of 1969, despite their strong antisegregation stance, were not. Rock had become a white genre, and the Rascals' announcement only underlined that change. From now on, when rock bands shared double bills with black artists or invited black musicians to join them as guests, it would be seen as an attempt to cross boundaries or add a touch of blues, soul, or funk, rather than because they were all part of a single musical movement.

The Beatles and their peers had made rock into the most popular concert and album category of their time, and in the process expanded the style beyond anything its previous practitioners had imagined. Indeed, the later 1960s brought a respect for popular music and a popularity for complex artistic experimentation that had not been matched in any previous era—Whiteman's symphonic excursions, famous as they were, were never as broadly influential as his dance music, and jazz attained widespread respectability only after it had ceased to be a mainstream pop style.

In the process, though, they had led their audience off the dance floor, separating rock from its rhythmic and cultural roots, and while the gains may have balanced the losses in both economic and artistic terms, that change split American popular music in two. When similar splits had happened in the past, the demands of satisfying live audiences had always forced the streams back together, but by the end of the 1960s live performances had lost their defining role on the pop music scene. So the Beatles and the movement they led marked the

47. "The Rascals: Won't Play Unless Bill Is Half Black," *Rolling Stone*, 1 Feb. 1969, 8. The seven gold records included both singles and LPs.

end not only of rock 'n' roll as it had existed up to that time but also of the whole process explored over the course of this book, in which white and black musicians had evolved by adopting and adapting one another's styles, shaping a series of genres—ragtime, jazz, swing, rock 'n' roll—that at their peaks could not be easily categorized by race. The shifts in recording technology, radio, television, race relations, global politics, and an infinity of other factors might have brought a similar result even if the Beatles had never met—as always, we can only know what happened, not what might have happened. But what happened was that they were the catalysts for a divide between rock and soul that, rather than being mended in later years, would only grow wider with the emergence of disco and hip-hop. And that fundamental split would create myriad splinters over the following decades.

When the Beatles appeared on the *Ed Sullivan Show*, it was the last time a live performance changed the course of American music, and when they became purely a recording group, they pointed the way toward a future in which there need be no unifying styles, as bands can play what they like in the privacy of the studio, and we can choose which to listen to in the privacy of our clubs, our homes, or, finally, our heads. Whether that was liberating or limiting is a matter of opinion and perception, but the whole idea of popular music had changed.

2009

▼

HILTON ALS

"How different is one's body from one's soul? Are they connected, and if so how does the body show what one feels?" These questions, from Hilton Als's meditation on Beyoncé's *Lemonade*, are typical of his open-ended and provocative writing on identity and culture. Als (b. 1960), a staff writer for *The Village Voice* and later *The New Yorker*, is the author of *The Women*, published in 1996, a dramatic book-length essay on racial and sexual self-definition that challenged gender archetypes within the African American community. The book takes the form of a triple portrait in which personal identity grapples with social identity, and with the elements of culture that inform both. His meditations on race and gender continued in *White Girls* (2013), which collects the post-mortem reflection on Michael Jackson's many contradictions included here. Als has been honored with a Guggenheim Fellowship and was a finalist for the National Book Critics Circle award in 2014. He has taught at Yale, Wesleyan, and Smith, and currently serves as an associate professor of writing in Columbia's School of the Arts.

▼ ▼

Michael

1.

THE FEMALE elders tell us what to look out for. Staring straight ahead, they usher us past the Starlite Lounge, in the Bedford-Stuyvesant section of Brooklyn, and whisk us across the street as soon as they see "one of them faggots" emerge from the neon-lit bar. This one—he's brown-skinned, like nearly every one else in that neighborhood, and skinny—has a female friend in tow, for appearances must be kept up. And as the couple run off in search of another pack of cigarettes, the bar's door closes slowly behind them, but not before we children hear, above the martini-fed laughter, a single voice, high and plaintive: Michael Jackson's.

It's 1972, and "Ben," the fourteen-year-old star's first solo hit, is everywhere. The title song for a film about a bullied boy and his love for a rat named Ben (together they train a legion of other rodents to kill the boy's tormentors; eventually Ben helps kill his human companion), the mournful ballad quickly became Jackson's early signature song— certainly among the queens at the Starlite, who ignore its Gothic context, and play it over and over again as a kind of anthem of queer longing. For it was evident by then that Michael Jackson was no mere child with a gift. Or, to put it more accurately, he was all child—an Ariel of the ghetto—whose appeal, certainly to the habitués of places like the Starlite, lay partly in his ability to find metaphors to speak about his difference, and theirs.

2.

The Jackson 5 were America's first internationally recognized black adolescent boy band. They were as smooth as the Ink Spots, but there was a hint of wildness and pathos in Michael Jackson's rough-boy soprano, which, with its Jackie Wilson– and James Brown–influenced yelps, managed to remain just this side of threatening. He never changed that potent formula, not even after he went solo, more or less permanently, in 1978 at the age of twenty. Early on, he recognized the power mainstream stardom held—a chance to defend himself and his mother from the violent ministrations of his father, Joe Jackson (who famously has justified his tough parenting, his whippings, as a catalyst for his children's success), and to wrest from the world what most performers seek: a nonfractured mirroring.

After "Ben," the metaphors Michael Jackson used to express his difference from his family became ever more elaborate and haunting: there was his brilliant turn as an especially insecure, effete, and, at times, masochistic scarecrow in Sidney Lumet's 1978 film version of the Broadway hit *The Wiz*. There was his appropriation of Garland's later style—the sparkly black Judy-in-concert jacket—during the 1984 "Victory" tour, his last performances with his brothers, whose costuming made them look like intergalactic superheroes. And there were the songs he wrote for women—early idols like Diana Ross or his older sister, Rebbie—songs that expressed what he could never say about his own desire. "She said she wants a guy / To keep her satisfied / But that's alright for her / But it ain't enough for me," Jackson wrote in the 1982 Diana Ross hit song "Muscles." The song continues: "Still, I don't care if he's young or old / (Just make him beautiful). . . . I want muscles / All over his body." The following year, Jackson wrote "Centipede," which became Rebbie Jackson's signature song. It begins: "Your love / Is like a ragin' fire, oh / You're a snake that's on the loose / The strike is your desire." In bars like the Starlite, and, later, in primarily black and Latin gay dance clubs like the Paradise Garage on Manhattan's Lower West Side, the meaning was clear: Michael Jackson was most himself when he was someone other than himself.

Ross was more than an early idol; she served as a kind of beard during a pivotal period of Jackson's self-creation. During the late 1970s and early 1980s, as he moved away from being a Jackson but was not willing to forgo his adorable child star status, Jackson "dated" a number of white starlets—Tatum O'Neal, Brooke Shields—but once those girls were exhibited at public events two or three times, they were never seen with him again. Ross, on the other hand, was a constant. Gay fans labeled her as the ultimate fag hag, or sister, who used her energetic feline charm to help sexualize Jackson. But intentionally or not, the old friends perverted this notion in the 1981 television special *Diana*. In it, the two singers wear matching costumes: slacks, shirt, and tie. The clip was shown over and over again in the clubs. Jackson dances next to Ross, adding polish to her appealingly jerky moves; he does Ross better than Ross.

The anxiety of influence is most palpable on the spoken-word introduction to his 1979 album *Off the Wall*, the first of his four collaborations with the producer Quincy Jones. Here, Jackson can be heard struggling against his own imitation of Ross's breathy voice (a voice canonized in *Diana*, her brilliant Bernard Edwards and Nile Rodgers–produced 1980 album featuring the militaristic hit "I'm Coming Out," which has subsequently become a gay anthem of sorts). It was during this period that a number of black gay men began to refer to Jackson as "she" and, eventually, "a white woman"—one of the slurs they feared most, for what could be worse than being called that which you were not, could never be? As his physical transformations began to overshadow his life as a musician, Jackson's now-famous mask of white skin and red lips (a mask that distanced him from blackness just as his sexuality distanced him from blacks) would come to be read as the most arresting change in the man who said no to life but yes to pop.

3.

The chokehold of black conservatism on black gay men has been chronicled by a handful of artists—Harlem Renaissance poet Bruce Nugent, playwright and filmmaker Bill Gunn, James Baldwin, and AIDS activist and spoken word artist Marlon Riggs among them—but these figures are rare, and known mostly to white audiences. In black urban centers across the US, where Jesus is still God, men who cannot conform to the culture's edicts—adopting a recognizably heterosexual lifestyle, along with a specious contempt for the spoils of white folk—are ostracized, or worse; being "out" is a privilege many black gay men still cannot afford. Bias-related crimes aside (black gay men are more likely to be bashed by members of their own race than by nonblacks), there's the bizarre fact that queerness reads, even to some black gay men themselves, as a kind of whiteness. In a black, Christian-informed culture, where relatively few men head households anymore, whiteness is equated with perversity, a pollutant further eroding the already decimated black family. So, in their wretchedness, and their guilt, the black gay men who cannot marry women, and those who should not but do, meet on the "down low" for closeted gay sex and, less often, love and fraternity.

During Jackson's childhood in Gary, Indiana, black conservatism would have reigned. Among US cities with a population of 100,000 or more, Gary—a steel town twenty-five miles southeast of downtown Chicago—has the highest percentage of black residents, mostly Southern transplants, mostly Christian, and steadfastly heterosexual. Both of Jackson's parents' roots were in the South. His mother, Katherine, was a devout Jehovah's Witness. She suffered Joe's various infidelities and cruelties to their nine children with the forbearance of one whose reward will come not in this world, but the next. (Joe Jackson has never adopted his wife's faith.) In her 2006 study, *On Michael Jackson*, the critic Margo Jefferson discusses this split in parenting, the fractured mirroring in the home:

> Katherine Jackson's pursuit of her faith was analogous to what she had been doing all along: housekeeping. Dirt and disorder were the enduring enemy in the household. Germ-free spiritual cleanliness was the goal in her religion. The Witnesses say you are not pure in heart unless you are pure in body. You *must* follow scriptural condemnation of fornicators, idolators, masturbators, adulterers and homosexuals. . . . So while Katherine works to lead their souls to God, Joseph works to bend their minds, bodies and voices to his will for success. Not that Katherine objects: she has her own suppressed ambitions. The boys become singing and dancing machines. And little Michael becomes a diligent Witness.

For her children ever to have raised the issue of Katherine Jackson's complicity with her husband's drive for his sons' stardom (and thus his own), and with his various cruelties—Jefferson writes, "He put on ghoulish masks and scared his children awake, tapping on their bedroom window, pretending to break in and standing over their beds, waiting for them to wake up screaming"—would have meant the total loss of family: she was the only emotional sustenance they knew. And who would object to the riches Joe Jackson's management eventually yielded, despite his hard-line style? Two years after his fifth son,

Michael, began to sing lead in the family band in 1966, they were signed to Motown Records, where they would remain for more than a decade. And despite their uneven career paths, none of the Jackson children would ever lack for financial security again.

4.

In his 1985 essay "Freaks and the American Ideal of Manhood," Baldwin wrote of Michael Jackson:

> The Michael Jackson cacophony is fascinating in that it is not about Jackson at all. I hope he has the good sense to know it and the good fortune to snatch his life out of the jaws of a carnivorous success. He will not swiftly be forgiven for having turned so many tables, for he damn sure grabbed the brass ring, and the man who broke the bank at Monte Carlo has nothing on Michael.

Baldwin goes on to claim that "freaks are called freaks and are treated as they are treated—in the main, abominably—because they are human beings who cause to echo, deep within us, our most profound terrors and desires." But Jackson was not quite that articulate or vocal about his difference, if he even saw it as such after a while. Certainly his early interest in subtext—expressed primarily by wordplay and choice of metaphor—receded after he released his synthesizer-heavy 1991 album, *Dangerous.* That album gave us "In the Closet," where an uncredited Princess Stéphanie of Monaco pleads, at the beginning of the song, for the singer not to ignore their love, "woman to man." (It's another link in the chain of influence; she sounds like Jackson doing Diana Ross.) In a later part of the song, Michael pleads: "Just promise me / Whatever we say / Or whatever we do / To each other / For now we'll make a vow / To just keep it in the closet."

But this would be his last engagement of this kind. Unlike Prince, his only rival in the black pop sweepstakes, Jackson couldn't keep mining himself for material for fear of what it would require of him—a turning inward, which, though arguably not the job of a pop musician, is the job of the artist. After *Dangerous*, Jackson became a corporation, concerned less with creative innovation than with looking backward to recreate the success he had achieved more than ten years before, with *Thriller*. In contrast, over a career spanning roughly the time of Jackson's own, Prince has released more than thirty albums, not all of them great, but each reflective of the current permutation of his musical mind, with its focus on sex and religion as twin transformative experiences. When not content to sing as himself, Prince has created an alter ego, Camille, to explore his feminine side, and thus help promote his stock in trade: androgyny (which is Prince's freakishness, along with his interest in bending racial boundaries without resculpting his face). For Jackson to have admitted to his own freakishness might have meant, ultimately, being less canny about his image and more knowledgeable about his self—his body, which was not as impervious as his reputation.

James Baldwin did not live long enough to see Jackson self-destruct. And the most interesting aspect of his essay in light of Jackson's death is Baldwin's identification with Michael Jackson, another black boy who saw fame as power, and both did and did not get out of the ghetto he had been born into, or away from the father who became his greatest subject. But the differences are telling. While Baldwin died in exile, he did not presumably die in exile from his body, and while Baldwin died an artist, Jackson did not. After 1991, Jackson's focus was his career—which is work, too, but not the work he could have done. And his tremendous gifts as a singer and arranger, and as a synthesizer of world music in a pop context, became calcified. He forgot how to speak, even behind the jeweled mask of metaphor.

In the end, the chief elements of his early childhood—his father, his blackness, the church, his mother's silence—won, and the prize was his self-martyrdom: the ninety-pound frame; the facial operations; the dermatologist as the replacement family; the disastrous finances; the young boys loved, and then paid off. Michael Jackson died a long time ago, and it's taken years for anyone to notice.

2009

Evelyn McDonnell

Though it has addressed many aspects of contemporary popular culture, the writing of Evelyn McDonnell (b. 1964) has had its greatest impact in calling attention to two undervalued resources in rock and pop history: the crucial contributions of women musicians and women writers. McDonnell is the author of four books, including a study of Icelandic/international star Björk and *Queens of Noise: The Real Story of the Runaways*. Her skills as interviewer, historian, and interpreter are all on display in her telling of the Runaways' origin story included here. She also co-edited two anthologies, the first of which, *Rock She Wrote: Women Write About Rock, Pop and Rap* (1995, with Ann Powers), marked an important step in making a place for the voices of women writers in the history of American rock and pop writing. McDonnell has served as editorial director for www.MOLI.com, pop culture writer at *The Miami Herald*, senior editor at *The Village Voice*, and associate editor at *SF Weekly*; her writing on music, poetry, theater, and culture has appeared in numerous publications and anthologies, including *The Los Angeles Times*, *Ms.*, *Rolling Stone*, *The New York Times*, *Spin*, *Billboard*, *Vibe*, and *Interview*. With a bachelor's in American studies from Brown University and a master's in specialized journalism from the University of Southern California, in 2010 McDonnell was appointed assistant professor of journalism and new media at Loyola Marymount University.

▼ ▼

The Runaways: Wild Thing

ON A summer day in 1975, a 16-year-old girl carrying a Silvertone guitar took four public buses from Canoga Park to a two-story house in Huntington Beach. At the door, she was greeted by another 16-year-old, a surfing beauty with piercing blue eyes, feathered blond hair and muscled arms. The two strangers climbed to the above-garage rec room, which doubled as Sandy Pesavento's bedroom. Sandy sat down at her red Pearl drum set. Joan Larkin plugged in her guitar.

"We just clicked; we locked in right away," says the guitarist. "She was so friendly and outgoing. She was like me: She was a tomboy, she loved sports, she was a roughhouser. I couldn't believe how she played. She was such a solid, strong, powerful, really good drummer. I don't even want to say for being 16—for being anything. She had this shit down and it was powerful."

That suburban rec room was ground zero for the Runaways, the all-girl teenage band that busted down rock barriers and took an unbelievable amount of shit. Sandy West and Joan Jett, as they would soon become known to the world, formed the nucleus of the group that is now the subject of a much-hyped feature film, *The Runaways*, directed by Floria Sigismondi and starring Kristen Stewart and Dakota Fanning as Jett and singer Cherie Currie.

Declaring themselves the queens of noise, Jett, West, Currie, guitarist Lita Ford and bassist Jackie Fox were pre-punk bandits fostering revolution girl-style, decades before that became a riot grrrl catchphrase. West, played in the film by Stella Maeve, was a powerhouse who proved that girls could play just as hard as boys. The band's breakup affected her more than any other Runaway, and during the following decades, as she created great, little-heard music with other players but fell into horrific, sometimes violent, drug-fueled episodes, she continued to advocate for the band's reunion—or at least their due critical appreciation.

Yet West is the one band member who is not around to see the Runaways get the kind of attention that eluded them when they were treated as a jailbait novelty act. On October 21, 2006, the strong, charismatic, bighearted woman succumbed to the lung cancer that first struck her while she was in prison on a drug charge. It was a tragic end for a bon vivant whose very entrance filled a room with energy, a drummer who beat a path for girl musicians, a tomboy whose skills and search for thrills included a facility with guns, a California dreamer who created, and was passed up by, musical history.

Sandy wasn't supposed to be there. She told her parents that she was going to Disneyland, but actually, she was at a happier place on Earth that Saturday night during the summer of 1975—the parking lot of the Rainbow Bar and Grill. Sandy knew this Sunset Strip spot was the place to hang out if you wanted to meet rock stars and/or their handlers.

"She was with her friends from Huntington Beach," says Kim Fowley, the pop-industry veteran who would become both the Runaways' manager and, to some at least, their villain. "They were up there standing around like everybody did that didn't have ID to get into the Rainbow or the Roxy. They were up there as tourists, weekend warriors coming to Hollywood."

Fowley speaks derisively of young suburbanites, but they were the demographic key to the Runaways, whose homes ranged from the San Fernando Valley to Orange County. On weekends, teenagers from all over L.A. converged on West Hollywood, first at Rodney Bingenheimer's English Disco, then at places like the Sugar Shack (teens only) and the infamous Starwood. There, they discovered the music of David Bowie, the New York Dolls, Sweet and Suzi Quatro (Jett's hero), and could even rub elbows with stars like Led Zeppelin.

"There's Sandy standing there looking like [Beach Boy] Dennis Wilson's sister," says Fowley. "She was with a bunch of musicians in a musician's stance. One of those, 'Hi, I bet everybody here should know I'm a musician.' Like Billy the Kid coming to town ready to have a gunfight. So I said, 'Are you a musician?'"

Sandy's timing was dead-on. Just that afternoon, Fowley had auditioned Jett. He gave her phone number to West and, not long after, Jett took that long bus ride to Huntington Beach, where the girls played basic rock progressions—Chuck Berry and Rolling Stones riffs—and "bonded over the straight, pure thing of rhythm guitar and drums locking up," says Jett. They played over the phone for Fowley, who was having lunch with a writer from *Billboard*. Fowley held the phone up, and the writer smiled at what he heard. "At that moment, I knew it would work," he says.

They auditioned musicians. One day, a sexy guitarist from Long Beach with long, blond hair came to the rehearsal studio on Sunset and Vine.

"I walked in and Sandy and I hit it off right away," says Ford. "I started playing this old Deep Purple song, 'Highway Star.' She knew the entire song; I couldn't believe it. We just jammed it out. As soon as we did that, we were like, 'I love you.'"

Fowley and Jett found Currie at the Sugar Shack. After trying out a few bassists, they settled on Jackie Fuchs, redubbed Fox. Once set, the Runaways were promptly signed to Mercury Records. For most of them, it was their first band. None of them was older than 17.

Until tragedy struck the Pesaventos, Sandy was an active, happy child from prosperous, middle-class suburban L.A. Maybe because he realized he was never going to have a son, father Gene bonded with the youngest of his four daughters, fixing cars and playing ball together. "They were close," says Teri Miranti, the second-oldest daughter. "She related to him and he related to her."

Second-wave feminism and Title IX were opening doors for women, and the youngest Pesavento eagerly rushed through them. That challenge to do whatever the guys did was both Sandy's lifelong drive and part of her downfall. She played tennis and basketball, swam competitively, ran track, surfed, waterskied and rode horses. "She was incredibly energetic, hysterical, very funny, athletic," says Lori, the third daughter.

Sandy was smart, but she struggled in school. Lori attributes her difficulties to conditions with which she was diagnosed decades later: "Early on, she had a lot of challenges with academic performances primarily because she had a lot of learning disabilities, which later on in life we learned that she had ADHD. She had challenges that were around things like mood disorders, bipolar disorders."

In fourth grade, Sandy made it clear that she was not going to follow in the classical path paved by her sisters. Ellen played violin, Lori viola, Teri cello. The family wanted Sandy to be a violinist, so the daughters could form a string quartet. Sandy lasted about two weeks. "She said, 'No way,'" her mother, Jeri, says. "'You know what: I can be the first girl drummer in Prisk Elementary School.' That's how it began."

On Jan. 25, 1971, Sandy had just returned from school when Gene Pesavento had a massive heart attack at home, and died. "It was very traumatic for my family," says Lori. "It was off the Richter scale."

Sandy, 11, took it especially hard. "When I first met her, she talked a lot about her dad, how much she missed him," says Pam Apostolou, who befriended West in 1980. "Her dad got her."

In 1972, Jeri married Dick Williams, a former colleague of Gene's, whose wife had also recently died—and who, oddly enough, had three daughters, including a Sandy. The new, blended family moved to Huntington Beach, a place where they could start over on equal ground, not surrounded by memories of lost loved ones. Some of the daughters were in college or lived elsewhere. Still, the Huntington Beach house held five girls, three cats and two dogs who were trying to navigate deep hurt, massive change, puberty and one another's spaces. This was no *Brady Bunch* story.

"We were struggling at first, getting to know each other," says Jeri.

Sandy was outgoing, fun, easy to get along with, popular enough to be elected governor of her seventh grade. But Lori recalls her transition into puberty as bumpy. "She was very androgynous. She was one of those girls who didn't develop very early. People used to call her a boy. That upset her."

Around this time, Lori and Sandy were realizing they had something in common: They both liked girls. During her lifetime, Sandy also had boyfriends, but her primary relationships were with women. "Early on," says Lori, "she was very clear with me about her orientation. I don't sense she ever really struggled with it."

Music and sports were Sandy's outlets. By the mid-'70s, she was listening to hard rock and playing in a local band. Her drumming heroes were Led Zeppelin's John Bonham and Queen's Roger Taylor. Sandy poured her athleticism into pounding those skins.

"Sandy early on was pretty determined that she wanted to play rock music," Lori says. "It was a way for her to translate the grief. And she was a phenomenal natural drummer. I don't think the boys in the business ever even saw that coming."

By 1975, pop music had a noble history of female-vocal groups, but not of bands made up of women playing the instruments. Such acts as Goldie and the Gingerbreads and Fanny broke ground culturally but did not have much impact commercially. And they weren't composed of five hot teenagers, three of whom, at least—Lita, Sandy and Joan—could seriously play. Another, Currie, was a Promethean ingenue, a rape victim who strutted in a corset like it was armor and sang like she was going to draw blood. The Runaways created a West Coast version of glam rock that was part metal, part bubblegum and proto-punk.

The five strangers got to know one another fast. Shoved into a van and sent touring across the U.S., and then England, they eventually made it to Japan, where they were greeted with something like mass hysteria. The Runaways were like a girl gang, or a deranged sorority. "Being on the road was like taking a small child and a few of her friends to the zoo for the first time," says Currie. "There was wonderment of everything we were experiencing, good or bad. We were a family."

They were forging and experiencing something woefully rare in American society: the power of females working, creating, living and loving together. Occasionally, the love was physical. Currie got intimate with both Jett and West. "Back then in the mid-'70s, that was just what happened," Currie says. "At that time—David Bowie and Elton John—everybody was coming out. We experimented together. We had fun. We loved each other."

The Runaways had to become one another's support, because by choice and by circumstance, they were separated from their families. Currie's parents had recently divorced. Jett's father had left. Perhaps caught up in their own sorrows, the others didn't even realize West had issues. Sandy's parents loved her, but they didn't care for the music—and they certainly didn't care for Fowley.

"When he walked in the door, I was not happy," says Jeri. "He was not good news."

The Williams' understandable parental concern could have felt to West like lack of support. The band's name was a gimmick, but maybe, in a sense, she was running away from a relatively conservative upbringing. In order to be closer to the band and the action, West was living in West L.A. with her sister Teri, who was in college and had her own life to live.

"I think that [her] family didn't know what to do with her need to be a drummer, her need to kick ass, her need to dominate the world of rock & roll and be a crusader," Fowley says. "I think that was her burning need to get out there. She escaped the golden ghetto."

West saw the Runaways as a team. While other band members were taking shots at each other, she was quick to punch out anyone who threatened or insulted her bandmates. She told her friend Jerry Venemann about an incident when the band was hanging out with the Sex Pistols in London. On a houseboat on the Thames, Sid Vicious kept pawing at Jett, who was in no mood, or condition, for love. West told him to quit. Vicious kept harassing Jett, so West picked up the skinny bassist and dropped him into the river.

And then it began to seem that the people the Runaways most needed protection from were the people with whom they were working.

In Sigismondi's cinematic version of *The Runaways*, which opens March 19, Michael Shannon's Fowley steals the film—as any good villain should. There's no doubt Fowley, who was 36 at the band's inception, was the Runaways' evil genius, picking their name and accompanying bad-girl image, priming and primping—and pimping?—them for rock stardom.

The girls went along with this to a degree, dressing and posing provocatively. But sometimes, the sexploitation went too far. An English ad for *Queens of Noise*, for example, featured disembodied crotch shots of the teenagers in fetishistic gear. In article after article, male journalists slobbered over the Runaways, asking them for their body measurements, passing over their musical talents.

West's family blames Fowley for exposing her to the chemical lifestyle that ultimately derailed her. West herself spoke bitterly of the manager, and most of the people who know her say she stayed angry with him for much of her life. There were serious money issues. Bun E. Carlos, the drummer for Cheap Trick, remembers when his band and Tom Petty and the Heartbreakers opened for the Runaways in Detroit in 1977. The girls were driving a rental car they hadn't returned and were "living off nothing, no advances, peanuts. The gild was off the lily for the band. We knew they were being taken advantage of." Still, Carlos says, "Without Kim, they wouldn't have been there at all."

Jett, who remains friendly with Fowley, firmly rejects the charge that the girls were his victims: "This whole abuse thing is maddening to me. I think in hindsight people have to create monsters, but they should look at their own shit and responsibility in not making it happen. If you feel abused, get the fuck out. Nobody was forced to stay."

Fox and Currie did get out of what by 1977 had become an overheated pressure cooker of underage sex, ready drugs and kick-ass rock & roll. In Japan, Fox cut herself with a broken glass and left the band, replaced by Victory Tischler, aka Vicki Blue. Currie quit a few months later, when the Runaways were in the middle of recording their third studio album, *Waitin' for the Night*. The final straw for the singer: a *Crawdaddy* article in which Fowley said that the best thing Currie could do would be to hang herself.

Fowley admits he was in over his head as the Runaways' manager, denying either knowledge or memory of many of the charges against him. He was not on the road with the band and puts much of the blame for unhealthy high jinks on the tour manager, Scotty Anderson (who got Currie pregnant, according to her book).

"Their age group was rebelling against parents, teachers, Sunday school," Fowley says. "The feminist movement started in the early '70s, here we were in '75. Suddenly I have five warriors, cheerleaders with atomic weapons, ready to kick ass."

In the end, it was Fowley's ass the girls kicked, firing him in '77. The band was a trio by '78: West, Jett (who also sang lead) and Ford (on lead guitar and bass). They hired a new manager, Toby Mamis, and a new producer, John Alcock, a Brit who had worked with Thin Lizzy. "They had a sense of frustration that they were previously not really allowed to develop as musicians," says Alcock. "They wanted to focus more on the music and less on the image."

But by the time they recorded their fourth studio album, *And Now . . . the Runaways*, their musical tastes were splitting. While West and Ford cut their teeth on metal, glam fan Jett was getting more and more into punk. "We all had dark stuff going on toward the end of the band, after Cherie left," Jett says. "I just sensed it was going to slowly die. . . . Look at any picture of us as a four-piece; you won't find one picture of us smiling. . . . We decided that New Year's Eve 1978 would be our last gig."

One song in the Runaways' live set focused on West's showmanship and singing: a cover of the Troggs' 1960s garage-rock classic, "Wild Thing," captured in a video moment in Japan. The instruments stop on the verses and West raises one of those long, sinewy arms—she had arms like Tina Turner has legs—and sings: "Wild thing, I think I love you." Then she smashes the sticks down for two beats. "I want to know for sure." She's pointing at the audience. "C'mon and hold me tight." Her hand is in the sky now, twirling the stick like a Wild West gunman. "You move me."

"Wild Thing" was West's signature. After the Runaways broke up, it became a way of life.

The Runaways introduced West to a lifestyle she never figured out how to move beyond. At the age when she should have been learning practical life skills, she was shooting heroin with Keith Moon (according to a story she told her sister Ellen). Careers and lives lost to drug abuse are unfortunately a dime a dozen in rock & roll, but West took an especially crazy turn. She freebased coke and took crystal meth. She became a drug runner and dealer's bodyguard. She carried a gun. She was involved in scary, violent scenes that she told only a select few friends about, memories of which probably only deepened her depressive states. She was arrested and jailed repeatedly.

Initially, West was excited to start a new, mixed-gender band with Ford, working with Alcock. But after a few months, when that failed to get off the ground and Ford moved on, she began to realize the enormity of what she had lost.

West saw the success Jett and Ford had as solo artists and was determined to compete. She formed her own group, the Sandy West Band. The music was good, but if labels thought the Runaways were dead without Currie, they certainly weren't interested in a band fronted by a drummer.

"She had a very healthy ego," says her sister Ellen. "She became delusional about how great she was. She had visions of being a really big star getting an enormous amount of attention. Meanwhile there was the deterioration of the addiction, all that going downward. It's such a Greek tragedy."

Family remained important to West. But she didn't see her parents and sisters that often. She seemed to feel alienated by how different her life had become. Instead, she built an alternative family. Often, West turned to fans for friendships. Some of those people were vital links in her support network, but there were also hangers-on who took advantage of her, who just wanted to party with a rock star.

"Because Sandy's life didn't move forward as well as the others', it was easier for her to fall back on drinking and drugs," says Alcock. "She started doing some fairly heavy partying with people I didn't know, somewhere down in the beach communities. Those were not great people."

She would disappear with these people, into black holes of drug-fueled behavior. Family and friends staged interventions; West went into rehab a few times. But she always fell off the wagon.

At one point, says Currie, "she came over to the house and she was freebasing cocaine, which I tried desperately to get her to stop. It was extremely difficult to watch her do it. Having been in her position, I knew all the begging in the world wouldn't stop her."

The thing that was destroying West, says Ellen, was "the evil drug . . . crystal meth. One time I drove her home. I just remember trying to relate to her. I looked at her and saw her teeth getting black. I saw the tremors. She was disconnected, couldn't have a coherent conversation."

Sometimes, when West disappeared from friends' and families' lives, it turned out she was in jail. Her life of crime had begun harmlessly enough: On a Runaways tour in Europe, she, Currie and Jett were arrested for stealing hotel keys. Her stateside arrest record starts in 1988, when she was picked up in Orange County for driving under the influence. There were at least six arrests after that, in multiple counties: more DUIs, possession of controlled substances, possession of illegal substances, driving with a suspended license. She was able to serve some of her sentences concurrently. Friends say she took her jail time in stride, that perhaps it was easier for her to be institutionalized.

"She told me that in some ways being in prison reminded her of being in a band," says Lauren Varga, who befriended and played guitar with West in the '90s. "She said, 'I was living in such a bad way that when I went away, that was the only stability I had for a year. When I got back out, it was back into the chaos.'"

In fact, West was lucky to get put away for minor charges when she was doing much worse things. "Sandy got involved with mob-type figures," says Tischler-Blue: "Because she had this all-American-girl look, people wouldn't red-flag her. She started running drugs into the recording studios. Sandy loved coke. That was this turn that took her down a very different road. That road led to the underbelly of the Hollywood music scene. At that time, there were some really bad characters moving around. Heavy-duty drug people. Gunrunning people."

Looking tough but emotional, West talks about "the dangerous adventures of me" in Tischler-Blue's 2004 documentary about the band, *Edgeplay*. "Maybe that was the self-destructive side of me. Maybe I was out to push it. I was fearless. You go down and break somebody's door down. They've got guns all over you, you've got guns all over them. You don't know who's going to get killed. . . . I had to break somebody's arm once. I had to shove a gun down somebody's throat once and watch them shit their pants. And then you look around and say, 'I just wanted to be a drummer in a rock band.'"

Near the end of her life, West lived in circumstances demeaning to a former rock star: in a trailer in San Dimas. She appeared to be getting her life together. She released a four-song EP that shows her multiple talents: singer, songwriter, guitarist, pianist, drummer. She shared the trailer with Jan Miller, a quiet widow nine years older than West with an adult son. They signed a domestic-partnership agreement, and with Miller's insurance, West was able to get a needed hysterectomy. She was playing with Venemann and had formed a band with guitarist Varga and others, which they jokingly called Blue Fox after the Runaways' bassists. She was also working different jobs—handyman, vet's assistant, drum teacher. She had a dog, CJ, her surrogate child. "I just want to settle down and have a family," she told Miller.

But then she was arrested again, for possession of drugs and paraphernalia. In the era of three strikes, this was one offense too many. This time, West was sent not to the relatively tame county jail for a short stint, but to state prison in Chowchilla for 18 months. She found herself surrounded by hard-core criminals.

Before she went in, she did rehab one more time, this time at a facility specifically for musicians. Friends say this stint may have succeeded better than others. "She really was a different person," says Varga. "She said, 'It's taken me almost 30 years to get over this band. I really just have to let it go.'"

But West didn't have time to find out if she was cleaned up for good. Not long after arriving at Chowchilla, she developed a bad cough. It was small-cell lung cancer—the deadly, aggressive kind.

West underwent chemotherapy while still in prison. When finally released, she returned to Miller's care, and they moved to a house in West Covina. By this point, West's family was back in her life, helping to take care of her. Currie, Blue and other friends were there often. Jett visited her. She and Ford talked on the phone.

West's last months of life were full of pain, as the cancer, which moved to her brain, ate away at her. She lost some of the things that defined her: her golden hair and the strength to drum. She gained religion and a determination to do good. When she recovered, she said, she planned to speak to young people about the perils of drug use. "Through her suffering, and she really did suffer a lot, she became closer to her faith and wrote quite a few songs that were spiritual," says Jeri.

West was moved to a hospice. On October 21, 2006, Ellen had the feeling she had to get there right away, so she drove like crazy from San Francisco. Half an hour after her arrival, Sandy "West" Pesavento died. She's buried at Forest Lawn cemetery in Cypress, next to her father.

West had two dying wishes, Miller says: to have her autobiography published and the music she was working on released. Varga is working on both, though West's family is not eager to have her secrets exposed. The family donates West's royalties to the hospice and to a scholarship fund at the Rock 'n' Roll Camp for Girls in Portland. So West is not only still inspiring other women to rock, she's helping to pay their way.

West did live long enough to sell her life rights to the producers of *The Runaways* and to know that the band might be immortalized on film. But Sigismondi's movie focuses on the relationship between Currie and Jett. Sandy West has only a bit part.

2010

▼

KELEFA SANNEH

Kelefa Sanneh (b. 1975) has been exploring music, race, and culture—and the myriad ways they intersect—since his tenure on Harvard's *Transitions* magazine. Sanneh built an impressive and diverse portfolio during the eight years he spent covering hip-hop, rock, and pop music as a *New York Times* staffer, while also contributing to publications such as *The Source, The Village Voice, Blender,* and *Rolling Stone.* His 2004 essay for the *Times,* "The Rap Against Rockism," took critics and readers alike to task for their reflexive dismissal of pop music and suggested that music not be so starkly divided into high and low art. In 2008, Sanneh joined *The New Yorker* as a staff writer; from that perch he has written about all facets of contemporary American cultural experience, from music to sports to politics and beyond. In the piece here, Sanneh uses the publication of four books (centrally, Jay-Z's *Decoded*) to think about the insights and limitations created by treating hip-hop as poetry. Sanneh's prose is eloquent without being ostentatious, passionately engaged without being preachy, and—above all—informed by a keen understanding that all stories worth telling are at their core human-interest stories.

▼ ▼

Word:
Jay-Z's *Decoded* and the Language
of Hip-Hop

LAST YEAR, an English professor named Adam Bradley issued a manifesto to his fellow-scholars. He urged them to expand the poetic canon,
and possibly enlarge poetry's audience, by embracing, or coöpting, the
greatest hits of hip-hop. "Thanks to the engines of global commerce,
rap is now the most widely disseminated poetry in the history of the
world," he wrote. "The best MCs—like Rakim, Jay-Z, Tupac, and many
others—deserve consideration alongside the giants of American poetry.
We ignore them at our own expense."

The manifesto was called *Book of Rhymes: The Poetics of Hip Hop*
(Civitas; $16.95), and it used the terms of poetry criticism to illuminate
not the content of hip-hop lyrics but their form. For Bradley, a couplet
by Tupac Shakur—

> Out on bail, fresh outta jail, California dreamin'
> Soon as I stepped on the scene, I'm hearin' hoochies screamin'

—was a small marvel of "rhyme (both end and internal), assonance,
and alliteration," given extra propulsion by Shakur's exaggerated stress
patterns. Bradley also celebrated some lesser-known hip-hop lyrics,
including this dense, percussive couplet by Pharoahe Monch, a cult
favorite from Queens:

> The last batter to hit, blast shattered your hip
> Smash any splitter or fastball—that'll be it

Picking through this thicket, Bradley paused to appreciate Monch's
use of apocopated rhyme, as when a one-syllable word is rhymed with
the penultimate syllable of a multisyllabic word (last / blast / fastball).
Bradley is right to think that hip-hop fans have learned to appreciate all

sorts of seemingly obscure poetic devices, even if they can't name them. Though some of his comparisons are strained (John Donne loved punning, and so does Juelz Santana!), his motivation is easy to appreciate: examining and dissecting lyrics is the only way to "give rap the respect it deserves as poetry."

This campaign for respect enters a new phase with the release of *The Anthology of Rap* (Yale; $35), a nine-hundred-page compendium that is scarcely lighter than an eighties boom box. It was edited by Bradley and Andrew DuBois, another English professor (he teaches at the University of Toronto; Bradley is at the University of Colorado), who together have compiled thirty years of hip-hop lyrics, starting with transcribed recordings of parties thrown in the late nineteen-seventies—Year Zero, more or less. The book, which seems to have been loosely patterned after the various Norton anthologies of literature, is, among other things, a feat of contractual legwork: Bradley and DuBois claim to have secured permission from the relevant copyright holders, and the book ends with some forty pages of credits, as well as a weak disclaimer ("The editors have made every reasonable effort to secure permissions"), which may or may not hold up in court.

Even before *The Anthology of Rap* arrived in stores, keen-eyed fans began pointing out the book's many transcription errors, some of which are identical to ones on ohhla.com, a valuable—though by no means infallible—online compendium of hip-hop lyrics. But readers who don't already have these words memorized are more likely to be bothered by the lack of footnotes; where the editors of the Norton anthologies, those onionskin behemoths, love to explain and over-explain obscure terms and references, Bradley and DuBois provide readers with nothing more than brief introductions. Readers are simply warned that when it comes to hip-hop lyrics "obfuscation is often the point, suggesting coded meanings worth puzzling over." In other words, you're on your own.

Happily, readers looking for a more carefully annotated collection of hip-hop lyrics can turn to an unlikely source: a rapper. In recent weeks, *The Anthology of Rap* has been upstaged by *Decoded* (Spiegel & Grau; $35), the long-awaited print début of Jay-Z, who must now be one of the most beloved musicians in the world. The book, which doesn't credit a co-writer, is essentially a collection of lyrics, liberally footnoted and accompanied by biographical anecdotes and observations. *Decoded* has benefitted from an impressive marketing campaign, including a citywide treasure hunt for hidden book pages. (The book's launch doubled as a promotion for Bing, the Microsoft search engine.) So it's a relief to find that *Decoded* is much better than it needs to be; in fact, it's one of a handful of books that just about any hip-hop fan should own. Jay-Z explains not only what his lyrics mean but how they sound, even how they feel:

> When a rapper jumps on a beat, he adds his own rhythm. Sometimes you stay in the pocket of the beat and just let the rhymes land on the square so that the beat and flow become one. But sometimes the flow chops up the beat, breaks the beat into smaller units, forces in multiple syllables and repeated sounds and internal rhymes, or hangs a drunken leg over the last *bap* and keeps going, sneaks out of that bitch.

Two paragraphs later, he's back to talking about selling crack cocaine in Brooklyn. His description, and his music, makes it easier to imagine a connection—a rhyme, maybe—between these two forms of navigation, beat and street. And, no less than Bradley and DuBois, Jay-Z is eager to win for hip-hop a particular kind of respect. He states his case using almost the same words Bradley did: he wants to show that "hip-hop lyrics—not just my lyrics, but those of every great MC—are poetry if you look at them closely enough."

If you start in the recent past and work backward, the history of hip-hop spreads out in every direction: toward the Last Poets and Gil Scott-Heron, who declaimed poems over beats and grooves in the early seventies; toward Jamaica, where U-Roy pioneered the art of chatting and toasting over reggae records; toward the fifties radio d.j.s who used rhyming patter to seal spaces between songs; toward jazz and jive and the talking blues; toward preachers and politicians and street-corner bullshitters. In *Book of Rhymes*, Bradley argues convincingly that something changed in the late nineteen-seventies, in the Bronx, when the earliest rappers (some of whom were also d.j.s) discovered the value of rhyming in time. "Words started bending to the beat," as Bradley puts it; by submitting to rhythm, paradoxically, rappers came to sound more authoritative than the free-form poets, toasters, chatters, patterers, and jokers who came before.

The earliest lyrics in the anthology establish the rhyme pattern that many casual listeners still associate with hip-hop. Each four-beat line ended with a rhyme, heavily emphasized, and each verse was a series of couplets, not always thematically or sonically related to each other:

> I'm Melle Mel and I rock so well
> From the World Trade to the depths of hell.

Those lines were recorded in December, 1978, at a performance by Grandmaster Flash and the Furious Five at the Audubon Ballroom, on Broadway and 165th Street (the same hall where Malcolm X was assassinated, thirteen years earlier). The springy exuberance of Melle Mel's voice matched the elastic funk of the disco records that many early rappers used as their backing tracks.

The rise of Run-D.M.C., in the early nineteen-eighties, helped change that: the group's two rappers, Run and D.M.C., performed in jeans and sneakers, and they realized that hip-hop could be entertaining without being cheerful. They delivered even goofy lyrics with staccato aggression, which is one reason that they appealed to the young Jay-Z—they reminded him of guys he knew. In *Decoded*, he quotes a couple of lines by Run:

> Cool chief rocker, I don't drink vodka
> But keep a bag of cheeba inside my locker

There is aggression in the phrasing: the first line starts sharply, with a stressed syllable, instead of easing into the beat with an unstressed one. "The words themselves don't mean much, but he snaps those clipped

syllables out like drumbeats, *bap bap bapbap*," Jay-Z writes. "If you listened to that joint and came away thinking it was a simple rhyme about
holding weed in a gym locker, you'd be reading it wrong: The point of
those bars is to bang out a rhythmic idea."

The first Run-D.M.C. album arrived in 1984, but within a few years
the group's sparse lyrical style came to seem old-fashioned; a generation
of rappers had arrived with a trickier sense of swing. Hip-hop historians call this period the Golden Age (Bradley and DuBois date it from
1985 to 1992), and it produced the kinds of lyrical shifts that are easy
to spot in print: extended similes and ambitious use of symbolism; an
increased attention to character and ideology; unpredictable internal
rhyme schemes; enjambment and uneven line lengths. This last innovation may have been designed to delight anthologizers and frustrate
them, too, because it makes hip-hop hard to render in print. Bradley
and DuBois claim, with ill-advised certainty, to have solved the problem of line breaks: "one musical bar is equal to one line of verse." But,
in fact, most of their lines start before the downbeat, somewhere (it's
not clear how they decided) between the fourth beat of one bar and the
first beat of the next one. Here they are quoting Big Daddy Kane, one
of the genre's first great enjambers, in a tightly coiled passage from his
1987 single, "Raw":

> I'll damage ya, I'm not an amateur but a professional
> Unquestionable, without doubt superb
> So full of action, my name should be a verb.

These three lines contain three separate rhyming pairs, and a different anthologist might turn this extract into six lines of varying length.
If Bradley and DuBois followed their own rule, they would break mid-
word—"professio-/nal"—because the final syllable actually arrives,
startlingly, on the next line's downbeat. In *Book of Rhymes*, Bradley
argued that "every rap song is a poem waiting to be performed," but
the anthology's trouble with line breaks (not to mention punctuation) reminds readers that hip-hop is an oral tradition with no well-
established written form. By presenting themselves as mere archivists,

Bradley and DuBois underestimate their own importance: a book of hip-hop lyrics is necessarily a work of translation.

As the Golden Age ended, hip-hop's formal revolution was giving way to a narrative revolution. So-called gangsta rappers downplayed wordplay (without, of course, forswearing it) so they could immerse listeners in their first-person stories of bad guys and good times. Shakur and the Notorious B.I.G. created two of the genre's most fully realized personae; when they were murdered, in 1996 and 1997, respectively, their deaths became part of their stories. (Both crimes remain unsolved.) As the anthologizers blast through the nineties ("Rap Goes Mainstream") and the aughts ("New Millennium Rap"), their excitement starts to wane. They assert that the increasing popularity of hip-hop presented a risk of "homogenization and stagnation," without pausing to explain why this should be true (doesn't novelty sell?), if indeed it was. There is little overt criticism, but some rappers get fulsome praise—"socially conscious" is one of Bradley and DuBois's highest compliments—while others get passive-aggressive reprimands ("Disagreement remains over whether Lil' Kim has been good or bad for the image of women in hip-hop"). Perhaps the form of their project dictates its content. They are sympathetic to rappers whose lyrics survive the transition to the printed page; the verbose parables and history lessons of Talib Kweli, for instance, make his name "synonymous with depth and excellence," in their estimation. But they offer a more measured assessment of Lil Wayne, praising his "play of sound" (his froggy, bluesy voice is one of the genre's greatest instruments) while entertaining the unattributed accusation that he may be merely "a gimmick rapper." Any anthology requires judgments of taste, and this one might have been more engaging if it admitted as much.

Jay-Z grew up absorbing many of the rhymes that Bradley and DuBois celebrate. He was born in 1969, and raised in the Marcy Houses, in an area of Brooklyn from which Times Square seemed to be "a plane ride away." (Nowadays, some real-estate agents doubtless consider it part of greater Williamsburg.) "It was the seventies," he writes, "and heroin was still heavy in the hood, so we would dare one another to push a leaning nodder off a bench the way kids on farms tip sleeping cows." He was a skinny, watchful boy with a knack for rhyming but no great interest in the music industry, despite some early brushes with fame—he briefly served as Big Daddy Kane's hype man. Besides, Jay-Z had a day job that was both more dangerous and more reliable: he says he spent much of the late eighties and early nineties selling crack in Brooklyn and New Jersey and down the Eastern Seaboard. He was no kingpin, but he says he was a fairly accomplished mid-level dealer, and though he hated standing outside all day, he found that he didn't hate the routine. "It was an adventure," he says. "I got to hang out on the block with my crew, talking, cracking jokes. You know how people in office jobs talk at the watercooler? This job was almost all watercooler." Then, almost as an afterthought, "But when you weren't having fun, it was hell."

Early recordings of Jay-Z reveal a nimble but mild-mannered virtuoso, delivering rat-a-tat syllables (he liked to rap in double-time triplets, delivering six syllables per beat) that often amounted to études rather than songs. But by 1996, when he released his début album, *Reasonable Doubt*, on a local independent label, he had slowed down and settled into a style—and, more important, settled into character. The album won him underground acclaim and a record deal with the very above-ground hip-hop label Def Jam, which helped him become one of the genre's most dependable hitmakers. He was a cool-blooded hustler, describing a risky life in conversational verses that hid their poetic devices, disparaging the art of rapping even while perfecting it:

> Who wanna bet us that we don't touch lettuce, stack
> cheddars forever, live treacherous, all the et ceteras.
> To the death of us, me and my confidants, we
> shine. You feel the ambiance—y'all niggas just rhyme.

Too often, hip-hop's embrace of crime narratives has been portrayed as a flaw or a mistake, a regrettable detour from the overtly ideological rhymes of groups like Public Enemy. But in Jay-Z's view Public Enemy is an anomaly. "You rarely *become* Chuck D when you're listening to

Public Enemy," he writes. "It's more like watching a really, really lively speech." By contrast, his tales of hustling were generous, because they made it easy for fans to imagine that they were part of the action. "I don't think any listeners think I'm threatening them," he writes. "I think they're singing along with me, threatening someone else. They're thinking, *Yeah, I'm coming for you.* And they might apply it to anything, to taking their next math test or straightening out that chick talking outta pocket in the next cubicle."

Throughout *Decoded*, Jay-Z offers readers a large dose of hermeneutics and a small dose of biography, in keeping with his deserved reputation for brilliance and chilliness. His footnotes are full of pleasingly small-scale exultations ("I like the internal rhymes here") and technical explanations ("The shift in slang—from talking about guns as tools to break things to talking about shooting as *blazing*—matches the shift in tone"); at one point, he pauses to quote a passage from *Book of Rhymes* in which Bradley praises his use of homonyms. Readers curious about his life will learn something about his father, who abandoned the family when Jay-Z was twelve; a little bit about Bono, who is now one of Jay-Z's many A-list friends; and nothing at all about the time when, as a boy, Jay-Z shot his older brother in the shoulder. (Apparently, there was a dispute over an item of jewelry, possibly a ring, although Jay-Z once told Oprah Winfrey that, at the time, his brother was "dealing with a lot of demons.")

Decoded is a prestige project—it will be followed, inevitably, by a rash of imitations from rappers who realize that the self-penned coffee-table book has replaced the Lamborghini Murciélago as hip-hop's ultimate status symbol. In his early years, Jay-Z liked to insist that rapping was only a means to an end—like selling crack, only safer. "I was an eager hustler and a reluctant artist," he writes. "But the irony of it is that to make the hustle work, really work, over the long term, you have to be a true artist, too." Certainly this book emphasizes Jay-Z the true artist, ignoring high-spirited tracks like "Ain't No Nigga" to focus on his moodier ruminations on success and regrets. (The lyrics to "Success" and "Regrets" are, in fact, included.) Readers might be able to trace Jay-Z's growing self-consciousness over the years, as his slick vernacular verses give way to language that's more decorous and sometimes less elegant. In "Fallin'," from 2007, he returned to a favorite old topic, with mixed results:

> The irony of selling drugs is sort of like I'm using it
> Guess it's two sides to what substance abuse is

Bradley has written about rappers "so insistent on how their rhymes sound that they lose control over what they are actually saying." But with late-period Jay-Z the reverse is sometimes true: the ideas are clear and precise, but the syntax gets convoluted, and he settles for clumsy near-rhymes like "using it"/"abuse is." For all Bradley and DuBois's talk about "conscious" hip-hop, the genre owes much of its energy to the power of what might be called "unconscious" rapping: heedless or reckless lyrics, full of contradictions and exaggerations (to say nothing of insults). If you are going to follow a beat, as rappers must, then it helps not to have too many other firm commitments.

One day four years ago, Jay-Z was reading *The Economist* when he came across an article bearing the heading "Bubbles and Bling." The article was about Cristal, the expensive champagne that figured in the rhymes of Jay-Z and other prominent rappers. In the article, Frédéric Rouzaud, the managing director of the winery behind Cristal, was asked whether these unsought endorsements might hurt his brand. "That's a good question, but what can we do? We can't forbid people from buying it," he said, adding, slyly, "I'm sure Dom Pérignon or Krug would be delighted to have their business." Jay-Z was irritated enough that he released a statement vowing never to drink Cristal again, and he started removing references to Cristal from his old lyrics during concerts. (He eventually switched his endorsement to Armand de Brignac.) In Jay-Z's view, Rouzaud had not only insulted hip-hop culture; he had violated an unspoken promotional arrangement. "We used their brand as a signifier of luxury and they got free advertising and credibility every time we mentioned it," he writes. "We were trading cachet." (Actually, the book, not free of typos, says "cache.")

It's hard not to think about Cristal when Jay-Z insists that his lyrics should be heard—read—as poetry, or when Bradley and DuBois produce an anthology designed to win for rappers the status of poets. They are, all of them, trading cachet, and their eagerness to make this trade suggests that they are trading up—that hip-hop, despite its success, still aches for respect and recognition. It stands to reason, then, that as the genre's place in the cultural firmament grows more secure its advocates will grow less envious of poetry's allegedly exalted status.

Another great American lyricist has just published a book of his own: *Finishing the Hat* (Knopf; $39.95), by Stephen Sondheim, is curiously similar in form to *Decoded*. Sondheim is just as appealing a narrator as Jay-Z, although he's much less polite. (While Jay-Z has almost nothing bad to say about his fellow-rappers, Sondheim is quick to disparage his rivals, subject to a "cowardly but simple" precept: "criticize only the dead.") But where Jay-Z wants to help readers see the poetry in hip-hop, Sondheim thinks poeticism can be a problem: in his discussion of "Tonight," from *West Side Story*, he half apologizes for the song's "lapses into 'poetry.'" And where Bradley and DuBois are quick to praise rappers for using trick rhymes and big words, Sondheim is ever on guard against "overrhyming" and other instances of unwarranted cleverness. "In theatrical fact," he writes, "it is usually the plainer and flatter lyric that soars poetically when infused with music." Most rappers are no less pragmatic: they use the language that works, which is sometimes ornate, but more often plainspoken, even homely. (One thinks of Webbie, the pride of Baton Rouge, deftly rhyming "drunk as a fuckin' rhino" with "my people gon' get they shine on.") Maybe future anthologies will help show why the most complicated hip-hop lyrics aren't always the most successful.

It's significant that hip-hop, virtually alone among popular-music genres, has never embraced the tradition of lyric booklets. The genius of hip-hop is that it encourages listeners to hear spoken words as music. Few people listen to speeches or books on tape over and over, but hip-hop seems to have just as much replay value as any other popular genre. Reading rap lyrics may be useful, but it's also tiring. The Jay-Z of *Decoded* is engaging; the Jay-Z of his albums is irresistible. The difference has something to do with his odd, perpetually adolescent-sounding voice, and a lot to do with his sophisticated sense of rhythm. Sure, he's a poet—and, while we're at it, a singer and percussionist, too. But why should any of these titles be more impressive than "rapper"?

In the introduction to *Finishing the Hat*, Sondheim explains that "all rhymes, even the farthest afield of the near ones (*home/dope*), draw attention to the rhymed word." But surely rhyming can deëmphasize the meaning of a word by emphasizing its sound. Rhyme, like other phonetic techniques, is a way to turn a spoken phrase into a musical phrase—a "rhythmic argument," as Jay-Z put it. *Bap bap bapbap*. Rapping is the art of addressing listeners and distracting them at the same time. Bradley argues in *Book of Rhymes* that hip-hop lyrics represent the genre's best chance for immortality: "When all the club bangers have faded, when all the styles and videos are long forgotten, the words will remain." That gets the relationship backward. On the contrary, one suspects that the words will endure—and the books will proliferate—because the music will, too.

2010

ANTHONY DeCURTIS

Among rock journalists a debate about writers and their relationship to those they cover has simmered since the beginnings. Robert Christgau insisted on keeping his distance from the acts he wrote about; his colleague Richard Goldstein could hardly get close enough. Anthony DeCurtis (b. 1951) is of the Goldstein camp. His best writing, like the carefully observed reassessment of the Rolling Stones' *Some Girls* included here, combines a deep knowledge of pop music and American culture with a fan's appreciation of what the music does well. He's also one of rock journalism's very best interviewers. DeCurtis is a contributing editor for *Rolling Stone*, where his work has appeared for more than thirty-five years. He has published two collections, *Rocking My Life Away: Writing About Music and Other Matters* (1998) and *In Other Words: Artists Talk About Life and Work* (2005). DeCurtis was the cowriter of Clive Davis's 2013 autobiography, *The Soundtrack of My Life*; he is also the editor of *Present Tense: Rock & Roll and Culture* (1992) and *Blues & Chaos: The Music Writing of Robert Palmer* (2009). His album notes for the Eric Clapton box set *Crossroads* won a Grammy Award in 1998. DeCurtis holds a PhD in American literature from Indiana University, and is a distinguished lecturer in the creative writing program at the University of Pennsylvania. He is currently writing a biography of Lou Reed.

▼ ▼

Love and Hope and Sex and Dreams:
Punk Rock, Disco, New York City
& The Triumph of the Rolling Stones'
Some Girls

FORD TO CITY: DROP DEAD. The headline blasted from the *New York Daily News* on October 30, 1975, and captured the desperation New Yorkers felt as their hometown teetered on the brink of bankruptcy and chaos. It hardly mattered that President Gerald Ford had never uttered the words "drop dead," or that he would eventually agree to loan the city money to stave off fiscal collapse. The tabloid tough talk had made its point: "We're dyin' here! Do something!"

That was the tenor of life in New York in the mid-Seventies. The town seemed dangerous and ungovernable. In July of 1977, most of the city lost electrical power, and looting erupted. Stores were stripped of their wares, and buildings were set ablaze. And in 1976 and 1977, a serial killer who called himself the Son of Sam prowled the city's outer boroughs, firing on couples who had come to lovers' lanes. "Hello from the gutters of N.Y.C. which are filled with dog manure, vomit, stale wine, urine and blood," he wrote in a letter to a newspaper columnist. It felt as if the wide-open sex of the free-wheeling Seventies in New York had found its psychotic moral avenger.

It might seem strange that an environment like that would provide such rich inspiration for one of the Rolling Stones' greatest albums: *Some Girls* (1978). In fact, it makes perfect sense. The Stones' most compelling work before then—the extraordinary run of albums between 1968 and 1972: *Beggars Banquet*, *Let It Bleed*, *Sticky Fingers* and *Exile on Main Street*—took shape as the utopian hopes of the Sixties yielded to violence and repression. So the travails of New York City provided an ideal imaginative setting. And as New York struggled economically, its cultural life burgeoned. People packed dance clubs to set their troubles aside, hear some spectacular music and maybe meet a delectable someone. And then there was punk rock. In its raw, guitar centric sound and shredded-clothes aesthetic, punk more directly reflected the strains the city was under than did the fantasy world of disco.

New York, disco and punk: The three emotional accelerants for *Some Girls*. Asked about the album in a 1995 *Rolling Stone* interview, Mick Jagger responded, "The inspiration for the record was really based in New York and the ways of the town. I think that gave it an extra spur and hardness . . . Punk and disco were going on at the same time, so it was quite an interesting period." In addition, in the Seventies merely being in your thirties raised issues about whether or not you were too old to rock. It was time for the Stones to prove that their best work was not behind them. Guitarist Ron Wood had joined the band, replacing Mick Taylor, and with *Some Girls* the newly reconstituted group set out to reclaim its stature.

Finally, the album had a more serious urgency for the Stones. In February of 1977 the band had gone to Toronto to record, and, after a police raid of his hotel room, Keith Richards was charged with possession of heroin with intent to sell. A conviction could have meant a stiff prison term. Keith's trial date loomed as the band recorded *Some Girls*. The very existence of the Rolling Stones hung in the balance.

The Stones began working at the Pathé-Marconi Studios in Paris in October of 1977, and they would stay there through most of December. After a holiday break, they resumed, and wrapped up the sessions in early March of 1978. Paris might seem like an odd choice in retrospect, given the New York focus of the album, but an environment can sometimes be imagined more vividly if you're not living in it.

The Stones decided to keep the sessions focused on the five members of the band, though Faces keyboardist Ian MacLagan, saxophonist Mel Collins, percussionist Simon Kirke and harmonica player Sugar Blue appear on various tracks. This stripped-down approach left more room for Jagger to play guitar, which made for a harder attack. Jagger liked to play loud and mean. "Oh, here comes Lou Reed again," engineer Chris Kimsey would say every time the singer strapped on his guitar.

Some Girls was released in June of 1978, but a few weeks before, "Miss You" dramatically announced that the Stones were back. The song, which rocketed to number one, reflected Jagger's subtle feel for the dance music current at the time. Richards' and Wood's winding guitars and Sugar Blue's moaning harmonica mix inextricably to provide an ideal backdrop to the intense erotic longing of Jagger's vocal. That yearning then gets a searing instrumental interpretation in Mel Collins's stuttering sax solo. It's a masterful performance, one of the Stones' finest singles.

"Miss You" opens *Some Girls* on a cinematic note of emotional drama, and then yields to the guitar roar of "When the Whip Comes Down." If the singer of "Miss You" wanders night-time New York in search of love, the young gay male hustler in "When the Whip Comes Down" does something at least a little bit similar. Having come to New York, like so many other young people, in search of a place where he can be himself ("I was gay in New York, which is a fag in L.A."), he ends up working as a garbage man during the day and turning tricks at night in the Loop, the notorious gay cruising area on East 53rd Street.

"Imagination" is the Stones' rough-edged cover of "Just My Imagination (Running Away With Me)," a number one hit for the Temptations in 1971. Delicate, orchestral and dreamlike in the Temps' version, the Stones toughen it up, replacing strings with guitars and lagging languorously behind the beat, an effect that is simultaneously unsettling and deeply satisfying. Jagger adds a New York reference to the lyrics, bringing the song further into the album's emotional space.

The title track shifts the mood again, this time into a realm where sexual relationships are defined, at least in part, by money, power and manipulation. A thick, molasses groove on which Jagger not only plays like Lou Reed, but sings like him, the song is a catalogue of world-weary observations about women, most notable for the singer's off-hand assertion that "Black girls just want to get fucked all night / I just don't have that much jam."

Primarily because of a threatened boycott of the album by the Rev. Jesse Jackson, who declared that the lyric "degrades blacks and women," the song ratcheted up complaints about the Stones' misogyny. Beyond political correctness, that critique of songs like "Some Girls" reveals an emotional tone-deafness that has little to do with the ways men and women relate to each other in love. "Some Girls" is like a Don-Juan-in-hell reminiscence, a recounting of battles won and lost in the erotic wars by a character who obviously loves women but is under no illusions about their moral superiority to men.

That the album's garishly colourful art work, designed by Peter Corriston, depicted the Stones in drag among a gaggle of celebrity women might have suggested to discerning viewers that *Some Girls'* gender roles weren't exactly fixed. Inevitably, the cover art only got the band into more trouble. Farrah Fawcett, Lucille Ball, Raquel Welch and the estates of Judy Garland and Marilyn Monroe all objected to their depictions. The unhappy women were removed, but not replaced, and Corriston wittily added the text, "Pardon Our Appearance—Cover Under Reconstruction."

"Lies" and "Respectable" relaunch the Stones' blistering, punk-style assault. Both songs are thought to be directed at Bianca Jagger, who had filed for divorce from Mick shortly before the album came out. While acknowledging the reference to "my wife" in "Respectable," Jagger brushed off that reading, however slyly: "My wife's a very honest person, and the song's not 'about' her . . . it's just a shit-kicking rock & roll number." In 1993, he would insist that "the lyric carries no fantastically deep message, but I think it might have had something to do with Bianca."

In keeping with the emotional dynamic of *Some Girls*, "Far Away Eyes," for all its parodic, country elements, again taps into the longing of songs like "Miss You" and "Imagination." Jagger recalled the song as originating in his actual experience. "You know, when you drive through Bakersfield on a Sunday morning or Sunday evening . . . all the country-music radio stations start broadcasting live from L.A. black gospel services," he said. "And that's what the song refers to." Of course, the broadness of Jagger's vocal complicates the impact of "Far Away Eyes," and introduces another note of humour—the most overlooked aspect of *Some Girls.* "The actual music is played completely straight," he explained, "but it's me who's not going legit with the whole thing, because I think I'm a blues singer not a country singer—I think it's more suited to Keith's voice than mine."

Keith put that Appalachian twang to perfect use on "Before They Make Me Run," which has become a personal theme song for him. He has described it as "a cry from the heart," and it derives from all the trials— in all senses of the term—resulting from his arrest. As jaunty as it is, the song is an unflinching look at addiction and its costs: the deaths of loved ones ("another goodbye to another good friend") and the pain inflicted on yourself and those around you. It is also Keith's prayer that the judge will let him off easy. "When you get a lenient sentence," he explained, "they say, oh, they let him walk." His wish was granted, and Keith's sentence was for the Stones to play a couple of charity shows in the Toronto area.

Richards came up with the riff for "Beast of Burden," which ranks as one of the Stones' most powerful ballads. He claims he came up with the title to express gratitude to Jagger for taking responsibility for the band while he struggled with his heroin problems: "When I returned to the fold after 'closing down the laboratory,' I came back into the studio with Mick . . . to say, 'Thanks, man, for shouldering the bur- den'—that's why I wrote 'Beast of Burden' for him, I realize in retro- spect." Both Keith and Ron Wood play acoustic and electric guitars on the track, and their interweaving, in Keith's words, "is a good example of the two of us twinkling felicitously together." The song expresses a desire for equal standing in a relationship, a wish to get beyond the power struggles of love and just be two people together.

Some Girls ends back on the ravaged streets of New York with "Shat- tered," which evokes the city's crisis ("the crime rate's going up, up, up, up, up!") but in a humorous way. Jagger speak-sings in the character of a New Yorker driven mad by the city's deterioration: "Go ahead, bite the Big Apple / Don't mind the maggots!"

But he also sings, "Love and hope and sex and dreams / Are still sur- viving on the street," and that exuberance and conviction, that deter- mination to survive, are the song's ultimate message—and the album's too. *Some Girls* became the Stones' most commercially successful album of original material; it went to number one and, to date, it has sold well over six million copies in the U.S. alone.

More important, though, *Some Girls* is an album that has only grown in stature. Its songs hold up, but, taken together, they amount to much more than the sum of their extraordinary parts. *Some Girls* is an album about a time and a place, and about an era, but it simultaneously transcends those categories. Timely and timeless, it's as rewarding—and as much fun—to listen to now as when it initially burst on the scene to remind us that, regardless of trends, the Rolling Stones would not be leaving the musical pantheon any time soon.

2011

DANYEL SMITH

Danyel Smith (b. 1965) began her career as a popular music writer in 1989 in the Bay Area, writing for *The San Francisco Bay Guardian* and *The East Bay Express*. She later worked as a freelancer for *Spin* and an editor for *Billboard*. Her first major appointment came in 1994 when she was made music editor—the first African American editor, and the first woman—and later editor-in-chief, for *VIBE* magazine. She has by now written for just about every high-profile music and culture magazine in the U.S.—*Time, Cosmopolitan, The Village Voice, The New Yorker*, and *Rolling Stone*. In her piece on pop crooner Barry Manilow, Smith eloquently makes the point that there's no such thing as a "guilty" pleasure, as long as the pleasure is real—a pleasure that her writing viscerally communicates. A frequent commentator on news and newsmagazine television, Smith has published two novels, and is currently at work on a history of African American women in pop music.

▼ ▼

After 30 Years, I Finally Went to a Barry Manilow Concert

AT THE St. James Theater—the velvet place where *Oklahoma!* first came sweeping down the plains in 1943—we get glow sticks with our programs. I haven't had a glow stick since seeing D.C. rapper Wale at New York City's Terminal 5 in 2011. Wale's galvanic show was for those 18-and-over. Kids had on plush animal-head masks and pajamas.

Manilow on Broadway, on St. Valentine's, was date night for those kids' burnished elders.

Certain my husband and I were the only two who'd been to both shows, we settled in with our Pringles and our peppermints, and geared up for my dream to come true. The night wasn't about kitsch for me. I wasn't in it for the probable camp. I'd done my hair as carefully as any of the other ladies from Long Island and Westchester and Jersey. I'd been thinking of seeing Barry Manilow, live in concert, for over 30 years.

I was that kid—molded in conditions split unequally between paternal fascism and maternal quiescence—who made a fetish of not just free will, but of the future. I didn't want to die or "to die" from my unhappiness. I wanted to get to legal adulthood. I wanted my freedom. In 1978, I was living through Manilow's new "Ready To Take A Chance Again," from the soundtrack to Chevy Chase and Goldie Hawn's *Foul Play,* which I had not and have never seen. I was at a good public school in Los Angeles, where I hung with the Shores and the Wunsches and the Gorens from around the way, and the Dianitas and the Candaces and the Portias bussed in from Watts. This along with the kids from my own Jewish and African-American Fairfax District neighborhood, which was just south of what was then a fading retail stretch known as the Miracle Mile.

We were a mile or two from the wealthy subdivision of Hancock Park, before it seemed like all the kids from Hancock went to private school. At John Burroughs Junior High, we mostly mixed. But we also segregated ourselves. The black kids thumped Heatwave and Chic. White kids bumped Lynyrd Skynyrd and Kansas. But in Band class, the talk centered on Queen, Earth, Wind & Fire, Donna Summer and Barry Manilow. My junior high was weird: Lou Rawls' son was at our school. Booker T. Jones' son was there. One of the Neiman-Marcus Marcuses. Governor Jerry Brown's niece. Our band teacher was a road and studio musician for EWF. I've little recollection of one Pope dying, and another rising to power. I have only vague memories of Camp David and people striving for "peace." I had my own peaces to negotiate. Had flute to practice. Had Manilow to listen to.

I thought Barry Manilow was not only singing truth to power, but was proving that life would be, eventually, my own. He was going to have a sweet life. And he didn't have to be cute—he was the awkward and undisputed truth of my tween emotions. Of course I wrote out, and memorized all the lyrics to Sugar Hill Gang's 1979 "Rapper's Delight." And I swore by *Right On!* magazine, where the Jackson brothers ruled. But Manilow was, for three or four intense years, my mindset. I liked pop and didn't know to call it that. Liked pop and didn't know that me liking it is what in fact made it *pop*ular. I didn't know to articulate anything about pop phrasings, straightforward melodies and the crisp, bold enunciations that with some luck and a promo budget meant millions would request a song at radio, meant millions would purchase singles and albums and T-shirts and lunchboxes, would contribute to the radio/sales/tour/merchandise quadruped that, until the internet and "views" and "free," meant a song could gallop to the top, and be, in ways that are more elusive now, a really big show. An artist could reach the kind of places that are, as Jay-Z says, "higher than weather." I didn't know that Barry Manilow made himself as much as he was made. I didn't know he was raised by a single mother in (Williamsburg) Brooklyn. I didn't know what Brooklyn was.

I was a kid. I cared about volume. And the tears that flowed as (in Band) we went for the crescendo. From the radio I wanted to hear the big chords, the big drums, the big horns. I didn't know there was such a thing as being manipulated by the right pauses—I liked Clive Davis' ear and Clive Davis' work and I didn't know yet who Clive Davis was. Michael Jackson was a world apart, a king, but my regular high school favorites were Prince and Rick James, and by the time I hit college, aside from Run-DMC, Sade and Luther Vandross, I was about Whitney Houston, who in 1978 was singing backup disco for the Michael Zager Band. This was seven years before Davis would re-apply what he'd learned making hit after hit with Manilow to the woman who would become one of the most loved and bestselling artists of all time. Listen to Manilow ballads, then listen to Houston ballads. Check, as we used to say in hip-hop, the technique. If it wasn't broke Davis saw little need to fix it. The songs Davis made with Manilow and Houston are the songs I loved. Besides, what other way had I to judge? My mother, after all, had to tell me when I was 13 who Booker T. Jones Jr.'s dad was. I thought like I used to think about all songs when I was young— that every artist's song was purely autobiographical, and so 100 percent meaningful. And if I categorized at all, it was based on what radio station played what. So I thought Barry was rock 'n' roll—and not rock in a "white" frame. Rock in a frame marked "real."

As a part of his 1978 Even Now tour, Barry Manilow did 21 sold-out nights at the Greek Theater in Los Angeles. That's what everyone was going to, and where I wanted to go. I was disappointed that I wasn't allowed. It was because there was to be no chaperone for the group attending—that was my mother's story. Nonsense. I'd been able to stay at home chaperoneless since I was seven. Took public buses by myself at eight. I rode my bike to Venice Beach, 15 miles round trip, with my younger sister, at 11. I counted sheets in locked closets. I catalogued bruises—on me, on my mother. I began to recognize the tenets of sociopathy, alcoholism, the bitter power trips born of disappointments suffered and missteps made. Plus my father figure's intense discomfort and long guilt for having been black and upper middle class in the era of segregation. He did not love anything really except his mother and my mother, and even them in ways so foul it tattooed us all.

My grandmother eventually told me why I couldn't go. I was not allowed to attend the Manilow show because I'd made it known in my household that it meant a lot to me. I'd played "Daybreak" a few too many times in a row. I'd asked what was special about the "New England" Manilow sang of. It wasn't a state—so I needed clarification. I'd expressed too much fascination at the fact that the O'Jays had a song called "Brandy" that was supposedly about a dog, and Manilow had a song called "Mandy" that was maybe about a dog. The apartment I lived in during junior high school was rarely "happy," but when music was played it was the classics: Motown and Streisand. It's wild, even creepy, how we become fans of artists. But love is love. *Whatever I am*, Manilow sings, *you taught me to be.* My eyes well up every time I hear the two minutes, 16 seconds that is his 1973 "I Am Your Child." They did so at the St. James.

After a long break, it was in 2007 that I began listening to Barry Manilow again. I was editing *VIBE* magazine, and was happily knee-deep in Rihanna, Gym Class Heroes, Akon and Beyoncé. I'd ended up, after all, the girl who goes to concerts for a living. And even still I avoided Barry.

Ridley Scott's *American Gangster* was in theaters, and was ricochet-ing through the music industry's creative cliques because Jay-Z had created a concept album, also called *American Gangster* (Roc-A-Fella/Def Jam) inspired by the film. James D'Agostino, better known as DJ Green Lantern, was especially moved. Green (as he prefers to be called) is a prolific producer as well as a DJ, has been the road DJ for Jay-Z, and for Eminem, and is currently the road DJ for Nas. He also has a show on Atlanta's often No. 1 rated V-103 (CBS Radio's WVEE 103.3 FM), which is also often ranked as the No. 1 urban station in the country. Green is from Rochester, New York. He grew up listening to a lot of Led Zeppelin, and a lot of hip-hop. "I can't say I'm a *fan*," says Green, "but I've definitely been exposed to Mr. Manilow, and can appreciate his hits, and the fact that he's a songwriter/musician/singer. I place those kind of artists on a pedestal, in the sense of creativity. And he's up there."

Unlike DJ Skee, 9th Wonder, and others who did entire *American Gangster* remix projects, in '07 Green created an unofficial remix of just one track from Jay-Z's *American Gangster.* "This is right around the time when the *Gangster* a cappellas were released," Green says of Jay-Z's move—like with his 2003 *The Black Album*—to make his vocals available for people to work with. "I like to use things that say the same thing, but from a different source . . . A continuity-type of thing." So Green electronically flipped through his dusty grooves, rooting around for a constancy in theme that would ring. "Jay-Z has a song called 'Sweet,'" he says, thinking back to the original, which was produced by Sean "Diddy" Combs, and Sean C. & LV. "And here's this Barry Manilow song, 'Sweet Life.'" The song was written by Manilow, and is on both his actual 1973 debut *Barry Manilow* (Bell) and the re-release of that album, as *Barry Manilow I* (Arista). *Sweet Life* is also the title of Manilow's 1987 autobiography.

"I'm really a fan of the 'Mama / Can you hear me' part, and wanted to focus in on that," Green says. "That was the reason I'd kinda tucked [the song] in my sample folder. But I went back, and the 'I'm gonna have a sweet life' jumped out at me, like *Oh that's it, that's the part. That's gonna work with that* . . . So sure enough there's a break in there and all I had to do was separate it, and loop it, and add just a little bit . . . I might've put a kick with it, and maybe a clap at the most." Green plays down his end result. The remix is a sound collage—interview snippet here, the odd Jay spoken moment there, all placed to emphasize rhyme, and swag, and bold bittersweetness, and almost-rhyme. *Sweet! And still there's pain,* Jay-Z says, *No shame / No sir.*

The two Brooklyn boys, Jay-Z and Barry Manilow are talking the eternal underdog struggle: the what-ifs, the I-ams, the thoughts of death and the desire for their own peaces. Manilow on piano comes careening through on Green's remix, four decades strong, like it was waiting to bear Jay-Z's lyrics, to be something else—yet a same thing. "It was sparse because I wanted the original sample to shine," says Green. "The piano, just the mood of it, the soulfulness of it." *Mama, can you hear me.* That's what Manilow sang. *I'm gonna have the sweetest life you've ever seen. And when the day is over, I'm gonna go to sleep in a field of green.*

There's a smallish riot going on at the St. James Theater. It's Glow Stick City.

Barry Manilow opens with 1975's "It's A Miracle." Never my favorite, it seems to be exactly where songs like Lionel Richie's 1985 "Dancin' on the Ceiling" were bred. The production for the show is low-key. The set is too dark, what lighting there is, is unimaginative and the back-up singer/dancers are both too much—and not enough. The question of backing tracks is easy to answer. Manilow speeds through "Could It Be Magic." There is a medley, and then a moment when he unbuttons his tux coat, and a lightweight pelvic thrust right on the beat. When he hurries through "Somewhere in the Night" I'm worried. "Looks Like We Made It" is too cabaret. The show itself is very cabaret. But except for when he performs some recent cover songs, I don't stop singing. My husband is astounded by the energy in the room. Confetti drops as the show ends. It's Valentine's Day. After all the years of not going, it looks like I've made it.

And so had he. Manilow was coming off a recent flu, and a recent hip surgery. He is 69 years old. He's in the Songwriters Hall of Fame. He's sold maybe 80 million records. No show now is going to be one of his nights at the Greek Theater in 1978. And Manilow—he knows this. You can say a lot about him, but you cannot say he didn't live to tell the story. He's so aware of the fact that he's not the weird arty boy he was on Burt Sugarman's syndicated *Midnight Special* variety show, he shows clips from it on Broadway. And he plays piano along with the clips. The self he is now sings along—not like a synch, but heartbreakingly and strikingly, like a duo. His low-tech collaboration with his former self says that Manilow knows who he is, and who he is to us—and he thunders through it the best he can. That's rock and that's hip-hop and that's soul, and we make it pop, or not. "You all have been here all along," he said, acknowledging our part in it, and giving us our props for it.

I was indeed waving my glow stick like a maniac, and it reminded me that the Wale song I'd been most excited to hear that night at Terminal 5 with the 18-and-overs was his 2009 "Beautiful Bliss" which features the rapper J. Cole, and the gorgeously melodramatic singer Melanie Fiona. The song is co-produced by DJ Green Lantern (with Mark Ronson), and it's one of the best rap songs of the last five years. If you're lucky, and negotiate your peaces, it all comes around. I'd told my mother I was going to see Manilow, and she was psyched for me. *When you feel like this,* Wale raps, *a beautiful bliss.* For a millisecond, on both nights, it was like I was 13 again.

2013

▼

Greil Marcus

Across a career that now spans nearly five decades, Greil Marcus (b. 1945) has expanded the possibilities of rock writing and provided it with an impeccable intellectual pedigree. Before turning his energies full-time to rock writing, Marcus completed a BA in American studies and an MA in political science at UC Berkeley; that training—the complex, interdisciplinary frames of reference they provided—has been crucial to everything he has written since. Marcus's writing is notable for the intellectual leaps and risks he takes in constructing a rich cultural context for his interpretations of rock and pop; he can hear—and makes his readers hear—Puritan theology in the background of a Robert Johnson recording, and the influence of the French Situationists in the shambolic noise the Sex Pistols made. Marcus may be rock writing's most literary writer. Other critics in rock writing's first wave (Christgau, Goldstein, Willis) showed what it would look like to take rock & roll seriously; no one else did it with Marcus's sensuous, allusive prose. Among his more than twenty books are the critically acclaimed *Mystery Train: Images of America* (1975), currently in its sixth edition; *Lipstick Traces: A Secret History of the Twentieth Century* (1989); *Dead Elvis: A Chronicle of a Cultural Obsession* (1991); *Like a Rolling Stone: Bob Dylan at the Crossroads* (2005); and *The History of Rock 'n' Roll in Ten Songs* (2014), from which this essay on Christian Marclay's *Guitar Drag* is taken. In addition to his books, his writing has appeared in *Rolling Stone* (where he was the first records editor), *Creem*, *Artforum*, *The Village Voice*, and *The Believer*, among many other magazines. He has taught as a visitor at UC Berkeley, Princeton, the University of Minnesota, New York University, and The New School.

▼ ▼

Guitar Drag

IT'S 2013, maybe 2014. You walk into one of the vinyl shops that are beginning to dot cheaper commercial neighborhoods—the Lower East Side in New York, Skid Row in Seattle, West Hollywood, maybe Stranded on Telegraph Avenue in Oakland. In a used bin you find a twelve-inch disc with a blurry photo on the cover. You can see rope and some kind of machinery. You turn the sleeve over and on the back there's a distorted but decodable picture: what seems to be an electric guitar with two leads attached, one taut, one loose, on a brown surface that might be a road. There are no words or even lettering on either side; the spine reads "Christian Marclay Guitar Drag Neon Records." You pay $7.95—"It's pristine," says the guy at the counter—take it home, slit the shrink wrap, take out the record, put it on your turntable, info label side up: "Soundtrack from the video Guitar Drag, 2000. Recorded San Antonio, Texas, on November 18th, 1999. Released by Neon Records, Sweden 2006." You cue it up and the tone arm slides right to the label. You adjust the weight and try again, with the same result: there are no grooves on the record. You turn it over, where the label again shows the blurry photo—now you can see the six tuning pegs of a guitar, a rope around the top of the neck, and a dirt road. 33 RPM, it says. Now it plays.

At first there's silence, then intermittent rumbling noises, scraping noises, the noise of something hollow. After a minute, you catch the high pings of a guitar being tuned, then feedback turning into a whine, bass strings being fingered, a quiet strum on the strings that echoes into more feedback, making a sound far too big for whatever it is you're picturing as the action behind what you hear.

At two and a half minutes there's the unmistakable sound of a car starting—the only unmistakable sound, it will turn out, that you'll hear. Immediately a harsh noise kicks up, relentless, monochromatic; then a second noise, higher, then under the surface of the first two tones a bass counterpoint, so much bigger than the other sounds it almost drowns them out, then a treble sound raised over the others and held.

Another minute and a half has gone. The higher tone has shifted under the lower. The harsh noise has disappeared. Then the guitar begins to screech and reach; you can feel it trying to make a chord. There's a bass rumble, then a scramble, the pace picking up: the simultaneous levels of sound are constantly changing position, fighting for primacy, bass versus treble, treble versus bass, scattered noise versus steady tone. You try to make a narrative out of it all, to see the music, because it is beginning to come across as some kind of music, going somewhere. Guitar Drag? For a moment you forget the label you read: maybe that's the name of the band, a drone band like Th Faith Healers, with their mesmerizing thirty-two minute "Everything, All at Once, Forever," which pretty much covers the territory. You hear the car engine again, revving up, increasing speed, until it vanishes under a furious sonic back-and-forth, yes no yes no yes no, that breaks any picture you were trying to make.

At seven minutes, the sound begins to fade, or seems to—the piece, or the documentary recording, or the computer manipulation, whatever it is you're listening to, seems to assume a kind of shape. If you can't find a story in the noise, or make one up, you can get used to the noise, stop hearing it, erase the story you can't decode. The sound rises slightly, more modulated, less frantic, dissonant but with direction. Then the noise doubles into a high screech, then it narrows, so that there's less to hear, and then you're looking straight into a chainsaw, everything cut and torn apart, then quiet, an object being pulled through water or gravel, and then a surge of speed and volume, then the volume up and the speed down, a moment of suspense, a breath drawn, and at eleven minutes you don't like where this is going.

Before that sensation can turn into a thought, the terrain the sound is making is invaded by the loud, focused sound of something boring into something else. Everything begins to break up. Even in the chaos you get used to it. The sound isn't quieter but it seems to be. The boring noise recedes, replaced by a high scratch, the sound band narrowing even further as the car again picks up speed, even sounds, feels as if it's swerving from one side of the sound, or the road, to the other. With the screech constant, for the first time you begin to hear as if you're listening from inside of the noise as it happens, as it is made, as it occurs—no epistemology rules any more than any sound does, but what you're hearing is alive, trying to speak, trying to form a language.

You can distinguish three levels of sound. As at the start there is rumbling, feedback, but without a sense of movement, a slowing down, the sound narrowing from a dark mass to a single line drawn in pencil down a page. The sound holds, and, at just over fourteen minutes, it disappears.

Colson Whitehead's novel *John Henry Days* centers on vastly different appearances of the ballad about the race between the great steel driver and the steam drill built to replace him, the story of how John Henry beat the machine at the cost of his own life: of how, as countless singers black and white have sung, from some time in the 1870s or the 1880s to this day, "he laid down his hammer and he died." Parading through Whitehead's pages are an unnamed singer searching the old song for new words, the Tin Pan Alley song plugger who at the start of the twentieth century becomes the first man to copyright it, a Mississippi blues singer recording it in Chicago in the 1930s, a crackhead singing it on the street in the 1990s. Alternating with their stories are the cynical adventures of a hack journalist named J., on a junket to Talcott, West Virginia, one of various places where the great race was supposed to have taken place in the years after the Civil War, now in 1996 celebrating the issue, right there in Talcott, of a thirty-two-cent first class John Henry stamp. The town is celebrating the first annual John Henry Day festival. It's going to put the town on the map.

Also in Talcott is Pamela Street, there to sell the town the contents of her late father's John Henry Museum, which filled her family's apartment in Harlem, a museum containing hundreds of recordings of the song, every sheet music version, lawn jockeys, paintings, theatrical programs and costumes, even five spikes a salesman claimed came from the Big Bend tunnel in Talcott, the very spot where John Henry stood side by side with the steam drill and a pistol shot sent them off. Her father bought all five—"the new school clothes could wait"—and hung them over the mantel. To a little girl they were five scary, threatening fingers:

"a railroad hand," a dead man's hand, reaching out to grab her in the night. She hates everything about John Henry: her father's obsession took away her childhood. But in spite of herself, she knows everything about John Henry.

She and J. approach the Talcott John Henry: a statue of a hugely muscled black man, stripped to the waist, with a hammer in his hands. They read the plaque: "This statue was erected in 1972 by a group of people with the same determination as the one it honors—the Talcott Ruritan Club." In Whitehead's novel, every time anyone confronts the song—a folklorist in the 1920s, seeking to prove the legend true or false, a little girl on Striver's Row in Harlem in the 1950s cheating on her piano lessons with what her outraged mother calls gutter music—they are, in their own way, singing it, and so Whitehead imagines the Talcott sculptor: "The artist was forced to rely on what the story worked on his brain. He looked at the footprint left in his psyche by the steeldriver's great strides and tried to reconstruct what such a man might look like."

"You see those dents in the statue," Pamela says to J. "People come around here and use it for target practice. One time they chained the statue to a pickup and dragged it off the pedestal down the road there. Then the statue fell off and they drove off so they found it the next day just lying in the road." "Probably not much to do here on a Saturday night," says J.

This isn't merely a story. The novel is made of accumulating detail, Whitehead researching down more than a century and then imagining every setting, every character's milieu, what a room looks like, how people talk there, what they wear, what the air is like. But there are also coded, hidden details, and this—"One time they chained the statue to a pickup and dragged it off the pedestal down the road"—is one of them. It's an illustration of the twists and tangles folk songs take as they emerge from real life, live on in the imaginative life of generations of singers and dancers, and then as the songs are pulled back into real, lived life, until you can't tell the song from the events behind it and in front of it, the real from the imaginative—when you can't tell if an event caused the song or the song caused the event. Here, the tale of people chaining the statue to a pickup truck and dragging it off of its pedestal is an inescapable, folk-fictional version of an actual historical event. For a novel published in 2001, there is no way that this is not a version of the murder of James Byrd, Jr., in Jasper, Texas, on 7 June 1998.

Byrd was forty-nine and black. He was walking home from a party. Three white men in a Ford pickup, John King, Russell Brewer, and Shawn Berry, offered him a ride; he climbed in. They drove behind a store, pulled him out, beat him with a baseball bat, chained him by his ankles to the truck, and dragged him to death. When they finally dumped the body at the gate of a local black cemetery, there was no head and no right arm. Investigators determined that Byrd had tried to keep his head off the ground until the driver swerved and smashed him into a culvert. King and Brewer were both white supremacists—King had a tattoo of a black man hanging from a tree. Berry was sentenced to life; Brewer and King were sentenced to death. Brewer was executed in 2011.

In *John Henry Days*, and in history, this event can be seen—heard—as an unsinging of "John Henry," with the black man stripped of his hammer, chained to the steam drill, and pulled through the tunnel like a coal car. It's an argument that any lynching of a black American is an unsinging of "John Henry." And it's an argument that the song itself—whether called "John Henry," "The Death of John Henry," "Nine Pound Hammer," "More About John Henry," "New Railroad," or "Spike Driver Blues"—is a symbolic unsinging of any and every lynching of a black person, an affirmation of the power of a single African-American to deny and defeat the white power set against him, even if it costs him his life, but not his dignity, with the song rolling down the decades from the 1920s, when it was first recorded, taken up by Uncle Dave Macon, Mississippi John Hurt, Paul Robeson, the Monroe Brothers, Woody Guthrie, in the present day by Bruce Springsteen, the Los Angeles techno duo Snakefarm, the Boston bluegrass combo Crooked Still, and, taking John Henry from a factless past into the historical present, the British punk singer Jon Langford. Christian Marclay's "Guitar Drag," emerging out of this complex of real and imaginary situations, is another version of this version of the song.

Born in 1955 in California, raised in Switzerland, Marclay is best known for *The Clock*, first shown in 2010: his twenty-four hour, minute-by-minute video collage of clips from thousands of movies that, playing only in real time—when you enter the viewing space in a gallery or a museum at 10:13 A.M., it's 10:13 A.M. on the screen—creates a picture of an entire, mythic day. With hundreds of projects behind him, Marclay is an inveterate visual and sound artist who has always worked with musical themes, at first taking commercial albums and fitting them with new covers and labels, breaking and reassembling LPs and fitting the pieces of different records together into one that would actually play, redesigning, deforming, and distorting every kind of musical instrument or sound equipment, even scouring cities to photograph music-themed signs, advertisements, tattoos, and sound holes in walls and elevators. He is an omnivorous assemblage artist drawn to destruction: everything in his work is about taking something out of one context and putting it into another, or recognizing the way in which an object has lost its original, seemingly defining context and occupied another, so that every element of a construction, or deconstruction, begins to tell a story it never told before—but, the feeling is, a story it always wanted to tell.

Marclay's real life as an artist began in 1977, when, attending the Massachusetts College of Art in Boston, he found a children's Batman record in the street, run over but still intact. It played; Marclay was drawn to the sounds made by the tire tracks on the grooves and the dirt and gravel embedded in them. "When a record skips or pops we hear the surface noise, we try very hard to make an abstraction of it so it doesn't disrupt the musical flow," he said years later. "I try to make people aware of these imperfections and accept them as music; the recording is sort of an illusion while the scratch on the record is more real."

On the art-world edges of the New York punk scene in the early 1980s, Marclay became a club disc jockey, a turntablist with as many as eight records spinning at once, scratching back and forth between them until a new music emerged and just as quickly erased itself. He invented the Phonoguitar, allowing him to scratch, distort, and remix a phonograph record while performing as if he were a guitarist, right down to bending the top of his body back in full guitar-hero mode. In 1983, at the Kitchen in New York, he first played "Ghost," a scary, trance-like version of Jimi Hendrix's utterly despairing "I Don't Live Today," from 1967. Nearly twenty years after his death, Hendrix remained larger than life, an unsolved mystery: "I think Jimi's gonna be remembered for centuries, just like people like Leadbelly and Lightnin' Hopkins," John Phillips of the Mamas and the Papas said in 1992. "He's really a folk hero, another John Henry." "Will I live tomorrow? / Well, I just can't say / Will I live tomorrow? / Well, I just can't say / But I know for sure / I don't live today." Marclay didn't sing those words—or he sang them in his own way. Moving the disc back and forth, he found tones in the grooves that had never been heard before. He turned words into echoes, and battered them in the air with complaints, criticisms, denials, all the sounds of distortion, until Hendrix could seem present, as a ghost presiding over the whole affair, and, as a ghost, as physically, cruelly dead as he had ever been. "Bands were being formed right and left," Marclay said in 1992. "Grab a guitar for the first time and start a band. You would get a club date before even starting rehearsals. That's how raw it was. A lot of it was bad but it didn't matter. It was the energy that mattered."

> I grabbed a turntable and used it like a guitar. *Ghost* was an homage to Jimi Hendrix. I was using a turntable-console strapped around my neck like a guitar . . . I'd play Hendrix records, scratch them bad, crush the tone arm through the grooves, and shove the thing in the amp to get feedback. I also used a wah-wah pedal. It was very loud. The portable turntable allowed me to move around and get into some Hendrix moves. What I always liked about Hendrix is the way he was pushing the limits of his instrument, looking for new sounds even if it meant burning his guitar. But *Ghost* was also dealing with the absence of the performer—the absence or death of the performer because of the recording technology. I was playing these records, going through the motions with my surrogate guitar. It was very ritualistic. I sort of became Jimi Hendrix. Instead of playing air-guitar, I was playing records.

What Marclay did onstage with "Ghost" is what he did on video with *Guitar Drag*. In 1998 he was on an airplane, reading *Time*; there was a story about the James Byrd murder. The only photo was of the back of the killers' Ford, rust covering the insides and outside of the truck, with the license plate dead center, smashed, bent, the paint scratched to the point where TEXAS was barely legible. The picture stayed in Marclay's mind as an image that wanted to be taken farther. A year later, in San Antonio as a resident artist, he determined to do it. He borrowed a truck—"from Linda Ronstadt's cousin," he said in 2013. "A Ford, a flatbed—or a Chevrolet, which has rock & roll resonance all over the place." He recruited two people to shoot from the truck bed; he scouted locations. He mounted a Trace Elliot amplifier in the back of the truck.

As the video begins, a thin man, his face obscured by a baseball cap, is holding a new Fender Stratocaster. He plugs it in; with forceful gestures, he knots a rope around its neck and secures it to the back of the truck. He gets into the driver's seat, starts the engine, and drives off. "I didn't know if it was right, as a white artist, with a race crime," Marclay said in 2013—even though, as the driver, he was throwing himself all the way into the story: he was the killer. Isaac Julien, a black British installation artist and filmmaker, was with Marclay in San Antonio: "Do it," he said.

Immediately, the guitar is jerking, turning over, every movement, every movement inside every movement, shouting out of the amplifier, and at first you are attuned to the guitar as an instrument, interested to see what kind of noise it will make, and how long it will last. There is no reference to James Byrd. But within seconds you are drawn into the destruction as a thing in itself, an act with its own imperatives, rules, values, and aesthetics, and that destruction soon casts off any perspectives not completely sucked into an irreducible violence.

Marclay takes the truck down a paved road. Even if no thought of James Byrd enters your mind, even if you are sorting through art-world or rock 'n' roll references—"the tradition of guitar-smashing," Marclay has said of his own sense of the piece, "of the destruction of instruments in Fluxus"—the guitar is becoming a living thing, an animal or a person, something that can feel pain, and you are hearing it scream. The truck turns onto what looks like a dead swamp, a field of scrub and weeds, as if to drown the guitar in dirt. The sound it is making is full, undiminished, shooting out in too many directions. The truck races into woods, down back roads. There are constant cuts—sometimes Marclay stopped the truck and changed places with one of the videographers and vice versa—but there is no feeling of that. This is a race, a race to see how long it will take to destroy the guitar and whatever symbols and allegories, along with leaves, vines, and rocks, are wrapping themselves around the neck and tuning pegs—allegories like Dock Boggs's stalker's version of the murder ballad "Pretty Polly": "He led her over hills and valleys so deep / He led her over hills and valleys so deep / At length Pretty Polly, she begin to weep."

You are watching torture. You begin to flinch. You might turn away, but even if you don't look there's no stopping the sound. There is no abstraction. The truck pulls back onto a paved road, swerving hard to the left, to the right, the guitar swinging on the rope from one side of the road straight to the other, and while there may be a thinning in the sound, a hollowness, there's no way to anticipate when the volume will shoot up, when a sound the guitar hasn't made before will rise up and die. The truck slows down, speeds up, pulls the guitar over railroad tracks, through rocks and ever rougher surfacing, the guitar still speaking. The truck turns onto a wider road, a highway, the guitar slamming the pavement, by this time perhaps all the strings gone, the tuning pegs broken, and sound still streaming out of the body. What was clandestine before—the swamp, the field, the back roads—is now public, a crime in progress, anyone can see it, and you think, surely the police will stop it? There is no one else on the road. Is the man still in the cab of the truck? Is this some drama now so caught up in its own momentum it can play itself?

"We could not kill it," Marclay said in 2013. "We tried to: that moment when the guitar goes over the train tracks, embedded in the ground, but it still jumps into the air—the tracks marking the racial divide." As the piece ends—and you can feel it ending, slowing down—

the truck crests a hill in a haze of sun and dust, like the end of a western, John Wayne framed in the light in the cabin door in *The Searchers*, any movie cowboy trailing off into the sunset with his horse. There is no resolution, no real ending at all. "Once you go down that road," Marclay said in 2013, echoing *Detour* or *Raw Deal* or so many other noir films of the 1940s, "there's no way out."

Guitar Drag is a scratch in the record—the historical record. If you put the soundtrack record back on with all of this in the front of your mind, other music begins to rise out of it. There is most of all Jimi Hendrix's Woodstock transformation of "The Star-Spangled Banner," the greatest and most unstable protest song there is: every time you hear it, it says something else. In the twisting abstractions of that performance, in the music of *Guitar Drag*—you can't call it chance music; you could call it forced music—you can begin to hear the droning abstractions in the blues. The gonging in Blind Lemon Jefferson's 1928 "See That My Grave Is Kept Clean." The intimations of the uncanny and the unknowable in the way Robert Johnson's guitar strings seem to stand apart from his fingers in his 1936 "Come on in My Kitchen." The push toward wordlessness, into a music of pure signs, the refusal to even approach a narrative, in John Lee Hooker's "John Henry," with a pace that, if the true context of Hooker's song is not a private recording for a record collector in 1949 but a video by a sound artist more than half a century later, can seem to match the pacing of *Guitar Drag* so completely that Hooker's own guitar could have been cut right into the noise made by the amplifier on the truck and the guitar on the road. "John Henry laid his hammer down / And headed back to his hometown / But someone turned the signpost round / Someone took the road signs down," Jon Langford sang in 2006 in his strongest Welsh accent in "Lost in America," a song about the American Dream as snake oil that the singer buys in spite of himself—and soon John Henry is everywhere, taking the place of the engineer in "Wreck of the Old 97" in Virginia in 1903, "Scalded to death by the dream," then, one September morning just two years short of a century after that, reappearing in the last verse to reveal Superman as merely one

more version of the superman who was there first, John Henry stepping forth, once more, to "turn the planes around today / Make them
fly the other way."

John Henry, the man who denied the machine, the machine that,
in the Disney version of the story, comes out of the other side of the
mountain as a single metal scrap, the former slave who traces his country's history in "Lost in America," is in *Guitar Drag*. "The record is
supposed to be a stable reproduction of time," Marclay said in 1991,
speaking of any recording, by anyone, "but it's not. Time and sound
become elusive again because of mechanical failure. Technology captures sound and stamps it on these disks. They then begin lives of their
own. Within these lives, technological cracks—defects—occur. That's
when it gets interesting for me, when technology fails. That's when
I feel the possibility of expression." Isn't that what John Henry says,
when he challenges the steam drill to a duel?

You can hear the heedlessness of "Shake Some Action" in *Guitar
Drag*; you can hear Little Richard's "Keep a Knockin'." I imagine Little
Richard alone in the setting Marclay designed for viewings of *Guitar
Drag*—"a projection, it has to be loud, it has to be experienced in a
black box where you can lose track of time and space, lose your balance.
The image is jerky and you may get dizzy. It has to be a physical expe-
rience you need to feel it through your body"—and I imagine Little
Richard tapping his foot. I think of the end of *American Hot Wax*.

In this 1978 movie, it's 1959. Tim McIntire's Alan Freed arrives outside the Brooklyn Paramount for his big rock 'n' roll extravaganza, with
Chuck Berry and Jerry Lee Lewis topping the bill—appearing in the
movie as themselves, Berry time-traveling effortlessly, Lewis making it
by sheer force of will. There's a huge crowd outside. As Freed heads for
the entrance, standing straight, moving to his own beat, snapping his
limbs like fingers, he's accosted by a Dion figure. He's got this group,
Mr. Freed, he wants to audition right on the street; Freed calls for
quiet and they go right into an acappella "I Wonder Why." Freed's
grin is tight, hinting at fear, fatalism, even suicide. His career is crash-
ing all around him. He's about to be kicked off the air, blacklisted for
payola; the D.A. is going to shut down his show and throw him in

jail. McIntire, like Freed an alcoholic, a drug addict, carried all that with him, dying at forty-one, eight years after playing Freed, who died at forty-three: "Dead frequency, Slick, over and out," Charles Wright wrote of McIntire in 2005. "It's mostly a matter of what kind of noise you make."

Through the window of the D.A.'s car, hovering on the edges of the crowd, you see a ragged figure, in a state of utter obliviousness, pounding on an overturned garbage can, his pompadour flopping into his face, shouting out "Good Golly Miss Molly" so tunelessly you can barely recognize it. This is less Little Richard not invited to the Brooklyn Paramount but showing up anyway than it's the Little Richard specter—the specter of the excluded, silenced, worthless music hovering behind every finished piece of rock 'n' roll, the unheard music that reveals the music that is heard as a fake. In his car, plotting strategy, the D.A. doesn't notice the bum in the alley, he isn't listening to him, but subconsciously he hears him, and what he hears is what he sees. "Look at that filth," the D.A. says of the boys and girls, black and white, crowding into the theater.

With Jerry Lee Lewis as the last act, standing on top of his burning piano and the stage covered with cops, teenagers grabbed by police as others are trampled as they rush down the stairs, the audience flees into the night. Freed clutches a small boy. In the last shot, the bum stands on the now-deserted street, playing for the sky, pounding his can: "I say a wop bop a loo bop a lop bam boom. Got a girl. Named Sue. She knows just what to do. Got a girl"—and the movie is over. That scene too is in the music of *Guitar Drag*.

2014

SOURCES AND ACKNOWLEDGMENTS

INDEX

▼ ▼ ▼ ▼ ▼ ▼ ▼ ▼ ▼ ▼ ▼ ▼ ▼ ▼ ▼ ▼

Sources and Acknowledgments

THE EDITORS would like to express their gratitude for the research and editorial assistance of Taylor Kingsbury.

The list below gives the source of each text included in this volume; the texts have been reprinted without change, except for the correction of typographical errors. Ellipses, spaces, asterisks, and brackets are the authors' own. If more than one source is named, the copy text for this edition is the first cited.

Vince Aletti, from *The Disco Files*: Aletti, *The Disco Files 1973–78: New York's Underground, Week by Week* (New York: DJhistory.com, 2009). Copyright © 2009 by Vince Aletti. Used by permission of the author.

Hilton Als, Michael: Als, *White Girls* (San Francisco: McSweeney's, 2013); originally published in *The New York Review of Books*, August 13, 2009. Copyright © 2009 by Hilton Als. Used by permission of The New York Review of Books.

Gina Arnold, from *Route 666*: Arnold, *Route 666: On the Road to Nirvana* (New York: St. Martin's, 1993): xi–xii. Copyright © 1993 by Gina Arnold. Used by permission of the author.

Eve Babitz, Jim Morrison Is Dead and Living in Hollywood: *Esquire*, March 1991. Copyright © 1991 by Eve Babitz. Used by permission of the author.

Carola Dibbell, The Slits Go Native: *The Boston Phoenix*, November 11, 1980. Copyright © 1980 by Carola Dibbell. Used by permission of the author.

Gerald Early, from *One Nation Under a Groove*: Early, *One Nation Under a Groove* (New York: Ecco Press, 1995): 74–88. Copyright © 1995 by Gerald Early. Used by permission of the author.

Chuck Eddy, The Ramones: *Rolling Stone*, September 20, 1990. Copyright © 1990 by Rolling Stone LLC. Used by permission. All rights reserved.

Donna Gaines, Sylvia's Husband: *The Village Voice*, June 9, 1987. Copyright © 1987 by Donna Gaines. Used by permission of the author.

Nelson George, The Power and the Glory: *The Village Voice*, May 8, 1984. Copyright © 1984 by Nelson George. Used by permission of the author.

Richard Goldstein, Master of Mediocrity: Goldstein, *Goldstein's Greatest Hits* (New York: Prentice-Hall, 1969); originally published in *West Magazine*, 1968. Copyright © 1969 by Richard Goldstein. Used by permission of the author.

Peter Guralnick, King Solomon: The Throne in Exile: Guralnick, *Sweet Soul Music: Rhythm and Blues and the Southern Dream of Freedom* (New York: Harper & Row, 1986). Copyright © 1986 by Peter Guralnick. Used by permission of the author.

David Hajdu, Ray Charles: Hajdu, *Heroes and Villains: Essays on Music, Comics, and Culture* (New York: Da Capo, 2009); originally published as "Unchained Heart" in *The New Republic*, December 13, 2004. Copyright © 2009 by David Hajdu. Used by permission of Da Capo, a member of the Perseus Books Group.

Devin McKinney, from O.P.D./*Deus Est Vivus*: The Beatles and the Death Cults: McKinney, *Magic Circles: The Beatles in Dream and History* (Cambridge: Harvard University Press, 2003): 254–275. Copyright © 2003 by the President and Fellows of Harvard College. Used by permission.

Richard Meltzer, from *The Aesthetics of Rock*: Meltzer, *The Aesthetics of Rock* (New York: Something Else Press, 1970): 5–20. Copyright © 2015 by Richard Melzer. Used by permission.

Paul Nelson, Valley of the New York Dolls: *The Village Voice*, May 26, 1975; collected in Kevin Avery, ed., *Everything Is an Afterthought: The Life and Writings of Paul Nelson* (Seattle: Fantagraphics, 2011). Copyright © 1975 by Paul Nelson. Used by permission of the Estate of Paul Nelson.

Geoffrey O'Brien, Seven Years in the Life: *The New York Review of Books*, January 11, 2001; included in different form in O'Brien, *Sonata for Jukebox* (New York: Counterpoint, 2004). Copyright © 2001 by Geoffrey O'Brien. Used by permission of The New York Review of Books.

Robert Palmer, Sam Cooke's *Night Beat*: Anthony DeCurtis, ed., *Blues & Chaos: The Music Writing of Robert Palmer* (New York: Simon & Schuster, 2009); originally published as liner notes, Sam Cooke, *Night Beat*, RCA, 1995 reissue. Used by permission of Scribner, a division of Simon & Schuster, Inc. Copyright © 2009 by Augusta Palmer. All rights reserved.

Jon Pareles, The Cars' Power Steering: *Rolling Stone*, January 25, 1979. Copyright © 1979 by Rolling Stone LLC. Used by permission. All rights reserved.

Richard Poirier, Learning from the Beatles: *Partisan Review* 4, 1967; reprinted in different form in Poirier, *The Performing Self* (London:

Index

White, Josh, 384
White Album (Beatles), 383, 391, 393
Whitehead, Colson, 546–47
Whiteman, Paul, 474, 476–79, 495
"White Rabbit" (Jefferson Airplane), 85, 92, 118
Whitesnake, 366
Whitfield, Norman, 352
Whitney, Marva, 408
Who, 26, 73, 87, 98, 297
Wichita Train Whistle Sings (Michael Nesmith), 121
Wild, the Innocent & the E Street Shuffle, The (Bruce Springsteen), 355
Wild Cats, 99
"Wild Thing" (Troggs), 512
"Wild Tyme" (Jefferson Airplane), 82, 85
Wilentz, Sean, 438
Williams, Big Joe, 2–4
Williams, Hank, 2, 245–46, 321
Williams, Hank, Jr., 292
Williams, Kae, 268
Williams, Martin, 144
Williams, Paul, 47, 484; "Outlaw Blues," 71–93
Williams, Rusty, 413
Williams, Viola, 268
"Willing and Able" (Prince), 209
Willis, Ellen, 293–94, 486, 543; "Janis Joplin," 227–33
Willis, Victor, 173
"Will You Still Love Me Tomorrow" (Shirelles), 299–300
Wilson, Brian, 42–61, 71, 480
Wilson, Carl, 48, 56–58
Wilson, Dennis, 48, 54, 56, 58, 506
Wilson, Jackie, 344, 408, 498
Wilson, Marilyn, 51, 54, 58, 60–61
Wilson, Mary, 345
"Windy" (Association), 78
Winfrey, Oprah, 525
Winger, 365

"Winter Melody" (Donna Summer), 170
"Within You Without You" (Beatles), 28, 39
With the Beatles (album), 383
Wiz, The (film), 499
WLAC (Nashville), 101
WMCA (New York City), 410
WMIS (Natchez), 245–46
Wolk, Douglas: *Live at the Apollo*, 405–14
Wonder, Stevie, 169–72, 205, 208, 434, 487, 494
"Wonderful, Wonderful" (Johnny Mathis), 348
"Won't You Try" (Jefferson Airplane), 81, 89
Wood, Ron, 531–32, 534
Woodlawn, Holly, 294
Woodstock Festival, 303, 493–94, 553
"Work with Me, Annie" (Hank Ballard), 349
"Wreck of the Old 97," 553
WSMB (New Orleans), 245
WVEE (Atlanta), 540
WWL (New Orleans), 245
Wyman, Bill, 77–78

X-Ray Spex, 307

Yardbirds, 25, 85, 151, 160
Yellowman, 443
"Yellow Submarine" (Beatles), 102
"Yesterday" (Beatles), 474–75
Yesterday and Today (Beatles), 27, 31
Yo La Tengo, 359
"You Are My Sunshine," 248
"You Better Leave That Liar Alone," 419
"You Better Leave That Woman Alone" (Ray Charles), 419
"You Can Make It If You Try" (James Brown), 285

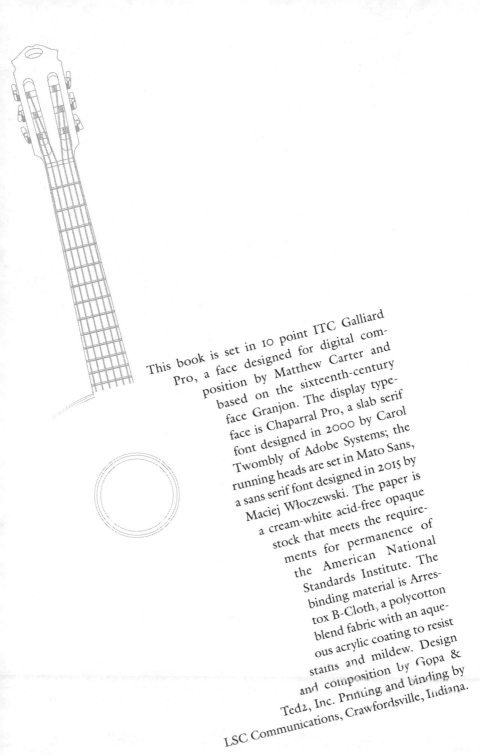

This book is set in 10 point ITC Galliard Pro, a face designed for digital composition by Matthew Carter and based on the sixteenth-century face Granjon. The display typeface is Chaparral Pro, a slab serif font designed in 2000 by Carol Twombly of Adobe Systems; the running heads are set in Mato Sans, a sans serif font designed in 2015 by Maciej Włoczewski. The paper is a cream-white acid-free opaque stock that meets the requirements for permanence of the American National Standards Institute. The binding material is Arrestox B-Cloth, a polycotton blend fabric with an aqueous acrylic coating to resist stains and mildew. Design and composition by Gopa & Ted2, Inc. Printing and binding by LSC Communications, Crawfordsville, Indiana.